Nomads in Postrevolutionary Iran

Examining the rapid transition in Iran from a modernizing, westernizing, secularizing monarchy (1941–79) to a hard-line, conservative, clergy-run Islamic republic (1979-), this book focuses on the ways this process has impacted the Qashqa'i—a rural, nomadic, tribally organized, Turkish-speaking, ethnic minority of a million and a half people who are dispersed across the southern Zagros Mountains.

Analyzing the relationship between the tribal polity and each of the two regimes, the book goes on to explain the resilience of the people's tribal organizations, kinship networks, and politicized ethnolinguistic identities to demonstrate how these structures and ideologies offered the Qashqa'i a way to confront the pressures emanating from the two central governments.

Existing scholarly works on politics in Iran rarely consider Iranian society outside the capital of Tehran and beyond the reach of the details of national politics. Local-level studies on Iran—accounts of the ways people actually lived—are now rare, especially after the revolution. Based on long-term anthropological research, *Nomads in Postrevolutionary Iran* provides a unique insight into how national-level issues relate to the local level and will be of interest to scholars and researchers in Anthropology, Iranian Studies, and Middle Eastern Studies.

Lois Beck is Professor of Anthropology at Washington University in Saint Louis. She has conducted anthropological research in Iran since 1969. Her books include *The Qashqa'i of Iran*; *Nomad: A Year in the Life of a Qashqa'i Tribesman in Iran*; and the coedited *Women in the Muslim World*; *Women in Iran from the Rise of Islam to 1800*; and *Women in Iran from 1800 to the Islamic Republic*.

Iranian Studies

Edited by:
Homa Katouzian, University of Oxford and
Mohamad Tavakoli, University of Toronto

Since 1967 the International Society for Iranian Studies (ISIS) has been a leading learned society for the advancement of new approaches in the study of Iranian society, history, culture, and literature. The ISIS Iranian Studies series published by Routledge provides a venue for the publication of original and innovative scholarly works in all areas of Iranian and Persianate studies.

1 **Journalism in Iran**
From mission to profession
Hossein Shahidi

2 **Sadeq Hedayat**
His work and his
wondrous world
Edited by Homa Katouzian

3 **Iran in the 21st Century**
Politics, economics and
conflict
*Edited by Homa Katouzian
and Hossein Shahidi*

4 **Media, Culture and Society
in Iran**
Living with globalization and
the Islamic State
Edited by Mehdi Semati

5 **Modern Persian Literature
in Afghanistan**
Anomalous visions of history
and form
Wali Ahmadi

6 **The Politics of Iranian Cinema**
Film and society in the Islamic
Republic
Saeed Zeydabadi-Nejad

7 **Continuity in Iranian Identity**
Resilience of a cultural heritage
Fereshteh Davaran

8 **New Perspectives on Safavid
Iran**
Empire and society
Edited by Colin P. Mitchell

9 **Islamic Tolerance**
Amīr Khusraw and pluralism
Alyssa Gabbay

10 **City of Knowledge in Twentieth
Century Iran**
Shiraz, history and poetry
Setrag Manoukian

11 **Domestic Violence in Iran**
Women, marriage and Islam
Zahra Tizro

12 **Gnostic Apocalypse and Islam**
Qur'an, exegesis, messianism,
and the literary origins of the
Babi religion
Todd Lawson

13 **Social Movements in Iran**
Environmentalism and civil
society
Simin Fadaee

14 **Iranian–Russian Encounters**
Empires and revolutions since
1800
Edited by Stephanie Cronin

15 **Iran**
Politics, history and literature
Homa Katouzian

16 **Domesticity and Consumer
Culture in Iran**
Interior revolutions of the
modern era
Pamela Karimi

17 **The Development of the
Babi/Baha'i Communities**
Exploring Baron Rosen's
archives
Youli Ioannesyan

18 **Culture and Cultural Politics
Under Reza Shah**
The Pahlavi State, new
bourgeoisie and the
creation of a modern society
in Iran
*Bianca Devos and Christoph
Werner*

19 **Recasting Iranian Modernity**
International relations and
social change
Kamran Matin

20 **The Sīh-rōzag in
Zoroastrianism**
A textual and historico-religious
analysis
Enrico G. Raffaelli

21 **Literary Subterfuge and
Contemporary Persian
Fiction**
Who writes Iran?
Mohammad Mehdi Khorrami

22 **Nomads in Postrevolutionary
Iran**
The Qashqa'i in an era
of change
Lois Beck

Nomads in Postrevolutionary Iran

The Qashqa'i in an era of change

Lois Beck

LONDON AND NEW YORK

First published 2015
by Routledge
2 Park Square, Milton Park, Abingdon, Oxon OX14 4RN

and by Routledge
711 Third Avenue, New York, NY 10017

Routledge is an imprint of the Taylor & Francis Group, an informa business

© 2015 Lois Beck

The right of Lois Beck to be identified as author of this work has been asserted by her in accordance with sections 77 and 78 of the Copyright, Designs and Patents Act 1988.

All rights reserved. No part of this book may be reprinted or reproduced or utilised in any form or by any electronic, mechanical, or other means, now known or hereafter invented, including photocopying and recording, or in any information storage or retrieval system, without permission in writing from the publishers.

Trademark notice: Product or corporate names may be trademarks or registered trademarks, and are used only for identification and explanation without intent to infringe.

British Library Cataloguing in Publication Data
A catalogue record for this book is available from the British Library

Library of Congress Cataloging in Publication Data
Beck, Lois, 1944-
Nomads in post-revolutionary Iran : the Qashqa'i in
an era of change / Lois Beck.
Includes bibliographical references and index.
1. Qashqa'i (Turkic people)--Iran--Ethnic identity.
2. Qashqa'i (Turkic people)--Government policy--Iran.
3. Iran--Politics and government--1979-1997. 4. Iran--
Politics and government--1997- I. Title.
DS269.K3B425 2014
305.894'36--dc23
2014012116

ISBN: 978-1-138-01561-6 (hbk)
ISBN: 978-1-315-79422-8 (ebk)

Typeset in Times New Roman
by Taylor and Francis Books

   Printed and bound by CPI Group (UK) Ltd, Croydon, CR0 4YY

Dedicated to

Borzu Qermezi
The Qermezi tribal group
The Qashqa'i people

Contents

Foreword	xi
Preface	xiii
Acknowledgments	xvii
List of terms	xix
List of identities	xxi
Timeline	xxiii

1 Introduction   **1**
  Interlinking perspectives 2
  The process of research 7
  With my daughter 12
  Organization of the book 14

2 Past and present: Forty-four years of transformation   **18**
  Circumstances in 1970 19
  Circumstances in 2013 22
  Transformational processes 28
  Demographic patterns among the Qermezi, 1970–2000 31

**3 The revolution and the Islamic Republic: Reflections on
    1978–2013**   **36**
  Experiencing the revolution 36
  Imprisonment of Qashqa'i leaders 42
  Martyrs of the Iraq–Iran war 58
  The state and the tribe 69
  *New revolutionary Islamic councils for nomads
    and villagers 107*
  New faces in the tribe 116

**4 Reclaiming culture: The politics of resistance and defiance:
    Reflections on 1992**   **144**
  Attire 144
  Religious belief and practice 149

x *Contents*

Ritual and ceremony 152
Nasir Qermezi's wedding 154
Ibrahim Qermezi's wedding 165

5 The hope of spring: Reflections on 1995—winter and spring   **174**
Struggles over land 174
Life in town 189
Welcoming the New Year 201

**6 Death and memory: The end of the life of a Qashqa'i
tribesman in Iran: Reflections on 1995—summer**   **211**
Borzu Qermezi's last spring 212
Borzu Qermezi's demise and burial 213
Third-day memorial 217
Seventh-day memorial 218
Adorning the gravesite 223
Thursday afternoon visitations 225
Fortieth-day memorial 226
Events in the year after the death 228
One-year memorial, 1996 229
Second anniversary, 1997 232

7 Life moves on: Reflections on 1996   **234**
Shahriyar Qermezi, parliamentary deputy 234
*Teachers, schools, and students: The promise of
    formal education 256*

8 Decisions and consequences: Reflections on 1997 and 1998   **303**
Mohammad Karim Qermezi sells his flock 303
A split in the family 312
Abbas Qermezi and his rifle 325

9 Facing the future: Reflections on 1999   **332**
Revolutionary Islamic councils for villages and towns 332
A wedding postponed 338
Assaults against their lands 348
A new settlement at Mulleh Balut 360

Conclusion   **372**

Glossary   376
Bibliography   379
Index   393

Foreword

With my mother

As a five-year-old child, with long ponytails and an impressionable mind, I was curious about the man named Borzu about whom my mother often spoke. We were sitting in a Shiraz courtyard garden and would soon travel to Hanalishah, the summer pastures of Borzu's tribe in southwestern Iran.

On arrival at Hanalishah, my first impressions (and lasting memories) focus on Borzu and his kindly, striking presence. Not yet understanding Qashqa'i Turkish, I was inspired by my mother's ease of communication with the man she had not seen in over a decade, a period I could barely comprehend, one twice my lifetime. Until myriad stars filled the sky and the embers in the firepit were glowing only faintly, they spoke about the events taking place during the years they were apart.

Four years later, arriving in Isfahan by plane from Europe (via Tehran), my mother explained the cause of her disquietude. She feared that Borzu might have succumbed to infirmity. If the worst had occurred, his grandson Masud, who was meeting us, would be dressed in black clothing, a symbol of mourning. Our previous visit that year to the nomads' winter pastures had been filled with joy at reuniting with our dear friends but had also been underlined with concern for Borzu's deteriorating health. When we reached the arrival gate at the Isfahan airport, tears filled my mother's eyes. Masud, wearing a black shirt and trousers, was waiting for us.

My mother was far more than a foreign scholar residing with the tribe. She was also a valued family member, warmly welcomed "home" each time she returned. As with David Bornstein and Muhammad Yunus, or Howard Cutler and the Dalai Lama, the effort of understanding another person and his or her life endeavors, particularly over a long period, is a *human* endeavor. The respect and affinity that develop motivate the researcher in her or his efforts. My mother shared the tribe's sorrow over Borzu's passing. I remember the moment when we arrived at Borzu's tent encampment. The women there began to wail in grief; this visit was my mother's first one without the headman greeting her. The next day, when we approached the grave to announce our presence, the women were once again bereft in the knowledge that the man we had come to see was no longer among us. The depth of emotion and

xii *Foreword*

empathy my mother shared with the tribespeople affected me profoundly, and I was now old enough to convey my own feelings of sadness.

Respected by this tribal community, my mother had always upheld people's confidences, and they knew they could speak candidly with her. She was perceptive about nuances in expression in people's personal lives. When she inquired about potentially sensitive matters, men and women often responded by saying, "Telling these stories is our way to ensure that our children and our children's children will understand our history and our unique culture." The people recognized her work and valued its importance.

Moved by Borzu's death, my mother wrote *Nomads in Postrevolutionary Iran* as a tribute to the man and the tribe he represented and loved. The book contributes to the field of anthropology and Iranian and Middle East studies, to the world's understanding of tribal life at the local level in Iran, and even to the future of the tribe itself, whose members will be able to revisit the experiences that otherwise now exist only in fading and soon-to-disappear memories.

Eighteen years after my initial visit to Iran with my mother, I sat on a sunny Delhi terrace reading her manuscript. I experienced mixed emotions and renewed appreciation and respect. During each visit while I had explored the nomads' camps and surrounding mountainsides with companions my age, my mother conversed with the tribespeople and learned about the issues currently pertinent in their lives. When we returned "home" at the end of each day, to the campmates who welcomed us so warmly, we would chat with them around the fire and eventually retire to our tent. As we listened to the nightly clamor of the sheep, goats, donkeys, dogs, and wolves, my mother would share with me the stories she had heard that day, and my understanding of the people's lives was enlightened in these incremental ways. While reading the manuscript, I recognized the details and saw how aptly they are interwoven in the broader context of the tribespeople's struggles with the circumstances that enmeshed them. My worldview was fundamentally shaped by my childhood experiences among the Qashqa'i nomads and with my mother, the woman who raised her daughter alongside the daughters and sons of the people with whom she had shared her life for decades.

A courageous, dedicated person passionate about her research and writing, my mother has accomplished a rare feat and has produced a record of lasting significance. I feel proud and thankful to have shared these experiences with her.

Julia Huang
London School of Economics and Political Science

Preface

My interest in Iran began when I was an undergraduate student at Shiraz University. As a graduate student in anthropology at the University of Chicago and then as a post-graduate scholar, I returned to Iran to conduct research on political and social change among nomadic pastoralists of the Qashqa'i tribal confederacy. Just after the revolution against Mohammad Reza Shah in 1978–79, I traveled to Iran to continue my studies of the Qashqa'i. I aimed to understand how this revolt and the emerging Islamic regime were affecting the lives of the tribal people. I focused on the ways in which these two, quite different, kinds of modernizing, centralizing states have impacted the community. I have returned to Iran on many occasions since then to further these studies.

I was motivated in part by being the only American anthropologist allowed by the Islamic Republic to conduct research there for long durations on multiple occasions. As someone who had experienced Iran at the local level under the shah's regime and then under postrevolutionary and Islamizing circumstances, I was privileged to be able to examine the impact of both regimes on the Qashqa'i. As another motivating factor, I saw that my perspective differed from that of scholars who focused on only (or primarily) national events. A local-level study offered opportunities to understand historical, societal, and cultural transformations in ways that an investigator from afar or even situated in Tehran could not. As a third motivation, the most personal one for me, I was closely affiliated with a tribal group with which I had lived over a span of decades. As a long-term, dedicated witness, I wanted to continue to chronicle the lives of these tribespeople and to detail the ways they were confronting new kinds of pressures brought about by the revolution and the Islamizing state.

Until the twentieth century, perhaps half of Iran's population was organized by nomadic and/or tribal groups of various sizes and political complexities. Historical, political, economic, and demographic factors since then have reduced this proportion, for those still practicing nomadism, to only a few percent. A much larger percentage of Iran's people is still tribally organized, for reasons I explain through the example of a still existing, partly nomadic, fully tribal community. The pressures and influences experienced by this group are similar to those of other people in Iran and the wider region but its responses are specific to its heritage and particular to its time and place. Through the

xiv *Preface*

study of one group, I discuss these broader issues as well as explain local practices and patterns.

I examine the ways in which people in this community are interlinked through kinship, marriage, tribal groups, tribal leaders, common ethnolinguistic identities, shared cultural systems, still-viable economic activities, geographic location, and social and cultural as well as physical separation from Iran's dominating population. Holding on to notions of a common collectivity, each person shares with others an array of affiliations with a family, lineage, subtribe, tribe, tribal confederacy, and unique ethnolinguistic group. These collective notions and their institutional structures offer people support and provide barriers against incursions. As a result, people are able to avoid some kinds of external threats in ways unavailable to many of Iran's other citizens. Following the practices of their ancestors and antecedents, they deploy certain strategies to protect themselves from disruptive forces emanating from outside their closely knit and cohesive communities.

These tribal people have experienced the efforts of modernizing, centralizing states in the twentieth and early twenty-first centuries to integrate and assimilate them. Yet they have seen that becoming citizens of the nation-state does not offer them the types of group solidarity that had sustained them in the past. State citizenship does not meet most of their requirements and expectations. Resilient, the people have devised creative ways to handle the circumstances confronting them, as they faced one state that aimed to disrupt their livelihoods, lifestyles, and customs and then another state proclaiming some of the same goals.

The ways of life inherent in nomadism and tribalism were once prevalent throughout Iran and the wider region but have fallen under pressures of diverse sorts. People understood that they could not return to the past, and yet the livelihoods, lifestyles, and value systems that had sustained them continued to influence their strategies as they faced outside pressures. They have found ways to keep the features that still supported them, and they have adapted former practices and developed new ones to help them cope with factors that seemed to be beyond their control. These interrelated issues are relevant to Iran's past, present, and future.

This work contributes an anthropological perspective to the field of Iranian studies, which is defined primarily by historians and political scientists. It also moves beyond Iranian studies to address issues that remain pertinent in the modernizing Middle East and areas beyond, such as popular resistance and defiance against non-democratic centralizing states.

The system of transliteration used in this book is a modified version of the format recommended by the *International Journal of Middle East Studies*. I exclude all diacritical marks except for the *hamza* (') in "Qashqa'i" and "Qur'an" and the *ain* (') in "Shi'i" Islam, to follow the usage of other scholars. The spelling of known figures, places, and entities follows conventional, customary use. The literature refers to Iran's new revolutionary Islamic committees as "*komiteh*," for example, a spelling I apply here rather than an unfamiliar "*kumitih.*" I spell some personal and family names according to people's preferences and/or to the way these people are already known in the literature ("Khomeini," for example). Some common Turkish, Persian, and Arabic words and names appear in anglicized form, such as "gelim" and "bazaar." I minimize the use of Turkish, Persian, and Arabic words in the text, but, when I include them, they fall in parentheses after the English translation. I italicize them on their first use but not thereafter. The English word is sometimes pluralized but I use the singular form in the transliteration. I spell "Qashqa'i" according to the *IJMES* system. Other spellings found in the literature and among some Qashqa'i include "Qashqai," "Ghashghai" (the spelling used by the formerly ruling Janikhani family), and "Kashkai."

I identify some Qashqa'i individuals by their lineage, subtribal, tribal, and/or confederacy labels (in this order). Mohammad Bahmanbaigi, for example, is a "Bahmanbaiglu Amaleh Qashqa'i" man. Each of these labels was significant to him in different contexts, and together they formed his primary identity. Most people about whom I write in this book are members of the Aqa Mohammadli lineage of the Qermezi subtribe of the Darrehshuri tribe, one of many tribes of the Qashqa'i confederacy. When I write about other Qermezi, I identify them by their lineage names. The last name of almost all Qermezi is "Qermezi." When I refer to other Qashqa'i, I add their subtribal, tribal, and/or family names.

Many people, including authors and even specialists in Iranian studies, often use the terms "Persian" and "Iranian" interchangeably. Yet only half of Iran's population consists of ethnic Persians, whose first language is almost always Persian and who adhere to broadly defined notions about "Persian" culture. The other half of Iran's population consists of many ethnic and ethnolinguistic minorities, including Azeri Turks, Kurds, Lurs, Arabs, Qashqa'i, Baluch, and Turkmans. In this volume, the term "Persian" refers only to ethnic Persians, while the term "Iranian" includes all citizens of Iran and those in the diaspora who consider Iran their homeland.

I do not usually qualify the term "Islamic" by placing it within quotes. Instead, I try to include the perspectives of different people concerning its meaning. Any given idea, action, object, institution, or personage could be "Islamic" or not, depending on varying points of view. Most Qashqa'i (as compared with many Muslim clergymen), for example, did not explain the clothing restrictions of the Islamic Republic of Iran by invoking Islamic values of modesty. Rather, they viewed the policy not as a religious duty, but as an expression of power and coercion by the ruling clergy and its supporters. Writers on the Middle East increasingly refer to the revolution in Iran in 1978–79 as "Islamic," a phrasing that has become conventional (and not always examined). Many Iranians who participated in the revolution were not affiliated with Islamic institutions and were not motivated by ideologies or other factors relating to Islam, and they object to the notion that the revolution was "Islamic." Even the Islamic Republic has been and continues to be less than "Islamic" in its implementation of some policies.

xvi *Preface*

Official, open-market, and black-market rates of exchange between the Iranian *tuman* and the United States dollar varied widely during the period under consideration. Annual rates of inflation after the revolution in 1978–79 have been high. I usually avoid reporting monetary sums; they lack meaning unless I include the multiple exchange rates each time and the people whom such rates affected. I would need to place these amounts (such as the monetary value of a year-old lamb given to the host of a wedding) in the context of the then-current regional and national economy as well as in the context of the household economies of the donor and the recipient.

The solar calendar of the Iranian year runs from 21 March to 20 March, and I try to be precise when I include the appropriate year according to the Western calendar.

My prior publications (especially Beck 1986, 1991) provide photographs, maps, genealogical charts, and other kinds of illustrations on the Qashqa'i tribal confederacy and the Qermezi subtribe. Huang (2006, 2009) includes additional illustrations relevant to this book.

Acknowledgments

"So many people have passed on, too many to comprehend." Among the Qermezi tribespeople, the places of Borzu, Falak, Mohammad Karim, Dariush, Murad, Jehangir, and Hajji Qurban are especially empty. Among other Darrehshuri tribespeople, Jehangir Khan, Sara Bibi, and their son Manucher Dareshuri are especially missed. These people are part of my family, and I will mourn them forever.

I am deeply indebted to my Qermezi hosts, especially Borzu Qermezi and his wife Falak; their sons Mohammad Karim, Dariush, and Bizhan; and their daughters Samarrukh, Zulaikha, Zohreh, Farideh, and Farida. Many other Qermezi welcomed me and contributed to my research, and I am grateful to them. I also appreciate the many other Qashqa'i who facilitated my efforts to chronicle their history, society, and culture.

The Bayat family, including Molki Bibi Solat Ghashghai, Kaveh, Nazli, Farhad, and Furud, were gracious hosts in Tehran and made the transition to and from Qashqa'i territory comfortable for me and my daughter, especially the year when Julia traveled by herself to Iran from the United States.

Iranian officials at multiple levels supported my interests in traveling to Iran and conducting anthropological research there, and I acknowledge their assistance. Some of them are of nomadic, pastoral, tribal, and/or ethnic-minority backgrounds, which contributed to their understanding of the purposes of my visits.

Erika Friedl and Philip Salzman commented on an early draft of the manuscript. Mehran Kamrava convened at the Georgetown University School of Foreign Service in Doha, Qatar, two workshops on identity in the Persian Gulf region, and Lawrence Potter and other seminar participants enriched my appreciation of the topic as it relates to Iran and its neighbors. Geoffrey Haig organized a seminar at the Christian Albrechts University in Kiel, Germany, on Iran's endangered languages, and its members, especially Donald Stilo, assisted in my understanding of linguistic transformations in the region. Shahla Haeri, Fatemeh Keshavarz, Naheed Dareshuri, and Masoumeh Nourani helped in transliterating and translating Persian, Turkish, and Arabic words. I thank those who answered questions and located infor- mation during the process of revision: Amir Ajami, Naheed Dareshuri,

xviii *Acknowledgments*

Sohrab Dolatkhah, Zahra Farhoudi, Ali Gheissari, Sasan Ghermezi, and Bernard Hourcade.

Beginning in 1991, my daughter Julia Huang has accompanied me during all my research trips to Iran (except one). She helped in significant ways and was always enthusiastic about the ever-transforming adventure. She published a book (*Tribeswomen of Iran: Weaving Memories among Qashqa'i Nomads*) in 2009 about her experiences. She said she had not wanted to read the manuscript of *Nomads in Postrevolutionary Iran* or other writings or publications of mine on the Qermezi until after she had completed her book. She said she had wanted to preserve her memories and images of life among the nomads during the times she lived among them. If, early on, she had commented on this book, she would have added information and insight and a perspective different than mine. When she did read this manuscript for the first time in 2009, she offered useful comments and helped me to focus my arguments. I thank Julia for suggesting the book's working title, *Nomads Move On: Qashqa'i Tribespeople in Postrevolutionary Iran*.

Friends and acquaintances in Switzerland (Geneva, Montreux, and Zermatt), Germany (Munich), France (Paris), Bangladesh (Dhaka), Turkey (Istanbul), and Qatar (Doha) offered companionship, space, and changes in scenery while I revised the manuscript and contemplated its wider significance.

The Graduate School of Arts and Sciences at Washington University in Saint Louis and its Department of Anthropology offered financial and other assistance during the research and writing of this book.

I thank Homa Katouzian and Mohamad Tavakoli-Targhi, editors of Routledge's book series in Iranian studies, for their support of this project.

List of terms

The book's glossary contains words in Persian, Qashqa'i Turkish, and Arabic.

Agricultural Jihad, Ministry of (since 2000) (*jihad-i kishavarzi*).
committee (*komiteh*). Revolutionary Islamic institution.
Construction Jihad, Ministry of (1982–2000) (*jihad-i sazandigi*).
council (*shura*). Revolutionary Islamic institution.
district (*shahristan*). Administrative and territorial unit within a province.
elder. Influential man at the local level.
endogamy. Preferential marriage within a group.
ethnic. Refers to cultural traits marking a people or group as distinctive; often
    a term used for minorities in a region or nation-state.
ethnolinguistic. Linguistic traits combined with other cultural characteristics
    that mark a people or group as distinctive.
foundation (*bunyad*). Parastatal or state organization.
Friday prayer leader (*imam jumih*). Leader of Friday prayers in a mosque;
    appointed as a politico-religious leader by Iran's supreme leader since 1979.
gendarmerie. Rural police.
headman (*kadkhuda*). Leader of a local group or community; often appointed
    or recognized by the government until 1979.
household. Nuclear or extended family whose members reside together; often
    economically and socially independent.
Islamization. Processes by which Muslims disseminate often standardized,
    often regime-approved Islamic beliefs and practices; methods of system-
    ization often aimed toward the (political) unification of the religion's
    adherents.
khan. Tribal leader; also a term of respect.
lineage. Kinship group defined primarily by patrilineal descent.
minority. Person (or group) who is not a member of Iran's dominating,
    primarily ethnic-Persian community.
modest dress (*hijab*). Clothing acceptable for a woman according to local
    standards, government regulations, and/or Islamic values.
national minority. Politicized community having its own sense of nationhood,
    separate from that of the nation-state.

xx *List of terms*

New Year (*no ruz*). Begins on the first day of spring; an event almost all Iranians celebrate.

nomad (*ashayir*, pl.). Person who is mobile seasonally or annually; often a migratory pastoralist.

Organization for Nomads' Affairs (ONA) (*sazman-i umur ashayir*). Service-providing agency for nomads within the Ministry of Construction Jihad (Agricultural Jihad since 2000).

paramount Qashqa'i leader (*ilkhani*). Leading khan of the Qashqa'i tribal confederacy; member of the Janikhani lineage and family group.

revolutionary guard (*pasdar*). Member of the paramilitary corps of the revolution's guardians.

subtribe (*tireh*). Section of a tribe; has a distinguishing name, leader(s), territories, reputation, and cultural traits.

supreme leader (*rahbar*). Preeminent leader of the Islamic Republic of Iran.

tribal. Entity or trait associated with a tribe or tribes.

tribal confederacy (*il*). Political affiliation of multiple tribes; has a distinguishing leadership; often recognized as a polity by the government.

tribe (*tayifih*, *il*). Sociopolitical entity having a distinguishing name, leaders, territories, reputation, cultural traits, and often occupational specializations.

List of identities

These identities refer to people living in southwestern Iran. The labels are self-applied and/or applied by others, are used according to situation and context, and are combined with other factors (such as geographical location, socioeconomic status, occupation, education, and gender). People are also Twelver Shi'i Muslims, unless noted otherwise.

Arab. Native speaker of Arabic; an ethnic Arab; adheres to cultural systems connected with other ethnic Arabs; regional, tribal, cultural, and linguistic variations occur among them; a minority of Iran's Arabs is Sunni Muslim.

Bakhtiyari Lur. Native speaker of Luri; an ethnic Bakhtiyari Lur; adheres to cultural systems connected with other ethnic Bakhtiyari Lurs; part of the Bakhtiyari tribal confederacy; member of one of many Bakhtiyari tribes and subtribes.

Boir Ahmad Lur. Native speaker of Luri; an ethnic Lur; adheres to cultural systems connected with other ethnic Lurs; part of the Boir Ahmad tribal group.

Darrehshuri. Member of one of five major tribes of the Qashqa'i tribal confederacy; politically affiliated with a hierarchy of Darrehshuri leaders (khans, kikhas, baigs, headmen, elders); member of one of 44 Darrehshuri subtribes.

Iranian. Citizen of the nation-state of Iran; person originating from Iran; nine to 11 percent of Iranians are Sunni Muslims; one to two percent of Iranians consist of religious minorities who are not Sunni Muslims.

Janikhani. Lineage and family group of the paramount Qashqa'i khans; those who descend from Jani Khan (paramount Qashqa'i leader in the late eighteenth and early nineteenth centuries).

Khamseh. Confederacy of five tribes (Ainallu, Arab, Baharlu, Basseri, Nafar); a political construct created by the government to counter the power of the Qashqa'i tribal confederacy; this polity (unlike its component tribes) has no distinctive ethnolinguistic or cultural identity; some Arab Khamseh are Sunni Muslims.

xxii *List of identities*

Lur. Native speaker of Luri; an ethnic Lur; adheres to cultural systems connected with other ethnic Lurs; regional, tribal, cultural, and linguistic variations occur among them.

Mamassani Lur. Native speaker of Luri; an ethnic Lur; adheres to cultural systems connected with other ethnic Lurs; part of the Mamassani tribal group.

Persian. Native speaker of Persian; speaker of a localized Persian dialect or accent; an ethnic Persian; adheres to cultural systems connected with other ethnic Persians; regional, cultural, and linguistic variations occur among them; part of Iran's dominating population; a term not interchangeable with "Iranian" (citizen of Iran); current or former resident of Iran who is not part of Iran's non-Persian ethnic minorities; some religious minorities (Bahais, Jews, Zoroastrians, and a small minority of Iran's Sunni Muslims) consider themselves Persians.

Qashqa'i. Native speaker of Qashqa'i Turkish; an ethnic Qashqa'i Turk; adheres to cultural systems connected with other ethnic Qashqa'i Turks; regional, cultural, and linguistic variations occur among them; part of the Qashqa'i tribal confederacy; member of one of many Qashqa'i tribes (major ones are Amaleh, Darrehshuri, Farsi Madan, Kashkuli Bozorg, Shish Buluki) and subtribes; "Qashqa'i" and "Turk" are often synonymous in southwestern Iran.

Qermezi. Member of the Qermezi subtribe of the Darrehshuri tribe of the Qashqa'i tribal confederacy; member of one of five lineages (Aqa Mohammadli, Imamverdili, Qairkhbaili, Qasemli, Kachili) and associated families.

Tajik. Native speaker of Persian; an ethnic Persian; someone who is not a Turk; term used by Qashqa'i for someone who is not Qashqa'i; the abbreviated term "Tat" is often used in speech.

Turk. Native speaker of Turkish; an ethnic Turk; adheres to cultural systems connected with other ethnic Turks; regional, tribal, cultural, and linguistic variations occur among them; often part of a named subgroup of Turks (such as Azeris, Qashqa'i, Turkmans, Shahsevan, Afshars); term often used in southwestern Iran for Qashqa'i; a small minority of Iran's Turks is Sunni Muslim.

Timeline

1905–11	Constitutional revolution
1921	Reza Khan of the Cossack Brigade leads coup d'état (February)
1925	Parliament abolishes Qajar dynasty and rulership by Qajar shahs Reza Khan takes oath as shah (15 December)
1926	Reza Shah Pahlavi is coronated (25 April)
1933	Reza Shah executes the Qashqa'i ilkhani, Ismail Khan Soulat ed-Douleh
1941	Invasion by Great Britain and Soviet Union (August) Reza Shah is forced to abdicate and goes into exile (16 September) Mohammad Reza Pahlavi (Reza Shah's son) takes oath as shah (17 September)
1943	Battle of Semirom (Iran's army against Qashqa'i and Boir Ahmad Lur tribesmen)
1951	Mohammad Mosaddeq is prime minister (takes office 30 April) Nationalization of oil
1952	Mohammad Mosaddeq is chosen again as prime minister (takes office 22 July)
1953	CIA-directed coup against Mohammad Mosaddeq, who is deposed as prime minister (19 August)
1954	Mohammad Reza Shah forces Naser Khan Qashqa'i and Khosrow Khan Qashqa'i into exile abroad, to punish them for their support of Mosaddeq
1962–66	Government seizes weapons from the Qashqa'i Government conducts surveillance over and restricts the political activities of Qashqa'i khans Qashqa'i rebels against the government are active in southwestern Iran
1962	Mohammad Reza Shah's land reform begins
1963	Mohammad Reza Shah launches his White Revolution (January) Ayatollah Ruhollah Khomeini enters national politics

xxiv *Timeline*

1964	Mohammad Reza Shah deports Khomeini (4 November)
1971	Mohammad Reza Shah celebrates anniversary of 2,500 years of Iranian monarchy
1978–79	Revolution against Mohammad Reza Shah
1979	Shapur Bakhtiar is prime minister (takes office 4 January; is deposed 11 February)
	Naser Khan Qashqa'i returns to Iran after 25 years of exile (10? January)
	Mohammad Reza Shah flees from Iran (16 January)
	Khosrow Khan Qashqa'i returns to Iran after 25 years of exile (26? January)
	Ayatollah Khomeini returns to Iran from exile (1 February)
	Mehdi Bazargan is prime minister (takes office 4 February; resigns 6 November)
	Provisional revolutionary government is formed (12 February)
	Referendum for the Islamic Republic of Iran (30–31 March)
	Seizure of U.S. Embassy in Tehran (4 November)
	Referendum for the new Islamic constitution (2–3 December)
	Ayatollah Khomeini becomes supreme leader (rahbar) of the Islamic Republic
1980	Abul Hasan Bani-Sadr is president (takes office 4 February)
	Khosrow Khan Qashqa'i is elected to the Islamic Republic's first parliament (March)
	Revolutionary guards arrest Khosrow Khan Qashqa'i (5 June)
	Paramount Qashqa'i khans begin their two-year defensive resistance (6 June)
	Qashqa'i ambush against revolutionary guards at Tang-i Jelo (south of Semirom)
	Revolutionary guards arrest other Qashqa'i leaders and imprison them in Shahreza (June)
	Parliament expels Khosrow Khan Qashqa'i as a deputy (13 July)
	Iraq invades Iran (22 September)
1981	U.S. hostages released after 444 days of captivity (20 January)
	Abul Hasan Bani-Sadr is impeached as president (21 June)
	Ali Khamenei is president (takes office 13 October)
1982	Paramount Qashqa'i khans end their two-year defensive resistance (July)
	Revolutionary guards execute Khosrow Khan Qashqa'i (8 October)
1985	Ali Khamenei is reelected as president (takes office 16 August)
1988	Ceasefire for eight-year Iraq–Iran war (20 August)
1989	Ayatollah Khomeini dies (3 June)
	Ali Khamenei becomes supreme leader (rahbar) (4 June)
	Constitution is amended (July)

Timeline xxv

	Office of prime minister is abolished (3 August) Ali Akbar Hashemi Rafsanjani is president (takes office 3 August)
1993	Ali Akbar Hashemi Rafsanjani is reelected as president (takes office 3 August)
1995	Ahmad Khomeini (Ayatollah Khomeini's son) dies (17 March)
1996	Election for the fifth parliament (March, April)
1997	Mohammad Khatami is president (takes office 2 August)
1999	First municipal council (shura) elections throughout Iran (February)
2000	Election for the sixth parliament (February, May)
2001	Mohammad Khatami is reelected as president (takes office 8 August)
2005	Mahmud Ahmadinejad is president (takes office 3 August)
2009	Mahmud Ahmadinejad is reelected as president (takes office 5 August) Popular protests against Ahmadinejad's fraudulent reelection; beginning of the Green Movement
2013	Hasan Rouhani is president (takes office 3 June)

1 Introduction

In this book, I examine the rapid transition in Iran from a modernizing, westernizing, secularizing monarchy (1941–79) to a hard-line, conservative, clergy-run Islamic republic (1979–) and the ways this process has impacted the Qashqa'i—a rural, nomadic, pastoral, tribally organized, Turkish-speaking, ethnic minority of one and a half million people who are dispersed across the southern Zagros Mountains. I focus on the relationship between the tribal polity and each of the two regimes, and I explain the resilience of the people's tribal organization, kinship networks, and politicized ethnolinguistic identities to show how these structures and ideologies offered the Qashqa'i ways to confront the pressures emanating from each of the two central governments.

Scholars often write about the rigidity of the policies of the Islamic Republic of Iran for its citizens. Yet state officials were remarkably lax about some social and cultural dimensions of these nomads' lives. They empathized with the nomads whom they viewed as the exploited and oppressed victims of the ruling shahs (kings) (1925–79), they regarded them as worthy of lucrative government services, and they praised them as "original" and "genuine" Muslims (whom they compared with Iranians who did not respect Islamic values, who did not observe Islamic rituals, who violated the Islamic regime's edicts, and who resisted the state's control).

I demonstrate how scholarly works on politics in Iran often differ from my descriptions of the local-level dimensions of life for these nomads. Many writers seem unaware of or unconcerned about Iranian society outside the capital (Tehran) and beyond the machinations and details of national politics, even though they imply or say that they generalize for the country as a whole. Local-level studies on Iran—accounts of the ways people actually lived—are now rare, especially after the revolution.[1] (The Islamic Republic has prohibited or restricted the work of foreign researchers since 1979, especially Americans, and Iranian researchers have experienced other constraints and have conducted other kinds of studies.) Scholars continue to write in broad terms about the revolution and its causes and effects and subsequent developments, but little has yet been published about places outside Tehran, about people other than the Persian ruling elite (which includes most ayatollahs as well as the shahs), and about postrevolutionary society in general. As a possible exception concerning

2   *Introduction*

society as a whole, writings on Iran's women are plentiful but are still limited by their persisting emphasis on the secular, modern, West-oriented, professional, upper-middle and upper classes of Tehran, most of whose members do not back the Islamic Republic or rule by clergy.[2] I urge a closer look at the diversity of Iran's societies and cultures so readers can understand the ways that different sectors of the population support, comply with, challenge, oppose, or resist the policies and practices of the Islamic state.

This work is not an ethnography about Qashqa'i nomads, although it contains ethnographic aspects. While the study is based on my long-term anthropological research in Iran, it also presents an account of the nation-state as it transitioned from the rule of the last shah to that of the ayatollahs, and it draws on the large literature on the topic. While this literature concerns macropolitics, the current work emphases micropolitics and the ways in which people at the local level faced, responded to, and resisted the impact of the state. General political studies as well as works on specific topics, such as Iran's constitution, parliament, and conservative politico-religious ideologies, do not demonstrate how these institutions and ideas affected Iranians nationwide in their cities, towns, villages, and nomadic camps. Such topical discussions are necessary for understanding circumstances in Iran and the ways they have changed from one regime to the next, but readers also need to know how national-level issues relate to the local level and to people's lives.

What difference did it make to Iranians that a popular revolution overthrew the shah's regime and that hard-line conservative Muslim clergymen took control? This book addresses that question. The multiple answers provide information about the Qashqa'i but also extend beyond them to Iran as a whole. In some ways, local-level facts offer more insight about the Islamic Republic than do generalized studies about a particular facet of the new regime. The new government adopted a code of penalties for criminals, based on Islamic law, but how did the courts handle a Qashqa'i man who loaned his rifle to a Persian peasant, who then murdered a rival with the weapon?

Interlinking perspectives

In this book, I describe, discuss, and analyze the transformations experienced by people of the Qashqa'i tribal confederacy brought about by Iran's revolution in 1978–79 and the subsequent formation of an Islamic republic. I base this study on long-term anthropological research and personal observations and interactions in Iran and among Qashqa'i nomadic pastoralists there. My book *Nomad: A Year in the Life of a Qashqa'i Tribesman in Iran* details the same people during the annual seasonal cycle—autumn, winter, spring, and summer—of 1970–71 and includes historical information. In some ways, this new book begins where *Nomad* leaves off. *Nomads in Postrevolutionary Iran* also stands as an independent study but readers interested in the same group during the earlier period will find *Nomad* informative.

The general aims of this anthropological study are threefold and inter-related. They concern a longitudinal focus, an analysis of the impact of changing regimes in Iran, and a perspective from the local level.

First, the account presents a longitudinal perspective on current and former nomadic pastoralists in Iran. Seasonal and annual fluctuations in their lives were common, and a long-term view provides a representative account of these nomads and the ways their lives have altered. I conducted research with a single group on many occasions over a span of 44 years and have a broader view of its circumstances than if I had visited only once during this period.

The mobility and dispersal of the Qashqa'i and their frequently varying seasonal patterns of livelihoods, migrations, and residences complicate the issue of observing, documenting, and interpreting transformational processes. A settled community also engaged in seasonal activities but nomads usually experienced a wider range of differing patterns throughout a year. A researcher present for only a short period would have difficulty sorting out such diversity, understanding the complex processes of change, and concluding about general political, economic, and social patterns. Which variations were due to seasonal differences, ecologically diverse territories, mobility, widely dispersed people, and often changing livelihoods and residences? Which were due to broader processes such as a national revolution, a change in central governments, new market demands, environmental degradation, and expansion of settled popu-lations in the region? How did these diverse variations interconnect? How did the decisions of individuals, families, and local and wider groups figure into the emergence of this diversity?

Anthropologists and other social scientists rarely have opportunities outside their countries of origin and residence to conduct longitudinal research on multiple occasions in a single location or with a single group, especially in the Middle East and particularly in Iran. Many researchers spend a year or so in one place or with one community and then never return. Changing, sometimes volatile, political conditions may make subsequent visits difficult or impossible, and individual careers and choices also often figure against further work there. Many anthropological studies on the Middle East are based on a scholar's single visit.[3]

When a researcher spends only a year or so in one locale or community, she or he has difficulty discerning if changes have happened during that brief period and if any such changes are short term or long term, minor or major, non-recurrent or recurrent, or locally induced or responses to wider processes. The person will not know how each of these different kinds of change relates to the others. A minor, seemingly idiosyncratic, incident one year, for example, may prove to mark the beginning of a fundamental transformation connected to national, even international, circumstances. Without having prior experience there, the researcher does not know what occurrences are usual or unusual, significant or insignificant, and why. The person may not comprehend situations as being anomalous or extraordinary. Some parts of society and culture may experience major alterations over the short or long term while other parts of

4 Introduction

the same society and culture may not. Certain continuities in political, economic, social, and cultural life exist and are eventually discernible, but a short-term researcher may not be able to separate them from other aspects, some or all of which may be undergoing change. Readers of a monograph based on a single, short-term visit may be uncertain if the situation described is specific to that year (which could have been typical or unusual) or more general.

Historical and comparative research of diverse kinds solves some of these problems. A scholar focusing on contemporary Shiʻi Muslim passion plays in a village or urban quarter, for example, benefits by reading accounts of such performances in other historical periods and in different places and can judge how past events compare with the ones he or she observes.[4] A researcher can also draw on the perspectives of individuals who remember or heard about past performances and who can explain why they are or are not currently different. Confronting the past in this way, a writer is more likely than not to specify the dates of his or her research in the community and to employ the past tense (as compared with the "ethnographic present" tense) in publications. Anthropologists increasingly rely on various kinds of historical and comparative research, and the insights they derive from the effort assist them in comprehending current societies and cultures. They do recognize the limitations in understanding past events and similar occurrences in other locations when the circumstances in their own sites have changed or are changing dramatically. For many anthropologists (including me), historical documents of any kind are lacking for the specific people or group they study.[5]

This work's second aim is to offer information and analysis about the impact of changing regimes in Iran. When I first began research among the Qashqaʼi in 1970, the centralizing, modernizing, and secularizing government of Mohammad Reza Shah exerted power and authority over some dimensions of the nomads' lives. The book *Nomad* emphasizes the relationships between the state and the tribe at the time. When revolutionary forces threatened the shah and his supporting regime in 1977–78, change for the nomads seemed likely. When the shah and his regime toppled in 1979 and new figures of power and authority seized control and declared an Islamic republic, further alterations for the nomads appeared imminent. The Iraq–Iran war in 1980–88 and the state's continuing attempts at consolidation and stabilization exerted far-reaching impact. Despite these dramatic events, many aspects of the nomads' lives have continued in ways similar to the past. I describe and analyze the extent of transformations occurring over four decades as I focus on the ways that the nomads and two different kinds of regimes interacted.

My third aim, related to the first two, concerns life at the local level in Iran during the shah's last years and the Islamic Republic's first 35 years. In reading scholarly publications on the revolution and the Islamic regime, I saw how general the accounts often are and how infrequently their authors consider the ways these generalizations relate to people in their local communities. Many writers had not lived in Iran recently, if at all, and lacked detailed and personally derived information to supplement their accounts, which they drew primarily from newspapers, other publications, wire-service reports, and, later, the Internet.[6] They wrote many hundreds of books and thousands of articles—on the revolution, the collapse of the shah's regime, the rise and fall of leftist movements, Shi'i Islam in Iran, power and authority in the Islamic Republic, politico-religious ideologies, Islamization of the state, American hostages in Iran, the Iraq–Iran war, struggles between conservatives and reformists, the personalities and outcomes of national elections, Iran's nuclear industry, and international economic sanctions. Yet these works offer readers little information about how Iranians lived during this tumultuous period. Few of these texts address the essential question of this study. How did these national and international events affect Iranian society at the local level and impact the lives of ordinary citizens?[7]

Given the focus here on one regime in Iran ending and a new one emerging, I examine how state policies are "carried out, contested, reshaped, resisted, or revised" at the local level.[8] This level is "a crucial arena of social struggle ... and a unit of analysis to examine social change. It is the local that serves as the essential criterion and locus of change. ... It is in the localities that oppression is felt and resisted, where the people actually experience the effect of national policies."[9] An investigation of a small town in the provinces, for example, illuminates the "interconnected processes that may otherwise be overlooked if one were to focus exclusively on macronational events."[10] "What takes place in the provincial periphery of Iran today can tell us a lot about what takes place in the country as a whole."[11]

Even specialized scholarly studies, such as one on Iran's parliament and another on modern formal education in Iran, rarely provide a local-level perspective.[12] Their authors seem disinterested in offering such an outlook, which perhaps falls outside their academic disciplines and the research they conducted. Still, readers would benefit by learning about the ways that national institutions and programs affected people across Iran in their urban quarters, large and small towns, villages, and nomadic camps. In the case of the parliament, how did electoral candidates emerge from local districts? How did these individuals relate to local and national political groups and movements? What categories of people were their local backers? What local and wider factors motivated citizens to vote for one or another candidate? What impact did the winners have on these districts? In the case of formal education, how did local Islamic schools give way to modern, secular ones? How were new teachers trained, and what impact did they have on their students? What opportunities were available for the newly educated, and how did the expanding choices affect local communities?

In both of these cases, what changes occurred when the shah's modernizing, secularizing regime collapsed and a new (or renewed) coalition of forces led by hard-line Muslim clergymen formed a conservative Islamic state? How have these changes been sustained during the subsequent 35 years, and what new patterns have emerged? Where specifically did Islamic ideologies, practices, institutions, and personnel enter into the lives of the

6 Introduction

residents of local communities? What was the reach of an Islamic regime, and how did it affect different sectors of society (such as the rural poor or the urban rich)?

In writing this book, I needed to reconcile local facts as I knew them with published accounts about Iran as a whole. Was the local group with which I am familiar unusual in its practices and at odds with national ones? If so, how do I explain the differences? Or did the general accounts gloss over or ignore regional and local circumstances? Did their authors lack experience there or consider such locations and settings unimportant? Were these general accounts perhaps wrong? Their authors might not have lived in Iran recently, if at all. If they did visit, they rarely traveled beyond certain parts of the capital of Tehran or perhaps several other large cities.

In my focus on regions distant from Tehran and on the rural, tribal, ethnic, and minority peoples there, I offer a different kind of perspective on Iranian society and culture during the revolutionary and postrevolutionary periods. In this local-level study, I avoid some problems evident in general studies on Iran, in which authors make sweeping statements about the entire country when they comment, for example, on the changing status of women, politicization of the ethnic minorities, or opposition against the Islamic Republic. Such statements may indeed apply only to certain sectors of Tehran.

Writers who address a Western audience already familiar with negative images about Iran, the Middle East, Islam, and Muslims often exaggerate how the shah, the revolution, the ayatollahs, the Islamic Republic, the Iraq–Iran war, and Iran's defiance against the West have transformed Iranian society. This study offers a more balanced perspective by demonstrating widespread and local-level continuities as well as major changes.

Julia Huang's statement in *Tribeswomen of Iran: Weaving Memories among Qashqa'i Nomads* (2009: 4) is pertinent to my study as well:

> The Qashqa'i, as speakers of Turkish and one of Iran's many ethnic and national minorities, do not represent all other Iranians but they do share traits with the wider society. For example, the Qashqa'i, along with many Iranians, expressed exhilaration about the mounting protests against Mohammad Reza Shah in 1978–79 but were uncertain about who or what would replace him. When Iran's Muslim clergy seized control in 1979 and took steps to form an Islamic state, the Qashqa'i wondered how and to what extent would the new government apply Shi'i doctrine and practice to their lives. The Qashqa'i suffered appalling personal losses during the Iraq–Iran war (1980–88). They confronted hostile hezbollahis (partisans of the party of God) and defied the state's prohibitions against supposedly un-Islamic behavior. They grappled with rampant inflation and the scarcity of jobs. They sought higher education to gain new occupations. And they hoped to bring about reform in the state and society by voting for a moderate presidential candidate. In their day-to-day lives, members of this small Qashqa'i group encountered many of the

Introduction 7

same difficulties that other Iranians faced, and they devised similar coping strategies. Thus, this detailed account of their community resonates widely.

The process of research

I began research among the Qermezi tribespeople in 1970 and lived with them during many subsequent visits. Some Qashqa'i asked me why I did not choose other Qashqa'i tribes and subtribes, for which I often received invitations. My reasons for staying with one group center on the historical and longitudinal perspectives addressed in this book. I was not isolated while living among the Qermezi; they were dispersed across a vast territory of the southern Zagros Mountains, a region with which I became familiar. I often visited other Qashqa'i groups and locations for comparative purposes, and the Qermezi frequently entertained visitors from the wider Qashqa'i tribal confederacy and from other regional, tribal, and ethnic groups. My long-term research with the Qashqa'i tribal elite in Iran and in exile abroad (an issue not discussed in this book) has also offered me contact with and knowledge about a wide range of Qashqa'i people. By focusing on the Qermezi, I avoid some problems inherent in generalizing for the Qashqa'i as a whole. Yet this group is a vital part of the wider Qashqa'i society and represents it in many ways, and thus I can extend some observations more broadly.

This book derives specifically from my research after the revolution but also relates to my earlier studies. Initially I conducted research among the Qermezi in 1970–71 and on two separate occasions in 1977 and then continued in 1979 just after the revolution and the Islamic Republic's formation. Constraining political circumstances in Iran in the 1980s limited the possibilities for work there: the seizure of American hostages in 1979 and their detention until 1981, the Iraq–Iran war of 1980–88 (including Iraqi missile attacks on cities distant from the front line), and the sentiments of some state officials and supporters against the United States. I could have visited the Qermezi in the 1980s, given what was even then our long-term relationship, but I did not want to draw attention to them because of their American guest. I resumed research in 1991, accompanied by my five-year-old daughter, Julia Huang, and returned 10 more times (in 1992, twice in 1995, and in 1996, 1997, 1998, 1999, 2000–01, 2001–02, and 2004), always with Julia except once. Julia and I were traveling to Iran for further research in 2009 when popular protests over the presidential election erupted. Political circumstances in Iran since then have made the research of Americans there difficult.

Since 1979 (and through 2013), I have maintained continual contact with the Qermezi and those who know them through letters, telephone calls, and, increasingly, the Internet. Naheed Dareshuri travels to Iran annually, visits the Qermezi, and gathers information for me. She is a member of the Darrehshuri tribe, of which the Qermezi group is a part, and has known its members all

8   Introduction

her life. Throughout the book, I update information through 2013, depending on the subject matter and my personal communications.

During my initial research in 1970–71 and 1977, I experienced the four seasons and many territorial locations. My 12 visits after the revolution were also spread over the four seasons (for example, one trip in the winter and spring, another in the summer and autumn) and in many locales. Such broad, long-term, multiple-site exposure facilitates a comprehensive overview of the people's seasonal mobility, changing places of residence, and diverse activities. It also provides the details of day-to-day life for people and their communities. I focused my research on change over time and relied on oral history. No archival or other written historical material is available for this specific Qashqa'i group.[13] The results of my continuing, wider research on the Qashqa'i tribal confederacy do not appear obvious in all sections of this book but do aid in my understanding of the ways that local events relate to broader circumstances.

Until the early 2000s, I was the only American scholar to begin or resume anthropological research in Iran after the revolution, and I enjoyed unrestricted access.[14] Iran's officials permitted my work (while systematically denying access to other American anthropologists), perhaps because of my long-term interests in Iran, the ways I interacted there, and my chosen topics and publications. I had attended university in Shiraz in 1963–64, returned to Iran to conduct doctoral-dissertation research in 1969–71, and developed new projects there in 1977 and 1979. Influential authorities responded positively when I expressed an interest in coming to Iran in 1991. If I had wanted to work in other parts of Iran or among other groups after the revolution, I might have experienced difficulty, but I chose to return to a familiar community. Some officials interested in nomads were of nomadic, tribal, and ethnic-minority backgrounds themselves (unlike during the shah's regime) and supported my intention to document economic and social changes. My wide-ranging publications did not seem to raise concern among any authorities. At least several writings drew their praise, including one they regarded as an explicit rejoinder to *Not Without My Daughter*, a book and film containing negative portrayals of Iran, Iranians, and Islam.[15]

From the beginning, the anthropological methods I used to conduct research among the Qermezi and other Qashqa'i centered on participant observation and informal discussion. During each visit, I resided with Borzu Qermezi (the political leader of the Qermezi subtribe) and his immediate and extended family, with whom I formed close relationships. Borzu's role as the headman enabled me to learn about and interact with the wider community. Many Qermezi frequently came to consult with him, and I often accompanied him when he traveled within the widely dispersed group. He often met with the Darrehshuri tribal khans, under whose authority his subtribe fell, and I learned about their place in the tribal hierarchy and their larger networks. Borzu enjoyed wide-ranging contacts within the Darrehshuri tribe, the Qashqa'i tribal confederacy, other regional tribes and ethnic groups, and the surrounding

Introduction 9

Iranian society. He often dealt with state agents of different sorts; I heard their discussions and occasionally visited government offices with him. Thus I came to appreciate more people and their diverse roles and settings than my residence in Borzu's tent and camp would imply.

After Borzu died in 1995, I continued my relationships with his immediate and extended family and his tribal group. Close to death, he had worried that my friendship with those he was leaving behind would end, and I assured him that I would remain in close contact. His sons, Dariush and Bizhan, now headed his household, and I lived with them during subsequent visits. My ties with other family and group members intensified, and I continued to observe and learn about their links with other Qashqa'i groups, other tribes and ethnic groups, government agencies, and the wider society. Although based in Borzu's family, I often visited other Qermezi in their diverse, widely separated locations and enhanced my knowledge of their tribal polity.

Participant observation centers on the task of participating in daily events while at the same time observing them. Over the years, as the process grew familiar, I hesitated less often about joining in, and my understanding of the group and its activities and attitudes expanded. When people asked my opinion, I was less likely than before to withhold my views. I knew they depended on many perspectives, of which mine was only one. Unlike some male anthropologists who lacked much access to women and children in the communities in which they lived or visited, I had always enjoyed unrestricted interactions with men, women, and children. A wide range of people participated in my research activities over the years.

I conducted informal interviews with people alone, with several others, and in small groups. I raised questions and topics and relied on their answers and comments. With these and other individuals, I listened to and joined general conversations in which issues arose that I might not have introduced on my own. Unanticipated events, such as the return of a prisoner of war from Iraq, provoked especially useful discussions. Arriving visitors brought information from outside, which my hosts (and I) welcomed. Being so widely dispersed, the Qermezi depended on news from beyond their small and often isolated residential communities to inform their decisions. Somewhat less mobile than men, women in particular sought external contacts.

When I first began research among the Qermezi in 1970, I found the thousands of personal names, multiple interlinking kinship connections, complicated personal and family histories, and many group and place names to be daunting until I began to compile lists of people, families, groups, territories, places, and activities. These lists had grown by the 1990s and early 2000s because of the expansion and dispersion of the group and the increasing complexity of its members' lives. I was no longer able to remember all these facts and increasingly relied on the data, which I updated during each research trip and after my return home when I reorganized the material. While interacting with the Qermezi, I kept the compiled data sheets close by and often consulted them for details, and I entered new information at the time and later. This

10   *Introduction*

assemblage intrigued people; it increasingly contained extensive data that no single person could possibly know. Each individual held information based on her or his specific background and set of experiences. Borzu Qermezi, for example, could readily recite the minute details of a tribal feud breaking out half a century earlier but needed to consult his wife Falak when I asked him the name of his one-year-old grandchild then running in circles around us. (At the time he did have 32 other grandchildren and several great-grandchildren to keep in mind.) Young people in particular lacked the comprehensive historical, territorial, and genealogical information so highly valued by their elders.[16]

The compiled data, frequently updated and reorganized, include lists and tables covering many categories. I added information whenever people and I interacted in person and by telephone, letter, and email.

This material includes a comprehensive genealogy of each senior head of household in the Qermezi subtribe, which contains his lineage affiliation, paternal and maternal ancestors and their spouses and other kin, siblings and their spouses and children, wife or wives, and children and grandchildren and their spouses. (I include junior heads of households in the father's entry.) I note personal information such as dates (birth, marriage, and death), formal education, military service, occupation, leadership position, and unusual circumstances (such as someone killed by lightning or abducted as a toddler). Given the society's patriarchal, patrilineal, and patrilocal characteristics, I list people by their connection to male heads of households.[17]

These extensive genealogies enable me to see at a glance the extent of a person's kinship, marital, lineage, tribal, and extra-tribal ties. I also assembled the genealogies of people affiliated with the Qermezi subtribe, usually through marriage and/or co-residence. When marriage linked a Qermezi person to another tribal group for the first time, other marriages were likely to follow, and the genealogies tracked these developments. When a Qermezi visitor to summer pastures delivered the news that Safdar Qermezi had just agreed to marry his daughter to a boy in another Darrehshuri subtribe, people protested that the boy's family was unrelated to her. They regarded the match as unfortunate, even tragic, for the girl, who would from now on reside with the boy's kindred far away. Yet, when we checked the details in the entry on Safdar's father, we saw that the genealogy proved a kinship link, although distant and two generations earlier. People seemed somewhat reassured.

Other data include:

A list of every household head (organized by his lineage or the group with which he was affiliated), the location of his winter and summer pastures, the existence (if any) of permanent dwellings, and his occupation and multiple means of livelihood. Many of these facts changed from year to year.

Every location in which the Qermezi lived, each locale listing the Qermezi there and their lineage and other identities. Most people resided in two or

Introduction 11

more places during a year (most commonly in multiple sites in winter pastures and in summer pastures), and these facts also changed frequently. A new government project in 1999 to build a village for some Qermezi nomads opened another topic of research for me, and I began to chronicle its development.

People's occupations other than nomadic pastoralism and agriculture. The most comprehensive entry covers schoolteachers. Organized chronologically and by lineage, it includes the dates and places of training and service. Other entries include information about army soldiers, revolutionary guards, *basij* militia volunteers, factory workers, women employed outside the home, and other wage and salaried employees.

The nine Qermezi primary schools, including their histories and teachers, compiled chronologically.

Students, including those attending the government's special elementary, middle, and high schools for nomads. One list contains all the university students and their institutions, years of study, disciplines, degrees, and resulting occupations. A separate list covers the subtribe's four students in theological seminaries. Through the years I tracked each student's educational trajectory and outcome.

Casualties of the Iraq–Iran war, including the dead, the missing, the wounded, and the prisoners of war, with information about the branch of service, experience, government assistance, medical care, and burial place.

Economic data, including the prices of commodities bought and sold, wages, and household wealth (sheep, goats, camels, horses, mules, donkeys, handwoven textiles, land, orchards, other agricultural plots, houses, and motorized vehicles). I compiled a new list every visit and compared economic facts from year to year.

Shorter lists cover pilgrims to Mashhad, Mecca, and Damascus; hezbollahis (partisans of the party of God); and elected members of local Islamic councils. Another list includes details about the Persian and Lur cultivators who seized Qermezi pastureland. I compiled information on the Qashqa'i candidates for Iran's national parliament (including a Qermezi man) and on the histories, locations, and leaders of the 44 Darrehshuri subtribes (of which Qermezi is one).

Over the years I considered opportunities to conduct research within other Qashqa'i groups. Yet I was reluctant to do so because of the importance of continuing longitudinal research among the Qermezi. The task of assembling for another group the kind of data I hold for the Qermezi would be impossible, especially given the constraints and unpredictability of doing lengthy research in Iran. If I had chosen another or other Qashqa'i communities, I would have limited my research to a specific topic, but I still would have needed to acquire a comprehensive understanding of the new settings. My long-term friendships with so many Qermezi were also a decisive reason not to shift my interest elsewhere.

12 *Introduction*

With my daughter

My daughter, Julia Huang, accompanied me first in 1991 when she was five years old. She has been with me ever since, except in 1992 when the trip conflicted with the start of her first grade in elementary school. Julia's enthusiasm for the evolving experience motivated me. Sometimes I joked that I accompanied her, rather than she coming with me, because she brought so much energy and focus to the trips.

Our first visit together transformed me into a "mother" when previously people saw me mainly as a scholar and a university professor. They watched how Julia and I interacted and treated me differently. When I visited without her in 1992, everyone worried about her well-being and the separation's impact on us. If I sat pensively, someone might declare, "You're thinking about Julia right now." I had told university colleagues at home that I was traveling to Iran alone because the trip coincided with Julia's beginning first grade, but no one expressed any sentiment about my leaving her behind. When I arrived at the nomads' summer pastures, I encountered a quite different, heart-warming response.

From Julia's first day among the Qermezi, the many animals in the camp drew her attention, and the nomads appreciated her spirited interest in their means of livelihood. Already responsive to animals, the children there quickly understood that they could include Julia in their activities without needing a common spoken language. Her first treks away from the camp were to accompany children on missions to find lost lambs, water thirsty donkeys, and track wild boars. Soon, people of all ages invited her to come along when they engaged in their tasks, especially unusual, often season-specific, ones (such as collecting plants growing high on the mountain slopes and used for dyeing wool for weaving).

Julia spent most of her time with women and children by engaging in their activities and interactions, and she moved more freely within and between camps than I did. She avoided the formality that sometimes restricted me (and other adults). When invited for a meal, we both received hospitable attention, but when she dropped by on her own to see friends, people treated her as they would their own children. As her skills in Qashqa'i Turkish and Persian increased, she expanded her relationships. Three close friends in particular—a woman, a teenage girl, and a man—wanted to learn English, and she helped them with basic vocabulary, grammar, and expression. In turn, they and others eagerly taught her Turkish.

Julia appreciated people's affectionate responses to her and benefited by her rich associations. Adults in the United States often ignore children in their midst, even in contexts ostensibly created for children such as school fairs and birthday parties, or they offer a routine greeting or a pat on the head before resuming their adult conversations. By contrast, the Qermezi paid warm and seemingly genuine attention to children, who learned from a young age that their place in the local society and the wider group was vital and that their

Introduction 13

activities and opinions mattered. Children participated fully in family and community work and leisure and held an intrinsic value equivalent to or greater than that of adults, who regarded these individuals as younger versions of themselves rather than as a separate category. The way they treated children demonstrated their interest in forming individuals who could successfully carry forward the society and culture.[18]

My daughter introduced new dimensions to my interactions with the nomads and brought a fresh perspective to my research. Many of the scenes I describe in this book have added significance because I also saw them through Julia's young eyes and often needed to explain them to her then or later. For instance, her excitement about watching the nomads surgically extract the gall bladder (to use as an antidote for snake-bite venom) from a dead wild hyena highlighted my own impressions of that day. Julia observed and participated in aspects of the nomads' lives with which I was not as familiar as she was becoming, and she relayed many of these experiences to me the same day or later, even years later. Until I read the first draft of her book (*Tribeswomen of Iran: Weaving Memories among Qashqa'i Nomads*), I did not know about many of her activities, observations, and insights.[19] Before Julia had learned much Qashqa'i Turkish, I saw that she was already skilled in interpreting body language and other nonverbal cues. When we visited nomads she had not met before, she would see evidence of the special tie between a person and her or his mother's brother, before I had the presence of mind to process the kinship links among the many individuals present. She also sensed people's moods and understood if they were distressed about some matter. I would see her sitting quietly beside someone, often holding the person's hand, as she offered comfort.

Julia's sense of humor and fascination with what the nomads would consider the ordinary details of the livelihood and lifestyle (such as a goat trapped by its curved horns in the branches of a tree) connected her with others and brought forth their spontaneous laughter. As a five-year-old, Julia asked me one noon about the "king" who had not yet joined our large luncheon gathering. When I translated for the others present, no one understood who she meant. I asked her to explain. She referred to a man who always wore a "crown," and with a stick she drew its outline in the dirt (a technique she had learned from the nomads). Someone then realized that she must mean the Persian man who lived in a small canvas tent in the valley below, tended his beehives there, and ate meals with us. His felt hat had sharp peaks, similar to the crown that Babar the Elephant wore, and she had assumed that he was Iran's king (or shah) who periodically ambled up the mountain slope to grace us with his presence.[20] The thought that this unassuming man could possibly be Iran's shah amused and delighted everyone, especially because he had sought refuge in their humble tribe and had evaded the disgrace of forced exile and an ignominious death in a foreign land.

Julia's spirited and emotional relationships with so many of the nomads drew us all closer, and now I cannot imagine living among the Qermezi without her.

14 *Introduction*

Organization of the book

My original idea for this book came in 1995 just after Borzu Qermezi had died. I saw how many people were troubled, even distraught, by his passing, and I decided to write an account that would detail this response as well as serve as a tribute to him. The research I conducted that summer focused on his funeral and memorial services and the many people who came to pay their respects to his family and group.

Then I recalled how each of my recent research trips had stressed one or more significant events, not necessarily those I had initially chosen to study but ones that had captivated people's attention during the months I lived among them. Each subsequent visit I concentrated on the situations that dominated discussions. Shahriyar Qermezi's election to Iran's national parliament in 1996, for instance, not only consumed people's interest but also held wider merit as an unprecedented event to document. Mohammad Karim Qermezi's strategy to abandon nomadic pastoralism, especially given the distress these efforts caused his tribesmates, is another example. Abbas Qermezi's implication in a murder is a third one. As ideas for this book took shape, I decided to organize its contents according to the events occurring each year I was present. I would emphasize the circumstances that people marked as noteworthy. The 11 opportunities for research in the 1990s and early 2000s meant that I could explore a range of diverse topics as they occurred chronologically, following the years I was present.

I had always lacked interest in writing typical ethnographic accounts, the kind still common in cultural anthropology. When some colleagues and friends wrote about the personal experience of conducting anthropological research, often using perspectives encouraged by postmodernism, I was not convinced that these approaches, for me, would produce material of lasting import. If I narrated my personal activities, I feared that the Qermezi would become mere backdrops to the anthropologist's supposed discoveries, insights, and mistakes. I was intrigued, though, by novel forms of writing and new ways of communicating information about people in different kinds of societies and cultures. My efforts to write *Nomad* had been satisfying, and I hoped to write in a similar vein in this new book. The previous book's format—the stages of the seasonal cycle—would not fit the current one because of the new dynamics of nomadic pastoralism, the diversifying experiences of the expanding group, and the multiyear research.

After reviewing my extensive notes, data collections, and daily journals and then preparing a detailed outline of the book, I began to write about what was then the most recent period of research, whose events and circumstances were most distinct in mind. When drafts of those sections were complete, I turned to the previous year. Before beginning to write, I again read research notes and journals for that year and reworked the outline of the topics I planned to cover. I continued to write in reverse chronological order. When I encountered information and observations in notes and journals that would fit in other sections, I filed them to add later.

Introduction 15

An early chapter needed to contain information essential to subsequent ones, and two of its six sections could not be explicitly event oriented. Its contents would cover the revolution's impact and the following two to three decades instead of only one year, and it resulted from years of research. I could not easily include these details in the focused accounts on which I based later chapters. As I continued research among the Qermezi in 2000–01, 2001–02, and 2004 and via telephone, letter, and email during this period and to the present day, I asked the questions emerging as I wrote the manuscript and updated each chapter. During annual trips to Iran and via the telephone and the Internet, Naheed Dareshuri gathered further data for me.

In this book, I integrate relevant historical, political, economic, social, and cultural information in each chapter's narratives, just as I did in *Nomad*. When I discuss Bahram Qermezi's postponed wedding, for example, I also explain changes in marriage ceremonies since the revolution, the nomads' defiance against the regime's attempts to prohibit music and dance, the roles of hezbollahis in society, and the rituals of death and mourning.

While I wrote and revised this book, I also read the growing literature on Iran, the revolution, the war, the elections, the popular protests, and other events. Information and interpretations coming from a range of scholars (and some journalists) assisted me in understanding better the wider context of the lives of the Qashqa'i. In the course of his or her account, an author may comment, for example, on Ayatollah Tahiri or the death of Ayatollah Khomeini's first son. Inclusions such as these helped me to establish a small part of the larger story I was telling. Thus, while relating material about Qashqa'i nomads, I was also attentive to the larger arena in ways that may help readers to fit the local narrative into a context they may already understand.

(Ayatollah Jalal ud-Din Tahiri, Friday prayer leader of Isfahan and later a parliamentary deputy, had intervened in 1980 in the arrests of Qashqa'i men who had supported the tribal khans [Chapter 3]. Some Qashqa'i nomads compared the national political response to the unexpected death of Khomeini's second son in 1995 with that following the untimely death of his first son in 1977 [Chapter 5].)

The format of this book is chronological and topic driven. If my overall aim is to examine the transitions these current and former nomadic pastoralists have experienced in Iran since the revolution, then the structure of the book itself also demonstrates a diachronic approach. Due to the format, readers will see broad changes as well as year-to-year ones and will understand that a major alteration one year might be reversed the next. For instance, Mohammad Karim Qermezi abandoned nomadic pastoralism in 1997 in ways that seemed definitive at the time, but in 1998 he reconstituted his herd and resumed the livelihood and lifestyle he cherished. His seemingly conflicting decisions represent the situations faced by all Qermezi during difficult times, and they express the continuities and transformations in their society and culture and within a broader Iranian context.

16 *Introduction*

Notes

1 Bromberger (1989, 2013), Friedl (1989, 1997), and I provide several exceptions. Iranians living in Iran or visiting from abroad have experienced more opportunities for research than foreigners have done but they tended to focus their attention on other kinds of studies. Local-level studies of nomadic pastoralists in Iran before the revolution include Barth (1961), Beck (1991), Black-Michaud (1986), Bradburd (1990, 1998), Irons (1975), Salzman (1992, 2000), and Tapper (1979).

2 Most authors who discuss women during and after the revolution generalize for all women in Iran despite the many socioeconomic, educational, occupational, political, linguistic, ethnic, religious, regional, and tribal variations characterizing their lives. Most of these publications are valid for only certain segments of secular, urban (usually Tehran), middle-class and upper-class Persian society. Journalists visiting Iran during and after the revolution sometimes provide glimpses of local-level life derived from their brief encounters with hotel workers, taxi drivers, and the family members and servants of their interviewees. Naipaul's books on Islam (1981, 1999) contain chapters on Iran that demonstrate these techniques.

3 Each of the three anthropological works on nomadic peoples residing near or among the Qashqa'i is based on a single, short-term visit. Barth's *Nomads of South Persia* (1961) is possibly the best-known anthropological study of Iran. Salzer (1974) and Swee (1981) wrote doctoral dissertations that are not widely accessible. Two Austrian anthropologists conducted research over a four-decade period in a Boir Ahmad Lur village in Iran (Friedl 1989, 1997, 2014; Loeffler 1988, 2011). Hegland (2014) revisited the Persian village in which she had earlier resided. Tapper (1997: 309–14) summarizes changes for Shahsevan tribespeople. Nadjmabadi (2004, 2009a, 2010) examines her continuing research among Iran's Arabs along the Persian Gulf coast. Digard and Karimi (1989) comment on change among the Bakhtiyari. Ajami (2005) (a sociologist) returned in 1999 and 2002 to a village northwest of Shiraz where he had conducted research in 1967. E. Hooglund (1982a, 1997) (a political scientist) studied land use in a Persian village near Shiraz in 1978–79 and briefly revisited in 1997. These kinds of studies, demonstrating the productive results of longitudinal, long-term, multiple-visit research, are not common.

4 Aghaie's (2005) collection on ritual expressions among contemporary Shi'i Muslims in multiple countries demonstrates such an approach.

5 General historical studies on the Qashqa'i include Beck (1986) and Oberling (1975) but no published work (other than my own) or archival records (other than its name in lists) offer historical information on the Qermezi subtribe I consider here.

6 Writers on postrevolutionary Iran can be grouped into three categories: "those who have been totally detached from the society though not necessarily from the events; those who have remained on the periphery, and thus have maintained some contacts; and those who have lived in the society with a keen interest in its development" (Amirahmadi 1990: xvii).

7 Chehabi (1997) offers an unusual, welcome account of local politics as expressed in the creation of a new province (Ardabil) in Iran. A. Bayat (1997) discusses rural migrants and their grassroots movements in urban Iran. Ehsani (2009) examines postrevolutionary developments in a small town in Khuzistan. Memoirs by Iranians contain the personal experiences of the authors before, during, and after the revolution (Ebadi 2007; Farman Farmaian 1992; Farmanfarmaian and Farmanfarmaian 2005; Hakakian 2004; Nafisi 2003, 2008). These last accounts pertain to Iran's modern, secular, urban, West-oriented, Persian upper and middle classes and provide little information about the rest of society. Amirahmadi (1990: 12) notes the difficulties in presenting a comprehensive, accurate analysis of Iran's

Introduction 17

economy. The "many unknowns about the complex forces influencing post-revolutionary Iran" include "information about the minute transformations that have occurred ... in the social relations at the class, family, and individual levels."

8 Chehabi (1997: 235).

9 A. Bayat (1997: 5).

10 Ehsani (2009: 39).

11 Ehsani (2009: 65).

12 Baktiari (1996), Menashri (1992), Nomani and Behdad (2006), and others offer national-level studies. They provide readers with a broad understanding of the chosen topics but do not consider how such issues affect average citizens or local communities. Schirazi's study (1993) of land reform in postrevolutionary Iran offers some local-level cases.

13 See note 5 in this chapter.

14 Mary Hooglund (later, Hegland) began research in Iran in 1978 and stayed until December 1979 but did not return until short visits in 2003–08. Tober conducted research in Iran in 2002. Two Austrian anthropologists (Friedl and Loeffler) periodically visited Iran since the 1960s, and several other European anthropologists (including Bromberger and Digard), also aided by their citizenship, went to Iran then. Several Iranian anthropologists (including Shahshahani), one a long-term resident of Great Britain (Mir-Hosseini) and another of France and Germany (Nadjmabadi), also worked in Iran. Fazeli (2006) discusses the work of Iranian (but not foreign) anthropologists in Iran, and Nadjmabadi (2009b) offers the wider perspectives of some anthropologists who conducted research there. Hegland (2009) provides details and a bibliography of anthropological works on Iran. Spooner (1984, 1998) gives overviews of cultural anthropological research in Iran based on participant observation.

15 Mahmoody (1987). Starring Sally Fields, the film of the same name was released in 1991. Parts were filmed in Israel with the support of the Israeli government and immigrant Iranian Jews who played roles as fanatical, violent Muslims conniving to prevent an American woman from leaving Iran with her American-born, American-Iranian daughter. Decades after its publication, *Not Without My Daughter* still commanded attention. At the airport in Doha, Qatar, in 2011–13, the book continued to be the most prominently displayed in a large collection of works in English on the Persian Gulf region. Another book, translated from the German as *Not Without My Husband* (Harun-Mahdavi 2006), aims to challenge Mahmoody's negative account.

16 I prepared multiple copies of the compiled data for key members of the group when many people expressed an interest in this—their own—history.

17 I also assembled genealogies of the Darrehshuri and other Qashqa'i khans, which are crucial in my studies of the wider Qashqa'i tribal confederacy.

18 My views differ from those of Friedl (1989, 1997) on issues concerning children and childhood. She conducted research among Boir Ahmad Lur tribespeople similar to the Qashqa'i. Friedl (1998) and her daughter Agnes Loeffler (1998) explain their different perspectives on a shared experience among these Lurs. Tober (2004) discusses the issue of doing research in Iran while accompanied by children.

19 Julia Huang (2009; see also Huang 2006) offers accounts of her interactions and experiences. Shryock and Howell (2001) offer similarly varying, thought-provoking perspectives on a shared anthropological research experience in Jordan.

20 Babar the Elephant is a fictional character originally intended for French children (de Brunhoff 1937).

2   Past and present: Forty-four years of transformation

In this chapter, I describe and explain transformations in the society and culture of the Qermezi subtribe of the Qashqa'i tribal confederacy from 1970 through 2013, a span of 44 years. *Nomad: A Year in the Life of a Qashqa'i Tribesman in Iran* covers a single year (1970–71) of the nomads' experiences, and the current book focuses on the postrevolutionary period (1979–2013). Thus, an account of the overall processes of change during the last three decades of the twentieth century and into the second decade of the twenty-first is warranted. *The Qashqa'i of Iran*, my socio-historical study of the Qashqa'i tribal confederacy and its three-hundred-year relationship with the Iranian state, presents yet another kind of wider view.[1]

The Qashqa'i are one of Iran's largest and most prominent tribal, ethno-linguistic, and national-minority groups.[2] Their Turkish language derives from their ancestors and affiliates who lived in Central Eurasia and the Caucasus Mountains many centuries ago. As a significant sociopolitical group, the Qashqa'i tribal confederacy emerged in southwestern Iran in the late 1600s and became prominent in the 1750s during Karim Khan Zand's rule (1750–79) just before Qajar rule (1796–1925) began. The Qashqa'i population in 1970 totaled approximately 250,000 individuals. In 2013 the numbers had grown to perhaps 1.5 million, a sixfold increase in four decades.[3] Iran's population nearly tripled in the same 40 years, from 28 to 79 million.[4]

Qermezi ("The Red Ones") is one of 44 subtribes (*tireh*) of the Darrehshuri tribe (*tayafih, il*), one of the five major tribes of the Qashqa'i confederacy (*il*).[5] The subtribe provided the people with their primary sociopolitical frame of reference and played a significant role in their lives. Each Darrehshuri subtribe had its own history, territories, leaders, economic activities, and reputations, and together they identified as the sociopolitical components of the Darrehshuri tribe, whose history, territories, and leaders were also distinctive. Twenty-three of the 44 Darrehshuri subtribes are mentioned in this book. These names, along with the names of tribes, are the primary identifiers of the Qashqa'i. I avoid including subtribal names when they do not add useful information for the reader, but the fact that 23 of them appear in the book speaks to the ways that the Darrehshuri subtribes relate to one another and form the larger tribal unit.[6]

Forty-four years of transformation   19

The Qermezi subtribe consists of five sections (*bunku, bailay*), each defined by patrilineal ties. These named lineages—Aqa Mohammadli, Imamverdili, Qairkhbaili, Qasemli, and Kachili—were the major frames of reference for the Qermezi in their daily lives and local communities. Each Qermezi lineage was preferentially endogamous but some marriages also occurred between them. The Qermezi did not often marry with members of other Darrehshuri subtribes and even less frequently with other Qashqa'i tribes. Strongly discouraged, marriage outside the Qashqa'i community was rare. The five lineages shared many features but each also was characterized by distinguishing practices and reputations.

The Qermezi subtribe in 2000 contained 401 independent households consisting of nuclear and extended families, more than a threefold increase since 1970. At any given time or season, the subtribe's members were dispersed in small residential communities throughout winter and summer pastures and the periphery. Many continued to practice nomadic pastoralism in the customary ways in 2013, while some others lived part time or full time in villages and towns and engaged in a variety of livelihoods including pastoralism, agriculture, wage and salaried labor, and textile production.

Circumstances in 1970

The Qermezi subtribe in 1970 fell under the political authority of a single headman (*kadkhuda*), Borzu Qermezi, chosen by group consensus. All subtribal headmen had been subject to the authority of the khans of the Darrehshuri tribe until 1962, when Mohammad Reza Shah (r. 1941–79) suppressed their political activities. These khans, along with the khans of the other Qashqa'i tribes, had come under the loosely structured authority of the paramount leader (*ilkhani*) of the Qashqa'i confederacy until 1954, when the shah forced him and his likely successors into exile from Iran. The subtribal headmen were the only leaders in these three levels of the political hierarchy who functioned fully in 1970. They still met with the khans of their tribes, despite the state's attempted interference.

Qashqa'i tribes and subtribes also came under the authority of the Iranian state in 1970, particularly the coercive forces of the secret police, nomads' security force, and rural police (gendarmerie). The shah aimed to consolidate, centralize, and modernize Iran in the 1950s and thereafter and tried to exert control over the Qashqa'i and other tribal and ethnolinguistic peoples whom he perceived as political and military threats. He did not deploy the brutal methods of his father Reza Shah (r. 1925–41), but he too wanted to settle the Qashqa'i and other nomads in villages and towns, control them politically, and integrate and assimilate them in a modernizing Iran.

Qermezi and other Qashqa'i nomads faced the disruptions of land reform and pasture nationalization begun by Mohammad Reza Shah in 1962 as part of his "bloodless" revolution.[7] Forcibly disarmed at the same time, they watched as state agencies seized control of land formerly regulated by tribal leaders.

20 Forty-four years of transformation

Conflict with non-Qashqa'i agriculturalists and other competitors over land escalated. Insecure about problematic land rights, some nomads decided to establish permanent residences. A Qermezi family founded Atakula village in summer pastures in 1966, and others were under pressure to settle there or elsewhere. Yet most members of the subtribe persisted with customary pastoralism and nomadism, regardless of any houses they might have built or rented.

Mobile residents of the plateaus, slopes, and valleys of the southern Zagros Mountains, Qermezi nomads, like virtually all Qashqa'i nomads, migrated seasonally between lowland winter pastures (*qishlaq, garmsir*) near the Persian Gulf and highland summer pastures (*yailaq, sarhad*) hundreds of kilometers to the north and east. Each Qashqa'i tribe and subtribe exercised rights over specific grazing lands in these two locales. The nomads relied on camels and other pack animals to transport their black goat-hair tents and the rest of their possessions on these arduous, semiannual treks, each lasting from one to three months.

The Qermezi economy was based on the annual sale of live sheep and goats in regional markets and on the periodic sale of other pastoral products, including dairy goods, handwoven textiles, sheep wool, and goat hair. Through barter, credit, and cash, the nomads acquired items they did not produce themselves. When drought struck in 1970–71, they could not sell enough healthy livestock to offset their expenses. They fell deeply in debt to non-Qashqa'i urban merchants and moneylenders who charged annual interest rates of 50 to 100 percent. Debt followed the nomads from season to season; they used any accruing income to pay off the expenditures and interest payments of previous seasons. Pressure to abandon nomadic pastoralism grew, but the nomads also doubted their ability to earn adequate livings as part of the rapidly expanding, often impoverished, rural and urban proletariat, especially in locations where they lacked supportive social systems.[8] For similar economic and social reasons, no men sought wage labor outside Iran, such as in nearby Kuwait or other Persian Gulf states. Other options and opportunities were either unavailable or considered impossible. The nomads' detailed knowledge of environmental conditions taught them that productive years followed disastrous ones, and so most nomads tenaciously maintained their customary subsistence practices while waiting for the drought to end.

Flexible patterns of mobility and residence characterized the nomads' local social organization. The basic social unit was a household containing a nuclear or extended family. Headed by the eldest man, this unit owned its livestock and independently chose its political, economic, and social endeavors. Gender patterns resulted in part from the demands of the arduous pastoral and nomadic livelihood and lifestyle, which required the intensive, inter-related labor of all men, women, and children, each of whom possessed the skills to perform all necessary tasks.[9] Women exercised some power and authority over their activities and those of others. They did not cover their heads or bodies in constraining ways, and they were not secluded or socially

Forty-four years of transformation   21

limited in their movements. Throughout the year, households formed temporary camps of varying size and composition depending on ecological, economic, and social factors. Ranging from one or two to twenty tents, camps were smaller when pasturage and water were scarce and larger during the migrations when security and defense were mandated. The remoteness and isolation of these camps in the mountains—combined with the benefits of the nomads' kinship and tribal organizations—provided protection for women, who thereby escaped some social restrictions that bound many other Iranian women.[10] As one woman said, gesturing around her, "These mountains, these tribes, these dispersed tent encampments. Why would we need to wear *chadurs* [veil-wraps] and stay secluded inside our homes?"

The Qermezi and other Qashqa'i shared sentiments about their wider culture. Their primary sociopolitical and sociocultural identities were as members of an extended family, a lineage, a subtribe, a tribe, the Qashqa'i confederacy, and Iran's Turkish ethnolinguistic minorities. People manifested each of these identities according to their situations and contexts. While attending an intra-Qermezi wedding, Qermezi men competed as members of families and lineages in the vigorous sport of stick fighting. Visiting a regional market to buy saddles, they described themselves as members of the Qermezi subtribe or the Darrehshuri tribe. Transporting their livestock to a slaughterhouse in the distant city of Isfahan, they told others there that they were Qashqa'i or Turks. People expressed their Qashqa'i cultural identity by speaking the Qashqa'i Turkish language, practicing what they considered was a Qashqa'i livelihood and lifestyle, enjoying certain aesthetic forms (as embodied in their apparel, goat-hair tents, other items of material culture, weaving, customary technology, ceremonies, rituals, music, dance, poetry, sport, and cuisine), and perceiving themselves as distinct from others.

Persians, Lurs, and members of the Khamseh tribes form the wider sociocultural context for the Qashqa'i.

The Qashqa'i often identify themselves as "Turks" and do not always call themselves "Qashqa'i" unless other Turks are present. The term "Turk" relates to the people's historical connections with other Turkish speakers in Iran and beyond its borders. The label "Qashqa'i" refers primarily to the people's sociopolitical identities as members of the tribal confederacy and its tribes and subtribes. The label also invokes ethnic traits, compared with the more general term of "Turk," which does not connote specific cultural traits in southwestern Iran other than the Turkish language and a sense of opposition to Tajiks (a term Turks use for native Persian speakers). The label "Qashqa'i" is culturally specific (as this volume demonstrates).

Persians are native speakers of Persian (Iran's official language) and adhere to broadly defined notions of "Persian" culture. They inhabit the region's cities, towns, and villages and are not tribally organized, and many of them do not perceive themselves as an ethnic group. Persians dominate politically in southwestern Iran. For the Qashqa'i and other minorities, Persians represent the state, the government, and the ruling regimes of shahs and ayatollahs.

22 *Forty-four years of transformation*

Lurs in southwestern Iran are affiliated with tribes and ethnic groups. Some Lurs are still nomadic, most are village based, and some live in the region's towns and cities. They speak Luri, an Indo-Iranian language related to Persian. The Lurs closest to Qashqa'i territory are the tribally organized Boir Ahmad, Mamassani, and Bakhtiyari. The political organizations and leaderships of the Bakhtiyari and the Qashqa'i have been similar.

The tribes (Ainallu, Arab, Baharlu, Basseri, and Nafar) of the Khamseh confederacy are located to the east of Qashqa'i territory. In creating this polity in 1861 as a counterforce to the Qashqa'i confederacy, the Iranian government drew from regional tribes having diverse ethnic and linguistic traits. Combined, the Khamseh tribes never formed the unifying ethnolinguistic identity that has been a key trait for the Qashqa'i. Members of the Khamseh tribes demonstrate patterns of mobility and settlement similar to those of the Qashqa'i.

The Qashqa'i are Shi'i Muslims, Shi'i Islam being the dominant sect and faith in Iran. Their religious expressions before 1979 were unlike those of many other Shi'i Iranians, especially in towns and cities. They unquestionably identified themselves as Muslims but few fasted during Ramadan or performed daily prayers. Few had made the pilgrimage to Mecca or shown any interest in the destination. They observed births, circumcisions, weddings, and deaths according to tribal customs with little or no reference to Islamic rites and duties.

Circumstances in 2013

The last year of the shah's rule, the Iranian revolution (1978–79), the Islamic Republic's formation (1979), the war with Iraq (1980–88), and national political and economic crises through 2013 help to explain the wider context for the Qermezi and other Qashqa'i. The political and economic disruptions caused by the sometimes repressive regimes of Reza Shah (1925–41) and Mohammad Reza Shah (1941–79) extended well beyond 1979.

The Qermezi and other Qashqa'i perceived the dramatic events occurring in Iran from 1977 into the early and middle 1980s as political in nature, as a political revolt followed by a change in state leaders. They did not explain them in simplistic terms, and they downplayed the so-called "revolutionary" and "Islamic" dimensions of these developments. As a minority group under any kind of central government, they stressed the commonalities they experienced from one regime to the next. Patterns of oppression and neglect alternated under both governments. Initially, the new regime meant not much more to them than the top leadership passing from one segment of urban, Persian, Shi'i Muslim society to another. Most people were as alienated from the shah's regime as from the emerging Islamic one. They viewed the first as corrupt and abusive of power and the second as rigidly ideological with negative political, social, and cultural consequences. Other than their new access to formal secular education, they had not benefited from the shah's modernizing policies. They expected even less from the rule of hard-line, ideologically minded, conservative clerics.

Forty-four years of transformation 23

Later the Qermezi and other Qashqa'i saw that they might gain from new state policies favoring nomads and other sectors of Iranian society that the shahs had exploited and impoverished. The close intermixing of religion and politics (each entity always having had some characteristics of the other) would distinguish the second regime from the first, despite the interests of both in asserting control over the tribally organized nomads.

In their three-hundred-year history, the Qashqa'i had experienced many changes in state rule, and they viewed the most recent as one in a long succession. Their tribal system—its institutions, groups, hierarchical leaders, customs, regulations, ideologies, and symbols—responded to the wider instability and provided people with the means to maintain some degree of autonomy, defend their interests, and cope with and adapt to changing political conditions. Such a system had served the interests of the tribal people in the past and continued to benefit them in similar ways in modern times under the Pahlavi shahs and in the new Islamic state.

Some scholars, if they acknowledge tribal society at all, do not include its vibrant institutions as a part of civil society—which they usually consider an outgrowth of modernization and globalization and a vital part of democratization, and not a remnant of what they would regard, often negatively, as "tradition." The shahs, followed by the ayatollahs and their new regime, restricted Iran's citizens, sometimes forcibly, from forming the kinds of institutions associated with civil society in other parts of the modernizing world. Yet these rulers seemed to ignore how the Qashqa'i and similar peoples continued to rely on their tribal systems to maintain their ways of life and to adapt to and resist outside pressures. In the process, they allowed, seemingly unintentionally, these systems to persist and in some cases to strengthen and prosper.[11]

The subtribe continued in 2013 as the primary sociopolitical group for the Qermezi. Members of each of the five lineages still resided together and cooperated in economic ventures. Intra-lineage and intra-Qermezi marriages remained the predominant form, and unions with outsiders, especially those who were not Qashqa'i, continued to be rare.

After the revolution, an earlier form of leadership continued at the local level, and new ones emerged. By popular consensus, Borzu Qermezi remained the subtribe's headman (until his death in 1995) but his formal, state-related functions diminished. Government agents still approached him as the group's representative, although less frequently than before the revolution. The subtribe's members and others asked his advice and considered him the final authority in settling disputes. He handled, as before, the problems that no one in the subtribe wanted brought to the government's attention. Rarely a day passed without a dozen or more people coming to consult with him about various pressing issues. They filled his tent from early morning to late at night.

Borzu's main competitor for leadership was Bahram Qermezi, the only hezbollahi (a strident supporter of the Islamic Republic) living in seasonal pastures. Such an identity intensified for Bahram when his eldest son was killed in the Iraq–Iran war. Son of the headman who had preceded Borzu,

24 *Forty-four years of transformation*

Bahram was also Borzu's brother's son (and thus a subordinate). His lineage mates appointed him as the head of a three-man Islamic council (*shura*), a local organization that the new regime created for nomads (and others). Of limited power and authority, the council helped to resolve conflicts and assisted in matters such as procuring legal documents. If revolutionary guards seized a Qermezi man, Borzu and Bahram would meet with officials, produce affidavits, and attend court to testify on his behalf.

From Borzu's death in 1995 through 2013, no one assumed his position as headman. Some functions of this role had disappeared or lessened in the context of changing regimes, new state agencies, and new local Islamic councils, while the group elders took on others. The subtribe's growing numbers and the people's increasing spatial dispersion and diversifying economic activities meant that a single leader was not as feasible as before, despite the continuing need for one.

New sources of power in the subtribe, competing with the power and authority of the headman and the elders, first appeared in 1979–80, grew significant during the Iraq–Iran war, diminished by the mid-1990s, and reemerged in the mid-2000s. Initially, a few young men became impassioned supporters of the Islamic Republic and were known as hezbollahis (loosely organized "partisans of the party of God"). Most of them volunteered as basij militiamen in the war against Iraq and, if they survived, returned to proclaim sentiments of revolutionary politics intermixed with Islamic ideology. All but several of the Qermezi hezbollahis resided in small villages and a nearby town. Some were government-paid revolutionary guards who performed state-related duties. The salary and benefits they received, at a time of high national unemployment and runaway inflation, sufficiently explained why some young men chose to become guards. Those who were not also dedicated hezbollahis said they paid a weighty political, social, and emotional price, especially in the 1980s. Fervent hezbollahis harassed them, and other people incorrectly assumed that they supported this politico-religious movement.

The few Qermezi revolutionary guards, basij militiamen, and hezbollahis of the 1980s failed to add to their ranks in the early 1990s. By the mid-1990s only several of the original men continued to maintain these identities and hold these positions. Government salaries and privileges seemed to motivate these few. No younger men showed any interest in assuming these identities and roles, despite the economic inducements. On the national level, guards, militiamen, and hezbollahis continued to be the coercive means by which hard-line conservative clergymen controlled the country's citizens, especially since the mid-2000s. The local ones could exert some power by virtue of their being part of these national forces. Almost all Qermezi continued to distrust these figures, just as they had done since the Islamic Republic's formation, and at times they barely tolerated their intrusive presence.

The highest levels of Qashqa'i political leadership (the ilkhani and the khans) remained inactive for much of the period between 1970 and 2013. Most tribespeople did stay informed about the ilkhani's exile abroad and his

Forty-four years of transformation   25

probable successors. They held the hierarchical political system in abeyance, just as they had done in the past whenever state rulers had executed, exiled, imprisoned, or suppressed these high-level leaders.

During the late stages of the revolution, Naser Khan Qashqa'i (the ilkhani) and a few close kin returned to Iran after 25 years of forced exile abroad to resume the confederacy's leadership. The ilkhani's brother, Khosrow Khan Qashqa'i, was elected by popular vote to the Islamic Republic's first parliament in 1980 but hard-line conservatives arrested and expelled him. For two years he, his family, and their supporters sustained an insurgency (better labeled as a "defensive resistance") in the Qashqa'i mountains against attacks by Iran's new paramilitary forces. Zealots captured Khosrow Khan in 1982, sent him to prison, accused him of pro-West and anti-revolutionary acts, and tortured and executed him. They also killed, imprisoned, held under house arrest, or forced into internal or foreign exile his relatives and supporters.[12]

The new Islamic regime also severely restricted the formal leadership of the khans of the Qashqa'i tribes, the political level below the ilkhani. Many of these khans had joined the ilkhani's defensive resistance, and the government subsequently punished them. Since then, the surviving khans have resided in towns and cities during the winter while also maintaining their economic interests in seasonal pastures. Most continued to interact informally with the subtribal headmen and other tribal members.

Qashqa'i nomads and villagers between 1979 and 2013 fell under the political and military authority of the revolutionary guards, other security forces, and Islamic committees and councils. The government merged and centralized some security forces in 1991, and afterward the Qermezi and other rural inhabitants came under the jurisdiction of more diffuse and less threatening and coercive entities. The Organization for Nomads' Affairs began to provide state services to Qashqa'i and other nomads in 1982, including veterinary care, new roads in remote areas, and wells.

Many Qermezi families continued to migrate seasonally between winter and summer pastures in 2013. In the spring, livestock owners and hired shepherds drove the animals by hoof on accelerated schedules. In the autumn, some rented trucks to transport the animals due to the scarce grazing and water along the migratory routes that season, while others risked these impediments by migrating on foot. Traveling by rented trucks, most families and their possessions made the once-arduous, months-long, semiannual trek in a single day, thanks to new and newly paved roads. People spending part or all of the year in villages and towns often sent their livestock to migrate under the care of relatives. Those with diminished or no economic interests in pastoralism anymore still enjoyed living in seasonal pastures, especially during summers and holidays.[13]

Only one Qermezi man had owned a motorized vehicle in 1970, and he often found its use to be incompatible with his rugged overland migrations and remote mountainous residences. By 2013 many families owned or used motorcycles, Land Rovers, pickup trucks, large-load trucks, tractors, or

26 *Forty-four years of transformation*

passenger cars. Disadvantaged, others hoped to buy one, but with inflation in the cost of these items sometimes approaching 100 percent a year, any vehicle, even a decrepit one, fell beyond practically everyone's reach. Spare parts, tires, and repair shops were often unavailable, thereby crippling many who now depended on modern transportation.

Some Qermezi nomads had finally acquired by 2013 long-term legal leases for pastures in winter and summer quarters. Since the shah's national land reform in the 1960s, they had struggled to gain such documents but not all succeeded. Some wanted to buy cultivable land, particularly for fruit orchards. After the revolution, new and revamped government agencies helped the nomads to procure land, although arable plots with adequate water grew scarce, and competition drove prices upward. Disputes with non-Qashqa'i cultivators and other outsiders continued, but newly documented land rights and agreeable state agents sometimes supported the nomads' claims. Efforts to resolve conflicts over land through government offices in far-flung towns and cities continued slowly.

Practically all Qermezi families had diversified their economies by 2013. Many continued their primary interest in pastoralism and its products while others invested more in land and agriculture including orchards. Women more often than before oriented their weaving toward the commercial market. Specific livelihoods marked each of the five lineages. Men in one lineage relied on migratory pastoralism and did not purchase land or build permanent dwellings, while men in another lineage invested in settlement, agriculture, and urban-based jobs. Formal education leading to new occupations meant salaried or wage employment for some young men and women, a growing trend by 2013. New livelihoods, sometimes performed away from tribal territory, changed people's patterns of mobility, residence, local social organization, and consumption.

Urban merchants and moneylenders had become less exploitative by 2013. Interest taking is forbidden by Islamic law (which is often ignored in practice), and revolutionary guards had publicly flogged some abusive moneylenders when the government changed in 1979. Soon merchants and moneylenders found creative ways to continue collecting interest despite the religious prohibition, and by the mid-1980s most Qermezi men were again in debt, although not to the extreme that they had suffered during the 1970–71 drought. Low-interest loans from state banks were newly available for projects such as raising camels for sale as meat and constructing irrigation systems for orchards.

Patterns of social organization were similar in 1970 and 2013 except that many families had now established homes in villages, towns, and cities (some only for the winter). The first Qermezi village, founded in 1966, drew more residents in the 1970s and thereafter. Another group created the second village in 1975. Some Qermezi resided (often only seasonally) in close proximity to one another in three towns, usually as neighbors, and formed small quarters of Qermezi or Qashqa'i people. At any given time or season in 1970, the subtribe's members had been widely dispersed across a vast territory, including winter

Forty-four years of transformation   27

and summer pastures and the periphery. The same dispersal continued in 2013 but was more complex because of diversifying economies, and people were more mobile and dependent on vehicular transportation than before. Those who were fully or primarily nomadic and those who were fully or primarily settled stayed in close contact through kinship ties, intermarriage, economic cooperation, visiting, and ceremony. Their differences were not necessarily distinctive because, for example, many nomads lived in semipermanent or permanent dwellings in winter or summer pastures, and some settlers spent part of the year in tents in seasonal pastures.[14]

Gender patterns in seasonal pastures and one of the two Qermezi villages were also similar in 1970 and 2013.[15] Practices did change for town and city dwellers, where the regime and its agencies and supporters forced both women and men to adopt the ostensibly Islamic practices of public modesty and behavior. Qermezi schoolchildren there, girls especially, quickly learned about acceptable dress and deportment, and their lives differed from those of their agemates in seasonal pastures and the one village. Reuniting at weddings and funerals, these students gave the appearance—through behavior, speech, attire, material possessions, and outlook—of being two separate groups. Marriage between a nomadic man and a settled woman, or the reverse, grew problematic for both their families. Continuing practices of patrilocality meant that the bride would experience abrupt changes in her livelihood and lifestyle, and the nomads did not appreciate the newly conservative postures of some settlers.

Qashqa'i culture also underwent some changes. Forms of expression in 2013 were similar to past ones except that people were now sentimental as they elaborated the meanings. They had seemed to take their expressive culture for granted in 1970 while in 2013 they were more conscious of and explicit about it. People often commented about how they had once lived and were nostalgic for certain customs and strove to practice them, especially during weddings. While few romanticized their arduous past life when they had migrated for months through rugged terrain and when only airy tents had sheltered their families during inclement weather, they did reminisce about their former autonomy and relative isolation. They understood that they were now an increasingly integrated part of the wider Iranian society and culture. Many expressed concern for their children, whom they said would never experience the life (in all its dimensions) that they, the parents, once knew. They worried about their children becoming "Persians" (Persian Iranians, Iran's dominating population), whose attitudes and behaviors, they said, were so different from theirs.

Some so-called traditional, tangible aspects of Qashqa'i society and culture had diminished or disappeared, such as migrating in large groups accompanied by heavily laden camels and attending crowded assemblies hosted by the tribal khans. Many Qermezi came to regard the intangible aspects more intensely. A nomad—sitting one night in 1999 by an open fire just outside his goat-hair tent, listening to the distant wolves howl and the camp dogs respond in a frenzy of barking, and preparing to roast the wild partridges he

28 *Forty-four years of transformation*

had hunted that day—commented wistfully as he gazed into the starry night. "Isn't this how it used to be?" Although he had engaged in 1970 in precisely these same acts, in exactly the same location, he would never have uttered such a remark then.

Attitudes toward Islam had also changed since 1970 when few Qermezi ever mentioned Islamic beliefs and practices, let alone engaged in any of its rituals. They were more aware of institutionalized religion by 2013, due to their growing exposure to the Islamic regime and its agencies and zealous supporters, the focus on Islam at all levels of formal education and in the government-controlled media, and the new state regulations concerning supposedly un-Islamic behavior. A range of expressions occurred among the Qermezi in 2013 but two forms prevailed.

Residing in or near urban areas, one group demonstrated religious behavior approximating what it witnessed among its non-Qashqa'i neighbors and associates. (I cannot accurately determine the changes in religious beliefs, as compared with visible practices.) Some people, men more than women, prayed and observed the Ramadan fast, at least publicly, and became interested in pilgrimage. Their funerals and memorial services were similar to observances in towns. Women and girls changed their dress and behavior according to new standards of modesty found in urban areas.

The second group, distant from urban locales, manifested patterns similar to those found decades earlier, except that many people were now openly critical of, sometimes hostile toward, and irreverent about Islamic ritual expressions. A nomad, watching a visiting kinsman (a village resident) begin his afternoon prayers, inserted an audiotape of festive Qashqa'i music into his cassette recorder and began to play it. When, naively, I pointed out to him that the man was praying, he flashed me a mischievous grin, raised the volume, and encouraged his two-year-old grandson to dance to the music accompanied by his boisterous whoops. On another occasion, young Qermezi men waited eagerly until an itinerant Persian peddler visiting their tent had nearly completed his evening prayers before they loudly interrupted him to warn that the direction he faced was not even close to the prescribed one (Mecca, to the southwest). The peddler paused, presumably to calculate the error's severity, and then finished off the prayer without adjusting his position. At the time, I saw these two incidents (and many others) as vividly expressive and especially symbolic of conflicting cultural systems. Many Qermezi explained their distaste for Islamic rituals by blaming the ruling clergy for exploiting the religion for self-aggrandizing political purposes since the revolution, especially during the devastating war with Iraq in which 13 of their boys had been tragically, pointlessly, killed.

Transformational processes

Certain aspects of the lives of the Qermezi had changed between 1970 and 2013, some by the policies of the two governments, others by the era's general

Forty-four years of transformation 29

transformations, and still others by variable, often unpredictable, individual, family, and community preferences and choices. Continuities in the tribally organized society, a significant part of which still remained largely unaltered in 2013 by external events, explain other circumstances. In general, as this study indicates, the new state's impact on the Qermezi was greatest in politics and economics, less in culture, and least in social life and its related values.

External factors explaining change for the Qermezi include the residual effects from half a century of often repressive rule by the two shahs as well as the implementation of new state policies (including special services for nomads). Modernization accelerated as did the people's greater integration in the Iranian state and society. Many interrelated factors stimulated individual and group responses.

During the eight-year war with Iraq, for example, the deaths of Qermezi boys meant periods of ritualized mourning in which people ceased or limited any festivities because of their sorrow and their sympathy for the grieving families. These internal restrictions happened to coincide with the Islamic Republic's prohibitions against dance and certain forms of music. When the war concluded and the stipulated mourning ended, most Qermezi pushed to resume their customary celebrations. Their efforts coincided with decreased surveillance from hezbollahis and revolutionary guards, who had previously punished people engaging in state-prohibited acts. These coercive forces were finding that many citizens (Qashqa'i and others) were resisting the regime's restrictions and that they could not continue their harassments to the extent they had earlier enjoyed. (Later—buttressed by changes in national leadership— hezbollahis, revolutionary guards, and a revitalized basij militia resumed their aggressions against the citizenry.)

Directly and indirectly, the Qermezi experienced the final decade of Mohammad Reza Shah's (failed) efforts to form a modern and secular centralized state, his forced ouster and the short period of local freedom that the revolution allowed, the Islamic Republic's formation, and the war with Iraq. The regime's attempted consolidation of power and the efforts of citizens to oppose and resist produced other local effects. The Qermezi grew more integrated, but not evenly, in the wider Iranian society. They welcomed the regime's decreased personal and cultural restrictions in the mid-1990s and hoped that the trend would continue, but they had often experienced fluctuating government policies. Along with most Iranians, they praised the election of a new, moderate president of Iran in 1997 and the climate of greater individual freedom it promised. The following few years saw no dramatic improvements. The bodies of government not elected by the citizenry impeded or prohibited the new president's proposed reforms. Subsequent elections of hard-liners and neoconservatives dashed their hopes. A new president in 2013 once again raised people's expectations about government reform and Iran's reentry in the global community.

Modernizing processes, present in Iran in 1970 but of limited impact on most Qermezi, have continued since then to affect many aspects of life. Some

30 *Forty-four years of transformation*

changes would probably have occurred under most kinds of regimes and circumstances, although modernization did escalate under the shah and then slow during the Islamic Republic's first decade, which coincided with the war's debilitating impact on the economy. After the ceasefire, the regime continued to struggle with national economic crises (rapid inflation, escalating rural-to-urban migration, unemployment, and the government's inability to rule on fundamental principles of land rights), the volatility creating widespread insecurity. Inflation prevented most Qermezi from materially improving their lives in substantive ways. Mechanized transportation was routine for nearly everyone but even dilapidated vehicles were too expensive for most families to buy and maintain. The market and cash economy expanded, causing many people to diversify their livelihoods in search of more reliable and frequent cash income. The processes leading toward settlement continued although some families resisted pressures to build permanent residences, and others could not afford land or procure legal deeds. Most of those who did build or locate houses continued to migrate between winter and summer pastures or at least to visit both territories frequently and to maintain economic and social ties with relatives there.

People's enhanced consciousness of their Qashqa'i identity derived from their further integration in Iranian society and their growing awareness of discrimination and minority status. These heightened perceptions became politically charged agents of change and frameworks for individual and group resistance. A Qermezi community, for example, was determined in 1992 to celebrate a wedding by featuring men's and women's dance accompanied by the musicians whom the regime had forced into silence for more than a decade. Such an act of defiance against the government exerted a liberating impact on other, previously cautious groups. Resolved to wear customary Qashqa'i headscarves (which display most or all of the hair, a violation of regime policies governing a proper Islamic appearance), young women attending the wedding influenced others who had hesitated to resume donning their former attire.

Family and kinship groups, tribal institutions, and remote territories sheltered and insulated most Qermezi in 2013, just as in 1970. People enjoyed barriers of protection that many other Iranians lacked. The apparent hands-off policy of the regime allowed the tribal people to exercise autonomy in many aspects of their lives. The Qermezi did worry about the local impact of the deteriorating wider economy, but they still expressed less critical attitudes toward the Islamic regime than many other Iranians. Buttressed by their supportive kinship and tribal networks and their relative political autonomy, and less restricted by new state policies than many urban and rural people, they were less disapproving of the government.[16]

Writers on Iran often stress the extensive transformations caused by the revolution, Islamic government, war, and international sanctions. They tend to ignore the ways that life has also continued in well-established patterns, and they often disregard or are uninformed about sectors of Iranian society that are beyond Tehran or perceived to be politically insignificant.

Forty-four years of transformation   31

Many continuities in Qermezi society and culture were apparent in 2013. Despite some possibly superficial trappings of change—such as motorized vehicles, permanent houses (humble as they were), and new material goods— the people still seemed to be governed by the same societal and cultural norms and expectations that had guided them in 1970.[17]

The Qermezi valued the institutions, sociopolitical organizations, customs, and codes of tribal society. The political groups with which they identified, the khans they still respected (despite their living in exile abroad or held under surveillance and control), and the rules they adhered to stood at the center of their lives. Long-held notions of tribal, kinship, family, and gender relationships endured. People continued to live within and rely on the types of social groups that they had formed in the past. Their ideas about their unique Qashqa'i culture, especially their notions of identity, remained resolute. The culture offered a supportive system for people's perceptions of themselves and their sense of differentiation from others. It provided the means for individual and collective action. Yet change was evident in the increasingly proud, assertive nature of people's awareness. People's consciousness of themselves as Qermezi, Darrehshuri, and Qashqa'i and the ways they marked these and other identities were more explicit in 2013 than in 1970.[18]

Still dominant attributes of the livelihood and lifestyle helped to perpetuate certain aspects of society and culture for many Qermezi. People retained their supportive social and cultural systems through the practice of political and economic individualism, nomadic pastoralism in remote and isolated locations, and physical separation from non-Qashqa'i society. Many Qermezi women, for example, did not abide by new national laws specifying modest dress because they lived within their own kinship and tribal groups. They were freer to behave in customary ways than if they had resided in towns and cities and had fallen under the constant critical gaze of the regime's enforcers and supporters.

Demographic patterns among the Qermezi, 1970–2000

The Qermezi subtribe contained 121 independent households in 1970, and in 2000 it held 401, more than a threefold increase in 30 years. All of the 280 new ones grew from the 121, as sons and their sons separated from their fathers and formed new households. Most couples were having fewer children in the 1990s and thereafter than their parents, and the rate of growth of new households will decrease over time as these children marry and become independent.

The numbers 121 and 401 do not include people who affiliated closely with the subtribe. People in 1970 had always identified the affiliates by their respective tribal groups of origin, which was still the case in 2013. Over time, some of these individuals considered themselves to be Qermezi. Each of them allied with one of the five Qermezi lineages, and some came to identify themselves by these labels as well. Still, the names of their original tribal groups stayed with them, and others did not regard them as fully Qermezi in

32 Forty-four years of transformation

the way that all males and females born into the five lineages were, even after more than 70 years of close association.

Only some Qermezi engaged in full-time nomadic pastoralism in 2000, the dominant occupation of almost all Qermezi in 1970. The economies of most households were diversified, with pastoralism—sometimes fully migratory—occupying the attention of only some members while others engaged in agriculture and wage and salaried labor. Ghulam Husain Qermezi's six sons provide an example common in the subtribe. In 2000 three were traditional nomadic pastoralists who migrated seasonally, one was a village schoolteacher who also migrated seasonally, one worked in a steel mill, and one was a government office worker. The six shared economic interests in livestock, pasture rights, and an apple orchard and met often to coordinate their activities. The youngest of the nomadic pastoralists hoped to attend university after completing his mandatory military service and then locate a specialized urban job.

Most pastoralists occupying specific seasonal territories in 1970 were still there in 2000, usually with their sons and grandsons, but many more people were dispersed in more places in 2000 than in 1970. Some of them often changed their seasonal locations because they lacked long-term grazing permits. With long-term seasonal residence came agricultural production, an addition benefiting people economically. For many, agriculture made pastoralism possible, and during distressed ecological conditions it could subsidize the effort. People who located new pastures every winter and/or every summer were less likely to cultivate and tended to be less prosperous than others.

Only a few Qermezi lived seasonally in permanent structures in 1970. Many more had built, bought, or rented houses by 2000 and inhabited them seasonally or year-round. These dwellings fall into two categories.

In the first, many pastoralists built one-room, stone-and-thatch houses, sometimes not much more than huts, in winter and/or summer pastures, where they tended their livestock. These structures were scattered throughout a wide area (and not grouped), and people occupied them during only one or several seasons. Often they pitched their goat-hair tents close by and used both dwellings simultaneously. Houses stood as a claim to land and strengthened the rights of their builders to certain territories. They also protected people from the extremes of climate and weather, conditions that all Qermezi used to endure while dwelling in their woven goat-hair tents. Houses offered places for storage, necessary for the people's new material possessions and their concern about theft and vandalism.

The second category includes houses constructed, purchased, or rented in existing or new settlements in which some people lived year-round and others only seasonally. Many of these inhabitants also practiced pastoralism. Leaving their families at home, some men migrated with the livestock. Others hired shepherds or contracted with kinsmen to tend the animals. Their settlements are four types: exclusively Qermezi or Qermezi-dominated villages (Nurabad, Atakula), other villages with many Qermezi inhabitants (Mehr-i Gerd, Dezeh, Naqneh, Narmeh), towns and cities where Qermezi men and several women were employed, and, rarely, other locations where only a single Qermezi family lived. The Qermezi in villages tended to practice agriculture and pastoralism, as did some people in places where they were the only Qermezi residents. Most of those living in towns and cities pursued urban-related occupations, but they still maintained economic interests in pastoralism and agriculture and continued to cooperate with their kindred.

People in all four types of settlement cited their children's formal education as the primary reason for choosing permanent or semipermanent residences. Many men reported that, if not for their children, they would have continued migrating between winter and summer pastures indefinitely, without seeking other places to live, and would have avoided moving to villages, towns, and cities. Yet nomadic pastoralism could no longer support all of their children, when they became adults, and some or many of them now needed the formal education that led to other occupations. Education beyond the primary level could be found only in towns and cities, thus necessitating new places of residence for some families.

Wherever the Qermezi chose to live, all of them stayed in frequent contact with relatives and fellow tribespeople in winter and summer pastures. Their most meaningful ties remained within their kinship and tribal groups. The Qermezi subtribe and its five lineages were still the dominant sociopolitical groups in their lives. The people continued to identify with their winter and summer territories and to enjoy a life there that was difficult if not impossible in the new settlements, where the Islamic regime imposed social and cultural restrictions and where non-Qashqa'i neighbors and associates intruded on them.

Notes

1 Beck (1986, 1991).
2 Beck (2013, n.d. a) discusses Iran's linguistic, religious, ethnic, national-minority, and tribal groups.
3 The increase in population comes primarily from within the Qashqa'i group (via biological reproduction and patrilineal descent) and not from outsiders joining it.
4 Iran's population was 25.8 million in 1966, 33.7 million in 1976, 49.5 million in 1986, 60.1 million in 1996 (Hourcade et al. 1998: 34; Statistical Centre of Iran 1991, 1999), 70 million in 2006, and 79 million in 2013.
5 The Qashqa'i often use the terms tireh, tayafih, and il interchangeably. The five major tribes of the Qashqa'i confederacy are Amaleh, Darrehshuri, Kashkuli Bozorg, Farsi Madan, and Shish Buluki. Smaller tribes include Kashkuli Kuchek and Qarachai.
6 I use the past tense in this book except when referring to permanent or long-term facts and circumstances. The past continuous tense is occasionally useful ("each Qermezi lineage has been distinctive") but is cumbersome to maintain throughout the text. The past tense is sometimes problematic, such as in general descriptions of social organization, when the discussion also applies to conditions that may still be current at the time of writing and publication. Yet the present tense is often more problematic and can be wrong, unlike the past tense. I try to situate events according to specific eras and years.

34 *Forty-four years of transformation*

7 Mohammad Reza Shah's national land reform began in 1962. The shah announced his White Revolution in 1963. One of its initial six points is the nationalization of forests and pastureland.

8 Studies of poverty in Iranian cities demonstrate the difficulties for migrants (Kazemi 1980, Kazemi and Wolfe 1997). A. Bayat (1997) explains how migrants in cities formed grassroots movements to better their conditions. Their survival strategies (involving kinship, friendship, and informal economic activities) were similar to those of the tribally organized Qashqa'i. Yet the urban poor lacked the leadership, other institutional structures, and the unifying sociopolitical and sociocultural identities that have been essential to the long-term survival of the Qashqa'i.

9 In this book, I refer to choices that "parents" made with regard to their children's education and other activities. The collective term refers to fathers who were the family's public spokesmen and to mothers who contributed to decision making at more private and domestic levels.

10 Beck (1978).

11 I discuss (Beck 1995b) the role of tribal organization as it relates to the development of civil society in Iran.

12 Beck (1980b, 1986: 296–347) offers early accounts of the resistance. My fuller account (Beck n.d. b) is forthcoming.

13 E. Hooglund (1982a) describes similar continuing ties to the land for villagers near Shiraz. The limitations and fluctuations of urban employment made it precarious to leave the land completely. Urban migrants kept their rural links active and, during the 1978–79 revolution, connected villages into networks of political turmoil (Tabari 1983: 30).

14 Beck (1981b, 1998, 2002).

15 Beck (1978, 2004) discusses and compares the two periods.

16 Sanasarian (1995: 262) heard more negative criticism of the Islamic regime from Muslim Iranians than from Christian Armenians in Iran. Similar to the Qashqa'i, Armenians were distanced from the regime due to their supporting, sustaining society and culture.

17 Abu-Lughod (1986: 74–7) draws similar conclusions about the impact of modern technology on settled, tribally organized Arabs in Egypt.

18 The scholarly and artistic efforts of some Qashqa'i to record their expressive culture began to affect the Qermezi group in the late 1990s. These books are in the Persian language and Perso-Arabic script. Qashqa'i Turkish is not a written language. A few authors use the Perso-Arabic script to render Qashqa'i Turkish, as in poetry. See Bahadori-Kashkuli (1985), Bahluli-Qashqa'i (1996-2000), Bahmanbaigi (1989, 1995, 2000), K. Bayat (1986, 2010), Danishvar-Kuhva (1992, 1995), Duzgun (1998), M. H. Ghashghai (2005), M. M. Ghashghai (2013), M. N. Ghashghai (1986), Jeddi (1999), Kiyani (1993, 1997, 1999, 2001, 2002), Mardani-Rahimi (1999), Menash (1996), Nadiri-Darrehshuri (2000), Naseri-Tayyibi (2002), Qahramani-Abivardi (1994), Ruhani (1992), Safari-Kashkuli (2000), Shahbazi (n.d.), Sohrabi (1995), and Yusufi (2001). Some Qashqa'i authors (and musicians and artists) use tribal and subtribal names as their legal surnames. Others attach such names to their legal last names. People increasingly valued these tribal distinctions, and authors wanted these names prominently placed. Some people adopted "Qashqa'i" as a legal surname or attached it to a tribal or subtribal name (as in Rahimlu-Qashqa'i). Since 1924, when the government instituted formal surnames, until after the 1979 revolution, only members of the Janikhani lineage (the paramount Qashqa'i khans and their families) used "Qashqa'i" as a last name. (Most of them transliterated it as "Ghashghai.") (Some Qashqa'i employed by the oil industry in southwestern Iran in the 1950s and thereafter are an exception. They used the "Qashqa'i" name to differentiate themselves from other ethnic and tribal peoples,

Forty-four years of transformation   35

especially Arabs and Lurs, who also worked there.) The same usage sometimes applied to the names of tribes (such as Darrehshuri and Kashkuli), with only the khan families adopting them. After the revolution, anti-khan sentiments, the khans' reduced public and political presence, new notions about social equality, and enhanced ethnic and tribal awareness expanded the use of these names to people other than the Qashqa'i elite. Many Qashqa'i of varying ancestry and social rank have applied the names officially and informally since the late 1980s. The names "Qashqa'i" and "Darrehshuri" no longer necessarily indicate the members of khan families. Qashqa'i contributors to Facebook in 2010–13 demonstrated the increasing significance of confederacy, tribal, and subtribal names.

3 The revolution and the Islamic Republic
Reflections on 1978–2013

In this chapter, I examine six facets of the revolution and the Islamic Republic as they affected the Qermezi: the revolution itself, the arrest and imprisonment of Qashqa'i leaders by the new regime's revolutionary guards, the Iraq–Iran war, new and transformed government agencies, local Islamic councils, and the people's changing educational and economic opportunities. Depending on the topic, each discussion covers part or all of the revolutionary and postrevolutionary periods.

Experiencing the revolution

When I asked the Qermezi in 1991 about their experiences during the revolution, I initially expected them to recount their memories of the rapidly escalating political revolt in Iran *preceding* Mohammad Reza Shah's departure on 16 January 1979, Ayatollah Khomeini's arrival on 1 February 1979, and the provisional revolutionary government's formation on 12 February 1979.

Yet most people stressed the actual days the shah departed and Khomeini arrived and sometimes subsequent national events. For some, the term revolution (*inqilab*) meant the forced end of the shah's regime, and many considered Khomeini's seizure of power and assertion of authority as a process separate from the anti-shah revolt. For others, the term signified the day Khomeini returned to Iran from exile abroad. Some people confused the day the shah left with the day Khomeini arrived when they mentioned a locally significant event occurring at the time. A few defined the revolution as the period between the shah's departure and Khomeini's arrival. For some, the revolution ended with these two events, while for others it concluded with the "day of the revolution" that followed the "10 days of dawn" between Khomeini's return and the declaration of a revolutionary Islamic government. Several people stated that the revolution ended when Iranian citizens voted overwhelmingly (on 30–31 March 1979) to accept an Islamic republic.

To my knowledge, no Qermezi played an active role in revolutionary activities in 1978 and the first three months of 1979. The shah's troops shot and killed one young man, Nuri Qermezi (the son of Sharif of Qairkhbaili lineage), in December 1978 while he and several other wage laborers watched

The revolution and the Islamic Republic 37

street demonstrations in Shiraz. At the time, given the tumultuous protests, the armed forces considered any gathering of people as a provocation. Nuri's family never recovered his body, and his burial place is unknown (which people consider tragic because his family lacks a place to mourn him). A few Qermezi listed Nuri when they recounted the names of the martyrs of the Iraq–Iran war (1980–88). Years after these two separate events (the revolution and the war), the Qermezi equated them in some fashion or considered the war an extension of the revolution. Their memories of the anti-shah protests, the shah's flight from Iran, Khomeini's return, the Islamic Republic's formation, and the war with Iraq were intertwined. People remarked that they were removed in time and space from all of these events.

The Qermezi also explained these local perceptions by their relative isolation in winter and summer pastures, their lack of participation in the political events overtaking the cities and some towns, and their skepticism about any meaningful change resulting. They and their ancestors had witnessed states and rulers (and their vestiges) rise and fall. Their tribal system reflected the vicissitudes in Iran's national and regional politics. Regardless of political change in Tehran and other cities, the sociopolitical systems of the Qermezi (and the Qashqa'i) provided the people with structure, meaning, and continuity.

Still, people detested Mohammad Reza Shah and his father Reza Shah for their disdain for tribes, nomads, and ethnic minorities and for their attempts to destroy Qashqa'i leaders, institutions, and culture. They opposed the Pahlavi dynasty or family rather than only Mohammad Reza Shah, and they often considered the two shahs as one when they expressed negative sentiments. "Shah" could mean either or both of the two kings and the regimes they had created.

The Qermezi and many other Qashqa'i played a negligible role in the revolution, a fact necessary to mention because many authors stress near-universal, Iran-wide participation.[1] Most Qermezi men, including the young and the formally educated, and almost all Qermezi women lacked any positive expectations for the revolutionary movement other than the shah's possible ouster. They differed from many urban and some village men and women who held wider ranging hopes.[2] They were skeptical about any new post-shah government, which they doubted would bring about beneficial changes in their access to land and their pastoral and agricultural livelihoods.[3]

The Qermezi were not interested in the conspiracy theories that many Iranians at home and especially abroad commonly expressed.[4] They did not assert that foreign powers directed political events in Iran before, during, and after the revolution. Influenced in other ways by their fellow students in towns and cities, even young Qermezi men were free of conspiracy notions. Other Iranians declared that if the American and British governments had wanted the revolution to fail and the shah to remain in power, they would have orchestrated these events. If they had wanted Khomeini to abandon his scheme for an Islamic state, then he would have done so.

By contrast, the Qermezi placed responsibility for events—and their heavy consequences—in the hands of Iran's leading and oppositional figures and on

38　*The revolution and the Islamic Republic*

ordinary citizens who were swept up in mass political demonstrations. They stated that if Iranian politicians and activists had been organized and motivated to do so at the time, they could have changed the course of events by any number of actions: keeping the shah in power, forcing him to be less oppressive, undermining escalating revolutionary activity, creating a secular democratic republic, preventing Khomeini from returning, stopping him from seizing power, obstructing the Islamic Republic's formation, freeing the American hostages, repulsing Iraq's territorial aggression, and ending the war quickly.

Many Qermezi noted in 1991 that, in spirit, they had opposed the shah and supported the revolution (by which they meant the effort to rid Iran of him). Better informed than most others, students in town observed escalating political activity there. The most "revolutionary" (*inqilabi*) individuals were six young Qermezi men who witnessed the local progression of events but did not engage in any overt acts. Some of them lived in a village where they taught school or studied, and one was an army soldier still working toward his high-school diploma. One man said that, considering everyone in the subtribe, "only teachers and high-school students" (all male) were revolutionary in attitude. Another said that literate people supported the revolution (and opposed the shah) while the illiterate were silent. Some men listened to the Persian-language radio broadcasts of the British Broadcasting Company, heard the statements of Khomeini from his exile abroad, and followed the escalating national crisis. Students were excited about schools closing because of the turmoil. When I asked men who were high-school students at the time about their memories of the revolution (which they defined as the shah's ouster, thus facilitating Khomeini's return), they almost invariably began by saying that their schools shut down and they went home to their families in winter pastures where normal pursuits continued.

Of the few Qermezi boys and young men who later avidly supported Khomeini and the Islamic Republic in their roles as hezbollahis, revolutionary guards, and basij militia volunteers, only several were revolutionary in attitude at the time of the shah's fall and Khomeini's return. All other hezbollahis, guards, and basijis emerged later, including Shahriyar Qermezi (later a war hero and a parliamentary deputy). Qermezi men noted that the first revolutionary participants in Iran were the urban poor, many of them discontented, unemployed rural migrants, who were also among the first to be recruited as hezbollahis, guards, and basijis.

Many townspeople of Kazerun near winter pastures supported the protests against the shah and responded emotionally to messages sent by Khomeini. At least once, the shah's troops fired on demonstrators there and killed civilians including women. Several Qermezi boys attending grades six through eight in Kazerun schools observed street demonstrations. Unlike the inhabitants of some other rural communities in the region, no Qermezi living in winter pastures at Dashtak traveled to towns or cities to protest.[5] The day Khomeini returned to Iran, some schoolboys witnessed the joyous response of Kazerun's citizens.

The revolution and the Islamic Republic 39

Soon after Khomeini arrived, the political forces that had cooperated to oust Mohammad Reza Shah fell into often-conflicting groups. Qermezi men listed the three political categories that the Qashqa'i found relevant at the time: khan supporters, "communists," and Khomeini supporters. They continued to employ these categories through 1982, yet two of them no longer represented any significant activity at the local level in 1983 and thereafter.

When the Islamic Republic executed Khosrow Khan Qashqa'i in 1982 and arrested or drove into exile his probable successors, active support for the paramount Qashqa'i khans ended. State pressure on them increasing, the khans of the Darrehshuri and other Qashqa'i tribes grew politically quiescent and sought no followers.

Paramilitary forces and supporters of the new regime killed (in ambush and battle and by snipers and execution), imprisoned, forced abroad, or otherwise rendered inoperative the few "communists" (that is, variously affiliated leftists) within the Qashqa'i tribes. No Qermezi individuals expressed any interest in leftist groups (at least 50 in existence during the revolution and its immediate aftermath) and ideologies, and the tribespeople did not distinguish between and among the major groups, including the Mujahidin, Fidaiyan, and Tudeh. A Qermezi man referred to their lack of sophistication in these matters by noting that if his kinsmen's sheep had been stolen in 1980, the tribesmen would have proclaimed that communists were the culprits (which he said was unlikely).

The third category, Khomeini supporters, included the hezbollahis, a term whose currency continued into the second decade of the new century. In discussing a particular Qermezi man's history, people argued about his former strident stance and disagreed if he had been a communist, a hezbollahi, or both. Combining traits common to the two affiliations, they lacked an understanding of these terms at the national level. Leftists as well as hezbollahis opposed the Qashqa'i khans, and anyone holding such attitudes could be labeled in either or both these ways.

Most Qermezi expressed some verbal support for Khomeini in his efforts to overthrow the shah in the last months of 1978 and the early days of 1979. They said they would have backed anyone who strove with some success to achieve this goal, especially if the person or group was democratic and secular in political orientation, such as Mohammad Mosaddeq and the National Front coalition supported by the paramount Qashqa'i khans in 1949 and the early 1950s.

The sentiments of many Qashqa'i concerning democracy, nationalism, secularism, and liberalism derived from the stances of the paramount Qashqa'i khans, who disseminated these attitudes to the tribespeople by the personal example they set. They also imparted these notions through the two lower levels (khans and headmen) of the tribal political hierarchy. The Qashqa'i at the local level understood "democracy" as local representation, an institution already present in their headmen and elders. They viewed Iranian "nationalism" as a concept that excluded them (and other ethnolinguistic minorities).

40 *The revolution and the Islamic Republic*

Persians controlled the state and government and applied the Persian language and culture in their dominance over the citizens. (The paramount Qashqa'i khans manifested some support for Iranian nationalism when they participated in national politics. Later they regretted the roles they had played there, none of which had turned out well for them in the long term.) The Qashqa'i at the local level already held "secular" values (without explicitly labeling them this way). They opposed the insertion of Islamic institutions and ideologies in the state and government. "Liberalism" was less accessible and understandable for them, given its foreign and Western origins, and was not relevant in their lives as nomads and pastoralists.

No Qermezi indicated any interest in 1978–79 in Khomeini's particular politico-religious orientation, and none of them expected (and only a few later accepted) a government run by Shi'i Muslim clergymen. Even Khomeini in exile had denied any intention of returning to Iran to be its supreme ruler. Along with many Iranians, the Qermezi did not anticipate that the clergy and its supporters would hijack the revolutionary process and seize control for themselves.[6] They and most other Qashqa'i disliked and distrusted local, provincial, and national religious figures. Hence, many Qashqa'i were puzzled when they heard that Naser Khan Qashqa'i, the tribal confederacy's paramount leader in exile since 1954, had visited Khomeini in France, apparently to endorse his efforts to topple the shah. They supported the process but questioned the means and worried about the implications and consequences.

By late 1979 many Qermezi and other Qashqa'i recognized the mistake that they and millions of other Iranians had made when they acquiesced to the Muslim clergy's takeover of the revolution and its rapid formation of a conservative Islamic state. For them, one avoidable political or military crisis after another—each one caused and/or exacerbated by the new Islamic government—dominated in 1979 and the early 1980s, including the arrests and summary executions of reputedly anti-regime individuals, persecution of leftists and religious minorities, restrictions on women's rights, seizure of the United States embassy, long-term detention of American hostages, military attacks against Khosrow Khan Qashqa'i and his supporters, Khosrow Khan's execution, and protracted war with Iraq and its mounting casualties.

The headman of the Qermezi subtribe, Borzu Qermezi, had verbally supported the revolution from the time of the first urban protests in 1977 but did not participate in any revolutionary activities. He often commented that he had grown up hating the shah for having killed his father. (The shah's troops had shot Shir Mohammad in the Semirom war of 1943.)[7] When the news came that the shah had fled Iran, Borzu fired his rifle into the air six or seven times in celebration. His son Mohammad Karim shot five wild sheep in one of the shah's formerly off-limits wild-game preserves and brought them home for a communal feast. Borzu and many others often noted that they had also detested the shah for having executed Ismail Khan Soulat ed-Douleh, the Qashqa'i ilkhani. (Periodically serving as the paramount leader since 1902, Soulat ed-Douleh was imprisoned by Reza Shah and died in captivity under suspicious circumstances in 1933.) In talking about the "shah," the Qermezi and other Qashqa'i often did not distinguish between the father and the son.

When Soulat ed-Douleh's sons, Naser Khan Qashqa'i and Khosrow Khan Qashqa'i, returned to Iran from involuntary exile abroad in January 1979 to resume their leadership of the Qashqa'i confederacy, Borzu offered his support. Other Qermezi men also expressed enthusiasm for the returned khans then (and the new regime later punished some of them for this loyalty), but they regarded Borzu as the staunchest supporter of the paramount khans, even well past 1982 when the regime had defeated the khans militarily and rendered them inoperative politically. When Naser Khan and Khosrow Khan stressed repeatedly that they did not seek supporters to surround them, Borzu returned his attention to local Qermezi politics and defended the economic base of his group against threats to its pastures and livestock. Most other Qermezi men did not stay fully informed about rapidly changing national politics, which they said played little or no role in their lives. The demands of nomadic pastoralism were constant, they frequently changed their often remote locations, and they lacked interest.

During the last several years before the revolution, Borzu had been more prosperous than ever before. He expanded his livestock, purchased a vehicle, and bought two plots of land in towns for possible seasonal residence. When the shah's regime ended, the future for nomadic pastoralism was more uncertain than it had been since the shah regained power in 1953 after the aborted coup d'état. When revolutionary guards threatened Borzu with arrest in 1980, he worried that they would seize his land and confiscate his livestock. The Darrehshuri khans were consumed with their own political problems and did not assist Borzu as they had formerly done.

At the same time, a few young Qermezi men emerging as hezbollahis turned against Borzu to criticize his past support of the khans and to challenge his continuing power within the subtribe. Their negative sentiments against him persisted, although gradually lessening, until his death in 1995. He in turn mocked their discovery of Islam, a newfound enthusiasm that he asserted was politically strategic in these changing times. He often ridiculed the men who had exhibited no interest in Islamic beliefs and practices before 1979 but who suddenly became devout practitioners eager to display their prayers and fasts in public gatherings, to denounce others for their negligence and un-Islamic conduct, and to impose their newly acquired socially conservative values on others.

Borzu's attitudes toward the revolution hardened when the Islamic Republic's revolutionary guards arrested and imprisoned him in 1980. His views solidified when the new state's paramilitary forces attempted to crush the defensive resistance mounted by Naser Khan, Khosrow Khan, and their supporters. When a clergy-run Islamic tribunal issued a death sentence against Khosrow Khan and swiftly implemented it, Borzu was distraught, and he said he despised the men who had forced this outcome. When provoked, he would proclaim that the new regime had given him no opportunity to avoid being anti-revolutionary (*zidd-i inqilab*). If the revolution meant that the state could execute the

42 *The revolution and the Islamic Republic*

paramount Qashqa'i leader, he wanted no part of it. If the revolution meant that paramilitary forces could illegally detain him and seize his pastures and livestock for their own profit, he would resist.

Borzu's brother's son and new son-in-law, Husain Ali Qermezi, noted, "I didn't do anything during the revolution," either before or after the shah fled and Khomeini arrived. People gathered in the streets but he said he was not interested in joining them. When basij militiamen seized the weapons of ordinary citizens (but avoided the Qermezi group because of its reputation for aggressively defending its interests), he was glad he had not joined the force. (Along with other nomads, he did volunteer for the militia later, after Iraq invaded Iran.)

As a primary-school teacher for nomads in a secluded location, Husain Ali escaped the pressures on urban and village teachers to join anti-shah demonstrations in cities. Activists accused teachers there of opposing the revolution if they did not participate. Soon after the Islamic Republic was declared, Khomeini and other clerics ordered elementary and secondary schoolteachers throughout Iran to focus their instruction on Islam, the Qur'an, and Arabic; lead students in prayers and fasting; and advise them about proper Islamic conduct including modest dress for girls.[8] Husain Ali minimally complied with the new directives. He was usually unsupervised in his teaching, and parents did not push for any Islamic content. Later, when students prepared to take new standardized examinations covering the revised required curriculum, including Islam and Arabic, he adjusted his teaching to help students perform effectively. Success in these tests determined the students' future prospects, and he said he did not want to impede them in an increasingly competitive environment.

Imprisonment of Qashqa'i leaders

Borzu Qermezi's arrest and detention in 1980 were related to the attempted resumption of tribal leadership by the paramount khans of the Qashqa'i confederacy after the revolution.[9] Borzu's own account and the information others offer about him demonstrate the local context and meaning, which this section stresses.

When I first asked a few Qermezi men in 1991 about Borzu's arrest, one stated that the event happened just after the revolution, that first year (1979). No one then explicitly connected the action with Khosrow Khan Qashqa'i's own arrest, which I knew had occurred in the late spring of 1980. Thus I did not initially link the two events. Soon I saw how interwoven they were.

Several days later, a Qermezi man carefully (and accurately) described the events in the chronological terms that were relevant to him and in ways with which I was familiar. "The revolution erupted during the winter while the tribe was in winter pastures. Then we migrated to summer pastures. Borzu wasn't arrested that spring or summer. Then the tribe migrated to winter pastures that autumn, and then we returned to summer pastures that next spring. That's when Borzu was arrested, when the tribe came to summer pastures."

The revolution and the Islamic Republic 43

(Qermezi schoolteachers and other professionals could recite the specific years of certain events, especially if they coincided with their personal history [such as the year of their high-school diploma], but most other men and women could not. Everyone, including the well educated, marked the passage of time not by specific years but by juxtaposing events. A certain incident, for example, took place before, during, or after another.)

A few people seemed reticent in 1991 to provide details about Borzu's arrest, a hesitation I had never encountered before (or since), about any matter. Borzu once whispered to me that "they" would kill him and his family if the details were more widely known. Later he said he wanted me to hear about the event so that his grandsons would understand the kind of man he had been. (He assumed that I would write about the arrest and that his grandsons would eventually read the account.) More than three decades have now passed since the arrest, and the implied danger represented by the story is minimal.

When Naser Khan Qashqa'i and Khosrow Khan Qashqa'i returned to Iran in January 1979 after 25 years of forced exile abroad, hundreds of thousands of Qashqa'i and others traveled to many locations to welcome them in person.[10] From the khans' arrival in Tehran until their defensive resistance beginning in June 1980, many people accompanied the khans on their journeys and visited them at their temporary residences. Mohammad Reza Shah had confiscated all their properties decades before, and the khans no longer owned homes or land. They relied on the hospitality of tribal and nontribal relatives, supporters, and friends while they traveled throughout Qashqa'i and adjoining territories. Sometimes the two brothers made these trips and resided together, but more often they did not, and over time separate groups of supporters crystallized.

When first Naser Khan and then Khosrow Khan arrived in Shiraz in January 1979, Borzu Qermezi went to pay his respects and renew his loyalty. During these meetings and many others to follow, Borzu offered to provide the khans any support they needed. He volunteered to sell his livestock if the khans required funds for weapons or other expenses. Each time the khans thanked him for his generosity and said they would send for him when necessary. Borzu told them that he was ready to join their personal entourage. They replied that he should return to his family and subtribe and handle affairs there, especially because emboldened revolutionaries were consolidating their power at the local level.

Khosrow Khan responded personally to Borzu because of a tragic historical event linking them. Borzu's father Shir Mohammad had fought alongside Khosrow Khan against the shah's troops in the battle of Semirom in 1943 and was killed there. Shir Mohammad had often told his sons, "If I have one wish, here it is. When the son [Naser Khan] of Soulat ed-Douleh returns to Qashqa'i territory [from exile and imprisonment in Tehran], I will join the battle and be killed defending him." He had fulfilled that wish, and Borzu tried to emulate his father in similar acts of loyalty. When a man introduced Borzu to Khosrow Khan during their first face-to-face meeting in 1979, Borzu said to him, his voice breaking with emotion, "You won't recognize me. I am the son

44   *The revolution and the Islamic Republic*

of Shiri, killed in the Semirom war." Khosrow Khan embraced and kissed him.[11] Despite other people pressing toward him with their own concerns, the khan began to recount the battle's details and Shir Mohammad's death. His account was one that only a person who had engaged in the conflict could offer, and Borzu had never heard some of the specifics before. Khosrow Khan told Borzu, "You have sacrificed for the Qashqa'i," meaning that Borzu had lost his father for a worthy cause. He added, "If I had stayed [in Iran], I would have continued to help you." The shah had exiled Khosrow Khan and seized his property, and since 1954 the khan had been unable to offer assistance to the son of a man killed in war. Under other circumstances, the khan would have provided ongoing economic support to the deceased man's family. Foreign exile had temporarily broken the bond.

On other occasions, Khosrow Khan, Jehangir Khan Darrehshuri (by whose side Shir Mohammad had died), and Borzu talked about the war and his father's fate, and their association intensified. Khosrow Khan's particular personal touch was prominent among his charismatic traits, as demonstrated in these informal meetings with a backer such as Borzu (who was not more important than thousands of others). Khosrow Khan took the time to talk directly with Borzu, despite the presence of more influential people and the necessity to discuss the immediate crisis (the role to be played by the Qashqa'i and their leaders in the new Islamic Republic). This personal attribute helps to explain the loyalty that so many people were ready to offer him.

Khosrow Khan journeyed to Kazerun where tens of thousands of the town's and region's inhabitants welcomed him and heard him speak. Borzu and other Qermezi men were among them. When spring arrived, the paramount khans traveled throughout Qashqa'i summer pastures to visit the khans of the Qashqa'i tribes and other local dignitaries. Naser Khan and his brother Malek Mansur Khan established camps at Zain Ali where they had resided seasonally until 1954. Borzu along with other Qermezi frequently traveled there, just west of their summer pastures at Hanalishah, to join the large gatherings of supporters and visitors. Borzu was among the many assembled guests when Naser Khan and Khosrow Khan visited the homes of the Darrehshuri khans in and near Mehr-i Gerd village. Closely affiliated with Jehangir Khan, Borzu was often there when one or more of the paramount khans were present. When the khans traveled to other, sometimes far-flung, Qashqa'i locations, Borzu and others of the subtribe occasionally joined them. These many gatherings served to reconnect the paramount khans with the dispersed Qashqa'i people and to renew political linkages and loyalties. The full political hierarchy, dormant for decades, now resumed its operations.

The Qermezi often mentioned a turbulent gathering in 1979 in the Mehr-i Gerd orchard of Muhi ud-Din Kashifi, a regionally prominent Persian man who had acquired land in Darrehshuri territory there. A wealthy industrialist based in Isfahan, Kashifi had known the paramount khans in the past and supported them now. Present in the orchard were three of the four paramount khans, other members of their Janikhani family, most Darrehshuri khans,

The revolution and the Islamic Republic   45

khans of other Qashqa'i tribes, Qashqa'i headmen (such as Borzu Qermezi), Qashqa'i leftists, and supporters and observers. During the meeting, influential men addressed the many emerging problems, particularly the role of the few Qashqa'i leftists in Iran's rapidly changing politics. The paramount khans tried to convince the leftists there to ally with them rather than with their own ideologically based, nontribal groups.

These Qashqa'i leftists, buttressed by a larger number of leftists of urban, ethnic-Persian backgrounds, had traveled together to summer pastures to exhort the non-elite tribespeople there to seize the properties (land, livestock, and weapons) of the khans of the Qashqa'i tribes. They urged a preemptive strike before revolutionary guards confiscated these resources for themselves. Attempting to incite the tribal masses, the leftists proclaimed that the paramount khans had returned to Iran so they could resume collecting the animal tax (*gallih bigirih*) that they had occasionally solicited from Qashqa'i nomads before 1953.

During the large meeting in the orchard, Naser Khan and Khosrow Khan cautioned restraint. Aware of the wider implications of a growing local conflict, they had repeatedly told the area's revolutionary guards that they, the khans, were handling internal Qashqa'i affairs. (Tension between these two powers was rising, and the foundations for their overt hostilities were built at this time.) The brothers held a broader view of the national political scene than the others present, and they urged the Qashqa'i attendees to avoid confrontations with external political and paramilitary forces. They worried that precipitous actions by the Qashqa'i leftists (urged on by the ethnic-Persian leftists) would cause zealous revolutionary guards to target all Qashqa'i, particularly Qashqa'i leaders. Naser Khan and Khosrow Khan often stated that they hoped to intensify the common ethnolinguistic and tribal bonds among the Qashqa'i, and they advised the Qashqa'i leftists in particular not to act rashly.[12]

In other parts of Iran at the same time and earlier, among other ethnic and tribal minorities, people were seizing land from wealthy holders. Leftists among these groups and especially from outside were encouraging such moves, and revolutionary guards were attempting to assert power, seize property for themselves and the regime's supporters, and suppress ethnic and tribal resistance.[13]

Present at the gathering in the orchard, Borzu Qermezi lacked much understanding of the various ideologies expressed by the leftists there, especially when they included foreign terms (and not Persian translations) such as "feudalism" and "socialism." Similar to other Iranians at the time, he tended to categorize and group all leftists as "communists." During these discussions and arguments, when he found an opening, Borzu supported the views of the paramount and tribal khans. Yet he also sympathized with the sentiments of the non-elite Qashqa'i who complained that the tribal khans had exploited them in the past. More than other Qermezi men, Borzu had profited economically and politically from his close association with Jehangir Khan and other Darrehshuri khans. Still, before the revolution, these khans

46 *The revolution and the Islamic Republic*

had always treated him as a subordinate and made sure that he maintained that posture in their presence. (The Darrehshuri khans modified their behavior toward him after the revolution, especially after his arrest and detention and the defensive resistance of the paramount khans.)

As tensions rose in the orchard, Borzu shouted at the Qashqa'i leftists there, "We will kill you!" (Thirteen years later, a Shish Buluki Qashqa'i man who had been present recalled with amusement that a stocky, red-faced tribesman—most certainly Borzu—had loudly threatened the leftists.) Two groups—"bailay-yi khan" and "bailay-yi kommunist"—physically separated their forces, all heavily armed and ready to begin shooting. Emotions ran high. Forcefully urging restraint, Khosrow Khan yelled, "We are all Qashqa'i here!" Soon everyone lowered the weapons they had brandished.

Later, Qermezi men noted that Borzu's conflict with the Darrehshuri leftist rebel, Allah Quli Jahangiri, had begun on this day, and soon Allah Quli was issuing death threats against Borzu and other khan supporters.

After the gathering in the orchard, Naser Khan and Khosrow Khan established a tent encampment in the Khosrow Shirin plain, their main summer headquarters before their exile.[14] Bringing several sheep as a tribute, Borzu traveled south to visit them for several days and then returned to his summer pastures at Hanalishah. (Such gifts went directly to feeding the hundreds of daily guests and did not provide the khans any income.) Again Borzu offered to give the khans any support they needed, and again they advised him to return home so he could care for his family and tribal group. He noted later that their remarks did not offend him. He saw that they were not building a large entourage and that they gave the same suggestions to other supporters.

In March 1980, the following year, Khosrow Khan was elected to the Islamic Republic's first parliament as the representative of Eqlid district (in the eastern part of Qashqa'i summer pastures), and he traveled to Tehran to assume his deputyship. More than other events or circumstances occurring since their return to Iran in January 1979, this one forced the paramount khans to reconsider their many roles. They regarded themselves as leaders of the Qashqa'i tribal confederacy but they could also be leaders of a coalition of some or many of Iran's other tribes, especially those nearby. They were still regional powers in Iran's south and southwest. Were they still national politicians, as they had been in the past? Khosrow Khan's election to parliament and relocation to Tehran demonstrated that they were. They were obviously some combination of these diverse roles. If they were to operate on different political levels, who were their primary constituents and how would they acquire financial support? As proponents of democracy, nationalism, secularism, and liberalism, how should they relate to an increasingly conservative, hard-line, repressive, anti-West, clergy-dominated Islamic regime?

(The paramount khans had participated in national politics by serving in parliament under Reza Shah and Mohammad Reza Shah, joining Mohammad Mosaddeq's National Front coalition in 1949 and the early 1950s, and allying

The revolution and the Islamic Republic 47

with Mosaddeq as prime minister. They had supported Shapur Bakhtiar, a Bakhtiyari Lur tribesman who served as Mohammad Reza Shah's last prime minister in early 1979.)[15]

By this time, some politicians in Tehran perceived the paramount Qashqa'i khans as serious threats to their own driving ambitions for power. As a strategy to undermine the khans' credibility before they could garner a base broader than their tribal constituency, these men questioned the khans' loyalty to Khomeini and their commitment to the Islamic state and its guiding politico-religious ideologies. They tried to gain support from those Qashqa'i who might oppose the khans' resumed leadership, such as leftists of varying affiliations, schoolteachers, professionals, and the formally educated, most of whom were now urban based and aware of national political currents. Although increasingly antagonistic toward one another, other politicians supported the Qashqa'i khans because of their unwavering, time-proven, anti-shah credentials. After all, the khans had lost their properties and had suffered for decades in exile because of the shah. Some politicians approved of the khans' pro-democracy, pro-nationalist stance. Some also perceived them as secular and liberal in political orientation and as allies of the United States and other Western powers, which were certain liabilities in uncertain political times, especially as viewed by the staunchest, most conservative, anti-imperialist, anti-West advocates of the new regime.[16]

In this volatile context, regional and local revolutionary guards intensified their harassment of the paramount khans, the tribal khans, and their closest allies. Some began to arrest lower-level khans and supporters, and Borzu Qermezi pondered the possibility of such a fate for himself. Guards posted in the region condemned the higher-level khans and urged their seizure and execution. When Borzu conducted errands in the town of Semirom, guards there chastised him for his overt support of the khans.

Revolutionary guards served as a coercive paramilitary force in support of the ruling clergy and were increasing in numbers, strength, and authority throughout Iran. In southwestern Iran, as elsewhere, they were the force with which citizens had to reckon, not Iran's other, weaker armed forces (the army, urban police, and rural gendarmerie), which were still discredited because they had backed the shah during the revolution.

Revolutionary guards tried to prevent Khosrow Khan Qashqa'i from taking his seat in parliament by arresting him in Tehran on 5 June 1980 and beating and imprisoning him there. A day later, fleeing his captors, he traveled south to Qashqa'i summer headquarters at Khosrow Shirin. Already residing there, Naser Khan had sent messages concerning the crisis to the major Qashqa'i khans, including the Darrehshuri khans in Mehr-i Gerd, who met at Jehangir Khan's house to debate their response. Guards laid siege to the home, arrested some men gathered there, and transported them to the town of Shahreza for detention. They ordered other khans (Darrehshuri and others) to submit to their headquarters in Shahreza, as part of their efforts to seize all influential tribal khans (*khan giriftari*, "khan seizure").

48   *The revolution and the Islamic Republic*

At the same time, Borzu and several other Qermezi men traveled south to Khosrow Shirin to demonstrate their loyalty to Naser Khan and the newly escaped Khosrow Khan and to hear their plans for handling the rising tensions. Direct conflict with the paramilitary forces of the new regime seemed imminent. Driving back to Hanalishah, Borzu and his companions stopped at Zarghamabad, south of Semirom, to visit Mirza Tai, a Persian acquaintance there whose wife is Qermezi. Fearing that revolutionary guards would try to seize Borzu as he neared home, Tai suggested that Borzu leave his recognizable vehicle behind, take an indirect route by mule, and stay off the main roads. Tai's son said he would deliver the vehicle to Hanalishah later.

During Borzu's absence, 10 to 20 heavily armed revolutionary guards posted in Semirom made their move against the Qermezi headman. At night they drove in darkened vehicles to Hanalishah, left the jeeps hidden by a distant hill, and came quietly on foot to encircle Borzu's tent. The camp's dogs alerted the nomads to the approaching trespassers. The guards harassed Borzu's frightened family and left a written order for Borzu to appear at guard headquarters in Semirom. Then they searched the nearby tents of Borzu's son Mohammad Karim and Borzu's brother Abdul Husain. Armed with rifles, both men were guarding their sheep in the mountains. The guards eventually located and detained the two men and confiscated their weapons. Then they captured Murad, Borzu's cousin and ally, and looked for but did not find his gun. Murad was not at his campsite at the time, and his family escaped the incursion that the three other families had already suffered. The guards escorted the three men to Semirom and then to Shahreza.

The three men then and later complained about the guns' seizure, an act they regarded as an assault against their rights. In the future, whenever Borzu and the others recalled any part of the episode, they always mentioned that armed guards had forcibly confiscated their weapons. They regarded the seizure as a military and political act charged with symbolism. Later, the regime would attempt to control, by means of permits, the ownership and use of firearms by civilians but, at this time (1980), civilians were not legally forbidden to have weapons.

Borzu heard that revolutionary guards were searching for him, and he returned cautiously to Hanalishah by mule, via an indirect mountainous route. He had bypassed Semirom to avoid the danger that the guards in that town posed to him. After quickly consulting with other Qermezi men, he decided to go to Shahreza to submit to the guards' headquarters there. Three of his close kinsmen were already in custody, and he said he was obliged to help insure their safety. If guards were hunting him, he could not effectively aid his kin from the outside. Guards might kill him, along with innocent family members, if he remained at Hanalishah. Sentiment among the guards in Semirom (and other staunch regime supporters) against the Qashqa'i khans had turned vitriolic, and Borzu worried about renewed acts of violence against his family.

Borzu rode by mule through a steep mountain pass to the east. Arriving at a village along a road, he located a man who offered to drive him to Shahreza.

He chose this difficult route to avoid a paramilitary force traveling along the main road from Semirom.

In Shahreza, Borzu turned himself in at the guards' headquarters where he was roughly escorted first to a hastily assembled Islamic tribunal and then to prison. If guards had located him at the khans' camps at Khosrow Shirin or Mehr-i Gerd, his obvious association with these tribal leaders would have proved damaging and might have provoked further threats against him. Instead, complaining loudly about the arrest warrant, he appeared on his own in Shahreza. About the same time, guards returned to Hanalishah to seize Borzu's gun. His family claimed innocence, and the guards failed to find it during a disruptive search of the tent and its piles of baggage. They impounded his Land Rover, which his Persian friend had tried to hide for him. When they interrogated Borzu in Shahreza, he swore that he did not possess any weapons.

Simultaneous to Borzu's arrest, revolutionary guards also apprehended prominent Qashqa'i khans, *kikha*s (lesser khans), and other figures. As part of their raids, they grabbed all the weapons they could find; they wanted to prevent any armed resistance. They also seized vehicles to prevent the people left behind from joining or seeking support from other khans, especially the paramount khans still residing safely at Khosrow Shirin to the south.

Iran's rulers through the centuries had feared the possibility of khan-led tribal uprisings. The new rulers now perceived the Qashqa'i khans as threats to their efforts to centralize power and exert force over Iran's citizens.

Revolutionary guards transferred the four Qermezi prisoners, and the other Qashqa'i detainees seized about the same time, to a heavily guarded facility, the expropriated private residence of a wealthy Persian family in Shahreza that had fled Iran during the revolution. It contained multiple dwellings and a large garden, the tall walls surrounding the property now topped with barbed wire. It was not Shahreza's regular prison but rather the political headquarters of the revolutionary-guard corps there.[17] As an entity separate from Iran's regular army, police force, and rural gendarmerie, the corps established its own prisons and other places of detention in order to assert its autonomy, exert control over the people it had captured, and apply extra-juridical procedures and punishments.

While Borzu was turning himself in, a small, armed group of young Qarachai, Farsi Madan, and Kashkuli Qashqa'i men ambushed a convoy of revolutionary guards (in seven or eight military vehicles) as it traveled through a mountain pass (Tang-i Jelo) south of Semirom. (Tang-i Jelo is the "first mountain pass" reached when Qashqa'i nomads in the north begin the autumn migration to winter pastures in the south.) The Qashqa'i men had positioned themselves there to block the pass and prevent any guards from traveling farther south to arrest Naser Khan and Khosrow Khan in their camp at Khosrow Shirin. They killed three or four, some say eight or ten, guards in this skirmish, the first of many overt hostilities between the regime's supporters and the Qashqa'i khans and their backers. Able to distinguish between the Qashqa'i and the ethnic-Persian guards in the convoy on the basis of their physical appearance

50 *The revolution and the Islamic Republic*

and behavior, the ambushers avoided shooting any Qashqa'i. Suffering no injuries, the Qashqa'i group quickly dispersed, using back roads that the guards feared because of the threat of another ambush. By radio the guards called for reinforcements and helicopters to remove the dead and wounded.

Then and later, revolutionary guards blamed Naser Khan and Khosrow Khan for inciting the attack against them. Yet the two khans, by then well protected at Khosrow Shirin, had not been present. At the time and subsequently, both khans denied responsibility for the ambush. Privately among themselves and their supporters, they blamed the young tribesmen who had independently undertaken the military action. Newly returned to Iran, the khans understood that their authority over young Qashqa'i men was not assured or automatic. These youth had been born after the khans' forced exile, had not experienced any personal contact with the khans before 1979, and might have lacked their fathers' loyalty. They were inspired, even impassioned, by the changing political scene and wanted to participate in a way that represented their heritage. Armed resistance against the government was a long-held tradition in Qashqa'i society. Periodically during the twentieth century, small groups of young Qashqa'i men had planned and executed military action, independent of or against the khans' orders and sometimes directed against the khans' interests. The Tang-i Jelo incident was the most recent example.[18]

Of the Persian revolutionary guards killed at Tang-i Jelo, at least two hailed from Semirom and one from Shahreza. Semirom residents were angry about the attack against their fellow citizens and held Qashqa'i men including Borzu Qermezi accountable. A prominent Persian townsman claimed that Borzu had been present at Tang-i Jelo during the assault. Borzu and his family and supporters knew that he was detained in Shahreza at the time, and any accusations against him could be proved false (if the authorities handled any forthcoming juridical procedures fairly). If Borzu had been located at or near Tang-i Jelo when the ambush occurred (which could have happened if he had traveled from Khosrow Shirin a day later than he had done), his accusers could have claimed that the paramount khans had sent him there to block the pass and intercept any guards attempting to travel south. Despite Borzu's imprisonment in Shahreza, some Semirom citizens still declared in the 1990s that Borzu was responsible for the guards' deaths. Guards in Shahreza accused the three other detained Qermezi men of being the khans' allies and participating in the attack at Borzu's side. Then and later, even in the late 1990s, some Persians claimed that Qashqa'i forces had killed "two hundred" or "hundreds" of guards at Tang-i Jelo.

Even if the revolutionary guards at Tang-i Jelo had intended to proceed south to arrest or kill Naser Khan and Khosrow Khan, these and other guards did not immediately attempt to seize the two men. The paramount khans remained unimpeded, surrounded by heavily armed Qashqa'i supporters coming from all parts of Qashqa'i territory. The Tang-i Jelo attack, especially the guards' deaths, might have prevented other guards from moving against the khans at this time. Yet the ambush filled many guards with a desire for

The revolution and the Islamic Republic   51

revenge, which they inflicted during the next two years and for some time to follow. They explained their continuing hostilities against the Qashqa'i as stemming from the Tang-i Jelo assault.

Revolutionary guards held the four Qermezi men—Borzu, his son Mohammad Karim, his brother Abdul Husain, and his cousin Murad—under arrest in Shahreza for the next one to three months. Then or later, they did not seize or arrest any other Qermezi men. Detained with the four were some 40 other Darrehshuri men, including major khans (Jehangir among them), minor khans and kikhas, and influential non-elite men of the Narii, Bahramkikhai, and Janbazlu subtribes. Other Qashqa'i men were also imprisoned with them, including Husain Farsi Madan, Irij Qarachai, and other prominent Farsi Madan and Qarachai khans. The summer pastures of these three tribal groups are located in Semirom's vicinity.[19] The guards declared that they would charge Jehangir Khan Darrehshuri, Husain Khan Farsi Madan, Borzu Qermezi, and others with the deaths at Tang-i Jelo and execute them. Unstable political times and the possibility of immediate retaliation meant that no one could predict the outcome. Islamic tribunals and revolutionary judges often suddenly ordered executions, sometimes following brutal torture and forced confessions.[20] The prisoners' families were distraught.

Revolutionary guards had also seized a few Persian dignitaries of the region who were allies of the Qashqa'i khans, and they detained them along with the Qashqa'i prisoners. Nine Darrehshuri leftists, including the brothers and a sister (the only female there) of Allah Quli Jahangiri, were also held in the same facility but in different quarters. They remained captive after the other Darrehshuri prisoners were released, and guards later executed them. Some guards drove their grotesquely swollen bodies, their open-eyed faces pressed macabrely against the vehicle windows, to the homes of the people they had murdered, to prove that the regime had indeed punished them.

Through the efforts of relatives of the high-status detainees, a mediator brought the case of the Qashqa'i men to Ayatollah Jalal ud-Din Tahiri, who was the Friday prayer leader (*imam jumih*) of Isfahan and Khomeini's personal appointee and representative there.[21] As a long-time friend of Khosrow Khan Qashqa'i, Tahiri strove to have the khan's supporters released. He interceded with Islamic tribunal judges, who ultimately never charged any of the prisoners with crimes, much less sentence them to death. The Qashqa'i credited Tahiri for this positive outcome and were grateful to him.[22]

A lesser cleric, known for his efforts to execute Jehangir Khan and Borzu Qermezi, was later killed in the war with Iraq. The Qashqa'i considered his death a just revenge. Perpetrators of violence against Qashqa'i leaders in this and earlier periods subsequently suffered violent deaths, a theme often appearing in oral narratives. As a recent example, each man in the firing squad at Khosrow Khan's execution in 1982 died brutally afterward, one after another over a short period. The Qashqa'i sometimes invoked "the hand of God" in these retaliatory acts.

52 *The revolution and the Islamic Republic*

Borzu Qermezi stated that revolutionary guards had seized and detained him for eight reasons, including that he owned a gun, backed Khosrow Khan Qashqa'i, allied with the Darrehshuri khans, and participated in the Tang-i Jelo ambush. When I asked the three other Qermezi detainees why guards had singled them out, they separately noted, "They said we supported the khans." Borzu often complained that his accusers chastised and swore at him for being a khan ally (*khan khast*, a term having negative connotations since the revolution). Other than his many visits to the paramount and Darrehshuri khans, he had not undertaken any specific actions to promote them, and the other allegations against him were unwarranted and false. He did not comment about the weapon.

A newspaper article published a week after Borzu's arrest reported that he was responsible for the guards' deaths at Tang-i Jelo. Qermezi men read the article posted in a glass case outside a government building in Semirom. This or another newspaper article about the same time wrote that "Borzu Qermezi threw stones at vehicles" at a certain place west of Semirom. Laughing, Borzu noted that anyone familiar with the area would know that the report was false because no road ran near that place. He even created a humorous rhyme using the article's words.[23] The published report about the stone throwing stemmed from the efforts of Allah Quli Jahangiri and other Darrehshuri leftist rebels to discredit Borzu.

Allah Quli's supporters had hidden in a defile between the villages of Galleh Qadam and Vanak, just west of Borzu's summer pastures at Hanalishah, and had cast stones at the vehicles of revolutionary guards and committees (komiteh) as they drove by. Stopping these vehicles with barrages of rocks, the rebels then threatened the occupants with wooden clubs (the utilitarian kind used by Qashqa'i nomads in their livelihoods but also handy as a weapon). In their escalating attempts to create confusion and disinformation, the rebels later reported to other state agents that Borzu Qermezi and his kinsmen were the perpetrators. By planning and implementing the incident, publicizing it, and casting false rumors, they reinforced stereotypes about Qashqa'i tribesmen being bandits and highway robbers and incited the regime to punish and subdue them.

Of the four Qermezi men detained in Shahreza, only Mohammad Karim was physically assaulted. A guard beat him and kicked him in the face, causing severe eye injury and permanent loss of vision. The attacker and 289 other passengers and crew were killed in 1988 when the U.S. military shot down an Iranian passenger plane flying over the Persian Gulf from Bandar Abbas to Dubai on a routine scheduled flight. The Qermezi cited the incident as another example of divine vengeance bestowed on the perpetrators of violence against the Qashqa'i.

Guards periodically threatened all the detainees, including the Qermezi men, with physical harm. With rifles and handguns, they shot at them to scare them. On three or more occasions, guards ordered Borzu to exit his cell, used force to remove him from the sight of the other prisoners, and then shot at him. At

The revolution and the Islamic Republic   53

first the other detainees thought he had been executed. Later they understood the ploy but were agitated that the next time the shots would be lethal.

The four Qermezi men reported that their conditions in prison were difficult during the first days but improved as time went on. When Borzu said that their place of detention was quite comfortable, I joked that a life exposed to the harsh elements in an airy tent in the mountains was probably more aggravating. Always outspoken and argumentative with state agents and other figures of authority (except for the Qashqa'i khans), Borzu occasionally restrained himself under these new circumstances. Because guards had already seized his Land Rover and still sought his rifle, he worried that they would return to harass his family and confiscate his land, livestock, and household possessions (the last signified by the word *pushan*, "handwoven textiles," a family's most valued items). The prisoners' relatives brought food on a regular basis. A Persian resident of Shahreza, Borzu's merchant-acquaintance Haidar Tahani collected pots of stew and steamed rice from Borzu's wife Falak at Hanalishah and delivered them to Borzu for some of his meals. The detained khans later joked about their success in having cooked food, clean clothing, cigarettes, and playing cards smuggled to them, to ease their stay.

Revolutionary guards ordered the many prisoners to perform the daily prayers of Islam. According to many detainees, only Borzu refused. He claimed that he had never learned the Arabic phrases or the stipulated motions and could not comply when the guards yelled at him. A small minority of prisoners who wished to pray did so, while the others did not pray unless forced. Once, during a tour of the facility, an Islamic judge who had heard about Borzu's act of defiance asked him why he refused to pray. Logical and precise, Borzu was always clever in understanding the frame of reference of any authority. He responded to the judge that, for two reasons, prayers were not valid (*qabul*) if conducted under these conditions. (God would not accept these prayers, and there was no point in doing them.) First, he said, private property is inviolable according to Islamic law, and yet the prison itself was an illegally seized personal residence.[24] Second, according to the prophet Mohammad, God does not accept religious rituals performed under compulsion, and yet guards forced the prisoners to pray. (Muslims should lead by example, not compel.) Some prisoners noted that these remarks seemed to impress the judge, who then ordered the guards to lessen the harassment. In this and other cases, people used knowledge about Islamic law and practice to argue against and oppose the agents of the Islamic regime.

During such occasions, Borzu stressed that he was "a Muslim from the past," a genuine, authentic Muslim, unlike those who had recently become practicing Muslims for politically expedient reasons. He often ridiculed those who had seized state power "in the name of Islam" but for reasons promoting their own self-interests.

At the time of Borzu's initial arrest in Shahreza, a revolutionary guard (a Bulvardi Darrehshuri man) had informed the presiding Islamic judge that, decades earlier, Borzu had collected taxes from some tribesmen on behalf of the Qashqa'i khans. (Supporters of the Islamic Republic and other detractors of the paramount khans denounced them for returning to Iran only to resume extorting these taxes.) Stationed with his kinsmen at a mountain pass at the beginning of the spring migration, Borzu—as the agent of a Darrehshuri khan—would stop each migrating group and brand with the khan's symbol one of every one hundred livestock. The owners were then obligated to submit these marked animals to the khan (via Borzu) when they reached summer pastures. The Qashqa'i guard complained to the judge that when his father had migrated a different route one year so he could bypass the khan's branding location, Borzu learned of the deception, caught up with the man later, and branded a flap of his Qashqa'i felt hat in punishment. Laughing at the man's story, Borzu told the guard in Turkish (so the judge and the surrounding Persian guards would not understand), "If your father had intentionally avoided paying the tax, I would have branded his *face*!" The Darrehshuri khans and other Qashqa'i men present snickered until the guards there told them to be silent. Borzu was known for this kind of clever retort, often humorous but also conveying deeper meanings and, as in this case, ridiculing his accuser and righting their respective statuses. The revolution had placed the young son of an ordinary tribesman in a position of state-authorized power over a mature, respected tribal headman. Through biting humor, Borzu drew attention to their former relationship.

Prison officials established Monday as a weekly visiting day, and hundreds of people (including many Qermezi) came to offer the prisoners support during their months-long detention. Overseen by armed guards perched on the high, enclosing walls, the two groups met in the vast courtyard and garden. Visiting her relatives jailed there, including her father-in-law Jehangir Khan, Naheed Dareshuri describes the garden as rich with pockets of vibrant colors. Women and girls in vivid, sparkling Qashqa'i dress sat in the grass, their voluminous skirts spread out around them. They surrounded their male relatives and moved about greeting others. She says she always stopped by Borzu's group to say hello.[25]

As visitors or fellow prisoners, many who had not encountered Borzu before met him under these conditions. Those who had heard about his complex, dynamic personality experienced a chance to see firsthand the man whose reputation had preceded him.

Borzu commented later that he had worried about his family, tribal group, and property during his imprisonment (although his Qermezi visitors did offer reassuring news). He and others disapproved of the direction that Iranian politics appeared to be taking—and sweeping them along with it. Still, they spent a unique, memorable time together. Gauging by his and others' remarks, I understood that this experience was a highlight of their lives. They knew that their detention demonstrated their solidarity with the newly returned paramount Qashqa'i khans. It particularly expressed their growing antagonism toward the Islamic state and its leaders, policies, and hostile forces, exemplified by the paramilitary guards who had tracked them down and detained them.

The revolution and the Islamic Republic 55

Later, their imprisonment served to mark—and to date—their early opposition to the rulers and supporters of the Islamic Republic. It authenticated in unambiguous fashion their rebellious political stance at a time when other sectors of Iranian society were unwilling or afraid to express their criticism publicly. Also, the detention of so many Qashqa'i men coincided with the paramount khans' own organized resistance (see later) and played a factor in its emergence, numbers of participants, and persistence.

During Borzu's absence, Husain Ali Qermezi spent every night in Borzu's tent at Hanalishah to help safeguard the family. He is Borzu's brother's son, and his wife is Borzu's daughter. Husain Ali worried about zealous revolutionary guards returning to Hanalishah to seize other men, terrorize their families with threats of the men's imminent execution, and confiscate weapons and other property. (Borzu owned the only vehicle in the territory then.)

Husain Ali was also troubled by the leftist rebel Allah Quli Jahangiri, a Janbazlu Darrehshuri man, who was still seeking sanctuary in the mountains of summer pastures and who threatened to kill Borzu on his release from prison, because of his pro-khan stance. Allah Quli and his small cohort of allies had already murdered at least 25 Darrehshuri men, including some dedicated teachers he detested (and he would kill others in the coming months). Husain Ali and other Qermezi took the threats seriously. Allah Quli held personal (and not necessarily political or ideological) grudges against each of his victims. (Such personally motivated violence discredited Allah Quli and leftist movements in general, and it discouraged other Qashqa'i from considering seriously leftist ideologies and actions.) Allah Quli's brothers and a sister were still detained in the same prison as Borzu, and guards would soon execute them.

(Allah Quli did intensify his threats against Borzu after Borzu's discharge from prison. Before he could inflict further violence against his perceived enemies, Iran's paramilitary forces killed him along with members of his small group when they sought refuge in a mountain cave near Isfahan. Exemplifying the changing times, Iranian television provided live coverage of the siege, attack, and rows of dead bodies.)

Husain Ali's elder brother, Bahram, and several of Bahram's supporters opposed Husain Ali's armed vigilance, which signified to them his allegiance to the khans. In his defense, Husain Ali asserted that he was simply protecting the family of his paternal uncle, a threatened, imprisoned man, which the codes of tribal honor required him to do. Bahram was emerging as a hezbollahi, a determined advocate of the Islamic regime and a detractor of the Qashqa'i khans. He sought to lead the Qermezi subtribe, particularly the nomads encamped at Dashtak and Hanalishah. Borzu's detention offered Bahram an opportunity to exert his influence in the subtribe without challenging Borzu directly. As Borzu's nephew, Bahram was subordinate to him.

Of the four Qermezi men, Murad was released from prison first (held for 19 days), then Borzu (held for 36 or 45 days), and finally Abdul Husain and Mohammad Karim together (each held for 75 days). The guards freed Murad

56 *The revolution and the Islamic Republic*

and Borzu before the other two because, they said, they had not found guns in the men's possession at the time of their capture. Murad was not implicated in the Tang-i Jelo ambush, while Borzu was, but Borzu could unambiguously prove that he was already under detention in Shahreza at the time. The two other men remained in prison longer because they were armed at the time of their capture. Afterward, whenever the four men mentioned the experience, they usually cited the exact number of days they were detained, each one a travesty of justice. After the men's release, revolutionary guards and other coercive state agents took no further overt hostile action against them. Armed guards in Semirom and during their travels through Hanalishah for the purpose of surveillance and intimidation did periodically harass the four men but did not try to capture them again. Borzu regained his vehicle after some months of effort, only to discover how much abuse it had suffered in the interval. After a year Mohammad Karim secured his rifle's return. A guard had confiscated it for personal use and then illegally sold it. Another guard had irreparably damaged Abdul Husain's rifle after its seizure and then reportedly destroyed it.

Revolutionary guards demanded bribes to speed the release of the imprisoned Qashqa'i khans and kikhas, whom they perceived as wealthy compared with the other tribal detainees such as the Qermezi men. They regarded the tribesmen as impoverished and seemed not to know about tribal custom, in which every household in a subtribe would contribute funds to gain the freedom of a fellow tribesman. A khan detained in Shahreza on other charges some months previously produced the stub of a check he had earlier given the guards as a bribe and noted that he had already paid them sufficiently. Other khans claimed they lacked any cash in the summer, a season not producing income for them. That autumn after the men's return home, the same guards, renewing their quest for bribery, arrived in Mehr-i Gerd with two large trucks, one to confiscate the Darrehshuri khans' just-harvested apples, the other their sheep. The khans noted that despite revolutionary ideals and their captors' newfound enthusiasm for Islam, the greed for bribery was the same as under the shah.[26]

The forced detention of the Qashqa'i men created intense solidarity among them, a trait found among political prisoners elsewhere in the world. The men enhanced their existing bonds and created new ones. If the guards had intended to punish them for their politics and to prevent their further politicization, they failed. After his release, Borzu often mentioned the men with whom he had been imprisoned, and his respect for tribal leaders at all levels deepened. Many of his fellow prisoners joined the defensive tribal resistance formed around Khosrow Khan Qashqa'i after his arrest (and subsequent expulsion from parliament). These men later explained their readiness to participate by the camaraderie they had experienced while detained together in Shahreza. Other members of the resistance who were imprisoned elsewhere about the same time cited the same reason.[27]

Borzu did not join the defensive resistance (*urdu*, a term meaning a tribal camp or military gathering) of the paramount Qashqa'i khans. The phrase

The revolution and the Islamic Republic 57

"defensive resistance" refers to the absence of planned offensive actions. For two years the paramilitary and military forces of the Islamic regime attacked and attempted to capture the group in a succession of remote, isolated, mountainous locales. The khans and their supporters did not orchestrate any counter-attacks except for several small-scale, opportunistic ones involving only a few men. (These few assaults ended disastrously for the Qashqa'i participants.) The khans and their companions viewed their actions as defensive ones that protected Khosrow Khan from further arrest and guarded his possible successors as the confederacy leaders. The resistance movement— beginning in June 1980 and ending after Khosrow Khan's capture in July 1982—drew only a small group of varying size and composition depending on the location and the wider events.

Borzu was already detained when the resistance began, and on his release the persistent threats of the leftist rebel Allah Quli against his life preoccupied him. The many men whom Allah Quli and his cohorts had already murdered gave Borzu cause to worry about himself and his family and group. Revolutionary guards threatened to seize Borzu again and return him to prison. Simultaneously Borzu was confronting the Persian villagers and townsmen who were exploiting the postrevolutionary disruptions to steal his pastureland at Hanalishah and convert it to agricultural use. He was trying to restore his livelihood, interrupted by his detention. While imprisoned, he had instructed his sons to sell most of the livestock, to prevent the animals' confiscation, and he was trying now to rebuild his herds. He experienced heart problems, soon to debilitate him, and he regretted that ill health prevented him from joining the khans' resistance camps. He noted that he could not travel such a distance for any extended period, given the threats he and his family faced at home. Still, he remarked that his absence did not indicate a decline in support or loyalty. As he grew more infirm and understood that he would not live much longer, he expressed regret that he had not participated directly in the paramount khans' defensive action.

Borzu had supported the idea of a revolution against the shahs. The father and the son had killed his father (1943), executed the Qashqa'i ilkhani (1933), imprisoned the next ilkhani (1930s–1941), drove the ilkhani into foreign exile (1954–79), and attempted to destroy the livelihood and identity of the Qashqa'i (1926–79). When clerics seized control and declared an Islamic republic, Borzu grew skeptical about their ideologies and the changes they were implementing. Then, during the events preceding his arrest until after his imprisonment, Borzu rejected the revolution because its zealots had endangered him and other Qashqa'i. As a victim of multiple death threats proclaimed by the revolution's guardians (clergymen, revolutionary guards, and Islamic judges) and by a leftist rebel who remained unchecked by the regime, Borzu said he lacked any reason to change his negative opinion. When the Islamic Republic publicly executed Khosrow Khan (1982), Borzu proclaimed that he would never support the regime in any way, a stance he maintained until his death.

58 *The revolution and the Islamic Republic*

Martyrs of the Iraq–Iran war

The Qermezi were anxious to inform me in 1991 about events occurring since my last visit. The first news they conveyed on my arrival concerned the group's many martyrs (*shahid*) in the Iraq–Iran war (22 September 1980 to 20 August 1988, one month short of eight years). When I inquired how many had died, several replied that 17 had perished. I feared asking their names; I would have personally known most if not all of them. They would have been schoolchildren when I first lived with the group. Later, when I learned their names, the list contained 14 boys, not 17. When I was able to ask details, I heard that one boy they identified as a martyr was shot and killed in revolutionary demonstrations in Shiraz before the shah fled. Of the remaining 13 boys and young men, eight were killed in battle and their bodies returned to their families, four were presumed killed in combat but their bodies were not recovered, and one died several years after suffering war injuries.

Then and later, when men listed or referred to the martyrs, they usually mentioned only the fathers' names. Sons represented fathers just as fathers represented sons. Women always identified the martyrs as the sons of their mothers, for example, "Maryam's boy." (Such patterns of reference extend beyond this particular context.)

One man noted later that Shir Mohammad was the Qermezi subtribe's first (and only previous) martyr, a specific identification I had never heard until the Iraq–Iran war caused so many fatalities. Riddled with bullets by Iran's army in the 1943 battle of Semirom, he was the only Qermezi ever killed in state-level armed conflict before the Iraq–Iran war's outbreak. Other Qermezi had died in tribal disputes, some of which expressed regional and national politics. No Qermezi were killed battling the British troops posted in south-western Iran during World War I.[28]

Of the more than 150 Qermezi boys and young men who volunteered or were conscripted to fight in the Iraq–Iran war, 13 were killed or presumed killed, two were seriously wounded but survived, five received less severe wounds, at least three more suffered acutely from chemical warfare, and two were captured by Iraqi forces and held as prisoners of war in Iraq.[29] No one ever reported any draft dodgers, deserters, or absentees, and I presume that such acts were rare or nonexistent. Qermezi and other Qashqa'i men were proud of their reputations as courageous, proficient, honorable warriors, traits that the participants aimed to emulate. (I include a possible case of defection later.)

These numbers can be compared with those of other small communities in southwestern Iran. With 700 residents, the Darrehshuri village of Mehr-i Gerd lost at least seven boys in the war. Shishdangi, a Persian village near Shiraz with 1,300 people, had six graves in its martyrs' cemetery.[30] Guyum, a Persian village of 2,500 inhabitants near Shiraz, experienced 26 war deaths.[31] One hundred martyrs originated from the Persian/Lur village of Vanak, near Semirom, with 2,500 residents. Some Qermezi noted that their subtribe suffered more

The revolution and the Islamic Republic   59

losses than many other Darrehshuri subtribes, each of which lost only a few or perhaps no more than six or eight boys.[32]

A Qermezi man serving in the volunteer basij militia reported that 800 Qashqa'i boys and men in this force were killed. The state agency in Shiraz for nomads' education listed 50 or so tribal teachers as war martyrs, many or most of them Qashqa'i. Two of them are Qermezi. Sixty-eight graduates and upper-level students of the prestigious tribal secondary school in Shiraz were killed, many or most of them Qashqa'i. Their photographs lined the walls of the school's entrance in tribute in the late 1980s.[33]

No accurate official figures for the eight-year war are publicly available. Perhaps 300,000 Iranians were killed (mostly combatants but also civilian casualties from Iraqi bombs, missiles, and ground assaults), another 400,000 to 750,000 injured, and two million displaced. Iraq took 30,000 to 50,000 prisoners of war, and Iran took 70,000. The total combatant casualties of the war range from 400,000 to two million.[34]

Well after the war began, a section of the corps of revolutionary guards (*sipah-i pasdaran-i inqilab-i islami*) provided soldiers with identity cards. Later, the martyrs' evacuation brigade, a subsection of this entity, collected injured and dead soldiers from battlefields. The government formed in 1990 (two years after the war's ceasefire) a committee for finding missing soldiers, and it began a foundation for the memorializing of identified, unidentified, and unknown martyrs.[35]

Iranian officials stated throughout the 1990s that they wanted to continue exchanging prisoners with Iraq, a process begun in August 1990.[36] Yet, in 1996 and periodically thereafter, Iraq's government declared that it no longer held any prisoners, a stance it still upheld in 2001. That year Iran acknowledged holding thousands of Iraqis but claimed that 97 percent of prisoners on both sides had already been released. Many Shi'i Iraqi prisoners chose to remain in Iran after their release, and the government there offered some of them jobs.[37] Iranian authorities in 2002 listed the names of 900 Iranian citizens still being held captive. The military occupation of Iraq by United States forces in 2003 allowed any remaining Iranian captives to return home (if they chose to do so). The fate of many of them still remained unknown in 2013.

Most Qermezi participants in the war joined as part of Iran's new volunteer militia (*niruha-yi basiji*), especially its nomads' division. Years after the war's end, these volunteers (basiji) stated that they had responded emotionally to recruiting by Iran's new revolutionary organizations; to entreaties from Khomeini, other clerics, and secular leaders such as President Abul Hasan Bani-Sadr (1980–81); and to growing sentiment within Iran. Some volunteered because national leaders appealed to men with military training. Unlike many other Iranian youth, practically all Qermezi males were skilled marksmen, hunters, and mountaineers and were accustomed to living outdoors under difficult conditions. Others registering as volunteers, particularly older men, received a militia card but were not called to serve.

Other Qermezi were conscripted soldiers in the regular army when the war broke out or were called up afterward. Of the 150 participants, perhaps only

60 *The revolution and the Islamic Republic*

30 were regular army soldiers. Fathullah Qermezi had completed his mandatory two-year military service as a "soldier-teacher" when the army added another six months to his duty.[38]

Still other Qermezi joined the corps of revolutionary guards or its special nomads' corps (*sipah-i pasdaran-i inqilabi-i islami ashayiri*). They were revolutionary guards before the war, or, more commonly, they entered the corps during the war and were sent to fight in this capacity or served in other ways. Members of the nomads' corps recruited among the tribal and nomadic groups with which they were affiliated and where they were posted. Some recruits reported later that they had responded to these appeals out of tribal loyalty, not Iranian patriotism per se.

Whenever I asked people to list those who had participated in the war, they usually included some older Qermezi men who held positions in the subtribe's local Islamic councils. The government's Organization for Nomads' Affairs and the Ministry of Construction Jihad took council members to view the war firsthand, not necessarily the front line but the vicinity, and they remained there for only 20 days.

Qermezi men referred to Islam, Iranian nationalism, the Qashqa'i, and their tribal and family groups when they explained why they had joined the war effort. The state issued intensive propaganda, mostly related to Islam, to which some men responded. Khomeini and other clerics claimed that the secularist, infidel Saddam Hossein would destroy Islam if the faithful did not defeat the Iraqi leader and protect the religion from attack. Some clergymen fanned the fires of Shi'i-Sunni conflict and exploited the emotions of Shi'i Iranians about Imam Husain, who was killed by anti-Shi'i forces in AD 680 in what is today Iraq. (Grandson of the prophet Mohammad, Husain is the third of 12 imams in the majority branch of Shi'i Islam.) Iran's secular and other leaders stressed that Saddam Hossein threatened Iran's independence and territorial integrity and that Iranians would fall victim to the domination of Iraq's Arabs and Sunni Muslims, which was already the experience of millions of destitute Shi'i Muslims in southern Iraq and millions of Shi'i (and Sunni) Kurds in northern Iraq. Several Qermezi men mentioned that Iraq would seize Iran's oil fields and installations if Iranians did not repel the invaders. When Iraq sent missiles against cities far from the front, including Tehran, many Iranians grew more patriotic. When I asked Qermezi men why they had responded to the appeals, especially when the risks had grown, most stated that they had wanted to emulate their tribesmate and kinsman, Shahriyar Qermezi, who demonstrated courage and resilience against the enemy. Others commented that Iraqi soldiers would assault Qashqa'i women and children if Qashqa'i men did not stop the incursions.

Most Qermezi men stated that, as the war dragged on, they understood that Iranian leaders—Khomeini in particular—were motivated by nonmilitary reasons to prolong it further. They were skeptical about the state's propaganda and perceived the conflict as an attempt to sustain revolutionary fervor and especially to keep these leaders and their regime in power. The war helped

The revolution and the Islamic Republic   61

Iran's political elite to weaken and silence any internal opposition.[39] After the war, with no military or territorial gains for either disputant, Qermezi men were even more cynical and often expressed regret that they had been so gullible.

For most Qermezi, their haste to adopt patriotic sentiments for Iran had backfired when so many of their boys were killed, wounded, or captured in seemingly random fashion. They said they should pay attention instead to their local and regional kinship, tribal, and ethnic ties. The war had served to strengthen these bonds for them; the tragic, pointless deaths of the group's boys had united the subtribe. People who were separated by new livelihoods and lifestyles renewed their contacts by attending the many condolence rites. The war's casualties demonstrated that no one could predict when any of them would need the support of others, and it alerted them to the overriding importance of having and perpetuating meaningful kinship, tribal, and ethnic affiliations.

Many war veterans volunteered information in 1991 about their experiences while they sat together with relatives and tribesmates, but by 1995 hardly any were doing so, and from 1999 through 2004 I never heard anyone speak spontaneously about the war. When I privately asked about the diminished conversation, people responded that too much time had passed and that they already knew the details. Many remarked that the war had not accomplished any positive results and that discussions about it were unproductive. Increasingly they stressed that the ayatollahs had exploited them by forcing them into the war and then sustaining the conflict for the purposes of their own power and the accruing economic benefits. Many of them complained that they had been duped.

Hearing the news

Khanum and her son's wife Zohreh were pursuing routine tasks at their summer campsite at Hanalishah one day in 1988. Khanum was weaving at her loom, her usual location, beside the family tent. A military vehicle appeared on the dirt road downhill and then slowly made its way up a rocky path toward the tent. The news the two women heard was devastating: Farhad Qermezi had been killed in the war. The boy is Khanum's grandson, the eldest son of her eldest son Bahram. Within minutes the sad news traveled throughout Hanalishah and within a day to practically every other Qermezi location. Hundreds of mourners came to grieve and to offer condolences to Farhad's family and kinship group.

Farhad's extended family visited the cold-storage morgue in Semirom where the boy's body had been transported four or five days after his death. Women kissed his cheek, which they remarked was cold. He lay on his side, as if he were sleeping, and a small patch of dried blood marked his shirt. No one had undressed or cleaned him in any way; he appeared as he had died, sweat stained and dusty and still wearing boots and his militia uniform. Later, the brother of another Qermezi martyr reported that he had met a soldier who

62 *The revolution and the Islamic Republic*

was standing near Farhad when he was shot in the back, the bullet apparently piercing his heart. He stretched out his arms in front of him and fell to the ground and died. This description matched the state of Farhad's body and attire when he arrived in Semirom, and his family was relieved to know that he might not have suffered.

Farhad's family wrapped him, still in battleground condition, in a single piece of white cloth and took him to Atakula village for burial. Clergymen positioned at the morgue had assured the martyrs' families that the boys had died in a holy war (*jihad*), their souls had traveled directly to heaven, and their bodies required no washing or preparing. Farhad's kindred (and others) were shocked, and they found the disturbing instructions difficult to obey. They were accustomed to following specific rituals for cleaning and handling bodies and attiring them in multipiece shrouds. His female kin worried especially about his boots. They lamented that for all of eternity he would be uncomfortable wearing them. They said they had desperately wanted to remove them but feared that the *akhund*s would publicly chastise them for not respecting Islam.[40] "Even when we die, the *mulla*s are still controlling us." ("Akhund" is an often derogatory term that the Qashqa'i and other Iranians use for clergymen of all levels.)[41] Increasingly, most Qermezi blamed akhunds and mullas for such incomprehensible rulings, rather than questioning the basic tenets of the religion.

The dead and the missing

Of the 13 Qermezi boys and young men killed or presumed killed in or because of the war, seven were basij militia volunteers, two were revolutionary guards, and four were conscripted army soldiers. Four came from Aqa Mohammadli lineage, three from Imamverdili, none from Qairkhbaili, one from Qasemli, three from Kachili, and two from affiliated families. No meaningful pattern relating to lineage affiliation appears in this distribution.

A young man's place of residence more accurately predicted his fate than his lineage. Many boys from Atakula, Dezeh, and Naqneh villages and the nearby town of Borujen volunteered for the militia, a higher representation than from other localized Qermezi communities. The residents there were more integrated in the larger Iranian society and culture, more familiar with institutional Islam, more subject to and influenced by state propaganda, and more susceptible to recruiting. These locations also held the Qermezi subtribe's staunchest supporters of the Islamic Republic. Practically all of the subtribe's hezbollahis and revolutionary guards came from there. The young men who were dedicated to the Islamic regime were possibly also the ones who exerted greater effort in the war and put themselves at higher risk than others. Of the 13 dead boys, 10 came from these settlements. Another one was a Mehr-i Gerd villager. Only two of the 13 originated from families who were at the time traditional nomadic pastoralists.

From an affiliated family, one martyr, Kuhyar, is the son of a Musuli Amaleh Qashqa'i man who had joined the Qermezi subtribe when he was a

The revolution and the Islamic Republic   63

boy. He married an Aqa Mohammadli girl and remained with the group since, most recently moving to Atakula village along with some Aqa Mohammadli men. The other martyr from an affiliated family is Nasrullah, the son of the Qermezi subtribe's ritual specialist (*ussa*), who is part of a larger group of specialists within the Darrehshuri tribe. A former resident of Mehr-i Gerd, the father had relocated to Dezeh village. By including these two martyrs, the Qermezi reflected the dynamic nature of lineage and subtribal affiliation and identity. The two Musuli Amaleh men who had first associated with the Qermezi subtribe in 1921 were by the early 1980s considered to be Qermezi on the basis of decades of co-residence, intermarriage, and political association. Without hesitating or being prompted, the men listing the Qermezi martyrs always included Kuhyar. A few did not mention Nasrullah initially, but when I asked about him, they replied, "Certainly, he is one of our martyrs too."

In 1991, a little more than two years after the war's ceasefire, four young Qermezi men were presumed to have been killed but their bodies had not been recovered and returned to their parents. Their families expressed hope that they were prisoners of war in Iraq.

Safdar, the son of Mukhtar of Imamverdili lineage, disappeared in the war in 1982, one of the first Qermezi casualties. He was a schoolteacher with a promising career. His wife had bore him one child and expected another. He is the only Qermezi martyr for whom people regularly used the martyr title, in his case "Shahid Safdar." The other young martyrs had not yet attained professions, and only one other individual was married. (One had trained as a teacher but had not yet begun to teach when he left for the war, and one who died later of war injuries had married and sired children after returning home.) People perceived Safdar's death as more tragic than the others because he had left behind a wife and small children. The widow's mother is Shahriyar Qermezi's sister, a kinship tie enhancing her daughter's status. Shahriyar is the Qermezi subtribe's preeminent war hero.

Some of Safdar's physical remains surfaced in 1995, or at least the government's agents presented them as his. Iran and Iraq had allowed their representatives to search battlefields for human remains, and they recovered thousands of bodies as well as body parts and possibly identifying objects. Iran's Martyrs Foundation notified Safdar's wife and parents about the recovery and later delivered a skull, long bones, a metal identity tag, and an undershirt.[42] The news spread swiftly throughout Qermezi territories, and hundreds of people hastened to Dezeh village, where Safdar's wife and two children lived, for the funeral.

While men talked mostly about the bones and the difficulty in determining their identity, women concentrated only on the undershirt. It was the sole personal possession recovered with the bones, and women reacted emotionally. They did not speak about the impossibility of identifying a particular piece of unmarked clothing, especially such a common one. They talked about the garment as if Safdar had actually worn it. They said they dressed their babies and small children in such attire and were heartbroken that this article was now

64 *The revolution and the Islamic Republic*

all that remained of the boy. Worn close to the body, the undershirt provided a poignant connection for the women in a way that the bones did not.

The family buried Safdar's skull and long bones in the cemetery of Dezeh village, an event occurring, people noted, "thirteen years and two months" after the young man had disappeared, a period that these mourners said was incomprehensible. No one washed the bones or prepared them for interment in the customary way. Clergy from the Martyrs Foundation had instructed the relatives that, because of the holy war, Safdar's remains did not require the purifying rituals otherwise conducted for deceased Muslims. Similar to Farhad's family, Safdar's kin chafed under these restrictions and wondered what harm would ensue if they observed the customary rites. The family did proceed with the same kinds of burial, funeral, and memorial services that the surrounding Persian-dominated society practiced. More Qermezi from their many dispersed locations attended these events than usually participated. They recognized Safdar's lamentable end, a tragedy for the entire subtribe. The foundation had returned the remains of two other martyrs from Dezeh, boys from another Darrehshuri subtribe, at the same time as Safdar's, and their services occurred separately but simultaneously with his. Each of the three families wanted a comparably large attendance at its ceremonies.

Husain Ali, the son of No Ruz Quli of Qasemli lineage, was the second Qermezi boy to disappear in the war, in 1982 or 1983. His family received no news about his fate until 1998. Delegations from Iran and Iraq had continued to search for bodies in one another's territories and the border region. The Iranian representatives located or received from Iraq a thousand sets of remains and transported each set in a simple wooden coffin to Tehran where the Martyrs Foundation distributed them throughout the country. Husain Ali's parents received only bone fragments from a foot, a hand, and the skull, along with a metal identity tag. The family buried the bones and observed the memorial rites.

Kuhyar, the son of Aqa Bua, a Musuli Amaleh Qashqa'i man who lived in Atakula village, disappeared in 1983. His body was still not recovered by 1999, despite the government's efforts to locate all the deceased, and the Martyrs Foundation released no information about him. His parents continued to hope during these 16 years that he was still detained in Iraq as a prisoner of war. His mother was especially distraught during the burial and memorial services for Safdar and Husain Ali, who were also missing for many years. Borzu Qermezi had employed Aqa Bua as a shepherd in 1970–71, and I knew his young son Kuhyar well. Aqa Bua had wanted his sons to achieve a higher standard of living than he had managed to have. The Martyrs Foundation informed Kuhyar's parents in 2000 that his remains (bone fragments along with a tag and a tattered shirt containing some papers in a pocket) had been found in one of many mass graves newly disclosed by the Iraqi military. The parents buried the bones.[43]

The fourth young man whose body was not recovered by 1991 was Abdullah, the son of Isfandiyar of Imamverdili lineage. He was presumed killed in

The revolution and the Islamic Republic   65

battle, and a year after his disappearance the Martyrs Foundation gave his parents a coupon book enabling them to buy basic commodities at state-subsidized prices. It offered this benefit to the parents and wives of all war martyrs. Two years later, without warning, the foundation confiscated the coupon book. Its officials refused to provide the parents with any information. They implied that Abdullah had not been killed after all but instead had defected. Some kinsmen suggested that he might have been captured as a prisoner of war and then, to save himself from torture, might have offered aid to the enemy. Whatever had happened, he did not return home. His parents were distraught. For three years they had mourned their son, and now they did not know his fate. They had still not received by 1999 any news from Abdullah himself or the two governments. The Qermezi often agonized about him. Either he had been a martyr all along and deserved their respect or he had defected, probably after capture, and had abandoned the ties of family, lineage, and tribe that were so meaningful to other Qermezi. The war had created or enhanced patriotic sentiments in many Iranians, some of whom were incredulous that a soldier could betray his country by serving the enemy. A cloud of grief, sorrow, and uncertainty hung over Imamverdili lineage. Several Qermezi reported that Abdullah's family had received a letter from or about him in 2000, but, beyond the news that he was possibly alive in Iraq, no details were forthcoming. The U.S. occupation of Iraq beginning in 2003 did not produce any further information about him.

The families buried the remains of 10 of the 12 recovered martyrs in the small cemeteries of Atakula, Dezeh, and Mehr-i Gerd villages, near where they had lived before the war. The eleventh is Farhad, the son of Bahram of Aqa Mohammadli lineage. One of two nomadic pastoralists in this group of 13 families, Bahram buried Farhad in Atakula's cemetery because he expected to build a house there eventually. Two other Qermezi martyrs were already resting there (with two more to follow), and the survivors appreciated anyone who could attend the graves. Farhad would not be alone. Bahram's brother Bahlul had died suddenly during the spring migration in 1958, and the family buried him where it camped that night. His kin always regretted being unable to visit his grave regularly.

The other martyr not buried near his family is Nasrullah, the son of Ali Mirza, the Qermezi subtribe's ritual specialist. Ali Mirza had recently moved to Dezeh village, and his relocation motivated him to place his son where he too would not be alone. He chose the Shah Reza shrine in Shahreza on the road to Isfahan. Hundreds of martyrs from the region were already interred in this enormous cemetery, with thousands yet to come, and their families received solace as they grieved alongside so many others.

Mehr-i Gerd village has its own cemetery where eight martyrs were buried by the war's end.[44] One of them is Shukrullah, the son of Kaka Khan of Kachili lineage. His grave is the first of the eight as they ascend the hill, and when relatives of the other martyrs visited their loved ones, they also stopped to pay their respects to Shukrullah.[45]

66 *The revolution and the Islamic Republic*

Since suffering their first fatality in the war in 1982, the Qermezi began to follow the customs of the surrounding Persian-dominated society concerning death, burial, and remembrance. To announce a forthcoming memorial, each family purchased printed posters depicting the martyr's photograph (and listing his tribal, subtribal, and lineage affiliations) and distributed them throughout the subtribe and among its associates in other tribes and the wider society. Relatives displayed these posters in their tents and houses for years after the announced events, and visitors paid silent tribute to these boys while they looked at their photographs. The survivors held memorials at the nearest mosques and hired mullas to recite from the Qur'an.[46]

The 13 families of the dead and missing boys received special state benefits and privileges over which the Martyrs Foundation exercised control. The family of Nuri, killed in anti-shah demonstrations, also obtained the foundation's aid. For Abdullah's family, the favors ended after two years, when the foundation began to doubt his martyrdom. Parents, wives, and children received initial death benefits, monthly stipends, and other funds with which they bought land, houses, tractors, and vehicles. The foundation gave Safdar's widow and children a house in Dezeh village and three monthly stipends for living expenses. If she remarried, her stipend but not those of her children would cease, and she would retain the house on their behalf. The martyrs' siblings and offspring received preferential treatment when applying for admission to university and seeking government jobs.[47] The foundation arranged subsidized or cost-free pilgrimages for martyrs' families to the tomb of the eighth Shiʻi imam in Mashhad in north-eastern Iran. It registered family members who wanted to go as pilgrims to Mecca. When state officials traveled to Zain Ali near Hanalishah in 1992 to preside over the government's festivities commemorating the national Day of the Nomad, they presented valuable gold coins to any fathers of martyrs who came forward.

The wounded

Of the surviving veterans, Nazar Ali, the son of Ghulam Shah of Imamverdili lineage, had been the most severely injured. A shell exploded above his head, and a fragment entered his skull. Conscious when removed from the battlefield, he knew he was incapacitated. Surgeons removed the fragment but it had damaged the part of his brain controlling his legs and feet, and he never walked again. The Martyrs Foundation provided him a wheelchair, a monthly stipend for living expenses, and occasionally a driver. After several years he grew bitter about the lack of proper medical treatment and vowed to leave Iran to seek help, but the government denied him permission. He complained that the regime wanted to prevent him from publicizing abroad the details of his poor medical care. (A Saint Louis neurosurgeon who examined Nazar Ali's X rays and other medical records noted that the man's hopes for rehabilitation were most likely unwarranted, given the extent of his injuries.)[48]

Shahriyar, the son of Sohrab of Imamverdili lineage, was also seriously injured. During his eight years of service in the nomads' volunteer basij militia,

The revolution and the Islamic Republic 67

he suffered 11 wounds in many parts of his body.[49] His battlefield companions report that he was courageous against the enemy, especially when he was injured. His most critical trauma was in the upper abdomen. A shell fragment ripped open his torso, and intestines spilled out. Recovering from the blast's shock, he reinserted the intestines in the abdominal cavity, tightly wrapped a long cloth around his midsection, and resumed fighting. Later that day he underwent surgery to close the wound. On another occasion, when a bullet struck his lower leg, he bound the limb to restrict the bleeding and continued with his military mission. Except to his immediate family in the first days after returning home from the war, he never spoke about his heroism or his injuries. Most of the stories told about him originated from men who had engaged in combat near him and witnessed his actions firsthand. His valor during the war helped in his successful campaign for a seat in Iran's parliament in 1996.

People cited another Qermezi boy as a war hero, and he too was injured. Ali Khan, the son of Fariburz of Aqa Mohammadli lineage, shot down an Iraqi plane as it flew over a battlefield at a low elevation. Iconography produced in Iran during the war includes images of a sole Iranian soldier downing an Iraqi aircraft as he aimed at it from the ground.[50] In rural Iran this scene was hand-painted on the exteriors of public buildings such as schools and mosques. Ali Khan's former classmates drew such a scene on his father's house in Atakula. Ali Khan sustained a severe foot wound, and after the war the state provided him a job in the Borujen prison.

Said, the son of Asadullah of Aqa Mohammadli lineage, fell victim to chemical weapons in Iranian territory near Abadan during his second tour of duty in the volunteer militia, near the war's end. The airborne attack covered him with a poisonous powder that adhered to his moist skin (the weather being excessively hot and humid). (Iraq used slow-acting mustard gas, quick-acting cyanide, and sarin and other nerve gases, beginning in 1983.)[51] Said suffered from severe skin rashes until the mid-1990s. He noted that he would have preferred a shell injury, which would have healed. Instead he had to face the long-term, still-unknown consequences of intensive chemical exposure. No state agencies or medical facilities tracked his health's status, and no medical practitioners informed him about possible future problems. His general health in 2004 was poor, and several doctors blamed the war's chemical hazards.

The son of Amir Husain of the same lineage as Said, Farajullah experienced Iraqi chemical attacks toward the war's end but was not debilitated at the time. Doctors diagnosed his recently deteriorating condition in 2001 as leukemia and noted that they were simultaneously seeing thousands of such outbreaks among veterans who had been similarly imperiled.[52] Despite the definitive diagnosis, Farajullah received little medical care, and people expected him to die soon. He passed away in 2003.

Men wounded in the war received special state services and benefits including preferential university admission. The Qermezi individuals who attended high-status state universities include Shahriyar, Said, and Farajullah, which they attributed to their having sustained injuries.

68 The revolution and the Islamic Republic

Prisoners of war

Iraqi forces captured two Qermezi boys, held them as prisoners of war (*asir*), and released them in or after August 1990 when Saddam Hussein finally agreed to begin an exchange. (Abdullah Qermezi might be the third prisoner but no one in the subtribe knew about his fate.)

Ghulam Hasan, the youngest son of Sohrab of Imamverdili lineage, was seized at the beginning of the war along with his volunteer militia unit of 30 to 40 men, some of whom the Iraqis shot on the spot after tying their hands behind their backs. Prisoners captured at night were often killed then; those caught during daylight were usually separated from their companions and sent to camps in different parts of Iraq. Ghulam Hasan was held in prisoner-of-war camps in Mosul in northern Iraq for nearly eight years. His family back home soon learned about his capture from his brother Shahriyar, who had been stationed nearby. Iraq released Ghulam Hasan as part of a prisoner exchange after the war's ceasefire, and he returned to his family bent over and emaciated. Similar to Shahriyar, Ghulam Hasan never spoke about his experiences except to his immediate family, and the Qermezi knew little about his ordeal. He suffered terrible conditions in prison, and guards often beat him. His sister said that he lived for months on eggplant peelings and melon rinds (remnants of the guards' meals) and that his cell's space was too small for the many captives there to lie down at the same time. In one cell, each prisoner's space was only "two tiles wide." Prisoners passed the time by telling stories, reciting poems, and, for some, reading the Qur'an.

Iraqi soldiers captured Husain, the son of Isfandiyar of Qairkhbaili lineage, and held him at Tikrit (Saddam Hussein's hometown) in north-central Iraq for four years. He sustained a leg wound in battle, and his captors debated shooting him. Instead they threw him into the back of a truck and took him for rudimentary medical treatment and then to prison. His distraught family heard no news about him for a year and did not know if he were dead or alive. Then the Red Cross or the Red Crescent (both serving in the area) gave Iranian authorities a letter in which Husain stated his and his father's names and their place of residence. After Husain's release, he did not mention his ordeal to anyone other than his closest family. People noted that his eyes told a story of privation and abuse.

Radio Baghdad broadcast the taped statements of some prisoners. Families also received news when released prisoners provided information to Iranian officials about those still in captivity. After their safe return home, some men visited the families of those still imprisoned to relay details about their loved ones, especially if the two parties shared tribal, ethnic, and/or regional ties. Families of martyrs also learned specifics in this way. I witnessed an emotional meeting, when a militia volunteer who had been standing alongside a Qermezi boy when he was shot came to offer condolences to the boy's family. As he apologized for having gone home to see his own family first, everyone broke into tears, moved by his kindness.

During the boys' captivity, parents obtained monthly stipends and other state benefits. On release, both men received an initial cash payment equivalent to lost salary, a house, a vehicle, monthly stipends, and bank loans. Similar to other former prisoners, they were given preferential treatment when seeking university admission and government jobs and were advantaged over others lacking their circumstances. For every year that prisoners spent as captives, they were entitled to retire on a state pension three years ahead of other employees in comparable jobs. Ghulam Hasan had nearly reached that retirement point in 1999, 21 years before his fellow workers, and he could earn income from other activities while simultaneously receiving his pension. Government favors meant that Ghulam Hasan and Husain were better placed economically than other Qermezi men their age, despite many lost years.

When I asked about the prisoners of war possibly still held by Iraq in 1999, Qermezi men mentioned two, Kuhyar and Abdullah (see earlier). Their families hoped that they were still alive while others presumed, on the basis of the many years gone by, that they had been killed in battle or had died as captives.[53] Kuhyar's parents received his remains in 2000 and were finally able to still their doubts about his fate.

The war's aftermath

As each year passed after the war's ceasefire, the Qermezi talked less about the tragedy unless a specific event, such as the retrieval of bones, drew their interest. When I periodically asked about Iran's official stance on the war, people said that the government still declared that the "imposed" or "forced" war (*jang-i tahmili*) was Iraq's fault and that Iran had needed to defend itself.[54] Some Qermezi had complained in 1991–92 about the financial, educational, and employment benefits the state offered to martyrs' families and war veterans. They seemed to have relinquished the issue by 1999. Time proved to be an equalizer. Regardless of receiving state assistance or not, all men faced challenges in sustaining existing livelihoods and finding new ones, especially given Iran's worsening economic crises.

The state and the tribe

The relationships between the agencies and agents of the Iranian state and the Qashqa'i changed significantly during and after the revolution in 1978–79. The state itself demonstrated dramatic transformations, thereby altering many dimensions of its connections with the citizens. Yet other features continued as they had done before the revolution (especially in the 1960s and 1970s), a "surprising continuity."[55]

The revolution halted or disrupted many state functions in 1978 and much of 1979. Multiple popular revolutionary organizations (*nahadha-yi inqilab*) emerged in response to the national crisis and articulated highly politicized revolutionary, Islamic, and populist notions. They took over where the state

70 *The revolution and the Islamic Republic*

had collapsed, they performed new tasks, and they competed and sometimes cooperated with still-functioning institutions and with newly founded ones.[56]

Khomeini, Abul Hasan Bani-Sadr, and Prime Minister Mehdi Bazargan attempted by late 1979 to control the operations of these new revolutionary organizations, and the deputies of the first parliament in 1980 tried to legislate their functions. Efforts by these and subsequent leaders to bring them under control often resulted in their further consolidation. These revolutionary organizations operated under the direct supervision of Khomeini and were "neither subject to the forces of the market, nor to the budgetary and accounting scrutiny of the government."[57] Some of them became independent ministries or near-autonomous agencies under the office of the supreme leader (*rahbar*), the president, or the prime minister, and many remained important for years to come. Others were merged with or subsumed in various state agencies. (The revised constitution in 1989 eliminated the prime minister's post and transferred its powers and responsibilities to the president.)

From Khomeini's arrival until Bani-Sadr's dismissal in mid-1981, two parallel national governments operated, often competitively and pursuing conflicting agendas, under the auspices of the conservative, clergy-run Islamic Republican Party (IRP; disbanded in 1987) and the more moderate, often secularizing leaders in the provisional government.[58] The IRP and its strident supporters allied with the increasingly powerful and popular revolutionary organizations and received assistance from them. Some agencies were centralized politically while others operated free from central control, a feature emerging with the revolution and persisting thereafter.

Power rested in parallel organs: the republican institutions of the regime (parliament, the presidency, and, from 1999, municipal councils) and the unelected Islamic institutions (supreme leader, Guardian Council, and Expediency Council).[59] The regime created the Expediency Council in 1988 to mediate between the parliament and the Guardian Council and to advise the supreme leader. Conflict between the elected and unelected bodies has stood at the center of Iran's political difficulties since 1979. (The "republican" institutions were popularly elected, compared with the "unelected" Islamic institutions. Still, a small number of carefully chosen men also "elected" these last bodies.)

Supporters of the new regime established ideological "cleansing" committees (*komiteh paksazi*) to rid all government organizations of people who were not Muslims (especially Bahais) and those they viewed as un-Islamic, dissenters, anti-revolutionaries, and associates of the shah's regime. After the initial, radical purges, Islamic societies (*anjuman-i islami*) in all government agencies tried to ensure that people there observed religious tenets and expressed loyalty to the regime, and they reported violations to revolutionary guards and committees. All state agencies, new or not, were compelled to add "revolutionary," "Islamic," and populist dimensions to their leaderships and operations, and each was required to have one or more overseeing clergymen and/or an Islamic committee. Such religious figures and institutions did not represent a single source of religious influence, thus resulting in a "pulverization of authority."[60]

The revolution and the Islamic Republic   71

Such decentralization created further institutional impasses, at-odds political agendas, and popular uncertainty. Ambiguous, often seemingly contradictory, notions of "state" (or "government"), "public," "cooperative," and "private" institutions were common. Public ownership in Islamic law is distinct from state or government ownership, and public properties are intended to strengthen Islam and the Muslim community.[61] Such public entities, largely unaccountable to the government, enabled many individuals to become wealthy and powerful and to contest and interfere with state governance. Some cooperatives were considered government or public entities, and others were independent and/or part of the private sector. Some nationalized industrial enterprises were part of the private sector, and some foundations that performed public functions were private or independent.[62] Khomeini considered confiscated properties as public entities, not state ones. The Islamic state defended private ownership but still promoted the seizure of private and other properties as a means for mass mobilization.[63]

The terms "state" and "government" also meant different kinds of institutions and policies during the Pahlavi regimes (1925–79) and under the Islamic Republic (1979–). Some continuity was apparent in the rule of the two shahs; other kinds of features (despite some continuity with the Pahlavi era) emerged with the Islamic Republic. The concepts of "state" and "government" and their practical applications varied through time and according to circumstances.[64]

More prevalently under the Islamic regime than under the shahs, non-state and parastatal entities applied state policies, and they also acted in their own interests regardless of the benefits or detriments for citizens. Hezbollahis since 1979, for example, have tried to enforce certain standards of personal behavior and appearance on citizens, without being formally connected with state institutions and by acting without legal underpinnings. Through violence, the basij militia quelled popular demonstrations after the disputed 2009 presidential election, thereby demonstrating the regime's reliance on such entities. Formal state institutions tried to exert control but were not always successful and thus depended on the regime's fervent supporters to undertake certain tasks themselves.

Writers (especially journalists) often wondered (before the 2009 protests) why popular resistance to the Islamic Republic's rule had not emerged sufficiently in 30 years to threaten its existence. (Defiance erupted and then diminished in 2009, and writers again pondered the absence of revolt despite growing opposition to the regime.) Many people voluntarily changed their behavior, not because of government policy but because they feared the intimidating, sometimes renegade, forces that upheld and sustained the republic. The regime's zealous advocates applied intense, physical coercion, and the growing risks in participating in public demonstrations motivated the opposition to focus its attention elsewhere, especially on electronic means of communication including social media.

The Iraq–Iran war, erupting in September 1980 and lasting for eight years, allowed conservative hard-liners to consolidate power and eliminate the internal opposition, and it strengthened the revolutionary organizations. (The

72 The revolution and the Islamic Republic

war also slowed the regime's stabilization, devastated the economy, destroyed essential infrastructure, caused massive relocations of people, created widespread insecurity, and eroded public morale.)

Most of these developments are beyond the scope of this book, and readers could consult other publications to gain a better appreciation of the tumultuous times.[65]

The Qashqa'i and the state

The Qashqa'i often used the terms "state" (*daulat*) and "government" (*hukumat*) when they referred to external agencies and agents. They rarely identified government leaders, such as specific presidents, or explicitly connected these individuals with certain policies. Unlike the rule of the two shahs over five decades, the rulers and offices of the Islamic Republic changed often and unpredictably. Many Qashqa'i did not distinguish between the parts of the parallel national governments or between often competing formal state agencies and the revolutionary organizations, some of which were part of the government while others were independent or private. The literature on postrevolutionary Iran often differentiates these many entities, yet the Qashqa'i—living as they did at the local level and variably subjected to such outside ministration— tended to regard them similarly. Certain services (and sanctions) they received came from competing entities, and people drawing this attention might not have been aware of the precise connections. Many continued to use the terms associated with the last shah's regime, especially when the functions of old and new entities were similar.

Many men and some women of Qashqa'i, tribal, ethnic-minority, nomadic, and pastoral backgrounds became officials and employees of government agencies— perhaps the most significant change in the links between the Qashqa'i and the state after the revolution. Many were members of the same subtribes, tribes, and confederacies of the people under their jurisdiction or were part of comparable entities. They were more compatible with the people they served than the shah's agents had been and were less likely to be corrupt.[66]

The state agents with whom the Qashqa'i had interacted before the revolution were almost always urban Shi'i Persian men who were hostile toward and discriminated against "primitive" and "backward" nomadic and other rural, tribal, and ethnic-minority peoples, especially those they perceived as potential threats to themselves and the state they represented. In contrast, most state agents visiting nomadic and other rural Qashqa'i communities from mid-1979 through 2013 were tribally affiliated, ethnic-minority, regionally based men (and some women) themselves. They conducted their business professionally, avoided the constraints of a culture of exaggerated ritual politeness (*taaruf*, an institution prevalent among urban Persians), and departed at the conclusion of their tasks without waiting for or demanding personal payments. Bribery of state officials and agents had been rampant throughout Iran during the shah's regime. After the revolution it diminished for the Qashqa'i at the local level.[67]

The revolution and the Islamic Republic   73

New notions about the government's obligations, especially to the sectors of society that the shah and his regime had oppressed and impoverished, inspired some agents. Some held idealistic notions about revolutionary Islam, whose faithful could improve the lives of those they served.[68]

As during the previous 50 years, the Qashqa'i were caught in a dilemma after the revolution. If they sought beneficial government services, they were likely to fall under increasing state surveillance and control. If they maintained some political autonomy, they might have to forfeit useful economic and social benefits offered by the state. People strategized to strike a balance while also coping with the unstable, unpredictable political environment.

During the disruptions of the revolution, its immediate aftermath (including seizures of their pastoral and agricultural land), and the Iraq–Iran war, the Qashqa'i were uncertain about the choices confronting them. The government stabilized to some degree under Rafsanjani's presidency (1989–97), and people grew more confident in their decisions. Moderating state policies in the mid-1990s, followed by Mohammad Khatami's elections as president in 1997 and 2001, furthered people's trust until they saw that the reforms they desired were unlikely to be implemented because of the power still exerted by the supreme leader, other unelected sectors of government, and paramilitary and parastatal bodies. Elections in 2005 and 2009 of the neoconservative, Mahmud Ahmadinejad, as president dashed their hopes and lowered their expectations, despite his promises to focus government attention once again on the "disinherited."[69] Iran's new president in 2013, Hasan Rouhani, raised some people's spirits while cynics pointed out that the country's unelected power holders, especially the supreme leader, remained in charge.

Here I outline different dimensions of "state" and "government" as they affected the Qermezi at the local level from 1978–79 through 2013. I do not discuss all aspects of government, especially those having minimal or no impact on the Qermezi. Some state agencies continued to function as they had done under the shah's regime in the 1960s and 1970s. Others were radically altered to address new perceived needs. Still others were newly founded. Some were politically centralized while others acted autonomously. Some competing agencies offered overlapping benefits while others implemented opposing policies. Some were dedicated exclusively to assisting or administering nomads while others also provided for the wider Qashqa'i society. Some dealt with nomadic pastoralists, agriculturalists, or rural society in general. Some focused on the exploited and deprived sectors of Iranian society. Each agency discussed in this section experienced its own transformations during these decades. I outline only the general operations and tasks, especially as they impacted the Qermezi.

Ministry of Construction Jihad (after 2000, Agricultural Jihad)

The Ministry of Construction Jihad (*jihad-i sazandigi*, crusade or campaign for construction, often called simply "jihad") began as a revolutionary organization

74   *The revolution and the Islamic Republic*

in the first months after Khomeini's arrival in 1979 and became an official ministry in 1983.[70] By then the clergy and the Islamic Republican Party had transformed some mass popular organizations (such as Construction Jihad) into more controlled, structured, and institutionalized instruments of dominance.

As a service-providing agency, Construction Jihad's task was to correct the neglect and abuse that rural Iran had suffered under the shahs, build or improve the infrastructure (roads, electrification, telephone links, drinking water, irrigation, housing, public buildings, schools including Quranic ones, literacy programs, clinics, and health services), enhance agricultural production (by providing seeds, tractors, and pesticides), reclaim and preserve pastures, increase the food supply, and raise standards of living. Khomeini proclaimed that anyone who contributed to such efforts received more extra-worldly merits than if the person had performed the pilgrimage to Mecca.[71] Construction Jihad participated in local craft production in the mid-1980s and began some cultural activities. In many areas, local Islamic councils coordinated its activities. Officials hoped that the public would contribute (*khudyari*) and participate. They expected local communities to finish or maintain the projects the government had started but were sometimes disappointed by the response.

Construction Jihad assumed "the dual task of expanding social services in the countryside and of taking 'true Islam' to the peasantry. Its cadres were told that they need to build mosques, schools and libraries, as well as bridges, canals and roads, because the vast majority of the peasantry do not know how to pray, how to fast, or how to observe simple Muslim rituals. 'The peasants,' claims one cleric, 'are so ignorant of Islam that they even sleep next to their sheep.'"[72]

Some politicians viewed Construction Jihad's work as essential for stemming the uncontrolled flood of rural migrants to the cities, already unable to care for their excessive and growing numbers of inhabitants. This demographic, economic, and social problem was one of Iran's most troubling and had contributed (some say substantially) to the revolution against the shah. If this agency and others could improve conditions in rural areas, narrow the income gap between rural and urban inhabitants, and raise the standard of living in rural areas, then people there might be motivated to stay, and some migrants might return home.[73] Escalating rural-to-urban migration was compounded by rising unemployment and underemployment, by incoming refugees from the Iraq–Iran war zone and from Afghanistan, and by Persians and Shi'is expelled by Saddam Hussein from Iraq.[74]

Construction Jihad expanded its operations to contribute to Iran's efforts during the Iraq–Iran war. It brought combat engineers and heavy machinery to the front line, rebuilt bridges and roads, provided water, and assisted in recovery operations in areas devastated by bombs and missiles. Its own combat units began organizing by 1986, and many of its men were killed or wounded.[75]

Aware of the special needs and circumstances of Iran's nomads, Construction Jihad supported the formation of a new organization (see later) dedicated to

The revolution and the Islamic Republic   75

improving their livelihoods and lifestyles. The ministry continued through 2013 to provide services to nomads, such as veterinary care and pasture reclamation, and its activities complimented those of the special nomads' organization. After years of debating the issue, parliament voted in 2000 to merge two ministries, Construction Jihad and Agriculture, in order to cut costs and manage overlapping and ambiguous responsibilities.[76] The entity's new title was Agricultural Jihad (*jihad-i kishavarzi*). The special nomads' organization retained its independence after the merger.

Organization for Nomads' Affairs

The new government established the Center for Services to Nomads (*markaz-i khadmat-i ashayir*), which it modeled after the shah's Organization for Mobile Pastoralists (*sazman-i damdaran-i sayyar* [or *mutaharrik*], part of the Ministry of Housing and Urban Development). It transferred the organization's offices, personnel, and equipment to the Ministry of Agriculture after the revolution.[77] Under the prime minister's authority, the new center was responsible for emergency funds for nomads.

About the same time, the regime formed another new organization, the Supreme Council for Nomads (*shura-yi ali-yi ashayir*), and also placed it under the prime minister's jurisdiction. Aiming to centralize issues relating to nomads, the council contained representatives of ministries and agencies as well as some formally educated men of nomadic backgrounds who displayed solid revolutionary credentials.

The prime minister and the supreme council created in 1982 the Organization for Nomads' Affairs (ONA; *sazman-i umur-i ashayir*) based on the Center for Services to Nomads. Initially, it fell under the prime minister's control, and then it became an independent agency within the new Ministry of Construction Jihad in 1983. Its director served on the supreme council. The organization soon became the chief state agency for delivering services to Iran's nomads and continued to function actively through 2013.[78] The work of the supreme council and related and other agencies merged in 1991 as part of President Rafsanjani's centralizations.

The Organization for Nomads' Affairs defined "nomads" (ashayir) as "those who travel between winter pastures and summer pastures" and "those who do not stay in one place." The 1986 national census indicates that of Iran's total population of 55 million, 1.2 million were nomads, defined as people having a tribal organization (*qabilihi*), a primary reliance on animal husbandry (*damdari*), and a pastoral (*shabani*) or nomadic (*kuch*) lifestyle.[79]

Officials sometimes used the phrase "tent dwellers" (*chadur nishin*) but understood that not all nomads lived in tents. Implicit and sometimes explicit notions about livestock production being the nomads' primary livelihood complicated matters. When nomads also engaged in agriculture, state agents sometimes reclassified them as "agriculturalists" or "villagers," and people could lose their "nomad" status and the privileges accompanying it. Many

76 The revolution and the Islamic Republic

nomadic pastoralists also practiced agriculture by the 1990s, sometimes extensively, and built or used permanent dwellings (usually for only seasonal residence), and any limited definitions were problematic. Often ambiguous, these and other terms varied according to context. Agencies classified Qashqa'i schoolteachers in towns, for example, as "nomads" if they traveled seasonally between winter and summer pastures (which many of them did) and if their close paternal kin were nomadic pastoralists. Officials and the people themselves sometimes used the term "ashayir" to refer to a person's descent, one who descends from nomads regardless of his or her current occupation and lifestyle. They labeled still-migratory people as *ashayir-i sayyar* (mobile nomads) as compared to those who were not mobile (*ashayir-i sabit*).

Tribal, ethnic, linguistic, and regional terms and identities were also relevant.

Many state agents in the 1980s regarded a "tribe" (il, tayifih) as a political entity and chose not to use the term in their formal duties. During and after the defensive resistance of the paramount Qashqa'i khans in 1980–82, authorities were especially suspicious about the term "tribe" and worried that the Qashqa'i and other tribal groups would pose further military and political threats to the new state. Officials of the shah as well as the Islamic Republic also found the label "Qashqa'i" problematic and wanted to avoid it for political reasons. Instead they deployed the phrases "ashayir-i Fars" (the province), "ashayir-i junub" (the south), and "ashayir-i Bushire" (the area near the Persian Gulf port of this name, which contained few Qashqa'i residents). Understanding these euphemisms, the Qashqa'i often created their own joking, self-mocking ones (such as "ashayir-i biabun," nomads of the wilderness) in response. State agents who categorized tribal people without explicitly referring to their tribes (their named sociopolitical groups) created confusing distinctions, such as "nomadic nomads" (*ashayir-i kuchandih*) and "settled nomads" (*ashayir-i sakin*). They supported "nomads" but not "tribes" and tried to distinguish between them; they often used the Persian term "nomad" as a (misleading) substitution for "tribe." Some officials preferred the phrase "livestock farmers" (*dam kishavarzi*) to attempt to bypass these semantic obfuscations and to veer away from any implied association between nomads and tribes.

Especially in the 1980s, authorities also used "nomad" as part of a different—and positive—kind of political reference, as in those whom the shahs had socioeconomically oppressed (*ashayir-i mahrum*) and politically oppressed or persecuted (*ashayir-i mazlum*) and who now warranted special state services that would improve their lives.

By the early 1990s, when further "tribal revolt" in southwestern Iran seemed unlikely, state agents worried less about employing the terms "tribe" and "tribal," especially because they had not yet devised more accurate ways of categorizing such people. By the mid-1990s, many officials routinely referred to the nomads' tribal organizations and employed these named sociopolitical entities (tribes and subtribes such as Darrehshuri and Qermezi) in their administrative tasks, thereby reaffirming these structures for the people and the state and facilitating their survival.[80]

The revolution and the Islamic Republic 77

Some authorities still remained cautious through 2013 about the "Qashqa'i" label because of its former and still-current political connotations and avoided it when possible. Others tried to restrict its meaning to what they viewed as "nonpolitical" cultural traits, especially appealing ones such as goat-hair tents and handwoven textiles. Yet the Qashqa'i regarded these material objects as essential representations of their political identity. When the new government displayed these items in its commemorations of Iran's rich cultural heritage, the Qashqa'i noted that the regime was officially recognizing their polity.

The Islamic regime continued through 2013 to face problems concerning tribal peoples elsewhere in Iran, especially along its western, northwestern, northeastern, and eastern borders and all along the Persian Gulf coast. The Qashqa'i suffered by association, as a result, and fell under greater scrutiny because of their own tribal institutions.

Ethnic and ethnolinguistic terms such as Turk, Kurd, Baluch, and Arab also meant "nomad" in different parts of Iran. Names of languages such as Turkish, Kurdish, Baluchi, and Arabic conveyed sociocultural and sometimes political information about the speakers. Regional and provincial labels, such as Fars, Kuh Giluyeh, and Bakhtiyari, also designated the tribal and ethnic peoples living there.

The scholarly literature on Iran still exhibits these confusions, despite decades of clarifications by anthropologists. References therein to "tribes," "nomads," "pastoralists," "ethnic groups," and "national minorities" may not accurately depict the people under consideration. Even a label such as "Qashqa'i" could mean one or more or all of these entities or attributes unless an author specifies the context. Writers who equate tribal people with nomads or pastoralists may be incorrectly assuming such associations.[81]

Local and regional offices of the Organization for Nomads' Affairs (ONA) determined people's status as "nomads" and their rights to certain state services because of this classification. The director of the permanent ONA office in Semirom argued with a Qashqa'i man whose official documents displayed stamps from ONA indicating that he was a nomad and stamps from Construction Jihad indicating that he was a villager. The petitioner was trying to register at both offices so he could obtain duplicate coupons (used for subsidized commodities) for a newborn child. Skeptical about the man's nomad status, the director queried him, "Are you ashayir? Where are your winter pastures? Do you migrate?" In the end, unhappy about the man's equivocal responses, he still stamped his papers. When Farzaneh Qarehqanli visited Shiraz's ONA office to register as a nomad so she too could receive coupons, she told a clerk that she needed to cancel her official status as a "town dweller" (*shahri*). The man responded that he had never before encountered that request. People, he said, always sought to change their bureaucratic designation from "ashayir" to "shahri" or "*rustai*" (villager), to indicate their rising socioeconomic status.

ONA established national headquarters in Tehran and regional headquarters (22 in 1991) throughout Iran wherever nomads were concentrated. Shiraz's ONA office was the operational center for many dispersed ONA

78 The revolution and the Islamic Republic

facilities in Fars province and the periphery. The heads of all ONA offices were tribal men of nomadic pastoral backgrounds. Many of them originated from the same groups they now served.

The new Ministry of Culture and Islamic Guidance (*farhang va irshad-i islami*) assigned young clerics, often continuing theology students, to each of the national and provincial-capital offices. In most if not all cases, these men too originated from and identified with the tribes their facilities served. The clergyman assigned to the Tehran headquarters in 1991–92 was Karim Bahrami Qarehqani of the Darrehshuri tribe, one of the first Qashqa'i theology students after the revolution and a wounded war veteran. When I asked Ali Qanbari, ONA's national director who originated from and identified with the Bakhtiyari tribal confederacy, about the cleric's duties, he stated simply, "To make sure that this office's affairs are conducted according to Islam." Then, trying hard not to smile, he explained that his organization's services were so fundamental that he could not imagine them to be contrary to the spirit of Islam.

For the Qermezi who resided in seasonal pastures at Dashtak and Hanalishah, ONA's closest local offices were in Kazerun, Chinar Shahijan, and Dogonbadan in the autumn, winter, and early spring and in Semirom from mid-spring to the end of summer. To provide services to Darrehshuri nomads, ONA chose Dogonbadan for its main office because most Darrehshuri winter pastures were close by. This office's director, a Janbazlu Darrehshuri man, and four Darrehshuri staff members traveled seasonally between Dogonbadan and Semirom (centrally located in summer pastures) in 1998, and they hired local workers of nomadic and tribal backgrounds in each locale to help deliver ONA services. In Semirom the office dealt primarily with distributing coupons for essential commodities. A second ONA office in Semirom, this one operating year-round, focused on construction (remote roads, small bridges, and public bathhouses), links with other state agencies, and veterinary services for the nomads living in the area all year or only in the summer. The permanent office occupied a newly constructed, well-appointed facility (including a veterinary clinic) while the seasonal office and its agents rented an empty house. ONA agents posted in Shahreza and a more distant Isfahan periodically visited Hanalishah to assess the nomads' needs and speed the delivery of services.

The Qermezi in winter pastures at Dashtak sought aid from the ONA offices in Kazerun and Chinar Shahijan, which primarily served the area's Kashkuli, Farsi Madan, and Qarachai Qashqa'i nomads. (The ONA office in Dogonbadan for Darrehshuri nomads was too far away for them.) The ties of the Qermezi with the Kazerun office grew significant in 1999 when ONA decided to build a village in the foothills below Dashtak for some of them. The previous year ONA had begun a similar settlement farther south of Kazerun for Farsi Madan nomads, and the office gained importance in Kazerun and the region because of these two long-term projects. Twenty men, all Qashqa'i including three drivers, staffed the facility in 2000, and its director was a Kashkuli Qashqa'i man.

The revolution and the Islamic Republic   79

ONA was a valuable, powerful ally for the nomads in their conflicts over pastoral and agricultural land with outsiders. All nomads with whom I spoke praised the agency's assistance, especially after the war's ceasefire in 1988, and said it was instrumental in negotiating their land rights and improving their economic standing. ONA officials and workers were personally acquainted with most if not all of the men among the nomads and interceded on their behalf. Such close connections proved vital in the nomads' confrontations with other state agencies where they were less known or unknown. In some places, even if ONA, Construction Jihad, Pastures Organization, and Ministry of Agriculture disagreed about jurisdiction and authority, their respective services still supported the nomads, even if they did occasionally overlap.

ONA officials outlined their responsibilities as twofold, to assist the nomads in their current livelihoods and in their settling (*iskan*). As this book demonstrates, "settling" meant a wide range of activities that did not necessarily cause the end of nomadism, seasonal migration, pastoralism, use of seasonal pastures, or tent dwelling. Aiming to solve some problems of "basic living" for the people who wanted to continue as nomadic pastoralists, ONA offered bank-loan assistance, pastoral and agricultural aid, construction materials, and subsidized commodities. The agency also helped those who were ready to establish more permanent residences, regardless of their intention to maintain or to change their current livelihoods and lifestyles.

ONA offered loans in the 1990s and early 2000s, via the state Agricultural Bank, to nomads who wanted to construct or improve water-delivery systems for livestock, human use, and agriculture. The bank charged three or five percent interest annually (compared with 24 to 60 percent demanded by private moneylenders in towns). The bank's official stance was that the small percentage covered only the costs of administering the loans and was not interest per se, which Islamic law forbids.[82] ONA handled the nomads' applications for loans and, if it accepted them, issued documents for the nomads to file with the bank. The process took at least several seasons, and the nomads' residences in multiple locales delayed the completion.

Some Qermezi men at Dashtak and Hanalishah received ONA's help in acquiring loans for improving their access to water. Two groups of men at Hanalishah each received loans of four million tumans in 1996 for constructing concrete water channels and reservoirs, the money used for materials and labor. They bought cement, gravel, and pipes at low cost; ONA provided other supplies without charge. The men hired several Aqa Mohammadli kinsmen as master builders and other kin as manual laborers. Interest on the five-year loans was three percent annually, with the government reportedly paying the bank an additional 10 percent for handling the loans.

Also in 1996, six men at Dashtak each received smaller loans to build concrete water reservoirs there, where water was always scarce. They received subsidized prices for construction supplies. Rain collected in these reservoirs, and, whenever supplies ran low, ONA workers brought tankers to replenish them free or at a nominal cost. They also filled them without charge just

80 The revolution and the Islamic Republic

before the nomads arrived in winter pastures. Otherwise the nomads would have been forced to remain with the livestock at lower elevations at Mulleh Balut, near several wells, to wait for autumnal rains to supply Dashtak's simpler, hand-dug, dirt-banked reservoirs. Prior to building the concrete reservoirs, ONA brought bulldozers and graders to widen and level the dirt road through Dashtak, in part to facilitate access for its tankers. The six men built these structures alongside dirt tracks leading from the road, so ONA could easily service them. They brought a Persian master builder from Galleh Qadam village near Hanalishah in summer pastures to supervise the construction.

ONA also engaged in its own projects to make and improve roads, wells, water reservoirs (underground or covered cisterns), public bathhouses, private outdoor toilets, and concrete water channels and basins for livestock. It helped the nomads to buy and install motorized pumps for the new wells. The agency relied on groups of nomads and their representatives, especially the new Islamic councils, to bring needed projects to its attention. Its agents handled operations promptly and efficiently. When the nomads at Hanalishah asked in 1996 if ONA could send a bulldozer and grader to level part of the dirt road leading into the territory, a team with equipment came within a week. Listing ONA projects for me, a Qermezi man mentioned that its agents would provide concrete blocks, cement, gravel, porcelain keyhole platforms, and labor for any nomads who wanted to build outdoor toilets. Overhearing, his wife complained, "Well, why haven't you asked for that help, then?" Finding water for irrigating his apple orchard insufficient in 1999, Bahram Qermezi borrowed a small, two-wheeled tanker from ONA so he could transport water from his cousin's nearby spring. Anticipating a demand for water during his son's wedding celebration, he kept the tanker at his campsite until the festivity's completion. Also low on water, his two brothers received ONA assistance in digging a well, including laborers (Afghan refugees), and hoped to buy a low-cost pump to facilitate irrigation.

ONA built a modest but adequate bathhouse at Hanalishah in 1990 for the use of the many nomads in the territory. Women and children, who usually lacked access to the public bathing facilities that men sometimes enjoyed during their trips to town, were appreciative. As soon as the nomads began the migration to winter pastures in 1991, Persian and Lur cultivators in the nearest valley sabotaged the water heater and stole the pipes and faucets. They were angry about the growing competition over land and water in the area. When the nomads returned to Hanalishah the following spring, they tried but failed to repair the heater. ONA had painted in large ornate letters "*hammam-i ashayiri*" (nomads' bathhouse) on the outside wall facing the dirt road, but the hostile cultivators had chipped away at the paint and underlying concrete to eradicate the word "ashayiri" (which still remained visible as a deep indentation). (My daughter Julia suggested to the schoolchildren that they could fill the indentation with black paint, to accentuate the word.) Women complained that their kinsmen did not inform ONA about the vandalism and no longer tried to fix the heater. ONA's director in Semirom

The revolution and the Islamic Republic   81

told me that his agency would repair the heater or provide a new one if the local community took some initiative. When I raised the issue with several nomads, the men responded that those living in the camps nearest the facility should take responsibility. The bathhouse remained unusable through 2013.

ONA established veterinary clinics in towns throughout Iran for treating the nomads' sheep, goats, camels, horses, cattle, and other livestock. Clinics in Kazerun and Semirom served the Qermezi at Dashtak and Hanalishah. Veterinarians provided free or low-cost treatments, drugs, and surgical services. Pastoralists brought ill animals for diagnosis and treatment and submitted excised organs for disease testing. If drugs against diseases were available, veterinarians inoculated the herds near the infected livestock. Traveling from camp to camp in tribal territory, they also periodically assessed the animals' health and dispensed routine inoculations at no cost.

From its origin, ONA offered coupons for purchasing essential commodities at state-subsidized prices, significantly lower than found in private shops in villages and towns. Its own and the government's other regional cooperatives stocked these basic goods. If the agency determined that a man and his family were nomads, it issued sheets of serrated coupons for raw rice, vegetable oil, sugar, and powdered soap and a coupon book (*daftarchih ashayiri*) for milled wheat flour. Each coupon depicted a mountain peak (poised in the background), a nomad's tent or yurt pitched in a grassy area, a woman in "tribal" dress carrying a milk jug, two sheep, silhouettes of three or five individuals (demonstrating the number of eligible people), and the word "ashayiri" centered prominently.[83] When ONA issued new coupons in 1999, men at Hanalishah assembled the identity cards of their family members and hurried to Semirom to claim the coupons before supplies ran low.

Darrehshuri nomads from dispersed summer pastures traveled in the mid-1980s to an ONA cooperative in Mehr-i Gerd village to collect coupon-controlled commodities. One of them, a white cloth sack draped over her shoulder for transporting the goods home, complained about the ironic reversal of fortunes. "Akhunds carrying white bags used to visit us to beg for donations. Now we come to them in the same manner." Before the revolution, darvishes and *sayyid*s (reputed or alleged descendants of the prophet Mohammad) had circulated among the nomads' camps to solicit charity, white cloth sacks laid over their shoulders to hold the acquired goods. After the revolution, the nomads came seeking the same kinds of commodities from a clergy-controlled government. (The Qashqa'i often used the term "akhund," usually pejoratively, to refer to different types of religious figures from low to high status.)

ONA's second primary function was to assist nomads who wanted to build permanent residences and/or establish group settlements.[84] The agency negotiated land rights with the Pastures Organization so nomads could place new houses and settlements on or near grazing land, and it dealt with the Ministry of Agriculture to develop or expand cultivable land. ONA planned and implemented a village in 1999 for Qermezi nomads at Mulleh Balut in winter pastures.

82   *The revolution and the Islamic Republic*

ONA and the Ministry of Construction Jihad sponsored celebrations of the annual Day of the Nomad (*ruz-i ashayir*) in the many provinces where nomads resided. The day fell during the week-long annual observance of the Day of Construction Jihad. (Other national days honor teachers and Palestinians. Another national week commemorates the Sacred Defense, the war with Iraq.) A Qermezi man joked that the Day of the Nomad was actually the Day of the Unfortunate (*ruz-i bad bakhti*), given the sad state of affairs for nomads in the 1990s. (Most nomadic pastoralists in southwestern Iran seemed to be doing well economically, compared with many middle-class and lower-class rural and urban dwellers during this period. They produced, gathered, and hunted much of their food and did not feel compelled to purchase the high-cost consumer goods that villagers and urbanites now considered necessary.)

The director of ONA's permanent office in Semirom wanted to borrow a Qermezi family's tent to use during the Day of the Nomad celebrations in 1991. The senior woman there jested that she would instead contribute a "dented, charred pot" to show how impoverished they were. Traveling through Hanalishah, the director sought other large tents, attractive knotted pile carpets, and other culturally significant objects. He announced that he wanted some women to attend, dressed in full Qashqa'i attire, so they could demonstrate weaving and butter churning. Similar to Qashqa'i and other tribal women performing publicly during such occasions, these women could ignore the standards of modest Islamic dress imposed on all other Iranian women. State officials would attend, the national media including television would document the ceremony, and the organizers wanted a festive display. Resisting the government's pressure, Qermezi men at Hanalishah refused on moral grounds to volunteer any wives or daughters for the event. They objected to having their kinswomen participate in this type of public spectacle, especially when the regime was still suppressing the actions and dress of urban women. The day before the ceremony, ONA's director dropped off large milk cans at most camps so the women there could fill them with donated sour milk (to be served with the dignitaries' lunch).

Across the country, ONA and Construction Jihad marked the Day of the Nomad with "seminars" (the word used) (on pastoral and agricultural techniques, protection of pastures, veterinary medicine, and new state services) and cultural performances and exhibitions. They centralized events in Tehran, with smaller programs in the provinces, or they stressed regional ceremonies. In coordinating these gatherings, local, provincial, and national ONA officials depended on material, logistical, and financial support from local nomadic and tribal communities. Regional and national officials, parliamentary deputies, and other influential people attended. Some speakers addressed the contributions of Iran's nomads to the wider society and culture while others emphasized the ways that the Islamic Republic assisted them.

The governor-general (*ustandar*) of Isfahan province attended the one-day event in 1991 at Zain Ali, just west of Hanalishah, along with dozens of other high-ranking provincial and regional officials and their entourages. A caravan of 51 laden vehicles (counted precisely by Qermezi schoolchildren) passed through Hanalishah on its rough dirt track. The day before, ONA workers had hastily built a small bridge over an irrigation channel in case the officials took this route. That evening a special team of sharpshooters entered the territory, its heavily armed men taking positions all along the mountain ridges overlooking the route. The government still feared the region's tribesmen.

Local ONA personnel invited some nomads, particularly members of the new Islamic councils, to attend regional and national events for the Day of the Nomad and provided transportation, housing, and food. Three Qermezi men from Hanalishah traveled in an ONA minivan to the three-day national celebration in 1991 in Tehran, and officials there arranged for them to visit Khomeini's tomb south of the city. Qermezi men visiting Shahreza saw television coverage of Tehran's event in which President Rafsanjani posed alongside men dressed in Qashqa'i, Turkman, Baluch, and Bakhtiyari clothes.

Cultural seminars and festivals

At other times of the year, the government sponsored or permitted cultural seminars to highlight the contributions of Iran's nomadic and tribal peoples. Most were privately organized and funded. Some were staged at the national level, in Tehran or provincial capitals, and focused on Iran's diverse groups or emphasized a single one. Others were local events, featured the groups nearby, and drew mostly local officials and participants.

Many Qashqa'i cultural festivals were held from 1990 through 2013 in Tehran, Shiraz, and towns in and near Qashqa'i territory (such as Dogonbadan and Borujen).[85] From the government's perspective, these gatherings were apolitical and stressed "culture" (farhang) as defined by specific visible traits: goat-hair tents, handwoven textiles, traditional dress, customary technology, instrumental and vocal music, poetry, oral narratives, stick-fighting competitions, and women's and men's dance. By contrast, the participants and attendees regarded these events as explicitly political. Some activities, especially women's dance, violated general state policies or those of specific agencies. Yet some government sectors regarded the "traditions" of what they called "regional" groups (without naming the ethnic minorities, tribal groups, and nomadic peoples there) as exceptions to statewide regulations governing music, dance, and dress.[86] Organizers of these events understood that they enjoyed some leeway (and could avoid censorship) if they phrased them in "regional" terms. The attendees recognized the ruse and identified the performers, who had purposely accentuated key defining traits, according to specific ethnicities and tribes. Despite its attempts to avoid politics, the government tolerated the Qashqa'i male performers and spectators who wore the distinctive felt hat, an explicit political symbol of the group. The renown Qashqa'i musicians, Farhad Gurginpur and Furud Gurginpur, played at many events as did other prominent Qashqa'i instrumentalists, vocalists, poets, orators, and

84 *The revolution and the Islamic Republic*

artists.[87] The preeminent Qashqa'i artist, Bijan Bahadori-Kashkuli, displayed his watercolor paintings of customary, nostalgically rendered Qashqa'i life.

These performances and exhibits inspired the Qashqa'i youth, some of whom had not previously witnessed all these cultural forms, partly because the Islamic regime had or still currently prohibited some of them. Art forms new to most Qashqa'i drew their interest, such as poetry depicted by ornate calligraphy (using the Perso-Arabic alphabet to represent Qashqa'i Turkish, an unwritten language) and miniature handwoven replicas of Qashqa'i tents and accessories. Qashqa'i writers, scholars, teachers, university students, and professionals attending these events encouraged the expression of traditional and emerging cultural forms, especially in the young. They began in the early 2000s to publish specialized magazines covering Qashqa'i history, society, and culture, and they included photographs taken during these cultural festivals.[88]

The government videotaped and photographed these events to present on national, state-controlled television and in other media forms. Private individuals also recorded their own videotapes, audiotapes, and, later, CDs and DVDs and circulated copies widely, especially among the Qashqa'i living abroad. (I saw and heard many of them in Europe and the U.S. in the 1990s and early 2000s.) Street kiosks and small shops in Shiraz and Shahreza sold these tapes, CDs, and DVDs.

Many Qashqa'i sought in the early 1990s to resume their customary ceremonial practices, particularly during wedding celebrations. They cited the state's explicit approval of these same customs, as performed during the public festivals, despite local hezbollahis (sometimes Qashqa'i ones) trying to thwart them. One woman asserted, "If the government broadcasts, for millions of strangers [in Iran], images of Qashqa'i women dressed in traditional attire while dancing to Qashqa'i music in front of men, then surely we can express ourselves in the same way within the privacy of our own kinship groups." Many Qashqa'i communities used the same logic, to prevail over those who wanted to suppress these cultural forms for their own political, purportedly Islamic, reasons.

When the Qashqa'i began to acquire mobile telephones with imaging capabilities, they spread these images instantly and globally. Qashqa'i in many countries learned about events in Iran in this way and supported the efforts of people there to resist the Islamic Republic's stringent regulations. As the use of cellular phones, digital cameras, computers, tablets, and the Internet spread in the early 2000s, increasing numbers of Qashqa'i in Iran posted cultural (and politically charged) material for a widening audience.[89]

The Islamic regime had tried since its execution of Khosrow Khan in 1982 to prevent any Qashqa'i from visiting his unmarked gravesite in Shiraz. Later a Darrehshuri khan installed an inscribed marble gravestone. Many Qashqa'i posted emotional video tributes to Khosrow Khan, one featuring a young Qashqa'i man pouring water over the stone and laying flowers while he sang a poignant song in Qashqa'i Turkish.[90] Some Qashqa'i disseminated images of other politicized ceremonies, such as the funerals and memorials of prominent Qashqa'i figures (including Mohammad Bahmanbaigi).

Several Qermezi men purchased in 1999 a large framed photograph of a huge Qashqa'i tent and hung it in their newly constructed one-room houses at Hanalishah. They had just abandoned goat-hair tents as everyday residences, in favor of rudimentary houses, and yet, almost immediately, they sought to display an image depicting a tent. ONA had pitched this particular structure for public appreciation at one of its cultural festivals and festooned it with pro-revolutionary and Islamic slogans. An empty shell, the tent shown in the photograph was devoid of people and the equipment that nomads would need to sustain a livelihood.

Cooperatives Organization

Initially part of the Ministry of Construction Jihad, the Cooperatives Organization (*sazman-i taavunat*) and its nomads' division (*shirkat-i taavuni ashayiri*) also worked with ONA to deliver needed commodities at subsidized prices to nomads. It established year-round, permanent facilities in places such as Chinar Shahijan and seasonal shops in district centers such as Semirom and Firuzabad, where people whom the government defined as nomads could buy items at rates cheaper than found in the bazaar. ONA coupons and coupon books were necessary for some goods while others such as barley and fabric were not regulated by coupons. The government created a new Ministry of Cooperatives in 1991 but by 2005 the nomads' cooperatives still fell under the control of ONA and Agricultural Jihad.

Meat Marketing Organization

Also part of the Ministry of Construction Jihad, the Meat Marketing Organization (*sazman-i gusht*) purchased live sheep and goats at prices usually higher than those offered by privately owned slaughterhouses in towns and cities. Its regional headquarters was in Isfahan in the spring and summer when the pastoralists ordinarily sold their livestock. Qermezi men trucked sheep and goats there for sale but occasionally the organization bought animals in tribal territory. Hanalishah's nomads heard one afternoon in 1999 that the organization was buying livestock at a good price in northern Darrehshuri territory and would transport the animals from there without charge. Men quickly selected some livestock and found transportation in order to arrive in time. Agents issued receipts to each seller, who collected payment a month later at a designated bank in Isfahan (necessitating a trip there).

Parliamentary deputy for the district of Semirom in 1996–2000, Shahriyar Qermezi urged the organization to establish local facilities, such as in Semirom, so that the nomads could avoid the expense and risk of transporting livestock the long distance to Isfahan. Animals lost weight during the trip and while crowded together outside the slaughterhouse (the price of each animal determined by weight), and some were crushed during transport. Men rode among the trucked livestock to prevent suffocation and to slit the throats if any were

86 *The revolution and the Islamic Republic*

close to death (to render the meat edible, according to custom and Islamic law, and not forbidden).

The Meat Marketing Organization also purchased the commodity abroad. Experiencing a high demand, Iran suffered a nationwide shortage and relied on external sources. The strategy struck the Qermezi as ludicrous. If the government provided more assistance in their livelihood, mainly fodder when natural pasturage was inadequate, they could produce more meat for regional and national markets at a cost lower than importing it from abroad. Meat procured at home was also more likely to conform to Islamic requirements for proper slaughtering and did not need to be frozen and stored for long periods.[91]

National Forests and Pastures Organization

The Department of Environmental Protection (*sazman-i hifazat-i muhit-i zist*)—an independent agency for the protection and regulation of natural resources—was responsible during the shah's regime for wild fauna, game preserves, and national parks. After the government changed, the agency fell under the jurisdiction of the president's office and remained independent. It sometimes conflicted with Construction Jihad, such as when this agency encouraged its clients to cultivate protected lands and graze livestock on forbidden pastures.[92]

The Islamic Republic placed the new National Forests and Pastures Organization (*sazman-i milli-yi jangalha va marati*) (in this book, Pastures Organization) in charge of Iran's designated forests and pastures. The entity, part of the Ministry of Agriculture (and since 2000 part of the merged ministry, Agricultural Jihad), continued to serve nomadic pastoralists as the shah's natural-resources agency had done. The Qermezi called the new agency "natural resources" (*manabi-yi tabii*) despite its official name.

By the mid-1980s, regional and local agents of the Organization of Forest Rangers (*sazman-i jangalbani*, part of the Pastures Organization) were issuing grazing permits (*parvanih*) to Iran's nomadic pastoralists and were filing reports on land expropriation and misuse for other agencies to investigate and adjudicate. Permits listed specific territories and numbers of livestock allowed to graze there. The Kazerun office assigned the pastoralists at Dashtak their grazing permits in the late 1980s, while the Semirom office had not yet done so for Hanalishah's pastoralists by 2005. Asserting conflicting claims, Persian and Lur cultivators had confiscated lands at Hanalishah officially designated as pastures and illegally converted them to agricultural use. A single, temporary, "arm-long" document (compared with the "hand-long" one for Dashtak) from Semirom's office authorized the grazing rights of Hanalishah's pastoralists in 1991 despite the expropriations. Forest rangers investigated abuses, determined land boundaries, filed reports, and helped the pastoralists to pursue claims in other state offices and the courts. The pastoralists at Hanalishah were anxious in the 1990s to receive the government's promised 30-year deeds (*qarardad*) to the land so that ambiguity about claims and usage would end.

ONA agents assisted the Pastures Organization in addressing the pastoralists' land problems.

Forest rangers seeded high-traffic areas along Qashqa'i migratory routes in order to lessen the impact of the nomads' livestock on surrounding lands and to decrease conflict with local residents. They included several sites at the southern border of Hanalishah and posted metal signs explaining the use of the territories. Rangers hoped that nomads who migrated through Hanalishah would first graze their animals in these posted areas and then travel quickly through Qermezi territory. Nomads also camped overnight on these lands to avoid trespassing.

The Pastures Organization regulated the collectors of gum tragacanth (*katira*, a shrub sap sold for export) on land it classified as pastures. After rangers obtained approval from the resident pastoralists, the agency set a seasonal (summer) fee, due when the workers sold the sap they had extracted from the living roots of the shrubs. The collectors in Darrehshuri territory belonged to two subtribes known for this specialized work. The effort was not lucrative unless environmental conditions were superb. Trying to stay clear of low-lying protruding thorny branches, workers excavated around and then nicked the shrubs' roots while avoiding long-term damage to them. Later they returned to collect the exuded, gummy sap. Every year the organization issued permits for or denied the collectors access to Hanalishah. Rangers inspecting the area determined when the plants required further natural restoration before the next extraction. These hardy shrubs, the dominant plant in many parts of Qashqa'i summer pastures, supported the growth of smaller, more fragile plants nearby and helped to prevent soil erosion.

Along with agents of Construction Jihad and ONA, the Pastures Organization sponsored a four-day instructional seminar for Qermezi pastoralists at Hanalishah in 1999. Presentations covered pasture use and pastoral and agricultural techniques and offered concrete suggestions for handling land disputes through state offices.

Mahmud Atazadeh directed the provincial headquarters of the National Forests and Pastures Organization in Isfahan in 1996–2001. (He had served as Semirom's parliamentary deputy in 1992–96.) He is a Darzi Darrehshuri man whose mother is Qermezi. The Qermezi regarded his presence in this job as an asset; they planned to appeal to him to resolve disputes.

Ministry of Agriculture (after 2000, Agricultural Jihad)

The Ministry of Agriculture initially expanded under the Islamic Republic when the government brought many functions of related agencies under its jurisdiction. Construction Jihad (first an agency and then a ministry) soon offered overlapping and competitive services. Agents of the Ministry of Agriculture advised and assisted nomadic pastoralists who also engaged in agriculture. They provided low-cost saplings, pesticides, fertilizers, and irrigation supplies to those wanting to plant fruit orchards. They helped to

88   *The revolution and the Islamic Republic*

plan the orchards at Mulleh Balut when ONA began a settlement project there for some Qermezi nomads in 1999. At the seminar mentioned above, several agents contributed agricultural instructions and advice about obtaining state services. On the last day the participants traveled in an agency vehicle to another part of Darrehshuri territory where they inspected a productive, government-approved walnut orchard. The nomads praised this novel excursion, which included lunch at the orchard. Parliament voted in 2000 to merge the Ministries of Construction Jihad and Agriculture, the former dominant in the years to follow.

Agricultural Bank and animal insurance

Agents of the state Agricultural Bank toured summer pastures in 1996, including Hanalishah, to inform nomads about a new government program for life insurance for sheep and goats. In exchange for an annual fee (140 tumans for a sheep, 100 tumans for a goat), the bank promised restitution for animals dying accidentally. For an accepted claim, the owner would receive 10,000 tumans for a sheep and 7,000 tumans for a goat. The bank intended to use the money it drew in fees to pay off claims.[93]

All pastoralists suffered losses every year from disease, predators, injuries, and theft, especially during the migrations. Rapidly expanding vehicular roads in southwestern Iran forced the nomads in certain locations to guide their livestock on, beside, and across roads, and animals sustained injuries and deaths from vehicles and thefts from passersby (who snatched animals as their cars and trucks drove slowly alongside them). The pastoralists, lacking pens at night during these treks, endured theft and predator attacks. If they transported livestock by truck, an expensive venture, several animals were likely to be crushed and asphyxiated.

After the bank's agents (one of them a Kachili Qermezi man) explained the program, some pastoralists at Hanalishah agreed to participate. On a second visit, the agents inspected the animals that the owners had chosen for insurance (ones they intended to retain for at least a year), tagged each with a metal ear clip (in later years, plastic), and recorded tag numbers.

The insurance program proved to be limited and complicated. If a loss occurred in winter or summer pastures, the bank usually required the owner to bring the dead animal to its agents in town. If the distance was far, the owner severed the tagged ear and presented it at the bank. If the animal died in a ritually pure state (halal) (if a man had slit the throat of the injured or dying animal in the required fashion), the owner brought its meat to the bank. If it died in an impure state (haram), the man brought the tagged ear. If the owner could not recover the animal after a predator dragged it away or it fell into a mountain crevice, several witnesses needed to testify at the bank about the incident. If the loss occurred during the migration when the owner could not abandon his herd in order to transport the animal, its meat, or its ear to the bank, the bank required the owner to produce multiple affidavits.

If a vehicle struck an animal, the owner needed witnesses, a signed statement, and an ear. The policy did not cover stolen animals unless several people other than the owner testified to the theft. Owners of insured animals could receive treatment at reduced fees at ONA veterinary clinics.

Mohammad Karim, Dariush, and Bizhan Qermezi insured some animals in this new program in 1996. They reported in 1997 and 1998 that the process of making claims was too unwieldy for them to obtain payment for most stricken livestock, and they stopped pursuing the matter. When the contracts needed renewal, the men were no longer interested. They complained that other Qashqa'i men might have deceitfully obtained payment for allegedly dead or lost animals. Bizhan commented about the program in 2000, "Written reports from revolutionary guards, letters from ONA, trips to gendarme headquarters, visits to the banks. It's just too much trouble." During the time he was covered by insurance, he had managed to obtain payment only once, for two wounded sheep.

Seven-Person Commissions

The Islamic regime founded Seven-Person Commissions (*hiyatha-yi haft nafari*) throughout Iran to transfer land according to a 1980 law for sweeping redistributions. Each commission held local state agents (particularly from Construction Jihad and Agriculture and also from Justice and Interior), participants in revolutionary organizations, religious judges, members of village councils, and large-scale cultivators. Based in towns and cities, the commissions functioned successfully for eight months as advocates for local agriculturalists, until Khomeini suspended the redistribution law. Parliament passed another land-reform law in 1982, which the powerful Council of Guardians vetoed. Limited land-reform legislation was passed and approved in 1986 on squatters' rights and the use of "wasteland" but not on many other outstanding land issues.

Even after the two suspensions and the approved (but narrow) legislation in 1986, Seven-Person Commissions continued to negotiate conflicts between cultivators and landowners (who were usually absentee and often lived in cities) and to handle sometimes conflicting ministries and agencies. They determined land rights and resolved disputes despite the government's persisting inability to rule on general, "Islamic," and "revolutionary" principles of land tenure and reform. "In postrevolutionary Iran, no other economic issue has been more intractable and divisive than the question of property ownership."[94]

Cultivators and landowners remained confused and uncertain for years about their rights after the revolution. Did (former) peasants have the right to seize the land they had cultivated for the profit of others? What was the status of land (formerly) controlled by those who had fled Iran during or after the revolution? When people who had left returned to claim their (former) rights, what were the legal procedures? Was all private property inviolable, according to Islamic law, or did special circumstances allow for a more equitable

90 *The revolution and the Islamic Republic*

redistribution of land? (If people had acquired property "illegitimately," seizures were sometimes justified.) How many hectares of cultivable land could owners retain, and could they distribute their other holdings among family members to avoid confiscation? What was the status of arable but uncultivated and fallow land (a crucial issue for those using pastureland)? Mohammad Reza Shah's land reform of 1962–71 posed other problems. People who were dissatisfied with changes in tenure during that era now sought to restore their former rights or to take land they thought they should have gained then.[95]

The Islamic Republic did not resolve these issues definitively, largely because of ideological (and personally motivated) rifts among the clergy over the issue of private property. The new regime had initially oriented its policies toward helping people whom the shah had oppressed and impoverished. Yet many leading clergymen and their financial backers (including influential bazaaris) were themselves major landowners who fought to retain their rights, regardless of the interests of those who labored on the land.[96]

Some Seven-Person Commissions issued temporary leases, while they waited for new laws, so that agricultural production could continue rather than being interrupted or hindered. Underground aqueducts (*qanat*), for example, could collapse if they were not maintained. Many cultivators hesitated to invest capital in irrigation and other improvements until legal issues were resolved. Parliament, ruling on land that farmers had received on temporary leases, gave them permanent rights in 1986 if they were poor, lacked other income, and were local residents.[97] Other farmers and landowners continued to wait impatiently for the government to rule on many remaining and vexing land-related issues.[98]

The Qermezi residing in winter pastures at Dashtak were familiar with Kazerun's Seven-Person Commission because of their disputes with the state agency for natural resources. Consisting of urban Persians, the commission visited Dashtak and offered constructive suggestions for settling conflicts. The group had not yet interceded in the nomads' struggles over land rights at Mulleh Balut below Dashtak. There, an absentee Persian landowner refused to release the deeds to land that the Qermezi men had cultivated continuously for over 50 years and that the shah's land reform had unambiguously allocated to them in 1963. The Qermezi at Hanalishah reported that Semirom's Seven-Person Commission—along with Mahmud Atazadeh, a Darzi Darrehshuri man who was then director of the state agency there for natural resources—had helped to settle disputes for Qashqa'i cultivators in the region.

Ministry of Education

The Ministry of Education disbanded in 1982 the program for nomads' education (*idarih-i amuzish parvarish-i ashayiri*), which had successfully operated independently since its origin in 1954. The ministry's regional and local offices assumed responsibility for providing education to nomads. The government restored the program for nomads' education in 1988 and placed it under the jurisdiction of the Ministry of Education in Tehran. Led by a subcommittee of five Qashqa'i deputies, parliament voted in 1997 to restore the program's independence and in 1999 to reestablish its national headquarters in Shiraz where it had previously been located from 1954 to 1982.

Bagh-i Eram (garden of paradise) housed the program for nomads' education after the revolution. One of Shiraz's major attractions, the ornate building surrounded by cypress trees and walled gardens had been the headquarters of the paramount Qashqa'i khans since the nineteenth century. Mohammad Reza Shah had seized the property in 1954 to punish the Qashqa'i khans for their support of Mohammad Mosaddeq, who as prime minister had nationalized Iran's oil. (He was overthrown by a CIA-directed coup in 1953.) Revolutionary guards confiscated the estate on their own behalf in 1979.[99] (I discuss the state's educational services in Chapter 7.)

Ministry of Health

ONA helped some nomads to receive health insurance offered by the Ministry of Health. The program paid 50 percent of the charges of certain hospitals and doctors. Those nomads who chose specialized facilities (such as private hospitals) and practitioners because they believed them to be superior (especially in critical cases) found that the government did not cover these expenses. As with other programs sponsored or supported by ONA, the qualifying card it issued listed each nomad's confederacy, tribe, and subtribe (thereby affirming these affiliations, especially for the state).

The Ministry of Health was alarmed by Iran's rapidly rising birthrate after the revolution (especially after the war's ceasefire in 1988) and offered family-planning classes, which became state-mandated for couples before they could receive legal marriage licenses.[100] Some classes were segregated by gender. A middle-aged Qermezi widower with many children received instruction in female anatomy when he sought to remarry, his shy bride-to-be at his side. Another bride was puzzled that the ministry did not offer information about male anatomy in the class she and her groom-to-be attended together.

Corps of the Guardians of the Islamic Revolution (Revolutionary Guards)

Three weeks after the shah's ouster, Khomeini formed a central committee that created a statewide independent militia, the Corps of the Guardians of the Islamic Revolution (sipah-i pasdaran-i inqilab-i islami, often shortened in Iran to "sipah" [corps] or "pasdaran" [guardians] and sometimes abbreviated in the literature as IRGC). This "people's militia" served as a counterforce to the regular army, which citizens and those newly seizing power still distrusted because of its recent anti-revolutionary and pro-shah actions. A new Islamic political entity, the Organization of Holy Warriors for the Islamic Revolution (*sazman-i mujahidin-i inqilab-i islami*), helped to organize the corps.

92 *The revolution and the Islamic Republic*

The revolutionary-guard corps was a special force of the faithful to guard the revolution against internal and external enemies. As an ideologically inspired and reliable entity, free from over-centralized control, it came to serve as the coercive paramilitary arm of the Islamic regime. It identified and suppressed opponents of the new rulers and helped them to consolidate power. Clergymen positioned in the corps offered Islamic education and indoctrination to all those who joined, thereby perpetuating the system that sustained them. (I discuss revolutionary guards earlier in this chapter, in its final section, and throughout the book.)

The revolutionary-guard corps attained ministerial status in 1982. It continued to be separate from Iran's other armed forces, including the army (*artish*), urban police (*shahrbani*), and rural gendarmerie (*zhandarmiri*). This division in the state's military forces caused difficulties after the revolution when competing contenders struggled to establish their own versions of state power and legitimacy. The strength and status of the corps rose when it quelled resistance against the new regime by Iran's Kurds, Turkmans, and Arabs in 1979–80 and again when the regular army proved ineffective against Iraq's onslaught in the war's early years. Khomeini instructed the corps in 1983 to supervise the war's volunteer militia (niruha-yi basiji), which enhanced its power. When Iraq deployed missiles against cities distant from the front line, guards ran military-training classes, often held in mosques, for men, women, and older children so they could learn basic defense. The formal leadership hierarchy of the revolutionary-guard corps was intentionally loose until after the end of the Iraq–Iran war (1988).

Revolutionary guards were less powerful during the early and middle 1990s than they had been in the 1980s. They again grew in national influence after 1997 when they competed against the rising tide of the reformists. They became central to the support of hard-line conservatives and were crucial to their survival, especially under the presidency of Mahmud Ahmadinejad (2005–13). Many cabinet members were revolutionary guards or men of revolutionary-guard backgrounds, as were many parliamentary deputies, governor-generals of provinces, and ambassadors abroad.[101] From early on, the corps was directly involved in exporting the revolution beyond Iran's borders. As military advisors and even combatants, revolutionary guards supported Iran's foreign policies in Lebanon, Iraq, and Syria in the 2000s. The United States placed Iran's revolutionary-guard corps on its list of "terrorist" organizations in 2007.

The army and the corps each controlled separate forces for land, air, and water. Some revolutionary guards were stationed in the army, while some army soldiers were assigned to the corps. When young men were called to their compulsory military duty, some could choose to be soldiers (*sarbaz*) in either the army or the corps. The corps was often able to select the best of the new conscripts. Young Qermezi men noted that being a soldier in the corps was more comfortable than in the army because of relaxed standards governing behavior, dress, and appearance. The corps did not recruit or

The revolution and the Islamic Republic   93

accept guards as its own recruits in the mid-1990s but conscripted soldiers continued to serve in the army or the corps.

Revolutionary guards enforced state policy in the 1980s and early 1990s, especially when they suspected anti-revolutionary, anti-regime, and un-Islamic activity, and then again after the mid-1990s. At least in rural Fars and Isfahan provinces, they functioned similarly to the shah's rural gendarmes, except that many guards appeared to be committed to the regime and its politico-religious ideologies. Citizens feared the guards because of their threatening, coercive actions. They did not trust them and exercised caution in their presence. For greater control, the corps usually posted guards in Qashqa'i territories who were not Qashqa'i, and it assigned Qashqa'i guards to non-Qashqa'i areas. In Qashqa'i summer pastures, a large unit of the corps was positioned in Padena south of Semirom, as a show of the regime's strength.

Persian revolutionary guards stationed in Vanak village came repeatedly in 1991 in small, armed groups to Qermezi summer pastures at Hanalishah to solicit funds. These predatory visits had begun soon after the revolution and had continued since then. The guards asked the men in each camp to help them build a guards' residence in Vanak. They claimed that Bahram Qermezi, head of the nomads' Islamic council, had told them to collect a goat at every tent. Soon, hoping to gain a more lucrative response, they changed the prospective building to a clinic. In their appeals, they noted that "the people" needed to help the government (that is, the guards). Irritated, the nomads responded that, by now, more than a decade into the Islamic Republic's supposed reforms, the government ought to be aiding them. Each of the men argued with the guards before reluctantly turning over an animal. Borzu Qermezi complained that such demands impoverished the nomads, who detested the forced obligations. The guards sold the coerced animals and divided the income among themselves. The buildings for which they had sought funds never materialized.

Referring to these periodic solicitations, a Qermezi man used the term for the animal tax (gallih bigirih) that the tribal khans had formerly extracted from the groups under their authority. He stated that the new tax represented a larger percentage of their livestock than the khans' percentage, especially considering that other guards in winter pastures and along migratory routes also periodically coerced animals from them. The khans' tax had been episodic and supported the confederacy leaders when they faced regional and national political crises. The guards' tax was semiannual if not more frequent and served only as bribes for personal gain.

Revolutionary guards still toured summer pastures extorting livestock in 1992, but these coercions had diminished by 1995–99 in conjunction with the regional decline in the guards' power. Their authority faded in some regions, and people feared them less. Still, through 2013, guards continued to demand payments of animals or cash whenever any Qermezi engaged in land disputes or other conflicts that drew the guards' attention.

94 *The revolution and the Islamic Republic*

When Darrehshuri tribespeople in Mehr-i Gerd village celebrated a wedding in 1997, Persian revolutionary guards posted there heard the music and went to investigate. They climbed a barren hillside to spy into an enclosed, high-walled courtyard (and violated customs found everywhere in Iran about personal privacy in secured domestic spaces). There they saw women dancing in the presence of men. Descending to the courtyard gate, they ordered the men there to stop the music and dancing immediately. They shouted that these activities violated Islamic moral codes. The women ceased dancing but the musicians later resumed their performance without incident. At another wedding that same summer in an orchard not far from Mehr-i Gerd, the Darrehshuri hosts boasted that a cash bribe to the Persian guards assigned to a nearby village allowed them to celebrate with music and dance without interference.

Revolutionary guards served as the enforcing arm of revolutionary committees (komiteh) in towns and cities, which investigated and conducted surveillance on people's personal behavior. If committee members learned that a woman did not observe proper Islamic dress (*bad hijabi*, "improperly covered" woman), they sent guards to harass her kinsmen into forcing her to correct her attire. Guards also instructed and detained women along the streets if they objected to their appearance. The regime established in 1984 anti-vice patrols to combat immoral behavior, and pairs of vehicles, each carrying "Islamic brothers" or "Islamic sisters," toured city and town streets to warn or apprehend people behaving or dressing inappropriately.[102] These patrols and the revolutionary committees often coordinated their activities. Considered the "religious" version of the hezbollahis, the Center for Propagating Virtue and Combating Sin (*dayirih-yi amr bi maruf va nahi az munkir*) also deployed mobile morals squads. Anti-vice courts (*dadgah-yi zidd-i munkirat*) issued fines and punishments.

Nomads' Corps of the Guardians of the Islamic Revolution

The Nomads' Corps of the Guardians of the Islamic Revolution (sipah-i pasdaran-i inqilab-i islami ashayiri; often shortened to "sipah-i ashayiri," nomads' corps) began in December 1979 when a small group of young Qashqa'i men in Shiraz protested against the resumption of power by the paramount Qashqa'i khans. They wrote letters to Khomeini and sent copies to revolutionary-guard headquarters in Tehran. These men became the nucleus of the nomads' corps and assembled recruits. As a separate entity, the nomads' corps developed simultaneously with the regular revolutionary-guard corps. It gained high-level, regional, and local recognition for its military prowess during the Iraq–Iran war and the defensive resistance of the paramount Qashqa'i khans. In its early years it affiliated with Construction Jihad and helped to deliver its services, and it assisted the nomads' semiannual migrations by supplying water and fodder at congested locations. As the nomads' corps grew more militarily active, it associated more closely with the regular guard corps.

The revolution and the Islamic Republic   95

Members of the nomads' corps noted, as did officials of the Organization for Nomads' Affairs (ONA), that Khomeini had praised nomads for serving as a corps (sipah) in defense of Islam. In his last will and testament, he extols Iran's armed forces (army, revolutionary guards, gendarmerie, police, Islamic committees, volunteer basij militia, and "tribes") and mentions the "tribal militia" that served in the Iraq–Iran war. The translator renders the Persian term "ashayir" as "tribe" in English, despite the regime's not acknowledging Iran's "tribes." Khomeini had also lauded nomads as the "treasures" (*zakhayir*) of Islam and the revolution.[103]

The nomads' corps was part of Iran's military forces and contained both revolutionary guards and army soldiers. It functioned similarly to the Security Force for Nomads (*intizamat-i ashayiri*) under Mohammad Reza Shah. During the Iraq–Iran war, the corps flourished, its members recruiting and training volunteers for the national militia (niruha-yi basiji), especially the nomads' branch, from among the nomadic and tribal groups in their regions. It issued registration cards to these volunteers. During the defensive resistance of the paramount Qashqa'i khans, units of the nomads' corps—under the command of a Shish Buluki Qashqa'i man—were part of the government's attacking armed forces. The corps coordinated its assaults from Shiraz, its headquarters in southwestern Iran. Later, the Bulvardi Qashqa'i head of the nomads' corps in Shiraz unsuccessfully sought to create a separate corps for the Qashqa'i, which he called sipah-i Qashqa'i.

In Qashqa'i territory, most members of the nomads' corps were Qashqa'i men. In other tribal territories, they usually originated from the groups there. (This policy is the reverse of that of the regular revolutionary-guard corps.) A unit of the nomads' corps was assigned to each major Qashqa'i tribe and moved seasonally between its winter and summer areas. Similar to the government's policy to assign an ONA office to each major tribe, the nomads' corps also served to legitimize, support, and perpetuate tribal structures.

For the Darrehshuri, their unit of the nomads' corps relocated seasonally. Shortly after spring began, the force moved from Chinar Shahijan in winter pastures to Semirom in summer ones, where it remained until the nomads migrated back to winter pastures. The unit in Semirom in 1998 contained six men, three revolutionary guards and three army soldiers. Its officer, a guard, was an Imanlu Darrehshuri man. The two other guards were Lurs. One soldier was Qashqa'i, and the other two were Lurs. This office moved in 1999 from Semirom to Mehr-i Gerd village, the former headquarters of the Darrehshuri khans and more central to Darrehshuri summer pastures than Semirom. (The winter office of the corps remained in Chinar Shahijan.) All its staff members in 1999 were Qashqa'i: a Bulvardi Darrehshuri man as the officer, two other revolutionary guards, and three or four army soldiers.

Units of the nomads' corps periodically traveled by vehicle through winter and summer pastures in the 1980s to establish the state's presence in tribal territory. By the early 1990s it no longer conducted such routine surveillance. By then, the Qermezi at Dashtak and Hanalishah experienced little or no

96 *The revolution and the Islamic Republic*

contact with the corps or its members. When I asked in the mid-1990s about the functions of the nomads' corps, Qermezi men replied that the members spent their days drinking tea in their offices and collecting their salaries. Some Qermezi were unable to identify for me the tribal and subtribal affiliations of the current members. If they had met them, they said, they would certainly know their identities. (After routine greetings, two previously unacquainted tribal men would exchange information about their tribal, subtribal, and lineage identities.) I did not see any nomads' corpsmen at Dashtak or Hanalishah after the mid-1990s.

Other government agents dispatched units of the nomads' corps to the scene when they heard about murders and other serious crimes. (As under the shahs' regimes, the Qashqa'i still preferred handling these matters through their own leaders, without notifying any state authorities.) The nomads' corpsmen (as compared with the regular security forces) knew local languages and dialects and could handle interactions in culturally appropriate ways. Nomad men invited the corpsmen into their tents for discussions (and women there seemed comfortable in their presence). The men dealt more formally with other kinds of security forces (if they were not tribesmen), beyond the confines of their tents, so that these outsiders would have limited contact with the nomads' personal lives (including the women there).

The nomads' corps in and near winter and summer pastures served as a liaison for its headquarters in Shiraz and filled a bureaucratic role. The men processed applications for gun permits and sold bullets and cartridges at state-subsidized rates. Open-market prices were higher, and ammunition was sometimes in scarce supply.

The nomads' corps sponsored marksmanship contests for the Qashqa'i in different parts of tribal territory in the 1990s. It provided weapons (so no one would have an unfair advantage using his own, possibly specialized, gun) and ammunition, placed targets, judged results, and awarded prizes (usually ammunition). Qermezi males of all ages eagerly participated in every announced event. Their history was one of excellent marksmanship, and many of them had won or placed in these competitions. The corps held a contest for Darrehshuri men at Tang-i Ahan in 1999, which a contingent from Hanalishah entered. Of the 70 entrants drawn from the large tribal territory, the top three winners were Qermezi (Filamarz, Ali Murad, and Mohammad Quli). Bahram Qermezi had won first prize in another contest the preceding winter. A Qashqa'i woman competing against men the previous year had earned first prize. In some areas, the corps held separate events for men and women. (No Qermezi women were skilled in using firearms.)

Gun permits

Since the 1950s and early 1960s, Mohammad Reza Shah's regime had banned the Qashqa'i from owning or possessing guns (or had strictly controlled their use) and had periodically seized them (*khal-i silah*) from individuals and

The revolution and the Islamic Republic 97

groups, sometimes as a form of collective punishment. With this state's collapse in 1978, many Qashqa'i regained their confiscated weapons and bought new ones. Since then, except for individual or localized seizures, they retained their guns. During and following the defensive resistance of the paramount Qashqa'i khans in 1980–82, Qashqa'i men everywhere expected that the new regime would confiscate their weapons or restrict their use, out of fear that the insurgency would spread. The Ministry of Defense instituted gun permits in 1981 but few Qashqa'i obtained them then. The Supreme Council for Nomads invited an "ordinary nomad" to a meeting in Tehran in 1983 and asked him, "If you could make one request of the prime minister, what would it be?" He instantly responded, "To retain our weapons." A week later, probably unconnected with this appeal, the prime minister announced that nomads could keep their weapons and that the military would not confiscate them.

Ayatollah Ali Khamenei, Iran's supreme leader after Khomeini's death, issued in 1996 a new, stricter ruling about guns. The government authorized the Nomads' Corps of Revolutionary Guards to process applications for and issue gun permits (*javaz-i tufangi*) to qualified nomads.

The statewide ruling ordered all gunowners to apply for permits by 11 August. It required each one to submit his weapon(s), file an application for a permit, and verify his identity. If officials approved the request, the owner would obtain a laminated permit and retrieve his gun. The permit holder was required to carry the document at all times and was forbidden from loaning his weapon to anyone. Khamenei reassured the citizens who worried about credentials and eligibility that the government would forgive them for past illegal or anti-regime activities and would issue them permits if they were currently in good standing with the government. Iran's security forces would arrest those who did not comply and would confiscate their weapons.

Qermezi men faced these new regulations with mixed sentiments. Since rearming in 1978, they had been troubled about retaining their cherished weapons. During the tense two-year period when paramilitary forces pursued the paramount Qashqa'i khans, Qermezi men feared that the regime would order all Qashqa'i, and perhaps all civilian Iranians, to be disarmed. The new ruling in 1996 reassured them somewhat and seemed to offer them the right to retain their weapons over the long term and to be pardoned for past illegal or threatening actions. The four Qermezi men who were imprisoned in 1980 for supporting the Qashqa'i khans might fall into this category, they said.

Yet Qermezi men worried that through gun registration they would fall under greater state surveillance and control. They said that the edict was expressly political, another attempt to fortify the regime's rule, especially over the heavily armed tribesmen. During the past century, state rulers had periodically subjected the Qashqa'i to gun confiscations, and men had hidden or denied owning weapons. Government agents had confiscated guns from the men they arrested or detained and never returned them. All Qermezi men told stories about weapon seizures. Under the new ruling in 1996, they were perturbed that by submitting and registering their guns, the state would now hold vital,

98   *The revolution and the Islamic Republic*

detailed information about them, including precise descriptions of each weapon. Thus, when they encountered trouble with any authorities, they ran a greater risk of having their weapons seized. They also knew that local officials could confiscate their guns under any circumstances. After they submitted their weapons, a required step in the registration process, they might never be able to reclaim them. Officials could hold them for their own purposes, especially to punish and intimidate, and could sell them for personal gain. Qermezi men also feared the state's incompetence. What recourse would they have if their weapons were lost, damaged, or destroyed? The revolutionary guards who had seized two Qermezi guns in 1980 sold one and irreparably damaged the other. Despite being the state's official headman, Borzu Qermezi had never been able to reclaim the gun that security forces had confiscated from him in 1964 as part of a Qashqa'i-wide seizure.

After heated discussions, most Qermezi men decided to comply with the new ruling and take their chances by submitting their guns. They had experienced unpredictable circumstances since 1978 and found decision making difficult, given that the future was unknown. They had delayed in making key choices about their livelihoods and lifestyles because they expected the current regime to collapse and another one to emerge. "Why is a regime run by hezbollahis still in power," they asked one another. "What kinds of people are out there to form a new government?" A new regime would force on them other, possibly contradictory, changes, and they might regret the decisions they had made earlier.

The weapons of choice for the Qermezi were various kinds of often antique rifles used for hunting wild game. Some men owning more than one weapon registered only the least valuable one so they could retain possession of the others in case the authorities seized the registered weapon for any reason. If a father and a son residing together each owned weapons, sometimes only one registered his, thereby offering both men continued access to another gun if the registered one was later confiscated. Men said that each household ought to possess at least one permit so they could produce it whenever any authorities came to harass them.

Possibly the last time any Qermezi men had aggressively deployed guns for defensive or hostile intent was in 1945 when a small group of them confronted Boir Ahmad Lur thieves.[104] Regardless of the fifty-some years that had passed, men asserted that they still needed weapons for protection against external enemies. They cited two recent events, the death threats against Borzu Qermezi by Allah Quli Jahangiri (the Darrehshuri leftist rebel who had murdered many others) and the hostile attacks of revolutionary guards who had seized three Qermezi men at Hanalishah with the intent to execute them.

Men always responded enthusiastically to any questions I asked about guns, which indicates the importance that weapons held for them. Guns were potent symbols of the Qashqa'i tribal confederacy, the people's political autonomy, and men's bravery and masculinity. They offered the Qashqa'i a

way to defend their interests against the state and other enemies and signified
their intention to maintain their independence.

Revolutionary Islamic committees

The regime placed a new security force—revolutionary Islamic committees
(*komiteh-yi inqilab-i islami*)—under the authority of the Ministry of Interior
soon after the revolution, to join the urban police and rural gendarmerie.
Headed by pro-Khomeini clergymen, these new units were based on the popular
committees emerging in the neighborhoods of Tehran and other large cities in
1978 and early 1979 to coordinate revolutionary activities. Often housed in
neighborhood mosques, they performed administrative and police functions.
Soldiers of the shah's armed forces submitted their weapons at these places
toward the revolution's end. Disputes between and within the early committees
caused Khomeini to order some structure and centralization.

Formally established in all cities and towns by late 1979, committees exercised
some jurisdiction over what their members perceived were anti-revolutionary,
anti-regime, and un-Islamic activities. Revolutionary guards posted to these
committees (*pasdaran-i komiteh*) served as enforcers. Khomeini issued a
declaration in 1982 to curb the excesses of these and other revolutionary
organizations, and parliament attempted to legislate their activities in 1983.
The efforts of these committees to instill law and order and guard the borders
often conflicted with those of the police and gendarmes. Their activities were
broad in cities and large towns; in small towns such as Kazerun and Semirom
they were less active. Their facilities served as polling places, and everywhere
they played a major role in voter turnout. When the government introduced rationing of basic commodities, committees administered the system in
many areas.

Everywhere, committees aggressively pursued issues that they connected
with proper Islamic behavior, including prohibiting the production, distribution,
and consumption of opium, heroin, and alcoholic beverages. They sought to
prevent the immodest dress and appearance of women and men. Committees
handled reports of un-Islamic behavior and dispatched revolutionary guards
to detain offenders. They stamped black marks on the identity cards of the
guilty and charged them fines. They mistreated the people they arrested whose
cards already exhibited such marks, and they denied them some government
services.[105] Committees sometimes coordinated activities with the Center for
Propagating Virtue and Combating Sin, which dispatched mobile morals
squads.

Semirom's committee provided financial and other assistance in the
mid-1990s to an impoverished woman and her family in the Qermezi village
of Nurabad. Kazerun citizens reported that their town's committee was less
active in 2000 than it had been earlier, especially in the 1980s when it had
aimed to impose strict moral codes. It still disciplined young men in 2000 who
loitered in public or inappropriate places (such as near a girls' school), and it

100   *The revolution and the Islamic Republic*

applied controls on noisy and polluting vehicles. It used to harass women, and every year it seemed to lessen the restrictions it enforced on their dress and appearance. Kazerun's committee had hassled women who wore headscarves and overcoats instead of veil-wraps (chadur), but some women in the early 2000s wore small scarves and knee-length or even shorter coats without much interference.

Nomads' revolutionary Islamic committees

When the defensive resistance of the paramount Qashqa'i khans ended in 1982, the government founded special nomads' committees (komiteh-yi inqilab-i islami ashayiri) in some cities and towns near the nomads' territories. These entities often fell under the auspices of city and town committees, but at least some acted autonomously, and they handled interpersonal and group conflicts, smuggling, and theft. A nomads' committee headed by a Kashkuli Qashqa'i man was located in Kazerun in the mid-1980s, moved to Chinar Shahijan, and then was disbanded in the late 1980s. The nomads' committee in Shiraz persisted until 1997-98 when it too was dissolved. The only Qermezi who participated in these entities was Dariush Qermezi, who served half of his two-year compulsory military duty as an office worker and driver for Shiraz's committee. Its director for a decade or more was a Bulvardi Kashkuli Qashqa'i man. Dariush received the choice posting because of the friendship of his father Borzu with the director's father.

When President Rafsanjani centralized some security forces to form a general one (*niruha-yi intizami*) in 1990–91, most or all of the nomads' committees were formally disbanded (but not Shiraz's). Since then, the Qermezi at Dashtak and Hanalishah fell under the more loosely structured authority of the reorganized security forces posted in Kazerun, Semirom, and Vanak village. The nomads' revolutionary-guard corps, nomads' volunteer militia, and nomads' Islamic councils continued to exercise other forms of authority over Qashqa'i nomads and other tribal people.

Volunteer militia

Khomeini wanted to mobilize Iran's citizens and sustain revolutionary fervor. He called for the creation of "an army of twenty million" during the American hostage crisis (1979–81) to confront a possible invasion by U.S. military forces and to protect the Islamic Republic. In response, a popular revolutionary organization, the Unit for Mobilizing the Oppressed (*vahid-i basij-i mustazafin*), was formed in early 1980. The concept of the mustazafin (the oppressed and deprived) proved essential to Shi'i populism, a movement to mobilize the masses and give power to those kept powerless under the shah.[106] Basij forces became one of the Islamic Republic's most powerful, politicized, populist, and parastatal bodies. Together with revolutionary guards and hezbollahi vigilantes, they suppressed opposition to the regime and imposed strict

Islamic codes of conduct on society. They were a "violent force of suppression" that was "unaccountable to the law."[107]

The new organization drew volunteers—"the mobilized" (basijis)—below the age of 18 (the age of men's conscription), young women, and middle-aged men. Many of them received weapons training at mosques, workplaces, and educational institutions. The revolutionary-guard corps and the regular army trained the Volunteer Militia (niruha-yi basiji), which grew in strength and numbers after Iraq's invasion in 1980. Volunteers performed services near home, such as distributing rationed commodities. Khomeini allowed them to fight on the war's front line for the first time in 1982, where each person usually served a maximum of three to four months. Towns, large villages, workplaces, state agencies, and even individuals (such as Khomeini's son, Ahmad) sponsored and contributed funds to volunteer units at the front.[108] The youngest volunteers were given plastic keys to symbolize their entry to heaven, and they served in human-wave attacks and cleared minefields before the better equipped and trained revolutionary guards and army soldiers entered the fray. (Such actions drew international media attention in ways that few other atrocities of the war did.) Khomeini instructed the revolutionary-guard corps in 1983 to supervise the militia.

After the war, the Organization for Militia Volunteers (sazman-i basiji) provided services to militia veterans, particularly former prisoners of war and the wounded. Volunteers were part of an increasingly institutionalized body, especially after 1994. In some towns and cities, those serving as a mobile morals police enforced dress codes on women and men and harassed women in public about their relationship with their adult male companions.

Even more organized and institutionalized during the first presidency of Ahmadinejad (2005–09), zealous basij forces violently suppressed protestors against his fraudulent reelection in 2009 and continued their assaults against peaceful demonstrators, many of them part of the new Green Movement.

Nomads' volunteer militia

Special volunteer units for nomads (niruha-yi basiji ashayiri) recruited in tribal territories and served with distinction in the war. A regiment for the tribes of Fars province included Qashqa'i, Boir Ahmad Lurs, other Kuh Giluyeh Lurs, and Khamseh. Bakhtiyari tribes to the north had their own regiment. Nomadic and other tribal men were often already skilled in weapons and defensive and offensive strategies and could cope with difficult living conditions. Invoking an unnecessarily quaint tone, one author notes that "tribals in their traditional costumes" volunteered for the war.[109] Such clothes would have been their everyday attire, not a fancy outfit donned for effect.

Many Qermezi men registered as volunteers in the nomads' militia in the 1980s but few of the older ones fought in the war. A Qermezi volunteer traveled three times to the office of the nomads' corps before clerks would take his photograph for his basij militia card. On his first visit he lacked a

102 *The revolution and the Islamic Republic*

beard, on the second one the hair was still too short, and on the third he met the specifications for proper beard length. After the photograph, he shaved off the beard. State agencies often required male employees to grow facial hair (to a certain length) as a sign of revolutionary and Islamic fervor and dedication to the regime. Men who were clean shaven were often demonstrating their opposition and defiance.

Revolutionary guards in the nomads' corps and volunteers in the nomads' militia shared a building in the town of Borujen, and volunteers in Mehr-i Gerd village occupied a large house confiscated from Ziad Khan Darrehshuri after the revolution.

The nomads' volunteer militia based in Kazerun summoned in December 2001 74 registered nomads (all Darrehshuri, Farsi Madan, and Kashkuli Qashqa'i) in the area's winter pastures to attend a four-day mandatory instructional seminar on heavy arms (including large machine guns mounted in the back of open military vehicles), political and religious indoctrination, and communal prayers. The militia excused salaried government employees, such as schoolteachers, from work for the duration, and those who participated hoped to receive a slight increase in salary. Those who refused or failed to appear expected punishment in the form of salary cuts and loss of state services. The militia selected teachers because of their influence over multitudes of pupils.

The letters requiring the nomads to attend the event came from the Organization for Nomads' Affairs, not the militia or the guard corps, which demonstrates the overlapping and collaborative functions of some government agencies (especially those responsible for nomads). ONA held information about the nomads' current locations and could search for the men who failed to show up. The nomads' volunteer militia, the nomads' revolutionary-guard corps, and the clergymen assigned as advisors to these agencies cooperated in staging and speaking at this function.

Some nomads at Dashtak and Hanalishah had attended similar events in the past but not since the war's ceasefire in 1988. The nomads' volunteer militia had held a 10-day seminar in 1986, at Zain Ali just west of Hanalishah, in the very location recently vacated by the paramount Qashqa'i khans, who had set up camp there in 1979 when they returned to Iran from exile abroad. The event's planners understood the symbolic importance of the place and took pleasure in supplanting the former leaders. The nomads participating in the seminar praised the free food and entertainment but disliked the event's compulsory nature and the propaganda, mandatory communal prayers, and efforts to recruit them as volunteers for service at the war's front line. One attendee, 14-year-old Farhad Qermezi, did volunteer. He was killed in battle shortly thereafter.

Security forces

President Rafsanjani in 1990-91 fused some of Iran's armed forces—revolutionary Islamic committees, urban police, and rural gendarmerie—into a single military organization called "security forces" (or law enforcement forces, LEF) (niruha-yi intizami) and placed it under the authority of the Ministry of Interior. (Many Qashqa'i continued to use the phrase, *niruha-yi amniyih*, from the shah's regime.) Some tasks of the nomads' revolutionary Islamic committees were now included in the new force. Revolutionary Islamic committees in cities, towns, and large villages continued to function as a police force somewhat independently despite the merger.

Iran's reorganized armed forces included the regular army and the revolutionary military (consisting of the revolutionary-guard corps with its paramilitary basij militia and the newly merged security forces). The basij militia was now the most powerful paramilitary force in Iran. As cultural liberalization became increasingly visible in society by the early 1990s, the supreme leader ordered the security forces and the basijis to apply the principles of "propagating virtue and combating sin" more stringently to Iran's citizens.[110]

The Qermezi had fallen under the authority of these and other separate, sometimes conflicting, security and military forces (particularly revolutionary guards) since 1979 but their circumstances improved in 1991. The nomads at Dashtak and Hanalishah came under the jurisdiction of the newly combined armed forces, with units based in Kazerun, Semirom, and Vanak. They received summonses to appear at the headquarters (which they still called "*pasgah* zhandarmiri") in these locales, and personnel there wrote reports and forwarded them to the Ministry of Justice and other agencies in towns and cities. The security forces handled land disputes and serious interpersonal conflicts.

Secret police

Virtually everyone in Iran had feared Mohammad Reza Shah's secret-police organization (known by its Persian acronym, SAVAK) and harbored suspicions about its supposedly omnipresent agents and informers. When revolutionary forces threatened and then overthrew the shah and his regime, they immediately targeted SAVAK officials and offices. The Islamic regime reconstituted the shah's intelligence organization as SAVAMA and placed it under the prime minister's authority in 1982. Revolutionary committees and guards collaborated with it and pursued surveillance and intimidation in ways similar to former SAVAK practices. All ministries and other large state and parastatal agencies also established their own internal intelligence offices, which conducted independent investigations and meted out punishments. People said that SAVAMA was not as intimidating as SAVAK had been, and in the following decades it did not emerge as an agency to be feared by most citizens.

SAVAMA appeared to have no impact on the Qermezi, and I never heard anyone mention its agents or informers, a change from the shah's era when many people were suspect. Some Qashqa'i residents of Tehran, Isfahan, and Shiraz did fall under SAVAMA scrutiny but not in ways comparable to the shah's time.

104 *The revolution and the Islamic Republic*

Ministry of Justice

Qermezi men frequently answered citations from and sought legal redress through the Ministry of Justice and its courts (dadgah) in towns and cities in the region. Many state agencies investigated conflicts and wrote reports to forward to the Ministry of Justice's local, regional, and provincial offices, and Qermezi men spent years, even decades, pursuing documents, obtaining signatures and official stamps, paying fees and bribes, and waiting for hearings.

The court in Semirom until the 1990s sometimes held a single judge and other times none, and Qermezi men usually had to travel to Shahreza for inquiries. Due to Shahriyar Qermezi's influence as a parliamentary deputy, Semirom was upgraded to having a public prosecutor's office (*dad sara*) in 1999, and three judges were seated, none of them clerics. In other places with two or more judges, often one was a clergyman, and in locales with many judges, sometimes half were clerics. Shahriyar Qermezi also raised Vanak's status from a village (*dih*) to a township (*shahrak*) in 1999, and people expected that the community would receive its own court. Much of Hanalishah fell under the authority of the security forces in Vanak, and a court there would expedite the processing of claims, or so people hoped.

A young Shaikh Lur woman married to a Qermezi man confronted the legal system on her own behalf in 1999, in what might be the first incidence for Qermezi women or other women closely tied to the subtribe. Her husband had threatened to take a second wife, a war widow with economic means, and the first wife prepared to file a legal claim in the Borujen court. If he proceeded with the second marriage, she vowed to return to her parents, obtain a legal divorce, and secure the payment of the fee (*mahriyih*) listed on her marriage contract. According to Iranian, Islamic, and tribal law, her husband and his family would retain custody of his young daughter unless they forfeited their rights, an unlikely occurrence.

State taxation

Iran's government did not collect taxes from the Qermezi unless they were its employees. It extracted taxes (as well as health-insurance premiums and retirement funds) from salaries before the workers were paid. When pastoralists sought low-interest loans from state banks for capital improvements, the government required some of them to pay a small tax based on the number of livestock they owned and would not process the loan documents until it received proof of payment. Bribery payments to state agents, "independent tax collectors for themselves," can be construed as "direct taxation without state intermediation" and continued under the new regime.[111]

The government's tax on apples exported abroad affected some Qermezi indirectly. Their own apples were usually not acceptable for export, and they lacked the facilities for storage and refrigeration often demanded by the external market. Many did not sell their apples directly. Instead, they sold ("rented") the yet-unpicked harvests to entrepreneurial middlemen, sometimes urban-based Qashqa'i men, for a negotiated fee. When the state export tax was high, Qermezi men did not obtain adequate rents. When the state lowered the tax, as in 1999, they received higher prices.

Some Qermezi occasionally gave small sums to local religious shrines and to the poor and needy in villages, but I never heard anyone acknowledge paying the annual taxes stipulated by Islam (*zakat, khums*). If anyone did offer these taxes, he would give the amount to a religious authority or a devout person of his choosing or would find his own charity. The Islamic regime tried to control these resources by establishing a central khums fund and by placing collection boxes for charitable donations in government offices, along streets and highways, and even in private homes.[112] The government might have required Shahriyar Qermezi to show proof of his payment of Islamic taxes so he could be ruled eligible as a candidate for parliamentary elections. The few Qermezi men who traveled as pilgrims to Mecca joked that Islamic law obliged *hajji*s to perform all religious rites and duties for the rest of their lives, including paying Islamic taxes annually. (They refused to pay any amount. They said that Iran's corrupt clergymen deposited the money in their personal bank accounts abroad.) Some people jested that they did not undertake this and other major pilgrimages (to Najaf, Damascus, and Mashhad) because they disliked the idea of such mandatory lifelong obligations.

Revolutionary foundations

Many independent, autonomous, and parastatal foundations (bunyad) dominated by the regime's powerful clergymen were created soon after the revolution.[113] Initially the aims of many of them were to subsidize and improve the living standards of the poor and needy, but all these foundations became wealthy entities from which their founders and supporters benefited financially and politically. As officially nonprofit enterprises, they constituted a third sector between state-owned (or "public") operations and private capitalist ones and mediated between them. They operated in parallel with official government institutions, which exercised no control over them, and they "interfered with and reduced the efficacy of government decisions."[114] They provided assistance to the urban and rural poor, the disabled and handicapped, former prisoners of war, and families of martyrs. They mobilized grassroots support for the Islamic Republic during elections, demonstrations, and popular unrest. Several foundations contributed to Iran's foreign policy by extending their operations beyond Iran's borders to Hezbollah in Lebanon, Hamas in Palestine, Shi'i institutions and communities in Iraq and the Persian Gulf states, and al-Assad's regime in Syria.[115]

These foundations were active in all sectors of Iran's economy. They were public institutions because they did not pay taxes, were entitled to state-subsidized loans and foreign currency, received funds from the supreme leader, and were responsible for many of the state's tasks of distribution. The supreme leader

106 *The revolution and the Islamic Republic*

appointed and dismissed their directors. These foundations were simultaneously private and semiautonomous entities because they were not accountable to or monitored by the government, and their financial affairs were not public. They received 60 percent of the state budget, and yet the popularly elected president and parliament lacked the authority to supervise their operations, expenditures, and performance.[116]

Martyrs Foundation

Khomeini decreed in 1980 that a Martyrs Foundation (*bunyad-i shahid*) be formed to identify and assist the victims of the shah's regime and to provide services to the revolution's casualties (the injured and the families of the fallen). When the Iraq–Iran war began later that year, the foundation expanded its activities to serve the wounded and the martyrs' families, and Iran's supreme leader, Khomeini (and, after his death, Khamenei), assumed authority over it. It issued certificates to the martyrs' families to authenticate the deaths of their sons. For the parents, wives, and children of martyrs, the entity provided initial cash awards, monthly stipends, housing assistance, discounted commodities, financial loans, privileged jobs, and special educational opportunities. For the wounded, it offered similar services as well as early-retirement options. The foundation constructed elaborate, uniform tombs for the dead in locations chosen by their families. It gave extra benefits to war widows, especially those with children, and encouraged widows with or without children to marry war veterans, especially the wounded who needed care.[117] It provided transportation on Thursdays and Fridays to martyrs' cemeteries. It organized and subsidized the pilgrimages of its clients to Mashhad, Damascus, and Mecca and took them on shopping trips to Kuwait and Dubai. All these services connected injured veterans and martyrs' families to the regime and encouraged them to support its policies.[118] Combined, these millions of individuals helped to keep the government in power, especially because many of them also participated— as revolutionary guards, basij militiamen, hezbollahi vigilantes, and Islamic council members—in other regime-supporting efforts.

This foundation served the families of the one Qermezi man killed in the revolution and the 23 Qermezi men killed, wounded, lost, or imprisoned in the war. It continued to function this way through 2013.[119]

Foundation for the Oppressed

Khomeini established the largest of these parastatal foundations, Foundation for the Oppressed (*bunyad-i mustazafin*), in 1979. Its initial task was to seize, consolidate, and administer the "illegitimately acquired" property of the shah's Pahlavi family (amounting to one-fifth of Iran's private assets)[120] and its associates. He placed it under the prime minister's authority in 1984. This foundation became a "huge quasigovernmental conglomerate" of companies, industrial plants, real estate properties, and newspapers.[121] "Established to

The revolution and the Islamic Republic   107

work alongside the government, this foundation became largely unaccountable to the assembly and so powerful it was able to act autonomously; thus while enforcing the power of the state, it also paradoxically undermined it."[122]

This foundation issued a loan of three million tumans in 2000 to Shahriyar Qermezi (a wounded veteran) for building or buying a house in Shahreza. By then its expanded title was the Foundation for the Oppressed, Wounded [or Disabled], and Veterans (*bunyad-i mustazafin va janbazan* ["self-sacrificers"] *va sargaran*), and its services overlapped with those of the Martyrs' Foundation.

One of the foundation's stated goals was to offer welfare services to people oppressed by the shah's regime and to improve their living and housing conditions. Many Qashqa'i would have qualified for inclusion if the foundation had chosen to direct its attention to them. Yet the Organization for Nomads' Affairs was probably more effective in providing specific services than this foundation could have been, given ONA's reliance on men of nomadic and tribal backgrounds and its focused tasks (such as roads, wells, and veterinary care).[123]

New revolutionary Islamic councils for nomads and villagers

The Ministry of Interior instituted revolutionary Islamic councils (*shura-yi inqilab-i islami*) in many Qashqa'i areas (and throughout rural Iran) in late 1979 and early 1980. These nomads' councils (shura-yi islami-yi ashayiri) and village councils (shura-yi islami-yi rustai) served as liaisons between local groups (nomadic pastoralists and villagers) and state agencies and agents.[124]

Iran's new constitution, approved by citizens in a national referendum in December 1979, stipulated the notion of local councils (in principles six and seven).[125] That month the new government began to support revolutionary Islamic councils as the representative bodies of nomads and villagers and urged their formation throughout Iran. These councils were intended to replace the bodies created during Mohammad Reza Shah's regime for villages, including rural courts (*khanih-yi insaf*, houses of justice) and village associations (*anjuman-i dih*).[126] Iran's Supreme Court abolished in 1982 any legal institutions still surviving from the Pahlavi era.[127]

Two new agencies, Organization for Nomads' Affairs (ONA) and Construction Jihad (to become a ministry in 1983), supervised the process of notifying local Qashqa'i groups, certifying eligible candidates, and overseeing selections or elections.[128] In helping the Qashqa'i to adopt the new institution of Islamic councils, these agencies recognized existing kinship, tribal, ethnolinguistic, and socio-territorial groups and, inadvertently or not, reinforced these entities and ensured their continuing significance not only for the people but also for the state. (The main government agency responsible for serving Iran's nomads underwent several changes in names and affiliations after the revolution. It was first called ONA in 1982, a label I use for convenience throughout this section, including the period before 1982.)

Many publications on postrevolutionary Iran state that the 1979 constitution mandated Islamic councils but that the government did not establish them

108 *The revolution and the Islamic Republic*

until 1999 (after Khatami was elected as president). Writers seem unaware that the Ministry of Interior and other government agencies had coordinated and overseen council elections in tens of thousands of villages and nomadic communities as early as 1979.[129]

Under Mohammad Reza Shah, the task of linking Qashqa'i nomads and many Qashqa'i villagers with state agencies and agents had belonged to the tribal headmen (kadkhuda). Some headmen continued as mediators after the revolution while newly elected council members replaced others. Some groups chose their existing headmen as council members. Both offices in some groups functioned simultaneously. State officials noted that the institution of headmen, belonging to the shah, had died with the revolution, but they still interacted with these men as the representatives of their groups.

Most headmen in Qashqa'i society had represented their subtribes until 1979–80. Other headmen represented sections of subtribes if these entities were large or if disputing factions arose within them. The emergence of a second headman could signal a subtribe's division. Rival tribal khans played roles in this process by supporting rival leaders in a subtribe. Over time the process could result in two subtribes or one reconsolidated entity. Likewise, state officials could support one man over another and place authority in his hands as the subtribe's sole representative. When some subtribes divided, some or all of their parts could join other subtribes and affiliate with new headmen. Under some circumstances, a subtribe functioned as a unified polity while under others its sections acted separately. (The Qermezi subtribe and its five lineages operated in these ways, sometimes united, other times not.) The exact number of subtribes within any Qashqa'i tribe at any given time was imprecise because of these ongoing processes.

Shir Mohammad was the headman of the Qermezi subtribe from approximately 1918 until his death in the Semirom war of 1943. By popular consensus, his eldest surviving son, Khalifeh, assumed the office and served until a younger son, Borzu, proved to be more effective in interacting with outsiders, the Darrehshuri khans, state agents, and competitors for local resources. For some years, the two brothers shared responsibilities, and they continued to do so after the government recognized Borzu as the official headman in 1967. Borzu faced political challenges from his cousin Sohrab but always eventually persevered in any struggle. Sohrab never achieved a body of followers beyond some of his Imamverdili kinsmen, while Borzu created a wide network of supporters within his Aqa Mohammadli lineage, within the subtribe as a whole (comprised of five lineages and associated families), and beyond.

Borzu served as Qermezi's official headman until December 1979 when the Islamic regime announced a new kind of local leadership for nomads and villagers, the revolutionary Islamic council. His powerful personality, aggressive behavior, ability to solve problems, and extensive networks enabled him to persist as the subtribe's leader until his death in 1995. State agents continued to rely on his authority, mediation, and knowledge, despite the state's ending of the headman position. During the last few years of his life, ill health often prevented Borzu from pursuing the type of proactive, assertive leadership that he had mastered over the years, but he still remained influential and respected by the subtribe and by those with whom its members interacted. At his crowded memorial services, speakers declared that Borzu's name and the subtribe's were synonymous. People outside the subtribe knew one because of the other.

In some places, officials deemed Islamic and revolutionary credentials to be mandatory or at least recommended for any potential candidates for these new councils. Where no such individuals could be found, as often seemed to be the case in these usually small and relatively isolated communities, officials were forced to consider others. Agents of ONA and Construction Jihad knew individuals personally, could attest to their principled character, and rarely tested them about their knowledge of Islam. They found that "revolutionary" credentials were difficult to assess and often ignored them.

Some Qashqa'i communities held both nomads' and village councils. In Khunj, in southern Qashqa'i territory, the nomads' council in 1995 held five members, two of whom also served on the town council. People there noted that the three other members were ineligible for the town council because Construction Jihad considered them insufficiently knowledgeable about Islam.

For nomads and villagers, the council's mandate was to function in small communities that lacked other forms of state representation, such as revolutionary guards or committees. The council's main purpose was to carry into these communities the politico-religious ideologies embodied in the other revolutionary organizations of the new regime and to eradicate older institutions associated with the regime of the despised shah. For nomadic pastoralists, the council became the official body to represent the government as well as the group. A headman had served a subtribe of mobile, dispersed, and diverse people while the council represented a local territorial community rather than a specifically sociopolitical one. A headman had handled many internal and external matters while the council's scope and influence were more limited.

Initially the council's tasks were general. Other state agencies began or continued to take responsibility for the specific needs of nomads and villagers, such as pasture allocation, veterinary care, and education. In some local groups, the council's activities were initially few and then ceased. In others, the council continued to serve in a narrow capacity. Any given council reflected its members, particularly its head; some individuals were more responsive to the task and their group than others. Councils seemed to be only as influential as their dominant figures were, and councils rose and fell accordingly.

In 1980–81, one to two years after the revolution, five Qermezi communities formed Islamic councils: Aqa Mohammadli nomads at Dashtak and Hanalishah; Imamverdili and Qasemli nomads at Chah Shirin, Famur, and Bid-i Qatar; Qairkhbaili nomads at Dashtak and Kuh Pahn; Atakula villagers; and Nurabad villagers. Councils represented four of the five Qermezi lineages, whose members tended to co-reside in winter and summer pastures. Members of the fifth lineage, Kachili, were concentrated in Nurabad, Mehr-i Gerd, and

110 *The revolution and the Islamic Republic*

Narmeh villages, each of which formed its own council. The lineage itself lacked representation. Aqa Mohammadli's council served the few Kachili nomads at Dashtak during the autumn and winter. Atakula villagers came primarily from Aqa Mohammadli lineage but also from other Qermezi lineages and other subtribes, tribes, and groups. Atakula's council acted for the village and all its residents, not just those who were Aqa Mohammadli or Qermezi.

Directed by ONA (serving nomads) and Construction Jihad (serving villages), residents of the five Qermezi communities each selected three members (*uzv*) as stipulated by the government's instructions for communities this size. Larger communities elsewhere elected five or seven. The odd number would produce a majority vote on issues coming to the council's attention. State regulations stipulated that each member must possess basic literacy and reside in and stem from the local community.[130]

After the election, state agents gave each council a stamp or seal (*muhr*) to authenticate its documents. It included a phrase in Arabic from the Qur'an, translated as "together, we consult among us," and the name in Persian of the particular council.[131] At least two of the three members needed to assent to the seal's use. One member was not supposed to deploy the seal in case the other two disagreed or were uninformed about the matter under consideration. ONA and Construction Jihad initially provided printed forms for councils to use in their bureaucratic tasks but the supplies were exhausted by the early 1990s, and council members wrote on plain paper, including blank pages torn from their children's exercise books.

The government did not provide funds, weapons, or ammunition to the councils or their elected members. The nomads' volunteer militia gave the head of the council at Dashtak and Hanalishah a rifle and ammunition for the stated purpose of security, and not only because of his council role. Five other Qermezi men, three of whom served on this or other Qermezi councils, also received rifles and ammunition from the same agency, which seemed to recognize leadership in general and not council membership specifically.

A council's power and authority were limited, a situation depending on the prior political standing of its members, the regard with which the community held them, the quality of their ties to ONA and other state agencies, and their effectiveness and personality. Council members were part of the group they represented but the community also saw them as state agents and did not always appeal to the council, to avoid bringing the state into local affairs.

A council served a community in its relationship with some sectors of Iran's new government. Its major task was to issue documents. It certified a child's birth so the parents could obtain its identity card (*shinas namih*), a document mandatory for determining the person's age and birthplace, acquiring coupons for state-subsidized commodities, enrolling in school, voting, marrying, being conscripted, and dying.[132] A council testified to a draftee's inability to serve in the army because of his health, family, or economic circumstances.[133] During the war it assisted families who did not want their sons to be conscripted or sent to the front line. (Some councils held potentially incriminating lists of boys who did not serve in the war.) In disputes, especially with outside parties, a council verified the details and assertions. It certified people's identity as "nomads" so they could obtain the coupon books necessary for acquiring other state services. The Qermezi families who wanted to build houses in the government's new village at Mulleh Balut in 1999 needed to be officially classified as nomads for the privilege. To obtain this status they needed a coupon book.

Nomads at Dashtak and Hanalishah noted that they were usually able to settle their disputes without the council's intervention because kinship, marriage, and other long-term ties linked them. Qermezi villagers in Nurabad reported the same situation with regard to their council. By contrast, residents of the Qermezi village of Atakula stated that they often sought recourse through the council because of problems erupting within their diverse, expanding community. Hostilities among them deepening, they were forced to live together in the village at all times, while the nomads could more easily avoid contentious interactions by "voting with their feet" and relying on their dispersed, isolated camps to keep them separated. Some villagers complained that Atakula had been more harmonious before the revolution and the creation of the council. People now brought issues to the council (thus involving the whole village) when previously they had handled them more discreetly through the kinship ties of the immediate parties.

Councils sometimes coordinated the services of Construction Jihad, especially before ONA became active, such as by issuing rationed commodities, providing fodder, holding classes on natural-resource protection, planting bushes to prevent erosion, and helping to fund wells, pumps, and bathhouses. Later, ONA assumed these and other tasks and relied less on the councils' assistance. One task of a council was to notify Construction Jihad and ONA about its group's needs for roads, schools, water, and other state services.

A council assisted people who suffered losses and injuries during the war. It organized support for those who needed other kinds of aid, and it collected livestock and money for those in serious difficulty. A Darrehshuri man of another subtribe, threatened with imprisonment if he did not repay his debts to urban moneylenders, traveled through Hanalishah to solicit charitable donations. The nomads there suggested that he first visit their council head to see if he approved. Such a deflection of responsibility enabled the people this man had contacted to pay no more than the small sums they had already offered. The derelict man might not have wanted to advertise his problems to a local authority, and he never did consult the council head.

Some councils in Persian and Lur villages in the region in the 1980s handled matters that the regime connected with Islam, such as music, dancing at weddings, women's attire, and the smuggling and/or use of opium. None of the Qermezi councils had formally addressed these issues since their origin (and through 2013).

Of the five Qermezi councils, three served nomadic communities. The first of these was created in 1980 for the Aqa Mohammadli nomads at Dashtak and Hanalishah.

112 *The revolution and the Islamic Republic*

One winter day all the men at Dashtak gathered in Bahram's tent to hear two ONA agents address them. After answering questions about the proposed council, the two asked, "Who is ready to serve?" Several attendees offered nominations. The agents said they needed additional names, and those present suggested several more, for a total of six men. Some days later the two agents returned to Bahram's tent to conduct the election, and 45 or 50 men and women assembled.[134] Each of them voted on a paper ballot for as many as five individuals. Five of the six were elected, Bahram receiving the most votes and becoming the council head. ONA did not test the six candidates or the five winners about their literacy, knowledge of Islam, or revolutionary fervor. Its agents were already acquainted with the men.

Borzu Qermezi, former official group headman and still the de facto leader, boycotted the event. Released from prison only several months earlier, he assumed that he was ineligible to run for the council. More pertinently, he disapproved of such a so-called Islamic institution and was not inclined to support the regime in this way.

Several weeks later the two ONA agents returned to Dashtak to report that their headquarters in Shiraz had notified them that a community this size, under a hundred adults, could have only three council members. One of the five men elected, a teacher posted in a nearby but non-Qermezi nomadic community, withdrew from the council. Another one, perhaps understanding that he would receive fewer votes than the other three in a new election, said he was no longer interested in serving, which left the council with the requisite number. Bahram remained the head, and Jehangir and Mohammad Quli continued as members. The first two were nomadic pastoralists, and the third was a young unmarried schoolteacher whose father Murad, with whom he still lived, was also a nomadic pastoralist. The electees named their council the "Islamic Council of Aqa Mohammadli Lineage" (shura-yi islami bunku-yi Aqa Mohammadli). ONA agents later placed the council's seal in Bahram's care. They stated that new elections would occur every five years, but no further ones took place in this group during the next 24 years, and the council still functioned in 2004 in the ways described earlier.

Bahram is the eldest son of Khalifeh, Qermezi's headman before Borzu. He was the only man at Dashtak and Hanalishah who was a hezbollahi and an ardent advocate of the Islamic Republic, both qualifications aiding him in his interactions as the council head with state authorities, especially revolutionary zealots. People who voted for Bahram said they despised all hezbollahis and regime supporters but thought that these connections might help him to represent their community effectively. After Bahram's eldest son Farhad was killed in the Iraq–Iran war in 1988, Bahram grew devoutly religious (at least outwardly) and harsher in his opinions about the community's behavior. When almost all other Qermezi pushed to resume their customary celebrations (featuring music, dance, sport, and women's traditional dress) at weddings in 1991 and thereafter, Bahram was often the only person present who disapproved. He did not explicitly invoke his role as the council head, but no one

The revolution and the Islamic Republic 113

forgot that he was also a state representative. Sometimes he allied with the few other Qermezi hezbollahis who resided in villages and towns, some of them appearing at weddings to support his cause when otherwise they would not have bothered to attend. Many Qermezi conducted their weddings as they chose after 1992, with a full expression of festivities, and disregarded Bahram's continuing opposition. The council's specific tasks did not diminish because of Bahram's weakening power in these other political and cultural matters. After all, he was also a close kinsman of all community members, who showed him courtesy because of the common bonds. He was linked by marriage with many of them. As a martyr's father, he deserved their commiseration.

The council's second member was Jehangir, a brother of Khalifeh and one of the eldest men at Dashtak and Hanalishah. He was the first Qermezi to receive training as a teacher (but he did not assume a teaching post). He had never played an overt political role in the subtribe, in part because his brothers, Khalifeh and Borzu, dominated and wielded power and authority, but everyone respected his opinions. Unlike all other Qermezi men in 1970–71, Jehangir kept informed about national and international events (via a small transistor radio). Khalifeh and Jehangir were the only Qermezi men I had ever seen praying in those years. They prayed irregularly, not daily, and rarely engaged in other Islamic rituals.

The third member was Mohammad Quli, a young unmarried man newly assigned as the nomads' schoolteacher at Dashtak and Hanalishah. Just after the revolution he had interacted with schoolteachers and secondary-school students who were said to be pro-Khomeini and anti-khan, and later a few Qermezi noted that he had been a moderate hezbollahi at the time. Some young Qashqa'i teachers as well as some high-school and university students had opposed the khans' leadership in 1979–80. Mohammad Quli, if he had fallen into this category then, was only one of many. I did not see Mohammad Quli pray or engage in other Islamic rituals in the 1990s. He was a child when I knew him in 1970–71.

Mohammad Quli's father, Murad, was influential at Dashtak and Hanalishah. His contacts with the tribal khans had resulted in his arrest and captivity in 1980, and ONA agents apparently deemed him unqualified for council candidacy, especially so soon after his release. When I asked Murad why he did not serve on the council, he quipped that he was a *taghuti* (a corrupt, West-oriented secularist) who represented the old era.[135] Then, more seriously, he noted that the regime wanted younger people to serve at the local level, a policy throughout Iran to inspire the ideologically committed and bring them into politics. People viewed Mohammad Quli's election as a demonstration of support for Murad, who was expected to influence his son's decisions as a council member. The two men lived in the same tent at the time, and Murad was always aware of the issues reaching the council's attention. Mohammad Quli moved to the town of Borujen in 1986, where he assumed a new teaching post and resided most of the year. He spent the summers at Hanalishah. He did not play an active role as a council member in the 1990s. No one in

114 *The revolution and the Islamic Republic*

ONA or the community replaced him, and the council consisted of only two functioning members through 2004.

Imamverdili and Qasemli nomads at Chah Shirin, Famur, and Bid-i Qatar elected their council in 1981. Its head was Bahmanyar, the son of the most prominent Qasemli man. ONA agents did test his knowledge of Islam and found him lacking but did not eliminate him as a candidate or a winner. The two other members came from Aqa Mohammadli lineage. "Couldn't the men of Imamverdili find at least one suitable candidate among them?" people joked. "They searched and searched but the only men who were qualified were members of another lineage." Qahraman and his brother Safdar lived at Dashtak with other Aqa Mohammadli kinsmen during the autumn and winter, but during the summer they resided at Bid-i Qatar with the Imamverdili. Based on this co-residence, people viewed them as representatives of Imamverdili lineage. These three council members lacked any special connections to Islam, including rituals. They did not pray or fast before the revolution and did not begin afterward. After Qahraman died in 1996, no one was elected or chosen to replace him on the council, which continued to function through 2004.

Qairkhbaili nomads at Dashtak and Kuh Pahn also elected their council in 1981, which ONA agents named after the missing twelfth Shi'i imam (shura-yi islami *sahib-i zaman*). (Shi'i Muslims say that the Imam of the Age is in a state of occultation until he returns to restore justice to the world.) The agents took the name from a regime-approved list.[136] They argued that the Qairkhbaili lineage name (which they said meant "40 leaders") was politically inappropriate and represented a bygone era. *Qairkh* means 40, and *bai* is short for *baig*, a title in tribal leadership.[137] The nomads responded that the application of a religious title, especially this one, to their representative body was absurd and lacked any meaning for them.

The council's three electees were the young adult sons of prominent Qairkhbaili men and included Sarhang and Ali Reza. The council's head was Zafar, whom other Qermezi jokingly called Mulla Zafar in the 1990s for his specialty in prayer writing. (Formally educated clergymen condemned this amateur activity, used for foretelling the future and curing.) Zafar lacked any expertise in other aspects of Islam and did not pray or fast. He was the subtribe's only prayer writer. The Qairkhbaili council survived for only five years. ONA agents saw that the lineage's men constantly disputed among themselves about the council's activities and members, and they withdrew their support and disbanded the entity. The agency had never issued a seal, or had quickly reclaimed it, because of its concern about the ways the council might use it.[138]

Supervised by Construction Jihad (and not ONA), the Kachili residents of Nurabad village elected three kinsmen as their council members in 1981, all sons of prominent Kachili men, Husain as the head and Darab Ali and Murad as the other members. Nurabad's council (named shura-yi islami rusta-yi Nurabad—rusta meaning village) still functioned in 1999. Their settlements

The revolution and the Islamic Republic   115

officially classified as villages, the residents of Nurabad and Atakula could vote for new councils that year in nationwide municipal elections.

Also under Construction Jihad's guidance, residents of Atakula village—officially renamed Islamabad by the government after the revolution—elected Khan Ahmad as the council head in 1980. He is Aqa Mohammadli and the son of a village founder. The second member was Sultan Ali, an early settler and one of three Kachili men living in the village. The third electee was Fereydun Sadiq, the son of a Persian man who controlled the land where the village was built. Sadiq's extended family resided in the village, which became predominantly Qermezi by the late 1960s. During the first few years of the council (named shura-yi islami rusta-yi Islamabad), Sultan Ali disagreed with the other electees and abandoned the post. Villagers chose another early settler, Khanbua of Aqa Mohammadli lineage, to take his place, and soon he too conflicted with the other council members and withdrew. For years, only the two remaining members served on the council, which still functioned in 1999 when Iran held new elections.

Most elected members of these five Qermezi councils were young, a trend found throughout Iran in both re-staffed and newly established state and parastatal institutions. (All existing institutions underwent purges and dismissals after the revolution.) Supervising eligibility for candidacy and overseeing elections or selections, agents of ONA and Construction Jihad favored younger men over older ones. They said that young men were more apt to support the Islamic Republic than their elders and would be more amenable to implementing state policy as it related to Islamic politics and ideology. (These expectations were not fulfilled for the Qermezi councils, except in Bahram's case. As elsewhere in Iran, especially in cities and towns, the youth had proved to be more actively resistant to the Islamic regime than their elders.) Other than the Persian landowner in Atakula, the men elected to the Qermezi councils were the sons of the most prominent men of their lineages. When I asked a senior Qermezi man about the five councils, he ridiculed them while motioning repeatedly with his hands, one hand over the other and then the reverse. "Such is the way of politics in Iran. First one [man] is on top and then another is, and then the one on the bottom is unaccountably on top again."[139]

The Qermezi councils lacked hezbollahis as members. Of the 16 men elected, people considered only one of them (Bahram) a hezbollahi. The councils representing the communities where the few other Qermezi hezbollahis resided did not include any as members. None of the 16 had participated in revolutionary activities in 1978–79, only several years before.

The councils' stability was a further characteristic. When they began the program, agents of ONA and Construction Jihad said they would conduct new elections every five years. Yet in no case did this process occur. The agencies lacked initiative, and the local communities did not request new elections. Qairkhbaili's council ceased to function after five years, but the four other councils continued to operate, and the same men remained in office

116   *The revolution and the Islamic Republic*

from 1980–81 until 1999 or later, except for the two resignations in Atakula. People in these communities, except for Atakula, did not attempt to expel any council members. Residents of the two villages voted again in 1999, as part of new, nationwide municipal elections. Not all members of their councils chose to run, and, of those who did, not all were reelected.

The power and influence of the councils among the Qermezi and elsewhere in the region were diminished by the early 1990s, a trend matching the decreasing significance of other state-related, "revolutionary," "Islamic," and potentially coercive forces such as committees, guards, basijis, and hezbollahis. (As many Qermezi were now noting, "revolutionary" and "Islamic" were terms for the regime's seizure of power and exertion of force over citizens and lacked the meanings they might once have had.) Elections in 1997 and 2001 of the moderate reformist candidate, Mohammad Khatami, as president of Iran furthered these trends, but the presidency of the neoconservative Mahmud Ahmadinejad (2005–13) once again reinforced these multiple intimidating and potentially violent bodies.

Inhabitants of villages, towns, and cities throughout Iran elected revolutionary Islamic councils in 1999 (see Chapter 9). These new municipal institutions (*shuraha-yi islami-yi shahr*) were sometimes distinguished from the earlier local councils in villages and nomadic communities (*shuraha-yi islami-yi mahalli*). Their significance meant that the longstanding councils of nomads also gained attention but the government did not permit nomads to hold new council elections in 1999. A Qermezi man noted that their existing councils still functioned adequately, and new elections were unnecessary. Another man reported that an official had proclaimed, incorrectly, that nomads did not need their own councils anymore because they were settling. Still another man stated, more correctly, that the authorities had not yet decided how to proceed with the nomads' councils.

New faces in the tribe

The Qermezi had expanded and diversified their activities considerably by the 1990s and had moved even further along these lines by 2013. While most members of the subtribe continued along the paths they had selected by the early 1970s, a significant number chose directions that no one in the group had ever attempted before or could have even imagined. In this section, I discuss hezbollahis, revolutionary guards, theological students, schoolteachers, university graduates, women employed outside the home, a national war hero, a parliamentary deputy, and pilgrims to Mecca and Damascus. None of these roles and activities had existed among the Qermezi in 1971, and only one of them (schoolteachers) had emerged between 1972 and the revolution in 1978–79. Changes in the wider state and society had created the possibility of these roles and activities but local circumstances and individual abilities and personalities explain their selection by certain people. Some Qermezi were more likely than others to respond to the new opportunities.

Hezbollahis (partisans of the party of God)

Hezbollahis, "partisans of the party of God," were the most striking of these new directions, especially considering the extent to which their attitudes and behaviors contrasted with those of other people in the subtribe. The Qermezi accepted or approved of the individuals who adopted the roles and activities discussed in this section, except for the hezbollahis, whom they distrusted and disliked. According to the Qermezi, hezbollahis who became revolutionary guards and basij militiamen tainted these institutions with their politico-ideological stances. Qermezi guards and basijis who were not hezbollahis strove to distance and differentiate themselves.

Throughout Iran, the label "hezbollahi" referred to recognized hard-line members of the formal state apparatus, the regime's unofficial hard-line supporters, and pressure groups of different kinds.[140] In common Iranian parlance, the term could mean any hard-liner. Men's identities as hezbollahis, as the "truly revolutionary," stemmed from multiple traits: fervent support of and loyalty to Khomeini, the revolution, and the Islamic Republic; xenophobic nationalism; opposition to the United States and other imperialist powers; conservative politico-religious ideologies and behaviors that they attempted to force on others; strict religious observances; and austerity. Iranians considered hezbollahis as "permanent revolutionaries" even decades after the revolution. In some parts of Iran, especially urban areas, hezbollahis engaged in violence in support of the hard-line clergy and were derided as "club wielders" (*chumaqdar*), "knife brandishers" (*chaqukish*), carriers of heavy chains, and thugs and ruffians in the service of the hard-line politicians. "The hezbollahi have been viewed by many as enforcers of the regime's writ and considered not revolutionary but, in fact, street gangs intimidating those holding views considered 'heterodox'."[141] Hezbollahis, a "shapeless crowd run by behind-the-scenes hardliners," joined others' demonstrations, shouted slogans, and attacked and broke up the meetings of liberals and reformers.[142]

The Qermezi hezbollahis were not (ordinarily) violent, especially within Qermezi society. They totaled 15 young men at the peak of people's interest. These men did not use the label "hezbollahi" for themselves or others. (Several lapsed hezbollahis did occasionally refer with derision to their former stance.) Rather, "hezbollahi" was a term that others applied to them, usually negatively.

Hezbollahis in Qermezi and the wider Qashqa'i society were not part of Ansar-i Hezbollah (defenders of the party of God), a Tehran-centered, hard-line, semiclandestine, vigilante group having leaders, some form of organization, and direct and indirect ties to hard-line conservative clergymen.[143] Yet some Qermezi did worry about the ruthlessness of this wider, more organized and structured group and its affect on the local hezbollahis. In "spontaneous" demonstrations supporting the regime, Ansar members often wore battle fatigues and draped Palestinian checkered kafiyas around their necks. Often also basij militiamen and veterans of the war, they demonstrated the formal and informal networks among the regime's most coercive forces.

118 *The revolution and the Islamic Republic*

Hezbollahis among the Qermezi influenced the subtribe as a whole, sometimes only by the mere fact of their often distant existence. Their numbers within the group were small and their distribution among the many localized Qermezi communities uneven. They were not formally organized as hezbollahis, among themselves or in the wider Iranian society, but they did express a common identity through their attire, appearance, and behavior. Within their families, kinship groups, and local communities and sometimes within the larger Qermezi and even Qashqa'i society as well, hezbollahis tried to impose their ideas about proper belief and behavior. When others reminded them that God forbids "compulsion" in Islam (that is, no one should *force* Muslims to believe or practice in certain ways), they responded that "Islam" required them to fight for the survival of their threatened religion by using any means.

Many hezbollahis among the Qermezi joined the revolutionary-guard corps, a state-authorized institution providing them with a distinctive uniform and some leadership, organization, and focus. As revolutionary guards, they could impose their will on others; simply as hezbollahis, they lacked any immediate supporting institution for intimidation and coercion.

The 15 Qermezi hezbollahis dressed in the attire seen also among hezbollahis and revolutionary guards in the wider Iranian society since 1979. They wore military-style clothing in khaki, military-green, and camouflage colors with multiple outside pockets on their pants, shirts, and jackets. They buttoned their shirts to the neck and did not tuck the tails into their trousers, and their shoes and boots were dark leather, not the multicolored sports shoes that other males their age preferred.[144] Hezbollahis grew facial hair (but not beards), which they kept trimmed to a specific length, just as they did for the hair on their head. They did not sport the prominent mustaches that some Qashqa'i men their age and older preferred.[145] They conveyed a stern manner and did not openly jest or laugh, at least while interacting with those who were not hezbollahis. Faced with this demeanor, other people said they felt uncomfortably constrained in their own behavior, despite their inclinations. Sometimes—inexplicably, reacting to the tense atmosphere, or intentionally— they would erupt in sudden, inappropriate, loud laughter. Hezbollahis often performed their daily prayers publicly and ostentatiously, instead of quietly slipping away to a secluded spot like the few others who prayed. Before and after these prayers, they would accusingly ask those nearby if they were not also going to pray. Most Qermezi hezbollahis modified their dress and behavior in the middle and late 1990s, some to the point that they were no longer immediately recognizable as hezbollahis.

Many Qermezi boys and young men preferred the same types and colors of clothing that hezbollahis (and revolutionary guards) wore, and they were irritated when others misidentified them. Thus they often signified their anti- or non-hezbollahi identity (and their defiance against the Islamic regime) by wearing chic Western clothes labeled with foreign brands and English slogans, fashionable sunglasses, caps with visors, sports shoes, and tightly fitted trousers. They left their top shirt buttons open and tucked in the tails.

The revolution and the Islamic Republic 119

They were clean shaven and attentively styled their long hair. They behaved exuberantly and irreverently in public. Similarly, older Qashqa'i men demonstrated their opposition to the regime (and to the hezbollahis who supported it) by wearing Qashqa'i hats and being clean shaven except for their exaggerated mustaches.[146]

Hezbollahis among the Qermezi emerged after Khomeini's arrival in February 1979. Many joined the revolutionary-guard corps or volunteered for the basij militia during the Iraq–Iran war and tried to exert power and authority in their local communities on their return. Their influence at home was waning by 1991, and by the mid-1990s they exerted a minimal impact on community affairs. After Khatami's election as president in 1997, hezbollahis further lessened their intensity. The government now held two legitimized factions (conservative hard-liners and reformists) instead of just one, and hezbollahis lost the commanding presence they had earlier enjoyed. Few Qermezi talked about the hezbollahis by 1999, and only several of the original ones continued to proclaim the superiority of their politico-religious ideologies. Some hezbollahis had seen that such a political stance did not profit them economically or was no longer doing so. "No money, no house" was one man's short explanation for his withdrawal from the movement. Hezbollahis might have benefited in the 1980s but not in the 1990s, and economic and social conditions in Iran had not improved but only worsened, at least for the middle and lower classes. A former hezbollahi noted that the clergy had lied to them about creating a new egalitarian Islamic society. A few of his former comrades were still reluctant to admit it, he said.

Along with revolutionary guards and basij militiamen, hezbollahis reasserted their power and authority during Ahmadinejad's presidency beginning in 2005. The three forces suppressed popular protests after the president's fraudulent reelection in 2009, and they all experienced a resurgence of power in Iranian society thereafter. Citizens now included the "plainclothes" paramilitary (*libas shakhsiha,* "civilian clothed") in these coercive forces, although these men usually originated from the three other units.[147] Pressure groups (*guruhha-yi fishar*) of different sorts also acted as street gangs in the service of the fundamentalists. These five forces, three of them loosely organized, quashed demonstrations in 2011, in which Iranians who opposed the Islamic regime were galvanized by the then-occurring successful popular revolts in Tunisia and Egypt (the beginning of the Arab Spring). These wider circumstances seemed not to influence the few remaining hezbollahis in the Qermezi group, and the national movement continued to lack much resonance at the local level.

Since 1979 the vast majority of Qermezi wanted nothing to do with hezbollahis and at times barely tolerated their intrusive presence. Often the two parties sat silently in one another's company during obligatory social events. Ties of kinship, marriage, co-residence, and economic cooperation—combined with the shared subtribal affiliation as Qermezi—still connected them, the bases of which had formed long before the revolution. Still, the one party's newly extreme views and practices complicated its interactions with the other.

120   *The revolution and the Islamic Republic*

Twelve of the 15 hezbollahis resided in Atakula village or Borujen town in the early 1980s, and political events and attitudes in the town and the region had influenced them. They held urban-connected jobs in the wider Iranian society or were students who pursued such livelihoods. Two of the three who did not reside in the Borujen area were serious students who also planned future urban employment. The one man out of 15 who did not match these patterns was Bahram, the only nomadic pastoralist among these hezbollahis, and he practiced the livelihood and lifestyle in the customary fashion. A husband and a father of many children, he was also older than the others. The rest were unmarried young men in 1979. The 15 hezbollahis represent two of the five Qermezi lineages and one of the subtribe's affiliated families. Their residential location and not their lineage membership help to explain their ensuing identity as hezbollahis.

These boys and young men had not demonstrated any interest in Islamic ritual or ideology before Khomeini's arrival in 1979. They did not perform daily prayers, observe the Ramadan fast, commemorate the martyrdom of the third Shi'i imam during the month of Muharram, or express interest in pilgrimage to Mashhad or Mecca. All of them were similar in belief and practice to other Qermezi boys and men. Their closest female relatives wore the same customary clothes of other Qashqa'i females. They minimally covered their head and hair with a thin diaphanous scarf and did not don the enveloping black veil-wrap (chadur) that many Iranian women wore at the time.

Only one of the 15 men, Bahram, had experienced any exposure to Islam that was unusual in the subtribe. Somewhat paradoxically, he was also the only nomadic pastoralist in the group. In general, the nomadic pastoralists were less interested in Islamic beliefs and practices than some of the subtribe's other members who had adopted livelihoods based in villages and towns.

Bahram's father Khalifeh had obtained a minimal religious education at home, under the tutelage of several mullas his father hired, and had expressed some practical interest in religious matters, unlike others in his local community. The only Qermezi man of his generation to possess much literacy, Khalifeh wrote marriage contracts, kept the group's financial records, and offered advice on personal matters. He was the Qermezi headman's son and became the headman himself after his father's violent death, and his initial and abiding interest in literacy and basic Islamic tenets related to these political functions. He did not try to force his beliefs on others, and the only proactive stance he took was to hire mullas to teach basic literacy to boys in his group. At that time, the nomads lacked any access to formal education other than hiring mullas.

Khalifeh's eldest son Bahram became literate and also engaged in local politics. Until he began to demonstrate hezbollahi traits after the Islamic Republic was declared, he had not expressed any special interest in Islamic ritual or ideology. After his eldest son was killed in the Iraq–Iran war, he became more extremist (*tundru*) in his hezbollahi stance and less tolerant of the lax behavior of others. He was moderating his severe views in the mid-1990s, although they reemerged when he planned his youngest son's wedding in 1999.

The four Qermezi who entered theological seminaries in the 1980s and early 1990s did not consider themselves hezbollahis, and neither did others. Except for Bahram, the same is true for the 11 Qermezi men who later conducted pilgrimages to Mecca and for others who viewed themselves as devout Muslims.

Some Qermezi by 2000 explicitly (and approvingly) contrasted devout, pious (*mumin*) Muslims to the highly politicized hezbollahis. Most Qermezi had scorned manifestations of overtly religious, Islam-related behavior in 1970, but after having experienced two decades of politicized and repressive Islam, many of them no longer rejected what they now regarded as genuine and authentic religious sentiment.

No Qermezi women were hezbollahis, including one girl who attended a theological seminary. None exhibited the conservative politico-religious values seen among some women in other segments of Iranian society. Qermezi's 15 hezbollahis controlled the behavior of any females residing with them, especially their mothers, sisters, wives, daughters, and daughters-in-law. These women now prayed and fasted according to the patterns and schedules these men established, and they dressed in the same fashion as did "religious" women in the town of Borujen. Depending on their age, they wore layers of dark clothing topped off by black cloaks and hoods and/or black veil-wraps held tightly around their faces and bodies when they left home, even within the small, kin-based village of Atakula. These women were more restricted in their movements and activities than other Qermezi women were, and they were more subdued in their verbal and nonverbal expressions. People in the subtribe, including these women themselves, complained that kinsmen had forced these behaviors on them and that they would not have made these changes on their own. The political reasons explaining why men had adopted Islamic ideologies and behaviors played no part in their own lives, women said. Most of these women were ignoring the severest of restrictions governing their behavior and attire by 2000. Some even began to dance at the weddings of close relatives, as long as no adult male outsiders were present.

Revolutionary guards

Four young Qermezi men joined the revolutionary-guard corps (sipah-i pasdaran-i inqilab-i islami) soon after the Islamic regime took power. Nine more young men joined in the 1980s, and all 13 stayed in the corps through the 1990s. (Guards throughout Iran generally served in the corps for four years and then found other occupations.) The 13 resided in Atakula village, Borujen town, and nearby villages. They represent four of the five Qermezi lineages and include two men of the affiliated families. They had not participated in any revolutionary activities before Khomeini arrived. None of them had completed high school when they joined the corps, and the association provided them with benefits they would have otherwise lacked. They received what proved to be legitimate

122 *The revolution and the Islamic Republic*

and steady jobs, adequate salaries, and financial and other advantages, including the right to exert power and authority in their jobs, the local community, and Iranian society in general. The corps required its recruits after the mid-1980s to be high-school graduates, and many continuing corpsmen attended night schools and studied for examinations in order to receive their diplomas. After Iraq invaded Iran (1980), all of these guards fought in the war or joined the effort in other capacities.

The corps was not recruiting nationally in the early 1990s in the ways it had done in the 1980s. The war was over, other security forces were reorganized and gaining in legitimacy and strength, and the Islamic regime was exerting power and maintaining or inciting support through other means. With Ahmadinejad as president (2005–13) (and as a former revolutionary guard), the corps reestablished its position as the coercive force behind the hard-line conservatives.

By the late 1980s no other Qermezi boys or men joined the corps except as part of their mandatory two-year military service or as part of a profession. Conscripts could choose to be army soldiers or revolutionary guards, and the corps enjoyed the privilege of choosing the best among them. Those joining the military as guards lacked the dedication that some long-term Qermezi guards demonstrated. They performed their required stint of service and then resumed the lives they had left when the military conscripted them. Three Qermezi men found professional or other jobs in the corps (as a health worker, a petrochemical engineer, and a low-status office worker). They too lacked the fervor of the original group of Qermezi guards, and people considered it unfortunate that the wider society often mistook them for zealots. Two guards held positions in Islamic committees in towns while most others served in the corps offices in towns and cities. When President Rafsanjani merged some of Iran's armed forces in a new unit (niruha-yi intizami) in 1990–91, several Qermezi men transferred from the corps to the reorganized force and were no longer guards.

The Qermezi and the surrounding society considered some of the 13 revolutionary guards as hezbollahis, particularly the four who had joined first. The hezbollahi guards viewed their duty as honoring Khomeini, serving the revolution, defending Islam, and protecting the Islamic Republic from internal and external threats. People did not regard the others as hezbollahis, at least by 1991, and these guards remained in their positions primarily for the salary and benefits. Their jobs were well paying and secure during a time of high national unemployment and inflation. The guards who were not hezbollahis seemed to hold the same opinions about the revolution, the Islamic regime, and the war that many other Qermezi men expressed.

A revolutionary guard enjoyed appealing privileges but the vast majority of Qermezi men shunned the opportunity because of the heavy politico-ideological associations. Most men, preferring what they considered as their "freedom" and unwilling to compromise their beliefs, labored at other, often risky, sometimes unprofitable, economic ventures.

The revolution and the Islamic Republic   123

Theological students

Four young Qermezi studied in theological seminaries (*huzih-yi ilmiyih*) in the 1980s and 1990s. Initially considered as theological students (*talib*), three of them attained other labels (such as *ruhani*) after some years of study. One of these seemed destined to become higher ranked as he pursued the paths taken by those who eventually became *mujtahid*s, *hujjat ul-islam*s, and ayatollahs. The three males created careers from this venture while the fourth, a female, studied for only several years. Similar to the subtribe's hezbollahis and revolutionary guards, these four individuals originated in Atakula and two nearby villages. They represent three of the five Qermezi lineages. Their communities of origin and proximity to Borujen rather than their lineage membership figured in their choice to study theology.

Ibrahim is the son of Alinaz of Aqa Mohammadli lineage, an early settler in Atakula, the first Qermezi village. Alinaz had decided in 1969 that agriculture offered greater potential for a reliable livelihood than pastoralism alone. His son Ibrahim attended the village's primary school for five years and a middle school in nearby Borujen for three years. After the revolution he expressed interest in religious education, which he sought first in Borujen's seminary. No ayatollahs or prominent religious figures taught there, and after three years of study he traveled to Qom (Iran's theological center) to continue his pursuit for the next 12 years. Religious foundations (vaqf) associated with the seminaries financially supported him.

During Ibrahim's trip home after donning clerical garb for the first time, his turban came unrolled, and he was unable to rewrap it properly. Amused by his efforts, his fellow villagers watched him reluctantly return to school in borrowed civilian clothes. Elsewhere in rural Iran (so I am informed), people told stories about new theological students coming home and then being unable to rewind their turbans there.

Early in his religious education, Ibrahim contributed his knowledge and skills during his village's weddings, funerals, and memorials. Such services (if any villagers had wanted them) had previously been procured from non-Qashqa'i outsiders and were somewhat tainted by their association with men who lacked any formal training in Islam. The villagers had often mocked these individuals. Yet when Ibrahim began his studies, he seemed to influence religious beliefs and practices in the settlement and to soften some people's harsh attitudes. He helped his kin to cope with their grief when he spoke eloquently and emotionally at Borzu Qermezi's memorial services.

At small all-Qermezi weddings, Ibrahim wore civilian clothes for dancing and competing in the choreographed, music-accompanied sport of stick fighting. He said he worried that his flamboyant behavior during these festivities would shock his fellow seminarians, their teachers, and the religious sector of urban society if they learned about it. Such performances, however, expressed his deep sentiments about Qashqa'i culture. Some Qermezi commented that Ibrahim had effectively blended his Qashqa'i cultural background with the

124   *The revolution and the Islamic Republic*

role and persona of a decent, ethical Muslim clergyman (as compared, they said, with the corrupt, venal clerics at the helm of Iran's government). Dressed in his cloak and turban, he could mediate for them when problems arose with staunchly religious state authorities. The Qermezi were reassured when he and the three other theological students did not assume a hezbollahi stance or associate with hezbollahis. People noted that, quite the contrary, Ibrahim understated any judgments he might have held.

Ibrahim completed 15 years of formal study in the middle 1990s and took a government job as a religious advisor in several urban prisons. By this time he often wore civilian clothes at home in his village. When I asked several people if Ibrahim had recited from the Qur'an at a relative's funeral, they seemed surprised and then remarked that his status (and that of the two other male seminarians) was higher than that of the less-trained Qur'an readers who came from the wider society and whom the villagers still employed for the purpose. (Ibrahim had not recited from the Qur'an at the funeral and would not participate this way in the future.) Most recently, Ibrahim secured a post with the Ministry of Construction Jihad, a bureaucratic job that did not relate directly to religion or politics.

Two other theological students in the subtribe were still engaged in study in 1999 and did not hold paying jobs. They received stipends from religious foundations.

Tahmasib is the son of Khanbua, also of Aqa Mohammadli lineage and another early settler in Atakula village. Similar to Ibrahim, Tahmasib completed primary school in Atakula and middle school in Borujen. Then he traveled first to Shahreza and then to Qom to pursue religious studies through 1999. He took a job in 2000 as a religious advisor and leader of prayers at the headquarters of the government's security forces near Borujen. He no longer wore clerical clothes at home in Atakula or when attending Qermezi events elsewhere.

Tahmuras is the son of Surkhab of Qasemli lineage. After he completed his primary education in the nomads' school of his migratory group, the competitive tribal secondary school in Shiraz accepted him for study, where he remained for three years. At the time, he was only the fourth Qermezi student selected for this prestigious program. Rather than finishing the three additional years there and earning a high-school diploma, he began study at one of Isfahan's theological schools (huzih-yi Zulfaqar), where he remained in 2001. He entered the course of study (*dars-i kharij*, which entailed research) pursued by advanced theological students and continued on the path toward higher ranking clergy status (unlike the two other Qermezi men).[148] He had changed his name in the 1980s to Muslim-i Qermezi-yi Nizhad (Muslim of the Original Qermezi). (The Qermezi subtribe originated in the Qasemli lineage, according to oral history.) He wore clerical attire at all times, apparently.

The fourth theological student in the subtribe, Zahra, is the daughter of Qalandar of Imamverdili lineage and a resident of Naqneh village near Borujen. She attended primary school in Naqneh and secondary school in nearby

Dehaqan. After studying for several years under female teachers at the theological seminary in Dehaqan for girls and women, she married and discontinued the pursuit. Resuming her secular education, she received her high-school diploma in 1997, one of 17 Qermezi females to do so by 1999.

Three of the four seminarians began study in the 1980s while the fourth started and then stopped in the early 1990s. No other Qermezi demonstrated any interest in pursuing theology as a course of study or a profession, although young men admired the income and benefits that religious students received. (After ceasing his formal studies and obtaining a state job, Ibrahim purchased a new-model vehicle, a possession that no other Qermezi man could afford.) As Iran's government grew more democratic and secular in orientation in the mid-1990s, especially after Khatami's election as president, Qermezi men noted that theological school was likely a dead end. The influence of clerics had steadily decreased in Iranian society (but not in all aspects of government) since the early 1990s, and people anticipated further trends in that direction.[149] Qermezi men also expected violence against clergymen when the tide of national politics turned against them and when citizens rose up to eliminate them. They equated the fate (execution or exile) of the shah's secret police (SAVAK) with the one looming for the Islamic regime's akhunds. Many Iranians had grown to despise the clergy, especially the high-ranking ones who had created and sustained the regime under which many citizens had suffered restrictions, privations, and personal losses. No one among the Qermezi (except for Tahmuras) admired or wanted to join the clerical profession.

A high-ranking cleric noted in 1998 that he could no longer wear his cloak and turban if he wanted to walk along some Tehran streets, because ordinary passersby cursed at and spit on him. When asked if these streets were in northern Tehran (where most secular upper-middle and upper classes lived), he responded that people there did not assail him. Rather, he said he suffered abuse in the lower-middle-class and especially lower-class neighborhoods of central and southern Tehran (where many people had experienced economic losses since 1979). He attended Tehran's annual international book fair wearing jeans, a tee shirt, and a baseball cap in order to blend in with the crowd and avoid harassment. If he dressed as a cleric, he said he would have intimidated some attendees in this rare public space that allowed citizens certain freedoms they lacked elsewhere. Also, if attired as a cleric, he would have been uncomfortable examining some of the books on display.[150]

Schoolteachers

Qermezi subtribe had produced 32 trained schoolteachers by 1991, and that number had risen to 62 by 2002. Many Qermezi boys and some girls had aspired to become teachers in the 1970s and early 1980s, but fewer sought that profession in the 1990s and early 2000s. The types of people who had chosen to be teachers in the 1970s and 1980s were instead pursuing university educations in the 1990s and thereafter so they could enter other kinds of

126 *The revolution and the Islamic Republic*

careers. Many existing teachers also went after further education. Those who had not completed high school or even middle school before becoming teachers wanted to pass examinations for the diploma, and some holding diplomas attended university hoping to obtain higher-level jobs or at least to raise their teaching salaries (see Chapter 7).

University graduates

Only six Qermezi boys (and no girls) had studied beyond elementary school (grades one through six) in 1971, and most of them were enrolled in the first years of secondary school then. No one in the subtribe had yet attended high school or university.

Only one Qermezi had graduated from university by 1991. Ibrahim is the son of Himmat of Kachili lineage, who at the time was one of a few Kachili men still practicing full-time nomadic pastoralism. Most other Kachili men lived seasonally or permanently in villages and towns by 1991. Ibrahim completed university in Shiraz with a degree in chemical engineering. He took a job as a petrochemical engineer with the revolutionary-guard corps in Shiraz and was still employed there in 2002 when he died in a petrochemical fire. Eight other Qermezi men were university students in 1991, and all of them completed degrees in the years to come. Only one Qermezi girl had earned a high-school diploma by 1991.

Thirty-nine Qermezi (including three women) had earned four-year university degrees by 2001, and 42 others had been or still were university students without having yet obtained four-year degrees. Their numbers had risen rapidly in the 1990s, unlike those of teachers. All university students understood that they would face problems in obtaining jobs matching their degrees and specialized fields but they did not hesitate to continue. For them, university education was the pursuit, above all others, that promised upward social and economic mobility and offered the possibility of respected, reliable, remunerative livelihoods.

The most highly educated Qermezi (through 2013) was Masud, the son of Asadullah of Aqa Mohammadli lineage. Masud was born and raised as a nomadic pastoralist. Along with children his age, he attended the nomads' elementary school in winter and summer pastures and then studied in secondary school in Kazerun with a few other Qermezi boys. He received his high-school diploma in 1987 and passed Iran's stiff university-entrance examination with high marks. He entered university in Tehran, the first Qermezi to study there. He obtained a bachelor's degree in aeronautical engineering in 1993 from Iran's most prestigious institution, Tehran Polytechnic University (renamed in 1978 Amir Kabir University of Technology). He completed his master's degree in the same field at the same institution in 1996 and prepared to pursue a doctoral degree. Masud is the first Qermezi to obtain a master's degree and hoped to be the first doctoral candidate. The professors who could have helped him achieve this goal, however, had left Iran to seek jobs with the

National Aeronautics and Space Administration in the United States, and he worried about his future. Young officers in the Iranian air force, such as Masud, had received years of state-paid higher education and were knowledgeable about Iran's military equipment. The government considered them to be security risks and potential emigrants and did not ordinarily allow them to pursue further education abroad.

During his nine years of university education, Masud spent as much time as possible at home with his extended kinship group in winter and summer pastures where his parents and nine siblings pursued the customary practices of pastoralism. He often endured more time on the bus traveling to and from Tehran than he managed to enjoy with his family. Masud never performed any physical or other labor during these visits, other than watering the lawn he was struggling to grow in front of his family's new two-room house in summer pastures, but he did seem well integrated in his group of origin. His high level of formal education apparently precluded him from engaging in any work at home, despite the need for it. His former classmates and age-cohorts of both genders gently kidded him about his lofty status and its symbolic trappings (a computer, a fancy briefcase, and unscuffed shoes). Qashqa'i in other subtribes and tribes asked exploratory questions about his plans for marriage. They viewed him as quite a catch.

When I wondered in the early 1990s what his professors and classmates in Tehran thought about him being Qashqa'i, Masud confided that no one knew, that he never told anyone about his tribal, ethnic, or linguistic identity. (Non-Qashqa'i people, especially urbanites, often considered any Qashqa'i to be uneducated, unsophisticated, and dangerous.) Devising a strategy that worked for him in the distant national capital, Masud had learned to blend in with his fellow students.[151] Back home, he criticized Persian Iranians for their duplicity and dishonesty and noted that he disliked having to pose as one. After 1996, when his cousin Shahriyar was elected to Iran's parliament and did not hesitate to identify himself as Qashqa'i, Masud became less circumspect in acknowledging his Qashqa'i origins and identity.

Masud was disgruntled and unhappy in 1997, at a standstill in the pursuit of his chosen career. His quest for a doctoral degree had seemingly ended by default. He worked as a teaching assistant in the same university, well below his qualifications and achieved status. He mused about his cousin, the parliamentary deputy, removing the barriers holding him back. Iran and Japan had agreed to allow a few advanced aeronautical students from Iran to study in Japan at Iranian-government expense, but Masud lacked the political and social connections in Tehran that might lead to such an appointment. Two of his colleagues received higher marks than his on a newly introduced doctoral-candidacy examination in 1998, and once again he could not continue his formal education.

Masud's attitude about life improved somewhat, despite the professional crisis. Long rejecting people's efforts to find him a suitable spouse, he finally married a university-educated Darrehshuri Qashqa'i woman, although not a

128 *The revolution and the Islamic Republic*

Qermezi. They produced a son in 1999, and Masud's life assumed another dimension. He retook the doctoral-candidacy examination with the same result and continued his teaching assistantship while studying for the next year's test. Now with a family to care for, he abandoned the notion of traveling abroad to pursue a doctoral degree, although the possibilities in aeronautical studies in Russia tempted him. Such programs in Great Britain, Canada, and Australia were unavailable for Iranian applicants who did not possess near-perfect knowledge of written and spoken English, and the ongoing political impasse between Iran and the United States precluded him from setting his sights on America. Less mobile with a wife and baby, Masud was unable to travel to winter and summer pastures as often as he had done when he was single, and his family and wider kinship group missed seeing him. Still, as a recipient of a master's degree and a resident of Tehran employed in an esteemed profession, Masud remained a role model for Qermezi youth.

The feasibility of doctoral studies in Russia was revived in 2002, and Masud and his family considered leaving Iran for a four-year sojourn in Moscow. He would have to dedicate the first year to learning to read and write Russian, which he considered a waste of time, especially at his advanced age. Not until 2004 did the Iranian government authorize his trip to Moscow, and his wife and son were eventually able to join him there. Masud completed his studies in 2008 and returned home to Iran, where he resumed teaching at a Tehran university.

Women employed outside the home

Afsaneh, the daughter of Akbar of Aqa Mohammadli lineage, is the first Qermezi woman to take a paying job outside the home. She was hired in 1992 as a schoolteacher in a village near Borujen. Soon several of her Aqa Mohammadli kinswomen also became teachers. Gulbas, the daughter of Nasir of Aqa Mohammadli, is the first woman to secure a salaried job other than teaching. A university graduate specializing in computers, she took an administrative job in Shiraz's Ministry of Education. Javahir, the daughter of Abdul Rasul of Aqa Mohammadli, was hired as a nurse in Borujen.

The government offered excellent benefits for maternity and childcare leaves, sometimes lasting a full year, and women could combine salaried jobs, childbirth, and motherhood.[152] Two of these employed females lacked children and spoke explicitly about the need to find alternative work. Other married women without children in the early 2000s were pursuing university educations to prepare them for productive employment. The Qermezi increasingly viewed higher education and professional jobs as acceptable options for women who did not marry (usually because satisfactory suitors of their own or higher status were not available) or bear children. They also said that women who were divorced or widowed could study and find jobs, although no cases of these scenarios had yet emerged by 2005.

The revolution and the Islamic Republic 129

A national war hero

At least 150 Qermezi boys and men participated in the war against Iraq in 1980–88. Thirteen were martyred or lost, seven were injured but survived, and two were prisoners of war. Of these, one emerged as a genuine war hero. The son of Sohrab of Imamverdili lineage, Shahriyar Qermezi demonstrated bravery and courage during the nearly eight years he served in the war. His fellow volunteer militiamen as well as the Qermezi and other Qashqa'i admired him, despite their universal negative sentiments about the war itself. Shahriyar obtained a degree of recognition within Iran that no other Qermezi in history had ever received. (I discuss Shahriyar's military career earlier in this chapter and in Chapter 7 on his parliamentary deputyship.)

A parliamentary deputy

Shahriyar Qermezi drew on his war-derived reputation, along with other qualities, in a successful candidacy for a parliamentary deputyship in 1996 (see Chapter 7).

Pilgrims to Mecca

Until the Islamic Republic, no Qermezi had taken the pilgrimage to Mecca in Saudi Arabia. The trip was expensive and the destination far, and no one had expressed any realistic interest in going. Ten men did travel there in the 1980s and early 1990s, eight from Kachili lineage and two from Qasemli. Other Qermezi joked that Kachili men enjoyed time on their hands. Living in villages, they had left behind the daily obligations of nomadic pastoralism. A Kachili man made the pilgrimage in 1987 when Saudi Arabian security forces killed (massacred, say some) more than 400 Shi'i Iranians in pro-Khomeini political demonstrations there. People jested about the man who had escaped the *hajj* with barely his life. He in turn laughed about being required to shout "Death to America!" and "American Islam!" hundreds of times a day in such an ancient, sacred place devoted to high religious and ethical standards.[153] One of the two Qasemli men took the pilgrimage on behalf of his deceased father, to whom the merit accrued (and not to the actual pilgrim). Another man went on the pilgrimage in 2004 in the place of his still-living father. With high inflation in Iran and an unstable economy, those who considered going decided to postpone the endeavor. Two men registered with the government in the late 1990s for the trip. The Martyrs Foundation facilitated their efforts and paid for some or most of the cost. His son dead in the war, Bahram of Aqa Mohammadli lineage was its first pilgrim. A former prisoner of war in Iraq, Ghulam Hasan of Imamverdili lineage would be its first.

People did not regard Qermezi's pilgrims (except for Bahram) as hezbollahis, and the hajjis did not demonstrate the behavior and stridency associated with these zealots. One ardent pilgrim was also the man who urged the subtribe in

130 *The revolution and the Islamic Republic*

1991 to resume the music, dance, sport, and dress that the Islamic Republic forbade as un-Islamic.

A pilgrim to Damascus

Farzaneh, the daughter of Akbar of Aqa Mohammadli lineage and the wife of Mohammad Husain of the same lineage, traveled to Damascus, Syria, in 1999 to visit the tomb of Hazrat-i Zainab (the daughter of Ali, the first Shi'i imam) and ask her assistance.[154] Remarkably, she traveled "alone," without relatives to accompany her. She made the pilgrimage with villagers near Borujen; she was their community's schoolteacher. Some members of her natal and affinal families viewed the trip as essential given her state of apparent infertility. She had been married for six years without a pregnancy. Her husband was an only son, and his family feared that the patriline would end if he did not produce a son or at least a daughter.

Farzaneh was also the first Qermezi woman to travel internationally. Mecca's pilgrims and the soldiers who crossed the Iraqi border were all men. She was the first Qermezi woman to ride an airplane. A few Qermezi men flew before she did, including the pilgrims to Mecca and a pilgrim to Mashhad. (Other pilgrims to Mashhad took the bus or train.) Shahriyar flew to Mashhad to perform a pilgrimage of thanksgiving after his election to parliament, and he sometimes flew to and from Tehran on parliamentary business.

Notes

1 Publications on the revolution focus on Tehran and, only rarely, other large cities. A comprehensive account needs to distinguish the many levels of experience and perspective (Abrahamian 1980, 1982; Halliday 1979, 1980). Hardly any authors do so. These levels include: urban and rural, center and periphery, upper and middle and lower classes, modern or cosmopolitan and traditional (*sunnati*) sectors, majority and minority communities, Persians and non-Persians, Muslims and non-Muslims, Shi'i Muslims and Sunni Muslims, tribal and nontribal communities, the political left and right, liberal and conservative, moderate and hard-line, secular and religious (*mazhabi*), court and bazaar, males and females, older and younger generations, material conditions and ideology, and Iranians and foreigners. Beck (1980), Friedl (1983, 1989), and Loeffler (1988, 2011) discuss the revolution's impact on rural tribal areas. Hegland (1983, 2014), E. Hooglund (2009), M. Hooglund (1980), M. Martin (1989), and Safizadeh (1991) discuss rural, nontribal communities. Parsa (1989: 238) notes that 5,000 armed people from Firuzabad (the former winter capital of the Qashqa'i ilkhani) and "the nearby Ghashgha'i tribe" gathered on 9 February 1979 to proclaim their readiness to begin a jihad if Khomeini issued the order. Parsa is perhaps the only scholar to mention the political role of the Qashqa'i people (as compared with the khans) during the revolution. He does not cite his source but frequently draws on Iranian newspaper accounts.
2 E. Hooglund (1980: 6) lists the expectations of young men in a Persian village north of Shiraz.
3 Persian villagers expressed similar attitudes about land (E. Hooglund 1982b: 25).

The revolution and the Islamic Republic 131

4 Abrahamian (1993: 111–31), Amirahmadi (1990: 284), and Halliday (1990: 248) discuss conspiracy notions in Iran.
5 Friedl (1989), Hegland (1983, 1987, 2014), E. Hooglund (1980, 1997), M. Hooglund (1980).
6 Some writers who stress Khomeini's superior organization and support and the importance of institutional Shi'i Islam for Iranians object to the notion that Khomeini and other clergy "hijacked" the revolution (Ghamari-Tabrizi 2008: 244). Foran (1993: 358–409, 1994) and Parsa (1989) weigh the impact of the components and social forces of the revolutionary movement.
7 In his history of the Semirom war derived from oral accounts, Yusufi (2001: 6–30) mentions Shir Mohammad Qermezi's death, perhaps the first time that the name of any Qermezi person appears in any publication (excluding my work and that of its reviewers and commentators). Newspaper accounts and other publications on Iran's parliament mention Shahriyar Qermezi, a deputy in 1996–2000. Drawing exclusively on government documents (and not oral history), K. Bayat (2010) details the Semirom war.
8 Clergymen newly posted to the Ministry of Education ordered new instructional materials on Islam for primary and secondary schools nationwide. Iranians were amazed by the speed with which the government prepared new curricula and published new textbooks, and they saw how intent the new regime was in Islamizing society.
9 Beck (1980b, 1986: 296–347, n.d. b) describes these events. The account presented in this section covers only a small part of local-level Qashqa'i participation. I mention only briefly the next level of activity, involving the Qashqa'i khans in the region and nation. Almost all scholars and journalists writing about the immediate postrevolutionary period appear not to know about any Qashqa'i activity, or they deem any events insignificant. A few rare writers include only several words—a "minor rebellion" among the Qashqa'i (Bakhash 1984: 223), "the Qashqa'is in revolt" (Sick 1986: 169), and a khan who "tried to defy the government" (Katouzian 2009: 330). They do not describe or discuss what this supposed rebellion or revolt entailed and who took part and why.
10 These huge gatherings were similar to ones after Naser Khan was released from prison in Tehran in 1941. Duncan (1982: 146–53) offers dramatic photographs for 1944. Such greetings are part of Qashqa'i culture (and the wider Iranian culture) for people returning from war or released from prison.
11 Standing with his arms at his sides, Borzu received the embrace and the kiss on each cheek. If the two men had met under more ordinary circumstances, Borzu would have bowed slightly as he tried to kiss the back of the khan's right hand, and the khan would have kissed his forehead.
12 Iraj Khan Kashkuli (Shokat 2000), a member of the Ranjbaran leftist group, offers his views on these times. Some Qashqa'i object to his portrayal, which they consider biased. Part of the Janikhani family, Azar Ghashghai (Ameri-Siemans 2009) offers her criticisms.
13 Some general studies of this period mention briefly such activity among Kurds, Turkmans, Baluch, and Arabs (Bakhash 1984, Chehabi 1990, Hiro 1985, Parsa 1989, Schirazi 1993). Mojab and Hassanpour (1996) discuss political activities among Kurds in revolutionary and postrevolutionary times. K. Bayat (2005, 2008) offers historical overviews of ethnic communities in Iran and the extent of their participation in the revolution.
14 Duncan (1982: 140–57) includes photographs of the site.
15 The Bakhtiyari tribal khans of Shapur Bakhtiar's family participated in Iran's national politics in the early twentieth century (Garthwaite 1983), and the Bakhtiyari and Qashqa'i ruling elites were interconnected by kinship, marriage, and political alliance.

132 *The revolution and the Islamic Republic*

16 Some writers, Iranians and others, seem unable to move beyond the notion that these khans had been and still were "feudal lords" who oppressed their subjects. They do not acknowledge the many dimensions of their leadership; for these attributes, see Beck (1986, 1991). The "tribal" label, for many writers, seems to preclude other identities and roles. Afkhami (2009: 392) classifies a Qashqa'i rebel against the shah as someone who opposed land reform in order to fortify his relatives' "feudal" claims.

17 The property belonged to the sons of Ali Reza Khan Kiyani, a Persian dignitary of Shahreza who died before the revolution. The title of "khan" is honorific and not tribally based. His son was a member of parliament under Mohammad Reza Shah. Revolutionary guards seized the property just after the revolution and made it their headquarters in Shahreza. Throughout Iran, guards seized properties belonging to the wealthy and enjoyed the comfortable facilities. Naheed Dareshuri (personal communication, May 2009), a schoolmate of Kiyani's daughter, played at this very house as a child. Years later she visited her relatives imprisoned there.

18 The Islamic Republic jailed many Qashqa'i men and women because they associated in some way with the paramount Qashqa'i khans in 1980–82. It held some Qarachai Qashqa'i men, implicated in the Tang-i Jelo incident, the longest. The state freed the final Qarachai man in 1998, an event for widespread celebration among the Qashqa'i.

19 Bakhash (1984: 198) does not cite a source or a date for his comment that villagers in the Semirom area seized the land of khans and petitioned the government to retain these khans in prison (so they could not expel the new occupants). These events may coincide with those I describe in this section. Bakhash does not include the affiliations, tribal or not, of these "khans," a term used for influential men, both tribal and nontribal, in Iran.

20 Abrahamian (1989, 1999), Talebi (2011).

21 Ayatollah Jalal ud-Din Tahiri and other Friday prayer leaders were important links in the chain of command between Khomeini and the cities and towns of Iran, especially in the provinces. They were more powerful and influential than the provincial governor-generals (*ustandar*) who had dominated under the shahs. They issued decrees, propagated doctrine, mobilized recruits, led local branches of the Islamic Republican Party, and provided ration cards. Some, including Tahiri, created private armies of revolutionary guards, and Tahiri's army fought against his rival's in 1983. Overviews of the 1978–79 revolution and its immediate aftermath occasionally mention Tahiri's activities (but do not include any links he might have had with the Qashqa'i khans) (Parsa 1989: 114, 213–14, 280, 288). Tahiri was a "faithful revolutionary with leftist-fundamentalist tendencies" who became over time an "advocate of liberalism and toleration" (Borjian 2008). He resigned in 2002 as one of Isfahan's parliamentary deputies. He died in June 2013 (before the election of the new president), and his funeral drew large gatherings of protestors against the regime. Separated by gender, marchers chanted "Death to the Dictator!" (Iran's supreme leader, Ali Khamenei). I met Tahiri several times in 1970–71 and 1977, when he came to Mehr-i Gerd to preside over religious gatherings sponsored by a Darrehshuri *bibi* (a woman in the khan family). People joked at the time that he was "Darrehshuri's ayatollah," a nonsensical notion for the tribespeople.

22 By this time most Qashqa'i detested the Muslim clergy but some now regarded Tahiri more favorably than the others.

23 I lack references for these articles, published by one or several newspapers in Isfahan, and no one I knew possessed copies. Many people, Qermezi and others, talked about the published articles they had read.

24 Ayatollah Mahdavi Kani, one of the few high-level clergymen who openly opposed the occupation of the U.S. Embassy in Tehran in 1979–81, declared that

prayers performed in the embassy compound were not religiously sanctioned because of the illegal confiscation (M. Milani 1994: 173). Clergy in Mashhad ruled that the prayers said by squatters in homes they had illegally seized were not acceptable (A. Bayat 1997: 69). Villagers in southwestern Iran stated that smoking, drug addiction, and fatal car accidents had resulted from mixing illicit (*haram*) land and legitimate (*halal*) land after the land seizures that had accompanied the 1978–79 revolution (Ajami 2005: 348*n*).

25 Naheed Dareshuri (personal communication, 28 May 1988). Years later, when I checked some details about the prison with her, she looked surprised and then retorted, "But the khans would never have been held in the same prison as the *raiyat* [non-elite tribesmen]!" According to her, revolutionary guards would never have confined the high-status khans alongside ordinary tribesmen.

26 The Qermezi said they had expected that men who adhered to Islamic principles would behave ethically in their government posts.

27 Mohammad Reza Shah had imprisoned political opponents (clergymen, leftists, journalists, university students, National Front politicians, and tribal and national-minority leaders), and they too formed strong bonds that contributed to their combined efforts to depose him in 1978–79.

28 Beck (1986), Oberling (1974), and Safiri (1976) discuss British troops in southwestern Iran during World War I and the Qashqa'i forces raised against them.

29 Few Qermezi were wounded, compared with their level of participation.

30 Amir Ajami (personal communication, 25 May 2011). The village name is a pseudonym.

31 E. Hooglund (1997: 77, 78). Safizadeh (1991: 322–23) reports two to three martyrs (two bodies returned, one unaccounted for) in a village of 1,700 people in northwestern Iran. He notes 125 draft dodgers and deserters in the same village. Cemeteries of villages throughout southwestern Iran featured a special section for martyrs' graves, whose numbers appear to correspond with the size of each settlement. Some villagers buried their dead at regional shrines.

32 The Qermezi explain their many losses, compared with other Darrehshuri subtribes, by their high level of participation due to the example set by Shahriyar Qermezi during the war.

33 Sohrab Dolatkhah (personal communications, 2009–2011), a Qashqa'i student there at the time, provides details about the war's impact on the school. He volunteered twice with the basij militia for service in the war.

34 Hiro (1991: 250, 268), Sigler (1990: 147). Iran's Ministry of Islamic Guidance (Amirahmadi 1990: 330, Hiro 1991: 250) lists 123,000 combatant deaths (revolutionary guards and army soldiers), 61,000 men missing in action (and presumed dead or held in Iraqi prisons), and 11,000 civilian deaths (a total of 200,000 for Iran, well below actual numbers). Many basij militiamen were also killed in the war and may or may not be included in these figures. Abrahamian (2008: 171, 175, 212*n*) lists the government's revised figures in 1988 as 160,000 dead in battle. Another 30,000 died later of wounds, 39,000 sustained permanent injuries, and 16,000 civilians were killed in the bombing of cities. Chubin and Tripp (1988), Cordesman (1987), Hiro (1984, 1991, 2005), Khosronejad (2013b), *Middle East Report* (2010), Potter and Sick (2004), O'Ballance (1988), Rouleau (1981), and Takeyh (2009: 81–107) offer different perspectives on the war.

35 Khosronejad (2013a: 10–15). Unidentified martyrs are called "lost-name martyrs" (*shahidan-i gumnam-i jang*). Talebi (2013: 120) distinguishes between the hyper-visibility of the "state martyrs" in Iran and the discriminatory invisibility and lack of recognition of the "dissident martyrs."

36 The Islamic regime brought Iraqi prisoners of war (presumably all Shi'is) to participate in Friday prayers at Tehran University, where they sat together in a special section.

134 *The revolution and the Islamic Republic*

37 Families of some Iraqi prisoners already lived in Iran. After the war, Saddam Hussein expelled tens of thousands of Shi'is from Iraq, especially those he identified as "Persians" ("Ajam," meaning not Arabs), and many sought sanctuary in Iran (Al-Ali 2007, Alahmad and Keshavarzian 2010: 27). Some of them returned to Iraq after 2003, when Saddam's regime fell.

38 Army conscripts served for two and a half years during the war.

39 Alahmad and Keshavarzian (2010: 17).

40 Gruber (2013: 77–78) mentions the poignancy inherent in the martyrs' shoes (and other "contact relics") in the exhibits in the Martyrs' Museum in Tehran.

41 Abrahamian (2008: xv) defines "akhund" and "mulla" simply, as derogatory terms for clerics (*ruhani*).

42 Soldiers were not equipped with identity tags in the first years of the war, and initially only army conscripts (and not revolutionary guards or basij militiamen) carried official identity cards.

43 Iran returned the remains of 1,200 men to Iraq in 2002, and Iraq handed over 570.

44 Seven were killed in the war, and the eighth was murdered by Allah Quli Jahangiri, the Darrehshuri leftist rebel who had threatened to kill Borzu Qermezi.

45 Chapter 6 (this volume) and Huang (2009: 205–08) describe the Mehr-i Gerd cemetery and the mourners there.

46 Adelkhah (2000: 122–27) and Khosrokhavar (1995) discuss Islamic and other customs concerning death. Armenians in Iran produced memorial posters in the Armenian language for their martyrs. Farhi (2004) explains how the war changed politics, society, and culture in Iran.

47 Since 1982–83 (when universities reopened after ideological "cleansing") through at least the early- to mid-1990s, the government reserved 40 to 60 percent of university slots for members of martyrs' families, war veterans (especially the wounded), basij militiamen, revolutionary guards, and others with special connections to the regime (see Chapter 7).

48 Dr. Richard Bucholz of Saint Louis University Hospital examined Nazar Ali Qermezi's medical records (such as they were) and asked a colleague to translate into Persian his diagnosis so that I could deliver a detailed letter to Nazar Ali.

49 Shahriyar's eight-year service in the war corresponds with the timing of his brother's captivity as a prisoner of war. Perhaps Shahriyar remained in the war for this duration so he could fight the enemy as long as his brother could not, honor his brother's sacrifice, and help to bring the conflict to an end.

50 Chelkowski and Dabashi (1999) illustrate war-related iconography.

51 Hiltermann (2007).

52 After the war, tens of thousands of Iranians received long-term treatment for exposure to mustard gas and other chemical agents (Alahmad and Keshavarzian 2010: 17). Before being elected as president in 2013, Hasan Rouhani noted that the war's chemical weapons had killed 20,000 Iranian soldiers and injured 100,000 others.

53 The bodies of prisoners of war (the camps spread out across Iraq) were less likely to be recovered than those of men dying in battles (which took place along the Iraq–Iran border).

54 The Islamic regime also called the war the Sacred (or Holy) Defense (*difai muqaddas*), a phrase I never heard any Qashqa'i mention.

55 "There has been surprising continuity with the old, pre-revolutionary, political institutions, many of which remain in existence: the parliament, ministries and armed forces of the Pahlavi regime have not been abolished. ... The reason why the old apparatuses of state can continue is that they have been taken over by the revolutionary regime's forces; ... they are flanked by new networks of control and distribution" (Halliday 1989: 20). "The structures established by the Constitutional Revolution [1905–11] and fortified under the Pahlavis survived and even

The revolution and the Islamic Republic 135

expanded under the Islamic Republic. ... Thus tradition met modernity, and continuity met innovation" (Martin 2003: 173).

56 Akhavi (1986: 60) includes a chart of revolutionary organizations. The new revolutionary tribunals, committees, and guards are "states within a state" (Abrahamian 1989: 50). During the first six months after the revolution, "a kind of 'control from below' prevailed" (A. Bayat 1988: 50). "The fundamentalists created a state within the state that remained outside the jurisdiction of the provisional government. Khomeini was its undisputed leader and its source of inspiration; the Islamic Republican Party was its parliament and brain; the Komites [committees] its local police; the Pasdaran [revolutionary guards] its national army; the Revolutionary Courts its judiciary; and the Mostaz'efin Foundation its auxiliary source of revenue. This mini-state ... was skillfully used by the fundamentalists ... to destroy their opponents and to pave the way for their own ascendancy" (M. Milani 1994: 151). Amirahmadi (1990: 89, 282), Amuzegar (1993: 320–21), and Takeyh (2009: 24) note the parallel institutions and duplicate organizations with similar functions: revolutionary council versus provisional government, Friday prayer leaders versus municipal governments, revolutionary guards/volunteer militia versus regular armed forces, revolutionary committees versus regular police/gendarmes, Ministry of Construction Jihad versus Plan and Budget Organization/Ministry of Agriculture, and semiprivate foundations versus regular state service-providing agencies. Intragovernmental coordination was absent, regulations were lacking, and links between and among these entities were ambiguous (Amirahmadi 1990: 89). "The regime has managed to ensure the fulfilment of its own mandates via its trusted institutions while not risking hazardous political instability or economic chaos by a wholesale replacement of inherited agencies" (Amuzegar 1993: 321). Clergy-dominated supragovernmental foundations (and other agencies) "cannot be prised free without shaking the regime's very foundations and threatening its power base" (Amuzegar 1993: 331). After three decades, parallel governments, dualities in leadership, and resulting conflicts have continued (Ehteshami and Zweiri 2007). The fundamentally unchanged status of the economy after the revolution (and until 1993) and compared with that during the shah's era remains puzzling, and the continuities are "astonishing" and "curious" (Amuzegar 1993: 320; also Halliday 1989). Nomani and Behdad (2006) offer a statistically based study that demonstrates how Iran's economy (and the hierarchy of its socioeconomic classes) had changed from the last years of the shah to 1996. Their analysis demonstrates more changes than continuities.

57 Behdad (2000: 127).

58 The Islamic Republican Party was a loose gathering of people who were politically like-minded, rather than a formal party (Cole 2002: 13).

59 Keshavarzian (2007: 158). Rakel (2009) divides the institutions of formal state power in Iran into three sectors: the religious supervisory bodies, the republican bodies, and the religious foundations (*bunyad*).

60 Amuzegar (1993: 321).

61 Behdad (2000: 102). Amirahmadi (1990: 114–15) discusses Iran's three economic sectors (which are listed in the 1979 constitution): government (which he considers "public"), cooperative, and private. The regime promoted cooperatives to impede merchants from hoarding and profiteering.

62 Amuzegar (1993: ix).

63 Nomani and Behdad (2006: 37–38). The state could authorize sweeping confiscations by declaring that certain properties were "illegitimately" acquired.

64 State officials, including clerics, accepted the leftist Mujahidin organization during the early years of the Islamic Republic, an example of how sociopolitical and religious perspectives within the new state were diverse then (Talebi 2013: 142).

136   The revolution and the Islamic Republic

65 The complex events, circumstances, ideologies, and personalities involved in the revolution and the Islamic Republic's formation are beyond the scope of this book. For informative, insightful accounts, see Abrahamian (1982, 2008), Amuzegar (1993), Ansari (2007, 2012), Bakhash (1984), Chehabi (1990), Cole (2002: 189–211), Dabashi (2007), Gheissari and Nasr (2006), Hiro (1985), Katouzian (2009: 288–394), Keddie (2006), V. Martin (2003), Menashri (1990), M. Milani (1994), Moaddel (1993), Moslem (2002), Parsa (1989), and Takeyh (2009). Abrahamian (1982), Halliday (1979), and Katouzian (1981, 2009) discuss the preceding regime.

66 Writers on the Islamic Republic do not consider the affiliations (ethnic, linguistic, religious, regional, and tribal) of the new regime's agents who brought services to and/ or administered local populations. Did the Islamic regime follow the policy of the two Pahlavi shahs to send urban, Shi'i, Persian agents throughout the country, or did it rely on agents who originated in the local groups they served? This factor is important for assessing the impact of the new government's policies on Iran's many sectors.

67 Corruption and bribery in Iran as a whole might have been as prevalent after the revolution as under Mohammad Reza Shah, especially at upper government levels and among the ruling elite. "Iran's institutionalized corruption became pernicious, debilitating, and inimical to progress" (Amuzegar 1993: 296). When economic conditions did not improve for the sectors of society that Khomeini and others deemed "deprived," even after twenty-some years of Islamic government, Iranians and outside observers blamed corruption and abuse of power (Menashri 2001: 105–30). Urban Iranians said that corruption and bribery at all levels of government and society were worse in 2011–13 than they had ever been. The ever-worsening national economy, suffering under tightening international sanctions, partly explains these trends.

68 As experienced by the Qermezi at the local level, the ideological, idealistic notions of state agents of urban, Persian background decreased in intensity in the late 1980s and thereafter and were only rarely apparent in the youngest government employees. The Islamic Republic's rule gradually changed from focusing on the needs of the "disinherited" to enhancing the interests of the powerful and wealthy (Nomani and Behdad 2006; Schirazi 1993). The transition is apparent in Khomeini's speeches and decrees as early as 1984.

69 Unlike previous presidents, and as he had promised during his two campaigns, Ahmadinejad traveled to many of Iran's provinces, ostensibly to assess their economic needs. Attacks and threats prevented him from visiting at least eight of the most underdeveloped provinces.

70 Nadjmabadi (1993). The literature also refers to *jihad-i sazandigi* as Construction Crusade and Rural Reconstruction (given the agency's focus on the rural sector).

71 Schirazi (1993: 148).

72 Abrahamian (1989: 71). Qashqa'i pastoralists objected when officials complained about the proximity of humans and livestock, and they wondered why the government did not find other issues to occupy its time. Construction Jihad's formal goals in 1979–80 were to unite volunteers (university and high-school students, unemployed people including high-school graduates), create lines of communication between intellectuals and the disinherited, assist rural economic development, increase literacy among peasants, and propagate Islamic culture and the Islamic revolution in rural areas (Ferdows 1983: 12).

73 Rural migrants in cities and towns maintained contact with relatives and others who had stayed behind, and each group knew the economic and social conditions experienced by the other and could make informed decisions about staying or leaving. Mobile telephones, even among some nomads, were the principal means for these communications by the late 1990s.

74 A. Bayat (1997) examines the conditions of life in cities for the poor and their coping strategies.

The revolution and the Islamic Republic 137

75 Jihad members and employees were exempted from military service but could still volunteer.

76 The merger meant abolishing the Ministry of Agriculture and incorporating its agencies and functions in Construction Jihad (Schirazi 1993: 153). Three agencies important to nomads and pastoralists—Forest, Rangeland, and Watershed Management Organization; Department of Extension and Farming Systems; and Veterinary Organization—were part of the expanded Ministry of Agricultural Jihad (also called Agriculture and Rural Development).

77 Centers for Services to Agriculture, Rural Areas, and Nomads had been part of the Ministry of Agriculture under Mohammad Reza Shah, and the new regime assumed control of them. Schirazi (1993) provides an account but includes no information about the nomads' center.

78 Tapper (1994: 194–96, 1997: 312–14) offers brief accounts of ONA activities among the Shahsevan in 1993 and 1995. He comments (1994: 203) that "the state, through ONA, has taken over the political and economic functions of the former tribal leaders," referring apparently to higher-level leaders. In south-western Iran, tribal leaders had not offered the many economic services and infrastructural improvements now provided by ONA, and the state's political functions differed from those of the tribal leaders.

79 Statistical Centre of Iran (1991). Tapper discusses reconstructing nomadism in Iran (1994, 2002, 2008: 108–10). Census figures for nomads are approximations, err on the low side for political reasons, and reflect the people's inaccessibility.

80 Such official recognition of tribal structures occurred elsewhere in Iran. Among the Shahsevan, "despite all the economic and political changes, the tribe (taifa) and the tribal section (tira) continued [in 1993 and 1995] to be the main pastoral nomadic communities recognized by both the tribespeople themselves and the government" (Tapper 1997: 314).

81 Prominent Iranian historians often confuse the terms (tribes, nomads, and pastoralists) and use them inaccurately and interchangeably. "Nomads" did not take over state rule in Iran in the premodern period; rather, men affiliated with tribes did. "Nomadic" and "pastoral" values (whatever these terms could possibly mean) did not affect how these new leaders regarded women; rather, the norms of tribally organized society might have influenced them.

82 The government passed laws for and introduced usury-free banking in 1983–85. Yet most banks continued to pay eight to nine percent interest (in the name of profit) (Amirahmadi 1990: 141). Amuzegar (1993) discusses interest taking and banking as they relate to Islamic law in the Islamic Republic. He and other authors state that the new government was unable to ban interest taking. "Beneficent" institutions including interest-free loan funds and Islamic credit associations helped to satisfy some needs for alternative economic services (Adelkhah 2000: 53–78). Participants in some ventures received "bonuses" (such as televisions, refrigerators, and pilgrimage trips) instead of "unlawful interest" (riba).

83 The woman depicted on some coupons wears a long flowing skirt, tunic, headscarf, and headband (which are composite features from Iran's diverse communities of nomads).

84 "If nomads can be shown to have settlements (buildings, bases, stations)—something all nomads are apparently happy to have—then, even though they may still migrate (by truck or by transport animal), they can be said to have 'settled' and to be pursuing a modern way of life" (Tapper 1994: 207). Elsewhere, Tapper (1979) describes the processes of migrating, settling, and modernizing as continua and not in the fixed terms he uses here.

85 The government's elaborate public commemorations of the war and its martyrs had inspired some Qashqa'i to create other kinds of public forums for celebrating their culture.

138 *The revolution and the Islamic Republic*

86 The Ministry of Culture and Islamic Guidance took stances regarding instrumental and vocal music that conflicted with those of some other government agencies. A Friday prayer leader in northeastern Iran objected to a ministry-supported performance of regional poetry and music (Youssefzadeh 2000: 36*n*). The Islamic regime allowed literary and cultural gatherings for the Baluch in Baluchistan, and regional television broadcast programs about local lifestyles, dance, and dress (Jahani 2006).

87 Qashqa'i vocalists, poets, and orators were not ordinarily subjected to government control over the content of their performances and did not submit Persian translations of their lyrics and texts (in Qashqa'i Turkish) for approval beforehand (cf. Youssefzadeh 2000: 41–42, 46–47).

88 At least five different magazines devoted exclusively to Qashqa'i topics and focusing on the people's Qashqa'i Turkish heritage were published by varying entities (including independent and correspondence universities in southwestern Iran) and sold in bookstores and news kiosks in Shiraz and Isfahan in 2004. Their titles are *Aghur il* (Glorious tribe), *Qara Aghaj* (Black Wood River), *Oyan* (Wake up!), *Il yad* (Tribal memories), and *Il sozu* (Tribal voices) (all in the author's possession). "Il" (tribe) in these titles refers to the Qashqa'i tribal confederacy, to challenge the regime's attempts to ignore or erase the existence of such a polity. Baluch activists published bilingual (Baluchi and Persian) magazines in Baluchistan after 1979 (Jahani 2006). Iran's Azeri Turks expanded their literary production after 1979 (Asgharzadeh 2007). Publications appearing in the provinces were usually exempt from the regulations that restricted the mainstream press (K. Bayat 2005: 44), although the regime did exercise more surveillance over and censorship of publications in Kurdish and Azeri Turkish than in some other languages.

89 Reflecting their intensifying sentiments about Turkish identity, Turks in other parts of Iran; in Turkey, the Caucasus, and Eurasia; and in the global diaspora responded positively to this content and inspired the Qashqa'i in Iran to become more active via this medium.

90 www.gachsaran.org and www.youtube.com/watch?v=XEWWeverx41&feature= email (accessed 30 April 2011). Khosrow Khan's immediate family had refused the Darrehshuri khan's request to install the gravestone. The khan implemented his plan anyway, to the family's annoyance. The Islamic regime wanted to prevent any further political resurgence among the Qashqa'i, and a marked gravesite would draw visitors, a possible provocation. Khosrow Khan's family noted that revolutionary guards might not have buried Khosrow Khan there after his execution. This and previous regimes had treated with contempt other deceased family members, especially if they had executed them, and grave locations were sometimes unknown.

91 The Meat Marketing Organization sent clerics to foreign countries to train people in the proper techniques for slaughtering. Still, some Iranians questioned the status of the meat they bought in butcher shops if the animals were not killed there. They also preferred fresh over frozen meat.

92 Bernard Hourcade (personal communication, 5 May 2001). See Firouz (1998) and Zekavat (1997). Multiple and sometimes conflicting agencies under the Islamic Republic handled complicated environmental and ecological issues.

93 The agency might have modeled the livestock-insurance program after the government's crop-insurance program against natural disasters (for the latter, see Amuzegar 1993: 186).

94 Baktiari (1996: 84). Schirazi (1993) discusses the government's vacillation in establishing laws governing urban and rural land after the revolution; see also Akhavi (1986), Amuzegar (1993), Bakhash (1984), Baktiari (1996), and Rahnema and Nomani (1990). One hundred residents of a Persian village near Shiraz seized

The revolution and the Islamic Republic   139

hundreds of hectares of wheat land from the largest landowner there, just after the revolution (E. Hooglund 1997, 1982a). The land's legal status remained unresolved for decades, and agricultural production suffered. Hegland (2014) and M. Hooglund (1980) explain the political dimensions of the crisis.

95 The Guardian Council proclaimed in 1984 that Mohammad Reza Shah's land-reform laws were invalid because they were contrary to Islamic law (Schirazi 1993: 69).

96 "The regime's inherent contradiction" was "wealthy *mulla*-bureaucrats preaching virtue to the poor" (Menashri 2001: 114). "Many of those who gained access to the power of the state found lucrative opportunities for personal gain, which they did not hesitate to take advantage of in spite of their puritanical revolutionary and Islamic claims" (Nomani and Behdad 2006: 204).

97 Amuzegar (1993: 183).

98 Continuing land disputes, economic insecurity, and a widening gap between the rich and the poor in a Persian village near Shiraz derived from vacillating and indecisive state agrarian policies, a process still ongoing more than two decades after peasants had seized land from wealthy owners (Ajami 2005).

99 After the failure of the U.S. military in 1980 to recover American hostages held in Tehran, the captors dispersed many of them throughout the country. Some were housed at Bagh-i Eram and in nearby houses on the same street. Qashqa'i khans living on the next street joked about raiding these buildings and releasing the prisoners.

100 Wright (2001: 160–71) describes these classes for couples. The Islamic Republic has encouraged family planning and birth control since 1987; previously it had proclaimed that population control was un-Islamic.

101 For the members of his first cabinet in 2013, President Rouhani chose technocrats with American or European graduate degrees and not revolutionary guards, unlike his predecessor.

102 The regime created all-female police and military units to serve in these capacities, especially to impose dress codes. It required separate entrances to government buildings and airport terminals for women and men, with female employees searching all females.

103 Khomeini's remarks (1989; n.d. [1990]: 26, 44) are part of his last will and testament and are also found in *Nomads from the Imam's Perspective* (Supreme Council for Nomads of Iran, 1987). ONA's journal about nomads, published periodically since 1982, is titled *Zakhayir-i inqilab* (Treasures of the revolution).

104 Before and after 1945, a few Qermezi men had used rifles when they robbed vehicles on highways, but by the late 1960s increased surveillance by police and gendarmes and harsh punishments made the activity too dangerous. When two armed Qermezi men stopped a truck late one night and confiscated the boxes it carried, only to find later that they now possessed thousands of crudely manufactured metal forks, they reevaluated the risks and rewards inherent in this activity. (At the time, they ate only with their fingers.)

105 Mahdavi (2009) offers examples of these sanctions.

106 M. Milani (1994: 146). Mustazafin is "a loose term used to depict the general populace": the poor, masses, powerless, disinherited, exploited, and dispossessed (Abrahamian 1989: 22). Writers often translate the term as the "deprived." Abrahamian (1993: 27) considers the term "a broad subjective category" and explains its expansion to include some sectors of the middle class. The Islamic Republic, set up initially by clergymen as the "rule of the oppressed," gradually changed its focus after Khomeini's death to be the "rule of the 'arrogants' of wealth and power" (*mustakbirin*) (Nomani and Behdad 2006: 196–97). Khomeini seems to have lost interest by 1984 in supporting the impoverished. After Ahmadi-nejad's election as president in 2005, the neoconservatives claimed they would

140 *The revolution and the Islamic Republic*

return the focus of government policy to the "oppressed" (Ehteshami and Zweiri 2007), but they did not do so. These kinds of terms—mustakbirin (palace dwellers, nefarious oppressors, proprietors) and mustazafin (shantydwellers, the disinherited)—often appear in rhyming pairs. The term "deprived" (mahrum) means that someone is responsible for the deprivation. The concept leads people to make demands on the state to repair past wrongs (Chehabi 1997: 248).

107 Talebi (2013: 141).
108 A militia unit of Ahl-i Haqq (members of an esoteric Shiʻi sect found primarily among Iran's Kurds) fought alongside other basijis during the Iraq-Iran war (Mir-Hosseini 1994: 224).
109 Hiro (1985: 168–69). "Tribal people were put under considerable pressure to join up and undergo what the government called 'training suitable to their temperament'" (Omid 1994: 118). Elsewhere in her book, Omid uses the term "tribal" to refer to ethnic minorities, only some of whom are tribally organized, and her reference in this and other statements is unclear. The journal *Zakhayir-i inqilab* (vol. 19, 1992) includes photographs of nomad militiamen (Lurs, Bakhtiyari, Arabs, and Kurds).
110 Rakel (2009: 87).
111 Amuzegar (1993: 324). Adelkhah (2000: 9–29) discusses taxation under the Islamic Republic. Iran is one of the lowest taxed economies in the world (Moghadam 2000: 257).
112 Adelkhah (2000: 114–15) and Harris (2010) discuss the application of zakat and khums.
113 Moslem (2002). The largest, most powerful of Iran's foundations, the Sacred Precinct of Imam Reza (*astan-i quds-i Razavi*), predates the revolution and has handled the assets bequeathed to the shrine of the eighth imam in Mashhad.
114 Katouzian (2009: 363).
115 Adelkhah (2000: 53–54), Saeidi (2004).
116 This paragraph summarizes a passage in Keshavarzian (2007: 167–68). Maloney (2000) compares religious endowments (*vaqf*) and bunyads. The office of the supreme leader (rahbar) was another "state within a state." It was not open to scrutiny by the elected bodies or the judiciary. It used public money but was not held accountable for its expenditures.
117 Charitable foundations provided social benefits to only one wife of a deceased or wounded man (despite Islamic and state laws allowing a man up to four wives simultaneously).
118 Schirazi (1993: 164).
119 Contemporary Iran became "a huge martyrs' Welfare State designed to help the hundreds of thousands of families who have lost their sons in the war against Iraq" (Abrahamian 1989: 70).
120 Hiro (1985: 253).
121 Banuazizi (1994: 5); also Amuzegar (1993: 100–102). The Foundation for the Oppressed dominated 40 percent of Iran's economy in the 1980s and early 1990s (Ansari 2007: 305), was Iran's largest real-estate developer, and may have been the largest economic entity in the Middle East (Nomani and Behdad 2006: 45, 197).
122 Martin (2003: 172).
123 Parastatal foundations with limited impact on the Qashqa'i include the Housing Foundation (*bunyad-i maskan*), which was formed in 1979 to assist in sheltering the poor, especially in rural, depressed, and "tribal" areas. After the war's ceasefire, it participated in reconstruction efforts. It did not play any role among the Qermezi but might have helped other Qashqa'i. The Imam's Relief Committee (*komiteh-yi imdad-i imam*, meaning Khomeini), established just after his return to Iran, offered cash and consumer goods to the elderly, rural poor, refugees, victims of the war's collateral damage, and people suffering from natural disasters (Harris 2010). The Fifteenth of Khurdad Foundation (*bunyad-i punzdah-yi Khurdad*)

The revolution and the Islamic Republic   141

provided aid to widows, orphans, and victims of the war. Mohammad Reza Shah had arrested Khomeini on this date in 1963. The Foundation for Economic Mobilization (*bunyad-i basij-i iqtisadi*) was established after the war's outbreak to administer the domestic distribution of consumer goods and to allocate coupons.

124 Schirazi (1993: 263–71) outlines two processes concerning councils as they pertain to Iran's rural populations. First, "local" councils were part of a broad scheme for Iran as a whole that was put into law in 1979, stipulated in the 1979 constitution, passed by parliament in 1982, and yet not implemented by the government until 1999, after Khatami was elected as president. Second, "village" councils were quickly set up by Construction Jihad and the Ministry of Agriculture throughout Iran after 1979, and they covered "ninety-six percent" (Construction Jihad's figure) of the rural population by 1987 (Schirazi 1993: 268). The government's inability until 1999 to implement "local" councils limited the functions of the "village" councils. With the government's focus on municipal councils beginning in 1999, "village" councils increased in importance in some areas.

125 Factory and oil workers had formed councils during strikes in 1978. Some of these councils persisted after Khomeini's arrival, and revolutionary guards replaced some of them with Islamic associations. Peasants in Kurdistan, Turkman Sahra, and Gorgan formed councils in late 1978 and early 1979, sometimes directed by outside leftists, and revolutionary guards suppressed them. Some of these councils expressed ethnic-minority demands. Industrial factories, oil-industry and railway workers, air-force cadets, state administrative offices, municipalities, commercial farms, and poor urban neighborhoods elected (or were appointed) councils as popular, grassroots, and decentralized organizations during or soon after the revolution (Anonymous 1980; A. Bayat 1983, 1988, 1997; Goodey 1980).

126 E. Hooglund (1982a: 126–30).

127 The Supreme Court also abolished any laws still on the books if they violated the court's understanding of Islamic law.

128 Farvar (2003: 6, 17) notes that Iran's parliament passed a new law in 2003 for "tribal" councils. He probably means "nomads'" councils.

129 Ehteshami and Zweiri (2007: 7; also pp. 29, 34) note incorrectly (as do other writers) that the February 1999 council elections "marked for the first time that the Iranian people had directly elected their mayors and other local representatives."

130 By contrast, the state did not require parliamentary candidates or elected deputies to live in or originate from the districts they would represent.

131 Some say that Islamic rule is based on consultation. A Quranic phrase derived from two verses (*ayat*) (*amrahum shurayih binahum*) is written in Arabic on the seal of the Islamic councils of Qermezi nomads.

132 A family needed to present the deceased's identity card before a hospital or morgue would release the body (and thus authorize its transport to a location for washing and preparing for burial). The burial itself (at least outside of cities) seemed not to require any formal government permission. The Janikhani Qashqa'i family did need state authorization (and bribery) to bury its members in certain Tehran and Shiraz cemeteries, even where it owned burial plots where other loved ones were already interred.

133 The only son of a deceased man was exempt from military service because he was responsible for the care of his mother and siblings.

134 The government lowered Iran's voting age from 16 to 15 in 1981, raised it again to 16 in 2005, and raised it to 18 in 2007 (in the last case to counteract the rising number of young voters who supported the reformists). Fifteen translates as 16 according to a Western system of calculating age. In Iran, a child is 16 during its fifteenth year of life; in the West, this same child turns 15 after completing the fifteenth year.

142   *The revolution and the Islamic Republic*

135 I had never before (or since) heard any Qermezi spontaneously utter the word "taghuti," a Quranic term (meaning "satanic" and false gods) used by Iranians, especially after the revolution. Khomeini and others deployed the word when referring to the hated associates of the fallen regime: the shah and the royal family, the West-oriented secular elite, and modernists without religious roots.

136 Clerics assigned to local ONA offices supplied appropriate, Islam-connected names from lists their superiors had issued.

137 Qairkhbaili men explained the derivation of their lineage name as "40 families" ("bailay" meaning lineage or family group).

138 Other Qermezi jested that the lineage name meant "40 voices, each saying something different." ONA's notion that the name referred to "40 leaders" confirmed the joke.

139 Amir Ajami (personal communication, 25 May 2011) notes that rich farmers influenced the shura in Shishdangi village near Shiraz in 2002.

140 Rubin (2001: 2).

141 Akhavi (1986: 67).

142 Katouzian (2009: 359).

143 Rubin (2001: 44–87). Ansar-i Hezbollah began acting as a distinct group in 1989, adopted its name in 1993, and became recognizable in 1995 when its members attacked Abdolkarim Soroush (a leading religious intellectual) and disrupted the funeral of Karim Sanjabi (an activist in the National Front and the Liberation Movement of Iran, a member of the first postrevolutionary cabinet, and a Kurd who supported ethnic-minority rights). The organization played an often coercive role in parliamentary and presidential elections in 1996 and thereafter, by supporting conservative hard-liners and by representing war veterans, martyrs' families, and the basij militia. Its members crushed peaceful demonstrations against the closure of pro-Khatami newspapers (such as *Salaam*) in 1999 and subsequently.

144 Loose, untucked shirts helped to conceal the outlines of the men's genitals and conveyed their concern about bodily modesty.

145 Qashqa'i tribal leaders often grew prominent mustaches, which were symbolic of Qashqa'i autonomy and men's pride in their military prowess.

146 Many Qashqa'i and other women resisted and defied the regime by wearing tight overcoats or long blouses, flimsy headscarves, heavy makeup, and open-toed shoes.

147 The assassin of Neda Agha-Soltan in the 2009 post-election demonstrations was dressed in ordinary street clothes. When the irate crowd searched him, they found and displayed his basij militia card. Her death became a symbol of the resistance movement.

148 The two earlier stages are *muqaddamat* (introductory, approximately seven years, equivalent to high school) and *sath* (intermediate, approximately eight years, equivalent to university). The third stage (kharij, equivalent to graduate school) leads the student toward becoming an Islamic canonist (*mujtahid*, equivalent to a doctoral degree). *Kharij-i fiqh* is the highest religious degree. Buchta (2000) discusses the hierarchy of Shi'i clergy in Iran.

149 The supreme leader continued to appoint his personal representatives (almost all clergymen) to all major government institutions at the national and provincial levels and to all parastatal foundations. Clerics also occupied high-level posts in the regular army, other security forces, revolutionary-guard corps, and the basij militia. As a prominent example of the decline in the influence of clergymen in some other sectors of society, the number of clerics elected to parliament after the revolution has diminished significantly, from clergymen possibly being a slight majority in the first session to only a few men in the last few sessions. Voters realized that clerical politicians were no better than their nonclerical counterparts (Hiro 2005: 48, 353).

150 This individual requested anonymity.

The revolution and the Islamic Republic   143

151 Pious dissimulation (*taqiyya*), the practice of concealing a person's religious identity under threatening circumstances, has been common in Iran through history. I explain (Beck 2013, n.d. a) that the practice also applies to people who want to hide their ethnic, linguistic, and/or tribal identities.
152 The government in the late 1980s and early 1990s restricted maternity leaves and other family benefits to only the first three children, in an effort to control population growth.
153 The chant "American Islam!" (islami-yi amrika) (as compared with islami-yi nabi-yi mohammadi, the pure Islam of the prophet Mohammad) expressed the Iranian regime's antagonism toward Saudi Arabia and its close political and military ties with the U.S. The phrase also means an imperialistic Islam.
154 Hyder (2005) discusses the importance of Zainab for Shi'i Muslims.

4 Reclaiming culture: The politics of resistance and defiance

Reflections on 1992

The Qashqa'i sharpened their sentiments about their cultural, ethnic, linguistic, tribal, regional, and national-minority identities at the time of the revolution and the Islamic Republic's formation and further intensified them during the following decades. They experienced a heightened sense of the Qashqa'i as a minority group and suffered political and social discrimination in ways similar to and yet different from that under the shahs' regimes.

The Qashqa'i endeavored after the revolution to preserve their Turkish heritage, especially their language, in the face of increasing Persian and Arabic incursions. They retained traditional Qashqa'i attire, despite state prohibitions, and grew more enthusiastic about Qashqa'i customs, especially music, dance, and rituals. Women revitalized the styles and designs used in the past for weaving. People accentuated and perpetuated what they regarded was a Qashqa'i lifestyle, including migrating seasonally, living in the mountains, dwelling in black goat-hair tents, tending livestock, relying on customary technologies and natural resources, and separating themselves from non-Qashqa'i society.

In this chapter, I examine Qashqa'i culture as people expressed it through attire, religious belief and practice, and ritual and ceremony, all of which reflected their contact with and attitudes toward the new regime. I describe two weddings in 1992 to illustrate changes and continuities in Qashqa'i culture.

Attire

A potent symbol of Islam and revolutionary change in Iran is people's attire, especially women's. How the Qashqa'i responded to new national regulations specifying modest Islamic dress pertains to the extent of the Islamic Republic's power and the degree of the people's integration in the wider Iranian society.

Since the late 1920s, Iran's shahs had prohibited or condemned some features of men's ethnic dress but not women's.[1] By contrast, the Islamic Republic did not forbid or discourage people from wearing ethnic dress unless the attire violated what the regime defined as Islamic values.[2] Still, Qashqa'i women asserted—and were allowed—certain freedoms of dress and appearance unavailable to most other Iranian women and for reasons having little or nothing to do with Islam.

The politics of resistance and defiance   145

Qashqa'i men's apparel during the first half of the twentieth century had consisted of loose pants, a simple collarless shirt, a sleeved cloth cloak secured by a wide cummerbund, and a brimless felt hat.[3] After 1941 most men adopted a beige or tan felt hat with two upstanding flaps above the ears, which became, and remains, the preeminent Qashqa'i symbol. Herders often used a long-sleeved felt cloak to protect them against the elements. During warfare and celebrations, men wore a diaphanous cloak bound by a braided, tassel-ended cord. By the 1960s most Qashqa'i men adopted for their everyday attire the clothes seen among the region's villagers and consisting of loose trousers and long-sleeved collared shirts. They often donned suit pants and jackets for trips to town and the khans' camps. Many men continued to wear the distinctive Qashqa'i hat, although state agents and other city dwellers sometimes harassed them for appearing as unsophisticated peasants or menacing highway robbers. The Islamic Republic's rules for male attire and appearance did not affect most Qashqa'i men, whose clothes already modestly covered the body. Young men adopting Western fashions and demeanors, including tight jeans, open-necked and short-sleeved shirts, and long hair, were accosted by revolutionary guards and mobile morals squads and were criticized by regime supporters.

Until 1979 most Qashqa'i women and girls had worn a thin diaphanous headscarf pinned loosely under the chin and exposing the hair around the face. After the revolution, enforcers and supporters of the Islamic Republic insisted that girls nearing puberty and all women should conceal all their hair, in line with what became national law.[4] Some Qashqa'i women and girls, especially those interacting with the wider Iranian society, responded by donning an opaque scarf to cover much of their hair, often worn in long braids. Now wearing a square scarf folded in half and knotted under the chin like many other women in Iran, they complained that they could no longer don the multicolored silk headband. Women had loosely tied this headband, a distinctive feature of Qashqa'i attire, at the back of the head, over the diaphanous scarf, its long ends trailing down the back. The new style of scarf also conflicted with the rest of their customary dress, which consisted of multiple voluminous skirts gathered at the hips, a loose tunic slit up the sides to the waist, and a short form-fitting jacket, all in vibrant, often sparkling fabrics and all adorned with sequins, beads, and metallic embroidery. "We are Turks [Qashqa'i] only from the neck down. We are Tats from the neck up." The Qashqa'i use the deprecatory term "Tat" for any Tajik, by which they mean anyone who is not a Turk or who does not follow a Qashqa'i Turkish way of life. "Tajik" is also synonymous with "Persian" for them.

Qashqa'i women did insist on wearing brightly multicolored, boldly patterned scarves, which they ornamented along the hems with fringe and beads in contrasting colors. Urban women, pressured or forced by the regime to wear somber, solid colors (black, navy blue, dark grey, dark brown), were unable to make these kinds of decision for themselves, especially during the first decade of Islamic rule. Qashqa'i women did not cover the hair around their face, as

146 *The politics of resistance and defiance*

the regime required urban women to do during the first decade, nor did they conceal their body in the ways demanded of urban women, even when they visited town.

The Islamic Republic compelled urban women to wear an enveloping head-to-toe veil-wrap (chadur) or a lengthy loose overcoat (*mantu*, from the French *manteau*) and hair-concealing hood (*maqnai*) or scarf (*rusari*) fitting closely around the face. Some institutions such as universities and state agencies (especially in provincial towns) required women to wear a black chadur over their overcoat and hood or scarf, for travel to and from school and work, and some other women adopted this style when in public.

By the mid-1980s most Qashqa'i women donned a chadur, usually light-colored and patterned, when they went to town but did not wrap it fully around their head and body. The garment did not cover them or the vivid clothes they wore underneath, especially the expansive skirts. Qashqa'i women living in cities said they admired the freedom of expression these other women were determined to maintain. Yet the wearers complained that they looked ridiculous, forced to put on a chadur over layered clothes that already covered them sufficiently.

At a state-sponsored Qashqa'i cultural festival in Tehran in 1996, middle-class urban Persian women viewing the ornate, appealing clothes of the female Qashqa'i participants and spectators denounced their own plain, restrictive attire. "Why does the government force us to be so concealed when these women are so independent? Why do only we (and not they) 'endanger Islam' if we don't cover our hair? Do we have to join a tribe to escape the government's harsh clothing laws?" Using the term "tribe" derogatorily, they grumbled that they could choose how they looked only if they demeaned themselves by joining a tribe. (Many urban Iranians viewed tribes as primitive polities threatening modern society, while others romanticized tribes and their quaint customs.) For these urban Persian women, wearing state-mandated modest dress seemed to be worse than being a tribal person. They lacked an understanding of tribal identity and assumed that outsiders could acquire such an affiliation if they chose to do so. Hearing these women's grievances, a Qashqa'i man protested, "Let these Persians fight for their own rights! We [the Qashqa'i] are living under restrictions because of *them*! *They* brought us this government, so let *them* figure out a way to change its policy if they disapprove of it!"

Many Qashqa'i blamed Persians, whom they sometimes called "Iranians" (*irani*), for the restrictive Islamic regime. Under most circumstances, they did not consider themselves "Iranians," whom they equated with the dominant Persian-speaking population. Persians did not necessarily object to this disassociation; they already equated "Persian" and "Iranian" (and often excluded those who were not Persians from the category of "Iranian").

The Islamic state required Qashqa'i girls to wear modest attire while attending the nomads' elementary schools, and some of them abandoned some features of customary Qashqa'i dress, at least on schooldays. Their teachers, almost all of them Qashqa'i and the rest from similar, neighboring tribal

The politics of resistance and defiance   147

groups, exercised discretion in this matter and could relax the standards if they chose. Hearing that a school inspector planned to visit, they instructed the girls to moderate their dress for that day. Some schoolgirls wore plain trousers, full-skirted overdresses, overcoats or long jackets, and headscarves, often unadorned and in drab, solid colors, and they were similar in dress to the region's non-Qashqa'i village girls. Others adapted Qashqa'i dress to meet the new rules. (The state required urban girls in elementary and secondary schools to wear concealing monochrome uniforms, sometimes with white hoods, and they were even more restricted in their style and color of clothing.) Qashqa'i girls did continue to attend the nomads' primary schools with boys, unlike urban and many village girls. When they completed their formal education, which for some girls meant finishing the fifth grade, many resumed wearing customary Qashqa'i dress full time, often including the translucent scarf.[5]

Employed as a schoolteacher, Afsaneh Qermezi dressed in full compliance with ministerial and provincial regulations, all her body except for her face and hands covered with layers of black cloth. If she had taught in a nomads' elementary school in seasonal pastures or in an all-Qashqa'i village, she could have dressed less severely, but she served a large village where other female teachers and most of her students were not Qashqa'i. At home with her family, she substituted a multicolored patterned scarf for her other head coverings and displayed the hair around her face.

An elderly Qermezi woman living in Atakula village stopped wearing the full version of customary Qashqa'i dress shortly after the revolution so she could adopt a form of Islamic dress as defined by the regime and as stipulated by her many sons, said to be extremist hezbollahis. Then her daughter's son was killed in the war against Iraq. Full of anguish for this cherished boy, she promptly resumed wearing full Qashqa'i attire. "I wore Islamic dress," she told her family, "but what difference did it make? Did it keep my grandson safe? Now, dressed in black, I mourn for him." She blamed the Islamic regime for the boy's death, which came years after Khomeini could have accepted a ceasefire, and she withdrew her support, despite entreaties from her sons. Many middle-aged and virtually all elderly women maintained their customary style of clothing including the diaphanous scarf, and the only change they allowed was to darken the colors. Elderly women, often widows, always wore black or other dark, often solid, colors both before and after the revolution.

Qermezi women did not attribute their changes in attire to Islam per se but rather to the demands of those who had seized state power. They said that religion was not an issue for these men, who wanted only to exert control over others. The government's enforcers during the 1980s, particularly revolutionary guards, issued stern reprimands to and threatened sanctions against the close kinsmen of these women, including physical coercion and denial of state services, if they did not comply.[6] Some women also blamed the inflationary economy for changes in the attire of their daughters. "Village" clothes (often loose pants, an overdress, and a headscarf) were cheaper to sew and easier to maintain

148 *The politics of resistance and defiance*

than Qashqa'i clothing, which required dozens of meters of expensive, often imported, sometimes fragile fabric and decorative trim.

Most Qermezi women escaped the regime's fluctuating attempts since 1979 to enforce dress codes because their locations were usually remote and often isolated. For urban women, a particular appearance—such as visible hair, exposed toes, evidence of cosmetics, or revealing or inappropriate attire—that one week provoked assaults by revolutionary guards, hezbollahis, and mobile morals squads might not provoke them the next week. These vacillations correlated with political struggles in Iran. When people opposing the regime threatened the dominance of hard-line conservatives, reactionary forces subjected urban women to increased surveillance, coercion, and control. A journalist notes, "Women are the barometers of Iranian politics. One look at how much ankle or calf is showing or how much hair can be seen beneath the veil and the colour of the headscarf tells a book about the regime's level of toleration."[7]

By the mid-1990s revolutionary guards and other state enforcers focused less attention on Qashqa'i women's clothing, and women now enjoyed even more liberties in the choice of style and color. Attending wedding celebrations, many dressed in full Qashqa'i attire including the transparent scarf, even if non-Qashqa'i male outsiders were present. Thousands of glittering sequins and beads, often sewn in the elaborate designs that women also used in weaving, decorated their scarves and tunics. These scarves conveyed multiple messages. Women were defying the regime by featuring their fully visible hair (which they now often wore loose and flowing down their chest and back, instead of in tight braids). They were also proclaiming their freedom to reassert their cultural heritage, as symbolized by these ancient designs. Increasingly, Qashqa'i women resumed wearing full Qashqa'i dress on a daily basis, especially when residing in or visiting winter and summer pastures.

Renewed national, often state-sponsored, interest in (even fascination with) Iran's ethnic minorities—especially nomads and others perceived as picturesque and exotic—contributed to the resumption of full Qashqa'i dress. (Almost all of these ethnic minorities are Muslim, and many are also Shi'i. Several of Iran's non-Muslim religious minorities, especially Bahais, received a less charitable response.) Public cultural festivals, statewide celebrations of the annually observed Day of the Nomad, television programs, films (such as *Gabbeh*), the popular print media, photography books, and postcards displayed in street-side kiosks prominently featured customarily attired Qashqa'i women and legitimized the images they presented.[8]

The Islamic Republic exploited images of the Qashqa'i and other ethnic minorities in its efforts to appeal to foreigners. For journalists, businessmen, diplomats, and tourists, women in full Qashqa'i dress contrasted stunningly with dour-faced women obscured by black chadors. Even the staunchest regime supporters said that Qashqa'i women softened the image of Iran for an international audience and made the country seem less threatening and angry.[9]

Still forced to wear restrictive, conservative, dark attire, urban women of all socioeconomic classes complained resentfully about the double standard.

Why, they wanted to know, were Iran's ethnic minorities able to dress as they wished, regardless of so-called Islamic notions of decency, while the government still forced the Persian "majority" to observe strict standards? Urban women were not suggesting that these minorities should dress like them, to be more covered. Rather, they, too, wanted to escape the restraints.

Mounted in airport terminals in Shiraz and Isfahan and available in handicraft shops and bookstores in urban centers in the 1990s, a popular photograph (rendered as posters and postcards) of three young Qashqa'i women at a wedding depicts them standing with their backs to the camera, their faces not visible. Initially I saw the image as one simply displaying the vibrant, exotic clothing, but then I realized that the officials in charge of such public spaces still maintained certain proprieties by not showing any faces. A scene in an Iranian film shown in Iran in the mid-1990s depicts an urban Persian woman returning home from work and making the initial gestures of removing her scarf as she enters a bedroom. Viewers imagine her inside the room completing the act, without the filmmakers risking censorship by actually revealing her scarf-less. Likewise, those seeing the photograph of the young Qashqa'i women could imagine them turning around and offering their faces and their only partially covered hair.

Public appropriation of the dress of Qashqa'i women took bizarre forms when people who were not Qashqa'i were inspired by these apparently alluring and yet liberating images. In one case, an upper-class Persian woman wore Qashqa'i dress to hide her "ever more ample figure."[10] Another upper-class Persian woman wore "a traditional tribal costume" (possibly Qashqa'i or Baluch garments) when she received a government award at a public ceremony.[11] By doing so, she escaped wearing the regime-mandated, dark, concealing attire while also demonstrating her disapproval of it. Handicraft stores sold Qashqa'i and other ethnic attire, and shops in urban bazaars displayed such clothing for tourists as well as for the Qashqa'i. The American actor, Elizabeth Taylor, posed alluringly as an oriental odalisque in the Qashqa'i attire she had purchased in the Isfahan bazaar in 1976.[12]

Outside Iran, people also perceived Qashqa'i women's dress as appealing. In Orange County, California, a "Persian" cultural festival in 1998 featured dances performed by non-Qashqa'i Iranian women wearing elaborate Qashqa'i attire. Some enthusiastic participants and spectators, many in involuntary exile, said that Qashqa'i dress symbolized Iran before the country succumbed to the Islamic Republic's restrictions. Some noted, incorrectly, the anti-Islamic message offered by the attire.[13] To celebrate the Iranian New Year, some Iranians living in the United States encouraged their children to wear indigenous ethnic dress from Iran, including distorted Qashqa'i versions, despite being ignorant about the groups represented by the attire.[14]

Religious belief and practice

The basic religious faith, as expressed in love of God and ethical behavior, of the Qashqa'i as Shi'i Muslims is strong. Yet many resented or opposed the

150 *The politics of resistance and defiance*

new government's efforts to exploit Islam for political purposes, and the Islamic beliefs and practices most reiterated by the regime became tainted in their view.[15] As devout Muslims feared, "the main threat in Iran today [1994] to Islam as a faith is the experience of people under the Islamic government."[16]

Qermezi nomads viewed cynically the state's attempts to provide an Islamic explanation or justification for every circumstance, including the scarcity of chickens for sale in the bazaar and the prohibitions against wedding music but not military music. "Thanks to the delicately nuanced contingency of Islamic thought, and the possibility of widely varied but equally valid interpretations of scripture, the regime [in the early 1990s] is still claiming Islamic legitimacy for all its policies and strategies."[17] Qermezi residents of the town of Borujen and nearby villages, less publicly vocal in their skepticism, worried that their Persian and Lur neighbors, especially the merchants and state agents on whom they depended, would criticize them if they spoke their minds. The nomads and many village and town dwellers explicitly distinguished between their religious faith and the Islamic government's politics, which they disputed and resisted.

Tribal codes and customs rather than Islamic law (*sharia*) regulated the lives of Qermezi nomads and many villagers. Islamic law and its underpinnings had influenced such codes and customs in a general sense during past centuries, just as they had affected the wider Iranian society, but most Qermezi were unaware of the details. Some stated that certain rules came from Islam even though they were not apparently connected. They claimed that other customs were tribal and specific to the Qashqa'i, when indeed they were compatible with Islamic values and might have derived from or been influenced by Islam. As elsewhere in Iran and in Muslim society in general, codified Islamic (and secular) laws might not have affected how people actually lived, an issue often unacknowledged in the literature on Islam.[18] Dissemination of religious information through schools and modern technology in Iran, particularly via the state-controlled media, was changing the ways that many Qermezi viewed Islam, and not always in the direction intended by the regime.

The Islamic Republic's formation altered the public and personal religious lives of only some Qermezi. Before 1979 very few nomads had performed the five daily prayers (often combined in Iran in three prayer sessions), and few began to pray after the revolution. A man explained that women in his community were unable to pray because their hard work and many children did not allow them any free time. He added that they lacked access to bathing facilities (and could not carry out required ablutions), and they did not understand Arabic (the required language of prayers, which most men who prayed also did not understand). After the revolution, some women residing in Atakula village began to pray (occasionally) because of pressure exerted by their husbands and older sons, who had fallen under the influence of the nearby town and who had also begun to pray. For the nomads, the term "hezbollahi" identified men who had "become religious" after the revolution, "the ones who now pray." (The term primarily signified a staunch regime supporter.) The closest

The politics of resistance and defiance   151

kinswomen of hezbollahis were the ones most likely to pray, at least when men were nearby, and not of their own choosing, they said. Religious instruction and programming in the media, particularly television, influenced the Qermezi villagers and town residents who had access to electricity. "The more we understand about the 'akhunds' Islam,' the more we are repelled," said one man in 1995. "The regime should have been advised to leave us alone with our religion. Now, we care less and less about Islam." All children in school received lessons in Islam, the Qur'an, and Arabic. Some nomads and most villagers and town dwellers held funeral and memorial rites at the nearest mosque, and women sometimes attended these gender-segregated services if space was provided for them.

Islamic law forbids compulsion in matters of religious practice, and yet the regime and its supporters often ignored the ruling. Some clergy instructed Iranians that, in "true Islam," Muslims should lead and not compel. Such an idealized situation was not the personal experience of many Qermezi, who said they sometimes felt obliged to obey the people who exerted control over them. Subjected to mandatory prayers and fasting in schools, children expressed confusion about their duties.

Few nomads fasted during the month of Ramadan, before and after the revolution. Some village and town men and women did fast, or at least they behaved publicly as if they did. Before the revolution, only several Qermezi men had gone as pilgrims to Imam Reza's tomb in Mashhad, and no one had traveled to Mecca. After the revolution, a few men ventured on these trips, and several women accompanied them to Mashhad. Unprecedentedly, two Qermezi newlywed couples took honeymoon excursions to Mashhad in the mid-2000s. These participants seemed more enthusiastic about the adventure than about any accruing religious merit.[19]

Women more than men before 1979 had invoked the names of a few historical figures in Islam in their daily speech, as in, "Oh Ali, help me to lift this load." They rarely did so by the 1990s. Some noted that they still revered these individuals but did not approach them as they used to do. Their formally educated sons sometimes chided them for these exclamations. Clergymen also discouraged people from calling on these individuals for mundane purposes, a practice they labeled as improper.

Islamic beliefs and practices also relate to healthcare. The nomads used to rely on their own herbalists, curers, and bone setters and on non-Qashqa'i itinerants who visited Qermezi camps and villages to dispense prayers, prepare amulets, counteract the evil eye, and assist people in making and fulfilling vows. After the revolution, some urban clergymen declared that any practitioners who asserted enhanced legitimacy because of their reputed status as darvishes and sayyids acted out of ignorance and superstition, and that their treatments were not part of Islam and were forbidden. Fewer women placed protective, Islam-related amulets on their young children as they had always done before 1979. They said they were not sure if these objects were efficacious anymore. Most clergy condemned the routine use of such religious

152   The politics of resistance and defiance

symbols, as women explained it. Women's use of indigenous—or what they considered non-Islamic—amulets, particularly auspicious shapes carved from special wood, increased.

Ritual and ceremony

Soon after the revolution, the Islamic Republic banned activities its ruling clergy considered immoral or un-Islamic.[20] The regime's regional enforcers and local supporters prohibited Qashqa'i music, dance, and the stick-fighting game (an aggressive yet choreographed dance performed to music), activities that had helped in the past to define the Qashqa'i as a distinctive group in Iran.[21] People experienced the loss of these expressive forms sharply. For more than a decade, coercive state agents had forbidden them to include these socially and symbolically meaningful performances in their wedding celebrations, one of only two occasions when the Qashqa'i gather in large groups. The other occasion is funerals and memorial services.[22]

Specialized Qashqa'i musicians (ussa) play Qashqa'i music on oboes and large and small skin drums, and its distinctive rhythmic sounds carry long distances. Revolutionary guards and committees declared that the sensually arousing rhythms of the drums stirred up illicit passions and that the drums combined with the oboe incited men's and women's smoldering desires. Thus they prohibited their playing. Outsiders—Westerners as well as some non-Qashqa'i Iranians—might view these amusements as trivial but they were vital expressions of cultural identity at a time when other aspects of the society were also threatened.

These restrictions, imposed primarily from outside, began to relax in 1990. A few Qashqa'i communities began to feature the oboe, without drums, at weddings. Men seeking close ties to the regime, however, did not permit the oboe at their weddings. In one group, only one man objected to the instrument on what he claimed were religious grounds. His motivations were, in fact, political. Acquiescing to his attempts to exert control, the other men held a wedding without music. When some men performed without interference the competitive stick-fighting game, accompanied by only the oboe, at several weddings in 1990, the news spread throughout Qashqa'i territory. People were exhilarated. In some places in 1991 and everywhere in Qashqa'i territory in 1992, musicians were again performing at many such gatherings, a response to decreased surveillance and control by the regime and increased local, Qashqa'i demands. They played the drums along with the oboe without major disruption, and men reveled in being able to compete in the choreographed sport after a hiatus of 14 years. Practicing on the sidelines, boys eagerly learned the steps and motions.

Falling under the government's restrictions, Qashqa'i women could still dance privately if no men were present. Some nomads joked that the women lacked any such privacy, owing to the open terrain and open tents. Dancing requires music, also forbidden during this period. Women in villages could

The politics of resistance and defiance 153

dance within closed rooms to tape-recorded music played at low volume but they complained that such limitations made the effort hardly inspiring or uplifting.

During a wedding celebration in a small Darrehshuri village in 1991, women danced on a porch within a high-walled courtyard while their kinsmen chatted inside an adjoining room. Coming from a nearby town to watch, Persian revolutionary guards stood for several hours in the lane outside the courtyard and peeked through gaps in the doorframe. Relaxing, they tapped out the rhythm of the music issuing from an audiocassette player. When the hosts served the men in the room a meal of meat and rice, they invited the guards to join them, as the rules of hospitality seemed to require. Leaving the room after eating heartily, the guards sternly instructed the women, still on the porch, that they were forbidden to dance and must stop immediately.

The Qermezi struggled with the conflicting pressures on them in 1991–92 and were uncertain about the consequences if they took matters into their own hands. Almost all of them wanted to celebrate as they had done before the revolution but they still feared possible government reprisals, especially because they depended on services from state agents. When they saw that other Qashqa'i groups were increasingly ignoring the regime's restrictions, without sanctions against them, they became more willing to act on their own behalf.

Practically all Qermezi weddings after 1992 featured live music, stick fighting, and men's and women's dance. (According to Qashqa'i custom, the recent death of a distant relative meant a simpler, less exuberant ceremony out of respect for the mourners. The death of a close relative forced a wedding's postponement.) The subtribe's few hezbollahis did not permit their immediate families to engage in these festive activities, still forbidden and condemned by the regime. As some of them grew less strict by 2000, they began to tolerate live music, but only for men's stick fighting and not for women's public dancing. Changing their ideological proclamations to support their changing behavior, they justified the music and sport as integral to the Qashqa'i culture, which they now said was not historically or inherently un-Islamic.

At a large jubilant wedding held by a wealthy Darrehshuri group in an orchard in summer pastures in 1997, the hosts boasted that they had bribed the Persian revolutionary guards assigned to a nearby village with cash and thus could celebrate with music and dance without interference. Even throughout the 1980s, a period of strictly enforced government restrictions, elite Qashqa'i families holding wedding celebrations in urban hotels, reception halls, and restaurants routinely paid the local enforcers so that the celebrants could enjoy live music, men's and women's dance, and no constraints on women's hair, attire, cosmetics, or interactions with men. On these occasions, most women wore customary Qashqa'i dress with translucent headscarves, their hair fully visible. Other Qashqa'i women, their hair completely uncovered, wore tight Western-style dresses and danced provocatively like urban Persians they had seen.[23]

The Qermezi and other Qashqa'i understood that the Islamic regime's attempted control over certain forms of music, dance, attire, appearance, and

154 *The politics of resistance and defiance*

male–female interaction since 1979 affected all Iranians and was not aimed solely at the Qashqa'i. They did note that their society and culture were harmed nonetheless and that their children were growing up without understanding the full meaning of being Qashqa'i. Persianizing, Islamizing, and Arabizing pressures and influences simultaneously bombarded these children through their schools, the media, and their intensified contact with the wider Persian-dominated society. Their parents said that this wider context made mandatory their efforts to enhance Qashqa'i culture, especially through symbolic means. They explained the regime's prohibitions as efforts to control and coerce Iran's citizens and further integrate them in a more unified, more complacent whole.[24]

Nasir Qermezi's wedding

Qermezi nomads celebrated two weddings in summer pastures in September 1992 just before they began the autumn migration to winter pastures. Separated by three days, the weddings differed in circumstances but still expressed the prevailing attitudes of the vast majority of the tribespeople. They highlighted the importance that the Qermezi placed on restoring and renewing their cultural life.[25] An account of these celebrations also addresses other substantive issues raised in this book.

Nasir Qermezi of Aqa Mohammadli lineage was a traditional nomadic pastoralist who migrated seasonally between Dashtak and Hanalishah. Over the years he had carefully considered the alliances he hoped to form through the marriages of his three sons and six daughters. He had linked all but one of them by 1992, and this impending union now drew his attention. Seven of his children had married their first or second cousin in the Aqa Mohammadli lineage and the eighth her first cousin (her father's sister's son) in the Imamverdili lineage.

Unlike most Aqa Mohammadli and other Qermezi men, Nasir had married a woman from outside the Qermezi subtribe. Humayil comes from the Shaikh Lur lineage whose members lived near Dogonbadan in winter pastures. (Shaikh is only a name and not a religious title.) Her group was once part of a Boir Ahmad Lur tribe, and some of its members had allied with the Qermezi subtribe when the two groups occupied adjoining winter pastures near Dogonbadan. As the Qermezi headman, Shir Mohammad had even given the Shaikh Lurs one of his daughters, the only one to marry outside of Qermezi. (His five other daughters and all seven sons married Qermezi spouses.) A fellow lineage mate, Bai Mirza had also wanted to ally with the Shaikh Lurs, and so he chose a Shaikh Lur bride for his son Nimatullah.

These two marriages were, in a way, a mutual exchange. When Qashqa'i men sought a bride from outside their immediate tribal group, usually for political reasons, they often had to promise to give a girl in return. If they did not pledge to do so, the other group would probably refuse to turn over its own girl. As a powerful headman, however, Shir Mohammad would have

The politics of resistance and defiance   155

been more likely to choose a Shaikh Lur bride for one of his sons and to arrange for a fellow lineage mate to give a daughter to the Shaikh Lurs. Sending a daughter away threatened a group's integrity; accepting a bride from outside was not as damaging, especially because her children would trace descent from their father. A one-way marriage could mean the girl's abandonment; a two-way marriage promised continued contact between the two groups.

The two brides, the daughters of Shir Mohammad and Shaikh Ali Haidar, spent the rest of their lives among non-kin, and the Qermezi often lamented their sad fate. When a blood feud with Boir Ahmad Lurs forced the Qermezi group to flee the Dogonbadan area in 1945, the two women were separated even farther from their kin.

In the hostilities precipitating the feud, Boir Ahmad Lurs killed Nimatullah. Bai Mirza feared attacks against his other sons, and he left Dogonbadan along with other Qermezi families. He married his next-eldest son, Nasir (Nimatullah's half-brother), to Nimatullah's widow, Humayil, the Shaikh Lur woman. A young widow, with or without children, customarily married the brother of her deceased husband.

When Nasir broached the issue of their final child's marriage in 1992, Humayil insisted that they find a bride among her Shaikh Lur kin. She wanted to be closer to her natal family and its group, and her one remaining child was her last chance for a marriage alliance in that direction. Nasir reluctantly agreed, despite his interest in yet another marriage with his own close patrilateral kin. He had married two daughters to the sons of one of his half-brothers, and three marriageable daughters of his other half-brother Murad still lived at home. Nasir lacked any full brothers or sisters, and a marriage with a daughter of his half-brother Murad seemed the closest, best possible link for him. Nasir and Murad lived as neighbors at Dashtak and Hanalishah, and Murad's daughter would be able to see her natal family frequently. Still, Humayil's desire for a Shaikh Lur bride prevailed. She reminded Nasir that he had already chosen brides and grooms for his eight other children from among his own kindred.

As I heard people discuss the impending marriage in 1992 and asked about the family of the Shaikh Lur girl, many commented only that she is Qermezi's distant kin. Soon I discovered the details. The girl is Mali's daughter. A Shaikh Lur man, Mali had camped close to Borzu Qermezi in summer pastures at Hanalishah in 1971. I had known him and his family quite well at the time.[26] Mali had persisted as a nomadic pastoralist longer than many of his Shaikh Lur kinsmen, and he had sought to share pastures with the Qermezi at Hanalishah because his own kinsmen did not migrate that far north for summer pastures anymore. He needed a trustworthy group with which to live during the summer. Then I remembered that Mali and Humayil are siblings, and the new match in 1992 seemed not as farfetched as I had originally thought. It too was a first-cousin marriage, a union between a boy and the daughter of his mother's brother. A glance at Mali's genealogy showed me other Qermezi links I had forgotten. Mali's mother is Qermezi

156 *The politics of resistance and defiance*

as are the wives of three of his four brothers and the husbands of two of his three sisters.

When all Qermezi were nomadic pastoralists, some of them had found it expedient to ally occasionally with other tribes and subtribes so they could gain temporary access to alternative pastures in case their own were inadequate. The potential for sharing pasturage in other locations was the main reason people gave in 1970 for out-marriage. Such a strategy was not as relevant in 1992 as it used to be, and sometimes it was not pertinent at all. Instead, specifically social considerations had risen in importance. Renewed and reinforced alliances between families seemed to be the key reason for most marriage choices if they involved people outside Qermezi. At the same time that the Qermezi and their long-term affiliates were increasingly diversifying their economic activities and growing more spatially dispersed, they sought to use their kinship and marriage ties to draw them closer together again. Economic factors (especially the use of pastoral resources) were still important but not as primary as they used to be.

In the case of Nasir's last unmarried child, the son attended university and would begin his teaching career in a secondary school in Khunj, far to the south, where no Qermezi or Shaikh Lur people held any economic interests. Mali's family was pleased that the suitor had prepared for a respected profession and could support its daughter adequately, but the attraction she held for Nasir's family was that she was a "mother's brother's daughter," a purely social link without the wider pastoral and economic attributes that alliances used to stress. The link was not at all practical. The two families lived widely separated, which the nomads now computed in terms of driving time (at least nine hours during the summer and at least 12 hours during the winter), and the young couple would live even farther away from their natal families. No Qermezi or Shaikh Lur men lived within the other's group anymore. When the two groups sought to meet, they would do so because of their kinship and marriage ties, not because of any pastoral or other economic interests.

Some of these Shaikh Lurs had "become Qashqa'i" in terms of language, custom, and culture. Yet the Qermezi and other Qashqa'i continued to identify them as Lurs (the other large non-Persian ethnic group in the region) in the 1990s. I had not thought of them as Qashqa'i until I heard them speak Qashqa'i Turkish fluently and watched them engage comfortably in Qashqa'i customs. One man said to me, "Of course we speak Turkish. Our *mothers* are Qashqa'i!" Until the 1950s and 1960s, "being Qashqa'i" had meant powerful sociopolitical affiliations with a subtribe, a tribe, and the confederacy and with the leaders of each of these three groups. Then, after Mohammad Reza Shah dismantled the upper two levels of the Qashqa'i political hierarchy, "being Qashqa'i" increasingly centered on the people's sociocultural identity. Since the 1970s some Shaikh Lurs viewed themselves as Qashqa'i, similar to the way the Qermezi saw themselves, but the Qermezi still asserted the identity of the Shaikh Lurs as Lurs and not as Qashqa'i. For this reason, marrying with them was still problematic for many Qermezi.

The politics of resistance and defiance 157

On 9 September 1992, Nasir and his campmates at Hanalishah prepared for the wedding of Alamdar and Fatemeh. The camp contained one large extended family consisting of Nasir; his two independent, married sons (Nadir and Bahadur); and their respective wives and children. Some weeks earlier Nasir, Alamdar, and other family members had traveled to the bride's home near Dogonbadan where they discussed the terms of the marriage contract and then signed the document. Now preparing for a second trip, Nasir chartered a comfortable bus to transport his family and its Aqa Mohammadli relatives to Dogonbadan and back. He would collect the bride and any of her Shaikh Lur kin who wanted to come along (a possibility rarely if ever considered before 1979).[27] While the travelers enjoyed a ceremonial early-evening meal together before departing, others at Hanalishah pitched tents for the celebration, assembled supplies, and delivered last-minute invitations. Nasir expected hundreds of guests to arrive that evening and the next day, and he had rented from the town of Shahreza 20 categories of items, including 200 plates and sets of eating utensils (to be used, washed, and reused), serving platters, long plastic ground cloths, salt and pepper shakers, and enormous cooking pots. He had contracted with a Persian cook in Semirom to prepare the two main meals.

Before the first Qermezi death in the Iraq–Iran war in 1982, the Qermezi had always contributed their own supplies to all ceremonial, communal gatherings, and groups of Qermezi women had cooked for the multitudes. Yet the deaths caused by the war drew so many mourners that people began to rent equipment and hire cooks from outside. The families of each martyr could not handle all the necessary tasks for the five large commemorative events.

After dinner, those who planned to collect the bride hastened in their preparations while others decided spontaneously to go along despite their prior plans. En route to the camp, the chartered bus stalled in an irrigation ditch cutting across the lone dirt road through Hanalishah, and men ran to free it and help the driver to reverse directions. They saw that the bus could not reach the entrance to the wedding camp, and women worried about the return trip when they would need to escort the bride and her family with respect and in comfort and style.

The trip to Dogonbadan took nine hours, the party traveling all night and arriving early the next morning. Nasir had brought along the Darrehshuri musicians who would play that morning for the bride's family and kin group, and then they would return to his camp to perform there. The bride's family prepared an early noon meal while the groom's mother and other female kin dressed and readied the bride. The wedding party left in the early afternoon, with the bride's dowry goods packed in the back of the bus, and entered Hanalishah 10 hours later. People had assembled at Nasir's campsite to welcome the group and to sport and dance, but the bus had come too late at night for much festivity. Everyone was already exhausted, and more guests would appear at dawn. The musicians played briefly to announce the bride's arrival.

While waiting for the bride earlier that evening, Hanalishah's women and children had gathered at Nasir's camp. Already in a festive mood, they sought

158   *The politics of resistance and defiance*

sanctuary in the empty, canvas bridal tent. Two of Nasir's close patrilateral kinswomen, Zohreh and Huri, had brought from their homes an audiocassette player and worn-out tapes of Qashqa'i wedding music, and they prepared to dance. After lighting a propane-gas lantern and closing the tent flaps, they began the slow initial motions of the traditional Qashqa'i dance. As other women rose, they urged the girls present to copy their motions and join in. Despite the constraints of the small dark tent, the women were elated.

For most of these women, this occasion was the first time they had danced in a group in 14 years. The previous summer, a few of them had begun to dance, secluded behind a large goat-hair tent, at Bizhan Qermezi's wedding, but hostile remarks by several Qermezi hezbollahis there had inhibited others. After only a few minutes, the musicians had switched tunes to accompany the men's stick fighting.

Seemingly unprepared for dancing, some women in the small tent snatched the headscarves of the girls sitting among them. They needed these colorful cloths to accentuate their hand motions. The girls tried to regain their scarves and then attempted to cover their heads with their hands. Unaccustomed to being exposed, they were suddenly self-conscious, despite only women and children present. Their tangled, matted hair formed an unsightly mess, and the girls seemed more embarrassed by the disorder than by simply being scarf-less. They tried unsuccessfully to fix their hair with their fingers.

Also waiting for the bridal party that evening, Hanalishah's young men had stopped hoping for sport and dance and hurried to another celebration they had attended the previous day and thought was still ongoing. Held in a village east of Semirom, the festivity commemorated the marriage of a Qarehqanli Darrehshuri couple. Prior marriages linked the Qarehqanli and Qermezi subtribes, an alliance that afforded the young Qermezi men an opportunity for practicing their skills before the next day's intense competition.

That night, guests arriving for Nasir's wedding filled every Qermezi tent and house at Hanalishah, and Nasir's camp too was crowded. By dawn, everyone was awake, and by sunrise hundreds of people, elated by the prospects of the day-long festivities, were assembling at the wedding site.

This wedding would be the subtribe's first one to include all the activities prohibited by the Islamic regime since 1979: live music with oboes and drums, stick fighting, men's and women's dancing, women's diaphanous headscarves, and men's and women's relaxed interactions. The state's restrictions remained in place but people throughout Iran, not just in this small Qermezi group, were increasingly resistant to and defiant of them. At the same time, the regime's agents who had enforced the injunctions during the previous thirteen years were now hesitating to act against any protesters. Eager to resume their customary celebrations after the long hiatus, the Qermezi were anxious about possible repercussions, both negative and positive, which contributed further to their heightened emotions about these still-forbidden pleasures.

Nasir's kinsmen had pitched two large reception tents, one made of goat hair and the other of canvas, for the guests. They placed the goat-hair one

The politics of resistance and defiance   159

near the camp's center; it would be the social and ceremonial hub of the celebration. Men settled in the canvas tent while women gathered in and around the bride's small tent, and the long goat-hair reception tent remained peculiarly vacant. After quickly greeting the newly arrived bride and her kin, Zohreh and Huri again took charge of the women's entertainment. They moved to a semisecluded spot just behind the bridal tent, set up the cassette player and tapes of the previous evening, and prepared to dance.

Except for one woman who wore a diaphanous Qashqa'i scarf, the women and girls present wore the modest headscarves mandated by the regime. (Yet they had draped them to exhibit their hair, and the colors, designs, and trim were flamboyant.) From the Shaikh Lur community near Dogonbadan, the one exception was the wife of the bride's brother, whom the Qermezi women considered an odd spectacle. While they admired her courage in donning the traditional scarf, which displayed all her loose hair, they disapproved of her gaudiness. She had applied cosmetics to her face to exaggerate her eyes, eyebrows, mouth, and cheeks, and she had fashioned the bleached-blond bangs of her hair to curl up and over the scarf's edge. While the style of her Qashqa'i clothes—a tunic and long, full skirts—was identical to that of the Qermezi women, she had sewn them and the scarf from the same pink-hued fabric. Some elite Qashqa'i women had initiated this fashion, not yet seen among these Qermezi women, who still liked to mix different colors, patterns, fabrics, and textures as they had always done. Oblong metallic disks ornamented the woman's tunic and outer skirt, also mirroring the dress of elite Qashqa'i women and differing from the Qermezi women's attire. As the disks caught the early-morning sun, the woman stood out from the others, who appeared drab and colorless by comparison.

Later in the morning, a brave young Qermezi woman arrived wearing a transparent Qashqa'i scarf, and women and girls surrounded her with exclamations and congratulations. On my next visit, when I distributed photograph albums documenting events of the previous visit, everyone invariably noted that the picture of this one woman was the most stunning of the collection. They praised her courageous gesture, now historically recorded.

As more guests arrived by foot, car, van, and truck, women and girls joined the dancing behind the bridal tent, and their circle grew larger until others in the wedding camp could not avoid seeing them. Zohreh and Huri's initial impulse might have been to prevent certain men from witnessing them dance, just as they had carefully orchestrated the previous evening, but as the circle expanded and the dancers became more visible, the women were no longer so cautious. Their separation—at the very edge of the camp and behind a tent— had become largely symbolic. They were now obvious to anyone who cast his eyes in that direction.

Before the Islamic Republic, dancing was one of two dominant activities at Qashqa'i weddings. Women, girls, and some men and boys—accompanied by musicians—danced together in one large circle in the center of the wedding camp. Dancing and stick fighting initiated the celebrations and continued

160   *The politics of resistance and defiance*

until the end. When I first saw women at Nasir's wedding begin to dance behind the tent, I was disappointed, just as I had felt the night before when women had restricted their dancing to the dark, crowded interior of a closed tent. By the wedding's end, I viewed the women as heroic for pushing against the constraints that outsiders had forced on them. They could have chosen not to dance at all, or only within the bridal tent, or in a tight group hidden behind that tent. Instead, as their circle grew, no one attending the wedding could miss seeing them. The brilliant, often metallic-threaded scarves they waved as they danced—raising them up suddenly and then pulling them down as suddenly—could not help but draw the attention of others in the camp. People caught a flash of color and looked inadvertently.

As I realized later, Zohreh, Huri, and other women had been eager to dance the previous night and early this morning because they wanted it "on the record." Immediately on their arrival this morning, they began to dance rather than to take the time to greet the many guests as was customary and expected. As Nasir's kin, as Aqa Mohammadli lineage mates, and as Hanali-shah residents, they were obligated to share the responsibilities of hosting, to make the many guests from other Qermezi lineages and from outside this territory feel welcome and comfortable. The quality and reputation of the celebration would reflect not only on Nasir and his sons but also on their extended kin group, lineage, and territorial community.

Once the women began to dance and then continued, any men so inclined would have difficulty telling them to stop. Once the women had danced for some interval, could a few men instruct them that dancing was forbidden? Why had any men waited to act, if they had opposed the dancing? Now, no one could ever say that women had not danced at this wedding. As I came to understand later, Zohreh and Huri had intentionally set a precedent for the benefit of the women, the lineage, and the subtribe.[28]

Only a few men (and not any women) wanted to restrict women's dress, appearance, and behavior, a point that women often raised among themselves. "What exactly is going on?" they wanted to know. "Why aren't women a part of this discussion? Why are men looming over us like this? Does religion play any role in men's decisions about us, or do men just want to exert their dominance?"

At the same time that women began to dance, the wedding's hosts pitched a small open-sided tent for the musicians, close to the men's canvas reception tent. Some Qermezi men donned ceremonial cloaks and tasseled cords while the musicians readied their equipment and began the customary welcoming tunes that invited people to attend the wedding and partake in its festivities. Then they transitioned into the music for the men's sticking-fighting competition.

Men and boys quickly formed a circle around the first two players who had rushed forward with their sticks, and soon the crowd was thick. Boys, who had never witnessed a full expression of these fierce games, watched and later practiced on the sidelines. They tussled with one another to retrieve the sticks snapped in two by the men's aggressive attacks, displayed them as trophies,

The politics of resistance and defiance 161

and deployed them in their own sport. Older men who had competed in years past were distinct from younger men who had never participated before (but who had practiced among themselves without the benefit of live music and real competition). Men in both groups blamed the regime's ban for their impaired or inexperienced performances. Invoking Iran's ruling clergy, an older man lamented, "Oh turbaned ones, observe my disgraceful playing! I am so ashamed. But it is your fault!"

Sitting in the hot sun with the women, without the comforts enjoyed by the male guests, I again grew disappointed. I had thought that one of the two large reception tents would be women's but it remained vacant. The bridal tent was too small for all the women and children; the bride's kindred and its Lur and Persian acquaintances from Dogonbadan had already filled it. The hosts frequently offered the men, who relaxed in the shade of their spacious tent, hot tea, cold water, fruit, and sweets. The women and children received nothing.

The next event proved to be the wedding's turning point. In retrospect, it signified that the celebration was nearly over (and before the festivities had barely begun).

Told that the noon meal was imminent, the musicians stopped playing so the dusty performers and encircling spectators could wash. The hosts would serve the men in one large group, and the sport needed to pause. Eyeing the women's dancing all morning, the musicians now instructed young men to carry their felt mats and heavy drums to a row of parked vehicles alongside the women's semisecluded location in the sun. Following their equipment, they obviously intended to play so women could dance to live music (which women preferred to the old, sometimes barely audible, tapes). They would perform for half an hour and then return to the small tent where they had played earlier. Cars and trucks would shield the musicians, which seemed peculiar because they had played in the open before. Women's dancing, and not the musicians themselves, was the activity that needed to be hidden. In the past, musicians had remained in one place and alternated between the two types of music so players and dancers could each participate in turn. On this occasion, coping with the imposed gender separation, they graciously uprooted themselves so women could dance. Just as they reached the new temporary spot, I saw an unusual flurry of activity among some men on the camp's other side. Suddenly the same young men carried the mats and drums back to their original location. The women stood stunned, interrupted as they prepared to dance. Someone had decided that they could not do so.

As the men settled down in the canvas tent to enjoy the meal, the women waited for instructions about their own food. Often men ate first at these kinds of massive gatherings but preparations for the women would occur simultaneously. Several young men laid plastic strips in the still-empty goat-hair reception tent but only a few lower-status men who were not Qermezi—hired shepherds and drivers of the chartered vehicles—went there to eat. No one invited the women for lunch. When several mothers sent their young daughters to ask the host family where they should go for the meal, its women replied

162   *The politics of resistance and defiance*

that their kinsmen were responsible for the details. More than an hour later, young men spread clean plastic in the goat-hair reception tent, and women and children quickly assembled there. Food came promptly, and everyone seemed to return to good spirits. Then, almost all women and children returned to their former spot in the sun, and only a few Hanalishah women stayed behind.

Oddly, without any farewells, some Qermezi men, women, and children from Atakula and Borujen quietly boarded their cars and a rented minibus and left the wedding. They had arrived only several hours before and still had not enjoyed a chance to greet all their relatives. Others puzzled over their premature, rude departure. The celebration was supposed to continue until midnight. The people leaving had apparently received a message and departed suddenly, without explanation. The cause for their exit soon became clear.

Finishing lunch in their small tent, the musicians resumed playing music for stick fighting. As was customary in the past, older boys and young men used this interval to practice the sport. Their skills were not yet refined, and people worried about them becoming injured. A well-timed, sharp blow could break a leg. The musicians offered the novice players a brief period to practice while their elders rested or napped after lunch. Boys again sported on the sidelines.

Practically in mid-note, the musicians switched to dance music. The two styles of music were distinct, and people never performed one activity to the tunes of the other. Warned ahead of time about this strategy, some young men standing too-nonchalantly along the sidelines pulled colorful scarves from their pockets, quickly entered the space, and began to dance. Not alerted ahead of time, women peeked from behind the bridal tent when they heard the music. Before they could rise, gather their scarves, adjust their attire, and walk toward the space, the music abruptly stopped. Someone had ordered the musicians to cease.

Simultaneously many men gathered, obviously angry, just beyond the wedding camp. They pushed at one another, waving their arms and shouting. Despite their fury, they respected the hosts sufficiently to move the argument across an unmarked boundary indicating the camp's edge. The heated dispute centered on only two men, who were trying to prevent women from dancing, an activity they declared was un-Islamic. No one else opposed the music and dancing but only some were willing to confront the two. Others perhaps worried about the consequences. Several irate men abruptly left for home. Later they noted they would have attacked the two men if they had stayed.

Qashqa'i men usually tried to prevent verbal anger from escalating to physical assault. Violence drew many into the fray, caused injuries and even deaths, and ruptured social ties. Verbal exchanges, even hostile ones, could be smoothened over later.

By now the musicians were irritated. They had spent 19 hours on a bus traveling along rough roads to and from the bride's camp and still had not entertained the participants and spectators at Nasir's camp with dance music. Revolutionary guards had prevented them from performing (and earning a livelihood) since 1979, and they had begun to play publicly again only in

The politics of resistance and defiance   163

1991, the previous year. This summer they had encountered no direct opposition, and the ceremonial season was nearly over. They noted that factions within a few Darrehshuri subtribes still disapproved of music and dance and did not invite them to their weddings. All other Darrehshuri groups now employed musicians. These men were the very ones who had played at weddings in all parts of summer pastures during the past four months.

The musicians directed several young men to store the equipment in their van, and then they drove off in a state of ritual avoidance (*qahr*). Nasir's son had pressed some cash into their hands as they stomped toward the vehicle. When I had asked a musician about their departure, he replied, "Qashqa'i women are free everywhere, except those who are Qermezi." In passing, he added that he and other Darrehshuri musicians would never play for the Qermezi again.

Without any apparent concern for the hosts, let alone the groom and bride, virtually all the wedding guests collected their children and left. Those visiting Hanalishah went to their relatives' camps or returned home. The contingent of Shaikh Lurs from Dogonbadan appeared uncertain about the behavior expected of them but soon they left too and sought sanctuary in various tents at Hanalishah for the day and night. They planned to return home early the next morning. I did not see anyone say farewell to the bride, still secluded in the bridal tent, but surely at least her closest relatives did.

Back in Borzu's tent and later visiting at Husain Ali's, I heard more details about the dispute. Only two men out of the hundreds present had objected to women's dancing. When the pair had arrived in mid-morning, women were already dancing in the semisecluded spot, and the two decided that they could not easily force them to stop. Then, when the musicians tried once and then again to play the music intended for dancing, the lone protesters interfered and irritated the musicians so much that they packed up their equipment and left. The furious debate about whether or not they could or should play became moot.

The two dissenters especially objected to women's dancing to live music. They had arrived too late that morning to stop women from dancing to audiotaped music, but they could prevent the musicians from performing live music, an activity the government condemned more than the act of listening to taped music. The regime also banned women's dancing but the women had already begun before the disputants arrived. By stopping the musicians from performing for women at the camp's edge, the two men might have thought that they had ended women's dancing. Yet the musicians proceeded to play a second time, and now in the camp's center, a more public space. The act of women's dancing to live music in the heart of the camp, for everyone to witness, was more than the two irate men could tolerate.

If Nasir, the wedding's host, had taken a stand, the music could probably have continued, people said. He had chosen to invite the musicians and had set up a special tent for them. He had asked them to accompany the group that had collected the bride and delivered her to the groom's camp. Why pay them

164   *The politics of resistance and defiance*

if they were not to perform? He could have resisted the two hostile men but was not assertive. Deferring to him, his two married sons were also unwilling to act, and the groom could not intervene. (Grooms and brides at Qashqa'i weddings were sidelined during the festivities and needed to behave with decorum and modesty.) The elders of Hanalishah and other Qermezi locations were present but none assumed authority. If Borzu had been well, he would have dominated as he had always done in these kinds of conflicts, but he sat ill in the canvas reception tent, uninformed about the details. Along with all Qermezi elders, he supported the full resumption of customary wedding entertainments.

The two young Qermezi men who had ruined Nasir's celebration were not from Hanalishah, and one was not even Aqa Mohammadli. The more determined one, Ghulam Husain, is the son of Ismail of Imamverdili lineage. During the argument, when several men from Hanalishah told Ghulam Husain that he had no right to interfere in Aqa Mohammadli's celebration, he retorted that he had taken an Aqa Mohammadli bride and was as entitled as any Aqa Mohammadli person. I was puzzled; his wife is his father's brother's daughter and is as much Imamverdili as he is. Later I understood that he had referred to his extended family in the collective. Its Aqa Mohammadli links include Ghulam Husain's grandmother (his father's mother).

Subordinate to Ghulam Husain, the second objector was Farajullah, the son of Amir Husain of Aqa Mohammadli lineage and Nasir's patrilateral relative. Ghulam Husain and Farajullah were two of the subtribe's few hezbollahis. They had attended the wedding so they could provoke conflict and seemed surprised at the time that only two of them could cause so much disruption. Young men at Hanalishah had liked Farajullah, their age-mate and cousin, and were perplexed when he had developed hezbollahi traits after the Islamic regime took power.

People at Hanalishah felt differently about Ghulam Husain. His father's father, Sohrab, had challenged Khalifeh and Borzu for many years in their roles as Qermezi headmen, and the men of the two extended families had always maintained some social distance. Yet people's disapproval of Ghulam Husain centered on another issue, a shameful, criminal act he had committed during the Iraq–Iran war while serving as a revolutionary guard. In an isolated place far from the front line, he had shot a young Iranian he suspected was a deserter and left him to die in the wilderness. Gendarmes later tracked him down on the basis of the government vehicle he had driven. All Qermezi men contributed money to prevent the state from executing him. Still, they universally condemned him and his inexcusable, cowardly act. After prison, Ghulam Husain continued serving as a revolutionary guard, which remained his occupation in 1992. He objected to women's dancing for supposedly religious reasons and wanted to force changes in people's behavior but his upsetting the wedding also stemmed from his role as a revolutionary guard and a paid supporter of the regime that forbade women's dancing. Given his prior dishonorable deed, he had lost the subtribe's respect and probably could not

The politics of resistance and defiance 165

have exerted power on his own if he had not been a guard. (Farajullah, also a revolutionary guard, worked as a healthcare provider and was not as extreme in his political views.)

Ibrahim Qermezi's wedding

The second Qermezi wedding in 1992 occurred in Nurabad village, one of the two Qermezi villages, three days after Nasir's. Similar to Nasir, Ibrahim was anxious to hold the ceremony before the nomads left summer pastures for winter ones. Despite the musicians' impassioned claims that they would never play for Qermezi again, they came to this wedding too and adjusted their performance in tune with local sentiments. The same people who attended Nasir's wedding also appeared at Ibrahim's (except for the Shaikh Lurs, their Lur and Persian companions, and the two Qermezi hezbollahis). Ibrahim's drew a larger crowd. The location is more central for the dispersed subtribe, the large Kachili kin group would support him, and sport and dance were likely.[29]

Ibrahim is the son of Mohammad Tahir (Matahar) of Kachili lineage. Along with his brother Zulfaqar, Matahar had founded Nurabad village in summer pastures where their two families and other close Kachili kin built houses beginning in 1975. (The government named the village Nurabad—"place of light"—after the revolution when it introduced electricity.) Until the mid-1960s all these Kachili families had been nomadic pastoralists. They exploited summer pastures in the mountains near the location of their eventual village, and they continued to dwell in tents in these mountains during the summer after they built houses in Nurabad. Borzu Qermezi permitted some of them to share pastures with him at Dashtak during the autumn and winter. His wife Falak is the sister of three Kachili men who later built houses in Nurabad, two of them for only part-time residence.

Nurabad contained 22 households in 1992, the original settlers and their sons and families. Other Kachili resided in the nearest village, Narmeh, where some who built houses in Nurabad had dwelled beforehand. Some Kachili lived in nearby Mehr-i Gerd village where many of them and their parents had served the Darrehshuri khans. A few Kachili rented houses in the town of Shahreza. Patrilateral, matrilateral, and affinal bonds linked these four Kachili communities. The residents of each were also closely intermarried.

Ibrahim and his wife Ziba are the children of Nurabad's founders and earliest settlers. They produced two daughters and four sons, the third son now ready to marry. They and other Nurabad residents usually found spouses for their children among the Kachili, but this boy had already made his own match. Taimur had attended the tribal teacher-training school in Shiraz and then taught in the Qarachai Qashqa'i village of Arabshah in Qarachai territory south of Semirom. He was attracted to an older student there and wanted her as his bride. When his parents talked about the possibilities for him, he told them that he was already determined to marry a certain girl. His family made inquiries. The girl's father was dead; her mother and her father's brother

166   *The politics of resistance and defiance*

cared for her. They and their kinsmen did not oppose the match. They knew Taimur personally, respected his occupation, and understood that he could support her. He was an affable, attractive young man. No previous marriages had linked the Qermezi subtribe with this Qarachai Qashqa'i group.

Taimur and Fatemeh's wedding celebration was scheduled to begin in the afternoon of 14 September and would continue until midnight of the following day. Many guests would stay for two days while others only one. The residents of Nurabad prepared their small settlement for hundreds of guests. Ibrahim's three-room house and its large, partly enclosed courtyard was the wedding site while the other houses would host overnight guests. His kin pitched two extra-long goat-hair tents, one at each end of the courtyard, and the long unroofed porch facing the yard—the arena for stick fighting and dancing—also offered places for sitting. Someone strung colored electric lights across the space to add to the festive mood. Dangling from another cord was a single yellow bulb, the yard's normal illumination. Similar to other Nurabad houses, Ibrahim's faced southeast, and the guests would enjoy an unobstructed view of the rolling hills and mountains in that direction. "It's just as if we were sitting in a tent," someone on the porch later remarked.

When all Qermezi had lived in tent encampments, the households in the camp of the groom's father shared responsibility for hosting a wedding, and they chose a central spot there for sport and dance. When some of them created villages, the groom's father's house and courtyard became the wedding site, and the task of hosting fell primarily on the single family living there. Depending on kinship ties and goodwill, others in the community and from outside volunteered labor, supplies, and cash.

Arriving in the afternoon, the musicians sat on the porch and talked with guests. Nurabad's residents and relatives attended to errands and other details. Families that had taken brides from or given brides to the Kachili residents here assisted. Murad, a prominent Aqa Mohammadli man at Hanalishah, had married his eldest daughter to a young man in Nurabad, a tie ensuring that he, his extended family, and other Aqa Mohammadli would help at this wedding. Likewise, his Kachili in-laws in Nurabad would aid him when he was ready to host his own son's marriage.

Contrasting with the women at Nasir's wedding, all Kachili women at this ceremony wore diaphanous headscarves along with customary Qashqa'i attire. The few coming from Shahreza changed their city clothes for Qashqa'i dress immediately after their arrival. Women moved freely in and about the house, courtyard, and larger site as they prepared for the festivity. Later, female guests would congregate in one reception tent, and male guests in the other, but most people regardless of gender moved comfortably within these two areas and across the open courtyard. Such an open, relaxed environment contrasted with that of Nasir's wedding, just concluded, where nearly total gender separation, by design as well as poor planning, was obvious from the start.

Nurabad lacked any hezbollahis, revolutionary guards, or other regime supporters, which helps to explain these differences. Unlike Atakula village,

The politics of resistance and defiance 167

Nurabad is not located near a town or city, and religious institutions and regime agents did not directly influence its residents. Many Qermezi in Borujen, Atakula, and nearby villages had adopted certain traits of the larger Iranian society but the Qermezi in Nurabad had not. Men and women there still practiced customary agriculture and pastoralism, some resided in tents in nearby summer pastures, and a few migrated to Dashtak and other winter pastures. Nurabad's women utilized the same technologies and natural resources and enjoyed the same lifestyle as women at Hanalishah and Dashtak. The presence or absence of village houses differentiated them but these physical structures did not affect the people's basic attitudes. Some residents of Atakula and nearby settlements no longer pursued customary livelihoods. Qermezi men living in and near Borujen often took jobs in the wider Iranian society and returned home influenced by behaviors and values they encountered outside. Thus village life itself did not necessarily change people's attitudes about gender distinctions, proper conduct, and customary celebrations.

As dusk approached, the musicians set up their instruments in a small tent facing the porch across the courtyard and began to play. Someone plugged in the two strands of lights as men entered the yard's center to begin stick fighting. Soon the activity drew hundreds of spectators, and people stood on the porch trying to peer over the heads of those congregating around successive pairs of eager combatants. After an hour, the musicians switched to music for dancing, and the courtyard cleared. Then, one by one, young men and soon older ones began their graceful moves around the just-vacated battleground. Women and girls formed their own circle of dancers next to the men's in the open courtyard. All dressed in customary Qashqa'i attire, all wearing diaphanous scarves, they offered a stunning sight for one another and the many bystanders. Soon the two expanding circles of dancers touched in the courtyard's center. The vibrantly colored scarves they raised and lowered crossed. Sometimes a hand brushed another's. The viewers stood transfixed. "The music sinks into our souls," someone whispered to me. A few middle-aged men and women cried, moved by a sight they had not witnessed for 14 years. Several commented, "Akhunds stole the best years of our lives." (People would have enjoyed these years as dancers and competitors at stick fighting but the regime had prohibited them from doing so.) Later, people laughed about the pretense of gender segregation and predicted that within a year men and women would dance together in a single circle, a prediction that proved true.

Men and women, boys and girls, joined and left the respective circles as the mood struck them but most continued to perform until the musicians stopped several hours later when word came that dinner was ready. Efficiently and abundantly, the hosts served hundreds of people (men and women mixed together) in many locations in the house and reception tents and on the porch.

Before dinner, two groups of distinguished outsiders had arrived. The first contained men of the Zahidi family of Mehr-i Gerd. Part of the Darrehshuri tribe, they had served the Darrehshuri khans as subordinate advisors, scribes, and teachers until the revolution, when they began to seize land and other

168   *The politics of resistance and defiance*

resources formerly under the khans' control. After the downfall of these leaders, the Zahidis had risen in socioeconomic status. They were now the area's elite. Ibrahim had invited them to the wedding as a courtesy. They did not participate in sport or dance but still seemed to enjoy themselves.

The second group held Murad Atazadeh, a Darzi Darrehshuri man and the brother of Semirom's just-elected parliamentary deputy. The close kin of such a prominent man represented him on such occasions, and Murad's presence was politically motivated, but Murad also attended because of kinship. His mother is Kachili, a source of pride for all her kin. By his clothes, facial hair, and stern demeanor, he demonstrated a hezbollahi stance. His brother's elevated position might have encouraged him to assume hezbollahi traits opportunistically, especially if he hoped to gain economic and political rewards stemming from the association. Yet, twirling a strand of beads, he sat without objecting to the activities around him and watched without apparent judgment the musicians performing, men sporting, and women and men dancing.

After dinner the musicians played again for both men and women, and then people retired for the night, either in Nurabad's houses or in nearby Narmeh or Mehr-i Gerd. Some guests reluctantly returned home, pressured by other obligations. The time to migrate to winter pastures was upon them.

At dawn the next day, the wedding guests prepared to repeat the previous day's activities. The musicians played briefly to welcome new arrivals and signal the festivity's resumption before they launched into music for sport and dance. Several chartered minibuses for collecting the bride stood outside in the lane. The previous day the groom's mother Ziba and other kinswomen had traveled to the bride's village to bathe and prepare the girl for marriage, and they and others now readied to bring her from her village to theirs. The group had planned to leave in mid-morning and return in mid-afternoon, but Ziba reported that the bride's kin group was not offering a noon meal. People discussed possible reasons for this apparent breech of custom but understood that the bride's economic position was undercut because she lacked a father. The wedding guests now planned to eat lunch in Nurabad and then travel to Arabshah.

The musicians played all morning, alternating tunes for stick fighting and dancing, and the courtyard was always crowded. People filled the reception tents, porch, and house while multitudes of children ran tirelessly about. When a large contingent of Zahidi women arrived (the region's new elite), the hosts prepared a special place for them in the women's reception tent. The women wore traditionally styled Qashqa'i attire but used finer fabrics and more decorative trimming and displayed abundant gold jewelry. The Qermezi women seemed almost shabby by comparison, especially without much if any gold. Under colored lights the night before they appeared elegant; under the harsh sun and in the crowded reception tent they did not. Unlike the Zahidi men the previous night, the Zahidi women did not hesitate to join the dancing, including one in the last month of pregnancy.

Qermezi women did not dance in public if their pregnancy was so obvious. Several wondered later if this woman was emboldened by her now-superior

The politics of resistance and defiance   169

social and economic status. Perhaps she cared little about propriety because the wedding's other guests were lower in status than she was. Just as the khans' wives had demonstrated in multiple ways their superiority over the Zahidi women, now these women could assert their own elevated position.

Lunch was ready at noon, and then people prepared to travel to the bride's village several hours to the south. Two minibuses filled with those who did not find places in the multiple cars and trucks. Many people decided spontaneously to go. Standing by a bus to say farewell, they suddenly jumped in as it pulled away. Forming a noisy caravan, the vehicles displayed vibrant scarves fluttering in the wind, passengers sang loudly, and the musicians accompanying them played their oboes. Cars in front periodically paused along the road's shoulder so slower moving ones could catch up. People remarked that traveling and arriving in a large group would impress the residents of the bride's village and any people they passed along the way.

Driving through Semirom, the travelers sang and clapped to announce that they were collecting a bride, and the Persian townspeople looked on with kind amusement. At first I was surprised by the excessive show of happiness but then understood that it demonstrated feelings of exhilaration after 14 years of deprivation. Through exuberant display, the tribespeople were also flaunting their opinion about those who had imposed an austere, conservative definition of Islam on them. They were asserting their freedom of expression as compared to the seemingly more constricted lives of the Persian townspeople. (When we passed through Semirom on our return trip late that night, we saw several other wedding processions, at least one of them carrying Persian celebrants, and these participants were as rowdy as our group. These revelers too might have wanted to annoy any townspeople who disapproved of such behavior.)

(In retrospect, I saw how often these and other Qashqa'i blamed town and city Persians for the Islamic Republic and its restrictions. To the postrevolutionary era, they applied the negative sentiments they had felt about such Persians before the revolution, now for new and more explicit reasons [mainly, the forced imposition of an Islamic regime on them]. Some of these urban Persians probably also held unfavorable opinions about the government. Still, even when the Qashqa'i heard Persians criticize the regime, they often avoided contributing their views for fear that the Persians were baiting them and would later report to the authorities what they had heard.)

Arriving in the small village of Arabshah two hours later, the travelers saw a huge crowd. Hundreds of Qarachai Qashqa'i people had assembled to welcome the wedding party. The intertribal union required each group to demonstrate its support by way of many attendees. I assumed the same kinds of spatial dispersion for this Qarachai group as characterized the Qermezi subtribe, and several people there confirmed my notions. These Qarachai had traveled from all parts of Qarachai territory to attend the event, just as the Qermezi would have done if the bride had been theirs.

The Qermezi women gathered in the house of the bride's uncle, and the Qermezi men prepared to compete against Qarachai players. While sporting

170 *The politics of resistance and defiance*

among kin, men exercised certain strategies reflecting their different lineage affiliations. While sporting in the Qarachai village, they competed as a unified force, as Qermezi and Darrehshuri against the Qarachai. Qermezi men honed their skills at home so they could succeed in intertribal competitions. When the musicians switched to music for dance, women began and then men joined in, each forming a separate circle but, as in Nurabad, with people and scarves mingling where the two circles intersected. Hundreds of spectators gathered to watch the amazing sight, and no one apparently objected to women's dancing.[30] These Qarachai Qashqa'i had resumed a full expression of festivities the previous year.

As the bride's kinsmen packed her dowry goods in a large open-backed truck, they reserved the most expensive and attractive items for the top, to display as the party traveled back to Nurabad. (When the nomads had used camels for conveyance, they loaded the most valued and pleasing goods last, to exhibit them while en route to the groom's camp.) While the Qarachai kinswomen left behind wailed, the groom escorted the bride to the back seat of a passenger car where she would ride in relative comfort. (Usually grooms did not play so direct a role.)

The trip back to Nurabad was as noisy as the outgoing one, the travelers anxious to proclaim their happiness about collecting a bride. Once again the many vehicles formed a caravan with drivers dangerously jockeying for position toward the front. The faster moving ones periodically halted on the roadside where men and boys danced and sang while they waited. The wedding party did not arrive at the village until midnight, and the travelers saw that some guests had already left or retired. The musicians played briefly to welcome the bride to her new family and then left for their homes in Mehr-i Gerd. The wedding was over.[31]

Notes

1 Chehabi (1993) includes Reza Shah's dress-code law.
2 The postage stamps first issued by the Islamic Republic in 1979 feature Kurds and other men in Iran in indigenous ethnic dress. Since parliament's first session in 1980, some male deputies of ethnic-minority backgrounds wore their distinctive dress there. Government schoolbooks from 1981 through 2013 include drawings of Iranian men in varying headgear (each style signifying a specific group) and Iranian children in regional dress (Yavari-D'Hellencourt 1988: 249, 253). Mehran (2002) discusses ethnic biases and stereotypes in primary-school textbooks published in 1999. State-sponsored Islamic dolls in 1996 featured Sara and Dara in regional ethnic dress, including a (distorted) Qashqa'i version. K. Bayat (2005, 2008), Beck (2013, n.d. a), Elling (2013), Mojab and Hassanpour (1996), Samii (2000), and Tohidi (2009) examine relationships between ethnic minorities and the Iranian state.
3 Beck (1992a) describes Qashqa'i attire in the nineteenth and twentieth centuries.
4 Literature on the subject of women in Iran and their attire is vast. Nashat and Beck (2003) and Beck and Nashat (2004) offer different perspectives on changes in women's roles in Iran through history.
5 Huang (2006) describes different kinds of school and the attire that Qashqa'i girls and women wore there.

The politics of resistance and defiance   171

6 Stretching her imagination, Alavi (2005: 167–68) notes that the morality police would never dare to approach tribal women who refused to observe state restrictions, "for fear of offending the strict 'Islamic honour codes' of the indigenous tribes and starting widespread tribal rebellions against the regime." This statement contains glaring misrepresentations of Iran's tribes, tribeswomen, and tribal resistance against the state.

7 Liz Thurgood, *Guardian* (Manchester), 1 July 1989.

8 The film, *Gabbeh* (1996) has an accompanying book (Makhmalbaf and Ahmadi 1996). N. Mottahedeh (2004) offers a feminist analysis of the film but does not discuss Qashqa'i society and culture. Naheed Dareshuri (personal communication, 6 November 2011) attended a cultural exhibition in Tehran in September 2011 that featured textiles and music of two Iranian groups, Lurs and Afshar Turks. Some Qashqa'i women also participated but government officials told them not to reveal their identity as Qashqa'i. All the women wore the customary dress of their respective groups, including diaphanous scarves that revealed their hair. Officials objected only to the women's partially visible necks. (The exposure of women's necks has not ordinarily been an issue in Iran before or after 1979.) The women adjusted their scarves to cover more of their necks but did not alter the rest of their dress. Officials came every day to inspect their appearance.

9 Tourist booklets produced by the Islamic Republic for use in Lebanon and other strategic areas for Iran display Iran as a country of diverse peoples and customs and include photographs of rural Iranians in colorful dress, which contrasts with the strictly normative, dark-hued dress associated with the Islamic regime. The government intended these representations to refute globally circulated images of Iran, and the multiculturalism depicted invoked a Western sense of liberal modernity (Shaery-Eisenlohr 2008).

10 Mosteshar (1995: following p. 170).

11 Esfandiari (1997: 109). She suggests that the dress might have been Baluch (personal communication, 20 April 2002).

12 www.lacma.org/art/installation/elizabeth-taylor-Iran-photographs-firooz-Zahidi (accessed 29 October 2013).

13 "The Iranian revolution has made many Iranians [in the U.S.] hostile, suspicious, or indifferent toward religion" (Mahdi 1998: 87–88). The brochure advertising this "Persian Festival of Autumn" includes a color photograph of non-Qashqa'i women performing in Qashqa'i clothes (document in author's possession).

14 "Children wearing traditional dress are to receive prizes, and here and there a child is dressed in the colorful, flowing skirts of Iranian tribal women. [A] little girl in native dress goes up for a prize. The master of ceremonies asks her a question in Farsi [Persian], but she does not understand. 'Well, at least she is wearing native dress,' the emcee says with an awkward laugh" (Asayesh 1999: 207–08).

15 Researchers in rural southwestern Iran during or after the revolution note the same attitudes about religion that I report here for the Qashqa'i; see Anonymous (1982), Friedl (1983, 1989), Hegland (1987, 2014), E. Hooglund (1982b), M. Hooglund (1982), Loeffler (1988).

16 Banuazizi (1994: 5). "With the clergy's direct involvement in the affairs of state, it was inevitable that they would come to be blamed for the ills of society and the failings of the government" (ibid.). "Corruption and hypocrisy … may have undermined Islamic values far more than any Western influences" (Roy 1998: 38).

17 Amuzegar (1993: 25).

18 For example, Islamic inheritance rights, stipulating that sons receive full shares and daughters half-shares of a deceased father's property, are often ignored in all parts of the Muslim world. Afshar (1985: 68) notes for Iran: "Even though women are theoretically still entitled to their Islamic rights, in practice few rural

172 *The politics of resistance and defiance*

women have the means of enforcing the Islamic law against patriarchal, traditional, social and psychological resistance to it."

19 Iranians spoke of these multipurpose trips as "pilgrimage and amusement" (*ziyarat-u siyahat*) and "pilgrimage and trade" (*ziyarat-u tijarat*) (Adelkhah 2000: 135, 2007).

20 Khomeini condemned music at the beginning of Ramadan in July 1979: "The playing of music is an act of treason to this country and our youth; therefore, musical programs should be entirely stopped" (Rahmena and Nomani 1990: 222). Later, the regime permitted Islamic and revolutionary martial music, patriotic hymns and songs, and Iranian classical music but continued to forbid any music thought to stimulate people's sexual feelings. It authorized some musical instruments in 1988–89. Simpson (1988: 182–95) examines ambiguities in the regime's attitudes toward television programming, music, games, sports, books, and films in 1986–87. "Traditional" and "regional" music recovered some legitimacy in 1992 because of the regime's concern about preserving national and regional heritages (Youssefzadeh 2000). Under Khatami as president, the government tolerated popular music sung by males but it continued to prohibit solo female singers. State-controlled television broadcast concerts of traditional music but sometimes did not show the instruments or their players (Youssefzadeh 2000: 57–58).

21 Many tribal and ethnic groups in the southern Zagros Mountains demonstrated similar kinds of dress, music, dance, and sport but they also showed significant as well as subtle differences among them. Cultural and other markers also distinguished people within tribal and ethnic groups. Tapper and Thompson (2002) offer photographic evidence of such cultural diversity.

22 A third occasion, the large gatherings at the camps of the Qashqa'i khans, had ended in 1982 when the regime's paramilitaries defeated and suppressed these leaders.

23 The Qashqa'i living and visiting abroad circulated videotapes of these celebrations, and others viewing them received the erroneous impression that the Islamic Republic no longer subjected women to restrictions on their appearance and behavior.

24 Even after the first decade of Iranians' being subjected to Islamizing, anti-West policies, observers noted the failures. "A sombre dress code, and a drastic ban on drinking, gambling, and display of affection in public, have been brutally enforced in order to fight Westernization; but the public's yearning for most things Western has hardly been dented" (Amuzegar 1993: 324). "After two decades of cultural oppression, the Islamic state could not succeed in bringing the population to submit to its traditionalist Islamic norms of personal and public conduct and to accept its idealized traditional Islamic cultural norms" (Nomani and Behdad 2006: 58).

25 *Nomad* (Beck 1991) describes marriage ceremonies in 1970–71. Huang (2009) offers the more recent social and cultural context. Weddings played key roles in Qashqa'i society and culture and articulated and symbolized the people's attitudes about significant aspects of their lives. "The richest area of symbolic potential for distinctive markers of identity is that of culture and ethnicity. ... But there is one area of culture that holds for nomads ... deeply rooted, and usually unarticulated, meanings: the realm of ceremonies and rituals, in particular those associated with marriage" (Tapper 1994: 204–05).

26 Beck (1991: 293, 315) includes information on Mali.

27 Before 1979, a bride had traveled to the groom's camp unaccompanied by any of her kin.

28 The next year (1993), a few Qermezi hezbollahis sternly instructed women before each wedding began that they could not dance, thereby seemingly preventing a

The politics of resistance and defiance   173

recurrence of this year's strategies. The issue of women's dancing was still not resolved by 1999, at least for parts of this Qermezi group (see Chapter 9).

29 Huang (2009: 18; plates 2, 10) includes photographs of this wedding.

30 Huang (2009: plate 10) includes a photograph of this event.

31 Taimur Qermezi was killed in 1999, six years after his marriage, when the tractor he was driving overturned. Supported by his teacher's pension, his wife Fatemeh was left with two small children. The next year, threatened by her father-in-law's attempts to marry her to her dead husband's brother who was already married, she returned home with her children to her mother and uncle. Her father-in-law took the case to court, which ruled that the children could stay with her for two more years, after which she must give them to him. Fatemeh still retained custody of her children in 2004. Isolated from her natal and affinal kin, she lived in a rented apartment in the town of Semirom without obvious means of support except for the pension.

5 The hope of spring
Reflections on 1995—winter and spring

Three issues drew the attention of the Qermezi in the winter and spring of 1995: their escalating struggles for land rights in the postrevolutionary era, the new circumstances for those living part-time in towns, and the upcoming New Year's festivities, now dampened by the death of Ayatollah Khomeini's son. In the three sections, I focus on Borzu Qermezi and his family but their activities were similar to those of many other Qermezi.

Struggles over land

Borzu Qermezi had always been troubled by issues concerning land. He hesitated to make changes that would obstruct his nomadic pastoralism in winter and summer territories. Yet he knew that other Qermezi men—first some and then many—were prepared to alter their practices to adapt to wider economic realities. Borzu saw that he would have to accommodate these men. He was their leader and needed them as allies. He negotiated some land deals aimed to provide potential supplementary or alternative livelihoods and residences for himself, his sons, and close kinsmen.

Borzu owned no land in 1970, and his rights over winter and summer pastures were insecure and contested. Some Qermezi on whom he depended for political support were building houses in Atakula village and elsewhere. He worried that others would join them and leave him behind. Against this backdrop, Borzu decided in the mid-1970s to increase his options by transacting for land. These plans did not proceed smoothly, and practically all the projects were still under dispute three to four decades later. His sons' efforts to solve these ongoing, separate conflicts were stressful and wasted time and scarce resources. Demand for land in these regions of Iran caused prices to escalate rapidly after the revolution, particularly after the war's ceasefire, and the parcels that Borzu had purchased in the mid-1970s, or thought he had purchased, grew increasingly valuable. These and other disputed plots were in towns (Semirom, Kazerun), in winter and summer pastures, and near Mehr-i Gerd village.[1]

Land in Semirom

Many Qermezi men considered buying land and building houses in Atakula, Borujen, Naqneh, Dezeh, Narmeh, or other places in the early 1970s.

The hope of spring 175

Reluctantly, Borzu decided that he also needed a place for himself, his sons, his brothers and their sons, and other close paternal kin, in case they and other Qermezi decided to construct houses and establish seasonal or year-round permanent residences.

If forced to choose a location, Borzu preferred the climate of summer pastures over winter ones. Summer pastures were cold and snowy in the winter but work was minimal then, and a house would shelter him. Winter pastures were scorching in the summer when work was plentiful, and escaping the heat was impossible. Borzu wanted to live with his group, and some other Qermezi men had already built in summer pastures. No one had yet built in winter pastures. Borzu favored Semirom over other places in summer pastures. His territory at Hanalishah was close by, and many men discussed living in or near a town because of schools, markets, government offices, and medical facilities. He was not happy about this situation but needed to act so he could prevent especially his closest kin from building elsewhere, especially in regions where he lacked any economic interests. He worried that kinsmen and supporters would establish residences in more distant towns, and he prepared to take what he hoped would be preemptive action. He would not build alone but he needed to be ready in case some kin and allies proceeded with their own plans.

Borzu decided in 1976 to purchase land in Semirom from Nadir Khan Sami, a prominent Persian townsman, and he encouraged his closest kinsmen to buy adjoining plots. (The title of "khan" is honorific and does not connote a tribal leader.) After prolonged heated discussions, Borzu and five of these men bought 3,000 square meters of land beyond the upper western outskirts of Semirom, in Hanalishah's direction. The town rested along the slopes of a steep mountain near a pass and was expanding into the plain below, but Borzu and the other Qermezi preferred the upper mountainous section. Perhaps they would build houses on the land but they also knew that they could sell the property, with or without houses, if they later chose another location. Borzu's section was 1,200 square meters, which he envisioned as four equivalently sized lots for himself and his three sons. Together, five close paternal kinsmen bought 1,800 square meters: Murad (Borzu's cousin and closest ally), Ghulam Husain (his full brother), Asadullah and Husain Ali (his half brothers' sons and his sons-in-law), and Nasir (his cousin). These men bought one or two lots for themselves depending on their plans for their own sons. Borzu and the five men paid Nadir Khan Sami the full amount for the land, 48,000 tumans in cash, and Sami gave them a signed and dated document detailing the property, its boundaries, and the amount paid.

Without informing the six Qermezi men, Sami then sold the same land, plot by plot, to other individuals, all of them Persian residents of Semirom. Later he sold these same and adjoining lots, for at least the third time, to the township of Semirom for its development plans. When the Persians who had purchased these plots began to build houses there, Borzu and his kinsmen saw that Sami had tricked them.

176 *The hope of spring*

For years, until he fell seriously ill, Borzu attempted to gain restitution for the illegal transaction by appealing to government agencies and the Ministry of Justice and its court in Semirom. Mohammad Karim and Dariush continued with the legal actions. Incurring great expense over the years, they were annoyed. At least twice every summer they received a date for a court hearing but the case dragged on, unresolved. When Sami died in 1996, his sons claimed that the six Qermezi men had never purchased any land from their father. Semirom officials agreed in principle in 1997 to exchange part of the land under dispute with other property the township owned, but the plot they designated was located where the Ministry of Roads was constructing a new highway skirting the town. Borzu's sons rejected the offer. A nearby section, 1,000 square meters, remained, and Dariush considered that portion for building a house. The township also proposed in principle to give Borzu's sons some land by a now-collapsed and abandoned chicken-raising facility in the valley to the west. None of these schemes proceeded, and Dariush was resigned to let the issue rest until he returned to the Semirom region each spring. When Sami's sons claimed they possessed no property of their own, Dariush remarked, always kindhearted, "How could I pursue a case against them?" Besides, the effort seemed pointless if the Sami family was impoverished. Yet wealth and social status were interconnected, and the family's assertions seemed implausible given its continuing prominence.

Whenever traveling between Hanalishah and Semirom, these Qermezi would often cast their eyes toward the land they had purchased. Just an uninhabited wasteland and dumping ground in 1970, the location had become one of Semirom's expanding, flourishing residential areas. Poised on the mountain slope and offering relatively cool weather in the summer, it provided a superb view of the plain below and the mountains beyond. Houses and vacant land there had grown expensive. The township asphalted some streets and provided electricity, natural gas, and running water to the residents. Even if the Qermezi men had decided not to build houses there, they could have profited by selling the land to others, at now escalating prices. The new highway bypassing the town ran through the land's upper reaches and would have disturbed any Qermezi who lived there. Traffic was sometimes heavy and always noisy. Twenty-four hours a day, trucks carried enormous granite blocks (often one per flatbed vehicle) from quarries west of Semirom to Isfahan, and they now avoided the narrow, often obstructed road through the town's center.

Land in Kazerun

In 1975, a year before he negotiated for land in Semirom, Borzu bought a small plot in Kazerun from Kalayaz (Karbalai Ayaz) Nazarpur, a blind Persian merchant and moneylender there. Kalayaz was a frequent visitor to Dashtak. Accompanied by his sighted brother, he traveled by donkey from camp to camp to engage in small-scale transactions; he bought pastoral products, argued over a dying camel's meat, extended credit, and offered cash loans of a

The hope of spring 177

few tumans. The nomads disliked doing business with him because he was dishonest and deceitful but he did provide services that most other merchants did not, such as personal visits to Dashtak. Only Kalayaz would transport a sheep carcass to town and later offer some market commodity in exchange.

Borzu decided that he might need land in Kazerun, for the same reasons he considered buying land in Semirom. Both towns were close to his seasonal territories with which he would not sever ties. He had always proclaimed that the best economic strategy was to continue sending livestock to his winter and summer pastures and to acquire, if necessary, land in the nearest towns for houses. There, his grandchildren could continue their formal education, with some of them preparing for livelihoods other than pastoralism. Borzu intended to maintain nomadism, to move seasonally between winter and summer locales, no matter where he also owned a house. No other Qermezi men planned at this time to buy land for houses in Kazerun. The severe heat and humidity during the summer deterred them. Yet Borzu hoped that at least a few would eventually follow his example.

Kalayaz offered Borzu a plot in what was still uninhabited land in 1975, beyond the upper outskirts of Kazerun toward the mountains to the town's east. Borzu wanted to be close to his territory at Dashtak, and the sight of the nearby peaks reassured him. He paid Kalayaz 5,600 tumans in cash for the 320 square meters and received a bill of sale from him. Kalayaz had bought the same plot from another man but, without telling Borzu, had never obtained the legal title. For the next 14 years, Borzu tried to force Kalayaz to complete the bureaucratic and legal procedure so he in turn could acquire the deed, but he failed. He lacked concrete bargaining tools to move the transaction forward. Similar to the dispute in Semirom, Borzu's only-seasonal residence in the area impeded the legal process.

When Kalayaz died in 1989, his wife and children claimed that Borzu had never paid Kalayaz for any land. They asserted that Kalayaz had left them landless. Borzu took multiple legal actions through the Kazerun court to obtain redress but did not succeed. When he became ill and then died, his son Dariush continued the legal struggle. The bill of sale from Kalayaz was the main obstacle. It did not contain his signature but only his inked fingerprint in three places. Blind, Kalayaz had never learned to write his name, or so he claimed. Court officers told Dariush to secure a copy of Kalayaz's application for an identity card (required of all citizens), which would display his fingerprint from the time he had applied for the document as a young adult. The court could then match this print with the ones on Borzu's bill of sale. Clerks told Dariush that the process would probably take a year. Dariush obtained a Shiraz-based lawyer who handled cases in Kazerun but he remained doubtful about any positive outcome. After Kalayaz died, someone had built a house on the land in question, further complicating the issue. Dariush attended many court hearings but the matter never proceeded. Kalayaz's survivors submitted a fingerprint that did not match the ones on Borzu's bill of sale but that also differed from the one on Kalayaz's identity-card application.

178 *The hope of spring*

The illegal orchard at Hanalishah

Outsiders exploited the turbulent times of the revolution and its immediate aftermath by seizing Borzu's legal pastureland at Hanalishah when he was absent. Borzu discovered that he would have little or no recourse regarding this assault. The theft of his pasture and its conversion to agricultural use tormented him during the last years of his illness, and he did not live to see adequate redress.

In the spring of 1980, a year after the revolution, Borzu migrated to Hanalishah to discover that someone had plowed and cultivated a sizable portion of pasture nearest his summer campsite. The culprit had destroyed (severed or yanked out by the roots) thousands of large, mature, hardy shrubs, which supported the growth of more fragile ground vegetation and prevented erosion. The campsite was the last of three he occupied in the spring and summer and was the only one supplied with fresh spring water. The surrounding territory had never been planted before.

Irate, Borzu spotted the perpetrators brazenly working the new wheat and lentil fields. The three men were Persian residents of Semirom who had harassed him and the other nomads at Hanalishah for decades. The land they had stolen was pasture legally allocated to Borzu under the terms of the state's nationalization of pastures in 1963. Borzu rushed to Semirom to report the incursion to various authorities.

After Borzu's repeated requests, rangers from the agency for natural resources in Semirom came to Hanalishah to investigate. They proclaimed that the land was indeed pastureland and forbidden for agricultural use. Seeing that Borzu was not going to ignore their territorial aggression, the three Persian cultivators presented their case to the bureaus of the Ministry of Agriculture in Semirom and Isfahan. Their officials also visited Hanalishah and reported that the land appeared suitable for cultivation, especially if someone could tap the groundwater for irrigation. Borzu traveled to Isfahan to report the violation to the natural-resources agency there. Its officials inspected the territory and reiterated that any agriculture on the site was illegal. These agencies, clearly at odds, were part of the reorganized Ministry of Agriculture. Under Mohammad Reza Shah, the natural-resources agency had exercised independent jurisdiction over Iran's nationalized pastures, and its new director wanted to continue its autonomy.

The three cultivators harvested the wheat and lentils in August 1980, sold the crops in Shahreza, and pocketed the income.

During the early stages of these events, revolutionary guards had arrested and detained Borzu for several months. Imprisonment, death threats, and the regime's continuing accusations about his complicity in the Tang-i Jelo ambush (in which revolutionary guards had died) impeded him from effectively pursuing the dispute over his confiscated pastureland. The Persian cultivators had exploited his vulnerability, his newly problematic status vis-à-vis the state, and the government's ongoing inability to rule on land rights here and elsewhere.

The hope of spring   179

At summer's end, Borzu and the other Qermezi nomads at Hanalishah left for winter pastures. Without informing him, the three Persian cultivators sold the land in question to the Persian Shahidani family of Semirom for 70,000 tumans. Knowing the land was legal pastureland, the two parties wrote their own bill of sale and did not conduct the transaction through any government office, which such land transfers required people to do, even during the post-revolutionary confusion. The original Persian cultivators resumed their efforts to expropriate other sections of pastureland at Hanalishah while also developing apple orchards closer to the valley bottom.

Borzu and the other Qermezi nomads, migrating to Hanalishah in the spring of 1981, were shocked by the transformations to his pastureland. Intruders had denuded the land under dispute and much of the surrounding pasture of their vital shrubs and had plowed the now-expanded tract, planted 900 apple saplings, and enclosed the area with a stone wall topped with barbed wire. Borzu was doubly irate and hurried to Semirom to notify various state agencies. Officials there were not prepared to handle this kind of complaint swiftly and did not take any conclusive action for years. Borzu's arrest and imprisonment the previous year, combined with lingering suspicions about the Tang-i Jelo ambush, continued to complicate his relationship with the new regime. With difficulty, he tried to seek redress through agencies in Semirom, Vanak, Shahreza, and Isfahan in hopes of expelling the new encroachers from his state-authorized, legal pastureland.

Five Shahidani brothers and their sister's son (Amir) had seized Borzu's land. The family was among Semirom's leading ones. (After several years Amir disputed with his mother's brothers and abandoned the claim. His mother, and their sister, told Borzu that the confiscation was illegal and improper.) Several of the brothers already cultivated land in the Hanalishah valley, and they and many other Persians and Lurs were steadily moving up the valley slopes and trespassing on the nomads' legal pastures in an attempt to expand their agricultural land. During the revolution's turmoil and its aftermath—including the purging and reorganizing of all existing government agencies and the founding of sometimes competitive new ones—the Shahidani men along with other Persians and Lurs from Semirom, Vanak, and Galleh Qadam had exploited the lack of definitive state authority at the local and regional levels.

When the Islamic Republic's hard-line clergymen repudiated the Qashqa'i khans in 1980, their local supporters also renounced the khans' associates. Perceived as a khan supporter, Borzu was trapped by the political situation. He said he could not expect any outside authority—state agents or khans—to respond effectively any time soon to his rightful complaints.

Unlike Borzu and all other Qermezi nomads, the Shahidani men enjoyed political influence in Semirom. Kinship ties with a local judge (a cleric) led to his testifying in court that the land in question belonged to them. After the revolution, citizens feared the potential power of any local figures who were connected in some way with institutional Islam, and they worried about

180 *The hope of spring*

the wider clout such individuals could possibly wield. Few seemed to know where the local judge stood in the regional hierarchy of clerics and how important he could turn out to be. Of negligible significance during the shah's regime, this "akhund" (a pejorative term) could now command some authority and power simply because of the rule by clergy in Iran.

The five Shahidani brothers had seized 16 hectares of Borzu's prime pasture, land that had never been cultivated until the previous year when the three Persians planted wheat and lentils on part of it. They had also usurped some natural springs issuing from Borzu's land. Initially using the resource for irrigation, the brothers soon dug an eight-meter well and installed motorized pumps to draw water. A battery-powered generator ran one pump; gasoline and oil ran another. The men dug channels to direct the water's flow through the new orchard. Facing periodic water shortages, they soon constructed a deep concrete reservoir to hold the pumped water until they were ready to irrigate. Together the brothers irrigated, applied pesticides and fertilizers, reinforced the surrounding wall, provided surveillance, and shared expenses. After seven years, when the trees began to produce a marketable crop of apples, they split the profits.

Whenever state agents visited because of this or other business, Borzu regaled them with the history of the theft, all the while detailing the perfidy of the Shahidani family, and then he gave them a tour of the nearby barbed-wire-topped enclosing wall. He appeared to draw some sympathy. He stressed that the brothers had stolen the land by force during the revolution when local authorities had fled their posts and when he was migrating or residing in faraway winter pastures. The lower part of the orchard stood just south of his tent and campsite and constantly reminded him of the seizure. The issue was not somewhat abstract in the way that his disputed lands in Semirom, Kazerun, and other places were. By law, his livestock were entitled to graze this land but the Shahidanis had illegally restricted and devastated the territory. As long as that family occupied it and fortified the borders, Borzu could not graze his animals there.

Tufts of sheep wool and goat hair snagged on the multiple strands of barbed wire topping the stone wall surrounding the orchard, which indicated that some livestock did gain access at night after the Shahidanis had left for their homes in town. As part of a children's brigade, my daughter Julia periodically collected these tufts to remove traces of the animals' "trespassing." Borzu's shepherds cut weeds for the livestock and gathered firewood in the orchard at night.

The Shahidanis had caused environmental damage beyond the pasture's permanent destruction. The output of the springs on which Borzu and his campmates depended was decreasing, and the deep well and motorized pumps created new patterns of underground and near-surface drainage. The concrete reservoir was always full and sometimes overflowing, and Borzu complained that the trespassers were pumping more water than they needed, simply to deprive him of this resource. The springs still under his physical

The hope of spring   181

possession were losing water, and his campsite was newly muddy from emerging changes in drainage. He would curse at the Shahidanis at night, when they usually ran their pumps, the annoying mechanical racket disturbing the territory's otherwise soothing natural sounds.

National and local government had become more systematic and lawful by 1991, and Borzu finally succeeded in drawing official attention to the case. Many delegations of state agents arrived to investigate and write reports. The land was still officially classified as pasture, and the state's new Pastures Organization was the main agency responsible. Men from its provincial headquarters in Isfahan and its regional and local offices in Shahreza and Semirom came to inspect the territory and interview the disputants. The power and influence that the Shahidanis had claimed to possess proved to be insufficient.

Late that summer, armed security forces entered Hanalishah with an order (*hukm*) from the Pastures Organization requiring the Shahidani brothers to relinquish the orchard's lower half and return the land to Borzu. If the brothers refused, they would go to prison. For Borzu, this compromise was not just but he feared losing this chance to regain some land. The two parties had argued for more than a decade about the territory's fate. Dramatizing their distress, the brothers threatened to raze the whole orchard if the government forced them to surrender any part of it. At the same time, they demanded restitution from Borzu for all the funds they had expended since they planted the first saplings.[2] They especially insisted on the cash they had paid for the land. Passing along the inside of the stone-and-barbed-wire barrier, they screamed insults at Borzu, peppered with the specific sums they claimed he owed them.

The Shahidani brothers had destroyed the pasture's naturally growing hardy shrubs and fragile ground vegetation and had plowed under and eroded the top soil. Borzu would find the task of restoring the land difficult, and his livestock would not derive any sustenance from it for years to come. (The land was still void of any vegetation in 2004, except for a few inedible thorny plants here and there in the dusty expanse.) The Pastures Organization discussed with Borzu a project for planting new shrubs and reseeding but the agency never implemented it.

Borzu considered claiming the lower half of the orchard and maintaining it but the land there lacked water. If he could not irrigate, the trees would dry up and die. The natural springs, well, pumps, and reservoir were all located in the upper half and remained under Shahidani control. Given the acrimony of the two parties, no chance of a water-sharing agreement seemed imminent. Borzu asserted, rightly, that the water also belonged to him. The well was located on his legal pastureland.

Government agencies still officially classified all of this land as pastures. If Borzu took the orchard's lower half as it stood, his acceptance could mean that he agreed to the reclassification of the territory as cultivable land. This move was not in his interest, given his stake in the still remaining,

182 *The hope of spring*

surrounding pastureland. The line that state agents drew between pastoral and cultivable land rarely allowed for this kind of diversion, a cultivated plot encircled by pastures. The pastoralists and cultivators at Hanalishah constantly disputed over the boundary between these two types of land, and Borzu and the other nomads did not want to grant any new advantage to the enemy. They all faced the determined efforts of the cultivators to expand their land at the expense of the nomads' pastures. The two-pronged strategy of the cultivators throughout Hanalishah was to claim land for themselves (to use then or later for agriculture) and to devastate the nomads' pastures. In his final decision, Borzu was mindful of the constraints that his kinsmen also faced. His compromise was motivated more by the needs of the larger group than by his personal livelihood. In this way, he demonstrated effective, altruistic leadership and heeded the difficulties of his supporters.

During a quiet moment, Borzu confided to me that he feared dying without resolving the problem. He said his sons were not prepared for the task ahead. If they could not confront the Shahidani brothers, these and other cultivators would increase their hostile incursions to the detriment of all the pastoralists.

When the Shahidanis saw that some state agencies were ruling against them, they brashly offered to sell Borzu half of the land for 600,000 tumans. Greedy, they upped the price to 700,000 tumans several days later when they considered that they might profit from the loss after all. Borzu steadfastly refused to buy his own land. (The Shahidanis had bought both halves for 70,000 tumans in 1981, only a decade earlier.)

Irritated by the delay, armed security forces returned to Hanalishah. They brought the Pastures Organization's document ordering the Shahidanis to release eight hectares of the orchard to Borzu. The decree allowed the brothers to retain the other eight. After the nomads departed for winter pastures in September 1991, the Shahidani brothers picked and sold the apples from all 16 hectares and kept the money. While the nomads migrated to and set up camps in winter pastures, government-paid laborers severed the trunks of 400 apple trees in the orchard's lower section and dismantled the stone wall there. In a last-minute attempt to retain some property, the Shahidanis dug up some cherry and walnut trees and transplanted them in the upper part.

When Borzu and his family returned in the spring of 1992, they discovered a devastated, denuded plot punctuated by tree stumps. In just a few months, the strong winds of this high-altitude territory and the runoff from the past winter's rains and melting snows had eroded the soil. Vegetation, including the essential sturdy shrubs, no longer secured any topsoil. Borzu gained back part of his land but in useless condition, and the winds constantly swirled eroding soil throughout his campsite.

The Shahidanis had constructed a new stone wall to mark the reconfigured border and again topped it with multiple strands of barbed wire. Acutely aware of the steadily lowering water table, they increased the well's depth to 15 meters and pumped quantities of water, thereby causing the area's springs to produce even less.

A single walnut tree remained in the lower part, and Borzu and Mohammad Karim asked the brothers to let it stand. The Persians agreed or at least did not destroy it. Dariush surrounded the trunk with wire mesh to prevent goats from gnawing on the bark and grazing on the lower limbs. The tree was tall and healthy in 1999, and women and children relaxed in its shade. As Hanalishah's largest tree, it stood as a symbol of the conflict and its partial resolution.

That same year, another Persian cultivator trespassed across Borzu's pastureland from the other direction and excavated a huge hole at the base of the walnut tree. He claimed he was only tapping into the underground water and improving the flow of the spring there. Yet his intention was to destroy the tree's roots and thereby, indirectly, kill the tree. For him, the walnut tree stood as a symbol of the threat posed by the nomads' competing interests in cultivation. Despite his other assaults, he was not brazen enough to chop down the tree during the nomads' absence.

Dariush noted that the Shahidanis had undertaken great expense to pursue the case against Borzu and that they could have purchased land legally at Hanalishah near the river and planted a more productive orchard. As it stood, even the illegal orchard lacked sufficient water and suffered an ever-lowering water table.

Dariush lamented in 1999 that his family had not bought the land's upper half from the Shahidanis, with or without trees, despite it still being classified as pasture and therefore Borzu's rightful property. For years Borzu had fought against the inherent injustice of having to buy land that was already legally his. Dariush was less emotional and more pragmatic. The upper half including the trees had been priced at 600,000 tumans in 1991, and its value had risen to 10–15 million tumans by 1999. The property stood just beyond Dariush's summer campsite and would have provided a convenient place to build a new house sheltered by trees. Borzu's existing location was the most unpleasant one at Hanalishah by the late 1990s. Most other Qermezi men had planted orchards and lived nearby, the trees cooling the nomads and forming barriers against heat, wind, dust, and erosion. Borzu's location eroded further every year, and blowing grit made life miserable for the inhabitants and their visitors. Large herds traipsing across the denuded campsite multiple times every day deteriorated the land even more. By this time, practically all the camp's springs were dry, and the remaining one was the nomads' sole source of water.

Facing their own decreasing supply of water in 1999, the Shahidanis were once again busy with excavation and construction after the nomads departed for winter pastures. They deepened their well to 20 meters, dug more lateral underground channels hoping to tap into new sources of water, and extended the above-ground channels farther into the orchard.

Orchard land at Mehr-i Gerd

In the mid-1970s, Jehangir Khan Darrehshuri of Mehr-i Gerd offered Borzu an economic share in a new apple orchard he wanted to plant on a three-

184 *The hope of spring*

hectare plot south of the village. If Borzu would supervise the labor and serve as overseer, the khan would give Borzu the rights to the fruit of two-thirds of the trees.

The two men had enjoyed a close relationship since Borzu was a boy. Iran's army had killed Borzu's father in the 1943 Semirom war as he fought alongside Jehangir Khan. The khan often expressed gratitude to Shir Mohammad's sons, his favorite among them being Borzu, whose vibrant personality he always enjoyed. Prior to this new agreement, Borzu had supervised Jehangir Khan's flocks and shepherds, a job proving lucrative for him until the khan divested himself of most of his livestock. Jehangir Khan expected that the new orchard would continue their economic relationship and maintain their political bond. Requiring allies among the tribespeople, the khan had supported Borzu in his role as Qermezi headman at a time when other khans had tried to elevate another candidate in the subtribe.

Borzu oversaw the planting of a thousand apple saplings and arranged for a Qermezi relative living in Mehr-i Gerd to serve as caretaker. After seven years, the trees began producing a marketable crop, and Borzu reaped profits from that and subsequent annual sales of fruit. Jehangir Khan retained ownership of the land and the rights to the water.

Jehangir Khan decided in 1986 to divide the land with Borzu who, according to the initial two-thirds agreement, now became the owner of 700 mature trees. The khan retained 300 and divided the rights to the water issuing from an underground aqueduct (qanat). No money exchanged hands. The khan regarded the "gift" of two-thirds of the trees, land, and water as fair payment for Borzu's many years of loyal service. Given the hour's drive from Hanalishah, Borzu continued to rely on a hired caretaker from Mehr-i Gerd to perform some tasks, and his sons traveled there periodically to irrigate, spray pesticides, apply livestock dung as fertilizer, and check on the ripening crop. Annually he sold the upcoming harvest to a middleman who employed and supervised the labor to pick, pack, and transport the crop to markets in Isfahan. This land was the only one under Borzu's supposed ownership or control that did not cause him legal difficulties, and he was grateful to Jehangir Khan.

After several years of dispute with his younger brother Bizhan, Dariush decided in 1997 to sell the orchard so he could purchase a house in Kazerun. (Borzu had died in 1995.) The orchard's water supply had diminished to the point of concern, and Mehr-i Gerd's residents ("the khans' servants") stole apples and damaged the trees. Nasrullah Rezai bought the orchard for seven million tumans, plus another million for that autumn's apples. He is a Persian man who had taken up residence in Mehr-i Gerd to work for the khans and who over time had assumed a Qashqa'i identity (an unusual occurrence). Within months of the purchase, Rezai was demanding a refund from Borzu's sons. The orchard had become a liability given the water shortage. Most of the trees died, and Rezai cut them down and planted saplings.

The hope of spring 185

Orchard land at Hanalishah

Borzu bought some land in 1987 near the narrow river where it entered the Hanalishah valley from the mountain gorges to the east. The plot was small, a hectare or so, and cost him 120,000 tumans. (To demonstrate rising land prices and the ravages of inflation, this sum would buy only two or three mature apple trees in 1999.) This purchase of land was Borzu's first and only one at Hanalishah. Some other nomads there had already invested in agricultural land and planted apple orchards. Borzu had always been reluctant to adjust his livelihood to include the purchase of cultivable land but he understood the need to provide for his sons and grandsons. He bought the land from Mohammad Taqavi, a Persian resident of Vanak village with whom he had disputed, sometimes violently, ever since the nomads first came to Hanalishah.

Borzu's initial plan was to cultivate the new land with alfalfa. He had been unable to grow enough of this fodder for his livestock's needs and was forced to buy more from Hanalishah's Persian cultivators. For five years his sons grew alfalfa on the plot and irrigated with the plentiful water issuing from natural springs and the river. They harvested the crop three or more times each growing season, fed fresh alfalfa to their animals when natural pastures were depleted, and dried the crop for use in the late summer and early autumn. They also transported dried alfalfa to winter pastures to help sustain the livestock until winter rains sprouted the natural vegetation there.

Dariush and Bizhan planted apple saplings on the land in 1992 and began an orchard that they hoped would eventually provide a welcome annual income. Many kinsmen at Hanalishah had previously planted orchards and were now reaping profits. Dariush and Bizhan's orchard produced fruit for the market for the first time in 1999; the small crop, packed in crates, filled a single pickup truck. Every year thereafter they expected the fruit to increase until the trees reached maturity. Alfalfa, clover, and wild grasses continued to grow between the trees, and the brothers harvested them often during the summer to use as fresh and dried fodder.[3] Borzu's decision in 1987 to buy this plot had proved to be productive. Then legal complications erupted to plague even this purchase.

Taqavi died in 1991, and soon his sons were claiming that Borzu had never purchased any land from their father. Borzu had obtained a signed bill of sale from Taqavi but Taqavi's sons disputed it. Since then, this case too traveled through government agencies and the courts in Semirom and Shahreza while Borzu, and then Dariush and Bizhan, tried to resolve it. They could not obtain legal title to the land.

Dariush sought the mediation of Taqavi's eldest son, whom he hoped would help him reach an agreement with the others. Similar to his family's other land disputes, Dariush understood that the previous owner might force him to split the property. He would probably not obtain the man's cooperation in transferring the deed until the division occurred. In discussions with Amir Amiri (the Persian husband of Taqavi's daughter), Dariush convinced him to

186 *The hope of spring*

testify that Borzu had indeed paid Taqavi fully for the land. In the meantime, Borzu's sons tended the orchard as if the land were their undisputed possession. Taqavi's sons made no move to seize it or to claim the harvest.

(Amir Amiri had visited Borzu in 1970 when we camped at Kuh Pahn toward the end of the autumn migration. A young conscripted soldier posted in Kazerun, Amiri came to spend his furlough with Borzu. Borzu was acquainted with his family, which resided in Vanak and cultivated at Hanalishah. Borzu and Amiri seemed to enjoy one another's company, and Amiri assisted Borzu in his disputes with the region's Persians and Lurs who tried to force him and his nomadic group to leave Kuh Pahn. Later, when I asked Borzu about his relationship with the soldier and the reasons for his hospitality, he remarked, "You never know when you're going to need a friend." [A "friend" can offer favors, especially assistance in navigating the complications of the government's networks and bureaucratic formalities.] At the time I thought that this uneducated, unskilled Persian boy would never be in a position to benefit Borzu, and I told Borzu I was skeptical. For all the kindness that Borzu had extended to people during his life, I often wondered how many recipients had ever reciprocated, even in a small way. Three decades later, I saw that at least one courtesy was possibly to be repaid. Amiri could prove to be the person who could resolve this particular, troubling land dispute).[4]

The case finally reached some closure in 2000. Unable to get Taqavi's sons to clarify the issue, the government's office of deeds in Shahreza printed two notices in Isfahan newspapers stating that anyone holding interests in the property needed to notify its agents by a certain date. When no response resulted, the office provided Dariush and Bizhan with a property deed (*sunnat*). "Perhaps Taqavi's sons don't read the newspaper," commented Dariush, still uncertain that this affair was definitively settled. Bizhan and he proceeded to plant apricot, almond, and walnut trees along with more apple ones and increased the stand to 400. Their second harvest of apples exceeded the first one, and their spirits about their economic situation rose.

Land at Mulleh Balut

Since 1945, Qermezi nomads had exploited the sparse grazing at Mulleh Balut (a downward sloping expanse of land in the foothills below Dashtak's mountains) after they completed the autumn migration and before they ascended to winter pastures at Dashtak. They also cultivated fodder crops there in the autumn and winter and relied on rain (and not irrigation) to produce harvests.

Iran's land-reform officials issued their ruling about rights at Mulleh Balut in 1963 and allocated the land in its entirety to 27 Qermezi men. They assigned more land to Borzu and several others than to some who also cultivated there. Borzu and his kinsmen had heard rumors in 1962 about the rules for distribution under the terms of land reform, and a few of them promptly hired workers and employed draft animals to plow the land. Previously they had

The hope of spring   187

relied on their own labor to cultivate and did not use draft animals as intensively. Lacking sons old enough at the time, Borzu had contracted with less fortunate kinsmen to cultivate his plot in exchange for a share of the harvest. According to land-reform officials, Borzu was now entitled to five hectares of land, as were Murad and Ghulam Husain, because of their efforts to intensify production. Most other Qermezi men received two or three hectares, and a few gained only one. Borzu and the others continued to cultivate the land. Again, Borzu relied on poorer kinsmen to perform the labor in exchange for a portion of the harvest. Sometimes the nomads produced a crop netting little more than the volume of seeds they had planted, but they understood that, under the terms of land reform, they needed to cultivate annually to retain their rights. If they did not work the land, the state would deed it to others. Competition over such rights was growing.

Borzu's sons and the 26 other men had still not obtained legal deeds to the land by 2000, despite more than half a century of uninterrupted cultivation and despite the definitive ruling of the land-reform commission in 1963. The last official landowner on record, Mehdi Tabib, is a Persian from Kazerun. For years, despite trying, he had not collected rent but he still refused to release the deed or facilitate the process through Kazerun's agencies and court. When he died in 1990, his sons maintained the same stance. They inherited the land and received the updated deed in their names. This case too moved slowly through court. Dariush worried that Tabib's sons might force him and the other nomads to split the land if they wanted to resolve the conflict.

Borzu's three sons had not yet divided Borzu's five hectares among themselves by 2002. The brothers used mules and tractors (borrowed from their Qairkhbaili kinsmen camped nearby) for plowing and continued to sow the land and feed the harvest (barley and straw) to their livestock. The Organization for Nomads' Affairs (ONA) had dug a well in 1990 at Mulleh Balut for use by the nomads there and at nearby Dashtak. Some Qairkhbaili men had begun irrigating their fields, thus increasing yields. Then four Qairkhbaili men received government loans to dig their own wells and were able to expand their production to include vegetables and melons for town and city markets. Borzu's sons and the other Aqa Mohammadli men relied as before on precipitation and derived often small harvests.

ONA began to implement plans in 1999 for a small village for some Qermezi nomads. For the project, its officials chose a section of Mulleh Balut farther down the mountain slope from the areas still cultivated by Borzu and his kinsmen. Instantly, the entire location became more valuable, especially because of the government's plan to dig wells and construct reservoirs for irrigation. The nomads there hoped that the issue of legal tenure would finally be resolved.

Pastureland at Dashtak and Hanalishah

Borzu's grazing permit issued by the Pastures Organization stipulated that he could tend 240 animals at Dashtak. When its agents divided Borzu's permit

188   *The hope of spring*

in 1996 to reflect his sons' economic independence, they allowed Mohammad Karim 140 animals, and Dariush and Bizhan 120. The organization promised to issue 30-year grazing deeds to the nomads at Dashtak soon.

Another agency, this one in charge of natural resources, reconfigured the grazing permits of Borzu's three sons in 2001 and allowed them only 50 total head of livestock (17, 16, and 16, respectively) on their combined Dashtak pastures, an impossibly low number for them to sustain their livelihoods. Dariush wanted his own permit, separate from Bizhan's, but expected that the agency might deny him one for only 16 animals.

An agent in Kazerun had drafted a formula for determining the carrying capacity of the territory of the three brothers: $N = S\ P\ K$ over $2n$ (N: number of total livestock, S: size of pastures, P: amount of edible vegetation per hectare, K: percentage of land having edible vegetation, and n: number of days spent in winter pastures). With the data entered (310 hectares x 120 kilograms x 40 percent over 2 x 150 days), N equaled 49.6 livestock. The agent noted that he could enter a larger number for the three brothers if they would agree to pay higher state taxes. The annual tax for every 50 head was 6,000 tumans; an adequate combined herd of 600 would cost them 72,000 tumans. If the nomads needed a government loan or other state services relating to their primary livelihood, they would have to demonstrate proof of animal numbers and payment of taxes. Sensing unhappiness on Dariush's part, the agent said that Dariush could hire a private engineer to map the territory and possibly achieve better results. The fee for such a task was exorbitant and out of the question.

The three brothers remained uncertain about their course of action. They considered raising camels for the meat market, inspired by ONA's promised assistance and the profitable venture of several Aqa Mohammadli kinsmen.

Agents of the Pastures Organization also visited Hanalishah in 1996 to discuss land use there. They asked each nomad to state his livestock numbers, reduced that figure by at least half, and explained that the land could not sustain as many animals as the men currently tended. Later that summer they issued grazing permits specifying boundaries and herd sizes. Mohammad Karim, Dariush, and Bizhan had fallen under Borzu's grazing permit but the agency now issued Mohammad Karim his own permit and Dariush and Bizhan a separate one. The brothers continued to tend the animals they needed, not the state-specified number, and other nomads at Hanalishah did the same. Herd sizes fluctuated significantly during the course of a year because of births, deaths, sales, and social and ceremonial obligations, and each nomad temporarily cared for the animals of others. State agents tolerated some flexibility in numbers on any territory at any given time. Mohammad Karim's permit allowed him 85 animals, the same on Dariush and Bizhan's joint permit.

Much of Hanalishah's pastureland was still disputed in 2000, as had been the situation since the mid-1950s when Persians and Lurs from Semirom, Vanak, and Galleh Qadam began to compete over land in the valley. (The

The hope of spring 189

paramount Qashqa'i khans had controlled the area until Mohammad Reza Shah forced them into exile in 1954.) As the cultivators' demands for more land toward the mountain slopes grew, so did the conflicts. Dozens of often overlapping legal cases languished in the courts in Semirom, Shahreza, and Isfahan and forced the nomads to wait for resolutions. The Pastures Organization promised to issue 30-year grazing deeds to Hanalishah's nomads, but this outcome seemed unlikely as long as so many Persians and Lurs pressed their claims through court. Every year these cultivators labored to improve the land, including constructing new irrigation systems. By doing so, they impeded further a beneficial solution for the nomads. In some ways fortunate for the Qermezi, the ever-decreasing supply of water necessary for irrigation slowed the territorial incursions of some cultivators.

Life in town

In the autumn, winter, and early spring of 1994–95, six Qermezi families lived in the town of Kazerun near Dashtak, their winter pastures and those of their closest relatives. In the middle to late spring they all migrated to summer pastures at Hanalishah where they occupied tents or small stone structures. They include five Aqa Mohammadli families (headed by Husain Ali, Ali, Jehangir-Fathullah-Amanullah, Filamarz, and Borzu) and one Imamverdili family (headed by Nasibullah). Fathullah was economically independent but shared a house with his father Jehangir and his younger brother Amanullah. Of the six, Husain Ali was the first to live there, followed by the others, and Borzu was the most recent.

In this section, I describe conditions as they existed in 1994–95. Occasionally I offer updated information [indicated by square brackets] from my visits to Kazerun in 2000–01 and 2001–02, my visit to Hanalishah in 2004, and personal communications since then.

Six men in five of the six families were government-employed schoolteachers in or near Kazerun, and their children attended town schools. Four of them had formerly taught in nomads' schools in winter and summer pastures. When they decided to teach in or near Kazerun, they established town residences. The state offered teachers help in finding houses to rent or buy and vacant lots on which to build, and the six (Fathullah and Amanullah jointly) exploited the opportunity. One of them, Ali, received a low-interest, state-bank loan to help finance construction. Another, Fathullah, sought a loan but the government denied his request because he had nearly finished his house. The six teachers (Fathullah and Amanullah jointly) owned their houses in 1994–95.

These teachers depended on income beyond their government salaries to sustain the new lifestyle. Life in town proved to be considerably more expensive than in seasonal pastures. Their wages comparatively low, the teachers often complained that they earned little more than hired shepherds and sometimes less. (The scarcity of shepherds in the region in the 1990s and the difficult

190 *The hope of spring*

work meant they could command wages commensurate with some factory and urban jobs, including teaching.) When I inquired why these teachers did not take jobs as shepherds, they looked shocked and then explained that the work was too arduous. Once they had adopted the comforts of urban life, they were unlikely to return to the daily chores of nomadic pastoralism that they and their fathers had performed since childhood. As beneficiaries of formal education and as teachers, their social status was high in Qashqa'i society and was elevated in the wider Iranian society. Hired shepherds in both communities held low status.

The six teachers used to own sheep and goats independently, or jointly with their fathers and brothers, but only one maintained a substantial herd in 1994. He hired a shepherd, earned a welcome annual income from animal sales, and benefited by producing meat, dairy products, and sheep wool for his family. The other five entrusted their diminishing livestock to their fathers and brothers, who continued to reside at Dashtak and to migrate. They informally contracted with these kin to share the animals' expenses and the income from the products, based on the number of livestock each party owned. Two of the five derived a small but steady income from livestock. The other three drew on their animals mainly for social purposes, such as offering freshly slaughtered meat to honored guests and contributing live animals to the hosts of weddings and memorial services.

Five of the six teachers also owned apple orchards in summer pastures and relied on the annual sale of fruit to augment their government salaries. As relatively young men, they lacked sons old enough to contribute independently to the family income. Their children were still schoolage, except for one boy who quit after the eighth grade. The army promptly conscripted him, and he was imprisoned in Kurdistan in 1995 for having deserted. The father of two teachers, Jehangir traded in handwoven textiles in Kazerun and the vicinity and contributed the income to his and Amanullah's joint household.

The sixth Qermezi family residing in Kazerun belonged to Borzu. Given his worsening illness, he and his sons had decided in 1993 that he would prefer living in a house in town for the winter rather than in the family's stone-and-thatch shelter at Dashtak. Most nomads at Dashtak had recently built more substantial (but still rudimentary) dwellings and were sheltered from some of the season's harshness but Borzu's family had not yet taken this step. The marriage of Borzu's middle son Dariush in 1993 was another factor in the family's choosing town residence. The new bride (who is Darrehshuri but not Qermezi) was raised in Shiraz and was not accustomed to Dashtak's rigors. Wanting children, she did not relish the task of caring for an infant in winter pastures without adequate refuge, heat, and water. Borzu's youngest son Bizhan and his wife and son continued to reside in the family's hut at Dashtak while they cared for Borzu's two herds, oversaw the hired shepherds, processed milk products, and cultivated fodder.

Assisted by Persian acquaintances in Kazerun, Dariush located a house to rent for six months during the autumn, winter, and early spring of 1993–94.

The hope of spring 191

Most homeowners rejected potential tenants who would stay for only a few months but Dariush was fortunate to find one who had recently built another house and was prepared to vacate the one his family currently occupied. After the six months, content with the new arrangements in Kazerun, Dariush hoped to rent the same house again when he and his family would return to Kazerun in the autumn. The landlord countered by raising the rent beyond a sum that Dariush's family could afford. After searching, Dariush located another house, smaller and not as nicely finished, to rent for the following two-plus seasons. Dariush settled Borzu there on the family's arrival from summer pastures in September 1994.

Five of the six houses inhabited by these Qermezi families were located in a new residential neighborhood in the northern outskirts of Kazerun close to the mountains rising high above the town. A rough dirt road from Kazerun to their winter pastures at Dashtak ran nearby, and people in each area could travel to the other without needing to pass through town and be vulnerable to the townspeople's scrutiny. The first Qermezi settler chose this section of town to be near the mountains, and five subsequent settlers including Borzu found plots close by. As residents of isolated mountainous camps, the nomads could usually keep outsiders at a distance. Now residents of a town, they worried about their security and privacy and were glad they could travel to their pastures without urbanites seeing when they went, what goods they carried back and forth, and who visited them.[5]

Husain Ali and Zohreh invited Borzu's family and my daughter and me to be their guests for dinner. Walking east (in our first excursion in town), we followed the narrow dirt lane in front of Borzu's house past the high courtyard walls of three other dwellings. In front of us stood vacant land, and a sharp ridge of mountains rose behind it. There, in the empty space, Qashqa'i nomads had pitched their tents, their few sheep and goats grazing nearby, and I was struck by the sight of the two lifestyles so close together.

Although not adjoining, the houses of the five Qermezi families were near enough that men, women, and children could easily visit one another several or more times a day. A walk of only minutes along narrow dirt lanes brought the residents of one dwelling to the others. High brick walls secluded all domiciles in the neighborhood, and passersby rarely encountered other people along the way. Some houses abutted the lane with an enclosed open-air courtyard standing behind the dwelling. Other houses stood along the back wall with an enclosed open-air courtyard in front and adjacent to the high wall along the lane. A new section of Kazerun, the neighborhood consisted of vacant lots, houses under construction, and newly occupied homes, one of these often right next to the others.

A small grocery shop owned or rented by a Persian man and stocked with seasonal fruits and vegetables, processed foods, and commodities such as laundry soap and plastic buckets was close to the five Qermezi dwellings. A low six-sided concrete frame, its blue paint peeling, stood in front of the shop where the lane made a turn. It held flowering plants in the spring but

192   *The hope of spring*

currently only weeds grew. I dubbed the place "Qermezi Center" (*markaz*-i Qermezi, *maidan*-i Qermezi); it stood equidistant from the five houses. Such place names are common in Iran's towns and cities, and the Qermezi laughed about their application to their small community. Women and children frequented the conveniently located store while men and older boys usually walked or hitched rides to the town center to buy goods in larger quantities and at lower prices. Kazerun's twisting covered bazaar and straight central streets offered a variety of shops, commodities, and services. A bread bakery was located near the five houses, and the residents sometimes purchased their daily supplies of flat unleavened bread there. The same women buying this bread always baked their own flat bread in summer pastures.

[All women baked their own bread at home in Kazerun in 2000–02. Only rarely, such as when guests unexpectedly arrived, did someone run to the bakery. People cited rising prices as the reason for the change but they also preferred the taste and texture of their own bread and valued the tradition of caring for their own needs. This bread was thinner than the bakery's and more pliable for grasping other foods with the fingers. The renewed emphasis on "Turki" bread was part of the concurrent revival of Qashqa'i customs.]

The sixth Qermezi house, its construction just finished, stood in a new neighborhood of northern Kazerun west of the main asphalt road running through town. Its owner, Ali (Ali Qurban), preferred being independent, and when inexpensive lots became available for schoolteachers there, he chose one rather than searching the neighborhood of the other Qermezi families. By doing so, he isolated his wife and daughters and, in effect, prevented them from enjoying the daily interaction experienced by the other Qermezi women and children in Kazerun. A few houses in his neighborhood were recently occupied while others were still under construction. Some potential house plots stood vacant while piles of stones and fired bricks marked others. Several Persian men had already opened small shops in the neighborhood and stocked them with basic items. (Updating my lists of the activities of all Qermezi men, I would ask if each man rented or owned a house. Most of them did not. Sometimes the respondent would answer, "He's piled stones." That is, he claimed a plot and demonstrated his intention to build. The stone heaps on lots in Kazerun served the same purpose.)

[A Qermezi man newly holding socially conservative values complimented Ali in 2000 for isolating his four preadolescent and adolescent daughters from the "corrupting" influences that the other Qermezi girls, frequently visiting one another, experienced in their own neighborhood. By this year, Ali's neighborhood had developed, with paved streets, streetlights, and public utilities servicing the homes. With shocking suddenness and high volume, a loudspeaker nearby, mounted on a tall pole, called people to prayer three times (not five) a day, announced when to begin and end the daily fasts during Ramadan, and advertised Qur'an readings and other Islam-related events. Not yet built by 2002, the mosque intended for the neighborhood would stand on a plot abutting Kazerun's main asphalt road, in line with regime policy to place new

The hope of spring   193

religious structures where a maximum of passersby would see and possibly frequent them and where people would be exposed to state regulations and ruling ideologies. Such public displays demonstrated and symbolized the government's ongoing efforts to Islamize Iran's citizens.]

The single-story houses of these six Qermezi families contained multiple rooms. One, two, or three rooms were used for sleeping and storage. A large reception room was covered wall to wall with knotted pile carpets from the family looms, and an entryway also seated visitors. A kitchen was equipped with a refrigerator and a propane burner, and a bathing room was connected to a water heater in the kitchen. All houses featured a skylight over a small, recessed or sunken, ceramic-tiled space where residents displayed a few live plants and the horns, mounted heads, and stuffed bodies of wild game.

The Qermezi families stacked their belongings in one or two sleeping and storage rooms in the same way they did in their tents. Large grain sacks and other filled woven containers sat at the bottom of the pile, which rested on a tent's wooden poles to raise the goods several centimeters off the floor—for cleanliness and the circulation of air and to inhibit mice and insects from dwelling there. Smaller woven containers and folded textiles occupied the middle of the pile, and bedding rolls and pillows rested on top—all but the pillows draped with a decorative handwoven *gelim* hung with dozens of tassels. People could vacate these premises almost as efficiently and quickly as they emptied and dismantled their tents. In both places, they kept most of their possessions packed in special containers of different sorts. While residing in houses or tents, they could easily or with difficulty locate any specific item, depending on their memory, organizational skills, and efforts to keep others from rooting around in their possessions.[6]

Residents usually kept the reception room empty except for the knotted carpets on the floor and the firm, square cushions leaning against the walls for guests. Some stored these cushions and produced them only when visitors arrived, the way they also treated their finest-quality knotted carpets. Only one of the six families possessed any furniture; two tall wooden cabinets held goods in a room used for sleeping. Everyone sat, ate, and slept on the floor. Women and girls squatted in the kitchen to prepare and cook food just as they did in and outside their tents. Some enjoyed the luxury of a few shelves or wall-mounted cabinets for the storage of equipment and supplies.

Families decorated the reception-room walls with small handwoven items, strings of multicolored tassels (otherwise used to ornament the entrance to their tents), posters, world maps, notices of memorial services, photographs of war martyrs, and fancy clocks kept perpetually wrapped in clear plastic. The posters depicted images meaningful to and symbolic for the Qashqa'i: wild game (especially animals with magnificent horns and antlers), weapons, galloping wild horses, and Bagh-i Eram (the ornate residence of the paramount Qashqa'i khans in Shiraz, confiscated first by Mohammad Reza Shah and then by revolutionary guards). Several families displayed reproductions of watercolor paintings of nostalgically rendered customary nomadic life by Bijan

194   *The hope of spring*

Bahadori-Kashkuli, the preeminent Qashqa'i artist. One family with young, schoolage children posted a government-issued drawing of the proper positions and attire for men, women, and children during daily prayers. School administrators in Kazerun required children to pray at school and urged them to do so at home.[7] [The poster was gone in 2000, and my daughter and I never saw any children praying during any of our visits.]

In two Qermezi houses, a completed interior staircase led to a nonexistent second story, and people used the individual stairs for storage. Similar to others in Iran, builders and owners anticipated eventually adding a second story, for rental income or accommodating family members such as a newly married son and his bride. The stairs facilitated the raising of the second level and minimized the disruption to the first.

[In the autumn of 1997, two years after Borzu's death, Dariush and Bizhan purchased a small house in Kazerun. It contained a small but well-made basement, the only one for these Qermezi houses. Giving me a tour in 2000, Bizhan joked, "Whew! Look at all the junk we nomads have to carry around with us! For this reason alone, we should settle permanently somewhere!" There, piled in the basement, were the belongings the two families had transported to Kazerun at the end of summer and were soon to carry back to summer pastures, including folded goat-hair tent panels, rolled reed screens (to surround the tent as protection against wind and to use as lamb and kid pens), splayed tent poles, felt mats, livestock troughs, goatskin bags, kerosene and propane-gas lanterns, and paraphernalia for milk and yarn production. The families lacked any trusted friends near Hanalishah where they could store these items, and, once they loaded them for transport, they said they might as well take them all the way to Kazerun.

In Bizhan's case, he had planned to spend the autumn and winter in the family hut at Dashtak and would have needed this gear for himself there. On arrival he decided instead to stay in Kazerun and to rely more heavily on his hired shepherd at Dashtak. Such sudden changes in plans and a desire to be prepared, whatever decisions they chose, led the families in Kazerun to transport all their property back and forth. If Bizhan had to herd the livestock to another winter pastures because of deficient grazing at Dashtak, all the necessary equipment would be at hand.

Some nomads now held weddings at the end of winter or in the early spring (and no longer just in the summer), and they needed their own and other people's tents, poles, and screens to pitch for the celebrations.

All families always carried their valuable handwoven textiles with them because Kazerun's high heat and humidity in the summer would irreparably damage the items. They also worried about theft if these goods were in storage.]

High-walled, open-air courtyards situated in front or behind the house featured one or several citrus trees and grapevines and a cold-water tap where women and girls washed dishes and clothing. (They lit the water heater inside only periodically and just for bathing.) Unlike the yards of many other Iranian homes, these lacked a small pool with a fountain or one stocked with ornamental fish. A small brick structure in a corner contained a cement or ceramic keyhole platform situated over a pit and used by squatting. Families employed the courtyard's space for multiple purposes just as they did the area around a tent. Women and girls rigged their looms there, sometimes under a piece of tent fabric stretched out for shade or on a platform under a porch roof. They often used metal poles for the loom's frame, ordinarily too heavy to carry to summer pastures. Only one family owned a vehicle in 1995, which Dariush always parked in the enclosed and locked courtyard at night to guard against theft. No one kept chickens, dogs, or other animals during the months-long residence because of the messiness and smell. Relatives and hired shepherds tended any such animals at Dashtak. Several families did purchase chicks and ducklings toward the end of winter, kept them caged, and transported them to raise to maturity outdoors in summer pastures, where they would slaughter them for guests. Some Persian neighbors in Kazerun turned loose chickens, ducks, geese, and turkeys in the public lanes during the day to scrounge on weeds and kitchen wastes.

High walls kept the activities in each courtyard private. Qermezi women ignored Kazerun's codes of modest dress while they occupied their homes and courtyards, even when next-door neighbors could see them from their second-story windows and balconies. Notions of social distance operated. A Persian man on a balcony remained seemingly oblivious to any women in a courtyard below, and unveiled women there could continue their activities as if they were unobserved. I saw someone exercise caution only once. Early one morning, Bizhan and Husain Ali lugged a dead wild hyena into Borzu's courtyard and laid it out for everyone's inspection. The two men had spent many vigilant nights at Dashtak while waiting to sight and shoot the predator. Later, when Bizhan spotted a Persian woman shaking a carpet on a neighboring balcony, he yanked a gunny sack over the hyena. I did not ask the reason but he might have worried that he lacked a government permit for his rifle.

Sometimes the Qermezi residents kept ajar the metal door leading to their houses and courtyards to facilitate children running in and out and to aid their frequent visitors. Infrequent callers tapped on the metal door with a coin or key to indicate their presence, despite the door being unlatched. Strangers waited in the lane for someone to emerge from inside. All houses were equipped with electric doorbells but only one functioned (its sound a lengthy, elaborate, annoying bird song). Sometimes people complained that they had waited a long time before anyone heard their knocking and came to welcome them. Some frequent visitors employed unique taps to signal their presence. Residents also recognized, by sound, specific vehicles belonging to relatives and acquaintances as they approached and stopped by the gate. When they heard an unknown one, women within hastily straightened the reception room, set up cushions, and checked their attire to ascertain if they were properly covered. Every Qashqa'i driver gunned his engine just as he drew to a halt, as if to proclaim his special (and masculine) presence. No Qermezi women drove, as of 2005.[8]

196   *The hope of spring*

The Kazerun municipality provided the six houses with running water, electricity, and natural gas, and once a month its employees delivered (by hand) bills for services rendered. Residents still depended on other sources of light and heat, primarily kerosene and propane gas (the same fuels they also periodically used in winter and summer pastures), because of frequent power outages and brownouts. Women baked flat bread on a convex metal pan resting over a charcoal fire outside in the courtyard, where men broiled meat on skewers over firewood or charcoal. Men collected the wood from the upper slopes of Dashtak's mountains and transported it by mules and donkeys to the nearest road. (The logs they burned in faraway Hanalishah came from the same place and were treasured for the nightly communal gatherings around a tent's central firepit—another activity that the Qashqa'i value as central to their culture.)

Once a week or so a private garbage collector (not a municipal employee), pushing a large wheelbarrow with extended sides, came by the houses and sorted through, for recycling, items discarded outside the front gate. Qermezi women complained about throwing away kitchen wastes such as bones and vegetable peelings, which always provided essential food for pack animals, goats, chickens, and dogs in seasonal pastures. Home mail service was said to be available but the residents continued to depend on merchant-acquaintances to receive and hold any rare pieces of mail. If a man needed to send a written message, he always preferred entrusting it to a visiting relative to deliver personally.

Every Qermezi family wanted telephone service but their homes lacked connections to outside lines in 1995. Long waiting lists and high charges (including bribery) kept practically everyone without phone service through 1999. The municipality required a large cash deposit, which all men had paid years previously. Ali was the first to receive a telephone line to his house but he sold the connection back to the township so he could have money to buy a pickup truck. Fathullah received his phone number in 1995 but still lacked a line to his house in 2000. During the interval he would check my address book to see if I still listed his number and would joke about my not phoning him from the United States. When these families needed to place a call, they visited a friendly merchant in the bazaar but disliked having people there overhear their conversations, even if they discussed only trivial matters. They avoided the town's public telephone office; they suspected that the regime conducted routine surveillance on all exchanges.

[Husain Ali finally received a home telephone line in 1998 through Shahriyar Qermezi's intervention (the parliamentary deputy). Building a political base in the subtribe, Husain Ali wanted a phone to communicate with the widely dispersed Qermezi. Soon the device disgusted him. All sorts of calls came day and night, most of which conveyed instructions for him to relay messages to others. Bizhan Qermezi purchased a secondhand cellular phone in 2001, the first one in Qermezi. Mountains obstructed any signals during his sojourn in winter and summer pastures, and, disgruntled, he had to drive to a town having the necessary access in order to place a call. Many young and middle-aged

The hope of spring 197

Qermezi men owned mobile telephones by 2013. Most of them were still migratory and resided in multiple places every year, and by phone they could contact relatives and business acquaintances and make appointments with state agencies.]

Most of the families in town owned black-and-white televisions although they infrequently watched this state-controlled medium. They accessed only two channels in Kazerun whose programming was virtually identical, limited to several hours every evening (with additional hours on Fridays and other holidays), and heavy in religious content and politically censored news. Both channels announced and listed the times of the three (not five) daily prayers and the daily schedule for fasting during Ramadan. Men speculated about national and international events that did not receive television coverage. A few sometimes discussed the nightly Persian-language reports from the British Broadcasting Company and the Voice of America and learned what the regime was trying to conceal. A man listening to news on Iranian radio snorted, "Lies, all lies." Men and boys enjoyed most the televised hunting and nature programs produced in foreign countries and rebroadcast in Iran. Veterans of the Iraq–Iran war sometimes watched Iran-made, propagandistic, outdated drama-documentaries about the hostilities and would comment caustically. The state presented melodramas in March intended to demonstrate the danger of playing with fireworks to celebrate the New Year. Actors proclaimed, "Fireworks will kill or maim your precious sons!" In these often-indirect ways, the state tried to prevent the celebration of pre-Islamic, Zoroastrian rituals. When Ahmad Khomeini, the son of Ayatollah Khomeini, was ill and then died, the government added hours of religious coverage every day.

Qermezi women showed little or no interest in the medium and often complained that their children seemed transfixed by idiotic Japanese cartoons. They groused that their evenings were destroyed. Visitors sat silently facing the flickering screen instead of sharing information and appreciating companionship after a work-filled day.

[Channels available in Kazerun had increased to five by 2002, with one from Shiraz carrying regional news and a regular Friday-afternoon program about Qashqa'i culture. A daily dramatic series from Tehran captivated some people's attention so much that they planned their early-evening activities by its schedule. Some women would not serve dinner until that night's story had ended. By now, most families had purchased a small color television equipped with a remote-control device, which they kept wrapped in protective plastic.]

The Qermezi in Kazerun and at Dashtak frequently visited one another. Men living at Dashtak traveled to Kazerun multiple times every week to buy supplies, sell products, and meet with merchants and government agents, and they often paused at their relatives' homes to share news, enjoy meals, bathe, and temporarily store goods. Men living in Kazerun went to Dashtak once a week or so, more often if they owned livestock and/or cultivated there, and they too saw relatives, exchanged news, and ate meals together. The Qermezi visiting from the subtribe's many other locations usually stopped first at the

198   *The hope of spring*

homes of their relatives and tribesmates in Kazerun and then traveled together with them to Dashtak.

All Qermezi were widely dispersed, and those living in Kazerun were similar to the others. Their residence there was seasonal, as were the residences of other subtribal members. They interacted with many Qermezi, remained an integral part of the subtribe, and were linked to associates in other tribes and locations. They discussed current and future plans with these individuals, especially the actions they each anticipated for the next few seasons. Each person's decisions depended on those of others, and they proceeded in these communal ways, despite the physical distances that often separated them, to forge their individual actions (which were thus interlinked with those of others). Practically everyone still moved seasonally, regardless of periodically inhabiting permanent residences or not.

Women in Kazerun were more integrated in the larger Qermezi community than were women at Dashtak because their homes were gathering places for the subtribe. At Dashtak, women were somewhat isolated in their widely separated camps and could visit one another only irregularly due to their daily, consuming tasks. They traveled to Kazerun less frequently than their kinsmen at Dashtak. When they did come, they accompanied these kinsmen and followed their schedules and whims. Dashtak's women and children hoped to bathe during their trips to town but did not always find time or have privacy. Water was a scarce resource at Dashtak, and the cold, rainy, sometimes snowy weather usually precluded women's efforts to heat water and find seclusion for bathing. Living outdoors at Dashtak, they could not wash thoroughly. Women's interest in seeing doctors and getting medical tests seemed partly motivated by their desire to visit female kin in Kazerun and enjoy a chance to rest and bathe. Men were more apt to take wives and daughters there for medical reasons than simply for baths.

Qermezi women at Dashtak always wore customary Qashqa'i clothes (multiple skirts gathered at the hips, long tunics, and diaphanous scarves) at home and during visits to Kazerun. They sometimes grabbed a veil-wrap (chadur) to throw around themselves in case they stopped at a clinic or the bazaar. When Qermezi women living in Kazerun called on their relatives at Dashtak, even for only a noon meal, they always donned Qashqa'i attire. At home, a few of them wore modified versions of this dress, including fewer and less-voluminous skirts and long, loose blouses rather than shin-length tunics. There they often used opaque headscarves when they entered Kazerun's public spaces, but they changed to thin translucent scarves when they prepared to travel to Dashtak. (While residing in summer pastures, they all donned Qashqa'i apparel including the transparent scarf for some.) Qermezi women from other locations, who visited kin in Kazerun and at Dashtak, also put on Qashqa'i clothes, even if they were city residents who dressed in versions of urban attire there.

When children at Dashtak successfully completed the fifth grade in the nomads' elementary school there, they either ended their formal education

The hope of spring 199

(increasingly unlikely by 1995) or continued in Kazerun's public schools while living with close relatives there. A third option for some of them was attending the selective tribal secondary schools in Chinar Shahijan, Nurabad-Mamassani, or Shiraz. Between 1967 (when the first Qermezi boy began secondary school in Kazerun) and 1984 (when the first Qermezi man established a residence there), secondary-school students—boys only—rented rooms together and subsisted as best as they could on market-bought foods. They always returned home to Dashtak on weekends and holidays, where they resumed pastoral chores.

After 1984, these students lived comfortably in their relatives' houses in Kazerun and took their meals there. A crisis of sorts had emerged by the early 1990s when growing numbers of students sought temporary homes in town. When a Dashtak resident, Mohammad Karim, decided in 1998 to send one, then two, then three, then four, and then finally five of his children to live with his younger brother Dariush in Kazerun so they could continue school there, Dariush's wife balked at the idea. She was tending her ill mother-in-law as well as her young son, and she was beginning her first year of university study. Her home was already the center of social life in Kazerun for the Qermezi residents, the nomads at Dashtak, other Qermezi visiting from elsewhere, and acquaintances in other subtribes, tribes, and urban areas. Just feeding and caring for the many daily visitors was a full-time responsibility. Unhappy, Mohammad Karim needed to devise alternative solutions for most of these children.

When declining enrollments jeopardized the nomads' elementary school at Dashtak, the Qermezi residents of Kazerun worried that they would be inundated by all its pupils. Housing itself was a negligible factor given plentiful floor space and blankets. Food, clothing, and medical and school expenses were another matter, as was the deafening noise of many children in small interior spaces. Yet no one was willing to force any child to stop schooling simply because his or her presence was inconvenient. As inflation ran rampant, the Qermezi residents pondered the economic impact of hosting so many children. If the government classified them as nomads, they received a few state-subsidized food commodities, but only for their own children and not for more than three. Obligations of close kinship and intermarriage seemed to preclude the parents from offering any substantial economic contributions in exchange for the care of their schoolage children.

The Qermezi living in Kazerun experienced limited contact in their homes and neighborhoods with other town citizens. Men met fellow teachers at school but rarely outside. Schoolchildren knew their classmates but these relationships stopped at the school gates or the doors of their homes. Even neighbors on either side and across the lane only rarely interacted. They did not go beyond a routine affable greeting when they happened to encounter one another in the lane. A Qermezi woman did cultivate ties with a neighborblessed with a telephone line so she could learn the fate of her son imprisoned in Kurdistan. Neighborhood boys played soccer and other street games but never entered one another's homes. Unveiled women and older

200 *The hope of spring*

girls were likely to be there. Qermezi girls including students were more confined to their homes than boys. The town's codes of modesty and proper female behavior and the close proximity of multitudes of male strangers restricted these girls.

[Dariush's next-door Persian neighbor for many years, a woman he said he had never even seen, sent his family and other neighbors bowls of noodle-and-bean soup to fulfill a vow she had made in 2000 for Ramadan. Several days later Dariush's sister Fariba delivered a container of thickened milk—a special treat, the first milk of the season—to the woman's door. The two parties engaged in the same exchange in Ramadan of 2001 but had not interacted in any way in the intervening year, other than to offer greetings on the rare chance they met in the lane.]

Qermezi men in Kazerun and at Dashtak and the Persian merchants with whom they transacted did not create social relationships.[9] Before anyone at Dashtak had owned vehicles or took up residence in Kazerun, a few merchants periodically toured Dashtak to conduct business, and the nomads hospitably invited them into their tents. Merchants came to know family members and inquired about their well-being. Qermezi men never visited the merchants' homes in Kazerun. When some nomads acquired vehicles, they traveled frequently to Kazerun to handle business in the bazaar, which ended the merchants' trips through winter pastures.

Some other Qashqa'i had also established residences in Kazerun, seasonally like the Qermezi, and some Qermezi formed limited relationships with them. They did not socialize together, and no marriages had occurred among them by 2013. A Farsi Madan Qashqa'i family sought a Qermezi girl as a bride for its son in 1997, but her family politely rebuffed the offer because of the distant, non-kin relationship. For several years, the two families had lived on the same lane separated by only three houses. They cordially greeted one another when their paths happened to cross but did not otherwise interact. When another Farsi Madan man became the nomads' teacher at Dashtak, a relationship opened up between his family and some Qermezi. Husain Ali Qermezi needed someone to guard his house during his family's sojourn in summer pastures, and he chose the teacher as the most reliable prospect.

When all Qermezi inhabited tents, they never left a dwelling empty, for fear of thieves. After these six Qermezi families moved to houses in Kazerun for the autumn, winter, and early spring, they retained the custom. They worried more about robbers in Kazerun, where practically everyone was a stranger, than in seasonal pastures, where they could exercise effective surveillance. When these families migrated to summer pastures, they took all of their valuables along. They each found an adult acquaintance to occupy the home during their absence, to safeguard the few possessions they were forced to leave behind (such as the refrigerator and water heater) and to lessen the chances of vandalism.

[Two days after the beginning of the New Year in 2005, some Qermezi families in Kazerun planned a two-day holiday excursion to the Persian Gulf coast (an unprecedented event for any Qermezi). All of them, except one, left a person behind at home for security. When Dariush and his family returned to Kazerun after the trip, they found their courtyard door slightly ajar and the house empty, stripped of *all* of their possessions.]

Welcoming the New Year

The Qermezi who migrated between winter and summer pastures approached the beginning of the New Year (*no ruz*) on 20–21 March (the spring equinox) differently than many other Iranians. They began the move to summer pastures around that time, usually on the very first day of the New Year. Spring meant a renewed chance to better their livelihood by leaving behind the soon-to-be-hot winter zone and exploiting fresh grazing along the migratory route and then in cooler summer pastures. Other than rituals connected with seasonal pastoralism, they did not engage in the New Year's customs found elsewhere in Iran.

The Qermezi residents of Kazerun approached the New Year with humor. They observed, but did not usually emulate, the heightened, holiday-related activities of other town dwellers, who cleaned their homes, bought clothes, purchased gifts and special foods, and prepared to entertain guests. The low-altitude climate of Kazerun was moderate and warming at this time of year, and the Persian townspeople expected to host relatives and acquaintances, often without prior notice, from colder, northern, and higher-altitude climes. The rapid spread of private vehicular transportation in Iran allowed people to travel quickly from one area of the country to another. Iranians regarded the south, particularly Shiraz, as a major attraction during the New Year holiday, and Shiraz residents and others sought warmer weather even farther to the south and lower in elevation.

For the Qermezi nomads at Dashtak, these national travelers had become a menace. Every year growing numbers of outsiders trespassed on their territories in search of green landscapes, running water, and camping and picnic spots. Once locating a site, they sought free food and supplies from the nearest nomads and offered little if anything in exchange except destruction: ruined trees and vegetation, trampled grain sprouts, and land and water polluted by garbage and human wastes. Since the war's ceasefire in 1988, many vacationers traveled in large open-back trucks filled to capacity with dozens of people, piles of belongings, and camping equipment shielded by canvas canopies.

Dashtak's relative isolation meant that few national travelers knew about the narrow dirt road leading from the northern outskirts of Kazerun. The nomads near that road were sometimes spared from confronting these despoilers. The newly improved dirt road leading to Dashtak from south of Kazerun, off the asphalt road, was another matter, and it drew more trespassers every year. Travelers camped along the road leading into the mountains where the nomads lived, and some drove to higher elevations to seek sites near the nomads' camps. Their growing presence agitated the nomads at Mulleh Balut and Dashtak, who worried about the danger to women, children, livestock, fields, and property.

202 *The hope of spring*

Mansur Qermezi's wedding and Sayyid Ahmad's unexpected demise

Borzu, his family, and their many Qermezi visitors ignored the television's glare in a corner of the reception room while they deliberated Mansur's intention to host the wedding celebration of his son Barat at Dashtak sometime in the days ahead. Mansur had not finalized the plans but people expected him to act soon. By now (1995), the Qashqa'i could usually ignore, with apparent impunity, the Islamic Republic's ban on musicians, men and women dancing, and women's customary head-coverings. The Qermezi welcomed the forthcoming festivities, which would draw relatives and tribesmates they had not seen for months.

Almost all Qermezi until the early 1980s had staged their weddings during the summer in summer pastures. Since then, some people planned them for late winter or early spring in winter pastures. Wanting to avert the expense of feeding hoards of guests, some scheduled celebrations well before the New Year or several weeks after it to avoid the Qermezi coming from other locales for the holiday. Others who embraced a large gathering waited until New Year's Day and the days immediately following to capitalize on the presence of Qermezi visitors. Residents of still-cold Atakula, Nurabad, Borujen, and nearby villages welcomed a visit to winter pastures and their relatives there. They had grown nostalgic about these winter territories and the migrations that signified seasonal changes. Teachers and schoolchildren were on vacation as were government employees and some hired workers.

[Wedding hosts had ceased by 2000 to worry about any Qermezi who chose to attend. Rather, the non-Qermezi, "city" Qashqa'i with whom they were linked, often only by marriage, increasingly caused them concern. Carloads of them would descend without warning on the residents of Kazerun and Dashtak and expect hospitality until their departure some days or a week later. More engagements and weddings now occurred near the New Year, and these unwanted visitors took advantage of their holiday from work and school to be entertained at no cost. For the first time, I heard the Qermezi express regret about these out-marriages precisely for this reason, and many were reconsidering the notion of renewing links and forming new ones with any Qashqa'i who were not Qermezi. They did not want, and could no longer afford, to tend these uninvited urban guests for such long durations, and the only way to prevent their visits from escalating was to refuse to make further such marriages.

Beyond the intrusion and expense, the Qermezi were also unhappy about these visitors and the cultural values that conflicted with their own. The outsiders were more urbanized, Persianized, and Islamized than the Qermezi, and they negatively affected the habits and attitudes of the subtribe's youth. During an engagement ceremony in 2000, uninvited urban Qashqa'i guests, male and female, stopped the Qashqa'i music so they could dance provocatively to Persian popular music, thus ruining the occasion for the hosts and their close kin. When the engaged couple considered a wedding date, they chose one that

The hope of spring 203

fell well before the New Year, to avoid the onslaught of outsiders. The Qermezi in Kazerun and at Dashtak also grew alarmed when a few urban Qashqa'i began to assert Islamic beliefs and practices and to observe the corresponding social and cultural restrictions, and they wanted to avoid these influences as well. These Qashqa'i were exposed to Islamic institutions in their cities and towns and exhibited the regime's Islamizing efforts.

The changes these urban Qashqa'i had brought about in their lives had drawn them for nostalgic and romantic reasons to the lifestyles and cultural practices of the more "traditional" Qashqa'i. They aimed to experience once again the life they had left behind, and wedding celebrations provided the occasions when customary expressions were most vivid.

Yet another kind of outsider intruded on Qermezi weddings by 2002. These uninvited visitors were urban Persians who were drawn by the spectacular sights and sounds and who no longer feared the armed bandits and outlaws associated with an excursion into Qashqa'i territory.][10]

His eyes lured by the television, Said Qermezi edged closer to adjust the volume. A still image of the Qur'an and an off-screen Quranic recitation had just interrupted a political drama about two 12-year-old Iranian boys captured as prisoners of war and tortured by Iraqi soldiers. The new programming indicated to Said that a prominent Muslim clergyman had just died. Someone casually wondered if the akhund had been "good" or "bad." Another person responded, "Iran has plenty of 'bad' ones, so we won't miss this one." When a black-attired newscaster appeared on the screen, he uttered the standard Arabic, Quranic exhortations and then solemnly announced that the son of Imam Khomeini, Sayyid Ahmad, was unconscious in a Tehran hospital. Hujjat ul-Islam Ahmad Khomeini was the ayatollah's sole surviving son, and the ayatollah had often used him as his spokesman. (Iranians did not refer to Khomeini as a sayyid, a reputed descendant of the prophet Mohammad. The titles of ayatollah and imam superseded it.[11] They customarily used the title of sayyid for Ahmad.)

Khomeini's only other son, Mustafa, had been reportedly in fine health when he died at the age of 45 under suspicious circumstances in Iraq in 1977, where Khomeini was in exile. Many said that Mohammad Reza Shah had ordered his assassination. Some urban Iranians observed 40 days of mourning for him, and these communal rituals intensified the escalating political revolt against the shah and his regime.[12] Khomeini died in 1989, and his son Ahmad was the person who announced publicly the demise to Iranians.

Visitors to Borzu's house, just then arriving, recounted rumors circulating through the Kazerun bazaar. Merchants there had declared that Ahmad's enemies, fearing that he would continue to absorb his father's charisma and limit their opportunities for power, had attempted to assassinate him. (Later some suggested that assassins had used a laser to cause Ahmad's apparent stroke.) Hard-line conservatives in Tehran, incensed about Ahmad's recent controversial statements, might have sought to eliminate him before he drew more attention to his radical views. As Khomeini's son, Ahmad was a force with which to reckon.

204 *The hope of spring*

Several days earlier Ahmad had stated publicly that Iranians ought to solve their own problems, that they should cease blaming foreign powers for Iran's difficulties. If Iranians wanted political and economic change, they needed to confront the task themselves. In his remarks, Ahmad blamed the structure of the current government and its high-level impasse (caused largely by Ali Khamenei, Khomeini's successor as Iran's supreme leader) for the country's continuing crises. Hearing this speech, many Iranians at home (and abroad) were impressed by Ahmad's honesty and courage. They understood his now-enhanced prominence and noted that consequences, beneficial or not, would soon emerge.[13]

By now, practically all Qermezi detested all levels of the Muslim clergy. Yet their attitudes about Khomeini had changed somewhat by 1995. When the revolution against the shah had erupted in 1977–78, they advocated the efforts to rid Iran of him. Then, when Khomeini seized state power, urged the formation of an Islamic republic, sought to destroy all opposition, and implemented restrictions on the personal lives of citizens, they withdrew their support, their sentiments growing more negative as the Iraq–Iran war unnecessarily dragged on. After Khomeini's death, though, they were dismayed by the hard-line conservative clergymen who struggled for ascendancy. They now said that Khomeini, even considering his unconscionable and deadly prolongation of the war, had been a better leader than the akhunds who followed him, especially because he seemed not to have exploited his high position for the purpose of amassing personal wealth. They sympathized with Khomeini's son, now stricken; his recent courageous speech had impressed them.

That evening and during the few days to come, the Qermezi in Kazerun discussed the developing situation. When visitors entered any of their homes, the residents asked them, "Is he still among us? Is he dead yet?" The New Year was less than a week away, and people speculated, perhaps based on talk they heard in the bazaar, that the government would extend Ahmad's life until after the holiday in order not to ruin anyone's festivities. On state-controlled television, they saw Ahmad lying unconscious in a hospital bed surrounded by doctors and connected to machines apparently keeping him alive. Newscasters reported that only one percent of Ahmad's brain still functioned.

Some Qermezi noted cynically that Iran's ruling clergy wanted to placate the citizens, whose discontent would deepen and who would sharpen their criticisms of the regime if the formalities of national mourning disturbed their New Year's celebration. As long as Ahmad remained alive, people could enjoy the holiday as planned and might momentarily set aside their grievances against the government.

When television announced that Iran had summoned a foreign doctor, a British neurologist, to examine Ahmad, the skepticism of the Qermezi grew. Since the revolution, Iran's rulers had blamed foreign powers for meddling in Iran's affairs and for causing its escalating political and economic problems. Yet, faced with a medical—and, more pertinently, a political—crisis, these men sought a foreigner as their only apparent solution. "Where are the

Iranian doctors?" people asked. Some suggested that the rulers had hastened to invite a foreign specialist, as a pretense, to pretend that they cared for Ahmad. If Ahmad died, as people now expected, the regime had proved its intention to help him. If a foreign doctor could not save him, no one could.

The Qermezi wondered what effect Ahmad's illness and death would have on Mansur's wedding. After discussing with kinsmen and the prospective bride's father, Mansur decided to proceed with his plans and announce a date. The days possible were limited, given the few auspicious days of the week for collecting a bride from her father's home.

Four days before the New Year, on 17 March, the government announced that Ahmad had died, that he had suffered irreversible brain damage and been removed from life-support equipment. As if to forestall doubts among viewers, television covered the scene from Ahmad's hospital room, where female relatives cried at the bedside and hospital-gowned male relatives sobbed into their hands.

Several Qermezi women wondered why only the male kin wore protective clothing. They speculated that if the women also wore hospital gowns, some viewers might wonder if they were properly covered underneath, according to the rules of hijab. If they were not wearing the regime's mandated attire, especially when millions of Iranian men were watching on television, then why should other Iranian women have to do so? Another woman noted that practical considerations seemed more likely. Hospital gowns do not fit well over women's enveloping hoods and chadurs, just as chadurs do not fit over Qashqa'i clothes.

Quranic recitations, Khomeini's visage, and religious messages replaced regular television programming, which the government suspended for three days. A small black band stretched across the upper-right-hand corner of televised images. Scenes of distraught men and women (oddly intermixed and not segregated) gathering in a Tehran mosque, frantically beating their heads and chests and tearing their clothes, alternated with peaceful images of mosques and shrines around the world. Overwhelming grief (however ritualized) temporarily suspended the requirements for gender separation and intact clothing. Qermezi women were amazed by the spectacle and its televised, regime-approved broadcast. Expressions of mourning over the death of Khomeini's first son had accelerated the opposition against the shah, while these new rituals seemed to help in sustaining the current regime in power. Anguish for a prominent cleric demonstrated support for the clergy-run government. Still, suspicions that the regime would keep Ahmad alive until after the holiday had not materialized, whether by chance or design, unknown by ordinary citizens in Iran.

As part of the nation's mourning, Kazerun's bazaar closed for three days. On the second day, from well before dawn, a mosque near the Qermezi residences began to broadcast by loudspeaker readings from the Qur'an. Later, some boys playing outside in the lane yelled, "Enough already!" until their mothers told them to be quiet. A state of mourning continued for seven days after the

206 *The hope of spring*

death, during which many Iranians curtailed their activities out of respect for Khomeini and his son.

Sharing a New Year's Day lunch, Borzu's extended family discussed the morning's radio broadcast in which Ahmad's son, Hasan, had urged Iranians to continue their festivities despite his father's death. He told them that he knew they mourned for his father but that his father would not have wanted them to cancel their plans. Several people at the meal noted that Hasan had been close to his grandfather ever since Khomeini's tumultuous return to Iran. Photographs and film clips often depicted the grandfather and the young grandson sitting quietly side by side.

Mansur postponed his son's wedding until after the beginning of the New Year but was unwilling to wait until Ahmad's fortieth-day memorial ritual had ended. By then, the nomads, Mansur included, would be well on their way to summer pastures. He wondered about possible constraints on the celebration. Before Ahmad was stricken, Mansur had discussed the still-current state prohibitions against certain forms of music, dance, and immodest attire but was ready to proceed with the full festivities. After Ahmad's death, he worried about the impropriety of celebrating before the seventh-day and fortieth-day rites. He did not fret about the reactions of the Qermezi; they would not be bothered about any apparent indecorum. The few Qermezi hezbollahis would reproach him but he could ignore their strident views, along with all other members of the subtribe. Rather, Mansur considered the few merchant-acquaintances and other Persians who might attend the wedding, invited or not. He assumed that they would disapprove of any levity, especially acts and appearances that seemed un-Islamic at a time of national mourning for Khomeini's son.

Mansur reluctantly reduced the wedding celebration to a single day. He had wanted to begin the event one day and bring the bride the next, but her father objected to a trip on a Friday, an inauspicious day for collecting a bride. By forcing the full wedding to fall on a Thursday, a day corresponding with the seventh day of mourning for Ahmad, Mansur unhappily canceled any live musical performances.

Many Qermezi from widely dispersed and distant locations attended the ceremony, which began at Mansur's camp at Dashtak. Taking advantage of the New Year holiday, they came to visit relatives at Dashtak and were pleased that the wedding coincided with their trip. People always regarded a large wedding to be better than a small one, despite the expense. If anyone refused to attend because of the national mourning for Ahmad, no one reported it. Even Bahram Qermezi came, the only hezbollahi resident at Dashtak, and interacted pleasantly with the guests. His mother, Mansur's wife (and the groom's mother), and the bride's mother are three sisters, a kinship tie that mandated his presence. His mother now dead, he stood in her place as the eldest son.

By withdrawing the musicians, Mansur had halted any public dancing by men and women. Some men and boys competed in stick fighting to the rhythm of music issuing from an audiocassette player. When the attendees traveled to the other end of Dashtak and into the foothills below to collect the bride, women and girls sang wedding songs and brandished bright scarves as they rode in large, open-back trucks. At the bride's camp, some men and boys again performed stick fighting to cassette music while women dressed the bride, sang ribald rhymes, and clapped. The groom's party then delivered the bride to Mansur's camp, she stepping over a freshly killed young goat, its blood glistening in the dirt. Women surrounded her, escorted her to the bridal tent, and serenaded her with song.

At the end of the day, while he thanked each guest for attending, Mansur noted that he probably could have asked musicians to perform and given men and women the opportunity to dance. He had expected that the Persians from Kazerun would object to these cultural displays on the grounds of Islam and/or the mourning for Ahmad, but they seemed unconcerned. The urbanites were effusive in their praise for this adventurous excursion into the mountains, and they relished the hospitality provided. Enthused by their own positive sentiments about celebrating the New Year, they adjusted to the event as it unfolded. Some of them seemed to regard Qashqa'i customary traditions just as the national media currently depicted them: quaint, exotic, picturesque precursors of modern Iranian culture. The issue of where these traditions—now highly politicized by the Qashqa'i—stood with regard to Islamic values seemed irrelevant to them, just as the issue seemed increasingly inconsequential for the regime.

Rites of the New Year

As the New Year approached, those Qermezi who had suffered personal losses during the previous year could lessen or end the social restrictions of mourning. A day before the New Year, despite his worsening illness, Borzu traveled to Chah Shirin (winter pastures of another Qermezi group, south of Dashtak) to visit the natal family of his daughter-in-law Maryam. He brought along a large goat as a gift. Six months previously, a truck had struck and killed Maryam's father Husain as he climbed off the back of a kinsman's motorcycle, his first ride on such a conveyance. His immediate family had worn black clothes since then. In his roles as the subtribal elder and the father-in-law, Borzu urged the family to end its formal mourning. The widow would remain in black or other dark colors for the rest of her life but the others could now resume wearing normal attire. Borzu told them to approach the New Year with gladness, despite sorrow residing permanently in their hearts. When men in a neighboring tent invited Borzu to come there, he refused, saying, "I haven't come to Chah Shirin on a social visit."

A few Qermezi in Kazerun and at Dashtak bought a new item of attire for each family member. Men used to buy tunic fabric for their married sisters as a traditional New Year's gift but I saw no evidence of this custom in 1995. Unlike their Persian neighbors in Kazerun and other Iranians in Iran and abroad, the Qermezi did not specially clean their homes, sprout wheat grains

208   *The hope of spring*

or lentil seeds, purchase goldfish, or assemble items for the "Seven Ss" (*haft sin*) to display as they ushered in the New Year.

Beginning six nights before the New Year, to commemorate Wednesday's Celebration (*chahar shanbih suri*), and on many nights to come, dozens of fires blazed on the mountainsides around Kazerun. After Muslim clergymen had seized power, they had forbidden this traditional New Year's activity because of its pre-Islamic, Zoroastrian, "fire-worshipping" connotations. Clerics increased their warnings and threats when they understood that many Iranians perpetuated the act—or practiced it for the first time—so they could express their opposition to the Islamic regime. For years, revolutionary guards and committees had conducted surveillance on these activities and had harassed and arrested celebrants. On New Year's Eve, young Qermezi men suggested an excursion to a Dashtak location shielded from Kazerun by mountain ridges so they could light these fires, but a torrential rain halted the idea. They noted that they had lacked any interest in the ritual until the clergy banned it.

On New Year's Day, the Qermezi in Kazerun met their Persian neighbors and acquaintances with the Persian-Arabic phrase, "Blessings on your holiday" (*aid-i shuma mubarak*). Among themselves, some repeated the partly Turkish-language version, "*Bairamings mubarak*," and struggled to find a Turkish substitute for the Arabic "mubarak."

Borzu's household prepared a special noon meal for the extended family living in Kazerun and at Dashtak. When Borzu's daughter, Zohreh, entered the house early in the morning, she greeted her father with a wide smile and a loud, exaggerated "aid-i shuma mubarak!" to mimic some Persian neighbors she had encountered on her short walk. Seconds later I saw her face lose its mischievous expression and freeze in sadness, and I understood that she had just realized that this year might be her father's last, that she had offered him New Year's greetings for the final time. Later, one of Farideh's four-year-old twin sons began to cry inconsolably for reasons no one could determine, and Farideh decided to take him home. Departing, she remarked, "It's not good to begin the New Year crying." By noon, dozens of family members had arrived. High spirited and chatting with one another, they shared oranges and other fruit that they did not ordinarily buy and discussed their plans for the brand-new spring season and the scheduling of their migration to summer pastures.

Sometime in the morning, people heard incessant tapping on the courtyard gate. Investigating, Borzu's daughter Fariba reported that three "gypsies" (*ghurbat*) had come asking for a New Year's gift (*aidi*). Two women and a six-year-old boy, all dressed in thin shabby clothes and ignoring Kazerun's modesty code, carried multiple gunny and cloth sacks in which they sorted the gifts (raw rice in one sack, flour in another) they received from people who responded to their appeals. They said they came from a town near Bushire on the Persian Gulf. Fariba noted that she could ignore their request for charity only with peril, especially on the first day of a new year, and she offered them a large bowl of raw rice. To perform a good deed on behalf of her own nuclear family, Maryam gave each person a few coins.

The hope of spring   209

After lunch when it appeared that Borzu was fatigued, several young men decided on a whim to go to Dashtak. They assembled many young adults and children and packed into multiple vehicles. At the family's winter campsite, Dariush prepared to graft the grapevines and wild-almond branches he had cut early that morning in a distant village, and soon he attracted an enthusiastic band of helpers who playfully delegated the different tasks. One became the "knife engineer," another the "shovel engineer," a third the "plastics engineer" (for wrapping and protecting the grafted branches), and so forth, to mock the kinds of grossly inflated titles that many men in the wider society liked to bestow on themselves ("engineer" being one of the most exalted).[14] Even when the cloudy sky began to drizzle, the young men's excitement went undaunted, their spirit deriving from the celebratory day. Planting, even small-scale efforts, signified an auspicious beginning of the New Year.

Several days later, on a Friday, a day considered propitious for the specific task, Bizhan recruited another volunteer force to brand the faces or ears of the winter's new lambs and kids. Qermezi men had customarily branded their young animals just before the spring migration, when the threat of theft was greatest, and they continued the custom in 1995 for the same purpose. Young men living in Kazerun left before dawn to begin the arduous work, to complete it before the day grew hot, and hired shepherds at Dashtak assembled the herds in anticipation. Borzu and other spectators, arriving from Kazerun to witness the event and acknowledge its importance to their livelihood, sat in the warmth of the sun on folded felt mats. Continuing their efforts, several men reheated the iron brands in a wood fire and prepared more cold tea to douse the wounds when they removed the brands from the still-burning flesh. While Bizhan pulled each of the reluctant young candidates from the herds, Husain Ali applied the searing brand, a figure seven (a V signifying the last digit of Borzu's birth year), and another man treated the wound. Despite the difficult muddy chore and the desperate cries of the now injured lambs and kids, the participants engaged in lighthearted, high-spirited banter. Especially for men such as Husain Ali, who no longer owned any livestock, such customary tasks linked them once again to the nomadic pastoralist tradition that they continued to cherish. Looking around at the scene, more than one man noted to me, "Isn't this how it used to be?"

The job finished, the group moved on to the camp of Hajji Qurban and Zulaikha, another of Borzu's daughters, where everyone enjoyed lunch and some hours of leisure sitting on knotted pile carpets in the sunshine of the new spring.

Notes

1 The section "the state and the tribe" in Chapter 3 provides background information about conflict over land rights in postrevolutionary Iran; see also Chapter 9. Amuzegar (1993), Nomani and Behdad (2006), and Schirazi (1993) offer wider perspectives. Ajami (2005), Hegland (2014), E. Hooglund (1982a, 1997), and Loeffler (2011) examine land seizures in villages in southwestern Iran.

210　*The hope of spring*

2　These kinds of threats were common in the area. When Persian cultivators fought with Borzu Qermezi over land, they often threatened to burn their harvested wheat piled ready for transport, sometimes to claim that Borzu had committed the crime and other times to amplify their desperation.

3　Huang (2006: 836) includes a photograph of harvesting and preparing to transport this fodder.

4　Beck (1991: 57–72) describes the disputes over Kuh Pahn.

5　These concerns seem exaggerated but relate to the ways the Qashqa'i separated themselves from others and tried to keep their activities private.

6　See Huang's descriptions (2009) and the detailed account in Dareshuri and Beck (2014).

7　Qermezi boys in the town's middle school joked about saving their farts for the noon prayers so they could blame the Persian boys kneeling and bowing on either side of them for distracting the others from their required recitations and thus nullifying everyone's prayers.

8　Farzaneh Qarehqanli took driving lessons in Shiraz in 2006 to be prepared when her husband, Dariush Qermezi, could not drive because of his worsening illness.

9　Unlike most other Qermezi men, Borzu relied on merchants (including Haidar Tahani and Mehdi Zahrai [see Chapters 3, 6, 8]) for multiple purposes extending beyond commercial transactions, due to his role as headman and his wide networks.

10　Beck (1982) and Beck and Huang (2006) describe these and other patterns of uninvited guests and reluctant hosts.

11　The title of "imam" for Khomeini superseded his other title as "ayatollah" and associated him with the 12 Shi'i imams (especially the last one, for whom some people regarded Khomeini as the living representative).

12　Clergymen and secular nationalists jointly organized a seventh-day memorial service in Tehran in 1977 for Mustafa Khomeini. This mass politico-religious meeting demonstrated the growing, coordinated opposition to Mohammad Reza Shah among otherwise disparate political forces in Iran. Pro-Khomeini clergymen organized a more explicitly political event in Qom for Mustafa's fortieth-day memorial service and issued a public statement containing political demands, including the immediate return of Khomeini to Iran from exile abroad (Chehabi 1990: 235, Parsa 1989: 207–08). Mustafa's son Husain, who is Khomeini's grandson and a reformist cleric, has urged the overthrow of the Islamic Republic.

13　Iranians in Tehran report that after newspapers published Ahmad Khomeini's remarks, people photocopied the speeches and distributed them, concerned that hard-line conservatives would soon censor these remarks or deny that Ahmad had spoken them. His death "fuelled public suspicions that he had been prematurely prevented from speaking his mind and exposing the profound ills of the developing 'Islamic Republic'" (Ansari 2007: 336*n*).

14　"In social class terms *mohandes* (engineer) is a revered title denoting high social standing, professional competence and proven ability." It can demonstrate technical expertise and modernity but it "also represents a title embedded in Iran's socio-economic hierarchy" (Ehteshami 1995: 71).

6 Death and memory: The end of the life of a Qashqa'i tribesman in Iran

Reflections on 1995—summer

The death of Borzu Qermezi on the first day of summer in 1995 caused widespread grief in his family and tribal groups. The rituals his relatives conducted for his burial and memorial services demonstrate customary traditions, increasing contact with urban society, and modernizing and Islamizing trends.

Borzu Qermezi found the last several years of his life difficult. As his heart disease and related illnesses worsened, he continued to lack adequate medical care. He visited multiple doctors in Kazerun, Shiraz, Shahreza, Isfahan, and Semirom; submitted to rudimentary examinations and poorly administered tests; and was diagnosed, accurately or not, as having varying problems. Sometimes he carried previous test results, X rays, and medications with him when he visited new doctors but more often he did not. He hoped that each new practitioner would discover the actual causes of his ailments and be able to treat him effectively.

Doctors and other healthcare providers prescribed conflicting medications for Borzu, some that pharmacies did not have or could not obtain. Based on their own superficial diagnoses, pharmacists sold Borzu other drugs that no doctors had specified. These medicines usually lacked any identifying labels, ingredients, dosages, or instructions, and they never listed possible side effects or dangerous drug interactions. When the packages did display labels, they specified illnesses and symptoms he lacked. If the medicines were imported, their expiration dates were years overdue. If they were made in Iran, who knew what ingredients they contained? Borzu haphazardly ingested these various pills and liquid concoctions depending on how ill he felt at the time. If he was well, he did not take any. After each visit to a doctor or pharmacy, he returned home with yet additional medications and added them to plastic bags already full of these supposed remedies, almost all of them unidentified.

Borzu was periodically hospitalized when he experienced shortness of breath and chest pain, and on many occasions he was close to death. Yet each time he returned home to Dashtak, Kazerun, or Hanalishah and resumed life there as best as he could. Weak at first, he would slowly regain some strength, and soon he was shouting insults at his inept shepherds and the Persians who had stolen his pastureland.

Throughout his illness, people from the Aqa Mohammadli lineage, Qermezi subtribe, Darrehshuri tribe, other Qashqa'i tribes, Lur and Bakhtiyari tribes,

212 Death and memory

and wider Iranian society visited Borzu out of compassion and to seek his advice and mediation. When they heard he was ailing, many came, and when the hospital discharged him, even more welcomed him home. These visitors helped to distract him from pain and discomfort. He continued to assist people in solving their problems, and they respected his opinions. Many remarked that if he had still been physically capable, he would have confronted the threats still posed by hostile hezbollahis, revolutionary guards, leftist rebels, and trespassing cultivators. He seemed frustrated that his three sons did not take his assertive approach in facing these difficulties. Mohammad Karim maintained some social distance from his father, despite the camps they shared, and, as young men, Dariush and Bizhan were cautious in his presence. The sons (as well as other close kinsmen) did not demonstrate the kinds of leadership that Borzu had exhibited for decades, and he grew troubled by the fate of the subtribe for which he had cared for many years.

Right up to the end of his life, Borzu remained anguished by the Islamic Republic's execution of Khosrow Khan Qashqa'i in 1982. He and others often attributed his illness to the day he first heard about the tragedy. He noted that he had never recovered after Khosrow Khan's murder. Continuing as a staunch supporter of the confederacy khans, Borzu regretted the unfortunate fates they had suffered during and after their defensive resistance in 1980–82.

Borzu Qermezi's last spring

As the spring of 1995 progressed, Borzu fell increasingly ill, and his family pondered the appropriate course of action. Kazerun's weather during the summer was scorching, and the best plan seemed to be to take Borzu to Hanalishah. The weather there was still too cold for him in mid-spring, and the family delayed its departure from Kazerun. The nomads left Dashtak in early April, traveled along customary routes, and arrived at Hanalishah a month later. The only Qermezi remaining in Kazerun were schoolteachers (and their families) and students, who were obliged to stay until the end of the school-year for its concluding, crucial examinations.

In May Dariush drove Borzu and his immediate family to Hanalishah where they resumed residence in their new one-room stone house. Mohammad Karim, Bizhan, and their wives and children already inhabited the campsite there and were tending the livestock. Borzu remained at Hanalishah for 10 days, his breath growing short and labored. People attributed the problem to the cold windy weather, not the high altitude, which might also have been a factor. Dariush decided he ought to return his father to Kazerun. He had already transported their household goods to Hanalishah, including the items needed daily, and he needed to rely on another family. He took his father to live with his daughter Farideh and her husband Filamarz in Kazerun, and later he and his father joined another daughter, Zohreh, and her husband Husain Ali there. Borzu's sons-in-law taught in Kazerun schools. As the heat and humidity

Death and memory 213

grew oppressive, Borzu became more uncomfortable, and the family worried about the weather's effect on him.

Borzu's closest Persian associate in Kazerun was Mehdi Zahrai, a wealthy landowner and businessman. Zahrai suggested that Borzu move to Shiraz where the weather was moderate and offered him the use of a vacant house. Saying that an ill person should not have to endure the Land Rover's bumpy ride, he drove Borzu there in his own car. Dariush did not want to depend too heavily on Zahrai and took Borzu instead to the Shiraz house of Dariush's father-in-law. Borzu stayed there a short time but was uneasy about imposing. His host, Khosrow Qarehqanli, frequently entertained visitors, and the house was often too crowded and noisy for someone suffering from a serious illness. Dariush moved Borzu to Zahrai's empty house.

Early in the morning on Wednesday, 21 June, the last day of spring, Borzu reported that he felt worse and wanted to go to the hospital. Dariush was reassured that his father could walk unassisted to the Land Rover. As Borzu pulled himself up into the vehicle, he lamented to his wife Falak, "I'll see you in heaven." He had suffered many medical crises during the past six years, any one of which could have ended his life, but he had never before uttered such a foreboding remark. According to his family, he had also never before expressed any apparently heartfelt religious sentiments.

Dariush drove Borzu to the emergency department at Nemazee Hospital, Shiraz's preeminent facility. Tests there indicated that Borzu's heart was not functioning properly, and his condition seemed to be worsening. After an initial examination, doctors placed him in a room with many other patients. Dariush stayed with him that night.

Borzu Qermezi's demise and burial

Early in the morning on Thursday, 22 June, the first day of summer, Dariush saw that Borzu's health was deteriorating. When Falak arrived, Borzu once again said farewell to her. He lapsed into unconsciousness, his heart beating erratically. At one point he sat up and cried, "Dariush! Dariush!" Again he was insensate. A few family members, who had hurried from Hanalishah, gathered. A female doctor twice deployed electric shocks to restore Borzu's lapsing heartbeat. Borzu's grandson, Said, manually pumped air into his lungs. Indicating that Borzu had suffered a brain stroke, the doctor cut his left arm to insert a wire or probe into his heart. Borzu's daughter-in-law, Farzaneh, saw that he was deathly ill. Traumatized, she left the room, and when she returned she saw that Borzu had died. His heart had finally stopped. It was four-thirty in the afternoon. Crying, she rushed to locate Dariush who was searching for a doctor who had treated Borzu in the past. Returning to the room, they sobbed together.

During the two days that Borzu was hospitalized, Farzaneh had telephoned to notify the family at Hanalishah about Borzu's declining health. Dariush said he could not call anyone; the person would have instantly perceived the

214   *Death and memory*

news from his tone of voice. Hanalishah lacked any telephone service, and Farzaneh had called the Semirom home of a Persian cultivator at Hanalishah with whom Borzu's sons maintained semicordial ties. She did not want to frighten the family with the abrupt message of impending death, and so she asked the man to deliver a message to Bizhan that his father was admitted to the hospital in Shiraz. Her second message later asked Bizhan to bring Borzu's identity card, necessary for bureaucratic formalities. The third message, finally, was that Borzu had died. She hoped that she had cushioned the final blow.

That evening Dariush handled administrative details and arranged to take Borzu home to his family. Doctors said he needed an official death certificate before they could release his father, and that document required the identity card. Borzu's eldest son and other close kinsmen drove immediately to Shiraz when they heard the sad news. Staying only briefly, they escorted Falak and Farzaneh back to Hanalishah in Borzu's Land Rover. All of them, along with many others, would meet in Shahreza to wait for Borzu's final passage though the town. Wearing a new black shirt, Dariush continued to pursue the death certificate the next day, Friday, and hired an ambulance to carry Borzu to summer pastures. Borzu's body remained in the hospital morgue.

The following morning, Saturday, 24 June, the ambulance carried Borzu and Dariush to the Qur'an Gate in the hills overlooking Shiraz where the highway to the north begins. Some wearing black shirts, a few of Borzu's Qashqa'i and Persian friends in their own vehicles accompanied the body from the hospital to the city outskirts there. At the Qur'an Gate they joined 40 or so others, including officials of the Organization for Nomads' Affairs who had come directly from work. Mahmud Khan Iskandari Kashkuli sang songs of mourning in Qashqa'i Turkish ("Brother, oh brother, why have you left us?"), and the 50 or so people there cried. Then the small procession departed. Dariush rode in the ambulance with Borzu. The men who had escorted Borzu from the hospital to the Qur'an Gate or who came there directly remained behind. It was the first day of the workweek for them.

After a five-hour drive, the ambulance arrived in the town of Shahreza. The weather was hot that afternoon, and Dariush was suffering from the shock of his father's passing. Relatives, friends, and acquaintances dressed in black were waiting alongside the Shah Reza shrine for Borzu.

Haidar Tahani, Borzu's Persian friend and a Shahreza merchant, had arranged for a sayyid to prepare the body for burial. Using facilities at the shrine, the sayyid and his assistants washed Borzu in the customary way there. Tahani provided a white, unadorned, cotton burial shroud (*kafan*), which the sayyid tore into four sections, each unhemmed. (Dariush later reimbursed Tahani for the fabric. He said a son should provide the cloth.) The sayyid wrapped one piece around Borzu's waist and legs, the second around his torso, the third around his head (as a turban, *ammamih*), and the fourth, the largest, around his body from head to toe. With cloth strips torn from the original fabric, he tied closed the openings at the head and the feet,

Death and memory 215

to be loosened after the body was placed in position in the grave. The process took several hours.

Outside, the mourners cried and consoled one another. Dariush provided details about Borzu's last days.

Borzu's body prepared for burial and placed in a simple wooden coffin, the procession moved on, now with dozens of vehicles bearing the grief stricken, the ambulance in the lead. Following the Shahreza-Semirom highway, the bereaved drove into the mountains west of Shahreza. After an hour's travel, at the road branching off from the highway and leading west to Mehr-i Gerd village, they saw hundreds of cars, vans, and trucks, many displaying black banners fluttering in the wind. The vehicles carried Borzu's family, relatives, other Qermezi tribesmates, and affiliated people. Hundreds of Qashqa'i, Persian, and Lur acquaintances were also present. People pressed against the ambulance and comforted the immediate family. More conveyances arrived as the mourners stood in the hot sun. With the ambulance again in front, a cortege of hundreds of vehicles traveled slowly toward Mehr-i Gerd 20 kilometers away.

At the village outskirts by the abandoned gasoline station, the procession halted, and everyone stepped out of the vehicles. As men removed the wooden coffin from the ambulance, wails of grief rose from the crowd. Borzu's sons draped a handwoven blanket (*jajim*) from home over the top and added a spray or "crown" of multicolored gladiolas (*taj-i gul*). Many of Borzu's kinsmen, assisted by his closest acquaintances in other Darrehshuri subtribes, took turns carrying the coffin up the long, meandering, dusty path to the cemetery at the top. Other mourners, bereft and keening, followed sadly behind, men, women, and children together.

Long before his illness and then periodically during it, Borzu had informed his sons that he wanted to rest alongside his father Shir Mohammad, killed by army soldiers in 1943. Shir Mohammad was buried above the then-small settlement of Mehr-i Gerd, and his gravestone still lay where his sons had placed it more than half a century previously. He was the only Qermezi person buried in this cemetery other than some Kachili residents of Mehr-i Gerd. (In this and other cemeteries in Iran, men sometimes moved or cast aside gravestones when they dug new graves.)

When they heard that Borzu had died, his closest kinsmen at Hanalishah (including Mohammad Karim, Husain Ali, Murad, and Bahram) dug a new grave alongside Shir Mohammad's. Several meters away, the graves of unrelated people lay on either side. After excavating a rectangular hole a little more than a meter deep, its long sides facing Mecca to the southwest, the men lined the four vertical sides with cement and prepared a concrete slab as a cover for the top. They did not line the bottom of the grave.

The procession of the grief-stricken slowly made its way uphill and through the cemetery to the prepared gravesite, and people gathered around, close kin the nearest. A few men recited brief verses from the Qur'an, and people uttered the familiar Arabic phrases of the Muslim prayer of mourning (*fatihih*). Borzu's sons and closest kinsmen removed Borzu's shrouded body from the

216   *Death and memory*

coffin, lowered him into the grave, and laid him gently on his right side facing Mecca. One of them loosened the bands holding the shroud closed at his head and feet "so he would be more comfortable" and then eased back the cloth by Borzu's right cheek so his face would rest directly on the dirt. Unlike some other burials, no one placed any personal items (such as those needed in the hereafter, including eyeglasses and canes) beside his body. People sobbed and wailed, especially Borzu's daughters and sisters, and some whispered prayers. Men carefully fitted the concrete slab over the narrow opening (to keep dirt from falling on the body), piled dirt into the remaining space, and heaped more over the grave. The mound would gradually subside. Men repeated the Quranic verses, and others intoned their own prayers and laments.

Heavy with desolation, the mourners slowly dispersed, most of them back to their vehicles on the road below and some to their homes in Mehr-i Gerd. Borzu's wife, sons, daughters, brothers, sisters, and other close kin remained at the gravesite to receive condolences from latecomers who had just heard the news. They did not want to leave Borzu behind. They said he should not be alone as the night approached. (In life, he had rarely been alone. His work as the headman and his vital personality, extended family, subtribe, wider tribal society, and broad networks had kept him in the company of others.) His kin were somewhat consoled by the knowledge that they would return the next day for the third-day memorial rites and again a few days after that for the seventh-day rites. The immediate family and others would visit every Thursday afternoon until they left Hanalishah at the end of summer.

Returning to Hanalishah, men, women, and older children continued as best as they could to prepare Borzu's campsite for the arrival of a thousand or more mourners. As people in their widely dispersed places learned of Borzu's death, they would come to grieve and to pay their respects to the family. To create shelters for them, men and boys pitched Borzu's and Mohammad Karim's goat-hair tents and other goat-hair and canvas tents provided by the nomads at Hanalishah.

Seated together on the handwoven carpets in these tents, men sobbed into their right hands as they covered their eyes. Borzu's sons called out, "Oh my father, what shall I do now? What shouldn't I do? Who is here to guide me?" Other men recalled their deceased family members as they cried. They bowed their heads as tears ran down their faces and through their fingers, and they murmured a few words. Then, with a single downward motion, they wiped away the tears and, after a moment of silence, commiserated with those nearby.

Also seated closely together, women covered their faces and sobbed into the ends of their scarves or their tunic hems. Many sang long sets of phrases usually different from those of the women sitting near them. Borzu's daughters and sisters called out, "My father, my brother, where are you? What do I do now? How can I live without you?" They added as they cried, "My father, you cared so much for your daughters." "All the Qashqa'i knew your name and respected you. You offered hospitality to so many people." Women such as Borzu's daughter Zohreh were skilled in expressing their grief, and others cried quietly as they listened to the words and shared the emotions. One woman would start to sing phrases, others joined in with their own phrases, and still others uttered only several words. They all remembered other deceased relatives. Women who had recently suffered deaths in their immediate families resumed their active mourning for these individuals. After some minutes, one woman after another ceased singing, and finally the last one sung more and more quietly until she abruptly stopped. After uncovering and wiping their faces and sighing, everyone sat motionless, and then a few began to whisper despondently with their neighbors. For new arrivals in these women's groups, the process began again until all were exhausted.

Men and women regarded crying and singing as essential to their attempts to cope with death and loss. They said they felt constricted inside unless they expressed their emotions, which helped to loosen the tightness and release the sorrow. Children did not show their feelings in any ritualistic or communal fashion.

The adults in Borzu's immediate family and his nearest adult relatives dressed in black, unembellished clothes until after the fortieth-day memorial rites. Children did not wear black. Men wore black shirts and dark pants while women's attire was completely or partly black. All women donned black headscarves and almost all of them black tunics. Some also dressed in black skirts but most wore other dark-colored ones lacking any fancy trim. As the new widow, Falak dressed completely in black. Two of her daughters-in-law, not related by blood to Borzu, wore black scarves and tunics and dark skirts. Women carried black veil-wraps to drape over themselves when they visited the mosque during the seventh-day and fortieth-day rites. After the fortieth day, most adults gradually changed from black to other dark-colored, non-decorative attire and later to normal clothes.

Third-day memorial

Borzu's family and relatives found the third-day memorial on the following day, Sunday, 25 June, distressing. Visibly suffering from shock, they depended on others to help them host the multitudes of people who would come in response to the news. Borzu's sons hired a Persian cook from Semirom to prepare the noon meal, attended mostly by Hanalishah's nomads and others closest to the family. Men, women, and children sat together at this event. Afterward men and women traveled to Borzu's grave to cry and to repeat the ritual prayers.

The Qashqa'i never observed the third (*sivvum*), seventh (*haftum*), fortieth (*chihilum*), and one-year (*salgard*) memorials on a Saturday, Monday, or Wednesday. Thus, sometimes these rites could not fall on the specified day after a death. Under ideal conditions, a body was supposed to be buried before sunset on the day of the death. Borzu had died on Thursday but his family did not bury him until Saturday because of hospital bureaucracy, the trip from Shiraz, and preparations at the Shahreza shrine. His sons did hold the third-day memorial on that day.[1]

218   *Death and memory*

Seventh-day memorial

Borzu's sons and other close kinsmen turned their attention to the seventh-day memorial. They scheduled the gathering for Thursday, 29 June, seven days after Borzu's death. Traveling to Shahreza, Dariush ordered from a printer some commemorative cards and posters stating the event's date, time, and place. The posters depicted Borzu's face—a photograph taken 30 years earlier when Borzu became the official headman—and followed the style and wording customary among Persians in Shahreza. Qermezi families had initially used these printed announcements in 1982 when the first Qermezi boy was killed in the Iraq–Iran war. They had wanted to commemorate their martyr according to the practices found in the wider Iranian society. Since then, many Qermezi have used similar cards and posters to announce memorial services.

The card's Persian text read:

> The Seventh-Day Rite. We thank you for the kindness you expressed toward the relatives of the late Borzu Qermezi (may peace be upon his soul). We request that you come on Thursday 29 June 1995 for lunch. Your participation will make his soul happy and will comfort those left behind. Qermezi brothers. Address: Semirom, Hanalishah, private home.

The poster was more elaborate. It led with a Persian poem often used by Persians in mourning rituals:

> Oh father, your stature was a support for me.
> Your words were like a light guiding me along a road.
> You have disappeared from our sight, and pain is still in our hearts.
> Whatever direction I look, I find your face.

A Qur'an reader would chant the familiar poem in his initial remarks to the gathered mourners, and the reading would elicit intense emotion and crying, particularly from women.

The poster's Persian text read:

> Seven Days Have Passed. We thank and appreciate all the respected and dear participants who attended the burial and funeral service of the late and forgiven Borzu of the recognized family of Qermezi and who wanted to share our sorrows. With heartfelt sorrow we wish to inform you that a gathering will be held seven days after the death. To commemorate Borzu's memory, simultaneous gatherings for men and women will occur at Borzu's home at Hanalishah from eight in the morning until two in the afternoon on Thursday 29 June 1995 and thereafter from four to six in the afternoon of the same day at Sahib al-Zaman (peace be upon him) Mosque in Mehr-i Gerd. We request that you honor us by having lunch at our home on that day. Your participation will please the departed soul and will comfort those left behind. Qermezi and other related families.

Death and memory 219

While the shop in Shahreza printed these cards and posters, men at Hanalishah planned their itineraries so they could notify practically everyone in the subtribe in their many locations. They would also inform associates and acquaintances of Borzu and the subtribe. Alone or in pairs, they delivered a poster and/or a card to each family they visited. They posted the notice in public places in Semirom, Shahreza, and Kazerun so people there would see the details and possibly attend. Borzu's merchant-acquaintances mounted the sheet in their shops.

More than a thousand adults and many hundreds of children attended the seventh-day memorial, the largest gathering of all the rites. Most arrived in the morning and ate lunch, and then some visited the mosque and the grave before returning home. Others came a day or more early and stayed for a day or more afterward, especially if they had traveled far and wanted to visit relatives. Borzu's three sons assumed the task of caring for these many guests. They were distraught by their father's loss, and the event was painful for them. Their relatives at Hanalishah volunteered their time and effort, as did many guests. Borzu's family was gratified that so many people offered condolences and assistance; the presence of others consoled its members. Dariush commented later that he had not fully comprehended his father's death until the seventh-day memorial ended and the guests were gone, so busy had he been in caring for them. He had worried about each person being as comfortable as possible.

As the headman of the Qermezi subtribe for 30 years and its most prominent individual for at least that long, Borzu had always diligently attended the burials, funerals, and multiple memorials of its members and acquaintances. If distance or work meant that he could not participate in a certain rite, he would visit the deceased's family soon thereafter. Even when ailing, Borzu frequented these rituals and called on others who were infirm. Three months before his death, he traveled some distance to Nurabad-Mamassani to attend the fortieth-day memorial of a Darzi Darrehshuri man who was linked by marriage to the Qermezi group. Mahmud Atazadeh, the Darzi man who was then Semirom's parliamentary deputy, would likely be present, and Borzu understood the political importance of the event. That same week he visited the natal family of his daughter-in-law Maryam so its members could conclude their formal mourning and be able to celebrate the New Year. Despite the many, sometimes violent, struggles in which Borzu had engaged over the years, he never hesitated to visit his disputants when they fell acutely ill. When an antagonist died, he always considered the family's needs. He offered economic support to grieving families and brought a live lamb or goat as a tribute. Borzu joined the fortieth-day memorial of Mohammad Taqavi, a Persian cultivator with whom he had battled over land at Hanalishah. When news of Borzu's death spread, people were quick to reciprocate the favors he had shown them and their families over the years.

For the seventh-day memorial, Borzu's sons hired two Persian cooks from Semirom to prepare the noon meal. Traveling again to Shahreza, they rented supplies that the cooks did not provide, such as plates, serving trays, utensils,

220   *Death and memory*

tea glasses, and water cups, and they leased a gasoline-run generator for a microphone and amplifier for the Qur'an reader and other speakers. Assisted by men and boys at Hanalishah and early-arriving guests, they pitched four goat-hair tents and six canvas tents for male guests and two goat-hair tents and three canvas tents for female guests. The small houses of Borzu and Mohammad Karim would also hold mourners, especially women and children. Only at such large events were separate sites provided for men and women, and the Persian attendees would expect such segregation. Smaller, all-Qermezi rites were not divided. Dariush ordered a black cloth banner with white lettering announcing the sad occasion, which young men hung from the roof of Borzu's house. They attached a plain black banner next to the lettered one. Later someone decided that the second banner was too stark, and he taped Borzu's memorial poster to its center. Other men pitched an open-sided goat-hair tent and cleared space for cooking by the natural springs on the slope between the two houses. Alongside Borzu's house, they set up a canvas tent for preparing tea.

Many people, particularly from the subtribe, contributed livestock for the meals necessary for so many guests. Some gave sheep or goats but most offered large lambs, which were more valuable, to signify their respect for Borzu. Men assisting the event slaughtered 16 animals for the meat prepared for the noon meal. (From the time of Borzu's death through the fortieth-day memorial, men killed 70 to 80 animal for the meals.) Some people contributed sugar cones and bags of raw rice. Helped financially by close kinsmen, Borzu's sons purchased fruits and vegetables and other necessary commodities.[2] They said the rules of hospitality required them to buy cigarettes for the Persian and Lur villagers and townsmen.[3] In the subtribe only several men (and no women) smoked cigarettes.

People began arriving early in the morning, and most were present by ten o'clock. As signs of mourning, some vehicles displayed black cloth flags mounted on sticks or tied to external rearview mirrors, and some men had taped Borzu's memorial poster to the windows. One hundred cars, vans, and trucks parked wherever the drivers could locate space along the dirt road and near the two houses. Exiting the conveyances, mourners approached those who came to welcome them and then walked uphill toward the reception tents. On the way, they shook hands with and kissed the faces of Borzu's closest kinsmen who stood in a long receiving line. One greeter later told me that the highlights of each mourner's relationship with Borzu had flashed through his mind as he touched and kissed the person. Some arriving women, especially close kin, also spoke to and kissed the men in the line, and then someone escorted them to Borzu's house and to the women's reception tents. Whenever relatives came in groups, some in chartered minibuses, Borzu's daughter Zohreh went to the porch of the house where she wailed songs of grief to greet them. To offer comfort, Falak and another daughter sat quietly beside her.

The main reception area for men consisted of two large goat-hair tents connected together to form a double-width tent. Dozens of knotted pile

Death and memory 221

carpets contributed by Hanalishah's weavers covered the interior. In the tent's right-hand front corner (facing out), a platform held the amplifier. Borzu's framed photograph stood near a Qur'an holder. Just to the right, resting against a stand, a large wreath of multicolored gladiolas displayed a black banner with white lettering announcing Borzu's seventh-day memorial.

Husain Sabiri, a Persian from Semirom who taught the Qur'an in public schools there, read from the sacred text and sang songs of mourning in Persian. He was not a clergyman or a religious figure and had never attended theological school. He had known Borzu and his family for years. The microphone and generator-powered amplifier broadcast throughout the camp his words and those of other speakers.

Between sessions of Sabiri's reading and singing, prominent male guests offered tributes to Borzu and spoke about his impact on the Qermezi subtribe and the wider Qashqa'i society. (No women spoke publicly.) A few Qashqa'i speakers addressed their remarks in Turkish and added that Borzu would have wanted them to do so. Others used Persian out of respect for those who did not know Turkish. Many commented that Borzu was the epitome of honor and that his words and deeds had always been consistent. If Borzu promised to take some action, he always fulfilled that pledge. He was a man on whom others could rely.[4] Most speakers noted that Borzu was unique; another man like him had never lived. Some reminded listeners that the government had killed his father and that Borzu had always mourned for him. Several commented that no one in the subtribe smoked opium and only several smoked cigarettes because of his leadership and the example he set.

The influential Qashqa'i men who addressed the gathering included Mahmud Atazadeh, the Darzi Darrehshuri man currently serving as the parliamentary deputy for the Semirom district. A few Darrehshuri khans and kikhas as well as some leading subtribal headmen also spoke. Jehangir Khan Darrehshuri, with whom Borzu was more closely allied than any other khan, cried as he sang, "Borzu, why have you gone? Why didn't you take me with you?" He delivered a special tribute to Shir Mohammad, killed while the two of them had fought the army side by side. Jehangir Khan's elder brother, Mohammad Hasan Khan, spoke eloquently about Borzu's courageous and honorable character. A respected man from another Qashqa'i tribe lamented, "Borzu Qermezi has left the Qashqa'i."

Carefully choosing and enunciating his words, Mohammad Quli Nadiri spoke the longest.[5] He entertained aspirations to run as a candidate for parliament and took this opportunity to assert himself. Still, he seemed embarrassed by this display, and he prefaced his remarks by noting that he was not speaking for political reasons. A Nadirli Darrehshuri man, Nadiri had taught children at Dashtak and Hanalishah in 1969–72 and had stayed in contact with Borzu, his family, and former students. Similar to several other speakers, he said that Borzu was so eminent among the Qashqa'i that a foreign scholar had written a book about him.[6] He held up the just-published issue of *Zan-e Ruz* (*Today's Woman*, a leading Persian-language magazine)

222 *Death and memory*

containing an article about Borzu's generous hospitality and later passed it among the gathered men.[7]

Ibrahim Qermezi was perhaps the only Qermezi man who spoke publicly via this amplified medium to the gathering. Trained for years in theological seminaries and considered a clergyman, he offered religious guidance in a town prison. Dressed in civilian clothes and speaking persuasively, Ibrahim remarked that Borzu had never feared the tribal khans (some of whom were present to hear his words) and had always protected and defended the Qermezi and their subtribe. To the surprise of some outsiders, he did not include any explicit or implicit religious or politico-religious commentary. Some attendees who were not Qermezi did not know that he was a cleric.

The only man wearing a cleric's cloak and turban at the rites was Bahram Qarehqanli, a Qarehqanli Darrehshuri man and possibly the first Qashqa'i theological student after the revolution. He currently served in the Nomads' Corps of Revolutionary Guards as the deputy of Iran's supreme leader. Having only a passing relationship with Borzu, he did not speak at the memorial. Borzu's sons had not invited any non-Qashqa'i clergymen, including those residing in Semirom, despite possibly negative consequences for their family and tribal group. Unlike some Darrehshuri khans and prominent Darrehshuri headmen before 1979, Borzu had never cultivated relationships with any clergymen, for any political, economic, or religious reason, and he considered none as friends. His sons noted that they had respected his principled attitudes and honored his memory by not including any outside clerics.

Dariush Khan Qashqa'i had sent a telegram to Dariush Qermezi to express his sorrow about Borzu's death. He wrote that he had wanted to attend the memorial but could not. He was one of the few surviving paramount khans of the Qashqa'i tribal confederacy still resident in Iran, and was the only one the regime permitted to live in Qashqa'i territory.

During the Qur'an reading, Persian songs of mourning, and speeches, young Qermezi men passed hot tea, water, and fruit among the assembled male and female guests. Others including Borzu's sisters' sons (a customary role for these particular relatives) assisted the two hired cooks in preparing lunch.[8] The meal, consisting of steamed white rice, two kinds of meat stew, chopped cucumber-and-tomato salad, and sour milk, was scheduled for noon, men being served first and then women and children. Men and older boys from Hanalishah and other close relatives from elsewhere served the guests, including women and children. When people finished the meal, they rose from their places along the long plastic strips laid inside the tents, and others sat down to eat.

As two o'clock approached, people prepared to travel to Mehr-i Gerd's mosque for prayers and Qur'an readings and then to Borzu's grave. The hour's trip took travelers through Semirom, their black attire, posters, and black banners proclaiming the sad occasion to all witnesses.

Observances at Sahib al-Zaman Mosque, named after the "hidden" twelfth Shi'i imam, ran from two o'clock until six. Husain Sabiri again read from the Qur'an. Men sat quietly without overt demonstrations of grief while women cried into their black veil-wraps to express their feelings about this death and others. Women's wailing rose and fell; each woman grew emotional when she identified with the sentiments expressed by others. Attendees stayed for a while and then departed, to make room in the small crowded mosque for new arrivals. Women, girls, and most young boys stayed on one side of a thin cloth barrier strung loosely along a cord. The curtain flapped in the breeze coming through windows and doors, and people on both sides could readily see one another. Gender separation seemed largely a pretense. When a toddler wrapped himself in the cloth and yanked it down, no one bothered to hang it up again. Qermezi men and boys who resided in Mehr-i Gerd served tea, fruit juice, water, melon, and a sweet mixture of ground dates, flour, and oil (*ranginak*).

After visiting the mosque, some people traveled by vehicle or foot to the cemetery atop the hill overlooking the village. The mound of dirt over the new grave was covered with a handsome gelim from Borzu's home and a white cloth on which sat bowls of small cucumbers, nougat candy, and the date-and-flour sweet. A spray of gladiolas stood at the grave's foot. Led again by Husain Sabiri, people uttered the Arabic prayer, sang songs of mourning, and sobbed in despair. Among the women, Borzu's daughter Zohreh was again the leading singer, her voice rising above the others. After the short service attended mostly by close relatives, some traveled home while others returned to Hanalishah. There, the cooks had readied their equipment to leave, and others had washed and assembled the rented supplies for their return to Shahreza. Qermezi visitors who lived far away spent the night at Borzu's site in the two houses and many tents or sought shelter at other homes at Hanalishah. That evening Borzu's family members sighed that they were exhausted and distraught. Dariush noted that he had not slept for days.

Adorning the gravesite

After the seventh-day memorial, Dariush ordered a marble gravestone for Borzu from a craftsman in Shahreza, to be incised with his name and his father's; his subtribe, tribe, and confederacy; the years of his birth and death; and a Persian poem.[9] He and his brothers decided to order a new marble gravestone for Borzu's father as well, so that the side-by-side stones would be the same size, shape, and quality. Shir Mohammad's marker would display the image of a rifle to signify his courageous death in battle.

Well before the fortieth-day memorial, men returned to the cemetery to build a tomb over Shir Mohammad's and Borzu's graves. They included Burj Ali Qermezi—the subtribe's master builder, a member of Aqa Mohammadli lineage, and a resident of Naqneh village. He chose his assistants from the Qermezi communities near Borujen, and Qermezi men from Hanalishah and Mehr-i Gerd also volunteered.

When completed, Borzu's tomb was larger and more elaborate than the cemetery's other gravesites. Most sites displayed markers laying flat on the ground or resting on low platforms. The simplest were plain concrete or

224 *Death and memory*

stone slabs while others included the deceased's name and possibly the year of birth and/or death. Others were granite or marble carved with these details, tribal affiliations, and sometimes Persian poetry, Quranic verses, and floral images. The graves of eight martyrs, seven from the Iraq–Iran war, stood prominently in an orderly row running uphill from the cemetery's entrance but were soon eclipsed by Borzu's fancy tomb.[10] Metal fencing and a peaked metal roof, of uniform design and color and provided by the government's Martyrs Foundation, enclosed each martyr's gravestone laying on a platform. At each platform's head, a glass-fronted case displayed the person's photographs, personal items, and plastic flowers. At one time new Iranian flags raised on poles stood alongside each grave but by 1995 they were sun bleached and tattered, their strips fluttering oddly, discordantly in the wind.

In front of and slightly downhill from Borzu's tomb, the gravestones of Ziad Khan Darrehshuri and his wife Azar Bibi Darrehshuri rested side by side on low separated platforms, unroofed but enclosed by an unlocked metal fence. Unlike other graves in the cemetery, a fence defined the borders of this plot (three times larger than the space occupied by the two platforms) and prevented others from burying their dead too close to the khan and *bibi*. Even in death, their privileged position was evident. Yet only former servants came to pay their respects, and dry weeds filled the neglected enclosure. Jagged pieces of the marble gravestone of Ziad Khan's sister, Sughra Bibi, lay haphazardly on his slab. When men had dug new graves, they had disturbed her site and broken the stone and did not know how to handle the fragments other than to place them on her brother's grave.

During many visits to Borzu's grave that year and ones to follow, I never saw anyone attending Ziad Khan and Azar Bibi's site. Once I overheard two of the bibi's former servants call out to her as they passed by her grave on the way to one of their own relatives. "Bibi! Bibi! I ate lots of buttery, crispy rice!" The other added, "Me too!" As servants, they had stood at attention while Azar Bibi consumed quantities of this particular treat. I sensed some ambiguity in their tone of voice. They remembered fondly her appreciation of this food and wanted to remind her of it. Yet they also proclaimed a shift in their relationship. No longer servants, they now entitled themselves to partake in this delicacy. And they were still alive (while Azar Bibi was not).

Working without a sketch, Burj Ali and his assistants constructed a square tomb over Shir Mohammad's and Borzu's graves. He used kiln-fired yellow bricks and cement mortar and topped the structure with a concrete dome supported by steel rods. The tomb's inside dimensions were nearly three meters square. Workers temporarily removed Shir Mohammad's original gravestone in order to build around the site. They constructed two adjoining platforms and placed the new marble gravestones side by side, Shir Mohammad's to the west and Borzu's to the east. As the father, Shir Mohammad lay closer to Mecca. Dariush did not intend to discard Shir Mohammad's original stone (its curlicued, raised lettering still visible) but was perplexed for a while. Then, with sudden inspiration, he decided to mount it upright in the wall above the grave's head.

Death and memory 225

Workers lined the sides of the platforms and the floor with stone tiles. Open metal fencing on three of the tomb's four sides allowed people to see the interior, the southern side holding a metal gate that could be locked. Burj Ali inserted electrical wires before cementing the dome's interior so the family could attach a light fixture if electricity were ever brought to the cemetery. He and his crew completed the work just before the fortieth-day memorial. The mourners that day would find a structure exemplifying Borzu's stature.

After the memorial, Dariush and Mohammad Karim prepared a niche in the plastered wall at the head of Borzu's gravestone so it could hold a framed photograph, a fabric flower, and several candles. Dariush had ordered in Semirom a small metal frame mounted with clear glass and containing a door. The color photograph (taken in 1991) depicts Borzu looking directly at the camera as he leans against the stack of baggage, draped with a gelim, at the back of his tent. His daughters call it the "gelim photograph." They said they felt close to him when they saw his eyes looking directly at them.[11]

Thursday afternoon visitations

Every Thursday afternoon until they departed for winter pastures, Borzu's family and others visited Borzu's grave to pay their respects and share their grief. Mourners for others buried in the cemetery also customarily came on this day in the late afternoon as the sun's heat was diminishing. Borzu's sons stopped first in Semirom to buy melons and nougat candy and then at a faucet at Mehr-i Gerd's outskirts to fill containers for washing the gravestones. Parking along the cemetery fence, they and their companions hoped to arrive when other visitors would also be present. They disliked coming too early or too late because they would be practically the only mourners.

Borzu's daughters and other female relatives opened the unlocked gate of the small tomb, touched Borzu's gravestone as they entered, and sat facing it along the metal fence. Covering their faces with scarves or tunic hems, one and then another began to sing and weep rhythmically, and others joined in with their own phrases. Never singing, Falak usually stayed outside and cried there. Borzu's son or another male relative lit a candle by Borzu's photograph. Men and older boys stood solemnly and cried along with the women, but they stopped before the women did and turned to the task of washing the gravestones, platforms, and floor. Children gathered bundles of dry weeds to sweep away dirt and excess water. After allowing the family sufficient time to cry for Borzu and begin their cleaning, mourners at other graves came to offer fruit and candy to the new arrivals, who were obligated to utter a Quranic prayer for the deceased person when they accepted the gift. Visitors touched Borzu's gravestone and added words of comfort and condolence for the family. After they finished crying, older girls and young women mourning at Borzu's grave took gifts of food to others at the cemetery, they in turn receiving promises of prayers for Borzu. They laid food on Shir Mohammad's gravestone for others to take and offered it when they came. Sometimes Borzu's female relatives sat

226   *Death and memory*

beside his gravestone to sing and weep again. The rituals, cleaning, and food exchanging completed after an hour or so, the mourners placed their fingers on Borzu's grave one last time and prepared to leave. They said farewell to people newly arriving at the cemetery. One man closed the tomb's gate. Riding back to Hanalishah, they remained subdued in their talk. At home they quietly shared information about the visit with those not accompanying them.

Fortieth-day memorial

Borzu's sons scheduled the fortieth-day memorial service for Thursday, 27 July, 36 days after Borzu's death. The rite resembled the seventh-day one. At a shop in Shahreza, Dariush ordered commemorative cards and posters to be printed, similar to the seventh-day ones, to announce the event's date, time, and place. The card listed the more inclusive "Qermezi family" instead of just "Qermezi brothers." The poster depicted flowers and a Qur'an resting on a holder and included the simple black bow used on the previous one. It thanked those who had participated in the seventh-day rites. This time the printer added the day and month (28 Safar) of the Islamic calendar. He complained that revolutionary guards had ordered him to include these dates on all such notices. Except perhaps for the few hezbollahis, the Qermezi paid no attention to the Islamic lunar calendar, which they said the clerical regime had inflicted on them (just as Mohammad Reza Shah had forced an imperial calendar on Iran's citizens).[12]

A week before the rite, Dariush and Bizhan invited Hanalishah's nomads to gather at their home for a meal. They would soon be busy with perhaps a thousand guests and their multitudes of children, and they wanted a more intimate gathering beforehand for the closest relatives. They pitched several goat-hair and canvas tents, and the group (men, women, and children sitting intermixed) shared a meal and planned the memorial's details. Borzu's sons thanked everyone for their assistance during the past month. Three days before the rite, men at Hanalishah traveled to all other Qermezi communities to announce the date and present the cards and posters to every family. Again, they mounted the poster in public places in Semirom and Kazerun, and Borzu's merchant-acquaintances there also displayed it in their shops.

Borzu's sons hired a Persian cook from Semirom who prepared the noon meal with help from his assistants and young men from Hanalishah and other locations. They rented items that the cook did not provide and a gasoline-powered generator and amplifier for the Qur'an reader and other speakers. Dariush purchased another black cloth banner to hang from the house's roof. In ornate calligraphic white letters, it included Quranic verses and a tribute to Borzu. "Forty days have passed since Borzu departed from among us. ..." Hanalishah's nomads again contributed goat-hair and canvas tents, knotted pile carpets, and cooking and serving supplies. They and many guests provided live animals for the meals.

Slightly fewer people attended the fortieth-day memorial than the seventh. Seventy vehicles parked along the road, by the houses, and downhill from the

Death and memory 227

reception tents, and others sat behind Borzu's house in the wasteland created by the Persian cultivators who had destroyed his pasture there. Only one vehicle (belonging to a Persian visitor from Kazerun) flew a black flag of mourning but many displayed the fortieth-day poster. Before lunch, guests uttered the formulaic prayer in Arabic for Borzu. Husain Sabiri, the Qur'an teacher from Semirom, read from the Qur'an and sang Persian songs of mourning. Male guests spoke about Borzu's impact on the subtribe and other people he had known. Some mentioned that the government had killed his father and that Borzu had mourned for him until his own death. Guests passed around copies of the Persian-language magazine *Zan-e Ruz* containing an article about Borzu.[13]

A few of Borzu's closest relatives could not attend this memorial. They had traveled south to extend support to Qamar Qermezi's family. Daughter of Khalifeh and wife of Amir Husain, Qamar had been distraught at Borzu's seventh-day memorial. Shortly after she returned to her camp in the mountains near Shiraz, she died suddenly from an apparent heart attack, "from the shock of her father's brother's passing."

Another person who wanted to come was Mahmud Khan Kashkuli, who had sung at the Qur'an Gate when Borzu's body was beginning the journey from Shiraz to summer pastures. He was assisting his relatives in Shiraz with the funeral and memorial services of a kinsman.

Around two o'clock family members, relatives, and guests traveled to the Mehr-i Gerd mosque to offer prayers for Borzu and listen to Husain Sabiri read from the Qur'an. Dariush brought the framed color photograph of Borzu and stood it by the Qur'an holder. This event also resembled the seventh-day one. Young men of the village served food and beverages, and people stayed only briefly because of the crowded interior. Afterward some drove or walked to the cemetery where they greeted Borzu and repeated the Arabic prayer of mourning. Then some returned home while others drove back to Hanalishah. One hundred men and women stayed the night in Borzu's camp, and others slept at nearby homes. Most dispersed the following day after visiting other Qermezi families there.

After the fortieth-day rites, Borzu's immediate family and closest relatives gradually changed from black to other dark, unembellished attire and, some days or weeks later, to normal clothes. Two of Borzu's three daughters-in-law were the first women to end wearing black; they did not share blood ties with him. The third daughter-in-law, a distant relative, remained in black. Dressing in black as before, Falak stated that she would approach her own death wearing the color. (Women as well as men were wrapped in white shrouds for burial.) Several weeks after the fortieth-day rite, she donned a new black skirt trimmed at the hem with a narrow, almost unnoticeable, strip of dark blue and silver.

Borzu's close female relatives had stopped weaving when they heard that Borzu had died, and they began again only after the fortieth-day observance. In the interval, they prepared wool and yarn for their next weaving projects. Until after the fortieth day, Borzu's relatives did not attend any wedding celebrations or other festive events. Borzu's nearest kin postponed weddings until

228   *Death and memory*

a later date, and more distant kin formally visited Mohammad Karim and Dariush to ask permission to proceed with weddings and to receive the sons' blessings. Accepting the customary gift of nougat candy and offering good wishes, Borzu's sons told the visitors that they could not attend but that their more distant relatives might.

Events in the year after the death

In the coming days, weeks, and months, many hundreds of people who had not attended the seventh-day or fortieth-day memorials traveled to Hanalishah, Dashtak, and Kazerun to pay their respects to Borzu's family. Qashqa'i custom requires people to visit as soon as possible after a death and certainly before the one-year anniversary, one year considered adequate to fulfill the obligation. Borzu's children and others often commented about those who had not yet appeared. They mentioned a particular Darrehshuri khan who had still not repaid a large debt to a Kachili Qermezi man in Nurabad village. Giving the khan more credit than he deserved, they suggested that he was too ashamed to offer condolences. The khan had brokered the sale of the villager's apple harvest but then kept all the income for himself.[14] When Borzu's kin heard about a new death and contemplated attending the rites, they considered the presence or absence of that person and his or her family at Borzu's memorials. They were likely to visit those people who had formally acknowledged Borzu's death. Borzu's wife and children were especially grateful to those who came often and offered assistance.

During the year after the death, Borzu's absence was constantly apparent, especially because he had been so dominant and aggressive. Whenever an unusual or unexpected event occurred, people speculated about his response. No one emerged to take his place as the subtribe's headman and as the leader of the nomads at Dashtak and Hanalishah. As the head of Aqa Mohammadli's Islamic council, Bahram (Borzu's brother's son) served in some official and informal capacities. His stance as a hezbollahi, the only one in these two territories, decreased his influence, power, and authority.

Borzu's sons, particularly Dariush and Bizhan who became heads of the household, claimed some of their father's possessions and offered others to close relatives. Husain Ali requested Borzu's new Qashqa'i hat and his hand-crafted cane, but Khosrow Qarehqanli, in whose Shiraz house Borzu had briefly stayed before dying, inexplicably refused to give them to him (for no reason anyone could fathom). Several other people expressed interest in some personal object. Before his death, Borzu gave a few possessions and items of apparel to his sons-in-law and daughters-in-law to demonstrate his appreciation for the special role they played in his family. As he once joked to me, "I did not choose the children that Falak delivered and raised but I *chose* my brides and my grooms [the spouses of his children]!"

Most nomads at Hanalishah left summer pastures in late August or early September in 1995. Just beforehand, many visited Borzu's gravesite to say

Death and memory 229

farewell until the next spring. The departure was distressing for Borzu's immediate family. His daughters were particularly distraught about leaving him behind and sobbed with despair at the grave. Some men returned to Hanalishah to pick apples or supervise the harvest, and they paid their respects at the cemetery. The parliamentary election (staged in two parts in March and April of 1996) drew Qermezi men and women from Dashtak and Kazerun; they rented minibuses or took private vehicles to vote in Semirom where a Qermezi man was a candidate. Most visited the cemetery, still covered in snow in March. Just before the New Year in March, to mark the end of the sorrowful year, Borzu's sons, daughters, and other relatives at Dashtak and Kazerun chartered a minibus so they could attend the grave. On their return, Zohreh and Farideh tearfully unpacked their father's remaining clothes, washed them, rinsed them in rose water, and wrapped them in a clean cloth to save.[15]

As soon as the nomads arrived at Hanalishah in mid-spring, 45 days into the New Year, they traveled to the grave to announce their arrival to Borzu. Once again the women were inconsolable about Borzu having been alone during the cold, snowy winter. They found his absence at Hanalishah disturbing.

One-year memorial, 1996

The family commemorated the first anniversary of Borzu's death on Thursday, 20 June, just before summer began. People noted the special ways in which Borzu had always marked the beginning of each new season, and they commented on the irony of the timing of his death. For one last time Dariush ordered posters to announce the memorial. Including a photograph of Borzu's solemn face, the poster resembled the fortieth-day one except that it omitted the gathering at the mosque. This time Dariush did not print commemorative cards. Qermezi men posted the sheets in public places in Semirom and Shahreza and traveled widely to deliver posters and verbal invitations to relatives and acquaintances of Borzu and his family, lineage, and subtribe.

(Many of these posters were still visible in Semirom through the end of summer. Over time, announcements for more recently deceased people fully or partly covered Borzu's posters. I was always distressed to see Borzu's face at eye level when any vehicle in which I rode turned a particular corner on Semirom's main route. There, on a wall, his poster was still uncovered. The following winter's rains and snows dissolved all of them.)

Mohammad Karim, Dariush, and Bizhan spent the days prior to the one-year memorial service preparing their camp for guests, helped by Hanalishah's nomads and early arrivals. They pitched four long goat-hair tents, and Borzu's four married daughters and other women contributed large knotted carpets for the interiors. The camp's women and girls cleaned the two houses. Some Qermezi guests would sleep at other Hanalishah homes to lessen the congestion in this small camp. The three brothers erected small goat-hair and canvas tents for preparing food and tea. They bought food and supplies in Semirom and Shahreza and hired a Persian cook and several helpers to make

230   *Death and memory*

lunch for the guests. From Shahreza they rented 300 plates, spoons, and forks and many large platters and trays for serving food and beverages. (Helpers washed these plates and utensils for reuse many times over.) As before, kinspeople at Hanalishah contributed supplies. All families now placed distinctive marks on often interchangeable possessions such as plates and tent poles so they could retrieve their own after communal events. The brothers leased a gasoline-run generator for the amplifier. The night before, taking advantage of the machine, they strung up light bulbs to illuminate the house and immediate grounds, an unprecedented event. Hanalishah's young unmarried men traveled hundreds of kilometers to deliver posters and to purchase, rent, and collect supplies. They and others put all their vehicles to use, including those belonging to early arrivals, many of whom had come precisely for this purpose.

As many people attended Borzu's one-year anniversary as the fortieth-day memorial and from as many locations. The seventh-day rite had been the largest of the five (the burial being the first of five gatherings). Hearing about Borzu's death, many people had immediately demonstrated their support for the family. Some attended only the seventh-day rite, thus fulfilling their duty to offer condolences after a death. Others regarded the one-year event as the final opportunity to pay their respects.

For the one-year anniversary, some people arrived the night before, particularly those living a distance away. Most others appeared in the morning. Ninety vehicles surrounded the campsite by mid-morning, and others arrived before noon. Residents of Atakula village, mostly Qermezi but also others who had formed long-term ties with the group, rented two minibuses and rode in private vehicles. All Nurabad villagers came; they were the closest kin of Borzu's wife. Qermezi residents of Naqneh and Borujen chartered two minibuses and used personal vehicles. Some Shaikh Lurs, connected by kinship and marriage to the Qermezi group, came from winter pastures near Dogonbadan. One of Borzu's sisters had married a Shaikh Lur man, and her sons accompanied her to honor their mother's brother, a key kinship tie in Qashqa'i society.

As with previous memorials, many Qashqa'i from other subtribes and tribes participated. Borzu had taken two Qarehqanli girls as brides for his sons, and members of that subtribe acknowledged the link by their presence. Some Darrehshuri khans and kikhas and their families came. The khan closest to Borzu, Jehangir Khan, arrived along with his brother Mohammad Hasan Khan. Other khans of Mehr-i Gerd were noticeably absent, including Sohrab, and the Qermezi talked then and later about the reasons. Borzu had suffered politically since the revolution and had endured death threats and imprisonment because of his alliance with the Darrehshuri khans. Thus, the Qermezi asserted, all these leaders ought to have acknowledged Borzu's loyalty by observing this and the other memorials. The kind of persisting support that Borzu had offered had defined the khans as the tribe's leaders, and they ought to have been grateful to him. Without such allegiance from prominent headmen (including Borzu), the khans would not have held such an elevated political position.

Death and memory 231

Many non-Qashqa'i people also attended, which demonstrated the wide span of Borzu's contacts. As before, the Qermezi and others remarked that they had not understood the full extent of Borzu's extra-tribal links until after he died. Persian merchants and their families in Kazerun came, despite the grueling 10-hour drive (if all went well) through mountainous terrain and the few comforts (no running water, toilets, or privacy for women) at the destination. Prominent citizens, merchants, and their families from Semirom offered support. Residents there who owned land and/or cultivated at Hanalishah arrived with their families, as did officials and employees of the Organization for Nomads' Affairs, Nomads' Revolutionary-Guard Corps, and Pastures Organization. Villagers from nearby Galleh Qadam and Vanak came, including those who owned land and/or cultivated at Hanalishah. Borzu's acquaintances in Shahreza and a distant Shiraz also paid their respects. Some people, not attending the earlier rites, said they had not wanted to intrude on what they assumed were family events. Coming now, they were fulfilling their obligation to acknowledge the death before a year had passed.

At noon the hired cook, his helpers, and Qermezi men and boys fed over 900 adults in three sittings, a number they ascertained by the individual serving plates used and reused. (Multiple children often shared a plate, as did mothers and their children, and the number of attendees was higher than the plates used and reused.) The cook steamed five huge pots of rice and prepared two types of meat-and-vegetable stew, and guests consumed fresh fruit and tea before the meal and sour milk during it. Men had slaughtered 12 large sheep and goats to provide meat for the stews.

Before and after the meal, Husain Sabiri, the same Persian man from Semirom who had served during previous memorials, read from the Qur'an and recited Persian poems of mourning. Many cried while they listened to his solemn, melodious voice. Women sitting in the houses and reception tents wailed and sang their own words of grief. Some men offered short speeches, including Shahriyar Qermezi, the newly elected parliamentary deputy for Semirom, who promised to visit the family later when it was not so preoccupied. One of Qermezi's three clergymen, Ibrahim Qermezi, spoke eloquently about the importance, especially for still-grieving families, of remembering those who had died. Speakers remarked that, although people usually forgot the deceased by the time a year had passed (a statement certainly untrue), no one had yet forgotten Borzu. They noted that Qermezi was "Borzu's tribe [tayifih]" and his presence there so significant that he and the Qermezi name were synonymous. When anyone outside the subtribe mentioned either one, people immediately thought of the other. Several speakers commented, as others had done at earlier memorials, that no one in the subtribe smoked opium and few smoked cigarettes because of Borzu's positive influence.

Then Borzu's immediate family, most other nomads at Hanalishah, most Qermezi visitors, and many other guests traveled to Mehr-i Gerd to attend the last of the services at the mosque and then to visit the grave. Some Mehr-i Gerd residents who had not gone to Hanalishah stopped by the mosque to

232 *Death and memory*

pay their respects to Borzu's family. Standing beside the tomb, Husain Sabiri recited briefly from the Qur'an, and most everyone cried and grieved. People paid tribute to Borzu's father Shir Mohammad, whose grave now adjoined his son's. Some guests left for home after this ceremony while others returned to Hanalishah for the evening. Many who had traveled a distance stayed the night with other families at Hanalishah and stopped by Borzu's camp in the morning to say farewell. Borzu's exhausted family members hugged and kissed each beloved person who had come to share with them the final day of this year of grief.

Second anniversary, 1997

The family marked the second anniversary of Borzu's death on Friday, 14 March 1997, a week before the New Year began. Dariush and other family members chose this date rather than the actual anniversary, the first day of summer. They wanted to remember Borzu at the end of the year so they could begin the New Year with happiness. Other families also selected this time to acknowledge their deceased loved ones, for the same reason. Some continued to mark the actual anniversary as well, but they did so simply, often with only a few Quranic phrases before an otherwise ordinary meal.[16]

The Qermezi residents of Kazerun attended the event along with Mohammad Karim and others from nearby Dashtak. Assisted by Borzu's married daughters, Farzaneh and Fariba prepared the lunch. After the meal Mohammad Karim as the eldest son briefly uttered Quranic phrases, and adults intoned the customary prayer in Arabic for the dead. No one wept or sang songs of grief. One of Borzu's daughters explained that the family cried and sang only at the grave now. With so many young children running through the house, the ceremony was noisy and hectic, and Farzaneh vowed that, for the third anniversary, she would send the youngsters outside after eating so the adults could perform the customary prayers more reverently.

Notes

1 An Arab novelist (Soueif 2000: 38) writes: "There are no rituals of mourning. In the twenty-odd years I lived in England, I never found out how the English mourn. There seems to be a funeral and then—nothing. Just an emptiness. No friends and relatives filling the house. No Thursday nights. No Fortieth Day. Nothing."
2 Family members knew exactly who had contributed what items and in what quantities during this and subsequent memorials, despite the crowds of people, responsibilities, and underlying sorrow.
3 Family members later said that they had refused to buy opium to support the habits of addicts among the Persian and Lur guests.
4 Some speakers contrasted these traits (especially consistent words and actions) with those found among the Persians with whom Borzu had interacted.
5 Nadiri-Darrehshuri (2000) published poems by the preeminent Qashqa'i poet, Mazun.
6 Beck (1991).

Death and memory 233

7 The timing of this publication was fortuitous. The original English version appeared in 1993, and many published Persian translations followed (all without my permission or prior knowledge), including the *Zan-e Ruz* one in 1995, corresponding coincidentally with Borzu's death. See Beck (1993, 1995a).

8 Borzu is their mother's brother, a key relationship in Qashqa'i society. The sons of a deceased man's sisters played this special role during memorial services. As in other ceremonies, specific roles and obligations of kinship emerged in concrete form. During day-to-day life, they were not necessarily always evident. The sons of a deceased man's brothers represented his lineage and served in other capacities.

9 Huang (2009: 207) includes a photograph.

10 Allah Quli Jahangiri (the Darrehshuri leftist rebel) had murdered the eighth martyr in postrevolutionary struggles.

11 When I took this photograph, I sensed that Borzu knew it might be his last one. He was already quite ill. He actually prepared for this photograph (by shaving, getting a haircut, and cleaning his Qashqa'i hat) before I even considered asking him. Since 1970 he had never liked me photographing him. He complained that he looked nothing like his photographic images.

12 Mohammad Reza Shah had introduced in 1976 an imperial calendar for Iran, which began with the foundation of the Persian Empire 2,500 years earlier. Most Iranians roundly denounced this calendar too. Iran's clerics disliked the Persian solar calendar in part because the names of the months and days were pre-Islamic and linked to Zoroastrianism.

13 See note 7 in this chapter.

14 The khan never did repay the Qermezi man, who died in 2001. The villager had lost the year's apple sales as well as the labor and expenditures (fertilizers, pesticides) incurred during the year.

15 These women might have adopted this custom from some Persians they knew. I had never seen this ritual among the Qermezi or heard about it. In the past, the closest family members distributed the clothing of the deceased person to others. When Borzu's sister, Samanbar, died at Dashtak in 2000, other sisters wrapped her in Borzu's blanket and took her to Atakula for burial. Her family later returned the blanket to Borzu's family.

16 I had shared such meals, without initially knowing they were commemorative ones, until men uttered a Quranic prayer.

7 Life moves on

Reflections on 1996

Two topics drew the attention of all Qermezi in 1996: the unprecedented and sudden national prominence of a Qermezi man who was elected to Iran's parliament and the rapid escalation of interest in all levels of formal education. Focus on these issues seemed to dull the pain of the loss of Borzu Qermezi, the group's headman.

Shahriyar Qermezi, parliamentary deputy

A young Qermezi man was elected to Iran's parliament (*majlis-i shura-yi islami*) in April 1996.[1] Who could this person be? I had lived with the Qermezi group the previous summer and had heard no one talk about anyone running for parliament. Who could have achieved this level of distinction in such a short period?

The new deputy is Shahriyar Qermezi, known also as Abu Zar for his heroic military leadership during the Iraq–Iran war. (A war hero, Abu Zar was a follower of Ali and Husain, the first and third martyred Shi'i imams.)[2] Shahriyar is the son of Sohrab Qermezi, an Imamverdili man who for decades had unsuccessfully challenged Borzu Qermezi for the subtribe's leadership.

Shahriyar is a living symbol of the past, present, and future, a mixture characteristic of the continuation of "tradition" in increasingly "modern" times, a trait also found elsewhere in contemporary Iranian society and culture. He was born and raised as a nomadic pastoralist in the customary fashion. His parents sent him to a nomads' school held in a tent in winter and summer pastures where he received five years of elementary education, the maximum available there. Then he attended middle school in Kazerun for a year and after that the tribal teacher-training program in Shiraz.[3] He became a teacher first for his own nomadic group in winter and summer pastures and then, after the revolution, for a village where some Qermezi resided seasonally. Shahriyar did not play any role in the revolution, and no one then considered him a hezbollahi.

When Iraq invaded Iran in 1980, Shahriyar joined the nomads' volunteer militia (niruha-yi basiji ashayiri, a branch of the wider basij militia), along with relatives and fellow tribesmen. He spent nearly eight years along the

Life moves on 235

front line, and, early on, he distinguished himself as a division commander (*farmandih*). Other Qashqa'i boys and men joined the nomads' militia to serve with him, his tribal identity being key in their recruitment. By reputation, Qashqa'i males possessed superb military skills, especially compared with urban and village males. Shahriyar was injured multiple times, twice severely, and suffered 11 wounds, but he always returned to the front to fight again, once fleeing the hospital where he was still undergoing treatment. By the 1988 ceasefire, his feats, especially his reconnaissance behind enemy lines at night, had already achieved an epic, even mythical, quality. He attributed his military aptitude and tenacity to his upbringing as a mountain-dwelling nomadic pastoralist who had never known the comforts of modern, urban life. Shahriyar's father Sohrab, a fierce and courageous fighter in tribal conflicts, had been wounded in the war against Iran's army in Semirom in 1943.[4] Shahriyar grew up hearing stories about these exploits.

Several Qashqa'i who served with Shahriyar reported that whenever they captured Iraqi soldiers, Persian militiamen (nontribal "townsmen") in nearby units wanted to kill them against Shahriyar's orders. In response, the Qashqa'i militiamen developed a code to communicate that they had apprehended Iraqi soldiers to submit them as prisoners of war. The Persian militiamen soon understood the code and searched for the detainees in order to execute them. Investigating several such incidents, Shahriyar found the Iraqis dead and urged the commander of the culprits to dismiss them from service. His attitude and behavior exemplified traits commonly exhibited by Qashqa'i fighters in prior wars.

In the past, Qashqa'i leaders had earned a reputation for their humane treatment of captives. During the defensive resistance of the paramount Qashqa'i khans in 1980–82, several enthusiastic young men had wanted to kill several Persian revolutionary guards who had doggedly pursued them. Khosrow Khan did not permit them to do so. Instead he instructed them to shave off the beards of each guard, but from only one side of the face, to humiliate them when they had to return to Shiraz. The captives feared being killed but continued to claim that their religion did not permit them to shave the other half, thus amusing their captors.[5] In battles during World War I, when Qashqa'i forces fought British troops sent to southern Iran, Qashqa'i leaders ordered their men to aim at the tall, light-haired British officers, not the short, dark-haired, often turbaned, Indian rank-and-file who held no grievance against the Qashqa'i.[6]

During the war, Shahriyar studied independently, completed high school by passing required tests, and prepared for the university-qualifying examination. After the war and recovered from his injuries, he attended state universities in Zahedan and Isfahan and received a four-year degree in guidance counseling. He continued his administrative job in the Ministry of Education in the town of Dehaqan north of Darrehshuri summer pastures while also serving as a counselor in a secondary school there. Taking classes in Quranic recitation in Dehaqan and Shahreza, he learned to recite some verses but did not memorize the entire Qur'an.

236 *Life moves on*

Kinsmen, tribesmates, militiamen, teachers, and civil servants urged Shahriyar in the autumn of 1995 to run for a seat in parliament. After discussing the benefits and detriments of several administrative districts in and near Qashqa'i territory, he chose Semirom, a rural district in Qashqa'i summer pastures, in the south of Isfahan province. The district contained the predominantly Persian town of the same name. He filed as a potential candidate. The government agencies that vetted all office seekers ruled him eligible to run. His supporters collected money to fund his electoral campaign and volunteered their services, including plastering visible surfaces in high-traffic areas with posters depicting his name, face, and slogans. He garnered more votes than did his opponents, including a clergyman who had campaigned as if he were the sure winner.

As a parliamentary deputy (*namayandih*), Shahriyar did not play any formal role at the subtribal level, in part because of his relocation to Tehran, but people noted that they expected him to be an effective representative for the district and a role model for Qermezi and other Qashqa'i youth. Qashqa'i and others throughout southwestern Iran knew of him because of his campaign, election, and service in parliament. He achieved a distinction unprecedented in Qermezi history, and the Qermezi and their associates were proud.

Iran's parliaments, the Qashqa'i, and other minorities

Reza Shah chose the paramount Qashqa'i khan and his eldest son to serve in Iran's parliament. Under Mohammad Reza Shah, the paramount Qashqa'i khan, his youngest brother, and several other Qashqa'i khans were elected as deputies of some districts in Qashqa'i territory.[7] Between the revolution in 1978–79 and 1992, only one Qashqa'i was elected—Khosrow Khan Qashqa'i to the Islamic Republic's first parliament in 1980—and his quest ended in his execution.

Iran's 1979 constitution (amended in 1989) permits five religious minorities (Armenian, Assyrian, and Chaldean Christians; Zoroastrians; and Jews) to elect their representatives to the unicameral parliament. The document does not offer similar predetermined quotas for the ethnic minorities (including Azeri Turks, Kurds, Arabs, Baluch, and Qashqa'i), who make up half of Iran's population.[8] It also makes no allowance for Sunni Muslims (9 to 11 percent of Iran's population and persistently marginalized), an issue that has become increasingly politicized for these often ignored or suppressed citizens. Still, more ethnic minorities and Sunni Muslims have been chosen in the general elections for parliament than if these groups had been granted predetermined quotas. Almost all of Iran's Sunnis are ethnic and linguistic minorities, and many are also tribally organized.

Parliamentary election in 1992[9]

The 1992 parliamentary election prepared the way for Shahriyar Qermezi. In sections to follow, I detail his campaign and election in 1996 and his deputyship.

Life moves on 237

For the first time in history, a non-elite Qashqa'i man, Mahmud Atazadeh, was elected to parliament. He ran as a candidate in 1992 for the district of Semirom. Other non-elite Qashqa'i had run unsuccessfully in other districts in 1984, 1988, and 1992. Atazadeh is a Darzi Darrehshuri man who originates from a village near Mehr-i Gerd. His father is Darzi, and his mother is Kachili Qermezi. A university graduate, Atazadeh served prior to the campaign as the director of the agency for natural resources in Semirom.

The Qermezi were proud of their kinship connection with Atazadeh, and his maternal link with the Kachili lineage helped to raise its status. The Kachili lineage had been the lowest-ranking Qermezi lineage until the early 1980s because many of its members had served the Darrehshuri khans in various capacities. Other Qermezi often derided them as "the khans' servants," which many of them had been. With the political demise of the Darrehshuri khans in 1982 and thereafter, many Kachili expanded their economic and social opportunities by adopting permanent residences, agriculture, formal education, and urban-related jobs. Soon some of them held economic positions that other Qermezi were only beginning to contemplate seriously. At the time, Atazadeh's sudden rise to prominence symbolized the changing fortunes of the Kachili and the strategies they were effectively devising to meet the changing circumstances that all Qermezi now faced.

Atazadeh's three opponents in the 1992 election for the Islamic Republic's fourth parliament are Persians from Semirom or the vicinity. One was Fazlullah Subhani from the Padena region in the district's south. Before running, he worked in a sugar factory in Isfahan. His father is a Persian from Padena who claimed at least one Qashqa'i ancestor. Some people noted that his mother is Qarachai Qashqa'i while others said she is a Persian from Semirom. Those stating that she is Qashqa'i noted that Subhani did not speak Turkish, which caused others to doubt her Qashqa'i identity. (A child of mixed ethnicity usually learned the mother's language as well as the father's.) Some reported that Subhani is a sayyid, a reputed descendant of the prophet Mohammad, but others doubted it. He did not wear a turban.[10]

Some people confused Subhani with another opponent, Imad ud-Din Imadi, who also originates from a village in Padena and whose father and mother are Persians. People were more certain about his identity. He is both a sayyid (marked by his black turban) and an akhund who instructed students in Islam. Considered wealthy, he derived his livelihood from landownership and agriculture. Relatives working in Kuwait sent money for his campaign. Imadi had run in every parliamentary election for Semirom since the revolution but had already lost three times. The third opponent was a Persian man from Semirom named Nadiri whom many citizens discounted as a viable candidate.

Atazadeh served a full term in the fourth parliament, 1992–96. Expecting him to implement major changes, people in the Semirom district were disappointed and began to complain. He announced in the autumn of 1995 that he would not run for reelection for a second term. Some said he knew that Shahriyar Qermezi was considering his own candidacy, and Shahriyar's

238 *Life moves on*

credentials exceeded Atazadeh's. At the end of the parliamentary term, the government appointed Atazadeh as the director of the agency for natural resources in Isfahan province.

At least three other non-elite Qashqa'i men ran in the 1992 parliamentary election but lost. Two ran as candidates for the district of Firuzabad, the Qashqa'i winter capital in the nineteenth and twentieth centuries, and they split the Qashqa'i vote there. A Persian man won the election. The first Qashqa'i candidate, Sohrab Bahluli Qashqa'i, is a Bahluli Amaleh man who worked as an industrial engineer before the campaign. People throughout southwestern Iran remembered his father, Sutvan (lieutenant) Masih, a famous rebel (*yaghi*) against the Iranian government in the mid-1960s. The second Qashqa'i candidate losing the election in Firuzabad was Aminullah Masumeh, a Shish Buluki man. He was the commander of the paramilitary force raised against Khosrow Khan Qashqa'i in 1980–82. Qashqa'i and non-Qashqa'i alike condemned him for this treachery, especially when his efforts led to Khosrow Khan's execution. Even those Qashqa'i who had not supported Khosrow Khan as a tribal leader after the revolution still regretted his violent, untimely, unjust death. The third Qashqa'i man running in 1992 was Jahan Bakhsh Sulaimani, a candidate for the district of Kazerun. He is a Kalbuli (or Murrul) Farsi Madan man. Before the campaign, he served as the director of the Ministry of Education in Bushire on the Persian Gulf coast.

Parliamentary election in 1996[11]

Shahriyar Qermezi expressed interest in the early autumn of 1995 in running as a candidate in the upcoming election for the fifth parliament. After considering possible districts, Shahriyar chose Semirom. Its town of the same name consists predominantly of Persians and some Lurs. Yet many Qashqa'i (Darrehshuri in the north, Farsi Madan and Qarachai in the south) inhabit the wider district and live in villages and/or are seasonal residents of summer pastures there.[12] Shahriyar said he needed to depend on his fellow Qermezi tribesmates for any degree of success, and he chose the one area where they are concentrated in the summer and where some live all year.

Nationwide electoral rules indicated that people should vote where they resided. Still, individuals could actually vote where they wanted (but only one time each election, including a necessary runoff race, as regulated by the stamp on a person's identity card).[13] Shahriyar depended on the Qermezi living outside the district during the autumn, winter, and early spring to travel to Semirom to cast their ballots, and many promised to do so. The government scheduled the general and runoff elections for late winter and early spring.

The vast majority of Iranians did vote where they resided, partly for convenience but also because the electoral process there represented their interests more directly than the process elsewhere. Migratory or mobile people such as many Qashqa'i chose to vote where they held political, economic, and social interests, especially where a fellow tribesman was a candidate.

Life moves on 239

The voting history of a Qermezi man provides an example common in the subtribe. He was a wintertime resident of Dashtak and Kazerun. In the first parliamentary election of the new Islamic Republic in 1980, he traveled to Eqlid (just east of Qashqa'i summer pastures) to vote for Khosrow Khan Qashqa'i, who won. In 1984, with no Qashqa'i candidates of interest to him anywhere, he voted in Kazerun for a Persian candidate, who won the race. In 1988 he again voted in Kazerun, this time for a Farsi Madan Qashqa'i man; a Persian man won instead. In 1992 he traveled to Semirom to vote for Atazadeh, the successful Darrehshuri candidate. In 1996 he returned to Semirom to vote for Shahriyar Qermezi, who won. In 2000 he campaigned for a Nadirli Darrehshuri candidate in Kazerun but then journeyed to Shahreza to vote for Shahriyar Qermezi; both Qashqa'i men lost.

The Qermezi and other Qashqa'i said they thought Shahriyar would have an advantage in Semirom because a Darrehshuri tribesman had won the previous election there. This man's success had proved that a Qashqa'i could win in what seemed to be a Persian-majority district.[14]

Five substantial assets aided Shahriyar in the forthcoming race: his war record, politico-ideological stance as a regime supporter and a hezbollahi, formal education and occupation, family and kinship ties, and, most important, tribal affiliations.[15]

Shahriyar had already achieved prominence because of his long service in the nomads' volunteer militia during the Iraq–Iran war and his military feats and heroic "sacrifices" (his many injuries). He was reputed to be an advocate of the Islamic Republic, a devout Muslim, and a hezbollahi, and he demonstrated these identities, especially their outer appearances, in his behavior, rhetoric, facial hair, and clothing. His formal training as a teacher, four-year degree from prestigious state universities, administrative work for the Ministry of Education, and employment as an elementary-school teacher and a high-school guidance counselor enhanced his reputation in a region where people valued such professional achievements. Former students in his nomadic group and in Dezeh village and Dehaqan town could speak authoritatively about his positive personal qualities and genuine interest in their educational development.

Of Imamverdili lineage, Shahriyar's father Sohrab, Sohrab's three brothers, and other lineage mates had formed an intermittently supportive group within the Qermezi subtribe. Shahriyar's mother is from Qasemli lineage, and her kin connections there expanded his networks in the subtribe.

Shahriyar's father's mother is Aqa Mohammadli, and his father's father had once sought refuge with members of that lineage.[16] Shahriyar attended the Aqa Mohammadli elementary school (at a time when his own lineage lacked a school), and he remained close with his former classmates in that lineage. Some Aqa Mohammadli considered Shahriyar as one of their own because of the years he had lived among them. His Aqa Mohammadli ties were stronger than those of his lineage mates, and these links contributed to his success as a candidate, given the sociopolitical preeminence of the Aqa Mohammadli lineage in the subtribe.

240   *Life moves on*

Shahriyar's extended family—his brothers and sisters, uncles and aunts, nephews and nieces, cousins, and all of their maternal and marital connections—consisted of loyal backers. All five lineages of the Qermezi subtribe were represented among these maternal and affinal kin, and each person served as a link for Shahriyar to one of the lineages and a way to expand his networks. Shahriyar's brother (a prisoner of war in Iraq for eight years), his brother's son, and his father's brother's son were hezbollahis who could potentially garner help from other hezbollahis (Qashqa'i and non-Qashqa'i) with whom they interacted in the district.

Shahriyar's wife is Darrehshuri but not Qermezi, and he lacked that added link within the subtribe. Yet he could now count on assistance from her relatives in the Talihbazli subtribe and from its fellow members, many of whom lived seasonally or year-round in the Semirom district. A few other Qermezi-Talihbazli intermarriages enhanced this connection for him.

(When the Qermezi contemplated the negative and positive attributes of out-marriage and the merits of careful planning, they sometimes cited Shahriyar's case. When Shahriyar had arranged his marriage with a Talihbazli girl, he was unaware of the details of his future, and he had not expected any special role for the extended family and subtribe of his prospective bride. Yet, years later, he now enjoyed potential backers from a subtribe that was larger than Qermezi. Shahriyar's father Sohrab, certain to forge his own alliances through his son's marriage, had died when the boy was still young.)

Of Shahriyar's multiple attributes, his strong tribal ties would prove to be the most significant in his campaign and election and would be the factor placing him ahead of his opponents. Three of the other candidates lacked any support from organized groups; the fourth relied on his role as a government administrator.[17]

Shahriyar could draw on the loyalty of people in his subtribe (Qermezi), tribe (Darrehshuri), and tribal confederacy (Qashqa'i). The Qermezi would vote for a man in their own group, especially because of the office's prominence. The Darrehshuri would vote for a fellow tribal member, and other Qashqa'i would vote for a fellow Qashqa'i. Even people in non-Qashqa'i tribes would probably vote for another tribal person rather than for a Persian. As part of the larger Iranian society, the Qashqa'i and other tribespeople faced negative attitudes and stereotypes about them and their military, political, ethnic, linguistic, occupational, and residential (rural and nomadic) backgrounds. They would probably support Shahriyar, with whom they shared common bonds, rather than someone who represented those who discriminated against them. From the start, the Qashqa'i and other regional citizens viewed the election campaign in polarizing terms that distinguished people by their ethnicities (as Persians, Turks, or Lurs), languages, tribal or nontribal affiliations, and rural or urban locations.

Of the five assets, only one was potentially problematic: Shahriyar's identity as a hezbollahi. Hezbollahis among the Qashqa'i were few and rapidly diminishing in the early and middle 1990s. Most local groups contained no hezbollahis by 1995, and people spoke negatively about the ones they encountered elsewhere. Still, people seemed to overlook Shahriyar's hezbollahi reputation because of his overriding tribal identities, his other attributes, and the possibility of his success. Shahriyar often tempered his public remarks (whatever his underlying sentiments were), and people increasingly viewed him, at most, as a moderate hezbollahi and not an extremist one. Some noted that, despite the way he had lessened the intensity of his politico-ideological stance over the past few years, he still had to maintain some degree of hezbollahi identity if he wanted the regime's vetting agencies and hard-line conservatives to allow him to run. If he intended to use the parliamentary seat as a step toward higher office and greater national influence, as many predicted, then he would probably require some traits connected with a hezbollahi posture.

If Shahriyar had not been judged a hezbollahi, the government might not have approved his candidacy. For the vetting agencies, his identity as a hezbollahi seems to have superseded his identities as an ethnic Qashqa'i, a Turk, and a tribesman, each one highly politicized in southwestern Iran and also seen by the state as a potential threat. These agencies viewed his hezbollahi persona as his current (and future) identity. His ethnolinguistic and tribal background was only that, his point of origin and his past. (Many high officials in the Islamic Republic had overcome their social and economic backgrounds by adhering to the regime's dominant institutions and politico-religious ideologies.) Yet many voters going to the polls ignored Shahriyar's hezbollahi reputation and focused instead on his ethnolinguistic and tribal identities. As a parliamentary deputy, Shahriyar could serve in beneficial ways for the district and its Qashqa'i and non-Qashqa'i residents, regardless of how the vetting agencies and the voters had initially classified him.

Officials declared five candidates as qualified for the election of the parliamentary deputy of Semirom district. Eligibility according to a 1984 law included spiritual and revolutionary commitment to Islam; loyalty to the Islamic Republic, Khomeini, and the institution of *faqih* (Islamic jurist); political and social intelligence; and proof of formal education.[18] The law required candidates to resign from their salaried government posts at least a month before the general election, the campaign's official duration.

Two of the five eligible candidates had run unsuccessfully in the 1992 election, Fazlullah Subhani and Imad ud-Din Imadi. (I discuss them earlier.) The third candidate was Abdul Rasul Tai, the only one of the five originating from the town of Semirom. His father and mother are Persians from there, and his extended family owned land and orchards in the region and was considered wealthy. Before the campaign, Tai was a teacher in Isfahan. Several Qermezi men heard one of his campaign speeches in Semirom. After the presentation, when Tai asked for questions from the audience, the first respondent queried him about some matter. Tai replied, "Ask me a less difficult question, one '*zir-i diplum*' [below the level of someone having a high-school diploma]." He added that he had studied for many years to finish high school. "No matter how hard I tried, I did not succeed." Another person then

242 *Life moves on*

asked him why he bothered to run for parliament if he could not manage to complete high school.

The fourth candidate, Behruz Jafari, hailed from Vanak village west of Semirom. His father and mother are Persian Vanakis. He had striven for years to prepare himself for the effort and was the first of the five to declare candidacy. Similar to Shahriyar, he held substantial credentials in formal education and employment. He was the director of the office of the Ministry of Education in Semirom. For seven years he had worked diligently in this post to draw support from the community he served, especially the teachers, students, and administrators in the district's many schools and their families. He potentially drew from a larger community than any other candidate (except for Shahriyar) because many district inhabitants already knew his name and position. Formal education provided opportunities and livelihoods that otherwise would be unavailable to them and their children. Especially since the revolution, upward mobility based on education was the cherished ideal and was more possible now for the district's townspeople, villagers, and nomads than it had been under the shah's regime. Many people had benefited from Jafari's efforts, and he counted on their votes and those of their families and acquaintances. His government post in Semirom created networks for him with other influential officials there. Initially Jafari enjoyed greater visibility than any other candidate.

The fifth candidate, the only Qashqa'i one (and the only one who is not a Persian), was Shahriyar Qermezi. During the autumn, winter, and early spring he lived with his wife and children in Dezeh village and worked in Dehaqan town, both located along the Borujen-Shahreza highway. Neither community was situated in the Semirom district but both were close by. The government did not require candidates to reside or work in the districts where they ran, although most of them probably did live and were employed there, if only to utilize their local ties and be known figures for voters. Semirom's four other candidates resided in the district year-round, two of them were employed there, and five owned land and held other economic interests there.

Shahriyar owned little property of his own. (No one of such low socio-economic status could have been a parliamentary candidate, deputy, or senator under the two Pahlavi shahs.) He shared a modest plot of orchard land with his brother Ismail at Bid-i Qatar in Darrehshuri summer pastures, where he and other family members spent that season. His family's winter pastures were at Chah Shirin south of Kazerun but he no longer owned livestock (unless partnered with his brothers) or spent much time there. His father, a traditional nomadic pastoralist, had died in 1974. His mother, still alive in 1996, lived with her son Ismail at Bid-i Qatar in the summer and in Dezeh the rest of the year. Shahriyar's multiple brothers, male cousins, and nephews seemed dedicated to the revolution and the Islamic Republic, and many of them held government jobs and/or received financial and other benefits from Iran's powerful parastatal foundations (bunyads). They were loyal, determined supporters willing to assist his campaign.

Life moves on 243

Shahriyar announced his intentions for candidacy five months before the election. According to a new regulation, he could formally campaign for a month before the general election.[19] This period corresponded with his resignations from two government jobs. People in the district of Semirom viewed him as a strong, viable contender, and increasing numbers knew his name, a crucial asset.

Hardly any Qermezi spoke about the political factions that drew people's attention in Tehran and other large cities, and they did not discuss Shahriyar's possible affiliations with any of them.[20] These factions and their dominant figures in Tehran, almost all of them clerics, did not seem to matter for the majority of voters in the Semirom district, who paid attention instead to local issues and the candidates' qualifications to address them.

When Shahriyar interacted with prominent people at the district and provincial levels, who were likely to be attuned to national political currents, he expressed support for reformists and moderates and disagreed with conservatives, fundamentalists, and hard-liners. He was not affiliated with any of the clergymen who dominated national politics. (He did ally with Mohammad Khatami when he campaigned for the presidency in 1997.) The Qermezi who were the most politically savvy concerning national politics agreed with Shahriyar. They included most of the schoolteachers and the university students and graduates who studied and worked in urban areas, where they came into contact with national political developments, especially via the modern media.

Shahriyar established campaign headquarters in the town of Semirom, as did the four other candidates. Possessing no substantial property of his own, he needed to rely on outside assistance. He received a government loan for his campaign, and many backers contributed and loaned money. Each Qermezi household offered 5,000 to 30,000 tumans depending on its economic situation. Notions of tribal solidarity resulted in universal participation, and no one seemed to object. Shahriyar's closest supporter at Dashtak and Hanalishah was Bahram, who loaned 50,000 tumans. Wealthy Qashqa'i men in other subtribes and tribes each reportedly provided interest-free loans of 300,000 tumans. (The Qermezi subtribe lacked any wealthy individuals.) People gave their contributions to Shahriyar's eldest brother, Ismail, who handled finances, rather than directly to the candidate. (As Shahriyar's deputy, Ismail managed the multifaceted task with sophistication and diplomacy, and some Qermezi suggested years later that he would have been a better candidate and parliamentarian than Shahriyar. Yet he lacked some of Shahriyar's essential credentials and might not have won an election.)

During the month of formal campaigning, Shahriyar delivered speeches throughout the district, particularly in the town of Semirom. Citizens credited him for being able to speak extemporaneously, without reading or relying on notes or written statements, unlike three of the other candidates. He also wrote succinct tracts on various issues, which his endorsers circulated.

After Shahriyar addressed a large gathering in Semirom, several Persian men there complained to him about the role of the Qashqa'i tribal confederacy in

244 *Life moves on*

recent history, particularly the 1943 Semirom war. (Qashqa'i and Boir Ahmad Lur forces had defeated Iran's army there.) One of them argued that the Qashqa'i, battling against the government, had seized and burned two army tanks. In one of Shahriyar's rare public comments about his extensive military service during the Iraq–Iran war, he responded, "I captured or disabled two hundred Iraqi tanks, 198 over and above the two seized in 1943. In exchange for the two, I offer you two hundred." His questioners did not reply, and the primarily Persian audience burst into applause. Some Qashqa'i present noted among themselves that Shahriyar had redeemed the reputation of the Qashqa'i by this brief spontaneous remark.

Shahriyar's supporters distributed his campaign posters within Semirom, throughout the district, and in bordering towns, and they posted them on many visible surfaces. On my initial drive from Shahreza to Semirom in 1996, I saw but did not pay close attention to the many campaign posters stuck on the backs of every highway sign and on buildings along the road. Only later, driving to and from a fortieth-day memorial service in Shahreza, did I see that the face on every sign and wall was Shahriyar's. His backers had even ringed, with dozens of large posters, the water tank atop a tall tower near the junction of the Mehr-i Gerd road. I did not see anywhere the remnants of posters of the other candidates, which perhaps indicates the weaker support for these men or the men's disregard for the potential impact of such a communicative medium.

Shahriyar's photograph on these posters showed only his face and neck (and seemed to emphasize his facial hair, which was the length preferred by hezbollahis and was their signature feature). His expression was serious and unsmiling (as a hezbollahi's ought to be) as he looked directly at the camera. His hair was carefully trimmed. His image seemed to contradict the printed messages about his kind nature.

One of Shahriyar's posters prominently displayed generic quotes from Iran's two supreme leaders (rahbar). From Imam Khomeini: "People will elect a religious person empathetic to oppressed people, informed about religious issues and politics, and a follower on the path of the less fortunate."[21] From Ayatollah Khamenei: "People may not know all the candidates but they know who to trust." Large bold letters urged, "Together, Vote for Brother Qermezi." The text read: "Someone who is an untiring struggler and who is the candidate of intellectuals, university students, employees of educational institutions, people who make sacrifices, families of our respected martyrs, athletes, merchants, nomads, and the majority of the esteemed and informed people of Semirom township."[22]

Containing a larger photograph, another of his posters also contained generic quotes. From Imam Khomeini: "[People should send] to the parliament a deputy who is responsible, intelligent, and kind to the people, particularly [someone] from the oppressed class who can serve Islam." From Ayatollah Khamenei: "An elected parliamentary deputy must be able to preserve this nation's power in the shadow of revolutionary values and must follow the path and be a follower of Imam Khomeini." The text read: "Together we will

Life moves on 245

vote for Shahriyar 'Abu Zar' Qermezi, a kind teacher, an untiring militia volunteer, a person who sacrificed for the revolution, a responsible educator, an informed university-affiliated person, a protector of the oppressed, and in one word a supporter of the supreme leader in strengthening and promoting the state."

Shahriyar also produced a multicolored, ornately bordered, wallet-sized card depicting his name and photograph and a 12-month calendar for the new year about to commence. He had learned that a usable item brought good publicity. The card read: "Together we will vote for Brother Shahriyar Qermezi, a kind teacher and a volunteer militiaman."

The government staged the parliamentary election of 1996 (for the fifth parliament) in two parts, a general and a runoff one, both held on Fridays when people were ordinarily off work or out of school. All citizens, male and female, 15 years and older were eligible voters. To participate, they needed to present their identity cards, which polling officials stamped when the voters received ballots. "All" Qermezi reportedly voted in this election, and "all" cast their votes for Shahriyar. Practically all Qermezi men and some women from their many dispersed locations traveled to Semirom, including all men from Dashtak and Kazerun and even a university student in Tehran. Some groups chartered minibuses and taxis for the journey while others rode public buses and private vehicles. Snow fell during the general election, closing some roads, yet everyone managed to vote. The government set up polling places in two buildings in Semirom, one in the town center and another in the outskirts. All those traveling to Semirom to vote could have cast ballots instead in the districts where they resided at the time. For some people (including nomads) in remote areas far from towns and cities, the government brought numbered ballots and sealed boxes on election days.[23] Another vehicle holding observers for the candidates often accompanied the state vehicle, to increase the chances for honest and open voting.

In the general election on 8 March in which 21,000 people cast eligible votes in the district of Semirom, Shahriyar Qermezi received the largest number, 8,300. (A winner needed an absolute majority to avoid the runoff election.) The first runner-up was Behruz Jafari who gained 7,000. Fazlullah Subhani and Imad ud-Din Imadi were the second and third runners-up, and Abdul Rasul Tai came in last. People said that Jafari was dismayed that he did not receive the most votes, given the seven years he had devoted to the process and the extent of people's familiarity with him as a leader in education. They noted that Subhani and Imadi were unsuccessful in gaining votes because they did not originate from the town of Semirom. "The townspeople did not vote for candidates who live elsewhere." Indeed hailing from the town, Tai lacked any backing.

In the runoff election between Shahriyar Qermezi and Behruz Jafari 45 days later, on 20 April, in which 24,000 people cast eligible votes, Shahriyar received 12,300 and Jafari 11,600. (In the second round, a winner needed a relative majority.) The Qermezi estimated that perhaps only one or two thousand of Shahriyar's votes came from the town. Other citizens had boycotted the

246 *Life moves on*

runoff election because neither candidate emanates from their settlement. Most of Shahriyar's votes reportedly came from the Qashqa'i—Darrehshuri in the north and Farsi Madan and Qarachai in the south. The government declared Shahriyar the official winner.

Once again, people said that Jafari was taken aback. As some explained, his loss resulted from a factor beyond his control rather than from his personal or professional traits. Jafari hails from Vanak village located in the district of Semirom, and many Vanak men already occupied influential government posts in the town of Semirom. Most had acquired these jobs because of their military service during the Iraq–Iran war, their roles as revolutionary guards and volunteer militiamen, and/or their kinship with war martyrs. More young men from Vanak village (2,500 residents in 2006) than from the town of Semirom (26,000 residents in 2006) had volunteered for the war, joined the guard corps and the militia, and became martyrs, despite Semirom's much larger size.[24] The influence these Vanak men now exerted in the town and district irritated Semirom's citizens. (War veterans, revolutionary guards, militiamen, and siblings and children of martyrs enjoyed preferential treatment from the government in university admittance and job placement. Vanak had suffered a hundred fatalities in the war compared with Semirom's 68.) Some Semirom towns-people who voted for Shahriyar said they had actually voted against Jafari and his Vanak connections. A vote for Shahriyar canceled someone else's vote for Jafari. They bore no personal antagonism against Jafari but did not want someone from Vanak to represent them on the national level. They hoped to prevent Jafari from appointing even more Vanak residents to vital posts in the town and district if he served in parliament. Surprised by the outcome, Shahriyar had benefited from this dimension of local politics without having to take any specific action himself.

During his four years as Semirom's deputy, Shahriyar appointed many Darrehshuri and other Qashqa'i men to key posts in Semirom and the district or exercised influence in these assignments. These actions proved a pattern that some Semirom residents said they had avoided when they voted against Jafari. Going to the polls, they had evidently not considered the possibility of Shahriyar's selecting people associated with him. They had focused on preventing further nominees from Vanak. Given persisting ethnic tensions in the region, the Persian and Lur residents of Semirom (the town and district) would have preferred a Persian or Lur deputy to a Qashqa'i Turkish one and would have tolerated Persian and Lur appointees more than Turkish ones.

Months after the election, some Darrehshuri khans remarked that they had not voted for Shahriyar, despite his Darrehshuri and Qashqa'i identity, because they did not want a hezbollahi elected. Since the revolution, the khans had suffered politically and economically from "hezbollahi politics" (the ayatollahs' regime). They had known Shahriyar's father, Sohrab, well. He had fought in battles with them, incurred serious injuries, and was their client, and they had been prepared to vote for his son. Yet, when they saw Shahriyar's face on his campaign posters, the image of an ostensibly zealous regime supporter

Life moves on 247

repelled them. The khans said they would not support the government in any way, especially after its execution of Khosrow Khan Qashqa'i. Hostile hezbollahis and revolutionary guards had harassed them ever since 1979. A few khans reported that they had not voted. Some who lived in cities during the winter did not bother to travel to Semirom to cast ballots there. Others who did make the trip said that Jafari's credentials in education had drawn their votes. By the middle of Shahriyar's term in parliament, these khans reported that they now regretted their actions. They saw that Shahriyar was serving the district effectively and was not instituting hezbollahi values in his efforts. They were gratified that he supported Mohammad Khatami, Iran's new moderate president, just as they did.

Other parliamentary elections in southwestern Iran in 1996

Shahriyar Qermezi's election took place in a regional context where four other non-elite Qashqa'i men also won parliamentary seats. Forming an alliance, the five deputies implemented changes for the Qashqa'i and other nomadic, tribal, and ethnic-minority people in their regions and the nation. Iran's constitution does not allocate special parliamentary seats to ethnic minorities, unlike five religious minorities (but not Sunni Muslims or Bahais).

(A sixth Qashqa'i man was also elected to parliament in 1996. The chosen deputy of the district of Veramin just south of Tehran professed Qashqa'i origins stemming from the nineteenth century, when the Qajar shahs had relocated some Qashqa'i nomadic pastoralists from Fars province to the Veramin region. This new deputy did not ally with the five Qashqa'i deputies from the south.)

The four other Qashqa'i deputies in the fifth parliament include Sohrab Bahluli Qashqa'i, a Bahluli Amaleh man, elected as the representative of the district of Firuzabad, the former Qashqa'i winter capital. During his four-year term, he published five volumes of his parliamentary speeches.[25] He had also run for election in 1992 and lost (see earlier).

Shapur (Khudadad) Qubadi won in the district of Eqlid, including the town of Eqlid on the Shiraz-Isfahan highway. Qashqa'i summer pastures are west of the town. Citizens had elected Khosrow Khan Qashqa'i as Eqlid's representative in 1980 but hard-line conservatives arrested him before parliament convened and later had him expelled and then executed. A Kuhali (or Qurd) Shish Buluki man, Qubadi was an agricultural engineer before the election.

Ali Sohrabi was elected as one of three deputies of the large city of Shiraz. He is a Talihbazli Darrehshuri man who had taught at the high-caliber tribal secondary school in Shiraz and later worked for the program for nomads' education there. Just before the election, he published a book on formal education among the Qashqa'i.[26] Some Qashqa'i considered him a moderate hezbollahi.

Ali (Mohammad Mehdi) Qahramani also won as a deputy for Shiraz. He is a Bulvardi Amaleh man. Many Turkish-speaking Bulvardi (Abivardi) people had moved from Khorasan in northeastern Iran to Fars in the nineteenth

248 *Life moves on*

century and joined the Qashqa'i confederacy. Since the mid-twentieth century, those living in Shiraz had integrated and assimilated in Persian-Iranian society and culture more than other Qashqa'i. That community is Qahramani's place of origin. When asked about his identity, people replied, "His father's father is Qashqa'i." They viewed Qahramani as two generations removed from a more traditional Qashqa'i background. Some Qermezi wondered if he spoke Turkish, a common question about any Qashqa'i who was a long-term urban resident. Before his election, Qahramani was an engineer for the Shiraz municipality.

Of Shiraz's three parliamentary deputies, two were Qashqa'i men, an amazing fact given the city's large size (over a million) and the overwhelmingly Persian-Iranian identity of its citizens.[27] The third elected deputy was Rasul Muntajabniya, a Persian man who listed his former occupation as a "building construction assistant" (possibly a manual laborer). He had served Shiraz in the first three parliaments (and would be reelected in 2000). People considered him a radical.[28]

At least two other Qashqa'i men were candidates in the 1996 parliamentary election but lost. They include Amrullah Zandi who ran in the district of Mamassani in Qashqa'i winter pastures. He is a Lak Darrehshuri man who worked as a natural-gas engineer. The second candidate was Habibullah Narimani who ran in Shiraz. A Kuhba Kashkuli Bozorg man, he was employed in intelligence in the revolutionary-guard corps. Narimani is linked by kinship to the Qermezi. He is the grandson of Nizukat, the sister of two men of Musuli Amaleh Qashqa'i origin who had joined the Qermezi group in the 1920s when they were boys and who now resided in the Qermezi village of Atakula.

Conservatives were the majority in the fifth parliament.[29] More than half (156) of the 270 deputies were new (and not incumbents), a pattern evident in every session since 1984.[30] As in all previous sessions, the majority of deputies came from small towns and rural and provincial areas. National politicians and the informed public at large in 1996 regarded the new deputies from the provinces as unknown figures, like "unopened melons"[31] (a quaint phrase perhaps indicating urban sentiments of superiority over rural peasants).[32] Voters in peripheral provinces, especially where ethnolinguistic minorities predominated, were increasingly influential in determining the outcome of national elections.[33]

Shahriyar Qermezi's term in parliament, 1996–2000

The government provided Shahriyar Qermezi a rent-free house in Tehran when he was elected. His monthly salary during the first year (with increases each subsequent year) was 180,000 tumans. (The monthly salary of a secondary-school teacher in Kazerun in 1996–97 was 50,000 tumans.) He required a durable vehicle for traveling mountainous dirt roads in Qashqa'i territory and the district, and he purchased a new Nissan Patrol land cruiser with money

Life moves on   249

from the sale of the passenger automobile that the government had given him. He sold his aged Land Rover to Filamarz Qermezi, a cousin and classmate from elementary school. If he wanted a driver, the government offered one at low or no cost. He could consider running for a second term in 2000 and for subsequent terms. Afterward he would probably receive a well-paying, influential post. The government had appointed his predecessor, Atazadeh, as the director of the natural-resources agency in Isfahan province.

During his term in office, Shahriyar improved conditions in the district, initially by increasing its budget, and his efforts led to many planned and implemented projects. Before Atazadeh's term in parliament, Semirom's annual budget was 350 million tumans. Under Atazadeh, it rose to 550 million. Under Shahriyar, it grew to 1,300 million.

Semirom district is located in the very south of Isfahan province and is shaped like a peninsula there. Its boundaries are Bid-i Qatar (south of Borujen city) in the north, Vanak village and Dena Mountain to the west, Hana village to the east, and Baizan and Padena (north of Yasuj city) to the south. A sign posted along the asphalt highway leading from Shahreza to Semirom listed the district's total hectares and citizens.[34]

Wanting to enhance the district's infrastructure, Shahriyar oversaw the construction of new roads and improvement of dirt ones, some now paved with asphalt. Crews raised, widened, and asphalted the road from Mehr-i Gerd to the Borujen-Shahreza highway, and travelers (to Borujen, for example) could now take this shorter route instead of the indirect one via Shahreza. (The highway from Shahreza through Semirom town and then westward fell under the jurisdiction of the Ministry of Roads, not the district itself. The ministry completed an alternate route skirting the town, which allowed traffic to avoid the business center. Work on another new highway from Shahreza to the oil and natural-gas fields in the west, also bypassing Semirom, proceeded slowly.) Workers straightened and widened the main road through the town of Semirom, demolished some shops, and relocated the owners at government expense. They repaired the district's bridges. Shahriyar sent an engineer to survey for a new dam above Mehr-i Gerd. Engineers began another dam near Qarehaqach to serve the agricultural needs of nearby inhabitants, most of them Darrehshuri. Shahriyar planned a new water supply for Vanak.

Shahriyar upgraded services in the town of Semirom. He expedited the work of bringing natural gas from Yasuj (to the south) and increased the number of telephone lines available to citizens. He projected a slaughterhouse for pastoralists (so they could avoid transporting their livestock to Isfahan) and a large refrigerated warehouse where cultivators could store harvested fruit until demand and prices rose. Shahriyar ordered computers for Semirom's high schools. He expanded the deputy's office so it could serve people more effectively, and he visited there when parliament was not in session.

Semirom's new deputy wanted to establish a university in the town so students could stay close to home. He noted that people there who gathered in the streets to "hoist shovels and yell 'Hoa! Hoa!'" needed educational opportunities.

250 *Life moves on*

(Using this image, he alluded to uneducated, uninformed farmers who participated in politics only by yelling slogans they did not understand.) Initially he proposed an independent university for Semirom but later succeeded in implementing a correspondence one. (I discuss the types later in this chapter).

Of the district's many villages, Fathabad (formerly Eshqabad, "abode of love," a name the Islamic regime promptly changed for moral reasons) received the most assistance during Shahriyar's term because it had contributed many martyrs during the Iraq–Iran war. The Ministry of Housing (and not the Organization for Nomads' Affairs) built compact rows of adjoining two-room houses for settling nomads there, and other agencies constructed an athletic field and an ornate library building along the newly asphalted road. The nomads' settlement remained unoccupied in 1999, and only half of the houses appeared inhabited in 2004. Shahriyar was instrumental in having Vanak village reclassified and upgraded as a community under a mayor's (*shahrdar*) authority. Under township status, the place would receive more state and district money for schools, roads, and parks.[35] Shahriyar proposed a high school for Padena, an area in the district's south with many large villages, so students there would not have to travel so far to continue their education. He brought telephone service for the first time to some villages, often a single line connecting to a shop or clinic where people could place and receive calls. By writing letters, he helped district citizens who were imprisoned or in other legal or financial difficulty.

Shahriyar filled key government posts in Semirom with Darrehshuri Qashqa'i people, including some agency directors: a Talihbazli man for the Ministry of Construction Jihad, a Nadirli man for the Ministry of Agriculture, a Darzi man for the Organization for Nomads' Affairs, and another Darzi man for the Pastures Organization.[36] The immediate predecessors of at least two of these men had been Persians.

Shahriyar also played a national role, especially in educational development. Allying with the four other Qashqa'i parliamentary deputies, he focused on formal education for Iran's nomadic tribal people.

From 1954 until the revolution, Mohammad Bahmanbaigi (an Amaleh Qashqa'i man) had directed a flourishing educational program serving nomadic tribal people in southwestern Iran, Fars province in particular. His attempts to expand the program to other Iranian regions succeeded only in the short term. With his ouster in 1979, the overall program declined and then changed course in 1982 when the Ministry of Education took control of the schools, teachers, administrative offices, and teacher-training facility. Efforts to educate and train nomadic tribal youth lost the momentum that Bahmanbaigi had inspired.

Parliament, guided by the subcommittee of the five Qashqa'i deputies, removed the tribal-education program in Shiraz from the Ministry of Education's control and returned it to independent status in 1997. These deputies proposed a national educational program for Iran's nomadic tribal people, and a parliamentary majority approved the plan. Deputies of other regions politicked to host the program's headquarters in their areas, which would gain

Life moves on   251

economically. Other parliamentarians argued that the headquarters should be centrally located in Iran, such as in Isfahan. The Qashqa'i deputies urged that Shiraz was optimal because a center was already established there, where the program had enjoyed a long, successful history. After three years of discussion, parliament voted in 1999 to retain Shiraz as the headquarters. People credited the Qashqa'i deputies with the legislation.

When prominent officials visited the Semirom district and other areas in and near Qashqa'i territory, Shahriyar often attended and spoke at the public gatherings. President Rafsanjani was scheduled to go to Semirom in 1996, and Shahriyar arranged for people to assist with the event. Rafsanjani went to Shahreza instead, and Shahriyar greeted him there. Shahriyar also delivered speeches during seminars and cultural festivals offered or approved by government agencies for and about the Qashqa'i.

In his public (and private) interactions, Shahriyar unambiguously identified himself as a Qashqa'i Turk. By contrast, several parliamentary deputies of Qashqa'i origin (all of them high-status khans) who had served under Mohammad Reza Shah had tried to assert more of a Persian-Iranian identity, especially in non-Qashqa'i contexts. Shahriyar also stressed his Darrehshuri and Qermezi identities. Depending on the context, some state officials in public arenas might have downplayed their tribal, ethnic, and non-Persian linguistic backgrounds or attempted to apologize for or excuse them, but Shahriyar did not.[37]

Shahriyar publicly defended the Qashqa'i reputation on many occasions, especially when a potentially negative or damaging issue arose. During his first visit with President Rafsanjani in Tehran, he reportedly said that "Khosrow Qashqa'i" (omitting the khan title) had not acted against the Iranian people. Alluding to Khosrow Khan's defensive resistance in 1980–82, Shahriyar explained that this "minor" event—"one of thousands caused by political scrambles after the revolution"—was not Khosrow's creation or intention. After Khosrow died, he said, no Qashqa'i anywhere had fought against the government. Continuing, Shahriyar told Rafsanjani that a book detailing a thousand years of Qashqa'i history contained no evidence that the Qashqa'i people (versus the khans) had ever threatened the state. On another occasion, Shahriyar responded to a BBC Persian-language newscast that had announced that five "Qashqa'i leaders" (saran-i Qashqa'i) were elected to parliament. He noted that he was not a Qashqa'i leader and that his only role was to serve the Qashqa'i people. His comment (included earlier) that he had substituted two hundred Iraqi tanks for the two Iranian tanks disabled during the Semirom war is another example of his public stance.

Shahriyar campaigned for Mohammad Khatami's election as president of Iran in 1997 by delivering speeches throughout Fars province and the wider Qashqa'i territory. His audiences appreciated his extemporaneous abilities. Speakers for Khatami's opponents answered questions with difficulty, relied on reading printed tracts, and recited worn-out, accusatory slogans that lacked substantive meaning. Shahriyar requested an official Khatami campaign

252 *Life moves on*

poster printed in Qashqa'i Turkish (using the Perso-Arabic script) for distribution and display in Qashqa'i territory and nearby towns and cities. When Khatami was the surprising winner, Shahriyar declared that Iran's citizens had proven their desire for substantive changes in the country. When the new president was selecting cabinet ministers, rumors circulated that he might pick Shahriyar as the Minister of Defense. He did not. Three other Qashqa'i parliamentary deputies also endorsed Khatami. The fourth, Qubadi, did not originally do so but was leaning toward him later.

As Semirom's deputy, Shahriyar frequented the town and district and often visited nearby Qermezi communities, including Hanalishah. Usually he went to Husain Ali's home after first paying a short, obligatory call on Bahram, Hanalishah's staunchest regime supporter. Almost all men and older boys at Hanalishah attended these gatherings at Husain Ali's, and women in this and neighboring camps prepared feasts. Men took turns contributing a sheep or goat for the well-attended meals.[38]

Many Qermezi, especially those appreciating this kind of personal contact with Shahriyar, were gratified and amazed that "one of them" occupied such a nationally prominent position. His agemates had studied and played with him as children, and older ones had watched him grow up. Now he was meeting on a regular basis with Iran's national leaders and making decisions affecting the country.

During his informal interactions with the Qermezi, Shahriyar related his parliamentary activities and kept people abreast of national politics. He attested to President Khatami's widespread support across Iran, thereby linking these somewhat isolated Qermezi with political currents in the wider society. After a year of Khatami's service, when the unelected branches of government and hard-line conservatives continued to oppose and obstruct his policies and when the expectations of citizens for reform were still unmet, Shahriyar clarified the circumstances for his constituents and urged them to continue upholding the president. He explained the politics behind press censorship, including the regime's closure of influential newspapers in 1998. He interpreted the factors underlying student protests in Tehran and other cities in 1999 and expressed anger about the violent suppression. He said the government should change its international policies so Iran would be less ostracized and play a more vital global role. Iran's economy would not improve until the nation's leaders restored relationships with the United States. Iran needed new technology, spare parts for essential equipment, and funds the U.S. had frozen after the hostage taking. Millions of Iranians, including highly trained specialists in all fields, who had fled Iran after 1977 would be unlikely to return until Iran reconsidered its international stance. Shahriyar was not caught in the time warp cultivated by some other national politicians, especially conservative hard-liners, who considered slogans such as "Death to America!" to be essential for maintaining political support.

Shahriyar attended many marriage-contract signings, weddings, funerals, and memorial services in the Qermezi subtribe, often by undertaking the long journey from Tehran by road. Anticipating his presence, people were motivated to join the gatherings, more of them attending than in the past. As in informal meetings, Shahriyar used these more formal occasions to apprise people about national politics. At a wedding in 1999, several people complained that Khatami had not yet implemented his campaign promises. Reaffirming his backing of Khatami, Shahriyar explained that the president persevered with his goals despite facing stiff resistance from Khamenei (the supreme leader) and other conservative hard-liners. His listeners seemed to accept his commentary. Shahriyar planned to run for reelection in 2000 and used these various events to assess local sentiments and reconfirm ties.

Shahriyar helped many Qermezi individuals during his four-year term. He asked his brother to telephone a Semirom merchant to convey a message to the Qermezi nomads at Hanalishah about the plans of the Meat Marketing Organization to buy livestock that afternoon at a location in summer pastures. Without the phone call, the nomads would have missed the opportunity. When Irij Qermezi completed university with a degree in agriculture, Shahriyar found a job for him in the Organization for Nomads' Affairs in Semirom. Completing his university degree in school administration, Said Qermezi hoped that Shahriyar would assist him in securing employment in the reestablished national headquarters for nomads' education. When security forces arrested Abbas Qermezi for owning a rifle used by a Persian peasant to commit murder, Shahriyar eventually wrote a letter on his behalf. He was also possibly influential in repealing Ali Qermezi's death sentence; the regime had charged Ali with opium smuggling. When Husain Ali Qermezi needed to break a years-long bureaucratic hold on securing a telephone line to his Kazerun house, Shahriyar wrote to the appropriate agencies in Shiraz and Kazerun and also negotiated a price lower than Husain Ali could have obtained on his own. Subsequently, some Qermezi worried publicly about the propriety of seeking Shahriyar's help in handling minor matters (such as a telephone link) and argued that they should appeal to him only when absolutely necessary (as in the case of someone accused of murder).[39]

Qashqa'i from other subtribes and tribes also sought Shahriyar's assistance in Tehran and other locations during his travels. Shahriyar's daughter reported that their house in Tehran was often filled with guests and visitors, many of them seeking her father's help.[40]

Parliamentary election in 2000

Halfway through his four-year term, Shahriyar Qermezi considered running for election in 2000 as the parliamentary deputy of Mamassani, a rural district in Qashqa'i winter pastures where he said he could be more influential. In 1999 he decided instead to run in Kazerun, a district also in winter pastures. Its population is four times larger than Semirom's, and the district would offer Shahriyar opportunities to expand his political base and bring about change.[41] Similar to other Qermezi, he noted that he preferred the citizens of

254 *Life moves on*

Kazerun to those of Semirom. They regarded Kazerun's culture (farhang) as superior to Semirom's, by which they meant the cultural center, university, and extent of literacy and sophistication among the residents. Some of Shahriyar's relatives lived in Kazerun and the wider district, on whom he could rely for support during the campaign. Except for a schoolteacher, no relatives or other Qermezi lived in Nurabad (capital of the district of Mamassani), and only a few dispersed Qermezi resided in the district. Yet Nurabad and its district contain many Qashqa'i, Boir Ahmad and Mamassani Lurs, and other tribal residents, while Kazerun is a predominantly Persian town. The Qermezi debated the merits of the two districts as they would affect a successful candidacy.

When told about Shahriyar's choice of Kazerun, Mohammad Bahmanbaigi (a prominent Qashqa'i man) noted that the town's overwhelmingly Persian majority would make Shahriyar's campaign difficult. Qermezi men replied that the wider district contains many nomadic and settled tribal people (Kashkuli, Qarachai, Farsi Madan, and Shish Buluki), all of whom would be motivated to vote for Shahriyar as a fellow Qashqa'i. These demographic facts had benefited Shahriyar in Semirom and would probably do so in Kazerun.

After continuing discussion in 1999, Shahriyar chose yet another district, Shahreza, whose town of that name sits astride the influential Shiraz-Isfahan-Tehran highway.[42] Shahreza citizens are predominantly Persians but growing numbers of Qashqa'i were building or renting houses there, including some Kachili Qermezi and, for the first time, some Imamverdili Qermezi (Shahriyar's own lineage). Inhabitants of the wider rural district are primarily Persian agriculturalists but some Qashqa'i nomads occupy summer pastures there and were expanding their cultivation.

Shahriyar entered his name as a candidate, and the government's vetting agencies certified his eligibility. As a current deputy who had undergone official scrutiny before his previous candidacy, he avoided some aspects of the rigorous qualifying process. More pertinently, he seems not to have alienated the hard-line conservatives who disqualified candidates who did not agree with them. Changes in electoral laws included new regulations about the maximum size of campaign posters (no large wall posters now permitted) and the number of colors allowed.

The government held the general election for the sixth parliament in February 2000, and many Qermezi traveled to Shahreza to vote. Some Qermezi and other Qashqa'i who had voted for Shahriyar in Semirom in 1996 seemed complacent this time around and did not make the effort to vote as before, perhaps because they expected him to win. Coming in second in the five-man race, Shahriyar received insufficient votes and would not continue in parliament. The winner was Husain Ramazaniyanpur, a Persian man who was a university teacher in Dehaqan and Isfahan.

Shahriyar had set his sights too high, and he and others turned their focus to second-guessing his choices. If he had run for a second term in the Semirom district, where he had already implemented beneficial changes for a range of urban and rural citizens (and not only the Qashqa'i), voters there would have probably reelected him. Once again, state regulations had permitted candidates to campaign formally for only a month, and people in the Shahreza district were unfamiliar with Shahriyar. Citizens there paid less attention to his credentials as a wounded war veteran and volunteer militiaman than Semirom's residents had done four years earlier. The war was more distant in time than it had been when he first ran for election in 1996. His lingering reputation as a hezbollahi might also have hurt him with voters.

At least nine men proposed their candidacy for the electoral slate in the Semirom district. Officials declared five of them eligible, and they ran in the subsequent general election. They include three of the four men who had run against Shahriyar in 1996. Behruz Jafari, who had placed second then, received the most votes in the general election but then lost in the runoff election to Imad ud-Din Imadi, the cleric from Padena who had run five times before, in every election since the revolution, and had always failed. People explained Jafari's defeat by his recent affiliation with politicians who opposed Khatami. If he had continued to support Khatami, they said, he could have easily won. Faced now with an akhund as their deputy, some Semirom citizens complained about their regrettable choice and waxed nostalgic about Shahriyar's good works for their town and district.[43]

Finishing his term in the fifth parliament, Shahriyar considered his future. Presented with several promising posts, he agreed to serve as a deputy to the Minister of Industries and Mines. Shahriyar had known the minister in his former role as the governor-general of Isfahan province. Eshaq Jahangiri originates from Sirjan in Kerman province, and his ancestors were tribally organized nomadic pastoralists there. Hasan Rouhani named Jahangiri as his First Vice President when he was elected president in 2013.[44]

Other parliamentary elections in southwestern Iran in 2000

Of the five Qashqa'i men elected to parliament in 1996, four were qualified to run for reelection but only two won: Sohrab Bahluli Qashqa'i for Firuzabad and Shapur (Khudadad) Qubadi for Eqlid, both long-time Qashqa'i centers. Shahriyar Qermezi lost in Shahreza, and Ali Sohrabi lost in Shiraz. Citizens of Shiraz (who are predominantly Persians) were reportedly displeased in 1996 when they discovered that two of their three elected deputies were Turks (Qashqa'i). This factor worked against Sohrabi in the 2000 election. Other Qashqa'i candidates were defeated in other districts, including Mohammad Quli Nadiri in Kazerun. He is a Nadirli Darrehshuri man, a resident of Shiraz, who had no prior ties to the town of Kazerun and only a seasonal connection with the district 25 years previously when he had taught in two Qashqa'i nomads' schools (including the Qermezi one at Dashtak in 1969–72). Two Qashqa'i deputies now served in Iran's sixth parliament, 2000–04, down from five the previous session. Turnover in deputies from one parliamentary session to the next was high (averaging 60 percent), and the incumbency-return rate was low (averaging 29 percent).[45]

256   *Life moves on*

Parliamentary elections in southwestern Iran in 2004 and 2008[46]

Shahriyar Qermezi submitted his name as a potential candidate for parliamentary elections in 2004 and 2008 but the Guardian Council and other vetting agencies disqualified him each time. He did not bother to file for candidacy in 2012. A Kizinlu Darrehshuri man was elected in 2004 as the deputy of Borujen, a town and district in the province of Chaharmahal Bakhtiyari, to the northwest of Darrehshuri summer pastures. He is a university graduate with a degree in history.

Teachers, schools, and students: The promise of formal education

Formal secular education for Qermezi children began in 1959 when the director of nomads' education in Iran, Mohammad Bahmanbaigi, assigned the Qermezi subtribe its first formally trained teacher. Previously, Qermezi headmen had hired teachers for the families close to them. These men instructed only a few boys at a time in only several subjects.

In this chapter and others, I sometimes use the term "tribal" when referring to Bahmanbaigi's educational program even though the Persian term (as used in southwestern Iran) best translates as "nomad" and "nomadic" (ashayir, ashayiri). The program extended to nomads, part-time nomads, former nomads, and other tribal people. "Tribal" is a term relevant for all these individuals while "nomad" is not. When I discuss Bahmanbaigi's primary schools in the nomads' winter and summer pastures, I use the phrase "nomads' schools." Some of his other primary schools were located in villages inhabited by former nomads or by those who were nomadic part of the year, and so the phrase "nomads' schools" does not always apply there (except in the sense that these schools derived from the "nomads' educational program"). When outlining his teacher-training program, I use the term "tribal." The school drew teacher-trainees from settled as well as nomadic families, and "tribal" refers to both categories while "nomad" does not.

A Bahmanbaiglu Amaleh Qashqa'i man, Bahmanbaigi assigned teachers from his tribal teacher-training school to the Qermezi subtribe from 1959 to 1979. That year he fled his post when revolutionary guards threatened to harm him as one of the shah's former officials. His educational program for nomads and other tribal people continued for three years after his departure, and his successors chose specially trained teachers for the Qermezi subtribe. These teachers originated from the subtribes or tribes of their students, which was also the case under Bahmanbaigi. The Ministry of Education disbanded the nomads' educational program in 1982 and, through its provincial and local offices, assumed responsibility for providing teachers to Qermezi and other nomads. The government reinstated the nomads' educational program in 1988 and attached it to the Ministry of Education in Tehran. Five Qashqa'i parliamentary deputies restored the independence of the program in 1997, and the government reestablished in 1999 its national headquarters in Shiraz where it had been located from 1953 to 1982. During and following the revolution, Qermezi children received uninterrupted educational services, and teachers continued to originate from the subtribe, tribe, and tribal confederacy of the students.[47]

Formal secular education dramatically altered the lives of many Qermezi. This factor more than any other one helps to explain the many economic and social changes that the subtribe and its members and affiliates had experienced since the late 1950s. Formal education did not reach all Qermezi equally, and people still saw in 2013 the results of this disparity among them.

Teachers and schools before 1959

Teachers hired by Qermezi headmen and elders since the 1920s offered instruction in their residential tents. They migrated with the nomads and taught the boys when they were free from chores. A few boys at a time learned the basics of reading and writing Arabic and Persian, and teachers recited from the Qur'an and other books while the pupils copied passages on their chalkboards. Each student's family paid a fee of one tuman in the 1930s and 1940s for a year's lessons. Similar teachers during the first half of the twentieth century, who taught the sons and daughters of Qashqa'i tribal khans and their entourages, received from the khans their upkeep, a small salary, and a canvas tent for the lessons. This kind of "religious" school (maktab) was prevalent throughout Iran before the emergence and spread of modern secular education.[48]

Qermezi headmen, first Shir Mohammad (d. 1943) and then his sons Khalifeh and Borzu, hired a succession of eight teachers before 1959 for their sons and a few other boys. They considered seven of the eight as mullas, men who possessed literacy and some knowledge of Islam and Arabic. All eight originated from Darrehshuri subtribes other than Qermezi. Four of the eight teachers established long-term residential, political, and social ties with the headmen and their group and were eventually regarded as Qermezi themselves. (The Qermezi valued the mullas who taught in local schools but not those who dominated Iran's politico-religious life since 1979.)

Four of these teachers were originally Ipaigli, a prominent Darrehshuri subtribe in the early twentieth century but virtually disappearing as a sociopolitical group by 1960. Shir Mohammad hired Mulla Qurban Khan, an Ipaigli, as Qermezi's first formal teacher. Mulla Qurban taught the sons of Shir Mohammad and several close kinsmen. Later Mulla Qurban's son, Mulla Zulkhumar, taught these and other students. Mulla Zulkhumar resided full-time with the Qermezi until he died in 1970. Perhaps for economic reasons, he did not educate his sons so they could carry forward his specialized knowledge. Borzu and his kinsmen hired the sons as shepherds in the late 1960s and early 1970s, and later the sons resided with other Qermezi in villages in summer pastures.[49]

Shir Mohammad employed several other teachers, two of them Osmanli Darrehshuri mullas and the third another Darrehshuri mulla whose subtribe

258 *Life moves on*

no one remembered decades later. Then he hired Kaldastan Ipaigli who was not a mulla and possessed only limited knowledge. Years later, Husain Qermezi hired Kaldastan's son, Khuda Karam, to teach his own sons at a time when the leader of his lineage (Sohrab Imamverdili) disputed with Bahmanbaigi about Imamverdili's secular teacher. Khuda Karam studied under a mulla, and people eventually regarded him as one. Some say he taught only the Qur'an while others report that his lessons were broader.

Sohrab Imamverdili hired Mirza Fakhr ud-Din Musavi, a Shaikh Abuli Darrehshuri man of Boir Ahmad Lur origins. Formerly, Fakhr ud-Din had taught children in the entourages of the Darrehshuri khans. (Later, Fakhr ud-Din's son, Nasir Musavi, received teachers' training in Bahmanbaigi's program and served as Qermezi's fourth secular teacher.)

Qermezi's first secular teacher (and not a mulla) was Sarfaraz Fazilat, a Persian man from Shahreza. The U.S. Point Four program (called *asl-i chahar* in Iran) had hired Bahmanbaigi, who offered the Qermezi group one of the new program's first teachers for Qashqa'i nomads. This program already assisted schools in cities and some villages, and its American director promised to bring formal education to nomadic and tribal children in Fars province.[50] Fazilat used the textbooks introduced by the Americans for the Iran-wide educational program, and these books were the first of this kind ever experienced by Qermezi children. Initially they were the same books used in the U.S., only translated in Persian; their illustrations depicted American society and culture. Fazilat taught for only a year. Until two to three years later, when Bahmanbaigi's own program first began to assign trained secular teachers to the Qermezi, the subtribe lacked any kind of teachers.

Jehangir Qermezi received a year and a half of teachers' training in Shiraz from the Point Four program in the 1950s but discontinued his studies just before certifying as a teacher. In telling the story, people (including Jehangir himself) said that he had quit the program because his mother, distraught by his absence, cried for him every day. He never served as a teacher but two sons and two grandsons did.

Mohammad Bahmanbaigi's educational program for nomads

With guidance and financial support from American Point Four officials in 1953, Mohammad Bahmanbaigi began a program for the education of nomadic children in Fars province. Almost all of these youngsters were Qashqa'i, and the rest were part of other nomadic groups in the region (Khamseh and Lur primarily). The following discussion focuses on the Qashqa'i.

Bahmanbaigi established 69 elementary schools for nomads (*madaris-i ashayiri*) in 1953. Two years later Iran's Ministry of Education endorsed the program. Initially ministry officials assigned Persian teachers but these urban-raised men could not tolerate the rigorous outdoors life led by nomadic pastoralists. Sociocultural and linguistic differences also separated these men from their pupils and impeded teaching and learning. The Persian teachers feared the Qashqa'i, who held reputations as armed bandits and outlaws. Undaunted, Bahmanbaigi reasserted his efforts to educate intelligent, motivated young nomads in basic teaching methods and a core curriculum and then to dispatch them to their own or other nomadic groups to teach young children. He opened a tribal teacher-training school (*danishsara ashayiri*) in Shiraz in 1957.[51] He preferred to assign teachers to their groups of origin, but not all groups wanting teachers had their own trainees, and some groups produced more teachers than sets of students.[52]

State edicts specified that the instructional language in the nomads' elementary schools was to be exclusively Persian, and the academic subjects were those of the national curriculum: Persian language, math, science, geography, and Iranian history. The Ministry of Education provided students with the same paperback texts used nationally, one per subject matter for the upper grades. Instructors in the training school told the trainees to ignore or treat summarily Islam, the Qur'an, and Arabic, according to grade level and textbook coverage. Obeying the state's mandate, instructors required the trainees to learn and to teach a correct, standard, loudly enunciated Persian. Teachers and students seemed to become "more Persian" than the native speakers themselves. Persians did not ordinarily speak in the ways that Bahmanbaigi's program taught, unless they were reciting classical Persian poetry for an audience. Teachers and students constantly exaggerated and mocked the style to show their defiance and dislike. Instructors forbade the prospective teachers to talk about politics or to criticize Mohammad Reza Shah and required them to lead the pupils in patriotic songs and slogans. They told the trainees to ignore the indigenous languages, histories, and cultures of their students but many teachers did insert such politically charged topics in their daily lessons and informal relationships with students.

Teachers served as crucial role models at a time when Iran was rapidly changing. Mohammad Reza Shah had exiled the paramount Qashqa'i khans from Iran in 1954, and the secondary tribal khans had suffered losses in power and authority after 1962. Formal education promised to open new opportunities for the Qashqa'i, the youth in particular, at a time when the shah was dismantling the top levels of their tribal system. The agents of change—the teachers—introducing these new options offered themselves as examples of the benefits of literacy. They received a year's specialized training in a city (at no cost to them), earned a modest but adequate government salary, bought admired personal possessions, traveled periodically to Shiraz for refresher courses and administrative duties, and gained respect at home, among the Qashqa'i as a whole, and in the larger Persian-dominated society. Precisely at a time when many Iranians viewed the Qashqa'i as dangerous bandits and outlaws who menaced civilized society, the debut of hundreds and then thousands of skilled, articulate, composed, well-groomed teachers did much to improve the Qashqa'i reputation and image, especially because the wider Iranian society respected them for their education, profession, and efforts to transform the Qashqa'i. Intentionally reinforcing negative stereotypes,

260 *Life moves on*

Bahmanbaigi often noted that he was substituting chalk for bullets and that the youth, now armed with literacy instead of rifles, could build—instead of threaten—the country.[53]

Bahmanbaigi's basic aim was to provide six (later, five) years of elementary education to nomadic youth, girls as well as boys. He expected that some students would continue their education, after primary school, in regular town and city schools. For a small, highly select group, Bahmanbaigi founded a coeducational, boarding, six-year, tribal secondary school in Shiraz in 1968. (At the time, and ever since, all public secondary schools in Iran, grades seven [later, six] through 12, were gender-segregated.) He named the school Forty People (*dabiristan-i chihil nafari*) after the first group he admitted. Later he created tribal middle schools elsewhere in the province and region.[54]

(Iran's government changed the national educational system in 1966 from an elementary level of grades one through six and a secondary level of grades seven through 12, to an elementary level of grades one through five, an intermediate level of grades six through eight, and a high school of grades nine through 12. The intermediate or middle level first began in some schools in 1971 when children who had entered elementary school in 1966 reached the next level.)

Bahmanbaigi's overall goal was to prepare Qashqa'i youth for integration in the wider Persian-dominated society and culture and for assimilation and full citizenship in the nation-state of Iran. From his program's beginning, Bahmanbaigi achieved success in his efforts. Mohammad Reza Shah along with his American advisors viewed Bahmanbaigi's program as essential for transforming Iranian society, particularly its often perceived primitive and disruptive tribal sector. In pursuing his aims, Bahmanbaigi received political and financial support from these two governments, and he also earned international acclaim. U.S. Peace Corps volunteers taught English in Bahmanbaigi's tribal secondary school in Shiraz in the 1960s and 1970s, and at least one ran classes in Qashqa'i territory (in the Darrehshuri village of Mehr-i Gerd).[55]

(Some Qashqa'i at the time and especially later blamed Bahmanbaigi for undercutting Qashqa'i society and culture and weakening the sociopolitical identities of the Qashqa'i youth. They said he tried, through his educational program, to depoliticize the Qashqa'i and render them subservient to Iran's dominating Persian society.)

A teacher completed a year's instruction in Shiraz at the specialized teacher-training facility, which then assigned him to a host group. (At the program's beginning, all teachers were male.) There, the teacher met with the headman and elders to choose the school's location. The group's households were dispersed across the landscape, and these men tried to select a site convenient for potential students. They often chose a place in or near the headman's camp; they hoped that the headman and the teacher would provide mutually beneficial services. Sometimes the headman possessed only rudimentary literacy, and a teacher nearby was useful. The expanding state bureaucracy increasingly relied on written documents. When government agents sought out the headman, the teacher could assist in deciphering and writing reports and serve as an

Life moves on 261

impartial mediator, whom the agents respected because of his literacy, education, and profession. The headman was often able to provide food, transportation, and other benefits for the teacher, unlike others in his group.

The teacher's initial task was to accommodate the academic schedule to the nomads' annual cycle of activities. The young man pitched the government's white-canvas school tent in winter pastures, recruited as many students as possible, instructed them until the spring migration to summer pastures began, set up the school tent in summer pastures when the migration ended, enrolled any additional pupils there, and taught them until the autumn migration to winter pastures commenced.[56] Unless the teacher was a member of the same or a nearby nomadic group, he and his school did not migrate along with the students and their families, contrary to published reports on this "migratory schools" program.

Some teachers stayed with one nomadic group for years while Bahmanbaigi reassigned others to new groups, sometimes every year or two. He was sensitive to each teacher's ability, personality, tribal affiliation, and socioeconomic and cultural background and adjusted his placements accordingly. Without prior warning, he personally visited every school to observe teachers and pupils in action, and he also obtained information about teachers from his school inspectors and from the students' annual examinations. Every year he held large celebratory gatherings of schoolchildren to motivate the participants and demonstrate his efforts on their behalf.[57] (Sometimes he invited state officials and foreign dignitaries to witness these events, and some visitors published their observations.) Labeling these assemblies "urdu," a term previously used for the khans' political and military camps, he reiterated his efforts to transform Qashqa'i society. His choice of the symbolically charged word was deliberate.[58]

Many teachers served first in their own groups and then perhaps in other nomadic groups. Some became school inspectors for Bahmanbaigi's rapidly expanding program or filled other administrative jobs there. Some taught in villages, towns, and cities under the Ministry of Education's auspices. Others continued their formal education in secondary schools and universities and located employment, some in respected fields, in diverse sectors of Iranian society. Tens of thousands of Qashqa'i in salaried jobs and professions throughout Iran and abroad by the 1990s owed their success and status to the educational opportunities first offered to them (as students and/or teachers) by Bahmanbaigi and his unique program.[59] Few of them resumed the customary nomadic pastoralism of their parents and previous generations. Many Qashqa'i came to view literacy as an essential asset in a changing, modernizing Iran, and they regarded teachers as the individuals who could bring them this skill.

Qermezi schools from 1959 through 2004

Bahmanbaigi did not select any Qermezi boys or girls for teacher-training between 1957 (when he established the training program) and 1971. Perhaps

262 *Life moves on*

he did not find qualified candidates among them. He tended to favor those tribes and subtribes that connected positively with him and his family. Many groups he chose had sought formal secular education earlier than did any members of the Qermezi subtribe. Qermezi was also not among the first subtribes that Bahmanbaigi designated to host his newly trained teachers.

In their roles as Qermezi headmen, Khalifeh and Borzu continued to hire teachers for a few boys each year. Simultaneously, they pressured Bahmanbaigi, who finally sent them their first formally trained teacher in 1959. (Point Four's teacher, Fazilat, came earlier but might have received only rudimentary training, and he stayed only a year.) The Qermezi subtribe lacked any teachers among its members, and Bahmanbaigi sent them an outsider, a young Nadirli Darrehshuri man. The Nadirli group had participated in formal education before all other Darrehshuri subtribes, and, early in his program, Bahmanbaigi selected some of its young men to receive training and become teachers.[60]

The Qermezi were dispersed throughout winter and summer pastures in 1959, and they based their socioterritorial groups on lineage affiliations. The largest group lived at Dashtak in winter pastures, and the primary residents there derived from the Aqa Mohammadli and Qairkhbaili lineages. Because the headmen, Khalifeh and Borzu, resided at Dashtak, Bahmanbaigi sent the first teacher there. The largest group of Qermezi in summer pastures did not reside at Hanalishah then, but Khalifeh and Borzu lived there, and the pupils to be instructed were those who had begun the school year at Dashtak. The school reopened at Hanalishah in the summer, and children could complete their grade level that season and then progress to the next level when they returned to winter pastures. Some Dashtak residents migrated to other pastures in the summer, and their children either did not attend school that season or their parents sent them to Hanalishah to live with relatives so they could continue. A few Hanalishah residents did not live at Dashtak during the winter, and they too made the same kinds of decisions about school that season.

The first Qermezi school was located at Dashtak and Hanalishah. Children residing there during the school-year of 1959–60, along with any others who were sent there, were the first to receive formal secular education.[61] Dashtak residents were primarily Aqa Mohammadli and Qairkhbaili, and Hanalishah residents were mainly Aqa Mohammadli. Thus Aqa Mohammadli children, and to a lesser extent Qairkhbaili ones, were favored over other Qermezi children in their access to formal education. The consequences of this early advantage, beginning in 1959, were still visible in the subtribe more than 50 years later. Considering all Qermezi, women as well as men, the vast majority of high-school graduates, teachers, university students and graduates, and trained, salaried professionals were Aqa Mohammadli. The impact of this opportunity could also be seen in 2013 among other individuals whose families had lived at Dashtak and Hanalishah. From the four other lineages and other groups, these children enjoyed the same access to early formal education as the other residents of these territories. Even some children of hired shepherds and camel herders, usually the poorest of all residents and from other tribal groups, acquired economic and social benefits in later life that many Qermezi still lacked.

This early educational advantage was also evident among the children of the first recipients, who—inspired and motivated by their educated parents—achieved higher levels than most other Qermezi their age. The first females, for example, to graduate from high school, attend and graduate from university, and attain salaried professions outside the home were the daughters of the very first recipients of formal secular education.

The first Qermezi school served the nomads at Dashtak and Hanalishah without interruption from 1959 through 2013.[62] This school and the eight others established later were coeducational throughout, even during the Islamic Republic's first three decades when most other schools in Iran, from elementary level on, were gender segregated. Primary schools in thousands of small villages in Iran were also coeducational due to low numbers of children in these rural communities.[63] Details about the teachers in the nine Qermezi schools follow in the next section.

The second Qermezi school originated in Atakula village in northern Darrehshuri summer pastures in 1974, 16 years after the first school. By this time, eight years after the first nomads had built houses there, some residents stayed year-round, and their numbers warranted a school of their own, according to state policy. Previously some of Atakula's children had attended school in the town of Borujen two kilometers away. For years, the community's founders had urged Bahmanbaigi to provide them with a teacher from his program. Their children had attended his school at Dashtak and Hanalishah before moving to the village. They and others considered his educational system and the teachers he specially trained to be higher caliber than those assigned by the Ministry of Education. At the same time, other recently settled and newly settling Qashqa'i groups also sought to have Bahmanbaigi's schools in their new locations. Bahmanbaigi did not develop any consistent policies.[64] Some new villagers continued to benefit from his program, while the government forced others to switch to the lower-standard schools and teachers of the Ministry of Education.

Mohammad Reza Shah established the Literacy Corps (*sipah-i danish*, "army of knowledge") in 1963 (and added females in 1968) as part of his White Revolution. (The program ended in 1979 with his ouster.)[65] Literacy Corps teachers taught in the Ministry of Education's schools in rural and remote areas of Iran. The government sometimes (but not always) assigned teachers of ethnic, ethnolinguistic, and tribal backgrounds to their own or comparable communities. For some groups, particularly the Azeri Turks, Kurds, Arabs, and Baluch, the shah did not want to heighten their politicization by sending them educated, informed compatriots as teachers, and so the corps posted teachers of Persian ethnicity there. The lesson of education was integration and assimilation in Iran, and Persian teachers were more likely to support and advance this policy than members of minority groups. Teachers of minority backgrounds were not likely to encourage their students to be patriotic toward Iran. The

264　*Life moves on*

government did not send many Literacy Corps teachers to settling or settled Qashqa'i groups. Bahmanbaigi's expanding program provided an alternative for some of these communities.

Literacy Corps teachers were usually better educated and trained and more amenable to serving in remote areas than were the ministry's regular teachers. As "soldier-teachers" (*sarbaz muallim*), they were high-school graduates who opted to teach instead of serving a mandatory two years in the military. The corps assigned them to specific communities after a month of basic military training and three months of pedagogic instruction. These teachers also conducted adult-literacy classes, often in the evenings (which was not a regular feature of Bahmanbaigi's program).

Two Qermezi boys served in northwestern Iran as Literacy Corps teachers in lieu of regular military service. The corps sent Askar to Kurdistan where he adopted Kurdish dress, and Fathullah taught Azeri and Afshar Turks in villages in the Zanjan area.

The Literacy Corps staffed Atakula's first school in 1974–78. As the villagers had wanted all along, Bahmanbaigi created a nomads' school there in 1978 and chose as its first teacher a young Qermezi man whose family lived in the settlement. Several years after the revolution, in 1983, the Borujen office of the Ministry of Education assumed control of the school and remained in charge through 2013. It named the school Miraj, after the prophet Mohammad's night journey to heaven. This name and similar ones, a central feature of the regime's Islamizing policies, were foreign to and alienating for the recipients. Other efforts to Islamize Iran's citizens were not as easy to implement as this one, but even a symbolic change was problematic and sometimes counter-productive.

The third Qermezi school began in 1975 after some Kachili Qermezi families built houses that year in summer pastures for seasonal or year-round residence. Earlier some of their children had attended school in the nearby Narmeh village but, as their numbers increased, the new community applied for and received a school of its own. The school began as part of Bahmanbaigi's program, and then the government transferred it in 1981 to the Semirom office of the Ministry of Education.

Sohrab Qermezi created the fourth Qermezi school after some difficulties. He was the dominant figure in the Imamverdili lineage and Borzu Qermezi's main competitor as the subtribe's leader. Most Imamverdili lived in winter pastures at Chah Shirin south of Kazerun and in summer pastures at Bid-i Qatar in northern Darrehshuri territory. Both places, especially Bid-i Qatar, were far from the school at Dashtak and Hanalishah, and Imamverdili children could attend only if they left home and lived with relatives there. One of them was Shahriyar Qermezi, later a teacher, war hero, and parliamentary deputy. His longstanding close relationship with the Aqa Mohammadli lineage originated from his residence and schooling among them during his childhood.

After years of prevailing on Bahmanbaigi to provide his lineage with a teacher, Sohrab finally succeeded in 1965. Yet, when the teacher arrived, Sohrab was incensed. The man's ancestors were former slaves of African

Life moves on 265

origin who had been employed by the Darrehshuri khans, and the descendants were still serving the khans.[66] Sohrab was disturbed by the subordinate standing of the man's family as servants, not by the African ancestry or darker skin coloring. He saw the assignment as an insult to his status. He presumed that Bahmanbaigi regarded him (Sohrab) as unworthy of a teacher whose social position was equivalent to his (Sohrab's). Sohrab and others held teachers in high esteem, and he perceived a teacher who traced descent from slaves and servants as a contradiction. Ancestry and ethnic and tribal identity remained meaningful despite other sociocultural changes brought about by formal education.

Hearing Sohrab's angry complaints, Bahmanbaigi refused to send Sohrab a teacher the following year. He exerted power as the Qashqa'i khans had often done. Many Qashqa'i had criticized him for trying to supplant the khans, exiled since 1954, and he sometimes behaved similarly to them. If he were only a state official and not also a now-prominent Qashqa'i man, he might have lacked the authority to punish a particular tribal group because of its leader's defiance.[67]

The Imamverdili lineage remained without a teacher for the next nine years while the dispute persisted. During this period, Imamverdili families hoped to send their children to the school at Dashtak and Hanalishah, but most of them could not afford to lose their labor for such a long period, and only a few of these youngsters were able to attend the school. During part of this time, Husain Imamverdili hired Mulla Khuda Karam Ipaigli to instruct his sons. (Several Imamverdili boys close to Husain's family became hezbollahis in the early 1980s. Some Qermezi blamed this politico-ideological orientation on the boys' early exposure to religious education.) No other Qermezi children at the time received any religious instruction.

Bahmanbaigi finally assigned the Imamverdili group another trained secular teacher in 1975, and the school functioned continuously through 2004. The school ceased operating in the mid-1980s at Bid-i Qatar in the summer, and some children who would have attended this school studied instead in Dezeh village near summer pastures where some Imamverdili were building houses for part-time or full-time residence. The school at Chah Shirin remained open during the autumn, winter, and early spring.

The fifth Qermezi school formed in 1979 to serve the Qairkhbaili students who attended or would have attended the Dashtak school, which was now overcrowded. For several years beforehand, Bahmanbaigi had assigned new teacher-trainees to Dashtak's instructor to ease the pressure on him. Still worried about too many pupils there, he decided to create a new school for the Qairkhbaili. Most of them now spent the summers at Kuh Pahn in northern winter pastures and were unable to use Hanalishah's school so far away. During the autumn, winter, and early spring the new school operated in a gorge in southern Dashtak. Qairkhbaili families lived nearby, and the new school there was convenient. In the summer it traveled to Kuh Pahn, and it functioned continuously through 2004.

266　*Life moves on*

Most Aqa Mohammadli occupied northern Dashtak, the site of the first school, while most Qairkhbaili resided in southern Dashtak. In creating a new school, Bahmanbaigi recognized and affirmed existing kinship, sociopolitical, and territorial groups.

The sixth Qermezi school, begun in 1981, served the Qairkhbaili families living at Mulleh Balut in winter pastures in the foothills below Dashtak, some of them year-round. It began as a nomads' school, and later the government transferred it to the Kazerun office of the Ministry of Education. It operated during the autumn, winter, and spring and was closed in the summer during the severe heat.

The seventh Qermezi school began after the revolution at the bequest of Qasemli lineage. Some of its children had attended the Imamverdili school but when that one closed for the summer, the Qasemli needed a full-time school of their own. The government established the new school at Famur near Chah Shirin in winter pastures, and in the late spring it moved to Alay in summer pastures. It operated only in winter pastures by 1998 and was closed during the summer. Since its formation, this school was part of the nomads' educational program.

The eighth Qermezi school was founded as a nomads' school after 1979 for the Qairkhbaili families spending the autumn, winter, and early spring at Chah Shirin in winter pastures, and it still functioned as a nomads' school in 2004. The other Qermezi school at Chah Shirin, originally created for Imamverdili nomads there and then taken over by Qasemli nomads, had become too crowded for all Qasemli and Qairkhbaili children in the area.

The ninth Qermezi school was created after 1979 as a regular government school for the Aqa Mohammadli and Qairkhbaili residents of the small village of Darreh Gazan in the mountains north of Shiraz. Children there had previously attended school in Qalat, the nearest village with a teacher, but students had to walk a long distance twice a day. The Darreh Gazan school closed in the summer when Aqa Mohammadli and Qairkhbaili families pitched their tents at higher elevations.

Teachers in Qermezi schools from 1959 to 2002

The first Qermezi school, the one with the longest history, was located at Dashtak and Hanalishah. There, the Qermezi's first formally trained secular teacher was Ghulam Hasan Nadiriyan, a Nadirli Darrehshuri man. For five years he taught in winter pastures at Dashtak and in summer pastures at Hanalishah. At least five of his pupils later became teachers themselves (including the Qermezi subtribe's first two), and they often attributed this opportunity to his positive role.

The second teacher at this school was Ardishir Nikbakht, a Boir Ahmad Lur from Yasuj, who remained less than a year and "fled" before his pupils could complete their respective grades. This posting was his first teaching job, and his skills were inadequate, especially compared with those of the previous teacher. Khalifeh and Borzu were unhappy that Bahmanbaigi had not assigned them an experienced teacher. They complained that he was not Darrehshuri or even Qashqa'i, and they grew more irritated when he abandoned his post. Students did not earn their year-end certificate (*karnamih*) as a result.

The third teacher was Nasir Musavi, a Shaikh Abuli Darrehshuri man who taught for three years, the first of which repeated the grade levels that Nikbakht had not finished. Originally Boir Ahmad Lurs, Musavi's ancestors had joined the Darrehshuri tribe, its men serving the khans as scribes and teachers. Musavi's father, Fakhr ud-Din, had been one of Qermezi's mulla teachers. The fourth teacher was Manuhar Amaleh, a Qarihjulu Darrehshuri man who also taught for three years. His family lived briefly with the Qermezi group, and his sister later married a Qermezi boy—both of them becoming teachers in Atakula. Then came Mohammad Quli Nadirli, another Nadirli Darrehshuri man, who was posted there when I first lived among the Qermezi, and he too taught for three years.

The Qermezi stressed in 1970 the importance of producing their own teachers instead of having to cope with outsiders. During trips to Shiraz, I visited Bahmanbaigi and urged him to consider accepting several young Qermezi men as teacher-trainees. One time I took with me Akbar and Husain Ali, whom I considered the best candidates. They are first cousins in the Aqa Mohammadli lineage. Akbar was the first graduate of Qermezi's first secular school, taught by Ghulam Hasan Nadiriyan. He completed seventh grade in Kazerun and then returned to nomadic pastoralism. Another former pupil in Nadiriyan's school, Husain Ali was currently finishing eighth grade in Kazerun. Both were eager to become teachers. After several months, Bahmanbaigi informed me that he had chosen them for that autumn's training program.

Bahmanbaigi selected Akbar, after his year's instruction, for a new teaching post among Shahsevan nomadic tribespeople in Azerbaijan in northwestern Iran. High state officials (some say the shah himself) had been impressed by Bahmanbaigi's results among the Qashqa'i and other nomadic and tribal groups in southwestern Iran, and they authorized him to institute similar educational programs among other nomadic and tribal groups. Bahmanbaigi said he chose Akbar to begin the program in Azerbaijan because he was the most intelligent and enthusiastic of the new trainees. Akbar was also older and more mature than the others and possessed a sophisticated attitude about the merits and methods of education. Unlike most other teachers, he was married. His wife stayed with his family during his absence.

Eight years younger than Akbar, Husain Ali also completed the year's training, and Bahmanbaigi designated him to teach at Dashtak and Hanalishah. At last, after waiting for 13 years, the Qermezi subtribe hosted its own teacher. Husain Ali remained at that school for eight years, and then Bahmanbaigi assigned him to the just-founded Qairkhbaili Qermezi school. Bahmanbaigi considered him the best candidate to begin a new school because he had matured during eight years of teaching. Some new students there had attended school at Dashtak and Hanalishah, and their transition as well as Husain Ali's went smoothly.

268   *Life moves on*

Bahmanbaigi's success over the years derived from this kind of astute decision making. He conducted his program with these sorts of results in mind, and he appeared to be genuinely interested in the fate of each group he served. His strategies and methods surpassed those found among the disengaged, uninspired administrators and teachers in the Ministry of Education. His tribal affiliations, ethnolinguistic identities, and positive sentiments toward the Qashqa'i and other nomadic and tribal peoples also connected him with the communities to which he offered educational and other opportunities.[68]

Bahmanbaigi might not have initially known that Husain Ali's mother is Qairkhbaili, although the kinship tie could have figured in his choice of Husain Ali as the teacher for the new Qairkhbaili school. Husain Ali was a "sister's son" for his new pupils and their families, which facilitated his tasks, especially recruiting new students. Men who would not consign their daughters to an unrelated male teacher were comfortable entrusting them to their "sister's son."

Bahmanbaigi selected 15 more young Qermezi men as teacher-trainees after Akbar and Husain Ali, and he wanted each of them to enjoy a chance to teach in his own group. To provide them with experience, he delegated some to assist Husain Ali at Dashtak and Hanalishah, and one of them led that school when Husain Ali founded the Qairkhbaili one. Impressed by Akbar's performance among the Shahsevan in Azerbaijan, Bahmanbaigi sent eight more newly trained Qermezi teachers to schools there. He was planning to instruct and place other Qermezi teachers when revolutionary politics forced him from his job. His successor posted Mohammad Quli Qermezi to the school at Dashtak and Hanalishah and sent newly trained Qermezi teachers to assist him and gain experience, before they received their own schools.

When the Ministry of Education assumed control of the nomads' educational program in 1982, its administrators assigned Bahadur Qermezi to teach at Dashtak and Hanalishah. Bahadur had not received the intensive training that Bahmanbaigi's program offered. He had failed the qualifying entrance examination and seemed unenthusiastic. Bahadur ended his teaching in winter and summer pastures in 1997. After he built a house in Atakula village, the Borujen office of the Ministry of Education assigned him to a teaching post there, where he continued to teach Qermezi pupils. During the school-year he lived in Atakula; during the summer he tended his apple orchard now growing where he had once pitched the school tent at Hanalishah.

The Ministry of Education in 1982–83 named the Dashtak and Hanalishah school for Mustafa Chamran, Iran's minister of defense who was killed in 1981 in the Iraq–Iran war. It followed a new state policy to rename institutions, streets, and other sites for early Islamic and recent revolutionary heroes, especially martyrs. Chamran lacked any connections with nomads, tribes, and formal education, and his name on this school was alienating to the students and their families.[69]

After Bahadur Qermezi, two Farsi Madan Qashqa'i teachers taught at Dashtak for an extended session during each of four school-years. Children traveled ahead to winter pastures to begin the new school-year while their

Life moves on 269

parents remained behind in summer pastures for another month. Then, toward the end of the school-year, children stayed behind in winter pastures to complete their lessons and examinations while their parents migrated ahead to summer pastures. With Bahadur's departure in 1997, the school had ceased to operate at Hanalishah during the summer.

Students at the Dashtak school dwindled because of lowering birthrates, and the nomads wondered if the school could remain open with fewer than the required 10 pupils. They worried about the education of children, girls especially, who lacked other options if the school closed. Some men would end the education of their daughters sooner than that of their sons if the immediate territory lacked a school. Boys could walk the long distance to the Qairkhbaili school at Dashtak's southern end but girls traveling that far raised issues of safety.

When the 1998–99 school-year began, 12 children at Dashtak were ready for school. The teacher, a Farsi Madan Qashqa'i man, lived in Kazerun where he also attended university, and he traveled by motorcycle every day to Dashtak to meet his pupils. The school's status for 1999–2000 was again in doubt. Eleven students enrolled, and the school once again remained open. The school flourished in 2000–01 and 2001–02 with 16 and 17 pupils, a few of them children of three other Qashqa'i subtribes whose families worked as hired shepherds for the Qermezi nomads at Dashtak.

This kind of school demonstrated its flexibility in 1999 when some nomads at Hanalishah decided to stay there into the autumn because of unfavorable pastoral conditions at Dashtak. After the nomads had harvested the apples, their livestock could graze the lush ground vegetation in the irrigated orchards, previously off-limits because of potential damage to fruit and lower branches. When most pupils could not migrate on schedule to Dashtak, the teacher pitched the school tent at Hanalishah and instructed the children there until the parents were ready to leave. Parents already living elsewhere sent their children to live with relatives at Hanalishah so they too could begin their new lessons. The teacher then reopened the school at Mulleh Balut in the foothills below Dashtak when the parents arrived there. Only when the parents ascended the Dashtak mountains did he move the school close by their encampments. If "school" meant a permanent building somewhere, these kinds of adaptations would be unlikely.[70]

The first schoolteachers in Atakula village in 1974–78 were a succession of Literacy Corpsmen, all Persians who each served only a year and was then posted elsewhere. When Bahmanbaigi created the first nomads' school there in 1978, he assigned as the teacher Dehdar Qermezi whose family lived in the village. Dehdar had just completed several years of teaching among Shahsevan nomads in Azerbaijan, as part of Bahmanbaigi's expanded program there. After his first year in Atakula, his wife Madineh (a Qarihjulu Darrehshuri woman) joined him as the second teacher. Her brother, Manuhar Amaleh, had been Qermezi's fourth secular teacher in the mid-1960s. The Ministry of Education placed the Atakula school under the jurisdiction of nearby Borujen

270 *Life moves on*

in 1983, and the school lost its affiliation with the nomads' program. When Akbar Qermezi concluded 10 years as a teacher and school inspector among Shahsevan nomads in Azerbaijan, he assumed a teaching post in Atakula where he and other family members had built houses in the 1970s. Three of his four brothers also became teachers, and two taught in Atakula, one becoming the headmaster. The Atakula school employed six teachers (five Qermezi men and the Qarihjulu woman) in 1999 and enrolled a hundred students. The number of children increasing, the ministry added two new teachers in 2001–02, both Persians from Borujen. Akbar, the first of all Qermezi teachers, fell subject to the government's mandatory retirement policy after 30 years of service, and he found a new job in a cooperative store in Borujen.[71]

Nurabad's school began in 1975 with several Dundali Darrehshuri teachers from Bahmanbaigi's program. When the government classified the new settlement as a village in 1981, the Semirom office of the Ministry of Education chose its teachers from among the Kachili Qermezi residents there. Other Kachili teachers living in Nurabad served in Mehr-i Gerd and other nearby settlements.

The Imamverdili school began in 1965 but the lineage's leader did not welcome the first teacher, whose ancestors were black slaves and khans' servants. To punish the leader for his intolerance and insubordination, Bahmanbaigi refused to send the group any teachers for the next nine years. Finally Bahmanbaigi chose a Shahinkikhai Darrehshuri teacher in 1975, and, after the man's three years of service, Bahmanbaigi assigned four Qermezi men (one after another) including Shahriyar (the parliamentary deputy). Shish Buluki and Farsi Madan Qashqa'i men were the schoolteachers in the late 1990s and early 2000s.

The first Qairkhbaili school began in 1979 under the expert leadership of Husain Ali Qermezi, one of the two original Qermezi teachers and the one who had taught at Dashtak and Hanalishah for eight years. Four more Qermezi men, two of them teaching together one year, followed Husain Ali. For several years, the government assigned outside teachers, two Farsi Madan Qashqa'i men and a Dushmanziyari Lur man. When Khuda Rahim Qermezi completed his teacher-training, the government chose him for the post. He was the only teacher the Qairkhbaili lineage had ever produced. Later, when he received a university degree, he sought a more prestigious (and comfortable) position teaching in the boys' middle school for nomads in the town of Nurabad-Mamassani. Several Farsi Madan Qashqa'i men taught in the Qairkhbaili school during the next few years.

The second Qairkhbaili school was originally a nomads' school and received Qashqa'i teachers. When it became part of the Kazerun school system in 1990, it drew Persian teachers from Kazerun, including two young, unmarried Persian women at the end of the 1990s. The school hosted a Farsi Madan Qashqa'i teacher in 2001–02.

The Qasemli school was first taught by Barat Ali, this lineage's one and only teacher. A Jarrukh Lur man from Kuh Marreh Surkhi followed, and then the same Jarrukh Lur man along with a Farsi Madan one served in 2001–02.

The third Qairkhbaili school (and the second school at Chah Shirin in winter pastures) was taught by a Farsi Madan Qashqa'i man in 2001–02.

The final Qermezi school, serving the Aqa Mohammadli and Qairkhbaili living in Darreh Gazan village near Qalat, hosted a Kashkuli Bozorg Qashqa'i teacher in 2001–02, a man who married the daughter of one of the Qairkhbaili residents.

Except for the Qarihjulu woman in Atakula and the two Persian ones, all the teachers in the nine Qermezi schools were male. The Qermezi subtribe had produced four female teachers by 2002, and they taught in village and town schools, not for Qermezi communities. None of them had attended Bahmanbaigi's training program, which had produced thousands of female teachers by 1979.

Elementary-school students in 1970–71 and 1976–77 and their futures

Twenty-seven boys in grades one through five studied under Mohammad Quli Nadiri at Dashtak and/or Hanalishah during the school-year of 1970–71. At the time, this school was the only one available for Qermezi children (unless they resided near villages or towns and walked there everyday). A few boys were pupils only at Dashtak or only at Hanalishah. Most students were Qermezi; they include ten from Aqa Mohammadli lineage, three from Imamverdili, one from Qairkhbaili, five from Qasemli, and three from Kachili. Five came from other Darrehshuri subtribes, their fathers sharing pastures with the Qermezi group or employed as shepherds and camel herders. An additional student, a Nadirli Darrehshuri boy, is the brother of the teacher's wife.

Before Mohammad Quli became the teacher in 1969, eight Qermezi girls had been pupils at the Dashtak and Hanalishah school. Five studied for a year or more, with two completing the fifth grade, while three remained for less than a year. Only two girls enrolled in Mohammad Quli's school during his three-year term. Mohammad Quli was an outsider, not related to his pupils, although he was a fellow Darrehshuri tribesman. Several families appeared ready to send their girls to school in 1970 but each worried that its daughter would be the only one in attendance. I tried to help them to coordinate their efforts so that at least two girls could attend school and be companions for the long walk to and from home, but the hesitation lasted the year. The previous year Nasir Qermezi had removed his daughter from school after her first year. Following Mohammad Quli's three years, Husain Ali (the first Qermezi teacher there) assumed the post. During his eight-year tenure, many girls were his pupils. Nasir sent two other daughters to school, and they eventually earned high-school diplomas and two-year or four-year university degrees. Bahmanbaigi's interest in training teachers who would return to their own groups to teach did not seem to be motivated by the issue of girls' attendance, but his policy did have this result among others.[72]

I was well acquainted with the 27 students in Mohammad Quli's school in 1970–71 and knew precisely what had become of them 30 years later. Most of

272 *Life moves on*

them had completed the fifth grade. This group's primary occupations in 1999 total more than 27; some individuals engaged in multiple but equally important livelihoods. Of the 27, a high number, 10, became teachers themselves and were still teaching in 1999. Fifteen graduated from high school. Four attended university, all earning two-year or four-year degrees. The eight pursuing livelihoods other than nomadic pastoralism and agriculture were a company employee, civil servant, shopkeeper, hired driver, laborer, revolutionary guard, and factory worker (2). Five continued as nomadic pastoralists, and three engaged in agriculture. Four others had died, one killed during the Iraq–Iran war, one dying later of war injuries, one drowning during the migration, and one falling ill.

I continued research among the Qermezi in 1977 when Husain Ali Qermezi was the teacher. Of his 36 students at Dashtak and/or Hanalishah during the school-year of 1976–77 (none of them overlapping with the 1970–71 group), 23 were Aqa Mohammadli, two were Imamverdili, and four were Qairkhbaili. Seven came from other Darrehshuri subtribes, their families sharing pastures with the Qermezi or serving as hired shepherds. Six of the 36 were girls, all of them Husain Ali's close kin. Their parents noted that they were comfortable sending them to his school. The educations and primary livelihoods of the 36 in 1999 were similar to, but more diverse than, those of the 1970–71 students. The six female students were wives and mothers who conducted their livelihoods (including textile weaving and dairy production) at home. Of the 30 male students, three were teachers, one at a university. Fourteen graduated from high school. Nine attended university, all graduating with two-year or four-year degrees. One pursued theology in an urban seminary. Eleven engaged in urban-linked occupations as an engineer, civil servant, healthcare provider, gas-company employee, transporter, hired driver (2), factory worker (3), and revolutionary guard (2). Eight continued as nomadic pastoralists while eight were agriculturalists. Two were unemployed in 1999; one of them had worked for a newspaper that the Islamic regime shut down for political reasons in 1998. Three had died, two in the Iraq–Iran war and one by drowning. Given some men's multiple livelihoods, these numbers do not total 30.

For each of these two groups of students (1970–71, 1976–77), and for earlier and later groups as well, they formed a cohort that persisted for life. Students identified with those in their grade and school. Fifth-graders served as role models for lower-grade pupils, who relied on those ahead of them for assistance and support. Older pupils guided younger ones when the teacher was busy with other schoolwork. Initially I was surprised when a person could easily name every student in his or her school after 20, 30, or 40 years had passed, but then I came to understand how intense the bonds among them had been during those early years. The educational experience was profound for all students, who also shared the physical limitations of these rudimentary single-space schools (a tent or hut), the often severe climate and weather, and the difficulties in learning and studying under these conditions. As fellow students, children knew one another intimately; they absorbed information and formed judgments that endured a lifetime. Many pupils in any given school were close kin with one another, even siblings and first cousins, and yet these attachments by themselves did not create the close ties that these students formed in school.

Even those who were not kinship related, all students experiencing a coeducational setting seemed then and later to be more relaxed in mixed-gender circumstances than students who attended single-sex schools in towns. The many boys and girls who studied with Husain Ali, for example, remained close friends and comfortable with one another more than 30 years later. Masud Qermezi's age cohort of both genders joked with ease about his elevated educational and social status.

Teachers and pupils also formed intense bonds, especially if the teachers were Qermezi. The meaningful, respectful relationships that students had built with their teachers were still evident after they matured to take their place in adult society, sometimes economically elevated above these teachers. Teachers expressed fondness for their pupils and remembered their mischievous pranks and antics. They often took partial—and probably deserved—credit for the future educational and professional achievements of some students. A succession of teachers proudly noted three particular cases: Ibrahim Qermezi who was the first in the subtribe to enter university, Shahriyar Qermezi who was elected to Iran's parliament, and Masud Qermezi who earned master's and doctoral degrees in aeronautical engineering.

Some non-Qermezi teachers maintained regular contact with the Qermezi groups in which they had taught. Although living in Shiraz, Mohammad Quli Nadiri often visited Qermezi winter and summer pastures, especially after he began to entertain notions of running for parliament. He would need a broad constituency, part of which would help to fund his campaign, and he viewed his former pupils and their families as potential backers. (He ran in the 2000 parliamentary election and lost.) His predecessor, Manuhar Amaleh, visited Dashtak and Hanalishah yearly and always inquired about his former students. Nasir Musavi became a judge in Shiraz, and the Qermezi hoped to seek his assistance when they encountered legal problems. Mohammad Reza Azad was a school inspector who administered many nomads' schools in winter pastures near Kazerun (including five Qermezi schools). He had assisted Bahadur Qermezi in a Qermezi nomads' school for a year and had taught for seven years in a Kuruni nomads' school. In 2002 he was the mobile super-intendent of schools attended by the children of his former pupils, for whom he said he felt special affection.

A teacher's biography

The biography of a Qermezi teacher illustrates points made in this section and elsewhere. Ali (Ali Qurban), the son of Ghulam Husain of Aqa Mohammadli lineage, was a third-grade student in the Dashtak and Hanalishah school in 1970–71.

Ghulam Husain is one of Borzu Qermezi's two full brothers. He camped close to Borzu but always maintained his independence, despite Borzu

274　*Life moves on*

haranguing him about his economic and social strategies. Ghulam Husain's wife is Rukhsar, the daughter of an influential Qurd (Wolf) Darrehshuri man. They produced eight surviving children, six boys and two girls. The eldest son was a traditional nomadic pastoralist in 2002, the second was Ali (a teacher), the third was employed by a steel mill near Isfahan, the fourth was an administrator in Shiraz for the nomads' educational program, and the fifth and sixth were traditional nomadic pastoralists. The sixth wanted to attend university after completing his compulsory military service and then secure an urban job but he did not pass the stiff entrance examination. Married, the eldest daughter lived as a traditional nomadic pastoralist. Until her marriage to a Qurd teacher, the second one remained at home with her mother and youngest brother. Ghulam Husain had died in 1994.

Ali was instructed by three teachers discussed earlier (Manuhar Amaleh, Mohammad Quli Nadiri, and Husain Ali Qermezi) and completed the fifth grade in the nomads' school. He attended the sixth, seventh, and eighth grades in a Kazerun public school while rooming during the school week with young kinsmen who were also students there. They all returned home during weekends and holidays to resume pastoral chores. Accepted as a teacher-trainee by Bahmanbaigi in 1977, Ali studied for a year at the tribal school in Shiraz.

Bahmanbaigi sent Ali and three other newly trained Qermezi teachers to eastern Azerbaijan (in northwestern Iran) in 1978, to continue his program for the nomadic and tribal people there. The three included Ali's paternal cousin Amanullah, Nurullah of Kachili lineage, and Barf Ali whose Ipaigli Darrehshuri father had joined the Qermezi subtribe. Bahmanbaigi understood the importance of sending young kinsmen and fellow tribal members together to distant teaching posts, a strategy that helped to ensure their success there. They supported one another and were less likely to be lonely and abandon their posts. He assigned the four teachers to a new village in Dasht-i Moghan, the inhabitants formerly nomadic, recently settled Shahsevan tribespeople, Turks similar to the Qashqa'i and related to them historically. Once the two groups understood their minor linguistic differences, they communicated well together. The four men lived in a small dwelling the villagers provided. They used one room for cooking and storage, the other for sleeping. The coeducational school occupied a nearby building. They were the community's only teachers. When the shah fled Iran in January 1979, schools throughout Iran closed, and the four men returned to their families in the south. After Khomeini arrived in Iran and formed a new government, the four teachers traveled back to Azerbaijan to finish the school year. Then, Ali said, "We rolled up our carpets and said good-bye."[73]

At that time (and possibly into the twenty-first century), Qashqa'i Turkish demonstrated more Persian and Arabic incursions than did Shahsevan Turkish. The four teachers said they were glad to learn what they considered a "purer" form of Turkish. On their return home they introduced their families and their Qashqa'i students to Turkish words and phrases that they could substitute for Persian and Arabic ones. These linguistic contributions were still evident

Life moves on 275

among the Qermezi 30 years later, and they acquired added significance when these and other Qashqa'i reasserted their Turkic language in the face of increased pressures from the Islamic Republic to adopt Persian and Arabic.

During the two years following his teaching in Azerbaijan, Ali assisted his cousin, Husain Ali, in teaching the fifth grade at Dashtak and Hanalishah. At the end of that grade, students took standardized examinations that determined their future educational options, and Bahmanbaigi wanted to provide them with additional assistance.

Ali aspired to earn a high-school diploma, and he transferred to a teaching post near Kazerun. During the day, for four years, he taught Gujalu Darrehshuri children in a nomads' tent school, and during the evening he attended night school in Kazerun and studied. At the end of the fourth year, he passed his examinations and received his diploma. A year earlier he had married Mahsanam, his second paternal cousin.

Ali's next teaching post was in Kazerun proper, and for two years he taught boys in several elementary grades in city schools. After passing the university-qualifying examination, he enrolled in Kazerun's independent university in 1988. After a month of classes and study, he saw that life would be complicated without any income, and he quit. He took jobs teaching elementary school in villages near Kazerun for three years. Then he taught for five years in a coeducational school in Davan village where the five other teachers were women. He moved to yet another village school for a year and then returned to Davan for a sixth year there. He instructed Kashkuli Bozorg Qashqa'i children in a village for a year, and, for the next three years, he taught in a nearby Persian village. During all this time, while maintaining his residence in Kazerun, he traveled every schoolday to and from the villages by minibus or motorcycle. At first he rented a small house in Kazerun, a different one every year, often together with another Qermezi teacher and his family. Later he built his own house.

Until early September of each year, Ali did not know what his next appointment would be. The Kazerun office of the Ministry of Education assigned teachers to posts on a yearly basis, and Ali said he was glad to go where a school needed him. He preferred teaching in villages rather than in Kazerun's large schools. He appreciated the small coeducational classes and the decreased workload of the village schools, where he said discipline was not a problem, unlike in large, all-boys classes in Kazerun. He found the boys in Kazerun vexing to teach. They were distracted by television and soccer and enticed by the town's culture ("pizza and motorcycles"). Most of his pupils were unrelated to one another and were having their first experience with a male teacher (who was stricter than the female teachers of the lower grades). Ali formed close ties with the villagers and talked with parents while he walked to and from school. In Kazerun, he lacked any contact with parents (except when they privately offered him bribes to raise their children's marks).[74] Villagers often invited him for lunch, a courtesy absent in Kazerun, and he encouraged them to help the children with their lessons. He noted that village

276 *Life moves on*

students worked harder than urban ones and took their education seriously. Formal education was their only opportunity for acquiring new kinds of jobs, socioeconomic mobility, and a life outside the village.

Ali built a two-room stone house at Hanalishah in 1989, alongside his extended family's apple orchard, but he and his wife and three, soon to be four, daughters lived there only one summer. Instead, they stayed in Kazerun, despite sweltering weather, where he supplemented his modest teacher's salary by transporting goods for hire in his pickup truck. No family could survive on a single income anymore, he complained. As a government teacher, he was entitled to a discount on land in Kazerun and a low-interest bank loan for constructing a house. When Ali completed the dwelling in 1995, he hosted the subtribe's first-ever house-warming party, and most Qermezi in the vicinity attended. After a nine-year absence, he decided in 1999 to take his family to Hanalishah for the summer, and his wife and daughters were relieved to escape the high heat and humidity in Kazerun. He and his five brothers had agreed to divide their interests in the natal family's apple orchard, and Ali set to work to improve his stand of trees.

Ali's eldest daughter, Fatemeh, was one of only three Qermezi girls in the subtribe's history to pass the entrance examination for the prestigious tribal high school in Shiraz. (Shiraz's tribal middle school accepted two other Qermezi girls.) After Fatemeh completed a year's instruction there and qualified for the second year, her father removed her from the school. He said he preferred for her to reside at home in Kazerun and continue school there, rather than to live in a crowded dormitory in Shiraz. If other reasons were part of his decision, he did not explain them. He did exercise greater control over his daughters than most other Qermezi men. The two other Qermezi girls continued as students in Shiraz's tribal high school.[75]

Government policies and education

The Islamic Republic continued the efforts of Mohammad Reza Shah to exploit education as a way to integrate the Qashqa'i and other nomadic peoples in the nation-state. While its stated goal was to improve the conditions of the "deprived and oppressed," to offer them services that the shah's regime had denied to them, it also wanted to decrease the likelihood that these people would resist or rebel against the state. Among other attributes, education provided a forum for indoctrination and a means of integration and assimilation.[76] While the two regimes did not view "nomads" as potentially threatening, almost all nomads were also tribally organized, and tribal polities did pose threats to centralized states.

The two regimes have held ambiguous attitudes about Iran's tribal, ethnolinguistic, and national minorities, as compared with nomads, and were conflicted about attempts to integrate and assimilate them. Iran's national minorities were usually part of larger nations across international borders and posed other kinds of threat to the government. The policies of the two regimes for Persianization—with formal education at the forefront—were not successfully implemented among many of the tribal, ethnolinguistic, and national minorities. The two governments did not press these communities for the changes that they expected in other kinds of group such as nomadic ones.[77] Without formal education and living under increasingly impoverished conditions, minority peoples were unlikely to agitate for reform, thus allowing governments to ignore them.

Education beyond the elementary level

Since the first formal secular school for Qermezi children opened in 1959, ever-increasing numbers of students completed six (after 1971, five) elementary grades, attended and graduated from middle and high school, received teacher-training, took university-entrance examinations, and studied at and graduated from universities. The options in each of these areas expanded over the years, especially after the Islamic regime took power in 1979, and many Qermezi took advantage of the available opportunities.

Throughout Iran, the many students completing successive levels of formal education, compared with the few jobs available for these graduates (especially in the fields in which they had specialized and trained), posed a national crisis in the 1990s and early 2000s. Yet this national problem did not halt the quest of growing numbers of young Qermezi men and women for formal education. Almost all of those who obtained two-year and four-year university degrees and completed other advanced programs succeeded in finding and retaining jobs.

Children in Iran officially began school at the age of seven.[78] Some Qermezi parents sent their children to the nomads' elementary schools a year early to prepare them for the first grade the following year. Even younger ones attended these schools, especially if their fathers were the teachers or if their siblings were enrolled pupils. These early opportunities were not available in town and city schools and in most village ones, and they demonstrate yet another advantage of the nomads' schools. The first Qermezi child to attend a formal kindergarten or another preschool program is Salar Qermezi, whose father worked as a driver and whose mother was a university student.

Practically all Qermezi children since the 1970s attended elementary school (*ibtidai, dabistan*), and almost all of these completed the fifth grade. Students performing poorly in any grade repeated it the following year. The Qermezi living in villages and towns (often only seasonally) were likely to send all their children to elementary school while a few Qermezi nomadic pastoralists were unable to do so for reasons of distance and/or labor.[79] The nomads' schools were sometimes far away, especially for girls (an issue of safety, not strength), and boys worked as herders and cultivators.

Most students who finished the fifth grade in the nomads' schools (after passing a standardized examination) took another standardized one to determine the course of their further education. Their lessons during the fifth grade

278　*Life moves on*

centered on these two tests, and parents and others judged teachers by their ability to produce positive results.

Students scoring the highest marks in the second examination earned admittance to one of two selective, tribal, boarding, middle schools (guidance level, *rahnamai*; grades six through eight) in Shiraz, one for boys and the other for girls. (Shiraz's tribal secondary school, grades six through 12, from 1968 to 1983 was coeducational.)

Students receiving slightly lower marks could enter one of 17 regional, tribal, boarding, middle schools, usually the one closest to their family's winter home. The government had founded these schools, beginning in 1991, in multiple locations in and near tribal territory to meet the demands for education beyond the primary level. Shiraz had hosted a coeducational, tribal, boarding, six-year secondary school since 1968, and it split into four entities in 1983: separate boarding middle and high schools for boys and for girls. The nomads' educational program in Shiraz and the Ministry of Education administered these tribal middle schools. For Qermezi children at Dashtak and in the region, the closest tribal middle school (separate facilities for boys and girls) was located in Chinar Shahijan until 1998 when the boys' facility moved to Nurabad-Mamassani to the north.

Students whose marks were lower than those of the two other groups (above) attended the Ministry of Education's regular, public, gender-segregated middle schools in the region's towns and cities. Those living at Dashtak and in the area attended these schools in Kazerun.

Many Qermezi boys and some Qermezi girls continued their education in these middle schools. Qermezi residents of villages, towns, and cities were likely to send all of their boys and some of their girls to these schools, partly because of the close proximity, while Qermezi nomadic pastoralists hoped to place their high-scoring children in tribal schools with dormitories.[80] The nomads' second option was for their children to live with relatives in town, where they could attend school. This strategy often meant a long-term commitment by the host families. Nomadic pastoralists were more likely than their settled tribesmates to need their children at home as workers.

At the end of each year in middle school, students took multiple, subject-related examinations to determine if they could advance to the next grade. Those with failing marks in any subject were required to retake the examination toward the end of summer if they wanted to move ahead in school that autumn. Students spent the summer worrying about these tests and trying to memorize their textbooks, on which the tests were solely based. Those living in or near towns and cities could attend remedial classes there during the summer, a government program begun in the mid-1990s to assist low-scoring students. If they failed again, they repeated the grade. The tribal boarding schools held high academic standards, and several Qermezi students could not continue there because of inadequate performance. They transferred to town and city schools where academic expectations were less strict.

Life moves on 279

These procedures created new statuses and hierarchies for children. Adults and students alike regarded as positive role models those who passed all examinations on the first try, compared with those having one or more failures. They praised youngsters who passed previously failed tests and contrasted them with those who needed to repeat a grade.[81] Everyone, children especially, knew the details precisely: how many failures, what subjects, and what scores (zero to twenty) students had received. Students admitted to the high-status tribal middle and high schools and then not able to continue there were devastated (as were their parents and kin groups). They understood that they had lost an irreplaceable opportunity. For Hanalishah's nomads, the weeks of memorization preceding these makeup examinations—followed by the off-season trips of students to distant testing locations in Kazerun, Nurabad-Mamassani, Chinar Shahijan, and Shiraz—punctuated and "ruined" the students' summers.

In the history of the tribal middle schools, 32 Qermezi students attended (22 boys, 10 girls), and 20 of them (14 boys, 6 girls) had graduated from there by 2000. Eight continued as students in 2000–01. The four who did not complete their studies at the tribal middle schools attended and graduated from regular middle schools elsewhere. (These figures include students who attended the first three years of the six-year tribal secondary school in Shiraz before it divided into middle and high schools.)

When students successfully completed the third year of middle school, they took national, standardized tests to determine three results: if they could advance to high school, where these schools were located, and what subjects these schools covered. *Dabiristan*, grades nine through 12, offered academic programs. *Hunaristan*, grades nine through 11 or 12, provided vocational courses.

The highest-caliber school was the nationally prestigious, coeducational, tribal high school in Shiraz, Iran's only tribal high school before 1996. Its requirements for acceptance were lofty and the qualifying examination stiff.[82] The government divided the tribal high school into separate boys' and girls' facilities in 1983.[83] Between 1996 and 2002 the nomads' educational program founded 10 new tribal high schools (five with dormitories) in small towns in Qashqa'i, Khamseh, and Lur regions to serve students there. Shiraz's tribal high school could no longer admit all qualified applicants, and the need was growing. It did retain its high status.

Some of Iran's policy makers understood that educating (and indoctrinating) these young people was better than ignoring them or casting them adrift in an already-discontented Iranian society. Unlike under Mohammad Reza Shah's regime, many middle-level decision makers now came from nomadic, pastoral, tribal, and ethnolinguistic-minority backgrounds themselves, which led to policies that favored these populations. By the time these students were ready to enter high school, they would not likely return home to be nomadic pastoralists. They needed the state to provide viable alternatives. Still, students were educated within a series of tribal institutions (the new tribal high schools

280 *Life moves on*

being the latest innovation), and they grew more aware of and attached to their political, social, and cultural identities. In each school, including the nomads' elementary ones, students encountered lineages, subtribes, tribes, and tribal confederacies that differed from their own. Despite these divisions and subdivisions, students appreciated the political, social, and cultural characteristics that united them, and they gained an understanding of the larger entities of which they (and others) were a part. By continuing their education, they also grew more exposed to the Persian-dominating society, and the contrasts they drew between themselves—as tribal and ethnolinguistic minorities—and the Persian majority heightened. As a result, they were less likely to assimilate fully in Persian-Iranian society. The Islamic Republic risked fulfilling its primary goal of integration when it offered contradictory messages about these students, their various identities and political affiliations, and their place in Iran.

In the history of the prestigious tribal high school in Shiraz, eight Qermezi students attended (four boys, four girls), and three (all boys) graduated from there by 2000. Four continued as students in 2000–01. One dropped out. Of the eight in this institution, five of them (three boys, two girls) came from a single nuclear family headed by Amir Husain and Qamar, both Aqa Mohammadli, neither of whom had experienced any kind of formal education when they were young. Of the five, three had graduated from university by 2001, and two continued in the high school.

Many Qermezi students who were not admitted to the tribal high schools attended high schools in towns and cities. Regular public high schools were two types, a four-year academic program (in six fields) focusing on university admission and a three-year or four-year technical training program relating to specialized jobs.

The Ministry of Education began by 2001 to permit pupils who had failed one or more subject tests at the end of the ninth, tenth, and eleventh grades to enter the next grade and retake these tests later. As a result, some students studied for two grade levels simultaneously, and their chances for passing either or both decreased. They enrolled in one grade but "carried books" for the previous one. Those who eventually failed both sets of tests dropped out of school or at least discontinued formal classes while they struggled to catch up.[84] Parents and others criticized the ambiguity created, and they faulted the regime for the confusion.

Guided instruction during the academic program's twelfth grade ("before university," *pish danishgah*) helped students to prepare for the university-entrance examination. Students who failed their twelfth-grade courses and did not receive their diplomas could not sit for this test. Some students reenrolled in the twelfth grade in order to qualify, and, if they failed again, many returned a third or even a subsequent time to twelfth grade. The government had begun the "before university" program in 1992 to help quell the growing discontent in Iranian society about the stiff university-qualifying test, the many takers, and the relatively few university slots available. Yet the number of students enrolled in the twelfth grade had grown steadily by 2002 (an increase

Life moves on 281

beyond the normal progression of students through the grades), with many often repeating the experience. University spots were still comparatively few.

The first high-school graduate in the Qermezi subtribe is Fathullah of Aqa Mohammadli lineage. He received his diploma in 1974. Many youth who wanted further education in the 1970s attended the tribal teacher-training program rather than continuing in secondary school and acquiring a diploma. At the time, the teachers' program offered an immediate job; a high-school degree did not necessarily do so.

Qermezi students found their lives from 1977 through the 1980s disrupted and unsettled by the revolution, the new regime, and the Iraq–Iran war. Confronting the difficult times and seeking strategies that would enhance their lives in the future, some sought further secondary-school education. Growing numbers of students earned high-school diplomas by the middle 1980s, and this number increased further in the 1990s and early 2000s.

Twenty-nine Qermezi girls and approximately 120 Qermezi boys had graduated from high school by 2001. People could readily list all the female graduates but not all the males (because of their higher number). Every female graduate was noteworthy, especially the first few, while male ones were more common. Girls who attended high school made more personal sacrifices than boys did and experienced greater pressure to quit. Their fathers worried about their prospects for marriage if they had not been under constant surveillance at home.

Many young people found their formal educations interrupted or postponed by the war, military service, marriage, children, and other family obligations, and they struggled, sometimes for years, to study for the tests that determined high-school graduation. Some planned to take the university-entrance examination once they received their diplomas. Schoolteachers in particular wanted to finish high school (and possibly continue in university). Their educational level determined the amount of their salary, and their social status rose with each step. High-school graduates who were conscripted by the army and/or who joined the revolutionary-guard corps received more comfortable, higher-status postings than those without diplomas, and some of them received specialized training that they could use in jobs and careers after the military. Boys could postpone or interrupt their military service if they gained university entrance. The government allowed formal study to take priority, on the principle that educated men could serve their country more effectively than could uneducated conscripts. Called up by the military after high school, Anushiravan Qermezi had completed a year of a mandatory two-year stint when the government granted him a leave to study accounting at a university. He was uncertain about his military obligations for the second year and hoped to perform alternative service, perhaps as a teacher.

Those who wanted to become teachers for nomads (or tribal villagers) could attend the tribal teacher-training school in Shiraz for a year, if they passed the difficult entrance examination and a personal interview with Bahmanbaigi, his successors, or others in the program. They could enter this school at

282 *Life moves on*

different levels of their educational career. When the school began in 1957, some trainees had completed only a few years in primary school. After the nomads' elementary schools became widespread, Bahmanbaigi raised the standards. Applicants in the mid-1960s were required to be sixth-grade graduates, and they needed a high-school diploma in the 1970s.

The Ministry of Education closed the tribal teacher-training school as a facility exclusively for tribal teachers in 1981. After the nomads' educational program resumed independent operation in 1997, the Qashqa'i hoped that the tribal teacher-training program would resume at the original facility or elsewhere, but it did not. The era of special teacher-training for nomadic and tribal youth had ended.

The other option for those wanting to become teachers was to receive pedagogical instruction in other specialized facilities and in high schools and universities. The government established teacher-training centers (*tarbiyat muallim*), and prospective students needed to pass a qualifying examination. The period of required study in all programs increased from one to two years after 1981. Some teachers received two-year or four-year university degrees in elementary or secondary education.

In the history of the tribal teacher-training school, 17 Qermezi men (and no women) completed the program. At least 36 other Qermezi received pedagogical preparation in other institutions, totaling at least 53 teachers (47 males, six females) in 2001. Practically all of them were still teaching that year, and a few others were educational administrators. Two were martyred in the war.

The government forced the original two Qermezi teachers, Akbar and Husain Ali, to retire on state pensions in 2001. They had taught continuously since their training in 1971–72. Akbar located a job in Borujen's cooperative store, while Husain Ali took time off to contemplate his options. Each received a state retirement bonus of several million tumans, which Husain Ali spent on a pickup truck so he and his eldest son (a middle-school dropout with no prospects) could transport commodities for hire.

University education

The founders of the Islamic Republic closed Iran's universities (*danishgah*) in April 1980 so they could launch a "cultural revolution" (*inqilabi-i farhangi*, beginning in June 1980). They aimed to rid campuses of leftists, anti-revolutionaries, shah loyalists, and other political opponents; revamp the curricula to conform with Islamic principles; examine the politico-religious and possibly West-oriented ideologies of all faculty; expel suspect students and staff; and create a proper cultural atmosphere.[85] Universities remained closed until December 1982 when medical and some other technical schools gradually resumed. All were again operating by October 1983.

Initially, on reopening, these institutions allowed only students whose university education had been interrupted to take classes. Later, they admitted new students based on revised entrance examinations. Since beginning the

Life moves on 283

cultural revolution and during the delay before facilities could reconvene and accept continuing and new students, the regime encouraged unemployed high-school graduates (*diplumiha-yi bikar*) to perform national service in Construction Jihad and the literacy campaign. Many high-school graduates and university students who had to postpone their studies joined the revolutionary guards and volunteer militia to fight in the war (a juxtaposition of events that proved harmful and even deadly for them).

The options for undergraduate study after 1982–83 include state, independent, and correspondence universities.[86]

The best universities, the "state" ones (*daulati*), were usually well established, staffed, and equipped and were located in many cities throughout Iran. The Pahlavi shahs had founded them, beginning with Tehran University in 1934–35 (with women able to enroll in 1939–40).[87] Twenty-three state universities operated by 1979, a number rising to 54 by 2010 (12 of which were considered the most prestigious).[88] Under the Islamic Republic, students admitted to the state universities paid no fees for tuition, room, or board. Those attending according to quotas and exemptions received additional scholarships and stipends.

Aspirants for the high-status state universities took the annual national qualifying examination (*kunkur*) to determine if they would be accepted, and where, and for what fields of study. The test had four categories (each student choosing one): physics and mathematics, empirical (natural) sciences, human (social) sciences, and the arts. After taking the examination, students were ranked in their chosen categories. Then they competed for entrance in their favorite universities and disciplines on the basis of their scores and national rankings. Students with the highest rankings could enter the top universities and disciplines. Students who performed poorly in the test often retook it the following summer and perhaps after that as well. They were said to be "following the test" (*pusht-i kunkur*). Students who were not accepted but whose scores were higher than average were placed on a waiting list.

Half a million students each year in the mid- and late-1980s sat for this examination, a number rising to two or three million in the early 2000s. Places in the universities for only 50,000 students initially and perhaps 150,000 later were available.[89]

Zahra Qermezi received her high-school diploma in June 2011 and continued to study for the national university-qualifying examination in her chosen subject, physics and mathematics. She took the test in July. Newspapers published the results in August. Based on her score and ranking, she listed her favorite universities and disciplines. Newspapers published the results in September. There she learned if she had been accepted for university study or not. She was pleased to see that a specific university and discipline were listed for her. She enrolled in that program there in late September.

State officials interviewed those who passed the entrance examination about their knowledge of Islam, politico-religious leanings, and socioeconomic and cultural backgrounds. They were more interested in the loyalty of these

284   *Life moves on*

individuals to the regime than in their religious beliefs and practices. They disqualified students who failed to meet the new standards and did not permit them to begin study.[90] Some students had to explain damaging reports in their files from unidentified individuals, and many were refused admission. Such widespread ideological scrutiny was prevalent in the 1980s, decreased in the 1990s, and increased again in the mid-2000s. People in Iran continued through 2013 to name certain individuals who were denied admission for unstated reasons, despite having passed the academic examination. A Qashqa'i woman told me that she had not known that a graduate-level university program in Tehran had admitted her until a friend reported that her name was on a secret list of accepted students. Her name was not on the published list of those chosen for study.

Of the Qermezi students subjected to such ideological questioning, no one was denied access to university, even if their responses were inadequate. Several students reported that they had intentionally overstated the limitations of their nomadic backgrounds, and interviewers had acknowledged that the students' upbringing prevented them from understanding Islamic ideology.

People in "privileged social groups" received priority in university admissions: war veterans (especially if wounded or disabled), family members of martyrs in the revolution and the war, revolutionary guards, basij militiamen, "crusaders" and "toilers" for Construction Jihad and the literacy campaign, some state-employed hezbollahis, family members of prominent clergymen, and the children of military and security officials.[91] The regime, aiming to draw support from these sectors of society, did not always require these individuals to take the entrance examination, and those who were admitted often lacked the qualifications of those who had placed highly in the test.[92] Similar quotas also applied to students from "deprived" regions (but no Qermezi or other people with whom I spoke knew about or profited from them).[93] Qermezi students complained about difficulties in the classroom because of the disparities. Some admittees were qualified (as determined by the rigorous academic test) while others were not. Also, some students expected that the privileges they received in special-quota admissions would also extend to the level of effort they would need (or not need) to apply in their academic work.

These and some other special quotas decreased in number by the early 2000s, from their high after 1988 (the war's ceasefire) of perhaps 50 percent of all university slots.[94] Those who had wanted to attend university under such quotas, such as men injured in the revolution and the war as well as veterans in general, would probably have already done so by 2000. Other categories of students (revolutionary guards, basijis, state-employed hezbollahis, and children of martyrs, clergymen, and military and security officials) continued through 2013 to be admitted under special quotas. Distinctions among university students between those who were qualified and those who were possibly unqualified persisted and contributed to the growing reality that society was polarized—people who did not support the regime and people who did. (Under the last shah's regime, students tended to view society through socioeconomic lenses—the advantaged and wealthy versus the disadvantaged and poor.)

State universities began to accept students in one of two programs in the early 2000s. Students who ranked high in the qualifying test entered the day program (*ruzanih*). Tuition was free for them. Lower ranking students enrolled in the night program (*shabanih*) and paid tuition (less than charged by the lower caliber independent universities—see later). The highest of the high-ranking students, a limited number, entered the Association of Young Iranian Elites and received special scholarships.[95] Males in this category could fulfill their military obligations concurrently (as compared with having to do so after graduation).

Students attending state universities were subjected to constant surveillance by hezbollahis and basijis and to politico-ideological screening, and they were expected to support and demonstrate loyalty to the Islamic associations on campus. They were expelled if their behavior and speech did not match expected patterns.[96]

Lower-caliber universities include the newly founded, independent, "free" (*azad*) ones (also called open and private universities). They were usually located in towns (and less so in cities) throughout Iran and were of varying but generally poor quality. The first one, the Independent (or Open) Islamic University (danishgah-i azad-i islami), began in 1981, and its many branches and other similar institutions followed throughout the 1980s and into the early 2000s to respond to the rising demands for higher education.[97] These universities introduced their own qualifying examination, which was reportedly less difficult than the state-university one. They also subjected applicants to politico-ideological screening but the criteria were less restrictive than for the state universities.[98] Students who did not gain entrance to the state universities (for academic or political reasons) were often admitted by the independent ones, where they paid high and escalating tuition fees. Such payments, along with donations, supported these universities, whose founders were closely affiliated with the regime's ruling elite. Directors of these institutions often required female students to wear enveloping black chadurs, which they considered more conservative than the overcoats and hoods or scarves that many women wore at the two other types of university.

The third option was the new correspondence universities (*payam-i nur*, "message of light"), government owned and run like the state universities. They are called "distant education" or "long distance" universities. The Islamic Republic had founded them, beginning in 1987, to handle further demands for higher education. Headquarters were in Tehran, and facilities were situated in 30 provincial centers and 500 local study centers and campuses throughout Iran. Students took the same national qualifying examination as those wanting to attend state universities. These correspondence schools enrolled over one million national and international students in 2010.[99]

Correspondence institutions helped to dampen resentment in the hundreds of thousands of failed applicants for state and independent universities every year. Their presence enabled the attendees to claim the title and role of "university

286 *Life moves on*

student," which members of society valued. For the duration, these students (along with those in the other types of universities) avoided the disgrace of being unemployed (bikar) and unable to support themselves. They also eluded the stigma of serving no function in society and having no profession or promising future. These issues affected Iran's socioeconomic classes differently.[100]

Students who registered for the correspondence schools received reading lists for specific subjects and disciplines, studied on their own, took examinations, and received degrees if they passed. They rarely attended any classes. These universities usually lacked professors, instructors, classrooms, libraries, computers, and other equipment, and they often provided only a minimal administrative staff housed in small quarters. In facilities in which classes were held, they often met only on Thursday afternoons and on Fridays, to accommodate students who held jobs, had other commitments during the week, and/or lived a distance away. People including university students often ranked the correspondence schools as superior to the independent (azad) ones, despite—or because of—the lack of teachers and class sessions (a negative judgment about the quality of the faculty and instruction in the independent universities). They regarded degrees from the correspondence schools to be higher in caliber than those from the independent ones.

Vocational (*amuzish-i fanni va hirfii*), technical, agricultural, industrial, business, and secretarial colleges and institutes provided other kinds and different levels of training for students, many of whom did not or could not enroll in any of the three types of universities. Sometimes people mentioned enrollees in these programs when I asked about current and new students but they did not rank these schools among the higher-level educational ones. Vocational programs faced difficulties because jobs appropriate to the students' training were often unavailable.

Students accepted by the state universities usually attended because of the high status of these institutions, lack of tuition, and enhanced potential of employment after graduation. Some students applied for admission only to independent or correspondence universities if they could not live in the cities where the state ones were located. Many female students, especially those with husbands and children, were unable to attend any universities other than the locally available ones, even if they passed entrance examinations.[101] Farzaneh Qarehqanli is a wife and mother who was responsible for a household based in Kazerun during the autumn and winter, and, despite her aspirations, she could not pursue higher education except at Kazerun's independent university. Its schedule did not correspond with that of nomadic pastoralism, and for each of four years she remained behind in Kazerun to complete courses and examinations while her husband and his family migrated to summer pastures. Her young son stayed with his grandparents in Shiraz for the duration. Some other families seemed unwilling to make similar accommodations for their education-aspiring female members.

In these various universities, students studied for a succession of degrees: a two-year post-diploma (post-high-school) degree (*fauq-i diplum, kardani,* or high diploma, sometimes called an associate degree), a four-year degree (*lisans, karshinasi*), a post-graduate degree (*fauq-i lisans* or high license, equivalent to a master's degree), and several other post-graduate degrees (doctoral, medical). Many Qermezi who obtained a post-diploma degree continued to study for a four-year one. Only one person, Masud of Aqa Mohammadli, had achieved a post-graduate degree by 2002, and he was the only holder of a doctorate by 2009. The subtribe lacked any medical-school students or graduates.

Students often extended their university education over many years, in part because jobs were scarce after graduation. Those attending state universities were most likely to follow a set schedule and course of study, and most graduated after the fourth or fifth year. Free tuition, scholarships, and stipends placed them under certain obligations. Students in independent universities were not as regimented by schedules and courses, and their passage through various programs was often prolonged and interrupted. Those enrolled in correspondence universities enjoyed the most flexible schedules, and a series of successfully passed examinations determined their progress.

Many Qermezi men and two Qermezi women who practiced full-time salaried professions in 2001 were simultaneously university students, often in different, sometimes distant, locations. Particularly at independent universities, students often visited campus only once a week during academic terms. Some programs required them to appear before a school administrator or perhaps a teacher once a week but not necessarily for any classes or instruction.

Undergraduate university students (as well as many higher-level ones) attended classes (depending on their programs) and took examinations periodically but other activities were lacking. They owned textbooks, often only one per course, but did not seem engaged or inspired by them. Similar to students in elementary and secondary schools, the scholarly activity of university students consisted of memorizing specific, sometimes single, texts. Academic exercises entailing research, analysis, comparison, original thought, logic, and effective and creative writing did not exist. Students did not engage in independent or collaborative projects, either on-campus or off.[102] Examinations in mathematics, physics, and chemistry were based on problems and formulae laid out in texts, and students were not given new problems to solve.

I observed only one student at any level (primary school through university graduate programs) who engaged in academic work other than the memorization of required texts. Her teacher in a university course on English translation asked students to find 20 examples each of similes, metaphors, personifications, and alliterations in John Steinbeck's *The Grapes of Wrath*. Even seeing these stylistic forms clearly explained on paper, the student was unable to complete any part of the assignment correctly, perhaps because of the novelty of figuring it out independently. The next year, another teacher assigned the same student 30 densely written pages (not sequential) for her to translate from English to Persian. He did not tell her the origin of these pages (from the final chapters of the novel *Middlemarch*), the author (George Eliot), or the date of publication (1871–72), and neither did he explain the story, historical or social context, or

288 *Life moves on*

main characters. (The teacher himself seemed not to know any of this information.) Her task was limited solely to the translation and proved impossibly difficult and defeating. Sentences at the beginning and end of each page were often incomplete. The student was stymied by antiquated usages and obscure literary, historical, and sociocultural references, and she lacked any scholarly resources to consult. (This assignment occurred before any students had access to the Internet.)

People in Iran often complained about state officials who were simultaneously university students and periodically absent from work. They joked that under Mohammad Reza Shah, students graduated from university and then found jobs relevant to their degrees and specialties, while under the Islamic Republic, people secured jobs and *then* began to study the relevant subjects. Under the shah, professional credentials—more likely bogus than not—were necessary for many posts, particularly high-level, high-status ones. Under the Islamic Republic, many individuals obtained high-level, high-status posts because of other factors—their ties to the ruling clergy, affiliation with revolutionary organizations, hezbollahi identity, politico-ideological stance, and war-veteran status—and then decided to acquire professional credentials. Many of them had not yet attended university. They were young and might have come from underprivileged backgrounds, and perhaps the revolution and/or the war had deflected them from educational pursuits. Except for eminent clergymen, many high-level officials of the Islamic Republic were young, originally lower-middle or lower class, inexperienced, and ideologically committed (at least outwardly), as compared with most officials under the shah's government.[103] (Many officials under both regimes claimed to have enrolled in certain institutions and to have earned degrees and titles that they actually lacked, a further complicating factor. The tendency to fabricate educational and professional credentials was not restricted to government officials.)

By the end of 2001, 92 Qermezi individuals had attended university (30 in state ones, 39 in independent ones, nine in correspondence ones, four in advanced teacher-training programs, and 18 undetermined). (Eight students had studied in two types of university, and these figures total 100.) Many students had received teacher-training in various kinds of institutions; the four listed here had taken advanced training in specialized schools. Forty-five of the 92 graduated with four-year degrees, and many of the rest were still university students, some having already received post-diploma degrees. Five of the 45 were women, all Aqa Mohammadli. Of the 45, 24 were Aqa Mohammadli, six Imamverdili, two Qairkhbaili, one Qasemli, 10 Kachili, and two of affiliated families.

The professions of the graduates holding four-year degrees varied widely. They included, for 2000, civil servants, several state officials, teachers (in elementary, middle, and high schools), a university teaching assistant, engineers, a healthworker, a media worker, company employees, revolutionary guards, and a member of parliament. These occupations had not existed for any Qermezi in 1970, when nomadic pastoralism had been the primary livelihood of practically everyone, and only six youngsters (all Aqa Mohammadli boys) had yet completed primary school. At least 30 students still attended university in 2000–01, with many more yet to enroll, and the kinds of occupations will expand and become more prevalent in the future.

High rates of unemployment for university students and graduates characterized Iran as a whole and posed a national crisis. Most young Iranians who desired higher education were not admitted to universities or could not afford the high tuition, thus constituting another crisis.

My data on the Qermezi do not follow these national patterns. Several of those who wanted to attend university were deemed unqualified by academic and perhaps other standards, but almost all of them ended up enrolling in some form of university or other higher educational programs. Almost all individuals who held two-year or four-year university degrees were employed or actively pursuing further education in 2000.

Of the four unemployed graduates in 2000, one had lost his job when the regime shut down a newspaper supportive of President Khatami, and he did not immediately locate comparable work. He was employed in 2001, this time by state-run television in Tehran, and he occasionally conducted on-air interviews, sometimes relating to ethnic minorities. Another graduate, who held a two-year midwifery degree, received a year of state-paid maternity leave and was unemployed in the interim. Two young men discontinued, perhaps temporarily, their pursuit of a higher university degree and remained at home to contribute to the family livelihoods there. Other than these four individuals, all other degree holders had secured salaried jobs pertinent to their specializations or were continuing students.

Three factors explain these patterns, which differ from the national norm. First, most Qermezi students were highly motivated to attend universities and locate employment and were willing to undertake all necessary efforts. They deemed the alternatives—nomadic pastoralism, agricultural work, and low-status wage labor—as unacceptable and knew they needed to persevere to avoid them. Each one's success served as a stimulus for others.

Second, these students were willing to relocate almost anywhere. Many others in Iran, raised in urban areas such as Tehran and other large cities, were averse to moving to less urbanized areas, especially underdeveloped regions and distant provinces. They were likely to be out of school and unemployed in their places of origin where slots and jobs were already scarce. With apparent ease, Qermezi students traveled to all parts of the country for higher education and employment. Perhaps their backgrounds in nomadism and their frequent changes in locations and residences for the sake of productive pastoralism made mobility for education and jobs a comparable, commonplace, and acceptable activity.

Third, practically all of these students lacked the social contexts for being uneducated and unemployed and were uninterested in the trivia of fashion trends, Western youth culture, and electronic gadgetry that dominated the lives of many Iranian youth in urban areas. (Modern technology, particularly

290 *Life moves on*

computers and mobile telephones, had become an essential tool for all university students by 2013 and did not distinguish urban from rural and nomadic youth.) Unlike urbanites, Qermezi students lacked places to gather with their agemates such as streets, parks, restaurants, cinemas, shopping malls, and, later, Internet cafes.[104] They did not stage the parties (for both genders or only one) that the urban middle and upper classes allowed, even encouraged, and where all sorts of behaviors were tolerated. If they stayed home, they were supposed to contribute to the family labor. Idleness was not a virtue, and especially the nomads condemned it when they saw it. Some teenage boys and young men (among the Persian families I visited in Tehran and Shiraz) slept until noon, napped after lunch, took care to adorn themselves, went out with friends until dawn, and engaged in risky, addictive behaviors. Such activities were virtually impossible for Qermezi boys and young men (and even more so for Qermezi girls and young women) in their nomadic camps, villages, and small towns.

Three circumstances underlie the first two factors. First, most students were initially exposed to formal education in the nomads' schools, an intense experience motivating them to work hard, compete, and find satisfaction and reward in their efforts. From the first elementary grade and even earlier, students learned to achieve under rudimentary, sometimes extraordinarily adverse conditions: a long trek to school and back home, sometimes abysmal weather, insufficient food, inadequate clothing, poor lighting for reading and studying, a canvas tent or thatched hut equipped only with a mat (and no desks or chairs) and a chalkboard, and supplies consisting of only chalk, a few tattered texts, and often a single writing utensil. Their teachers, coming from similar if not identical backgrounds and often their own kinsmen, proved to be exceptional guides and role models and were not the detached, even hostile, teachers often found in other kinds of schools. Families of these students expected them to contribute fully to the tasks at home when they were not studying, and students learned early in life to combine school and work, despite difficulties.

Second, students resolved to overcome the obstacles of discrimination. Urban Iranians often viewed rural-dwelling nomads and villagers as backward, unsophisticated, and stupid, and the Persians among them treated this ethnic minority (the Turkish-speaking Qashqa'i) with disdain. Students strove to prove that they could integrate themselves in urban, educational, and professional settings and among the Persian-speaking, dominating majority. They appeared to be more motivated and harder working than many other Iranians who competed for the same slots and posts, and they were often more successful than many others.

Third, despite their strategies to blend into the wider society, these students retained a strong sense of their ethnolinguistic and tribal origins. No matter where and for how long they studied and no matter where their new jobs took them, they were still firmly grounded and integrated in their family, kinship, socioterritorial, lineage, tribal, and ethnolinguistic groups. Their identities as members of these various communities sustained them in sometimes trying circumstances. They admired and modeled their behavior after those who had achieved success in both arenas—those who drew status and income from one setting and social cohesion and emotional support from the other setting.

The immediate families and close kin of these university graduates and continuing university students were often still nomadic pastoralists. The parents and siblings had sacrificed for these students from the time they began formal education in elementary school. Some sent their children for extended periods to live with relatives who resided near schools. These children were lost as laborers at least for the interval and perhaps permanently, and others assumed the burden of work that the students left behind. Families were supportive and patient while these students studied for a series of exacting examinations and progressed up the academic and then professional ladder, one year at a time. Once these graduates obtained professions and jobs, they provided financial and other aid to their families and served as role models for siblings and other young relatives and tribesmates. Practically all of them lived some distance from their kin groups but they managed to visit home often, and they hosted people who periodically sought services in the towns and cities of their employment. Virtually all of these graduates married their cousins or other close relatives, and these extended ties also fortified the bonds with their families and groups of origin.

Formal education had become a viable, accepted option for different categories of Qermezi women by the mid-1990s and early 2000s: those who delayed in marrying or might not marry at all, those who married but did not produce children, and those who were divorced or widowed. An unmarried individual in her late twenties attended an adult-literacy school for women who wanted to advance their education. As a child, she had studied through the fifth grade in a nomads' tent school but had never received a certificate of completion, and she retook the fifth grade along with other adults. Then she entered a women's middle school, hoped to continue through high school, and even began contemplating university. Education was now a valued, legitimate activity for women who did not or were unable to fulfill societal expectations through marriage and motherhood.

Overview

I began this discussion of teachers, schools, and students by noting that early exposure to formal education, even including religious instruction, had privileged the members of Aqa Mohammadli lineage and those living with them, over people of other lineages who had not enjoyed this early access. The disparity also stems from the position of the Qermezi headmen in the Aqa Mohammadli lineage, that group's ties to the Darrehshuri khans and the benefits they offered, and the group's success in obtaining land rights and its resulting economic well-being. Members of the four other lineages found it difficult to reach the educational achievements of the Aqa Mohammadli, given the accelerated pace of this lineage's members. One of Qermezi's first two teachers, Akbar, had produced three teachers among his offspring by

292 *Life moves on*

1999, and many children of other early teachers studied in universities and secured professional jobs. Teachers provided roles to emulate, and this second generation of highly motivated students is already surpassing its parents' achievements.

Notes

1 Parliament, formerly named the National Consultative Majlis, was renamed in 1989 as the Islamic Consultative Majlis.

2 Abu Zar (Abu Dharr) (d. 652) was a famous companion of the prophet Mohammad and a warrior for Imam Ali. He criticized the early caliphs for their extravagance and accumulation of wealth, and he traveled to the desert to lead a simple life. The caliph, Uthman, had possibly banished him to exile there. Ali Shariati (d. 1977) translated from Arabic to Persian an account of Abu Zar's life (1978). He considered Abu Zar the "first Muslim socialist" (Chehabi 1990: 188). Some Iranians called Shariati, a prominent lecturer and writer on Islam in the 1970s, the "Abu Zar of modern Iran" (Abrahamian 1989: 106, 112). Some considered Ayatollah Taleqani (d. 1979) to be "Abu Zar-i zaman" (Abu Zar of the Age). Fellow basij militiamen bestowed the name Abu Zar on Shahriyar Qermezi in recognition of his battlefield prowess. Part of all militia units, clergymen offered classes on Islam, the Qur'an, Arabic, and early Islamic heroes. Shahriyar's original name is Isfandiyar. He had wanted to attend the tribal teacher-training school in Shiraz but was too young (not yet 17, the minimum age), and he acquired a new identity card under a new name and birth year so he could enroll.

3 Many tribal teachers at the time had similar educational histories, with only a few years of formal education before they began their jobs.

4 Whenever I visited Sohrab, he would mention the battles and ask me to feel the shrapnel permanently lodged in his arms and legs. His photograph is in Beck (1991: 83).

5 Islamic custom requires men to trim (and not shave) their facial hair. Shaving off someone's beard shamed a man perceived to be guilty of a transgression (Najmabadi 2005: 279).

6 The Indians also wore shorts, a novel form of dress for the Qashqa'i. Bahadori-Kashkuli illustrates the combatants on the cover of Yusufi's book (2001).

7 Two of these deputies were khans of the Darrehshuri tribe. Parliament under Mohammad Reza Shah had been bicameral with an upper house (senate) and a lower house (majlis). Meeting for the first time in 1950, the senate was filled mainly with shah loyalists. The Islamic Republic's new constitution eliminated the senate.

8 Armenian Christians in northern and southern Iran were each entitled to elect a representative. Assyrian and Chaldean Christians jointly elected one deputy, and Zoroastrians and Jews each elected one (Sanasarian 1995, 2000). The state denied the Bahais a representative. Non-Muslim religious minorities are one to two percent of Iran's population and have undergone high rates of emigration since 1978. Schirazi (1997) discusses the provisions for religious and ethnic minorities during the deliberations for Iran's new constitution in 1979. Ethnic minorities are half of Iran's population; the other half consists of ethnic Persians (Beck 2013, n.d. a).

9 Sarabi (1994) and Moslem (2002: 181–86) discuss the 1992 election for the fourth parliament.

10 Many citizens were newly claiming sayyid status after the revolution, and Subhani might have alluded to such an identity for himself when he considered ways to

Life moves on 293

draw attention to his candidacy. The sudden, widespread fabrication of sayyid status in the region (and in Iran as a whole) alerted the Qermezi as early as 1979 to the kind of chicanery they would face in their interactions with the wider, newly Islamizing Iranian society.

11 Adelkhah (2000: 79–104) provides a largely Tehran-focused perspective on the important 1996 parliamentary election, which served as a preamble to the presidential election in 1997 (in which the popular reformist, Mohammad Khatami, was the unexpected winner). Menashri (2001: 67–73) and Moslem (2002: 227–40) also discuss this election.

12 Iran's administrative divisions are provinces (*ostan*; 26 in 1996; 31 in 2013), electoral districts (*shahristan*; 195 in 1996; 202 in 2007), smaller districts (*bakhsh*; 501), cities (*shahr*; 496), and rural districts (*dehistan*; 1,582) (Hourcade et al. 1998: 25). The 270 parliamentary deputies (290 since the 2000 elections) come from these districts (shahristan), the non-Muslim minorities, and cities. Of the 290 deputies, 202 come from Muslim-majority, territorial, electoral districts; five from Christian, Jewish, and Zoroastrian communities; and 83 from cities. According to Iran's 1986 census, Semirom district had a population of 61,000 (Hourcade et al. 1998: 26). The 1996 census lists its increase to 65,000 (Statistical Centre of Iran 1999). The district, located in the very south of Isfahan province and shaped like a peninsula there, had 123 (or 139) villages and four "cities" (including Semirom) in 1996 and was one of the province's least urban (and most rural) districts. Chaharmahal Bakhtiyari is the province bordering the district to the west, Kuh Giluyeh va Boir Ahmad province is to the southwest, and Fars province is to the southeast. Isfahan province had 19 districts, a number rising to 22 by 2005. The government named one of the new districts in the province as Lower Semirom. People also refer to this district as Dehaqan, its central town. The town of Dehaqan had been part of Shahreza district in 1996. Semirom district is also known as Upper Semirom because of the mountains there. (Lower Semirom is north of Upper Semirom; the adjectives refer to elevations.) Citizens in Semirom district protested in 2003 when the central government tried to reallocate the territory of Vardasht to the new Lower Semirom district. Security forces killed and injured many people, and the conflict received international attention as evidence of growing opposition to the Islamic Republic. The conflict, instead, represented a local administrative dispute and was not explicitly anti-regime.

13 Citizens needed to vote in the same district for the primary and runoff elections; they could not change locations from the first round to the second. Total votes in any area could exceed the number of qualified voters there because people could vote outside their place of residence. The Western press often regards any such disparity as indicating fraud, which might not be the case. Politicians and others with special interests did transport voters from one locale to another (such as to Tehran where the stakes were high) to try to alter the results.

14 No population figures for districts, broken down by ethnicity, are available.

15 Adelkhah (2000: 83) notes the positive qualities of successful candidates in Tehran and other cities in 1996, qualities that Shahriyar also possessed: "exceptional personalities, outstanding because of their youth, their looks, their professionalism or efficiency, their academic qualifications, their energy and their independence."

16 Interlineage marriage enabled a person to find sanctuary in another group and to have access to alternative pastures.

17 Even as a sayyid and an akhund, Imadi seemed not to be significant in the clerical establishment in the town and district. He continued to play the roles that such figures had exhibited under the shah's regime. District residents did not view him as a rising figure in the new clerical elite.

18 Baktiari (1996: 109–10). He includes (on page 244) a chart of the complicated, highly politicized approval process for parliamentary candidates in the first four

294 *Life moves on*

elections (1980, 1984, 1988, 1992) and discusses (on pages 65–66) the operations of supervising the early elections. To maintain the power of hard-line conservatives in government, the Guardian Council increasingly exercised strict control in its use of politico-ideological factors to determine eligibility, especially for parliamentary elections in 2000 and thereafter. Its selection was "equivalent to a real pre-election in advance of the people's choice" (Adelkhah 2000: 80). Candidates who were otherwise eligible lost the chance to run because of politics and ideology. The council barred in 2004 87 current deputies (80 of them reformists) from running for another term. Such manipulations in 2005 and 2009 tainted the primary and runoff presidential elections, contributed to low turnouts, and helped to elect and reelect the neoconservative Ahmadinejad.

19 For the election of the fourth parliament (1992), candidates could officially campaign for only a week, a period ending 24 hours before polling began.

20 Sarabi (1994) analyses the 1992 parliamentary election as a contest between two prominent factions, the Association of Militant Clergy (*ruhaniyat*) (a long-standing pragmatic conservative group, then led by President Rafsanjani) and the Society of Militant Clerics (*ruhaniyun*) (a new group in 1988 advocating the continuation of Khomeini-era policies). Writers describe the principal tendencies as they emerged and changed in Iran's national politics since 1979 as radical fundamentalist, conservative, pragmatist, and reformist. These leanings appear in a wide range of political associations, which changed from one election to the next. Moslem (2002) discusses the period from 1979 to 2000. Such tendencies and political associations did not resonate at the local level of Qashqa'i nomads and villagers, who seemed uninformed and disinterested.

21 For the title of imam for Khomeini, see Chapter 5 (note 11).

22 Shahriyar's seemingly random list of categories is similar to Khomeini's in his arrival speech in Tehran in 1979: religious scholars, students, merchants, traders, youth in the bazaar, youth in university, professors, judges, civil servants, workers, and peasants (Algar 1981: 252–53).

23 The Iranian film, *Secret Ballot* (Payami 2001), depicts a female election official coming by boat to an island off Iran's Persian Gulf coast to receive the inhabitants' votes. A plane dropped the ballot box there early in the morning.

24 In northwestern Iran, more volunteers for the war came from the villages and small towns of Ardabil (which became a province in 1993) than from the large city of Tabriz (Chehabi 1997: 240–41). More volunteers and enlistees from Tehran came from the lowest socioeconomic groups, including migrant laborers, which was probably also the case with Tabriz. Fromanger (2013) discusses migrant workers in a largely Azeri Turkish community south of Tehran and their participation in the war.

25 Bahluli-Qashqa'i (1996–2000). Bahluli is the only one of the five Qashqa'i deputies having "Qashqa'i" as part of his formal name (according to one list, Sohrab Bohluli Ghashghaei).

26 Sohrabi (1995).

27 Many candidates were on the ballot in Shiraz, and voters seem to have selected the most qualified ones without necessarily being familiar with their ethnolinguistic backgrounds. The names of most candidates (such as "Husain Muradi") offered no clues about their ethnic and tribal identities. Other than the Qashqa'i who voted there, people in Shiraz did not go to the polls planning to elect Qashqa'i candidates. Even Qashqa'i voters were astonished by the improbable result.

28 Muntajabniya was elected as Shiraz's deputy at least five times (Baktiari 1996: 104, 151, 156), including in 2000. A list of the three elected parliamentary deputies for Shiraz in 1996 includes the two Qashqa'i men and Ahmad Nejabat (and not Muntajabniya). www.iranonline.com/iran/iran-info/government/Majlis/Majlis-members-1996.html (accessed 2 January 2014).

29 Reformists gained the majority in the sixth session of parliament (2000–04).

Life moves on 295

30 All deputies in the Islamic Republic's first parliament (1980–84) were new. No members of parliament under Mohammad Reza Shah ran for election under the new regime; the government would not have permitted them to do so.
31 Menashri (2001: 72); see also Baktiari (1996: x).
32 These kinds of sentiments also appear elsewhere. Referring to parliamentary debates on everyday concerns, "deputies, particularly those from obscure villages," speak their minds (Sciolino 2005: 299). Rafsanjani warned that a constituent assembly that would write the constitution in 1979 "would be packed with backward and ignorant delegates from far corners of the country" (Katouzian 2009: 336).
33 This national trend has brought new scholarly attention to areas outside Tehran; see Gheissari and Sanandaji (2009) and Tohidi (2009).
34 See note 12 in this chapter, for other information on Semirom district.
35 Vanak is one of the district's largest villages and was deserving of services, but Shahriyar might have also wanted to build goodwill among its citizens. A Vanak resident had lost the deputyship to him. Chehabi (1997: 237–40) discusses the process of upgrading territorial divisions in Iran and the resulting administrative and economic advantages for local populations.
36 These and other appointments of Darzi men might have stemmed in part from Shahriyar's obligations to his predecessor, a Darzi man.
37 Many parliamentary deputies came from rural areas and the provinces where ethnic minorities predominated, and often they (and other officials) did not hesitate to link themselves to their regions of origin (Adelkhah 2000: 88, Chehabi 1997). Deputies introduced their provincial and ethnic identities during speeches on the floor (Sanasarian 2000: 6). Gheissari and Sanandaji (2009) and Sanandaji (2009) list provinces where more than 50 percent of the population consists of ethnolinguistic minorities. Other provinces may also have over 50 percent, depending on how the term "minorities" is defined.
38 Bahram was too frugal to host these gatherings and was not well integrated at Hanalishah because of his hezbollahi stance.
39 A Qashqa'i student who periodically visited Iran set aside one day every week to handle the problems, usually minor, of his relatives and their acquaintances (such as mailing a letter and buying a bus ticket, tasks they could have managed on their own).
40 The daughter of a Qashqa'i khan (of the formerly ruling Janikhani family) visited Shahriyar Qermezi to ask his help in securing the return of confiscated land (an issue fraught with legal and political complications). He addressed her as "Hajji Khanum" (Pilgrim Lady), a generic term of respect for a married Persian woman. He did not utter her Qashqa'i title, Bibi, used for women in the khan families (anonymous, personal communication, 5 August 2011).
41 Iran's 1986 census lists 158,000 people for Mamassani district and 213,000 for Kazerun district (Hourcade et al. 1998: 26). The 1996 census lists 161,000 people for Mamassani district and 255,000 for Kazerun district (Statistical Centre of Iran 1999). See note 12 in this chapter, which lists the population of Semirom district.
42 Shahreza (Qumshah) district held 151,000 people in 1986 (Bernard Hourcade, personal communication, 5 May 2001). The 1996 census lists 164,000 people for Shahreza district (Statistical Centre of Iran 1999).
43 Imadi's first name is listed as Keramatullah in the news accounts of the conflict over redistricting in Semirom in 2003. He opposed the efforts of the Ministry of Interior in Isfahan province to attach Vardasht (a key area of Semirom district) to the new Lower Semirom district. In supporting the citizens of Semirom, he appears to have acquitted himself well.
44 As First Vice President, Jahangiri is first in the line of succession for the presidency. He was elected as a parliamentary deputy for Jiroft district in Kerman province in 1984 and 1988. Most people there are ethnic Baluch.

296 *Life moves on*

45 Turnover of deputies averaged nearly 60 percent for the second, third, and fourth parliamentary sessions (Baktiari 1996: x). In the first nine elections (1980–2012), this pattern held, and the incumbency-return rate was low (averaging 29 percent) (Farhi 2010). Twelve deputies survived the first four elections; 10 survived the first five (Baktiari 1996: 219, Menashri 2001: 77). The Guardian Council disqualified some or many deputies who wanted to run again (for example, 87 of them in 2004), other deputies chose not to be candidates or boycotted the election or were forced to withdraw under pressure, still others were not reelected, and a few who were reelected had their election contested and/or annulled. Baktiari and most other writers do not offer statistics on these four separate categories. Sarabi (1994: 101) does note that, of the 269 deputies in the third parliament (1988–92), the Guardian Council disqualified 39 of them from running for the fourth parliament, 20 did not seek reelection, and more than 126 of the rest lost in the election. Only 80 deputies in the third parliament took seats in the fourth, a rate of 30 percent.

46 Limitations of space prevent me from discussing parliamentary elections in southwestern Iran in 2004, 2008, and 2012, as they pertain to the Qashqa'i. Sanandaji (2009) discusses the eighth parliamentary election in 2008.

47 The final sentence of the *Encyclopaedia Iranica*'s subentry on rural and tribal schools (under the entry, Education) (Bahmanbeygi et al. 1998: 212) is misleading and possibly incorrect: "All these schools were closed after the revolution of 1979." This sentence follows a statement about Bahmanbaigi's programs in other parts of Iran but seems to refer to his entire program, much of which remained in place in southwestern Iran (although under other auspices after 1982) and operated with little interruption through 2013. The subentry peculiarly identifies the schools Bahmanbaigi directed as *maktab*, a term not used at the time by him, his program, or his teachers or students. The encyclopedia's editors must have added the word but their reasons for doing so are unclear.

48 For accounts of Quranic schools (maktab) and other forms of traditional Islamic education in Iran, see Akhavi (1980), Dustkhah and Yaghmai (1998: 180–82), Fischer (1980), Menashri (1992), and R. Mottahedeh (1985). Abedi (Fischer and Abedi 1990: 3–92) provides an autobiographical account.

49 One son, Khuda Bakhsh, appears frequently in the book *Nomad* (Beck 1991).

50 Point Four was a social and economic program intended for many third-world countries in which the U.S. held strategic and other vital interests. President Truman began the program in 1950 with Iran as its first recipient. Point Four teams were implementing a wide array of projects throughout Iran by 1952. Its many alumni served as Iran's managerial elite in public and private institutions. Helen Jeffreys, grandmother of Davar Ardalan (2007: 53–57), participated in a mobile health unit. Monir Farmanfarmaian (2007: 159–64) worked in Point Four's traditional handicrafts project. Gagon (1956) and Warne (1956) discuss Point Four's educational program.

51 Bahmanbaigi (2000: 263–64) includes photographs of female teacher-trainees taking examinations. All wear the elaborate dress of their tribal groups. They sit on folding chairs and write their answers on papers resting in their laps. The cover of Keddie and Baron's book (1991) on Middle Eastern women shows a young Qashqa'i woman reading.

52 For accounts of Bahmanbaigi and his educational program for nomadic and tribal children, see Bahmanbaigi (2000), Barker (1981), Beck (1986: 271–85), Gagon (1956), Hendershot (1964), Sabahi (2003), Shaghasemi (2011), Shahshahani (1995), and Sohrabi (1995). A. Milani (2008: 953–58) includes an entry on Bahmanbaigi as one of Iran's 150 "eminent Persians." Other individuals in this collection are also not Persians but Milani intentionally omits their actual ethnicities and identities. I periodically interviewed Bahmanbaigi in 1969–1971 and 1977 and observed his activities in the administrative headquarters, tribal secondary school, tribal

Life moves on 297

teacher-training school, weaving school, and many elementary schools. I also interviewed him in 1991–99 after his forced retirement. I conducted research on Bahmanbaigi's teachers, students, and school inspectors and talked with others who were familiar with Bahmanbaigi and his program. Despite many published accounts of this successful educational project, including widespread newspaper and periodical coverage in Iran and abroad from 1953 to 1979, Menashri (1992) does not mention it or the influential U.S. Point Four program in his comprehensive history of formal education in twentieth-century Iran. He notes incorrectly (on pages 170–71) that Iran's nomadic tribal people showed no interest in education and that government programs among them failed. Bahmanbaigi's program for the nomadic and tribal people of southwestern Iran (which he expanded to other parts of Iran) was one of the most outstanding educational projects in the entire country in the twentieth century, even without considering the difficulties in introducing formal education to a rural, dispersed, mobile, and often non-Persian-speaking population. Photographs of Iran during the shah's regime often include images of Qashqa'i children and their tent schools, an emblematic portrayal of the modernizing times and the enthusiastic acceptance of formal education by even the "uneducated" ethnic minorities. Thus Menashri's omission is puzzling. The film *Gabbeh* (Makhmalbaf and Ahmadi 1996) features a school for Qashqa'i nomads.

53 A Qashqa'i tribal teacher figures in a fictionalized short story about Iran (O'Donnell 1999: 135–49). A Qashqa'i teacher also appears in the film *Gabbeh* (1996).

54 Bahmanbaigi did not accept any children of the Qashqa'i khans for his tribal teacher-training program or for the tribal middle schools and high schools. He said he needed to give opportunities to non-elite Qashqa'i, not the elite, who would succeed on their own because of their privileged socioeconomic position. He had no way of knowing that the next regime (Islamic Republic) would also discriminate against the Qashqa'i elite and that the youth of both eras would be similarly disadvantaged. Three generations of these elite families have now lacked the opportunities that many non-elite Qashqa'i have enjoyed. Many non-elite Qashqa'i (such as some Qermezi) have attained socioeconomic positions that are superior to those of the (former) khans and their children. Some elite women have been enterprising in their entrepreneurial strategies to support their families. Their male age cohorts, often unskilled, undereducated, and perpetually unemployed, have faced problems with alcoholism, drug addiction, and other risky behaviors.

55 U.S. Peace Corps volunteers teaching in the tribal secondary school in Shiraz include Brad Hansen and Paul Barker (1981), the latter of whom published an article about Bahmanbaigi.

56 Bahmanbaigi (2000: 259–62) includes photographs of teachers and students in schools.

57 Bahmanbaigi (2000: 216) includes a photograph of such an assembly in which at least 14 white school tents are pitched for students.

58 As a university student in Shiraz in 1963–64, I attended such a gathering along with the governor-general of Fars province, other Iranian authorities, and a bevy of foreigners including American officials. While Bahmanbaigi examined the pupils' expertise, the officials and foreigners wandered about looking at camels and goat-hair tents. He had instructed a tribal headman to transport eight tents to the location just before our arrival. No debris marred the pristine terrain, and the shelters lacked all the equipment necessary for nomadic pastoralism. Camels provided an exotic background for photographs, and the headman, after Bahmanbaigi's suggestion, had positioned them for effect, too. Bahmanbaigi had staged this elaborate, contrived scene for his guests, none of whom understood the deception. By pairing a semblance of traditional life (as represented by camels and tents) with modern formal education, he suggested two scenarios simultaneously.

298 *Life moves on*

Spectators could choose which one better fit their interests. Formal education was compatible with this way of life, or it held the power to supplant this life and integrate the people in modern society. Bahmanbaigi invited me to travel with him for a day in 1977 while he inspected three Qashqa'i nomads' schools southwest of Shiraz. No dignitaries or other foreigners were present, and he conducted his task professionally and without the grandstanding I had seen in 1963–64. Teachers, students, and he seemed to have a genuine mutual respect and appreciation.

59 Bahmanbaigi (personal communication, 27 July 1999) listed prominent individuals in Iranian society who succeeded in life after having been students and/or teachers in his educational program. He was especially proud of—and took partial credit for—the parliamentary deputies, high-level ministry officials, and published authors. Hundreds of Qashqa'i abroad whom I have interviewed over a 40-year span had been Bahmanbaigi's students and/or teachers, and they all stressed the positive impact of these experiences on their lives.

60 The Nadirli claim that their ancestors had been the original leaders of the Darrehshuri tribe, before the Darrehshuri khan family established its pre-eminence. Generations later, members of this subtribe turned to formal education as a way to (re)assert their status.

61 Between 1959 and the year their communities received schools, a few Qermezi students living near villages or towns attended school there.

62 The school at Hanalishah closed in 1997 but its students continued at the Dashtak school during a lengthened school year.

63 Journalists and scholars often note that the Islamic Republic in 1979 and thereafter forced all schools in Iran to be gender segregated. They rarely add that secular, government-run, elementary and secondary schools in Iran had usually been segregated since their formation under Reza Shah (1925–41) and throughout the modernizing reign of Mohammad Reza Shah (1941–79). They also do not note the exceptions in all three eras, such as thousands of nomads' schools and many thousands of small rural schools. On this issue (enforced gender segregation) and others (such as coerced veiling), writers sometimes seem to be motivated by political agendas when they advance particular points of view that might not conform to reality on the ground.

64 Bahmanbaigi enjoyed considerable latitude in decision making and might not have wanted to press the government to introduce inflexible policies. He exercised power in the choices he made to grace one group with a school and to deny another one the same advantage.

65 Sabahi (2001, 2002a, 2002b, 2003) discusses the Literacy Corps. Bahram Soroush (personal communication, 4 July 2009) taught as a Literacy Corps teacher in the town of Nurabad-Mamassani in the 1970s, and the close ties he established with his students were still evident decades later. As a Bakhtiyari Lur, he said he felt close to his Mamassani Lur students. After the revolution, the Islamic Republic developed a similar literacy ("anti-illiteracy") campaign and also employed "soldier-teachers" who served in lieu of their military obligations. Construction Jihad took on many tasks that the shah's special corps had handled.

66 The Qashqa'i call these individuals *kaka siah* (black brothers) and *dada siah* (black sisters).

67 Bahmanbaigi's father had served as a subordinate to the paramount Qashqa'i khans, which sensitized Bahmanbaigi to issues of status.

68 Bahmanbaigi's teacher-trainees entered the program already motivated to bring education to children, and they encountered students who responded enthusiastically. These students were often their own relatives and tribesmates, and teachers had a vested interest in their success.

69 Chamran had engaged in military attacks against Iran's Kurds in 1979 (including summary executions), and the Qashqa'i opposed having a Qashqa'i primary

school named after him. One teacher complained, "Won't these young children learn that Chamran could have turned his gun against them?".

70 Huang (2009: plate 5) includes a photograph of the Dashtak school and some of its students in 1995. Students there ordinarily studied outdoors or used a canvas tent. The stone structure was for inclement weather.

71 The school principal in 2011 was Aliyar Qermezi, and most teachers were Persians from Borujen. Eighty students were enrolled in the elementary school, and Atakula's middle-school and high-school students continued to travel to Borujen. In the elementary school's history, 15 students had received a four-year university degree and one a master's degree. Ten more were still attending university in 2011, and three more were master's-degree candidates.

72 By segregating schools according to gender throughout Iran and making modest coverings for girls compulsory, the Islamic Republic lessened the sociocultural impediments against girls attending school. Jahani (2006) makes the same point for Baluchistan. The spread of modest dress among middle-class girls and women throughout the Islamic world has enabled females to pursue formal education and work outside the home, when otherwise their families might have restricted them.

73 Handwoven textiles often play a role in Qashqa'i-told narratives. The Qashqa'i use the language of weaving and textiles as a vital part of their stories (Dareshuri and Beck 2014).

74 Students with low marks could not enter the next grade. Ali said he refused on moral grounds to raise students' marks, especially if parents or others tried to offer him illicit payments.

75 Huang (2009: 107–48) provides a detailed account of the life of Nahid Qermezi, one of these tribal high-school students.

76 Mehran (1989: 35–50, 2002) discusses the indoctrination of schoolchildren. Siavoshi (1996) compares the content of high-school textbooks under the shah and in the Islamic Republic.

77 Beck (2013, n.d. a) discusses these issues. Members of tribal, ethnolinguistic, and national minorities are highly politicized and are often organized to resist state incursions, even in the guise of formal education. "Nomads," without considering their other identities, are not politicized and organized in these ways (unless their mobility and dispersal across the landscape are taken into account). These different kinds of often-overlapping identities complicate a discussion of Iran.

78 A seven-year-old is six according to Western calculations. Children officially began school according to the age listed on their identity card, which often included incorrect and intentionally misleading information. Whatever their ages, children tended to be mature because of their heavy work responsibilities and the ways adults treated them.

79 The Qermezi newly residing in villages and towns were motivated by the opportunities that education could provide, not by the state's regulations for universal primary education.

80 Secondary education for all boys and some or most girls was the norm in villages and especially towns and cities. For boys these ages, activities other than idleness or manual labor were lacking.

81 Under pressure from parents and kin groups, students in elementary and middle school usually repeated grades rather than dropping out. Those in high school were more likely to withdraw (perhaps temporarily) than to suffer the shame of repeating a grade they had earlier failed.

82 Practically all students graduating from the tribal high school from 1968 (its founding) through 1979 passed at high levels the national qualifying examination for state universities. No other high school in Iran had such an exceptional record. Often the top-scoring students nationwide came from the tribal high school in Shiraz.

300 *Life moves on*

83 The regime renamed the tribal school as Shahid Beheshti Boarding High School (*dabiristan-i shabaniruzi Shahid Beheshti*). ("Martyr" Beheshti, a leading cleric and politician in the Islamic Republic, was killed in a bombing in 1981.) Sohrab Dolatkhah (personal communication, 8 June 2011) was a Qashqa'i student in this "ashayiri high school" in 1985–89. At the time, he saw no physical traces of Bahmanbaigi's (former) program. The Ministry of Education had confiscated its facilities and equipment for its own schools. Dolatkhah and his classmates searched for the high school's piano and projector, retrieved them, and brought them back to their school.

84 For years, even for a decade or more, some individuals asserted that they were still preparing for tests they had earlier failed. Those living in houses placed these books on living-room shelves, as if to demonstrate their persistence to their family and visitors.

85 Iran's clerical leaders needed to find "a way to entirely remould the educational process so that it would produce obedient individuals subservient to Khomeini's vision of society as interpreted by the IRP [Islamic Republican Party]. The call for a cultural revolution which would completely transform education and render it compatible with the needs of Iran's post-revolutionary Islamic state became a perfect excuse for closing and conducting a thorough purge in the universities" (Rahnema and Nomani 1990: 224). Mir-Hosseini (2009: 182–83) describes the harsh ideological interview she underwent after her successful academic interview for a university teaching post in Tehran. Nafisi (2003), who taught in universities in Tehran at the time, offers a personal perspective on the impact of this cultural revolution.

86 Two further types of university are *ghair-i intifai* (nonprofit) and *ilmi karburdi*.

87 Reza Shah founded the Ministry of Education in 1936. Tehran University was still Iran's only such institution in 1943. Iran's first provincial university was established in Tabriz by Azerbaijan's autonomous government in 1946.

88 Sharif Polytechnic University in Tehran was the most distinguished of the state universities. Only students earning the highest scores on the national entrance examination were admitted. Its graduates often emigrated, tempted by education and employment abroad, a significant "brain drain" (*farar-i maghzha*) for Iran.

89 The scholarly literature lists contradictory numbers for the students each year taking the university-qualifying examination and for the university slots available then. Some writers consider only the state universities while others include the independent and/or correspondence ones, which accounts for part of the discrepancy. International news services and the foreign press reported a large political demonstration in front of the locked gates of Isfahan's state university on 15 July 1999. They connected this event with protests on and near university campuses in Tehran and other cities during the previous days, later said to be Iran's largest political crisis since 1981 (and until the 2009 presidential election). Yet the Isfahan event consisted only of crowds of families and friends anxiously waiting for students to emerge after having completed their qualifying examination for university admittance (personal observation that day).

90 Habibi (1989) details the scrutiny. Neighborhood committees (komiteh) and imams of local mosques provided information on candidates. Such data were usually not available for applicants of rural and especially nomadic backgrounds.

91 These "privileged social groups" received preferential treatment because of their contributions to the regime. To gain university entrance, they competed only with other applicants in their social group, and they were more likely to be admitted than regular applicants (Habibi 1989: 28).

92 Rastegar (1996) discusses the impact of this policy on the training of often unprepared and unqualified students in medical school and the low quality of

Life moves on 301

their eventual medical services. Mohammad Muradi, a Darrehshuri Qashqa'i man, joined the volunteer militia only to be able to enter university. With average marks on the entrance examination, he would not have been admitted otherwise (Naheed Dareshuri, personal communication, 6 November 2011).

93 Habibi (1989) does not discuss quotas for students from "deprived" regions, and this category might have emerged after 1988. Some sources, perhaps covering later periods, mention such quotas but offer no specifics (Amuzegar 1993: 280, Omid 1994: 163). A predetermined number of university entrants every year included applicants from Iran's "less developed provinces" (Amirahmadi 1990: 216, 218). These entrants received state scholarships and were required to work in their home provinces for a specified period after graduation. The government in 1993–94 assigned 500 university places to high-school students from "deprived regions" (*manatiq-i mahrum*) (six provinces listed) (Mojab and Hassanpour 1996: 243). This number is smaller than the government had intended in the late 1980s. Some well-off urban families sent their children to economically underdeveloped provinces for the twelfth (and final) grade of high school, to increase their chances for university admission. A prominent Tehran family (personal communication, 1999) sent its university-aspiring son to live in a remote rural village near Kerman in hopes that his location would improve his chances for admission.

94 Habibi (1989: 32–33) lists the percentages of university seats reserved for "privileged social groups" in various educational fields for four academic years (1985–89). All percentages rose during this four-year span. The social groups he lists are handicapped veterans, families of martyrs, basij militia veterans, and "crusaders" for the literacy campaign. Sohrab Dolatkhah (personal communication, 8 June 2011) reports that the quota for war veterans alone (basijis who had participated in the war for at least six months) was 40 percent until a few years after the war. Then the number dropped to 20 percent. He says that no quota existed in 2011 for any basijis who fought in the war.

95 Khamenei founded this elite association (*bunyad-i milli-yi nukhbigan-i iran*) in 2003 for the highest ranking university students.

96 Habibi (1989). A paramilitary organization affiliated with the revolutionary-guard corps—Jihad for Universities—recruited Islamists in universities (Ehteshami and Zweiri 2007: 185).

97 Seventy-three independent universities operated in 1988 in 70 towns and cities throughout Iran. These open or "free" universities constituted a powerful national network by 1996, when they were found in 130 towns and cities, had teaching staffs of 10,000, and held 530,000 students (Adelkhah 2000: 86). Branches increased to 400 in 2010. Some independent universities offered master's and doctoral programs. These institutions are "the country's equivalent of a community college" (Rubin 2001: 101). Soon these private institutions were the major producers of Iran's growing numbers of unemployed university graduates (Kian-Thiebaut 1998: 237). They accepted more new students in all fields in 1990 than did all the state-run universities put together (Rastegar 1996: 224). The Ministry of Science and Higher Education recognized the certificates issued by the independent universities. Iran's Azad University established branches in 2010 in many other countries, with more scheduled for the future. The plan of the shah's regime for an open university, for mass general education, had not been realized at the time of the shah's ouster.

98 Habibi (1989: 28n).

99 Government officials declared in 2008 that Arabic would be the second language of the correspondence universities and that all services would be offered in Arabic as well as Persian.

100 University education and degrees for the lower and lower-middle classes led to economic and social mobility. Many prominent figures in the new Islamic

302 *Life moves on*

government came from these classes. For the middle classes, education and degrees meant that people's economic and social positions might remain stable, yet Iran's persisting economic problems decreased the size of these classes. The upper classes now held two components, individuals whose families had been prosperous under the shah's regime and those who were among the Islamic regime's new elites. The Islamic regime often forbade admission to Iran's universities to the children of the former elites, and many university-aspiring youth emigrated. The regime gave the children of the new elites favorable treatment in university admission through special quotas and did not ordinarily require them to take the university-entrance examination (which they might have failed).

101 For several years a Qashqa'i woman living in Tehran flew weekly to Mashhad in northeastern Iran to complete requirements for her master's degree at the state university there. She enjoyed ample support at home, including her husband, her aunt and mother-in-law, and several household assistants, and her children were already of school age.

102 Every year for many years, Julia Huang (2009) organized her classmates in the U.S. and the nomad children in elementary, middle, and high school to write letters to one another. The nomad children had difficulty understanding the project and writing their individual letters, despite having copies of letters (translated into Persian) that the U.S. students wrote. They had never before faced a creative exercise like this one.

103 Mahmud Ahmadinejad (Iran's president in 2005–13) exemplifies these traits. Not a cleric, he had served in the revolutionary-guard corps, which led to his appointment as Tehran's mayor. The alienation of established technocrats and their replacement by ideologically motivated revolutionaries—an exchange of technical expertise (*takhassus*) for ideological commitment (*taahhud*)—was one outcome of the revolution (Amirahmadi 1990: 90). Habibi (1989) discusses the immediate and long-term negative consequences for the Islamic Republic of favoring unqualified candidates (at the expense of qualified ones) for university admission and high-level public-sector jobs.

104 Alavi (2005), Basmenji (2005), A. Bayat (2010: 115-58), Khosravi (2008), Mahdavi (2009), and Moaveni (2005) describe the social activities of urban youth. Technical and engineering students from the lower and lower-middle classes performed better than higher-class students because they were less distracted by an affluent modern social life (Chehabi 1990: 97).

8 Decisions and consequences
Reflections on 1997 and 1998

The changing economic and political context placed demands and pressures on all Qermezi families. Three examples of individual choices illuminate the wider environment in which these nomads lived. A nomadic pastoralist decided to abandon the livelihood, two brothers struggled to devise strategies to meet their divergent economic and social needs, and Iran's security forces arrested a man implicated in a murder.

Mohammad Karim Qermezi sells his flock

Mohammad Karim Qermezi decided in the spring of 1997 to sell all his sheep and goats and find a livelihood other than nomadic pastoralism. Qermezi nomads at Hanalishah, their visitors, and Qermezi elsewhere found his plan of action a topic of consuming interest.[1]

While people's wide-ranging conversations covered the details, their focus on Mohammad Karim's intentions concentrated on two issues. First, all Qermezi faced economic problems and sought to find ways to increase their options and opportunities. Each season was a time to evaluate their just-implemented plans and to consider new approaches for seasons to come. Mohammad Karim's decision suggested drastic changes that few people wanted to make this suddenly for themselves but his struggle to find new ways to provide for his family was similar to their own. If he proved successful, he offered a model for people perchance to follow. He might even open possibilities for others, such as young men needing income-producing work until they found more permanent livelihoods. If he failed in the new venture, he demonstrated the pitfalls for others to avoid.

Second, people worried about the impact of Mohammad Karim's "departure"—or even his "flight" or "desertion" as many phrased it—on their own integrity. They all depended on others in the pursuit of their chosen livelihoods and lifestyles. If Mohammad Karim ceased nomadic pastoralism, he posed a threat to their interests and to the solidarity of their kinship, tribal, and socioterritorial groups. The Qermezi viewed a man who removed himself from any of these groups, for whatever reason, as a person who undermined the efforts of other members. If Mohammad Karim chose not to reside in

304 *Decisions and consequences*

winter and summer pastures for economic reasons, he was withdrawing his political, economic, social, and emotional support from the residents there. By setting a path for himself, he ignored the needs of others. People saw his decision as a refusal to engage in the normal course of life that the others shared. If he succeeded in changing his livelihood, they feared he might tempt others to take similar routes, to the further detriment of existing kinship, tribal, and socioterritorial groups. One person "fleeing" might cause others to leave. This scenario had occurred in 1971 when first one nomadic family and then another and another had built houses in Atakula village.[2]

The impact of Mohammad Karim's absence would be harshest on his mother and two younger married brothers. Even in the presence of her other sons, Falak would often lament, "Borzu's hearth is extinguished!" (A tent's central firepit is a family's preeminent symbol.) Since Mohammad Karim's birth, she had expected that her eldest son would maintain the nomadic pastoral tradition carried forward by his father, his grandfather, and their ancestors. Mohammad Karim had always focused on the details of the livelihood and was not often distracted. Falak had worried more about Dariush who leaned toward urban livelihoods and lifestyles and whose wife was raised in a city. Her youngest son Bizhan, the one in Qashqa'i society who customarily cares for the parents as they grow elderly, was temperamental and prone to sudden, unpredictable actions. Dariush and Bizhan had also anticipated that their elder brother would continue nomadic pastoralism, and they depended on him to maintain the extended family's valuable pasture rights at Dashtak and Hanalishah. They based their own ongoing decisions on their confidence in Mohammad Karim. Their brother's announcement threw them all into confusion and reconsideration.

The year's adverse physical conditions for pastoralism and the escalating costs of fodder, hired shepherds, and transportation for the livestock provided the broader economic context for Mohammad Karim's choice to sell his animals and find an alternative livelihood. "If commodities are expensive and sheep are cheap, then a man must make some changes," declared Murad Qermezi. Men sometimes spent more money to care for the animals during the year than they netted in their sale. Their annual expenses covered the entire herd; they sold only a portion of these animals each year. In a favorable year, the sum they gained from livestock sales more than offset these annual costs and provided sufficient cash for the family's upkeep.

On a trip home from his university teaching assistantship in Tehran, Masud Qermezi asked his father Asadullah to tabulate the past year's expenses for his livestock and the money he received in animal sales. Asadullah anticipated that the amounts would be equivalent, given the year's environmental inadequacies, and he and others were surprised by the extent of the disparity. He had spent two and a half million tumans and had netted only two million. By earning an annual income from his apple orchard, he saw that this other venture, at least for the past year, had subsidized his pastoralism.

Mohammad Karim lacked much supplementary income to support his main livelihood when physical and market conditions for pastoralism were

Decisions and consequences 305

not productive. The idea of a regular income or a weekly or monthly salary appealed to him and seemed to be his primary motivation.

Mohammad Karim's strategy centered on selling all his livestock and spending the cash on a new vehicle. Then he would travel to Dogonbadan north of Kazerun to find work in the oil and natural-gas industry there. This venture was new for the Qermezi although they were acquainted with other Qashqa'i who had secured jobs in various capacities in the enterprise, including many Darrehshuri and Kashkuli whose winter pastures were nearby. Some Qermezi were related by kinship and marriage to Shaikh Lurs in that region, some of whom were similarly employed there. Mohammad Karim hoped for a job as the personal driver for an engineer, work he regarded as acceptable and comfortable. He was loath to perform low-status manual labor for the benefit of others. (He had always readily accepted the unrelenting physical labor that nomadic pastoralism entailed. This work he did on his own behalf.) To entice such an employer, he now needed sufficient money to purchase a new-model, attractive vehicle with a spacious cab. Several young Qermezi men were currently drivers for state agencies and received steady salaries and benefits.

As an alternative strategy, Mohammad Karim said that merchants and farmers could hire him to transport their commodities, and for that reason too he needed an appropriate conveyance. In this scenario, he would require a sturdy pickup truck suitable for large, heavy loads, and its appearance was less important. He understood that such work sometimes meant physical labor (such as loading and unloading goods) and long hours of driving but at least he would probably receive payment at the end of each job. Some Qermezi, including a cousin, used their vehicles for paid transport. Yet income from this livelihood was not regular or guaranteed, and he would have to circulate among merchants and producers to drum up each day's work.

Drivers looked for men wanting rides or transport at a traffic circle just north of Kazerun near three major routes (to the port of Bushire on the Persian Gulf, to the northern oil fields, and to Shiraz in the east and from there points north). Mohammad Karim was not necessarily interested in long-haul work, especially because he lacked contacts for finding loads for the return trip, but he was open to the possibility, especially if fees were rewarding. Glad for the extra income to supplement their modest salaries, several Qermezi teachers periodically drove to the traffic circle before or after school and on weekends and holidays to pick up local riders and short-haul work.

As a third possible strategy, Mohammad Karim explained that his eldest son Kurush could help with transporting goods or driving when he ended his two years of mandatory military service the next spring. Gradually Kurush could take responsibility for the job so that Mohammad Karim could either find other work or begin to restore his herd. Kurush had refused to continue his formal education beyond the eighth grade (just like his father, who had quit after the seventh). The army was not teaching him any specialized skills, and his options were limited. Mohammad Karim had long assumed that Kurush,

306 *Decisions and consequences*

as the eldest son, would assume the daily responsibilities of nomadic pastoralism but the boy had grown independent and obstinate, and this option seemed increasingly unlikely. The son acted as belligerently as his father had done at the same age. Dismayed, Borzu had also held high hopes—often unrealized—for his eldest son (Mohammad Karim).

As the Qermezi raised their concerns about Mohammad Karim, they often mentioned his wife and eldest daughter. They cited Mohammad Karim as an example of the negative consequences of marrying outside the subtribe. Mohammad Karim's ties with his wife drew him in the direction of her extended family and subtribe, and some people now blamed her for his interest in abandoning the Qermezi group to find a new livelihood. If his wife were a relative and a fellow Qermezi, he might have been more inclined to persist as a nomadic pastoralist under these trying circumstances. People noted that a fourth feasible strategy for Mohammad Karim was to cooperate economically with his wife's extended family, such as by helping them in their expanding apple orchards. He did not mention this possibility when talking about the future with his Qermezi kindred but they still worried that some action in this direction might be forthcoming.

People knew that Mohammad Karim was not responsible for marrying outside the subtribe. Borzu had sought that link 20 years earlier. Even when Mohammad Karim was a child, Borzu strove to establish ties with influential men in other Darrehshuri subtribes, to enhance his political and economic status, and he hoped that one of them might eventually give him a bride for his son.[3] Thus permanently linked by this intermarriage (and its promise of grandchildren for the two allied men), Borzu would strengthen his interests. Yet he was rejected at least twice, and he settled on his third or fourth choice, the granddaughter of Amrullah, the former (and deceased) headman of the Qarehqanli subtribe. The girl's father, if he had also been alive, would probably not have married her to someone of slightly lower status. Her paternal kin reluctantly agreed to the match, perhaps worrying that someone of their own or a higher status would not request her.[4]

From the beginning, Bulqais regarded her marriage to Mohammad Karim as a fall in prestige, and she refused to engage in the customary responsibilities of a new bride, some of which she viewed as beneath her. She was Falak's first daughter-in-law, and Falak had unattained intentions for this young woman. Within the first month, the two women were engaging in bitter disputes, and Falak regretted Borzu's quest to ally with a higher-ranked family. Borzu had increased his status by affiliating with a leading Qarehqanli family but by doing so he had accepted a bride who did not fit in and would not comply.

When Farahnaz, Mohammad Karim and Bulqais's eldest daughter, neared marriageable age, the Qermezi wondered who Mohammad Karim would regard as acceptable suitors. The subtribe's large size meant many potential matches, although the Aqa Mohammadli lineage suffered a shortage of young men, especially those whose natal families continued as nomadic pastoralists. Many Aqa Mohammadli now lived in Atakula village but few of the lineage's

Decisions and consequences 307

other members wanted to marry with them, and they especially avoided giving them daughters. When Bulqais's Qarehqanli kin began asking about the possibility of Farahnaz as a bride for one of its sons, Mohammad Karim did not reject them outright. Angered when they heard about this possible development, his own kin complained about Bulqais's overriding power. She served her natal family, not her affinal one.

When a Lur family from Baghan (a productive agricultural region north of Shiraz) came to ask for Farahnaz as a bride, the Qermezi were even more disturbed. The intended suitor is the son of Muzamfar (a Boir Ahmad Lur man) and Amlak (a daughter of Amrullah Qarehqanli, a Darrehshuri). The intended match would reinforce already existing ties between Mohammad Karim and his Qarehqanli in-laws (through Bulqais), especially because Bulqais is Amlak's niece. Bulqais's mother, also Qarehqanli, had remarried after her husband (Bulqais's father) died, and her second husband is Amlak's brother (another tie connecting the three women). Qermezi women were initially reassured by these multiple links through females, while Qermezi men remained angry about the suitor's Lur (and not Qashqa'i) identity.

Mohammad Karim agreed to the union, and the wedding soon followed. Agitated, many Qermezi, women especially, now complained that Mohammad Karim had discarded his daughter, lost forever from the Qermezi group. According to the rules of patrilineal descent, Farahnaz's children would be Lurs and not Qermezi or even Qashqa'i, and she and they would live far away from any Qermezi. Mohammad Karim's new father-in-law, Muzamfar, was wealthier than any Qermezi man. He owned fertile land, cultivated lucrative crops, and possessed homes in Baghan and Shiraz. The Qermezi were distressed that Mohammad Karim seemed to be more enamored with the economic consequences of the new alliance than he was in his daughter's fate.

Mohammad Karim now (1997) enjoyed potentially profitable economic ties with two groups outside the Qermezi subtribe: Qarehqanli subtribe (with key individuals based in a village east of Semirom) and Baghan Lurs (north of Shiraz). These links offered him possible advantages that other Qermezi at Hanalishah lacked but they came at the expense of amicable relationships within the subtribe. People viewed Mohammad Karim as someone who had rejected the Qermezi group. He had taken a wife from outsiders, through no fault of his own, but then he gave a daughter to even more distant outsiders.

Mohammad Karim and Bulqais had produced eight children, a common enough number in the past when perhaps half of them would die young but too many for the economic constraints of the 1980s and especially 1990s. In discussing Mohammad Karim, people always mentioned the excessive number of his offspring. The eight children helped to explain his desire for a more remunerative, dependable livelihood. As they grew older, expenses for their care increased. In part because his eldest son had refused to continue schooling, Mohammad Karim was determined to provide formal education for his other children and to increase their opportunities for future livelihoods.

308 *Decisions and consequences*

His eldest daughter Farahnaz had not continued beyond the fifth grade, and he had arranged her marriage when she was still young.

Mohammad Karim turned his attention in the mid-1990s to the education of his six other children. Three daughters completed the fifth grade in the nomads' school at Dashtak and Hanalishah. They all scored high enough in the qualifying examination to attend the tribal middle school in Chinar Shahijan north of Kazerun. They lived in a girls' dormitory there and visited their parents at Dashtak on holidays and long weekends. Two of them finished the eighth grade in this school in 1997 but did not qualify for admission to the tribal high school in Shiraz. They enrolled in a public high school in Kazerun and lived there with Dariush, their father's brother. That same year the third daughter began the seventh grade in the Chinar Shahijan tribal middle school.

Some people commented that Mohammad Karim had timed his decision to end nomadic pastoralism to coincide with his second eldest son's concluding the fifth grade in the nomads' school. Surush would have to continue his education elsewhere, and Mohammad Karim hesitated to ask Dariush to care for him in Kazerun during the school year. He preferred that option but was troubled that Dariush's wife would balk at the prospect of hosting another of his children. In June and July, Surush and other fifth graders took the examinations necessary to complete the grade and determine their eligibility for tribal schools in Shiraz and Chinar Shahijan. If they failed the qualifying test, their only other educational option was to attend public school in Kazerun. Taunting Surush about his poor academic performance, Mohammad Karim simultaneously expressed hope that his son could enroll in the prestigious school in Shiraz.

Until the program for nomads' education released the results of Surush's examination, Mohammad Karim was uncertain about his family's place of residence when the time came to leave summer pastures. Initially he said he would maintain his family in their stone-and-thatch one-room dwelling at Dashtak, where he had always spent the autumn and winter. The four children who would study in town could live with Dariush in Kazerun or in school dormitories elsewhere. The two youngest sons would continue studying at the nomads' school at Dashtak and live at home. If Mohammad Karim found work in the oil industry, his wife could manage their home at Dashtak where expenses were low. If he sought a house in Kazerun for Bulqais and the children, he would need money for rent. The Qermezi living in Kazerun complained that costs escalated rapidly, not just for rent and the public utilities that Dashtak lacked but also for increased purchases of food, clothing, and other commodities; more medical expenses because of clinics and pharmacies there; and more guests to entertain.

When Mohammad Karim had migrated with his livestock from Dashtak to Hanalishah in the spring of 1997, he had already decided to sell them, despite still being uncertain about the full consequences. After fattening the animals on spring pastures at Hanalishah, he rented a truck to transport 80 sheep and

70 goats to Isfahan to take advantage of the relatively high prices this early in the year. Most pastoralists in the region waited until summer to sell their livestock but by then prices had fallen because of the market's glut. By getting rid of many animals early on, Mohammad Karim also avoided the high cost of fodder, necessary when natural pasturage diminished and then disappeared. At the same time, he forfeited the possible advantage to be gained by selling heavier animals later on.

During the weeks to come, Mohammad Karim negotiated with his kin at Hanalishah about selling them his remaining livestock. Men wanting to purchase animals preferred buying them from known individuals, especially relatives, rather than from strangers. They acquired reliable information about their genealogy and history and knew about the quality of their care to date. Qurban Ali bought 25 goats, Ali Murad 12 goats, and Bizhan 40 sheep. Amanullah purchased six ewes and four lambs, which his young sons tended until the animals damaged his apple trees. He told his sons to return them to Mohammad Karim for him to supervise there. Surprised by the maneuver, the nomads responded that a man buying livestock should not expect the former owner to continue to care for the animals afterward, especially given the escalating cost of fodder. Mohammad Karim's daughters surreptitiously cut weeds in the nearby orchard of a Persian farmer, to feed the 10 animals, which roamed the camp and irritated people by their presence. Mohammad Karim could have temporarily reintegrated them in his diminishing herd but refused to do so on principle. Soon learning that others disapproved of him, Amanullah sold the animals to a kinsman.

From these and other livestock sales, Mohammad Karim netted three million tumans. By July's end, only 50 goats remained in his herd, and he planned to sell half of them soon. He found that he was unable to divest himself of the final 25. His identity hinged on owning livestock, and too many social obligations required him to contribute live animals. He asked Dariush and Bizhan to tend this final group in their joint herd.

Mohammad Karim's other assets were a decrepit Land Rover, his wife's and daughters' handwoven textiles, and a worrisome apple orchard. He intended to sell the vehicle as soon as he decided on the model he wanted to purchase. The disruptions he was causing in his life required him to have continuous vehicular transportation. Under pressure from the urban merchants to whom he owed money, he periodically gave them newly woven knotted carpets. These textiles were usually "gifts" that temporarily halted the merchants' harassments and did not provide any monetary return. Mohammad Karim seemed unable to sell these weavings more profitably outright, such as in the Shiraz bazaar to shopkeepers who dealt exclusively with "tribal" products. Bulqais vehemently argued that her three maturing daughters needed these carpets and other textiles as dowries and that he should not try to mollify his creditors this way.

Mohammad Karim's maternal uncles had divided their apple orchard, located near Narmeh village, in order to give him half when he married.

310   *Decisions and consequences*

Twenty years later, his parcel was not producing well. Water was in short supply, and he lived a long distance away and could not tend the orchard properly. He fertilized the trees with dung from his livestock, sprayed pesticides, and irrigated but he still needed to employ an overseer (who often proved inattentive). (Having disposed of his livestock, he would now have to purchase dung, another unexpected expense.) The fruit was low in quantity and quality, and for each of the last several autumns he had sold the crop for less than a million tumans. Many Qermezi who owned orchards sold the annual crop before the harvest to middlemen who hired a labor force to pick, pack, and transport the fruit and who later paid the owners installments of cash. The Qermezi always found the arrangement unsatisfactory but the harvest fell at a time when they were en route to winter pastures or already encamped there.

Mohammad Karim wanted to sell the orchard but could not find a buyer. He had hoped that the property would generate enough money for him to buy a new Nissan Patrol land cruiser, currently costing between nine and sixteen million tumans, depending on the model. Lack of sufficient water reduced the orchard's value, and, until he solved that problem, he would not gain any substantial income from either the apples or the orchard's sale. Unlike some other nomads at Hanalishah, he did not own an orchard there. He had not purchased cultivable land when prices were low, and by the mid-1990s values had risen beyond the reach of all the nomads.

People seemed to talk endlessly about Mohammad Karim's decisions and actions. He (and everyone else) operated within a constantly changing and unpredictable context, and every day brought new developments. Kinsmen grew reluctant to ask Mohammad Karim directly about his plans and, instead, judged for themselves by the activities they observed in his camp and during his excursions if they encountered him away from home. Aware that most people disapproved of his choices, he hesitated to discuss his full ideas with anyone. Women were less cautious in their queries to Bulqais, and soon she reduced her visits and even stayed out of sight when guests arrived at Dariush's house uphill. Perhaps because she was not Qermezi, some women rudely questioned her and pointed out the obvious. They asked if Mohammad Karim was selling his livestock when they already knew he had done so, and they could see for themselves that the herd was gone. They inquired about Farahnaz's health when they knew that Bulqais had not seen her married daughter for months.

Several months earlier, just after Mohammad Karim had reached summer pastures with his flock, his hired shepherd fled without warning and never returned. Qermezi men joked, with a trace of malice, "Mohammad Karim's shepherd bolted, and so he had to sell his sheep." They all faced problems with their hired shepherds, and desertion was common. Thus the loss of any particular shepherd was a trivial reason to abandon pastoralism. Through their negative comments, people impugned Mohammad Karim's ability to make sound, rational decisions.

When I first arrived at Hanalishah in 1997 and was learning about events that had transpired since the previous year's visit, I overheard several people mention that Mohammad Karim had spent the prior day hunting a wolf that had attacked two lambs belonging to a kinsman. From their facial expressions, I saw I had missed some wider point. Then someone's casual remark clarified the situation for me. A man who was divesting himself of livestock no longer needed to worry about wolves. One person queried, "Why traipse up and down rugged mountain slopes from before dawn until well after dusk if the predator is no longer a personal threat?" Later, people insinuated that if Mohammad Karim still possessed so much energy, he ought to have directed it toward caring for his flock. From his perspective, he might have wanted to demonstrate (to himself and his kinship and tribal groups) that he still valued physical prowess and obligations toward family and neighbor, despite the seemingly contradictory changes he was making in his livelihood.

People did not criticize a judgment that Mohammad Karim had made the previous winter to build a concrete reservoir at Dashtak, although he sometimes expressed irritation that he had undertaken that expense. The Organization for Nomads' Affairs had offered financial and material assistance to the men at Dashtak, who constantly faced water shortages. The nomads were always prevented from moving into Dashtak's mountains until the rains of late autumn had begun to pool in the dirt basins they had dug there. The government now agreed to fill the new concrete tanks before the rains began and then whenever needs arose. Rather than faulting Mohammad Karim, people considered him astute for exploiting the state's aid.

By the end of August, Mohammad Karim had taken most of the actions necessary to abandon nomadic pastoralism and prepare for another livelihood. He still pondered his decisions and often commented that if forthcoming seasons offered dismal conditions for pastoralism, then he had chosen wisely. If conditions were favorable, then he would suffer the outcome. He mentioned other sequences of years, such as seven ruinous ones falling in a row or a disastrous one followed by a superb one. All is "chance," he noted stoically. The previous summer, animal prices were high, and he said he should have sold his herd then. The cost of some vehicles had doubled in a year, and the extra two or three million tumans he would now have to pay represented several hundred sheep and goats and a year of hard labor.

At the end of summer, Mohammad Karim rented a small house in Kazerun for his family. His children would attend school there or, if admitted, at the tribal school in Chinar Shahijan. He sold his Land Rover for 1.7 million tumans and bought a new-model Saipa pickup truck for six million. As the prospects for finding employment as a driver for an oil engineer faded (and he seemed not to have exerted enough effort in the quest), he turned his efforts toward transporting fresh produce and other commodities within and near Kazerun for negotiated fees. Bizhan and his family moved into Mohammad Karim's one-room dwelling at Dashtak, and Dariush and Bizhan agreed to

312   *Decisions and consequences*

rent their brother's pastures there. In lieu of rent, they tended Mohammad Karim's remaining 25 goats without remuneration.

Mohammad Karim's story continues in the next section.

A split in the family

The three sons of Borzu Qermezi continued to devise economic strategies that would respond to changes in the local, regional, and national economies; satisfy expectations within their extended family and tribal groups; and meet their personal needs.

Until the 1980s the economic separation of a son from his father usually proceeded according to the rules and procedures that most Qashqa'i followed. As Qashqa'i households grew more diversified economically in the 1980s and 1990s, young men began to seek some greater degree of independence. A son's detachment from his father became complicated and emotional. Borzu's absence drew out and exacerbated the breakup of the household now belonging to his two younger sons.

Borzu's eldest son was already independent. According to established customs, Mohammad Karim had received a third of his father's herd and pack animals and some material goods when he formed his own household. His livestock had grown from 133 sheep and goats in 1985 to 250 in 1997, a number that should have adequately met the needs of an average-sized nomadic, pastoral household.

As Borzu's youngest son, Bizhan was "the son of the hearth" responsible for remaining with his parents to care for them as they aged. More accomplished in school than his elder brother Dariush, Bizhan had ended his formal education prematurely, well short of a high-school diploma, when his father fell ill and needed someone to assume full-time responsibility for the livestock and the cultivation of fodder crops. He avoided military service. Also not finishing high school, Dariush discharged his military obligation by serving with the nomads' revolutionary committee in Tehran and Shiraz.

Borzu arranged in 1991 for Bizhan to marry Maryam, the daughter of Husain, an Imamverdili kinsman. Sons and daughters usually married according to birth order but because Bizhan was taking on added responsibility, Borzu decided that his youngest son needed a wife to assist him. Borzu's wife Falak was burdened by household tasks, especially those connected with the hospitality that Borzu's role as the subtribe's headman required, and she welcomed a new daughter-in-law's support. Mohammad Karim and Bulqais now lived independently, and Bulqais no longer performed any chores for Falak. During the autumn, winter, and early spring, Bizhan and Maryam (and soon their infant son) lived in the family's hut in winter pastures at Dashtak, where Bizhan supervised the family's livestock tended by two hired shepherds. Then he migrated for a month with the herds and shepherds to summer pastures at Hanalishah where he rejoined his wife and natal family who had traveled there by rented truck. Under Borzu's instructions in 1993, Dariush and

Bizhan constructed a one-room stone house at Hanalishah, in part to coincide with Dariush's marriage that year to Farzaneh, a Qarehqanli Darrehshuri girl. When Borzu died in 1995, Dariush and Bizhan became heads of the household and joint owners of its property, along with their mother Falak and their unmarried sister Fariba, who still lived at home.

Dariush and Bizhan divided the labor that related directly and indirectly to their livelihoods. Bizhan managed the livestock and shepherds and cultivated grain and fodder crops while Dariush tended the newly planted apple orchard, negotiated with state agents, ran frequent errands in towns and cities, and hosted guests and visitors. Both could perform the full range of tasks, and one of them assumed all the work when the other was absent on business. Their wives shared other facets of the household labor based on preferences and skills, and the four individuals worked together effectively. Borzu had been embroiled in many long-term, as-yet-unresolved legal disputes, and Dariush took on their tedious, time-consuming details.

Dariush and Farzaneh, soon with an infant son, planned eventually to form an independent household. They wanted to reside in a town during the winter to escape the cold outdoors weather and then rejoin the family when it migrated to summer pastures. Dariush's livelihood in town was still uncertain, and his natal family was reluctant to support financially what it considered a leisurely and expensive life for him there. After several attempts, he still had not passed all the examinations necessary for completing high school. Until he did so, he would be unlikely to procure an urban job to his liking (one that would require at least a high-school diploma). If the two brothers agreed to separate, close-kin mediators would negotiate the division of family property and the duties of each man. The brothers had not yet settled the issue of which one of them would assume responsibility for Falak and Fariba.

Quite unexpectedly, Bizhan declared in 1997 that he wanted to become independent from his natal household and find urban work. Implicit in Bizhan's decision, Dariush would have to stay behind to care for pastoral and agricultural tasks in winter and summer pastures. Stunned, Dariush quickly agreed. He feared the family would otherwise lose its valuable pasture rights in the two territories. Yet he and especially his urban-raised wife were unhappy about this sudden reversal of plans. When Maryam gave birth to twins some months previously, Bizhan had reconsidered how and where to live, but the high costs of sustaining nomadic pastoralism and Iran's disturbing economic fluctuations drove him to his decision. Dariush, faced with the specter of performing all the tasks connected with nomadic pastoralism as well as the other responsibilities the two brothers currently shared, changed his mind about becoming independent. He hoped that Bizhan would also see the wisdom of staying together.

Dariush's and Bizhan's vacillating notions about how to proceed were complicated in 1997 by the abrupt decision of their elder brother, Mohammad Karim, to abandon nomadic pastoralism. The three brothers shared pasture rights at Dashtak and Hanalishah. They had inherited them from their father,

314   *Decisions and consequences*

and state regulations required that, singly or together, they tend livestock on these lands. When Mohammad Karim announced that he would quit animal husbandry, Dariush and Bizhan fell under growing pressure to sustain it.

Dariush and Bizhan's conflict escalated. They disagreed about how to share the work and expenses or, alternately, how to divide their property while still preserving their claims to pastureland. They grew progressively disgruntled about each other's financial decisions, every one of which now affecting them jointly. Dariush was dismayed when Bizhan bought unnecessary items such as sweets and soon-broken plastic toys while Bizhan compared the low economic demands of his wife with the relatively lavish ones of Dariush's urban-raised wife. Remarkably, Farzaneh and Maryam continued to be compatible, despite their close quarters, four rambunctious children, and the dispute expanding in their midst. During the years I lived with them, I never saw or sensed any unpleasantness between them. Fariba, whose fate was tied to her sisters-in-law, cooperated with both of them in handling household chores. Falak periodically complained about one or another of her sons or daughters-in-law and was disturbed about the consequences if her sons could not agree about the future.

The main assets of the two brothers in 1997 were their pasture rights, livestock, two apple orchards (in Mehr-i Gerd and Hanalishah), a decrepit Land Rover, and a motorcycle. Together they owed money to a state bank for a loan they had assumed, and they were in debt to Mehdi Zahrai, a Kazerun merchant. They engaged in many expensive legal disputes over land, their resolution probably not forthcoming.

By mid-summer Dariush and Bizhan tended 310 sheep and goats, the fewest of the year. They had sold 140 in the late spring and early summer. Bizhan wanted to buy more ewes before the autumn migration, to have new births in the winter and a larger herd by the spring, but Dariush responded that the herd's current size was adequate and that they lacked income to purchase livestock. He worried that more animals, particularly pregnant ewes, meant escalating costs for fodder.

At the same time, Dariush began in earnest to seek a buyer for the family's apple orchard near the village of Mehr-i Gerd. He wanted the money so he could buy a house in Kazerun, the town nearest his winter pastures at Dashtak. Before his death, Borzu had instructed his sons that they should not sell this orchard for any reason—unless they used the income exclusively for purchasing a house in a town. The current cash values of the orchard and a suitable house were approximately the same, eight million tumans.

Bizhan vehemently opposed both actions. He considered the orchard's annual income, one million tumans, to be essential to the household and wanted to retain it indefinitely. Yet the orchard was not producing well, and the brothers could not tend it adequately given its distance from Hanalishah. They unhappily relied on an overseer, a distant relative in Mehr-i Gerd who assisted with irrigating and pesticide spraying. Villagers and picnickers stole apples and damaged the trees. Irritated by Dariush's shortsightedness, Bizhan could not fathom how his brother could sacrifice the orchard for a momentary financial

Decisions and consequences 315

gain when otherwise they would profit from a healthy annual income for years to come. The inflationary rise in the value of cultivable land, especially a plot already productive, meant that they would forfeit the chance to profit even more in the future. Land prices in the area were doubling every few years. Bizhan often commented, "I struggle to *maintain* the value of the livestock while the orchard *rises* in value without any effort at all." If they needed to sell the Mehr-i Gerd orchard because of its distance from Hanalishah, then they should use the money to purchase an orchard or the land for one at Hanalishah. An orchard produced an annual income; a house in Kazerun certainly did not, and its running expenses would consume their limited funds and push them further into debt.

Bizhan also saw no need for buying a house that he would not use. Dariush considered renting a house in Kazerun for the autumn, winter, and early spring, just as Borzu and he had done since 1993, but he lacked the money for rent and the other expenses required by urban life. If he sought a loan from a moneylender, he would be unable to pay the high interest and to repay the principle. State banks offered low-interest loans for only specific projects such as construction and irrigation. Exaggerating their young son's needs, Dariush and Farzaneh claimed that they could not possibly reside in the family's thatched hut at Dashtak during the cold, windy, rainy, snowy weather because of inadequate shelter, heat, and water. Dariush argued that the orchard's sale would solve the housing problem for the winter. Bizhan retorted, "If my family with not one but three young children can live in a hut at Dashtak all winter, then you and your smaller family could also do so."

The status of Falak's health seemed to resolve this particular dispute. She was elderly, often ill, and diagnosed—correctly or not—with a heart ailment. Dariush and Bizhan had recently suffered through their father's prolonged illness and then death due to heart disease, and they were reluctant to subject Falak to the rigors of a harsh winter at Dashtak. They said she should rest comfortably in town. In cases similar to this one, an elderly parent lived temporarily with a close relative such as a married daughter. Yet, mindful of the still-elevated social status of Borzu's family, Dariush said he could not possibly expect Falak to live with anyone else. His responsibility was to care for his mother and provide her with suitable living conditions. On these grounds, his plan to sell the orchard superseded Bizhan's desire to retain it. (Without Falak, Dariush's claims for needing a house in Kazerun were undercut. She did have four married daughters, two of whom lived in Kazerun during the winter and agreed to care for her.)

Dariush negotiated the orchard's sale to a Mehr-i Gerd resident for eight million tumans (seven million for the land, water, and trees and one million for the impending harvest). He planned to spend practically all the money for a house in Kazerun. In his and Bizhan's names, he would assume a bank loan for the difference. Bizhan was irate but did not offer other viable options for the problems they both faced. By this time, they were unable to discuss calmly these economic decisions together.

316 *Decisions and consequences*

Another asset, Borzu's apple orchard at Hanalishah (planted in 1992), was not yet producing a marketable crop by 1997. The value of arable land there was soaring, and the brothers did not consider selling this orchard. During the spring and summer, they irrigated every 12 days, and other tasks were not yet onerous. Periodically they harvested the alfalfa, clover, and wild grasses growing between the trees for use as essential animal fodder. Dariush's assessment of his economic role did not include daily pastoral tasks, and so the orchard provided him with the semblance of a legitimate livelihood and a future income.

Dariush could choose to reside in Kazerun all year, especially because he was now purchasing a house there, but the summers were scorching, and he was accustomed to the cooler weather of summer pastures during that season. Summertime was the Qermezi subtribe's critical season for social and political activities. The group usually celebrated its weddings in summer pastures, and Dariush would be excluded or distanced if he did not continue to live there. He confided that he would never be the kind of leader his father had been, but he still aspired to a prominent role in the subtribe.

The family's run-down Land Rover and motorcycle were further assets for the brothers. The value of vehicles rose rapidly in Iran, despite their often dilapidated condition, because of inflation, scarcity, and high demand. Qermezi men fantasized about buying a decent vehicle, barely driving it, and then selling it for twice the purchase price the following year. Yet few possessed the means anymore to acquire a vehicle, and no one could avoid using an available one. Dariush relied more regularly on the Land Rover than did Bizhan because he handled errands and government business in town, including legal disputes, but Bizhan needed to transport livestock and fodder and arrange the family's economic affairs in other seasonal pastures. They used the two vehicles constantly. Every day each brother took multiple trips for various purposes, often without first consulting the other about his own possibly conflicting plans. Mohammad Karim occasionally borrowed the Land Rover and the cycle for errands, and sometimes others at Hanalishah requested their use. Many nomads there owned no vehicles or at most only a motorcycle.

The two brothers never seemed to confront these multiple economic issues directly. Co-residents of the same camp, they tended to avoid one another for days until a problem erupted, such as simultaneous needs for the Land Rover or an urgent demand for cash. Then they would argue about short-term and sometimes long-term but often seemingly random issues. Their temperaments differed. Dariush often retreated when an argument loomed while Bizhan lashed out in abrupt anger and fled before any resolution was possible. Borzu's mediating presence was gone, and the brothers' paternal uncles did not assume the authoritative role that such men often played in Qashqa'i society. In other families, an independent elder brother would likely intervene, but Mohammad Karim avoided the growing crisis, in part because his own problems consumed him. Any decision he made about his economic quandary would affect his brothers. Delegations of Qermezi men from Hanalishah and

Decisions and consequences 317

elsewhere sometimes consulted with him, but the visitors seemed motivated by their obligation to respect his status as the elder brother and not by any expectation that they could settle the dilemma with his help.

Before vacating summer pastures in 1997, the nomads at Hanalishah spent an intense month completing activities there, making crucial economic decisions, and preparing for upcoming seasons. Bizhan had spent weeks searching for a reliable hired shepherd and negotiating the rights to graze the stubble of newly harvested fields to the south. Finally he solved both problems and announced that he and the livestock were ready to depart from Hanalishah. He could not remain there any longer; their pastures were depleted. Dariush worried that Bizhan would leave before they could agree to stay together or to separate.

Following tense meetings with kinsmen willing to listen and arbitrate, Dariush and Bizhan separately accepted some compromises about their split and its economic consequences. Dariush requested two close kinsmen to mediate, Asadullah and Husain Ali, both his paternal first cousins as well as his brothers-in-law (his sisters' husbands). Dariush and Bizhan agreed to some basic principles, the details they would negotiate later. They would create three equal shares, one each for Falak, Dariush, and Bizhan, for some assets (livestock, Kazerun house), and Dariush and Bizhan would divide other assets equally between them (pasture rights, two vehicles). They would maintain joint ownership of the Hanalishah orchard for the immediate future and continue to share its labor and expenses. They said they would eventually divide the orchard into two shares, a decision omitting the economic interests of Falak and Fariba, both of whom were displeased. Everyone considered the Hanalishah house—the building and its contents, including all the valuable handwoven textiles—as Borzu and Falak's home, and it would remain with her and the son who provided for her. All items (such as dowries) that Maryam and Farzaneh had each brought into marriage were their own, as were any personal possessions of the six adults involved.

The Qashqa'i consider the youngest son to be responsible for his parents and unmarried siblings, but Dariush and Bizhan finally agreed that Dariush would care for Falak and Fariba. Their mother's health would benefit if Falak lived in the Kazerun and Hanalishah houses instead of the hut at Dashtak. Falak preferred Dariush to Bizhan in the matter of her care. Bizhan was too temperamental for her peace of mind. She enjoyed hosting guests and staying informed about wider events, and Dariush was more suitable than Bizhan because of his greater sociability.

Falak did express concern about her two sons' wives. She worried that the non-Qermezi wife who was not related by blood to her would "abandon" her. She often asserted that Dariush's wife Farzaneh, a member of another subtribe, would always serve the interests of "the youngest generation" (her son Salar) at the expense of "the oldest generation" (her husband's mother). Farzaneh was sometimes more attentive to her own natal family and lineage than to her husband's. Falak expressed more confidence in Bizhan's wife Maryam,

318   *Decisions and consequences*

a fellow Qermezi and a blood relative with whom she shared interlinking kinship and marital ties (such as Falak's brother's daughter being Maryam's brother's wife). Sometimes more responsive to Falak's needs, Maryam also possessed the necessary skills for nomadic pastoralism and textile production (many of which Farzaneh was still learning) and was willing to work hard for hours without complaining.[5]

Fariba preferred to live with Dariush, especially if he resided in a house during the winter. Her daily tasks there were less strenuous and wearisome than if she lived with Bizhan in a mountain hut where adequate shelter, heat, and water were lacking. Still, she was disgruntled about her circumstances. At 27, she had long passed the age when most girls married, and she complained about being the family's servant, without any acceptable prospects for escape. Yet, as a new daughter-in-law in someone else's home, she would serve the interests of the family there and not her own. Her elevated age meant that she might have to marry a divorcé or a widower who needed a new wife to care for his first wife's children. (According to tribal, Islamic, and Iranian law, a father retains custody of his children after his divorce or the death of their mother.) These scenarios did not please Fariba either. At least three families had formally requested her as a bride but she rejected them outright. She exaggerated the boys' undesirable traits by claiming that each suitor was insufficiently educated, held a menial occupation, originated from a low-status tribe or lineage, lived in an unacceptable place, and had a peculiar family history.[6]

Despite some discussion about selling Borzu's Land Rover, Dariush was unconvinced. It played a vital role in their daily lives. Then Bizhan suddenly sold the vehicle, without his brother's explicit approval, for a sum (2.1 million tumans) that many men considered was too low. All household members depended on motorized transport, and the loss caused a crisis. The sale especially disturbed Falak and her daughters, for the Land Rover was a visible reminder of Borzu, whom they had watched leaving camp and returning each and every day. With tears in their eyes, they mentioned the cloud of rising dust that followed Borzu's departure but that also signified his imminent return. The Land Rover symbolized the wide extent of his political, economic, and social networks. The women were distraught whenever they saw the vehicle in Semirom, now in a stranger's hands. Bizhan had claimed he needed the income to buy pregnant ewes, and the time to buy was now, before the migration began in earnest. He gave half the money from the Land Rover's sale to Dariush and used the other half to buy livestock and pay off debts.

After a trying month without any vehicular transport, Dariush bought another, cheaper Land Rover, the very one his brother Mohammad Karim had recently sold to an outside party. The vehicle was small, with room for only the driver and two adult passengers in the cab and an open back for loads, and could not hold the four adults and one child in Dariush's newly composed family. Borzu's Land Rover had been larger, with additional seating in an

Decisions and consequences 319

enclosed back. All men worried about buying a used vehicle whose history and condition were unknown. Hardly anyone possessed the cash to purchase a new model, and everyone lacked the mechanical expertise necessary for assessing the quality of a used vehicle. As a partial solution, men preferred to buy the conveyance of a relative or acquaintance. At least then they knew the kinds of abuse it had suffered. The same attitudes applied to buying camels, horses, and rams.

Soon after Bizhan sold Borzu's Land Rover, he found a buyer for the motorcycle. He had never obtained legal title from the former owner and thus needed to sell the cycle illegally (and cheaply). He gave half the money to Dariush and spent the other half on another cycle.

Dariush used the proceeds from the sale of the Mehr-i Gerd orchard, plus a bank loan of half a million tumans, to purchase a small house in Kazerun for eight million tumans. The structure, built several years previously by a Kazerun resident, had a shallow, high-walled courtyard. Equipped with running water and electric and natural-gas lines (but not always electricity or natural gas), it held five rooms, a kitchen, and a bath. After migrating from Hanalishah, Dariush and his family, including Falak and Fariba, took up residence there. The house was located at the town's edge near the mountains, and within walking distance sat the houses of the Qermezi men who taught school in or near Kazerun. Maryam and her three young children stayed with Dariush there while Bizhan migrated with the livestock from Hanalishah to Mulleh Balut, where he grazed the animals and prepared to enter the Dashtak mountains above. Then Bizhan moved his family into Mohammad Karim's stone-and-thatch dwelling at Dashtak. Searching for a paying job, Dariush finally found work as a driver for an engineer whose company was building an asphalt road south of Kazerun through the mountain passes to the east (a shorter route to Shiraz than the current road to the northeast). Dariush was unhappy about using his newly purchased but run-down Land Rover in the job but he did appreciate acquiring health insurance for his family through the construction company. During the autumn and winter, Bizhan took responsibility for caring for the livestock of the two brothers and for cultivating barley.

As planned months earlier, Dariush and Bizhan formally divided their jointly owned herd just before the New Year, the beginning of spring, at their campsite at Dashtak in 1998. The brothers chose a Sunday, considered the most auspicious day of the week for such a momentous undertaking. They and others said that an unpropitious day would jeopardize the health and well-being of the participants and the livestock. They again summoned their cousins and brothers-in-law, Asadullah and Husain Ali, along with a second cousin, Nadir, to mediate and supervise the separation. One of Dashtak's most senior men, Murad, watched the proceedings. Dariush could not attend because he was driving his employer that day. He said he trusted Husain Ali to guard his interests.

The negotiators assembled the sheep and goats of the two brothers and uttered the Qur'an's opening phrase ("bismillah al-rahman al-rahim," in the

320 *Decisions and consequences*

name of God, the compassionate, the merciful). Then they began the division. Similar to the other pastoralists, Bizhan knew the precise genealogy, age, history, condition, and habits of every animal.

First, the men located and separated the 25 sheep and goats belonging to Bizhan's wife Maryam. Then they did the same for the five ewes and lambs belonging to Dariush's wife Farzaneh. They added all the goats to Maryam's small herd. Dariush and Bizhan had earlier agreed to divide them later. Remaining were the sheep, the most valuable animals. The men found the ones that Bizhan had recently purchased with money from the Land Rover's sale and included them, along with their newborn lambs, in his (and Maryam's) herd. Then the mediators selected all the other lambs born that winter and created groups of three lambs similar in sex, size, and physical shape. Two of the three lambs in each group went into Dariush's herd, Dariush and Falak each receiving one. The third lamb went into Bizhan's herd, and he marked the back of its head with red dye or white flour (if the wool was dark) to distinguish it. When the men had distributed all the lambs this way, they allowed them to return to the still-undivided sheep to rejoin their mothers, and then they directed the nursing pairs to Dariush's or Bizhan's herd. The men urged the remaining 75 animals into an enclosed pen, including the rams, ewes without lambs that winter, and lambs of two winters past. Again, the men formed groups of three animals, each group having a similar composition, with two of the three going to Dariush and Falak and the third to Bizhan. Bizhan again marked his animals with dye or flour. The men noted that Bizhan did not need to label them; he knew the new status of each animal. The division complete, the men once again intoned the Arabic phrase.

Bizhan's newly constituted herd contained 170 animals (including the goats that the two brothers would divide later) while Dariush's held 100. The total, 270, was suitable for a single herd and shepherd, and Dariush preferred sharing the expenses with Bizhan, but Bizhan balked at performing all the labor. Regretting the extra expense, Dariush hired a shepherd to care for his small herd. Pastoral resources at Dashtak were unusually favorable that spring, and Dariush and Bizhan kept their herds there for two more months and then rented trucks to transport the animals to summer pastures. If conditions at Dashtak had been adverse, Bizhan and the shepherds would have herded the animals by foot to Hanalishah, a overland trek lasting a month. Dariush's salaried job would have precluded him from accompanying them.

When Dariush and Bizhan arrived in summer pastures at Hanalishah in 1998, their negotiated contracts with their respective shepherds ended, and both employees left. The brothers each hired a Persian teenager from nearby Galleh Qadam village to tend their separate herds for several months until they could locate more qualified and experienced shepherds for the autumn migration and the winter and spring seasons. The extra expense of two shepherds, when one sufficed, irritated both brothers, especially Dariush. Bizhan had been determined to divide the livestock and now said he must live with the consequences of that decision.

Decisions and consequences 321

The specter of the Kazerun house constantly grated at Bizhan. Still regarding the dwelling unnecessary, he grew anxious to reap his half of the purchase price, which had originated in the sale of the Mehr-i Gerd orchard. Dariush wanted Bizhan to consider the Kazerun house as his own, so that he, Dariush, could continue to reside there. If Bizhan forced Dariush to sell the house in order to gain half the price, as he now began to press, the other half was not sufficient to buy another house, even a smaller one. Dariush would be forced to rent, yet another unsound expenditure. Falak worried publicly that she would be expelled from the house, cast adrift by her sons and their quarrels. Sympathizing with her, people noted, "All mothers want their sons to live together." In these and later arguments, everyone seemed to ignore her one-third share of the house. According to the prior agreements of all parties, Bizhan was entitled to only a third and not a half of the house.

Bizhan's agitation heightened. He was preparing for the autumn migration to winter pastures but needed to act on the issues still confronting the two brothers. Sometimes alone, other times in pairs or groups, mediators met with one and then the other. Motivated by the approaching end of summer and the pressure to plan specifically for the autumn and winter, Bizhan demanded that Dariush pay him half the price of the Kazerun house. He argued that he needed the cash to buy livestock (again, more pregnant ewes) before the autumn migration. Knowing such an ultimatum was probably fruitless, Bizhan then insisted that Dariush give him all his sheep and goats in partial exchange for Bizhan's half of the house. The prices Bizhan listed for the live-stock and the house were unfavorable for Dariush. He set the house's value at nine million tumans and enumerated the animals' value below the current market price, which would force Dariush to relinquish his sheep and goats cheaply in exchange for half the inflated sum of the house. By this point most nomads at Hanalishah sided with Dariush and Falak against Bizhan, whom they viewed as posing troubling, even ridiculous, demands.

Dariush suggested that he could sell his animals in Isfahan for a price higher than Bizhan offered and then pay Bizhan his demanded sum. Bizhan flatly rejected the idea. First, urban slaughterhouses gave post-dated checks to sellers of livestock, and cash would not be available for a month, well past the time when Bizhan needed it. Second, Bizhan preferred to take Dariush's animals instead of buying others of unknown genealogies and histories. He had tended these same animals only a few months before and was ready to resume care of them.

For several days, many kinsmen visited the two brothers, separately, hoping to prevent the dispute from escalating. Nasibullah played a crucial mediating role while he alternately sought out each man and calmly chatted with family members nearby. He seemed to be Bizhan's only ally. His sister was Bizhan's wife, and he represented her interests; he also stood in the role of "mother's brother" to her three children. Yet his wife was Falak's niece (her brother's daughter), and in that role he represented Falak and both her sons. The many negotiators employed various arguments to force an agreement. They especially pressured Bizhan,

322 *Decisions and consequences*

the one who appeared to be making unreasonable, frequently changing demands. They stressed that brothers ought to support one another, and they invoked Borzu's memory to try to force a resolution. Dariush had already agreed to care for Falak, and the mediators urged Bizhan to consider her welfare. If Bizhan took Dariush's livestock, Dariush would be unable to support Falak financially.

Throughout, Dariush was more amenable to negotiation than Bizhan, who harbored resentments over past events, large and small. Bizhan often complained that, alone, he tended the livestock under arduous conditions while Dariush led a comfortable life. He was the one who rose before dawn every day and supervised the herd "in the cold and wind and rain and snow" until after dark. He was the one who jolted awake during the night to fend off predators and thieves. He was the one who suffered privations twice a year during the overland migrations. Interspersed with these reasonable complaints, he broached comparatively minor ones, such as Dariush and Farzaneh's "wearing out the tires" of the Land Rover when they drove to Semirom to telephone Farzaneh's father in Shiraz.

Finally, Bizhan reluctantly agreed to a negotiated settlement, and Dariush complied. Dariush would immediately give Bizhan practically all of his sheep, valued at 45,000 tumans a pair, except for the rams, each valued at 40,000 tumans. He would temporarily retain the past winter's lambs so he could fatten them on fodder cut from the orchard, and then he would sell them before leaving Hanalishah and give Bizhan 300,000 tumans from the sale. Dariush would retain the ownership of 50 goats, which he would divide between Bizhan and Mohammad Karim, who would tend them in exchange for the use of Dariush's pastures. The following year, after selling most of these goats, Dariush would pay Bizhan another 300,000 tumans to complete his financial obligations to his brother. In exchange, Bizhan would give Dariush (and Falak) his share of the Kazerun house, thereby ending their joint ownership. Dariush offered Bizhan and his wife and children the chance to stay there whenever they needed but Bizhan abruptly rejected the offer.

Dariush and especially Farzaneh were distressed that they would soon no longer own any livestock. They seemed surprised by the extent of their attachment to the animals, even though neither had fully participated in their care. Dariush remarked that he had owned animals since his birth and had never lived without them. Farzaneh lamented, "We like our sheep so much." When Mohammad Karim's young sons taunted Salar about his father's losing all his livestock, Farzaneh reassured Salar that nothing had changed, that Bizhan would simply tend them for a while.

At dawn the next morning, everyone in the camp silently watched Bizhan drive the combined herds from Hanalishah on their way south to the harvested fields he had rented for grazing. Sitting on her front stoop and inconsolable, Farzaneh sobbed at the sight.

After concluding their tasks in summer pastures, Dariush and his family transported their possessions to the house in Kazerun. Maryam and her

Decisions and consequences 323

children dismantled their tent and moved into the Hanalishah house until Bizhan was able to return there to escort them to winter pastures. After the four-week migration, Bizhan grazed the herds at Mulleh Balut below Dashtak. A month later, he and the livestock ascended Dashtak's mountains where his family stayed through the winter in the thatched hut that Borzu had built. They remembered the comforts they had enjoyed the previous winter in Mohammad Karim's dwelling, larger, cleaner, and better insulated than the hut. Mohammad Karim and Bulqais were back in residence.

Dariush was now the sole owner (along with his mother) of the Kazerun house. The road engineer for whom he had worked for several months the previous autumn, winter, and spring rehired him as a driver. Required again to provide a vehicle, Dariush worried about further deterioration of the worn-out Land Rover. His income did fund the family's basic expenses, and he hoped to buy some sheep and goats of his own in the near future. He sighed that he had not grown accustomed to living without livestock. Again his job provided health insurance for the family, a critical benefit given the traumatic news he had just received concerning his young son. A Shiraz heart specialist had diagnosed a life-threatening defect that required immediate open-heart surgery.[7] Passing the qualifying examination, Dariush's wife Farzaneh commenced study at Kazerun's independent university and hoped to secure a salaried job teaching in the girls' tribal middle school in nearby Chinar Shahijan after her graduation.

The three families returned to their shared campsite at Hanalishah in the late spring of 1999. Tending their still-jointly-owned orchard, Dariush and Bizhan were glad to see evidence of what might be their first marketable crop of apples. Mohammad Karim had formed a brand-new herd over the past year and was once again a fully practicing nomadic pastoralist. The presence of two large herds in the camp reassured everyone.

I rejoined the Qermezi group in winter pastures at Dashtak and in nearby Kazerun in 2000. On arrival, I was shocked to see Bizhan, Maryam, and their three boisterous children inhabiting Dariush and Farzaneh's now-crowded Kazerun house. I recalled the difficulties that Bizhan had caused when he demanded all of Dariush's livestock in exchange for releasing his (Bizhan's) rights to the house. Yet here he and his family resided, disrupting the life that Dariush and Farzaneh had planned for themselves. Bizhan seemed to contribute little to household expenses. He did buy a second refrigerator too elaborate for their needs, and he sometimes provided fresh fish from the Persian Gulf and other fresh produce. The brothers took turns slaughtering a goat for meat.

Against the advice of his kinsmen, Bizhan had just sold all of his sheep so he could purchase a pickup truck to transport commodities for hire. The weather uncommonly favorable for pastoralism, the other nomads at Dashtak watched the landscape turn a lush green and contemplated the ample income they would receive from the coming summer's sales of fattened livestock. Bizhan still retained his goats and hired a shepherd who lived at Dashtak, and he would sell some animals in the summer. He complained about not yet

324 *Decisions and consequences*

finding adequate work in Kazerun. He said his new livelihood as a transporter would improve when vegetables and fruit in this low-altitude zone neared harvest later in the winter.

Dariush once again resumed his job as a driver for the road engineer while Farzaneh entered her third year of university studies. Their son Salar, now six, entered a private nursery school, the first Qermezi child ever to do so. Falak's health grew steadily worse. She did periodically join animated discussions about current controversial issues (such as Mohammad Karim's intentions to marry his barely educated, unemployed eldest son to one of the Qermezi subtribe's few female university graduates). Fariba remained at home, unmarried, with no prospects on the horizon. As a child, she had completed the fifth grade in the nomads' school but had never received her graduation certificate. She was now repeating the fifth grade in an adult-literacy school for women and hoped eventually to pursue at least a high-school diploma.

Exuberant that he had returned to nomadic pastoralism, especially given the year's superb conditions for livestock, Mohammad Karim was pleased to own a vehicle again after spending a year without one. To buy livestock, he had sold the pickup truck he had purchased in 1997 when he abandoned nomadic pastoralism. The eight months he had spent transporting market commodities in the Kazerun area and to and from the nearby Persian Gulf ports had been tiresome and frustrating, especially those days when he was unable to locate any work. He spent all the income from this venture on rent, living expenses, vehicular repairs, and gasoline, and after eight months he was more in debt than he had ever been as a pastoralist.

Mohammad Karim's eldest unmarried daughter returned home after having graduated from a public (not tribal) high school in Shiraz. She had lived with her married sister there and would soon be engaged to the son of her father's father's sister, a boy employed by a helicopter factory. Her younger sister stayed with the married one in Shiraz to study for her high-school diploma. A better student than any of her siblings, the youngest sister was in her third year in the prestigious girls' tribal high school in Shiraz and lived in a dormitory there. Mohammad Karim's eldest son was soon to be betrothed to a close patrilateral kinswoman. He was still undereducated and unemployed, and the path he would follow was unclear. He continued to resist his father's attempts to keep him at home where he should be assisting his nuclear family in its pastoral and agricultural chores. Instead he lived with a Farsi Madan Qashqa'i family in Kazerun while he took vocal music lessons. (Both circumstances were unprecedented among the Qermezi. Young unmarried men did not live with other tribes, and they did not pursue singing as their only vocation. Only the revitalization of Qashqa'i culture and its expressions—including the music that the Qashqa'i cherish—saved him from unambiguous scorn.) The second son lived with Dariush and Farzaneh in Kazerun while he attended regular high school there. The third son, a recent elementary-school graduate who had not qualified to attend the tribal middle schools, stayed at home and seemed to be cast adrift by his poor academic performance.

He served his father as the family's shepherd. The youngest son continued as a pupil in the nomads' elementary school at Dashtak.

Abbas Qermezi and his rifle

Iran's security forces arrested and imprisoned Abbas Qermezi in the summer of 1997 for having loaned his rifle to a Persian villager who used it to commit murder. Similar to other events depicted in this book, the Qermezi discussed this odd circumstance at every gathering, and it formed one of the summer's leitmotifs.

Abbas is the son of Abul Hasan of Aqa Mohammadli lineage. Along with his father and elder brother, he was a traditional nomadic pastoralist who migrated seasonally between winter pastures at Dashtak and summer pastures at Hanalishah. They based their livelihood on sheep and goats and a small apple orchard at Hanalishah. Seeking a wife for Abbas, Abul Hasan asked his patrilateral kinsman, Murad, for his daughter Tahmineh, and Murad agreed. Abbas and Tahmineh were the parents of two young children in 1997. Abul Hasan's affinal link with Murad proved helpful in the summer's crisis and demonstrated the benefits of marriage between supportive relatives who lived in close proximity to one another. If Abul Hasan had sought a bride from distant kin, another Qermezi lineage, or another subtribe, he would have lacked the practical and moral assistance that Murad and his extended family provided.

Mohammad Reza Shah's ban forbidding most Qashqa'i to possess guns had lasted from 1962 or so, until the shah lost power in 1978, when many Qashqa'i men quickly rearmed themselves. The new regime's Ministry of Defense announced in 1981 that civilian gunowners should apply for permits, and it introduced more stringent rules in 1996. Qermezi men spent months (which extended into years) trying to obtain (or to avoid obtaining) such documents. Qermezi women were often irritated that men's quests in distant cities for weapons and permits took precious time away from crucial pastoral and agricultural pursuits and often left them, the women, performing men's tasks as well as their own.

Similar to other Qermezi men at Hanalishah and elsewhere, Abbas owned a rifle. He acquired his gun permit without complications in 1996 and periodically used the single-barrel rifle (inscribed as manufactured in the U.S. but probably an eastern European copy) for hunting wild game. He was proud of his gun and enjoyed a personal and emotional attachment to it. The possession of guns testified to men's determination to live autonomously, free from the control of a centralizing state. Guns also symbolized men's bravery and their tribal and gender identity.

A Persian villager from Vanak west of Qermezi pastures at Hanalishah visited Abbas's camp in the early summer of 1997 to request the temporary loan of Abbas's rifle. Talking pleasantly with Abbas over tea, Ali Nasiri explained that a sharp-tusked wild boar with an injured leg had sought refuge

326 *Decisions and consequences*

under a shrub by a pond in his apple orchard near Galleh Qadam village. He said he worried about not being able to open the irrigation ditch and release the flow of water to his trees if a dangerous predator lurked nearby. He needed a weapon to kill it. He added that his young daughter feared the boar's tusks, and for this reason too he wanted a gun. (In telling the story, Qermezi men emphasized the disrupted irrigation while Qermezi women focused on the daughter's fright. Women sympathized with the girl but noted that their own daughters would not cower if confronted by a boar.) Stories about wild animals always intrigued Qermezi men, and they often fell into near-obsessive states while they planned the pursuit and death of the beasts that preyed on their sheep. Nasiri's story did not strike Abbas as peculiar. The region's wild boars often harassed the pastoralists and cultivators, and he loaned Nasiri his rifle.

Along with other Qermezi men at Hanalishah, Abbas was troubled by the need to establish semicordial relationships with the region's Persian and Lur cultivators. The nomads detested them for their illegal incursions and resented the competition they created over land and water. Yet they needed acquaintances to supervise their interests during seasons when they were absent. Ties between the two sets of men were stressful because of the cultivators' ongoing efforts to seize the pasture and water of their Qermezi neighbors. The cultivators' claims had lingered in the region's courts for years, and as a result the Qermezi had not yet obtained clear, definitive title to their pastures. So, when a Vanak resident came to ask an ordinary favor, Abbas was reluctant to refuse.

Ali Nasiri had fabricated the story about the boar. Now armed, he lay in wait for Qarib Ali Jafari, an orchard owner with whom Nasiri had been disputing over irrigation. The Persian Jafari, who also hailed from Vanak village, shared water rights with Nasiri and other nearby cultivators. Every 12 days, they each held exclusive rights to the flow of water for 12 hours. Without this resource, their trees and crops would not survive. Nasiri and Jafari had argued for days about the schedule. Thinking that his water ought to be running by now, a perplexed, unsuspecting Jafari went to the junction of his channel to discover the obstacle. With Abbas's rifle, Nasiri shot Jafari dead and fled with the weapon.

Other cultivators in the vicinity heard the unmistakable blast and hurried to investigate. They were accustomed to gunfire in the surrounding mountains but not in the cultivated valley. They found Jafari dead. Several reported the incident in the nearest village (Galleh Qadam), and others traveled up the road to Vanak village to notify Jafari's family. Investigating, Vanak's security forces discovered that the murder weapon belonged to Abul Hasan Qermezi. Ascertaining his location, they arrested the men there, Abul Hasan and his son Abbas, and took them to prison in Semirom.

Prison guards did not physically attack the elderly Abul Hasan during his detention but they did severely beat Abbas. A Qermezi man visiting Abbas the third day reported that his face was ashen and distressed, and Abbas had whispered in Turkish that the guards had badly beaten his bare feet (*falak*; bastinado, a common method of torture in Iran). Prison guards would tie a

Decisions and consequences 327

rope around a victim's ankles, string him upside down from the ceiling by using a pulley, and beat the soles of his bare feet with a thin stick until he confessed or fainted. They would also spin him around until he vomited and fainted. They designed these and other methods to weaken the victim's resolve so he would confess and implicate others.[8] In Iran, "violent, corporeal, and humiliating penalties are used to control and limit liberties and natural rights and not to control crime per se."[9] For Abbas and other detainees, these beatings were not punishments stipulated by the court or regulated by law-enforcement officials but, rather, were dispensed by the guards at their discretion, as a form of coercion and control. Long-standing tensions between the Qashqa'i and the Persian residents of the town and region contributed to the guards' violence. Several of Abbas's guards hailed from Vanak, the murdered man's village. They held Abbas personally responsible for the killing.

As soon as the Qermezi men at Hanalishah heard about the arrest, they consulted with Husain Quli (Abul Hasan's eldest son) and then traveled to Semirom to offer support. Murad, Abbas's father-in-law, kept Abul Hasan's family and the other nomads at Hanalishah informed about events. With his youngest son at home to pursue daily pastoral tasks, Murad was free to spend time assisting his kinsmen. His middle son driving the pickup truck, Murad often transported men to and from Semirom and Shahreza. (Abul Hasan and his sons owned no vehicles.)

As the head of Hanalishah's Islamic council and one of the territory's senior men, Bahram Qermezi tried to visit Abbas in detention and eventually succeeded. Along with Jehangir Qermezi (another council member), Bahram wrote a document on the council's behalf to certify as true the statement that Abbas had made shortly after his arrest. It declared simply that, although Abbas was the gun's legal owner, he had not committed the crime or held any foreknowledge of the assault. Bahram applied the council's inked seal to authenticate the statement. Murad's eldest son (the third council member) lived in the distant town of Borujen and was not present to sign.

After seven days, security forces in Semirom released Abul Hasan and transferred Abbas to prison in Shahreza, the nearest town. Abbas's mother and wife welcomed the move. Living conditions there were better and physical abuse less common and severe. Shahreza's prison was more regulated and responsive to judicial procedures than Semirom's, where local officials and guards exercised leeway in their assaults.

Attempting to see their son, Abbas's parents traveled often to Shahreza. Prison officers told them that they could come only on visiting days held once a week. They timed their second trip for that day but a holiday canceled the event. A legal maneuver obstructed their third visit; their fourth finally succeeded. Abbas appeared tired and depressed, and the injuries inflicted on him by his jailers in Semirom were still visible.

Women at Hanalishah worried about Abbas's circumstances, his food and sleeping space. They knew about the experiences of other prisoners and hoped he would not suffer as much as they had. They sympathized with Abbas's wife

328   Decisions and consequences

and young children, unjustly punished by events beyond their control. When a visiting kinsman asked for an update, one woman commented, "He's sleeping there," meaning that no progress had yet been made to secure his freedom.

Bahram, Jehangir, Abul Hasan, and other Qermezi men attended the fortieth-day memorial service for Qarib Ali Jafari in Shahreza. He originated from Vanak but had built a house in Shahreza where he taught high school. Two years remained before his retirement. In a modernizing Iran, citizens were newly attuned to a formally defined retirement when a person ended a salaried government job and began receiving a pension. When someone died prematurely, as in Jafari's case, before harvesting the fruits of a life of labor, people considered it unfortunate.

The Qermezi men attending the memorial service regarded their presence as mandatory. They did not express privately any particular sorrow for the deceased, other than to talk about the odd twists of fate, but they did regret being drawn into the precipitating circumstances. They said their subtribe must be represented at the rites, to demonstrate group solidarity to the deceased's family and kin group and to show their lack of complicity in the murder. The Qermezi attendees especially wanted to draw a positive response from the murdered man's immediate family. They hoped that the Jafari family would ask for a pardon or a minor sentence when its members testified in court. Abbas was still in prison, and the court had not yet issued any ruling about his punishment.

Under Mohammad Reza Shah's regime, homicide cases had fallen in the public sphere. The Islamic Republic adopted an Islamic code of penalties and retributions in 1982, and the private nature of homicide cases became law. A private party, usually the victim's family, alone determined the fate of the accused. It could demand reparation identical to the harm suffered (*qisas*, *lex talionis*, an eye for an eye, the law of exact vengeance), require other forms of punishment, specify monetary compensation (*diyya*), grant forgiveness, or combine any of these actions. The Islamic regime changed the law in 1991 so that perpetrators were once again accountable in the public sphere. Judges and other officials had seen too often that a suspected (and likely) murderer was released from prison after his family paid off the victim's family. The new law stipulated mandatory prison terms of three to ten years for anyone found guilty of murder and who had paid compensation to the victims or been granted forgiveness by them.[10]

Another murder had implicated a Qermezi man in 1984 (see Chapter 4). Qermezi men made frequent individual and collective appeals to the Persian family of the victim so that its members would ask the court to release the accused man from prison. In an act of tribal solidarity, all Qermezi men contributed to the funds paid to the victim's family even though they expressed disgust among themselves about the murder and its circumstances. They had purchased a pardon; the state's rendering of Islamic law entitled them to do so.

According to Qashqa'i custom, a killer's family paid blood money to the victim's family. If both parties were Qashqa'i, the guilty party sometimes also

Decisions and consequences 329

offered a girl in marriage. The expansion of formal legal procedures under the shah's regime in the 1960s and 1970s had modified or replaced some of these tribal codes for the Qashqa'i, and tribal leaders were no longer always able to conceal crimes from state authorities. Then, when the new regime instituted Islamic forms of restitution, including the payment of blood money (diyya), formal state laws matched Qashqa'i customs.[11] Following the details of Islamic law, the courts determined the amount of financial compensation and fines according to the current price of a camel. The nomads laughed about the changing times. The shah had forced them to abandon their camels, and yet camels had now become a form of legal tender for the citizens.

In the 1984 case, the court publicly endorsed the payment of 1.3 million tumans from the Qermezi men to the victim's family, rather than the matter remaining a private affair among the parties as had been necessary under the shah's regime if all sides wanted to avoid involving the government.

In Abbas's case, the Qermezi men had not yet determined their course of action because Abbas was not the murderer. They did expect to have to pay cash to Jafari's family, either privately or through formal legal processes, to gain its support in court and secure Abbas's release.

Weeks later, the authorities freed Abbas from prison. Qermezi men and women visited Abul Hasan's camp to welcome Abbas, a customary gathering whenever kin and fellow tribesmates return home after falling victim to an external crisis. The assembled men considered the next steps. No case like this one would end quickly; it would drag out for months and then years, just as all others of this type did. The new problem would mesh with ongoing legal disputes over Hanalishah and would involve multiple state agencies.

Soon thereafter, Vanak's security forces came to Abul Hasan's tent to seize Abbas again, and they returned him to prison in Shahreza. Abbas's family was shocked by the turn of events until they heard that the murdered man's family had instigated legal action against Abbas and that the Shahreza court had ordered his capture. Iranian (and Islamic?) law stated that a person supplying a lethal weapon was responsible for the crime committed with it. The government's gun permits state that holders may not loan their weapons to anyone. The court noted that if Abbas had not provided Nasiri with a gun, Jafari would still be alive.

The flight and disappearance of the actual murderer also tarnished Abbas. The court held Abbas responsible for the murder in lieu of the killer. If the killer were caught, the court might charge Abbas with illegally loaning his gun and then issue a minor punishment and perhaps a fine.

If the Jafari family in Vanak had not initiated legal action against Abbas, he might have remained free until the issue of the weapon came to court. On hearing the news of Abbas's second seizure, Qermezi men traveled to the Shahreza courthouse to appeal to the authorities there. The case had assumed a new dimension when the Jafari family sued, and the Qermezi were amused, despite their underlying sentiments of concern for Abbas and his family.

330 *Decisions and consequences*

Readers may remember the name Jafari from the previous chapter. A relative of the murdered man, Behruz Jafari had run for a seat in parliament in 1996 after years of preparatory campaigning and had lost to a newcomer, Shahriyar Qermezi. According to the Qermezi, the Jafari family was now punishing Abbas out of revenge and retaliation for the loss of the deputyship and was hoping to gain financial restitution. If Behruz Jafari had won the election, his relatives would have profited economically and politically, and they viewed his loss in these wider, self-serving terms. Some people, especially Semirom citizens, had even voted for Shahriyar in order to cancel votes for Jafari and obstruct the privileges that Jafari would have bestowed on his kin and other Vanak residents.

Hanalishah was a second point of discord between the Qermezi and the Vanakis. Many Vanak men already cultivated there and wanted to increase their access to land and water, and others from Vanak also hoped to obtain plots. (Under Mohammad Reza Shah's regime, Vanakis had profited from poppy cultivation and opium production. When the Islamic Republic banned these activities, Vanak men sought to expand their cultivable land. A lucrative income from a small plot was possible in poppy cultivation, not in growing food and animal fodder.) Qermezi men at Hanalishah had not yet secured clear title to their pastures or to some sections of their cultivable land. The conflicting claims of men from Vanak had tied up the quest in state offices and the courts. Abbas's case became part of these wider conflicts, his fate entangled in them.

Qermezi men traveled to Shahreza to assist Abbas but were unable to schedule a court hearing for weeks. When they finally did face a judge (who was based in Isfahan and came to Shahreza only occasionally to hear and adjudicate cases), they stated that they wanted Abbas released. His imprisonment meant that they were all imprisoned, that he and they were the same body. They stressed how different they, as Qashqa'i tribesmen, were from Persian villagers who deployed violence to solve trivial problems such as a delay in the release of irrigation water. They said they were not responsible if a Persian villager had lied when he claimed that he needed a gun only for killing a wild boar. They would all benefit by the boar's death, and so Abbas loaned the gun.

In this and other legal cases, I often thought that the Qermezi petitioners should stress their most solid defense, which in Abbas's case was that he had not committed the murder and had been innocent in intent regarding the gun. I thought they should avoid other, sometimes peripheral, details, especially if they involved tribal customs that the court did not recognize and might not understand. Yet I did not conduct research in courts where any Qermezi were embroiled in cases and am unable to judge the effectiveness of their strategies.[12]

Abbas remained in prison for seven months and then was released in 1998. He was still free in 2002 but the legal case was unresolved. Whenever Abbas returned to Shahreza to check the court's scheduling, clerks told him that if he located the murderer and the gun, the matter against him would simplify.

The rifle remained missing and so was the murderer. Over the years, when I periodically queried the Qermezi about the case, they often stated, "The gun is still missing," and did not bother to mention the killer's fate unless I specifically asked. Rumors circulated that the fugitive was an office worker in Tehran and that his family in Vanak was in contact with him.

After the murder, relatives of Qarib Ali Jafari seized control of Ali Nasiri's orchard, performed the necessary tasks there, and commandeered the harvest. When Ali Nasiri's wife complained to Vanak's security forces about the confiscation, they were unsympathetic. "The government said nothing" about this local response to the inherent injustice of a murderer still at large.

Notes

1 I have known Mohammad Karim since he was 13 years old. Huang (2009) adds information and a different perspective on the activities of this extended family.
2 Beck (1991) describes the process of moving to villages in 1971.
3 Borzu gave these men many of the gifts I had brought from the U.S. for him. He cherished the presents for himself but thought that by offering them to these men, they might give him a daughter.
4 As subtribal headmen, Borzu and Amrullah were roughly equivalent in political status, but Amrullah had owned land and been wealthy, advantages that raised his socioeconomic status above Borzu's.
5 Huang (2009: 185–215) discusses the life circumstances of Falak Qermezi.
6 Huang (2009: 149–84) provides an account of Fariba Qermezi's life.
7 Two doctors in Saint Louis reviewed Salar Qermezi's medical record (such as it was) from Iran, including two echocardiograms, and diagnosed his situation as a common one that did not require surgery. They are Dr. Sessions Cole of Saint Louis Children's Hospital and Dr. Ernest Strauss (formerly at this hospital).
8 Abrahamian (1999) and Talebi (2011) describe these and other methods of torture in Tehran's prisons before and after the revolution.
9 Kar (2005: 52).
10 Afkhami and Friedl (1994: 180–87), Kar (2005), Niknam (1999: 19–20).
11 The Islamic Republic's security forces did not act in 2011 when the male kin of a Qashqa'i girl, who had eloped with a Qashqa'i boy, caught the pair and burned them alive. They accepted the family's actions as a personal application of Islamic law.
12 A documentary film about women's attempts to secure divorces in Tehran's Islamic courts demonstrates some of the same strategies (Longinotto and Mir-Hosseini 1998).

9 Facing the future
Reflections on 1999

Relationships between the Qermezi and Iran's state agencies waxed and waned in intensity in the postrevolutionary period. Once again I examine specific events and their impact on the Qermezi at the local level: nationwide municipal elections, renewed conflicts about state-mandated Islamic codes of behavior and dress, continuing efforts to prevent land seizures, and the government's intention to construct a village for the nomads at Dashtak.

Revolutionary Islamic councils for villages and towns

Iranians throughout the country heralded the nationwide elections in February 1999 for village, town, and city revolutionary Islamic councils (shura-yi inqilab-i islami). Iran's new constitution in 1979 stipulated the formation of these councils but the regime did not permit any elections in most places for 20 years. During his presidential campaign in 1997, Mohammad Khatami had promised to hold municipal elections if he won. Chosen by a groundswell of support from virtually all sectors of Iranian society, Khatami began preparations for council elections in Iran's "250,000" communities.[1]

The state agency that later became the Organization for Nomads' Affairs (ONA) was charged in 1979 with the responsibility of bringing services to Iran's nomads. One of its first actions was instituting revolutionary Islamic councils, as specified by the new constitution, for nomadic communities. Councils were to serve as a liaison between the nomads and the state. Construction Jihad, later becoming a ministry, planned to do the same for Iran's villages, and many of them—including two Qermezi villages—elected councils. Scholars writing about Iran's councils report that elections did not occur until 1999 under Khatami's presidency. They seem unaware of the thousands of nomads' councils and the tens of thousands of village councils, all of them elected decades earlier (in 1979–81) (see Chapter 3).

When the Islamic Republic prepared in 1998 for elections in Iran's other communities (all villages, towns, and cities), officials expressed mixed sentiments about the already existing nomads' councils. Some stated that they currently functioned, and new elections were unnecessary. Others, particularly those familiar with these communities, noted that members of existing councils might have served since 1979–81 and that new elections were essential to reflect changing attitudes and intragroup politics. They worried about anti-regime sentiments among growing numbers of Iranians and wanted to reevaluate the members of each council and eliminate troublesome ones (in a process similar to the state's wide-ranging purges just after the revolution). The politico-religious sentiments of current council members troubled some officials. Some electees might have misrepresented themselves back then or, two decades later, might have changed their views. People's attitudes toward Islam were in flux because the regime had politicized religious beliefs and practices, and citizens were increasingly hostile toward any forms of religion, institutionalized or not. The government had also deemed "revolutionary" credentials to be essential for council members in 1979–81, a trait difficult to ascertain and verify decades later. Still other officials stated that new elections were unnecessary because the nomads were settling and had joined or would soon join permanent settlements where the government now planned elections. In their view, the new municipal councils would represent many settled and settling nomads in their more-fixed places of residence.

ONA agents in and near Qashqa'i territory supported new elections for the nomads' councils at a future date. They said the government had not yet decided if existing councils would continue and, if they did, what importance they would play. The nomads noted that their councils would become more significant when all villages, towns, and cities elected their own, and their functions would be clarified and strengthened. Proposed new legislation would enhance their operations.

New elections for councils in 1999 affected some Qermezi living in villages but not those in towns and cities. The size of towns and cities meant that the few Qermezi residents there exercised a negligible role in the elections, and the new councils occupied a small or no role in their lives. By contrast, Qermezi residents of villages, especially where their subtribe was heavily represented, did play crucial roles in the elections, and the new councils influenced village affairs. Construction Jihad had previously allowed the two Qermezi villages (Atakula in 1980, Nurabad in 1981) to elect councils, and their residents had maintained them since then. New elections in 1999 demonstrated the extent of changes occurring in these villages during the preceding two decades.

The government allowed settlements it classified as villages to select five candidates to run for the election of a three-person council. It permitted settlements defined as towns more candidates, who would run for a council of five, seven, or more members. City councils could have up to fifteen as in Tehran, Isfahan, and Shiraz. The process was complicated in large communities but was manageable in the two Qermezi villages. Agents of Construction Jihad helped to select the designated number of candidates there. The individuals chosen for these local council elections were not vetted by any external supervisory agencies and did not need to win approval (unlike in towns and cities).[2] Electees would serve four-year terms.

334 *Facing the future*

Possibly wanting to broaden his support in regions in and near Qashqa'i winter and summer pastures, Shahriyar Qermezi (parliamentary deputy, 1996–2000) did not play any particular partisan role in assisting Qermezi or other Qashqa'i candidates in these many elections.

The government held council elections on a Friday in February 1999 in possibly 35,110 settlements throughout Iran.[3] Many voters turned out in most places, and the process attracted national and international attention.

Iranians and others viewed these elections as a referendum for Mohammad Khatami. Iran's moderate president had faced opposition to his reformist policies from Khamenei as the supreme leader and from other hard-line conservative clergy and their supporters since his election in 1997. People within and outside Iran hoped that citizens would elect moderate candidates to the new councils and that Khatami's intended reforms would receive their support. Reformists wanted to expand on their win in the 1997 presidential election and demonstrate the growing enthusiasm of a diverse citizenry for substantive change in Iran's government. Khatami and other reformists promoted these councils as a step toward developing the institutions of civil society[4] and furthering the democratization of Iran. Conservatives also welcomed these municipal elections. They hoped to establish links with their traditional power base in the provinces.[5]

Nationwide, reformists triumphed in these new elections. They hoped the results would lead to victories in the upcoming parliamentary election in 2000 and in subsequent elections.

Hundreds of Qashqa'i were elected in the many settlements where they now resided.[6] I discuss the communities where more than a few Qermezi lived in 1999.

Atakula village was founded in 1966 when Hajji Bua Qermezi of Aqa Mohammadli lineage constructed a house on land owned or controlled by two Persian men. Three of his brothers also built there in the next few years, and more Qermezi families joined the community in the 1970s. The village contained 40 households in 1980. When ONA and Construction Jihad encouraged nomads and former nomads to elect Islamic councils, beginning in 1979, Atakula was the first Qermezi community to do so. Its residents chose Khan Ahmad (son of an early Aqa Mohammadli settler), Sultan Ali (of Kachili lineage), and Fereydun (son of the Persian landowner). With two personnel changes, this council was still in place in 1999 when the village had grown to 100 households, half of them belonging to Aqa Mohammadli men.

The residents, allowed to participate in the 1999 election as a recognized village, offered the names of at least six men as possible candidates. Construction Jihad selected five from among them to run for the three-person council. Son of the Persian landowner, Fereydun wanted to be reelected but was rejected as a candidate. Sultan Ali of Kachili lineage decided not to run again. He had recently assaulted several villagers, and the Borujen court would probably sentence him to prison.

Atakula's five candidates include three Aqa Mohammadli men: Khan Ahmad (member of the original council), Siavash (son of the village founder,

Facing the future 335

Hajji Bua), and Dehdar (son of Ali, an early settler; also the village's first indigenous teacher).

The fourth candidate, Kushtas, is Ipaigli Darrehshuri. His father and several other Ipaigli men had affiliated with the Qermezi subtribe in the early 1930s when their own subtribe was disintegrating, in part because of Reza Shah's enforced settlement policies. Qermezi headmen offered them work and pasture. Several of them settled in Atakula in the late 1960s and the 1970s, and in 1999 seven Ipaigli families lived in the village.

The final candidate, Abbas Ali, is a Musuli Amaleh Qashqa'i man. Several young Musuli men had joined the Qermezi subtribe in the early 1920s after the Qermezi headman married a Musuli woman, and some of their descendants settled in Atakula in the 1970s. The largest group in Atakula by 1999, after the Aqa Mohammadli, consisted of 12 Musuli families. The 19 Ipaigli and Musuli men there enjoyed close mutual ties in the mid-1990s, built on their intermarriages since the 1930s, and Qermezi everywhere tended to call all of them "Ipaigli." As the Ipaigli group rose in status, some other Qermezi in the village (members of the subtribe's original five lineages) were threatened by the change, and they denigrated its members as low-status "yarn twisters," the apparent derivation of the Ipaigli name and group.

During the 1999 campaign, the two Ipaigli and Musuli candidates and their relatives privately promised Dehdar that all Ipaigli and Musuli people in the village would vote for him if he and other Aqa Mohammadli residents voted for them. Agreeing, Dehdar conveyed this strategy to his Aqa Mohammadli relatives, who approved the plan. When the villagers tallied the votes, they saw that the agreement had failed. Receiving the most votes, Abbas Ali of Musuli was declared the council's head. Kushtas of Ipaigli came in second, and Khan Ahmad of Aqa Mohammadli was third. Bitter, Dehdar complained that he had been tricked and betrayed. As the village's majority, the Aqa Mohammadli were dismayed by the results. Men representing only seven Ipaigli families and 12 Musuli families now occupied two of the three council seats, a majority vote for the council, which would act for the village's one hundred families. Even Khan Ahmad was not the first choice of Aqa Mohammadli voters. He won because other people in the village preferred him to Dehdar and/ or Siavash or thought that votes for him would cancel out others' votes for Dehdar and Siavash.

The village's hezbollahis, although steadily losing stridency, were noticeably absent as candidates in Atakula. Sentiment increasingly turning against them and the regime they supported, hezbollahis there (and elsewhere) had lost much of the power and authority they had tried to wield in the 1980s and early 1990s. They wanted positions on the council but understood that village voters would not elect them, and they avoided a public, official display of the community's disapproval and resistance.

Choosing candidates and electing a three-person council was not as problematic in <u>Nurabad</u>, the second Qermezi village. Founded more recently, in 1975, the village consisted of 33 households in 1999, almost all from the

336   *Facing the future*

Kachili lineage. Three households were part of other Darrehshuri subtribes and did not represent any interest group. The villagers elected to the original council in 1980 were all Kachili: Husain (son of a village founder) as the head, his cousin Darab Ali, and Murad (son of a village founder). For the new election in 1999, only three men wanted to be candidates, a decision emerging from private discussions among the villagers. Voters reelected Murad and named him as the head, and they chose Hasan (son of a village founder and brother of a previous winner) and Imam Quli (grandson of a village founder). Given close kinship ties and amiable interrelationships, the three men shared responsibilities equally.

Darrehshuri khans had founded the settlement of <u>Mehr-i Gerd</u> in 1941 for themselves and their servants and workers, practically all from the Darrehshuri tribe. Village politics had changed dramatically since the revolution when the Islamic regime eliminated the khans' power. Rapidly diminishing in influence, the khans withdrew from active politics in the village and concentrated on managing their remaining properties, mainly apple orchards. They resided in the village only in the late spring and the summer. After overseeing the apple harvest in early autumn and worrying about the approaching cold snowy weather, they moved to nearby towns and cities until late spring. Living in Mehr-i Gerd year-round, the village's other inhabitants originated from many Darrehshuri subtribes. Their ancestors had served the khans in various capacities, almost all of them as servants. Fifty to 60 of the village's 200 households were Qermezi in 1999, all of them Kachili. A few Persian men also resided in the village now, and at least several had taken Darrehshuri wives.

Residents of Mehr-i Gerd produced the names of many potential candidates for the 1999 election. Construction Jihad declared five of them eligible. Nadir Shujai received the most votes and became the council head, a position he had also held since 1980. Unlike the two other electees, he is not from the Darrehshuri tribe or the Qashqa'i confederacy. A Persian originally from Shahreza, he had purchased land in Mehr-i Gerd in the 1960s, moved there, and took a Kachili Qermezi wife. Shujai owned an orchard, a grocery store, and a minibus running between the village and Shahreza carrying paying passengers. He played a prominent role in village life.

Fathullah Zailabli, a Zailabli Darrehshuri man and the son of a khan's servant, was also elected. He worked for the village cooperative. The third winner was Abdul Reza Panahpur, the son of a Kachili Qermezi man who had served the khans. He was a paid laborer. The fathers of these two electees had formed part of the khans' personal entourage. When I asked several khans in 1999 about the new council members, they gestured with a dismissive, downward motion and offered only one word, "entourage" (meaning servants), to indicate that the subordinate status of the men's fathers was the only relevant issue. Mehr-i Gerd residents explained Abdul Reza's success simply: all Kachili in the village had voted for him because of his lineage identity.

<u>Narmeh</u> village had attracted some Kachili settlers in the 1960s and 1970s, some of whom left to found the nearby Nurabad village as an exclusively

Qermezi settlement in 1975. Some Kachili residents of Narmeh remained there, and their numbers grew to 13 households by 1999 when villagers voted for the new council. Winning, two long-time Lur residents and one Darrehshuri resident formed the new council. Two Kachili residents, both teachers, stood as candidates but were not elected.

Dezeh, a predominantly Darrehshuri village expanding on both sides of the asphalt road between Borujen and Shahreza, had also attracted Qermezi settlers. Imamverdili men built houses there in the early 1970s and thereafter, and some Qasemli men joined them. Dezeh contained 150 households in 1999, 66 of them Qermezi and 60 or so from Shahinkikhai, another Darrehshuri subtribe, some settling there before any Qermezi. In the 1999 council election, Lashkar of Imamverdili lineage was elected as head of the three-person council, and the two others chosen were Shahinkikhai. Ten to 15 Bahai households were also Dezeh residents; they had lived there since the village's founding. They did not play a role in village politics and did not raise any candidates.[7] A few other Dezeh residents were "one by one," each representing a different Darrehshuri subtribe, and did not form any interest group.

Shahr-i Majlisi, a town Mohammad Reza Shah's regime had built for workers at the steel-mill industrial complex near Isfahan, elected five members to its council. The candidate who came in sixth was Allah Murad, the son of Ghulam Husain of Aqa Mohammadli lineage. He had moved there when he secured a factory job. His family and another one were the town's only Qermezi residents in 1999.

Of the 112 qualified candidates running for election in the town of Kazerun, five men won seats on the council with two runners-up serving as alternates. Two of the five were teachers, two were engineers, and one was a retired army officer. Four of the five are Persians and the fifth a Kashkuli Qashqa'i man. Two other Qashqa'i men were unsuccessful candidates, both Farsi Madan teachers. Three women were unsuccessful candidates: a teacher, a university student, and "the wife of a revolutionary guard." During the campaign, supporters of the 112 candidates affixed their posters—photographs, credentials, and slogans included—throughout the town. The seven Qermezi families residing there in 1999 described the campaign as a time of confusion and commotion as they and other citizens tried to decide among the too-many candidates. The government constructed, in the town center, a new building for the council's meetings and administrative affairs in 2000, which speaks to the importance of the Kazerun council for the regime and its Islamizing efforts.

The town of Dogonbadan (in the district of Gachsaran) is situated along the highway leading north from Kazerun to the oil and natural-gas fields. The government judged 24 candidates as eligible for the election, and five were selected, all Darrehshuri and Kashkuli Qashqa'i men. The director of the Ministry of Education in Dogonbadan had guided the campaign of the Qashqa'i candidates and successfully strategized to prevent any Boir Ahmad Lur candidates from winning. The two main ethnic and tribal groups in the town are Qashqa'i and Boir Ahmad Lurs. Persians also reside there, but most

338 *Facing the future*

of them were recent arrivals who had responded to the availability of jobs in the oil industry. They did not (yet) form any interest group. Qashqa'i and Boir Ahmad tribespeople regarded them as unwelcome intruders who represented the state's attempts to Persianize this strategic region and its crucial economic base.

Semirom elected five council members and two alternates, all Persian men residing in the town. Said to be a sayyid and a shaikh, the elected head was the Friday prayer leader (imam jumih) of Semirom.[8] Not elected, several Darrehshuri candidates complained that Semirom's citizens were hostile toward them because of their Qashqa'i identity. "We don't want Turks [Qashqa'i] here. Turks have no business being in our town," townsmen had proclaimed. Only one Qermezi family lived in Semirom; the man was a state employee there.

In all these locations (except for a minority of Kazerun citizens), the terms "reformists" and "conservatives" did not seem relevant to most voters. (These and other labels were crucial in elections in Tehran and other cities.) Throughout southwestern Iran (excluding Shiraz), voters instead chose candidates based on local kinship, tribal, ethnic, linguistic, and socioeconomic ties and judged them according to their expected competency in addressing community needs. The candidates themselves also avoided the labeling and asserted instead their educational and professional achievements. Those who supported the policies of the new president (Khatami) seemed to be more successful in these elections than those who opposed him. Khatami's presidency was still new, and citizens could not yet gauge how effective he had been in implementing his reformist polities.[9]

A wedding postponed

The wedding celebration of Bahram Qermezi's son was supposed to be the social highlight of the summer of 1999. Bahram was the main contender for the subtribe's leadership but most people were reluctant to support him because of his political leanings. As the only hezbollahi at Hanalishah and Dashtak, he was also one of the subtribe's few remaining ones. Although said to be moderating his stridency, he still demonstrated some hezbollahi traits, which continued to foster people's negative attitudes about him.

Still, Bahram was perhaps the subtribe's second most prominent person (after Shahriyar Qermezi, the parliamentary deputy), and any wedding he would host would draw hundreds of Qermezi tribespeople and their wider Qashqa'i associates and acquaintances. Regardless of the identity of its sponsor, a wedding was an intense, exhilarating occasion, especially given the continuing defiance of the Qashqa'i against the regime's edicts about proper Islamic conduct and attire.

During the previous winter, Bahram had asked his second paternal cousin, Nadir, for Nadir's daughter Mahtab as a bride for his youngest son Bahlul. Bahram's eldest son Farhad had died in the Iraq–Iran war in 1988, and his

Facing the future 339

second son Mehrdad had married in 1991 and had recently become economically independent from his father. Bahram's request pleased Nasir (Nadir's father). Nasir had already given three sons and six daughters in marriage to close patrilateral and matrilateral relatives. Mahtab was the first of his sons' children to marry. Bahlul and Mahtab are paternal third cousins and maternal first cousins (their mothers are sisters), an ideal set of linkages.

Bahram and Nadir were neighbors at Hanalishah and co-residents at Dashtak, and both had built houses in Atakula, the main Qermezi village. Now elderly and ill, Nadir's father Nasir spent the winters in Atakula while Bahram traveled periodically between Atakula and his winter pastures at Dashtak to check on livestock and fodder crops there. A full-time nomadic pastoralist, Nadir migrated between Dashtak and Hanalishah. His house in Atakula was still vacant.

Mahtab had just completed two years of university courses and received a two-year degree. She was one of the subtribe's 27 female high-school graduates and one of its four female university graduates by 1999. Her intended groom had a fifth-grade education. As Bahram's youngest son, Bahlul lived with his father, mother, and unmarried sisters and would care for his parents as they grew elderly. Already he took responsibility for the family's livestock and cultivation in winter and summer pastures. Similar to Nasir, Bahram had carefully chosen spouses for his other children from his close patrilateral kin, and this new match was like the others. He had married his eldest daughter to Bahadur, another of Nasir's sons, and the new bride represented the reciprocal part of an exchange of daughters.

During the spring and early summer, the Qermezi eagerly anticipated the wedding celebration. In every gathering, its topic erupted almost immediately in the exchange of news. "Has Bahram set a date yet? Did he announce the signing of the marriage contract?" People referred to the event as "Bahram's wedding," rather than Bahlul's, and they identified Mahtab as "Bahram's bride."

Qashqa'i everywhere since 1990 had resisted and defied the Islamic Republic's prohibitions against live music, women's and men's dancing, the men's stick-fighting game performed to music, and women's supposedly un-Islamic, immodest dress. The Qermezi were no exception. Hanalishah had not hosted a wedding festivity since 1997 and had held only six such events since 1990, and people wanting more often to enjoy such cultural performances had to attend weddings elsewhere. Their eagerness to celebrate and revitalize their culture—and to reject the regime's injunctions and austere behavioral norms—often distracted people, men mostly, from their economic pursuits, leaving women and children to labor in their absence. Throughout the 1990s many men were gone for days, often traveling from one wedding to another, even if only the most distant kinship and affinal ties connected them with the hosts.

Agitated, people conversed about Bahram's impending celebration. What activities would Bahram—a hezbollahi—permit? Would he allow live music, women's and men's dancing, men's stick fighting, and traditional Qashqa'i attire for women? Or would he forbid these activities so he could hold a more

340 *Facing the future*

solemn, correctly Islamic observance? Would he proclaim his politico-religious stance and subject everyone to it? Would he force his values on those who would co-host the event? Large kinship and tribal groups, not individual families, staged weddings.

People spoke of group honor and the best ways to uphold and enhance it. If they denied support to Bahram—a fellow kinsman and tribesmate—in this event, they would undermine the reputation of the lineage and the subtribe as groups that supported all fellow members regardless of circumstances. If they acquiesced to a wedding that Bahram deemed acceptable according to Islam, they would damage their reputation as groups unified in opposing and resisting the regime. In either case, they would undercut the stature of the lineage and the subtribe. The wedding would evoke many issues wider than simply Bahlul and Mahtab's union.

Since the Islamic Republic's early years, Bahram had publicly asserted his opposition to music, dance, and women's customary dress. (Before the Islamic regime took power in 1979, he had welcomed a full expression of Qashqa'i culture and was no different than other Qermezi men in his matter.) Buttressed by his leadership of Hanalishah's Islamic council, he would denounce certain behaviors. He especially disapproved of women's dancing and their wearing of transparent headscarves.

When Borzu Qermezi's son Dariush had married in 1993, Bahram was the only close relative to thwart women's dancing. Despite his anger about the edict, Borzu reluctantly proceeded with a wedding without the activity. Ever since then, Dariush's wife Farzaneh had bitterly complained about Bahram's interference. She noted, "I'm going to marry only once!" That is, she had already lost her chance for a festivity. As a bride somewhat secluded during the ceremony, she would not have danced but would have known that others were doing so, and people would have praised the event afterward. If she did happen to marry again, her wedding—like that of any previously married woman—would lack musicians and other customary jubilations.

Bahram and several other Qermezi hezbollahis had successfully stifled any overt manifestations of local sentiment on these issues during the 1980s. They were unexpectedly assisted in their cause by the unfolding tragedy of the Iraq–Iran war, which was devastating Qermezi families and groups and deflecting their attention from celebration. The extent of the forced Islamization of Iranian society was still uncertain, and no one yet knew how this broad policy would affect the different dimensions of Qashqa'i society and culture. People pondered, "How has this odd turn of events come about? Why are we even facing these issues?" Of all the possible futures in store for them, no one had ever considered that a harsh Islamic regime would be dominating their lives in these ways.

After the war's ceasefire, and intensifying in 1990 and thereafter, the Qermezi found obvious and subtle ways to defy government restrictions, and the hezbollahis among them were losing the power they had earlier exerted. The wedding of Bahram's son marked a turning point for the Qermezi as they discussed the ways they could respond to a decrease in external pressures.

Facing the future   341

As the weeks of spring and early summer passed, news of other marriage negotiations reached Hanalishah, and soon invitations began to arrive.

Until the late 1980s close kinsmen of a groom's father had traveled by horse or vehicle to deliver verbal invitations to all Qermezi families in their widely distributed locations. Usually weddings followed immediately. A family received a summons one day for a ceremony beginning the next or the following day.

Emulating practices they observed in the wider Iranian society, the Qermezi had adopted printed notifications for the memorial rites of the martyrs of the Iraq–Iran war. They found this new form of communication convenient and began in the late 1980s to distribute printed invitations for weddings as well, a method they had grown to admire among urban acquaintances. Practically all Qermezi (except for the poor) were issuing such formal invitations by the late 1990s. Despite the expense, the procedure proved advantageous, given the subtribe's growing population and people's increasing territorial dispersion. Such invitations were only for first marriages. When the previously married formed new unions because of death or divorce, the groom's family held a small wedding lacking the festivities characterizing first marriages.

Relying now on this new medium of communication, a groom's family needed to plan ahead rather than rushing from the final negotiations with the bride's family to the actual fete. Invitation cards, folded in half, displayed a picture on the front and contained space inside for the details. Copied from Western sources, the images featured light-haired brides and grooms dressed in fancy Western wedding attire, flower-bedecked horses and carriages, multitiered wedding cakes, chandeliers, and entwined lovebirds.[10] A few families paid printers to include the ceremony's details inside the cards while most others purchased cheaper generic ones and entered by hand the information on the blank lines provided.

Inviters, now often teenage boys who lacked their parents' familiarity with all Qermezi, quizzed the people they visited about the names and locations of other families. Often they did not recognize major figures such as the subtribe's elders. On this and other issues related to geographic and social distance, the Qermezi increasingly stated their lack of knowledge about the totality of the subtribe's members. "If we don't see them, we don't know them." The teenagers sat in the first tent, hut, or house they encountered in any given Qermezi territory and addressed the envelopes one by one according to information offered there. They might have already entered the details inside, but sometimes they sat writing the specifics as well. Some requests came addressed only to "Qermezi family" without any personal names attached, which demonstrated a breech of custom that many remarked was shameful.

By mid-July, Hanalishah's nomads had received invitations for five Qermezi weddings occurring within the next week. Several fell on the same days, and people discussed which ones they would attend and whether or not they would travel from one to another. Until the late 1970s weddings had lasted three days but since then they usually began one afternoon or evening and then ended the following evening, a change caused by the need to decrease

342 *Facing the future*

expenses and by people's busier schedules and complicated dispersals. Some weddings were even one-day affairs such as Mansur's (discussed in Chapter 5). Two-day events allowed people to attend more than one wedding if they chose. Sometimes the distance was too great, such as simultaneous rites near Kazerun in winter pastures and in Atakula in summer pastures. People in each territory decided among themselves who and how many would attend. Each Qermezi section, defined in both lineage and territorial terms, wanted adequate representation. The Aqa Mohammadli at Hanalishah, for example, embodied their lineage as well as their location, and at least several men among them were obliged to attend every Qermezi wedding. They also cooperated in providing the group's gift, usually a live goat or lamb that the hosts would sacrifice for the ceremony's meals. Close ties of kinship and marriage often connected some people in each territory to any particular host, and they would contribute additional livestock and other supplies and would assist at the event.

In Semirom on business, Dariush heard that a young Qermezi man who had been delivering wedding invitations had just died. From Imamverdili lineage, Ghulam Husain and two male cousins had been riding a motorcycle, just as they had arrived at Hanalishah the previous day. They were traveling at night to Hana village to present the last set of cards. Ghulam Husain struck the metal struts of a tractor-pulled wagon as the tractor driver turned off the asphalt road onto a dirt track. He had not seen the unlit vehicles and had probably been driving too fast, given the late hour as he neared the task's end. The impact threw the passengers from the cycle, and both were badly injured. Ghulam Husain died instantly, suffering severe head trauma.

Dariush conveyed the sad news when he returned to Hanalishah. Maryam, the deceased man's cousin (her father's brother's son), was the person there most closely touched by the death. Grieving, she prepared to travel to the man's family home. Others decided to accompany her, to offer support, and her husband Bizhan went to inform the several Imamverdili families at Hanalishah and others in the vicinity. After the initial shock, people began recalling their brief encounters with the three men. They regretted the now-pathetic jokes they had told one another, including one about the hennaed hands of the just-deceased man. Some expressed a fatalistic outlook; they said they never knew which conversations would be their last. People understood that this wedding was now cancelled and that all others, if not called off, were postponed. Later they awkwardly referred to the cash gifts they had given Ghulam Husain to help offset the celebration's expenses.

Then someone mentioned the wedding of Bahram's son. What would become of it? To determine Bahram's obligations as a mourner, people calculated the precise degrees of his kinship with Ghulam Husain, first finding the closest paternal ties and then moving on to maternal and affinal ones. Multiple kinship and marriage ties connected any two Qermezi individuals, and people sometimes entertained themselves by finding as many different links as they could. Women tended to stress the ties between and among women and to focus on

Facing the future 343

maternal and affinal connections. They referred to the bride as "Nurijan's daughter" (and not Nadir's). Men often limited their comments to ties between and among men unless a particularly close connection to a woman was relevant, such as their mother.[11]

The closest tie between Bahram and Ghulam Husain was somewhat distant. Bahram's third daughter had married an Imamverdili man whose brother's son's wife was Ghulam Husain's brother's daughter. (It took me several minutes to determine this connection as I scanned the relevant pages of the Qermezi genealogy. Most Qermezi adults knew the closest tie instantly.) While people discussed the kinship, they also considered Bahram's political ties with the subtribe's few remaining hezbollahis—many of them Imamverdili. These connections, rather than kinship alone, would probably determine how Bahram would proceed.

Out of respect for the grief-stricken, Bahram could not announce a wedding date for the next week or so. Yet would he consider holding the event after an appropriate period had passed? What would be the status of music, dance, sport, and festive attire? Would a state of mourning prohibit these activities if Bahram decided to schedule the wedding soon? Several people cynically suggested that Bahram no longer needed to announce how celebratory the wedding would or would not be (each scenario alienating some Qermezi). He could (reasonably) restrict his remarks by saying only that he would offer a simple event without music, out of respect for Ghulam Husain's family and lineage. The terms for a wedding with music (*tuy*) and without (*kurkish*) were distinct, and people often decided not to attend a wedding if they heard that no one would play music. As the Qermezi pondered the possibilities, they shuffled through the invitations they had received for other weddings while saying "cancelled" or "postponed" as they glanced at each one and then tossed it aside.

People discussed their plans to attend Ghulam Husain's burial, which they assumed would occur the next day. They did not know if the coroner had yet released his body from the Semirom morgue. Perhaps his relatives would take him to the Shah Reza shrine in Shahreza for washing and preparing for burial, or they might transport him to his home in Dezeh village for washing there. Most men at Hanalishah traveled together to Semirom to determine the details and then proceed to Dezeh where they would help with the funeral and burial and the many expected attendees. Others at Hanalishah decided to wait until the third-day or seventh-day memorial service. Some suggested that the family might combine the two rites for economic reasons—given that Ghulam Husain had been a manual laborer and his wife and four children were now impoverished. In this case, the event would probably fall between these two days.

That day and during the next few, men and women at Hanalishah and the other Qermezi territories traveled to Dezeh to join the rites. The large numbers attending, including many women, surprised me. Usually a small delegation of Hanalishah's men participated in distant funeral rites for someone in

344   *Facing the future*

another lineage. Often Falak, the senior woman at Hanalishah, traveled with them, despite her ill health. Then someone's casual remark provided an explanation. The new widow is the daughter of the sister of Shahriyar, the parliamentary deputy, who was certain to be present. The nomads at Hanalishah were determined to demonstrate their support for him. Any gathering, even a mournful one, allowed for a full range of discussions, and no man or woman wanted to be excluded and then later forced to hear about the proceedings secondhand. Women's sympathy for a young widow with four small children also drew their attention more than, for instance, an elderly man whose family had long anticipated his demise. An unexpected, violent death, especially of a young man having a family to support, would draw attendees.

All the men, and the closest kinswomen of the deceased, accompanied Ghulam Husain's body to Dezeh's small cemetery. After the burial, they paid their respects at other Qermezi graves, including those of three war martyrs. Then the men visited the village's small mosque to utter the Arabic prayer for the dead and to listen to Quranic recitations. Women said their own prayers at Ghulam Husain's home; the mosque lacked a women's area. Several days later, combining the third-day and seventh-day memorials, people gathered again to mourn and to utter prayers for Ghulam Husain, men at the mosque and women at home. As before, Ghulam Husain's family hired a sayyid to read from the Qur'an at the mosque. "Sayyid, mulla, akhund, ayatollah, grand ayatollah. What's the difference?" several people curtly responded when I asked about the man's identity. Demonstrating their disdain for religious figures, they implied that a low-status Qur'an reader, a man with no formal religious education, was equivalent to an ayatollah at the helm of Iran's government.

Family members postponed indefinitely the wedding of Ghulam Husain's paternal cousin, for whom the deceased man had delivered invitations. Some talked about cancelling it altogether because of the ill-omened beginning, which could potentially signal future problems such as infertility, serious illness, or even another death. They were unwilling to risk further disasters. Another Imamverdili wedding, for which men had purchased and rented supplies just before the death, proceeded but without music or dance.

A wedding between a Qairkhbaili groom and bride went forward according to plan. The groom's immediate kin group lived near winter pastures during the summer, and its celebration there included live music and men's and women's dancing. The hosts explained the festivity by their only-distant kinship with the deceased Imamverdili man and noted that they had sent a delegate to ask permission. Several Aqa Mohammadli men and women at Hanalishah who attended this wedding would not have ordinarily gone. They justified the long trip by saying that the bride is the daughter of Borzu's sister.[12] (Usually the groom's relatives, and not the bride's, frequented weddings. The bride's closest kin often claimed that shame kept them away, a notion that seemed less important in the late 1990s than in 1970. Attitudes about "shame" refer to the impending physical consummation of the marriage.) The Aqa Mohammadli travelers also noted that they needed to reaffirm their ties with the Qairkhbaili, with

Facing the future 345

whom they would soon co-reside (only seasonally) in the new Mulleh Balut settlement (see later).

During the next few weeks, the nomads at Hanalishah and their visitors often asked about Bahram's wedding. Bahram's brothers were almost as uninformed as others, and everyone relied on brief encounters with Bahram in Semirom and observations of his camp's activities. Bahram maintained some social distance from his co-residents at Hanalishah, largely because of his hezbollahi stance, and he held his family closely under control. His sons Mehrdad and Bahlul did not participate in the social life of Hanalishah's other young men, who often went visiting and who sought companions for hunting, distant weddings, and errands in town. No one, women especially, routinely visited Bahram's camp as they did all the others. Nadir and his father and two brothers also kept to themselves, and little or no information was forthcoming from the bride's side either. One day, some men delivered a large load of firewood at Bahram's camp, and people understood that the celebration was approaching. (Weddings needed quantities of firewood for cooking and nighttime illumination.) Bahram borrowed a small water tanker from the Organization for Nomads' Affairs to irrigate his orchard, and his brother reported that Bahram had said he would keep it until after the wedding. The event could be imminent.

People debated Bahram's options, even though they still lacked any firsthand information. If he postponed the wedding for several weeks, he could still avoid having musicians, dancing, and sporting because of the Qashqa'i rules of mourning. A wedding falling before a fortieth-day memorial service was supposed to be solemn and should first have the blessing of the eldest male relatives of the deceased person. After the fortieth, a fully celebratory event was possible, especially if the groom's senior kin visited the deceased's kin to ask permission. If Bahram waited until after the fortieth day, apparently the appropriate gesture given his sentiments about proper behavior, he would then face difficulty explaining the lack of music, dance, and sport on any grounds based on Qashqa'i custom. People anticipated his ostensibly religious reasons for omitting these activities. These days, they said, any action could be justified on the basis of Islam, especially because a single source of religious authority in Iran was lacking.

People noted the inconvenience and even impossibility of trying to reconcile Qashqa'i beliefs and customs with those said to be Islamic. The first were part of their centuries-old heritage and were intertwined in all aspects of their society and culture. The second, in their view, were part of a newly introduced political strategy deployed by Iran's rulers to repress and control the citizenry.

Some Qashqa'i had access to, and perhaps interest in, the state-controlled media (newspapers, magazines, books, and television), where they saw that even the ruling clergy did not censor images of Qashqa'i women dancing at weddings and dressed in customary attire, including the translucent headscarves that reveal their hair. (The regime and its vigilantes still outlawed, censored, and punished such behavior and dress for other Iranian women, especially in cities.)

346　*Facing the future*

Women at Hanalishah commented, "If the akhunds don't object to our dance and dress, why should Bahram? Is he more Muslim than those wearing turbans?"

One woman avowed, "If I attend Bahram's wedding, I will wear a transparent scarf, no doubt about it. If he wants to slit my throat for Islam, well, let him! I am ready to be his sacrifice." Bahram had forbidden women to dance at her wedding, and she was still bitter. (Following Islamic law, Muslims cut the throats of the living animals they intend for eating or ritual sacrifice, to drain the blood.)

On a hiatus from his university teaching assistantship in Tehran, Masud Qermezi announced that he would return for the wedding if Bahram hired musicians, allowed men and women to dance, and permitted men to perform stick fighting. If Bahram forbade these activities, he would not bother to come. "What is a wedding without music?" he asked rhetorically.

The dead man's paternal uncle heard about the controversy and wanted to settle it before it grew more disruptive. Traveling some distance, he formally visited Bahram to urge him to proceed with a musical celebration. He said he felt somehow responsible for the impasse. Others noted the strange turn of affairs. A man planning a wedding should visit a grieving family to ask permission to go ahead. The mourners themselves, fighting back their sorrow, should not have to make these appeals.

Rumors circulated about the impending signing of the marriage contract, an event that would precede the celebration. One evening, Bahram, his nuclear family, and a few close kin gathered at Nadir's home. The groom's brother, Mehrdad, had traveled from camp to camp the previous day and had awkwardly invited the men to attend. Some women did not realize the slight until after he left, and they were angry. Contract signings had always included everyone in the community and were festive affairs, often with singing and dancing. Families received general invitations, not gender-specific ones, and they now worried that Bahram was signifying his intentions for the forthcoming event.

At the signing, Bahram and Nadir good-naturedly argued about the household articles that Bahram was supposed to provide the new couple and about the payment due the bride if the groom divorced her. Bahram did object to buying several items already present in his Atakula house where perhaps the bride and occasionally the groom would reside for brief periods. (The groom would continue to migrate between Dashtak and Hanalishah with the livestock and would occupy the customary dwellings there.) Then Bahram's hezbollahi nephew wrote the marriage contract stipulating the agreement's details, and the groom offered the bride a gold ring, a watch, and a set of Qashqa'i clothes (minus the transparent scarf). Bahram and several other men took turns singing solo some traditional Qashqa'i songs, and the small gathering enjoyed a meal prepared by the bride's family. The next day the groom and bride traveled to Semirom where a low-level clergyman, a shaikh, certified the marriage contract.

Bahram told Nadir (who informed others) that the wedding would fall after Ghulam Husain's fortieth-day memorial and that he would hire musicians.

Facing the future 347

He noted rather obliquely that he would not permit women to dance or to wear diaphanous scarves, both of which he claimed were anti-Islamic acts. Women speculated how he would enforce his injunction about headgear. Would he rip the offending transparent scarves from their heads (thus exposing them even more)? Would he throw more concealing scarves over their hair? Women noted that both actions would bring Bahram into close physical contact with them, which would seem to be forbidden according to his notions about proper Islamic behavior. Would he demand that improperly covered women leave the celebration? All these actions, they said, seemed exaggerated and out of character, for Bahram was not a violent man. Still, they wondered how he would react if they chose to defy him.

The families celebrated the wedding several weeks later. Bahram did not invite any musicians after all. People conjectured that his earlier, unambiguous statement about employing musicians had been a ploy to ensure a large attendance. Some suggested that he had intentionally lied, which they noted was contrary to Islamic principles. They compared his behavior to that of bazaar merchants who proclaimed their piety through public prayer and fasting but who cheated and deceived them in their economic practices. Bahram needed many guests to come, to prove the extent of his political clout, and only the promise of live music (and hence dance and sport) would draw them. Yet he had misled them, or, worse, he had lied, and all in the name of Islam. (If any musicians began to play, Bahram would have been unable to prevent men and boys from dancing and sporting, and so he refused to hire them. People attended weddings to participate and not just to listen to music.) At the wedding, some young men did perform stick fighting to audiotaped music but complained about being uninspired.

One female attendee had considered boycotting the celebration but decided instead to wear a black, tightly buttoned overcoat and an opaque headscarf rather than Qashqa'i dress. Bahram's decrees had forced her wedding some years earlier to omit women's dancing. She said she refused to wear Qashqa'i attire if she had to add a regime-imposed headscarf. The items of apparel contradicted and "fought" with one another, she noted. For her, Qashqa'i dress symbolized freedom, while a dark, concealing scarf proclaimed oppression. As a further act of protest, she chose a dark navy-blue scarf instead of the regulation black one mandated by Bahram and the conservative sector of society (a subtle distinction I might have missed if she had not pointed it out). She always wore flamboyant Qashqa'i dress at weddings, and she knew that others would understand her attitude about this one. Women praised her courageous stance. Several remarked about the irony of a woman wearing conservative dress only to demonstrate her hostility toward it.[13]

Most wedding participants traveled the short distance from Bahram's camp to Nadir's, nearby on a hilltop. Women and girls joined the bride in her father's home as she prepared to leave, and they serenaded her with song. One inserted an audiocassette of Qashqa'i music into a player they found there. In celebration they began to dance in the closed-door, confined quarters of the

348 *Facing the future*

house's single room. Within seconds, a belligerent Qermezi hezbollahi—the one who had written the marriage contract—banged open the door, rushed into the room, and ripped the audiotape from the machine. He ordered the women there to stop dancing. They reluctantly complied, not wanting to disrupt the event any further for the despondent bride. Later they said they had remembered another wedding at this site, which had ended abruptly when two young Qermezi hezbollahis had forbidden women's dancing (discussed in Chapter 4). Women commented that the man must have been lurking just outside the house to spy on them. One joked about yet other ironies. The only man who had eyed their supposedly un-Islamic, provocative motions was the one who violated women's private domestic space and who claimed that Islam prohibited men from seeing such a spectacle because it aroused them sexually.

After dispiritedly escorting the bride to the groom's camp, the wedding participants dispersed to their own camps and homes.

Assaults against their lands

Qermezi nomads, as they left winter pastures every year, steeled themselves against the probability of new assaults against them. On their arrival at summer pastures in 1999, they saw that Persian and Lur cultivators had staked new claims on the land, water, vegetation, buildings, and roads of Hanalishah during their absence. Despite the nomads' stated intentions to hire guards to protect their interests, they never managed to do so. No one lived at Hanalishah year-round, and the only guards potentially available resided among the assailers and could not be trusted. During their stay in summer pastures, the nomads confronted the threats these cultivators orchestrated. During their absence, they worried about new incursions and further destruction of natural resources and material goods. The cultivators and other trespassers undercut their confidence in being able to protect their property and other investments.

Disputes at Hanalishah were caused and exacerbated by conflicting state and local definitions of land, by new and modern technology, by competing state agencies, and most of all by the Islamic regime's persisting inability to rule on land reform and redistribution despite 20 years of promises. The government continued to lack any clear policies or laws for the ownership of property, especially land.

The nomadic pastoralists and the settled agriculturalists each held their own notions about land and its use. Since Mohammad Reza Shah had nationalized pastures in 1963, the presence of water usually marked the legal boundary between pastoral and cultivable land. The government defined as pastures any land above—at higher elevations from—a natural source of water. It defined any land below as (potentially) cultivable. In this semiarid region, agriculture was difficult, uncertain, or impossible without irrigation, and the availability of water determined the cultivable areas. Land without water determined the pastoral areas. Yet new and modern forms of irrigation had transformed these categories by bringing water to formerly dry land, and prior customary and

Facing the future 349

legal definitions grew muddled. State agencies established competing interests in either pastoral or agricultural land and rarely both. Conflicting policies defined specific areas at Hanalishah as one or the other. If land was cultivated, herders could not graze their livestock there during the growing and harvest seasons (a period filling the herders' sojourn at Hanalishah). If land was pasture, no one could cultivate it. The vested interests of the pastoralists in pasture and the cultivators in cultivable land meant that disputes between them were inevitable. Complicating the situation, many pastoralists also cultivated and grew dependent on the water that the cultivators also needed.

Hanalishah's 60 or so cultivators in 1999 resided in the town of Semirom (25–30 of them) and the villages of Vanak (16–20) and Galleh Qadam (16–17). These numbers represent the land's alleged owners, at least the men who claimed they owned or held rights to the land they worked. (I use the term "cultivator" here to represent these men only and not their dependent sons or the laborers they sometimes hired. I use the term "pastoralist" here to represent the nomads even though many of them also cultivated.) Some cultivators employed laborers to perform all or much of the work, and most relied on them for the harvest. During the agricultural season, the cultivators and their male relatives and laborers traveled to Hanalishah every day.

The Qermezi had never intermarried with the Persian and Lur cultivators at Hanalishah (or in the region), and no kinship or marital ties connected them. Only men and boys from Semirom, Vanak, and Galleh Qadam worked Hanalishah's land, and Qermezi women and girls experienced little or no contact with the females in the cultivators' families. If these families had lived at Hanalishah, relationships among the men might have been less antagonistic than they were. The two groups of women would have possibly engaged in social and economic exchanges for the betterment of their respective families.

The cultivators did not build dwellings for their families at Hanalishah, not even for use in the summer. As they increased their investments in the lands they claimed, they too worried about incursion, destruction, and theft, more from passersby and fellow cultivators than from the pastoralists, who were present only when the cultivators worked the land. Some cultivators built thatched huts where one or more men slept some nights, particularly during the harvest, and where they temporarily stored equipment. Unlike the pastoralists, they fortified their claimed plots with stone walls, barbed wire, fences, thorny bushes, boulders, rock piles, and dirt embankments.

Although all the pastoralists at Hanalishah held the government's exclusive, legal grazing permits for specifically delineated territories, they found that during their absence the cultivators had converted part of this land to agricultural use. Depending on rain and melting snow (and not irrigation), the cultivators often produced a harvest only equaling the amount of seed they had sown. Still, they had established a precedent for cultivating these plots that might lead to their obtaining legal deeds in the future. Over the years, the farmers had moved steadily closer to the nomads' campsites. A cultivator planted barley a stone's throw from Mahmud Qermezi's tent in 1999 and incrementally

350 *Facing the future*

expanded other areas he had sown in years past, as he had done every year.[14] Three other cultivators destroyed part of Mahmud's campsite when they constructed a large concrete reservoir to hold the water issuing from his camp's springs. The pastoralists who were less affected by these illegal maneuvers were those who purchased land and brought it under cultivation themselves. They were better able to control their rights to grazing land by buying portions of the adjoining territory and planting apple orchards there, which served as buffers. Yet many lacked sufficient water to sustain these new ventures.

Poppies for opium production had been the major cultivated crop of Vanak village before the Islamic Republic. (Vanak cultivators reported that the new regime had executed some 30 villagers in the 1980s for opium production, sale, and consumption.) When this lucrative source of income diminished and then ceased after 1980, the cultivators there turned their attention to other crops and to expanding their arable land. One nearby region they particularly sought was Hanalishah, thus increasing competition and raising values. Even if the pastoralists had wanted to buy land there in the 1990s, prices had risen beyond their reach.

Water was more precious than land. Without water, only two livelihoods were possible at Hanalishah: pastoralism and non-irrigated cultivation with unpredictable harvests. (Gathering of natural resources and hunting were supplementary activities.) With water, various kinds of cultivation were possible, and the market value of this land rose rapidly. Modern technology had opened up new parts of Hanalishah to agriculture, and the cultivators anticipated further such developments when they staked their claims to currently unusable land. They plowed pastureland (thereby destroying the natural vegetation for the long term) but did not yet plant there because water was lacking, and for the same reason they left fallow other land they had earlier claimed, plowed under, and sown (perhaps only once).

Hanalishah's four sources of water were a small river issuing from springs and melting snow in the mountains to the east, two man-made underground aqueducts (qanat) predating the arrival of the Qermezi group, many natural springs, and winter rain and snow. The river had flowed naturally through the Hanalishah valley in 1970, and the few cultivators there at the time had dug small irrigation channels toward their fields along the banks. These cultivators, their sons, and many new claimants had destroyed the river's flow by 1999, by sculpting the landscape with bulldozers, backhoes, and cement. Ceasing to exist, the river now took the form of dozens of narrow concrete channels snaking their way steadily downhill from the eastern mountain pass through pastureland to the valley floor. By constructing canals in the hillsides, the cultivators had raised the river from the valley bottom to the hill slopes and let gravity bring water to their new fields there. These new cultivated areas were (former) pastures still legally belonging to the Qermezi.

The pastoralists and cultivators also competed fiercely over Hanalishah's uncultivated vegetation, especially the lush growth along watercourses, within orchards, and at field verges. The more men relied on irrigation, the more

Facing the future   351

profuse this wild vegetation became. Cultivators staked their claims to this growth on the principle that their efforts had created it. Pastoralists claimed the territory as theirs and said they were entitled to harvest what they chose. They depended on the wild growth, especially from mid-summer on, when most natural pasturage distant from water sources was depleted and when they could not yet migrate to winter pastures.

As the pastoralists increased their investments by constructing on and improving their sites, they risked the wrath of the cultivators, who viewed any sign of permanence as a threat to their interests. During the pastoralists' absence, the cultivators severed the trees that the nomads had planted to create shade, cooler microclimates, erosion control, windbreakers, and raw materials for structures they eventually intended to build. The cultivators hauled away the cut trees for use as firewood or left the trunks where they fell. They stole any items they could find, including livestock fencing and troughs, and they broke into huts and other dwellings to pilfer goods the nomads had stored there.[15]

After the nomads left Hanalishah in the late summer of 1995, some cultivators broke the wooden door of Mohammad Karim Qermezi's new one-room house, carried off all the articles he had left there, and cached hay inside. For warmth inside the chimneyless house, they built fires that coated the walls with smoky residue. The invaders used charred sticks to scrawl obscenities on the walls. During Shahriyar Qermezi's campaign for parliament, trespassers wrote offensive remarks about him peculiarly intermixed with Quranic phrases. (Shahriyar's main competitor hailed from Vanak, where some cultivators lived.) Despite repeated efforts by Mohammad Karim and Bulqais to whitewash the walls, many words and phrases were still visible years later, including an insulting rhyme. "If a Lur becomes prosperous, at the end he's just a donkey. If a Turk [Qashqa'i] earns a high-school diploma, at the end he's just a first-grader." Before they left Hanalishah in 1998, Mohammad Karim and Bulqais tacked a miniature Qur'an to the door after locking it. On their arrival in 1999, they saw that the trick had actually served as a deterrent. For the first time since they had built the dwelling in 1993, no one had broken in, and the possessions they had stored there were untouched. They laughed about the superstitious cultivators, who seemed to believe that God would punish them for disregarding His word. Without God's warning (the Qur'an), the cultivators might have proceeded to trespass, steal, and destroy.

The roads and paths at Hanalishah were also a source of contention between the pastoralists and cultivators. A rough dirt road ran into the territory, descended into the valley, and ascended the hills to the west. Halfway through, a branch forked toward the eastern mountain gorges. Narrow dirt paths angling off the main route led to each of the nomads' campsites. Most pastoralists had only periodically relied on motorized vehicles until the 1980s but afterward they came to depend on them. Always needing roads, the cultivators were now even more dependent on tractors, earth-moving equipment, trucks for transporting supplies and produce, and personal conveyances for

352 *Facing the future*

daily travel to and from their fields and orchards. They took shortcuts through grazing land and even through campsites, to the pastoralists' annoyance. Piling mounds of stones and dirt, the cultivators were quick to block any paths they wanted restricted near the land they claimed, but they promptly dismantled any barriers that the pastoralists constructed for the same purpose. They also rendered the main and side roads often impassable because of their irrigation ditches, which they dug alongside and across roads, and water oozed and overflowed from them.

Persian vacationers and local tourists also used the dirt road running through Hanalishah, and these trespassers irritated the pastoralists in other ways. Some pilgrims traveling to the Zain Ali shrine to the west took the Hanalishah road instead of the new asphalt one bypassing the territory. They usually drove straight through without stopping unless to refresh themselves at a spring. Other types of travelers were more disruptive. The territory's cultivators invited families and friends to their orchards on Fridays and other holidays. Residents of Semirom and the distant Shahreza came uninvited on these days too and, intruding, searched for shady sites near water for their entertainment. These travelers sought Hanalishah's relative isolation and seclusion so they could enjoy the activities that the Islamic regime defined as illegal, immoral, and un-Islamic. Outsiders wanted refuge and privacy so they could consume alcohol, smoke opium and take other drugs, play games of chance (playing cards, backgammon, and chess) and gamble, listen to and sing and play forbidden music, dance, form relaxed social groups of unrelated men and women, and violate the state's mandates for women's and men's dress, appearance, and conduct. The pastoralists knew that some trespassers engaged in illicit sexual activities, including male homosexuality.[16] "While the official policy has consistently aimed at imposing an ascetic and puritanical 'Islamic' value system onto traditional Persian culture, objective reality has triumphed over ideological dogma. The 'cultural engineering' seems to have produced *contradictions, deception, and escape* instead of spiritual unity ... or social harmony."[17]

The regime issued severe penalties in the 1980s and early 1990s against people violating Iran's new laws and regulations. Inspired by restrictive conservative values, members of Semirom's revolutionary Islamic committee conducted surveillance and wrote reports, local revolutionary guards arrested and detained people, and local courts determined sentences. These institutions had decreased their scrutiny and arrests by the mid-1990s but citizens still feared that the regulators would catch them engaging in regime-prohibited activities. Ahmadinejad's presidency (2005–13) emboldened these state agents to police, restrict, and punish people's social activities once again.

Persian visitors and trespassers at Hanalishah sought precisely these forbidden pastimes, sometimes engaging in all of them virtually simultaneously. The noise they made could be heard long distances. Every Friday morning from late spring until early autumn, car after car loaded with exuberant passengers arrived to seek shelter in any secluded location under trees belonging to an acquaintance or a stranger. Reveling in the orchards, they damaged trees and stole fruit. They polluted the water and the surrounding area with human wastes and garbage. They stole firewood, even dismantling fences and huts for fuel, and risked burning trees and structures.

Trying to avoid the revelers, the nomads were annoyed when delegations came to their tents and huts to request spring water, free pastoral products including fresh meat, and charcoal for the braziers used in opium smoking. A Persian group, all strangers to the Qermezi, asked for charcoal, then a brazier, then an opium pipe and its implements, and finally, hesitatingly, the opium itself. Customary codes of hospitality required the tribespeople to treat guests respectfully. Yet the Qermezi did not smoke opium or possess the substance or its paraphernalia, and the intruders transgressed behavioral norms and were not even their guests. Still, the nomads hoped that these outsiders could prove to be "friends" who could help them navigate the wider Iranian society, and they sometimes handed over the requested item if they possessed it. If alone and unacquainted with these unwelcome visitors, women sometimes gave small quantities of food or fuel or claimed they lacked the sought-after goods. They often told the strangers to return when the men of the camp were present, thereby cynically exploiting notions found in Iranian society about gender separation and women's inability to act independently.[18]

The coroner's outing

Mahdi Quli Sami of Semirom bought an apple orchard at Hanalishah in 1998 so he could enjoy a pleasant place outside of town to entertain family and friends privately. Containing 300 mature trees, the orchard cost him nine million tumans. The seller was the son of Ghazanfar, one of Hanalishah's first cultivators. Sami was the coroner at Semirom's hospital.

One Friday in August 1999, while the nomads nearest the dirt road were performing their usual tasks, a rising cloud of dust appeared to the south. Then they saw one car after another, 13 in total, speeding toward them. As the first vehicle came abreast of Mohammad Karim's spring, the driver slammed on his brakes, causing the second to crash into him. The others screeched to a halt, the only motion being the dust cloud rising in the air. Leaving the engines running, the drivers and passengers rushed downhill to the spring to fill containers. Full of spirit, they laughed and joked, already enjoying their exciting outing with its forbidden pleasures. Several women pushed Bulqais aside so they could splash water on their faces. She was washing clothes there, but the 50 or so trespassers said nothing to her and pretended they did not see her. Hastening back to their cars, the vacationers sped toward Sami's orchard in the valley bottom. They acted as if they had already lost precious time from their planned illicit activities.[19]

I asked Mohammad Karim, who witnessed this onslaught from his porch, why he did not protest against the incursion. He shrugged his shoulders as if to say that any action against them was ineffective, even impossible. I similarly queried his brother Dariush, also present. Receiving no answer except another

354   *Facing the future*

shrug, I remarked, "You know, the bridge you're now constructing at the entrance to your orchard will benefit these kinds of trespassers. You'll have hoards of vacationers coming from as far away as Isfahan to steal your apples and destroy your trees with their antics." His eyes widening with understanding, Dariush looked at me with dismay. I asked again why he did not try to restrict the trespassers. His answer was identical in form to the ones I had heard his father Borzu utter over the years when faced with similar uninvited guests and other intruders. With a sigh, Dariush responded, "Perhaps we will need Sami if we're hospitalized in Semirom or if we need someone's body released from the morgue there."

I never expected any such reciprocity. Yet, not even a year later, Mohammad Karim and two other Qermezi men proved to be the only ones able to help Jehangir Khan Darrehshuri when his son Bahman suddenly died en route to Semirom's hospital. Only Mohammad Karim knew where Mahdi Quli Sami was that afternoon. He went to Sami's orchard at Hanalishah to extract him from his entertainments so he could return to Semirom to issue the death certificate and release the body. The Qermezi men were then able to take Bahman first to be ritually washed and then to Mehr-i Gerd's cemetery to be buried. Elderly, alone, and unable to perform these tasks, Jehangir Khan depended absolutely on these Qermezi men to assist him.

The illegal walnut grove

In the disruption and turbulence during and following the revolution in 1978–79, a Persian man from Semirom seized a small plot of Borzu Qermezi's legal pastureland by plowing and planting grain. Unlike a few other cultivators in the Hanalishah valley, Abbas Shahbazi and his father had not been peasants (raiyat) who had farmed the land on behalf of the paramount Qashqa'i khans and who had then (perhaps) obtained title to it through the land reform of the 1960s. He lacked the advantages these other cultivators enjoyed.

Abbas Shahbazi selected this piece of land because a small spring issued forth there, which he used to irrigate the new crop. The plot sat on a steep mountain slope above the dirt road leading into the Hanalishah valley. Shahbazi chose a time, after the nomads had migrated to winter pastures, that enabled him to complete the job without interference.

On his return the following spring, Borzu filed complaints with the natural-resources agency. Its rangers were supposed to protect nationalized pastureland, but the case lingered for years in this and other bureaus. At the time, Borzu was more troubled about the seizure of a larger, richer piece of land next to his summer campsite (discussed in Chapter 5). As his illness worsened, he was unable to pursue adequately the case of the small plot. If he had been healthy, he would have forcibly expelled the man, as he had often done in his life, perhaps by destroying the crop just before harvest or by burning the piled grain and straw afterward.[20]

Two decades later (1998), encouraged by legal delays and the Islamic Republic's persisting inability to rule on land disputes, Abbas Shahbazi

Facing the future 355

planted 60 walnut saplings on the same small plot of grazing land. The time he chose was early spring before any nomads had arrived from winter pastures, and he used the natural spring there to water the trees. The land now belonged to Borzu's sons who held exclusive legal rights to graze livestock there. On their arrival they were disturbed by Shahbazi's trickery.

One day Shahbazi climbed the slope to tend the trees and saw evidence that livestock had visited the small orchard. He filed a complaint with the Ministry of Justice in Semirom that Dariush and Bizhan's goats had eaten all the new leaves. Irritated that "a new crisis like this one erupts every day," Dariush considered his options. He shouldered these burdens so Bizhan could devote himself to the animals, and he had grown troubled by the waste of money, time, and energy that new and ongoing disputes caused him. Countering with their own legal claim, the Qermezi brothers stated that Shahbazi's objections were invalid because the land was their pasture and the orchard was illegal. Besides, they queried, where is the proof that their goats ate the leaves and not someone else's? In their document, they detailed an elaborate (but implausible) scenario whereby a mystery herd had wandered over the jagged, impassable mountain ridge to the east. (They did not emphasize the main issues, that the land was legally theirs, not Shahbazi's, and that it was legal grazing land, forbidden for agriculture.) Shahbazi stacked stones around the grove to prevent goats from further bothering the trees. Annoyed by animals climbing over the wall, he continued to pursue the case with local authorities. When several trees dried up from insufficient water, he blamed the goats for the loss. Encountering Dariush one day on a Semirom street, he yelled, "My walnut trees don't have a single leaf left."

Shahbazi, and some unrelated men who also carried the family name Shahbazi, regularly used the dirt road running in front of Dariush and Bizhan's camp. Until Shahbazi planted the walnut orchard, he and the other Shahbazis had maintained sociable ties with the Qermezi brothers. They waved when they drove or walked past the camp en route to and from their orchards and beehives, and they sometimes dropped off gifts of produce. They reported news, such as the death of a prominent Semirom citizen or the theft of the town's single water pump (which left the townspeople without water for days). The Qermezi brothers in turn patronized the Shahbazi shops in Semirom and offered their own pastoral products when the men passed by. These "friends" were the types that the nomads tried to foster, individuals who could provide them with goods and services. The brothers hoped that the men, as they traveled along the road by their camp, would serve as deterrents against thieves and vandals, and they relied on them during the spring and autumn when the nomads migrated or resided elsewhere. During the winter, deep snow covered the land, and no one lived in or passed through the area.

Abbas Shahbazi's determined efforts to retain the plot and protect his fledgling walnut grove ruined, at least for the time being, the cordial relationships from which both parties had profited. Whenever Shahbazi passed by the nomads' camp in 1999, he faced forward and ignored the people there. Dariush waved dispiritedly without earning a response.

356 *Facing the future*

Despite the labor he was investing, Shahbazi did not care about the orchard itself, especially given its small size and inadequate water. Rather, Dariush and Bizhan knew that he and the other Shahbazi family harbored designs on the rest of their land. Similar to Hanalishah's other cultivators, the Shahbazi men constantly tried through often small-scale, incremental efforts to gain greater access to the land, water, and other resources. They fought against the nomads, who were simultaneously attempting to enhance their own ties to the land. They engaged in an aggressive policy on these two fronts, to expand their interests and to restrict and eventually expel the nomads. They held the advantage because they lived year-round in the area. They also benefited by their residence in Semirom where they had developed ties and created networks in township offices and with prominent authorities. The cultivators, willing to expend their energies these ways, hoped that pastoralism was a declining livelihood and that agriculture was the best strategy for the future. Knowing that the course of events would eventually justify their aggressive efforts, the cultivators could afford to be patient. The longer they worked these lands and expanded their territories, state agencies were more likely to support their claims.

Only two willow saplings stood in the orchard in 2000. Goats and insufficient water had deprived the walnut trees of their life-sustaining leaves. Natural-resource agents came twice to assert that Shahbazi lacked any rights to the land, that it was still legal pastureland. Yet Dariush and Bizhan feared that Shahbazi would renew his efforts to fortify his claims to the territory (and the surrounding lands), aided now by a lengthy, state-created bureaucratic record of his having cultivated on the site for more than two decades. The brothers noted that they needed to be vigilant. In many such cases, the state eventually ruled on behalf of those who possessed proof of prior cultivation. In this instance, the state itself had created the official record through the visits and reports of its agents (even though many of the documents actually favored the Qermezi brothers).

The walnut tree

A large walnut tree grew on Borzu's pastureland just south of his primary summer campsite.[21] It had been part of the orchard planted illegally in 1981 by the Shahidani brothers, Persian residents of Semirom (see Chapter 5). The Pastures Organization had forced the Shahidanis to return half of the land to Borzu in 1991, and its workers severed the apple trees there. Just beforehand, the brothers transplanted some cherry and walnut trees to the still-standing upper half of the orchard, which the government now apparently entitled them to keep. One walnut tree remained, perhaps too large to transplant, and Mohammad Karim and Dariush urged the brothers not to destroy it. Its young trunk protected against goats by a metal mesh cage, it continued to grow, fed by a small spring near its base, and Borzu's campmates relaxed in its shade. Children played there, improvising as they built miniature

Facing the future 357

camps and assembled pebbles as their sheep. Borzu's daughter Fariba especially appreciated the spot. She slipped away to sit there alone in the late afternoon, to rest from the day's work and to prepare for the tasks yet at hand. The light at this time was striking; the harsh glare of midday was gone, and the sinking sun illuminated the slopes and peaks of the surrounding mountains.

Natural springs had bubbled from the ground of Borzu's campsite and the surrounding pastureland until the 1980s. Persian and Lur cultivators in Hanalishah's valley in the early and middle 1980s had dug deep wells and installed motorized pumps to raise groundwater for use in irrigation. They had also exploited the small river flowing through the valley bottom. As they seized additional land away from the river and up the surrounding mountain slopes, they sought other sources of water. Steady use of the new pumps had diminished the area's spring water.

The flow of Borzu's springs had dwindled by 1990, and during the decade to come their output grew less every year. Some of them producing water in mid-spring were dry by summer. Dariush's and Bizhan's families were soon forced to transport water from Mohammad Karim's spring downhill. The three families of this site now possessed only one dependable spring, and its yield also steadily declined. They wondered what they would do without locally available water. The (former) abundance of free-flowing, clear, clean spring water had always been primary among the pleasures of summer pastures, especially compared with winter ones.

A Semirom resident, Pashutan Sadiqi, planted in 1980 an orchard of 2,500 apple and apricot trees just below Borzu's campsite to the northeast. His father Ghulam Reza was one of the first Persians to cultivate at Hanalishah. He had seized the land's lower portion in 1963 during the confusing early days of land reform, and his son confiscated adjoining sections farther up the slope during and just after the 1979 revolution.

Initially Pashutan irrigated the large orchard by using the natural springs in the land's upper reaches. When output diminished, he channeled water from the springs just above the orchard. When this flow also decreased, he constructed a massive concrete reservoir above the orchard to collect water from the springs there. Some springs now issued within the dirt-bottomed reservoir while others were outside it, their water entering through narrow concrete canals. Whenever Pashutan wanted to irrigate the trees, he released water from the reservoir and used gravity and a network of dirt channels to carry it throughout the expansive orchard. When he finished, he closed the pipe valve and allowed the springs to replenish the reservoir's supply.

The land that Pashutan had stolen for the reservoir in early 1995 was Borzu's pasture. Knowing about Borzu's worsening illness, he exploited the opportunity it gave him. He made sure to complete the construction before any nomads returned to Hanalishah that spring. When Borzu's sons arrived from winter pastures, they were outraged by the Persian man's bold move and reported the invasion to the Pastures Organization.

358 *Facing the future*

The reservoir, and the assault it signified, was Borzu's last impression of the territory he loved. As he rode away from Hanalishah for what proved to be the last time, he cast his eyes first at his family gathered forlornly by his house, then at the reservoir and the devastation that its construction had caused to the surrounding landscape, and finally at the bleak and dusty road ahead of him.

Pashutan grew more agitated about his orchard in 1996 and 1997. The output from the springs he had commandeered was steadily diminishing. Using deep wells and pumps, his fellow cultivators in the area were extracting more groundwater for their orchards than rain and melted snow annually replenished. Without sufficient water, the trees would die and the land would lose its value. Pashutan had long desired to seize further territory just uphill where other springs were located but Borzu's sons were well entrenched on the site. Two stone houses and a stone-fortified livestock pen stood there, visible year-round evidence that others already claimed the territory. Unable to grab the land, at least for the time being, Pashutan sought to control the water issuing from there.

When Pashutan arrived by vehicle from Semirom to begin the day's work in his orchard, he would shout abuses from his car window as he slowly drove by the nomads' camp just uphill from the reservoir. His tirades increased in hostility if he spotted anyone handling water. Even women washing clothes in a trickle below a spring incited him. When he saw shepherds filling livestock troughs with spring water, he would leap from his car and rush downhill to yank out the plastic hoses. "That water is mine!" he would scream repeatedly. Spring water flowed downhill and would eventually enter his reservoir unless the nomads used it first. (Seepage into the streambeds and banks, as well as evaporation, also reduced the supply of water for him.) The camp's residents learned to ignore him but the tension he created grated on everyone.

When I suggested retaliatory action, the nomads initially and persistently responded that Pashutan would destroy their houses and pens as soon as they left Hanalishah for winter pastures. When my daughter Julia proposed that the nomads could construct their own concrete reservoir on their own land, just uphill from Pashutan's reservoir (which also sat on their land), so they could collect what was their own water, they looked wide-eyed at her. They held full legal rights to take this action but feared the Persian's revenge. Julia and I remained puzzled by the nomads' restraint and good manners when they faced the greed of others for land and water that was not legally theirs. Borzu would have physically removed Pashutan from his land if the man had dared to commit any aggression against him or the other nomads.

The water problem grew more severe by the spring of 1998, and Pashutan developed new tactics. The nomads migrating from winter pastures discovered that he had dug new channels leading from the springs at their campsite toward his reservoir and had straightened and deepened existing ditches so water would flow more directly downhill toward the land he claimed. He repaired and redirected the channels in the nomads' presence, without uttering a word, whenever the reservoir's supply was threatened.

Facing the future   359

By the spring of 1999, algae obscured the reservoir's thin layer of stagnant water, and its surface did not reach the mouth of the pipe that should have directed the flow from the catchment. Pashutan was in despair. His orchard was doomed.

Every day Pashutan marched along the ditches to inspect the flow from the springs. One morning when the three Qermezi brothers were away on business, Pashutan intruded on the camp so he could break open a small pond there (used by the camp's animals for drinking) to allow its water to flow downhill. By this time he seemed obsessed. The minuscule quantity he tried to claim would not make any difference to the orchard, even if it did reach the reservoir. Returning to the camp, Dariush restored the pond's banks so water could again slowly collect there, and Bizhan directed his shepherd's son to fill the ditch leading downhill. They performed these chores as if they were ordinary, daily ones not charged with tension.

Early one morning several days later, Borzu's daughter Fariba shouted toward the nomads' camp that Pashutan was cutting the roots of the solo walnut tree. Women and children came running, to find two of his hired workers removing dirt from a hole they were digging alongside the tree trunk. As usual, Pashutan wore a white shirt to distinguish himself as a landowner, superior to the hired workers who dressed more suitably for the muddy task. "Pashutan is killing my tree," Fariba sobbed. Continuing, she noted that he hated any sign that nomads lived here. "One tree is the beginning of an orchard!" he had yelled at her, blatantly ignoring the history of this particular tree and the lack of water for any orchard. Perhaps suspecting that the camp's men would find recourse through the state, he did not cut down the tree. As he chopped at the roots he and his workers had exposed, he claimed he was only assisting the output of the spring there.

The camp's men were gone for the morning, and no other men were nearby to confront Pashutan. By the time Dariush and Bizhan assessed the damage, Pashutan and his laborers had excavated a huge hole at the tree's base and had unearthed, severed, and cleared away all the roots they could find. The hole was so deep that the nomads could not see, from a distance, the men inside. Pashutan again insisted that he was only improving the spring's flow and was not damaging the tree. The brothers saw that the hole's depth and width and its close proximity to the tree trunk were not warranted if better access to water were his only goal. They told him to stop. Seemingly ready to quit for the day anyway, due to the noontime heat, he and the workers returned to his orchard downhill.

Several times later that summer, the camp's inhabitants found Pashutan digging in the hole, and again the Qermezi brothers insisted that he cease. They regretted that whatever action they took against him now, they were powerless once they left for winter pastures. They expected the tree to be dead by the next spring, the limbs and trunk hauled away by villagers to use as firewood during the frigid winter.

When the nomads arrived at Hanalishah in mid-spring in 2000 they were disheartened. Incurring great expense, Pashutan had hired specialized workers

360　*Facing the future*

to excavate an underground aqueduct (qanat) from the tree's base toward his reservoir.[22] He intended to take the qanat all the way to the reservoir but the Qermezi brothers forced him to stop construction. The three aeration holes surrounded by mounded dirt (a qanat's distinguishing external sign) gaped open and were a lethal danger to children and animals, and the brothers insisted that Pashutan provide covers.

Angry about the new assault against their property, Mohammad Karim and Dariush reported the incursion to government agencies in Semirom. They were not optimistic about the outcome of any new legal pursuit. Dariush noted, "We could fight it. We could spend years traveling to and from Semirom following the legalities of the case and end up achieving no positive result." More than his two brothers, he had grown fatigued by the family's many disputes over land, few of them ever ending well, even after decades of effort and expense. Tensions between the two parties remained high.

The camp's residents had now lost all use of the water formerly issuing from the springs near the new qanat. Excavations had forced underground the water's downhill flow. Women, somewhat shielded from view by bushes, rushes, and the land's dip between the stream's banks, had always washed clothes, dishes, and yarn along the narrow water course and had welcomed the privacy they achieved in this way. Hidden by vegetation, they could even bathe without notice. Now, the huge mounds, the destruction of all the plants, and the mess left behind totally altered the terrain. The women's only access to water was to haul it from the campsite's sole-surviving spring just below Mohammad Karim's house. They preferred to do some washing there, to avoid carrying quantities of water uphill, but Mohammad Karim—and perhaps Bulqais—did not want others' clothes and dishes cluttering the site. Dariush and Bizhan purchased several wheelbarrows so the women could more easily transport heavy goatskin bags and plastic containers back to their homes.

The walnut tree looked weak and decimated but continued to survive through the summer. The camp's inhabitants were not optimistic about its survival, given the recently enlarged hole at its base, more roots severed, massive excavations in the immediate vicinity, and spring water directed deep underground. They noted that if sufficient rain and snow fell that winter and if Persians ceased digging at its base, the tree could grow new lateral roots.

A new settlement at Mulleh Balut

The Organization for Nomads' Affairs (ONA) of the Ministry of Construction Jihad formalized plans in the winter of 1998–99 for some Qermezi nomads to build houses as part of a new settlement (shahrak) in the foothills below their winter pastures in Dashtak's mountains. ONA had begun similar settlements since 1992 for other groups of Qashqa'i nomads in winter and summer pastures.[23] The Qermezi did not know why the government had selected their group, out of many hundreds of comparable Qashqa'i ones, for this kind of project. Shahriyar Qermezi's prominence as a parliamentary deputy was perhaps a factor.

Facing the future   361

ONA chose Qermezi men from the Aqa Mohammadli and Qairkhbaili lineages for the Mulleh Balut ("gorge of the wild oak tree") project. Almost all nomads at Dashtak since 1945 had derived from these two lineages. Most nomads in the three other Qermezi lineages occupied winter pastures elsewhere. The 22 Aqa Mohammadli men selected lived at Dashtak during the winter and held grazing permits there from the Pastures Organization. Some of the 22 Qairkhbaili men chosen also resided at Dashtak during the winter while others lived at lower elevations below Mulleh Balut and used pastures there. When officials announced the plan and released some details, other Aqa Mohammadli and Qairkhbaili men expressed interest in joining the settlement.

Before starting the Mulleh Balut project, ONA had begun another one south of Kazerun on the road to Farrashband, this one intended for Farsi Madan Qashqa'i nomads. Some Imamverdili and Qasemli Qermezi nomads occupied winter pastures nearby, and ONA suggested that some of them could join this new settlement. Practically all of them refused, despite enticements, and cited their unwillingness to live in a community of strangers. One Qasemli man and his newly independent son were the exceptions, and they proceeded to build two houses there. They stressed the economic benefits of exploiting this unexpected windfall, while other Qermezi men were appalled by their readiness to separate themselves from their kin.

Mulleh Balut, the territory ONA chose for the Qermezi, is located at lower elevations from their winter pastures at Dashtak. The nomads utilized Mulleh Balut for grazing in the autumn, at the end of the autumn migration, before they ascended into the Dashtak mountains. By occupying Mulleh Balut then for a month or more, they could conserve their pastures at Dashtak. Mulleh Balut was also closer to several wells and more convenient for livestock and people. The nomads waited for rain and runoff to fill their hand-dug, dirt-fortified reservoirs at Dashtak before they left Mulleh Balut. Mulleh Balut was also the area where Dashtak's nomads planted fodder and grain crops. After plowing in the autumn, often by mules but increasingly by borrowed tractors, they sowed and then hoped that sufficient rain would germinate the seeds and grow the crops to maturity. (In the early winter of 2001, they first sowed barley seeds and *then* plowed, a procedure that protects the seeds, first from birds and then during germination.) No springs or other surface water sources here, they did not irrigate.

The Qermezi group had fled Qiz Mazarih ("girl's tomb" in Darrehshuri winter pastures to the north) and traveled south to Dashtak in 1945 because of a blood feud with Boir Ahmad Lur tribesmen. The nomads rented pastures at Dashtak from landowners in Davan village across the mountains to the northeast. They needed agricultural land for fodder crops and rented some at Mulleh Balut from several landowners in Kazerun, one of them a woman.

When Mohammad Reza Shah began his national land reform in 1962, Mulleh Balut's landlord was Mehdi Tabib, a Persian living in Kazerun. Land-reform officials prepared to distribute the land to the actual cultivators in 1963 but Tabib deployed his political clout to prevent the transfer. Borzu and

362 *Facing the future*

Khalifeh Qermezi struggled to settle the case in the 1960s and 1970s and attempted to negotiate a compromise. They eventually suggested that Tabib retain two-thirds of the land at Mulleh Balut and release one-third to the Qermezi. The nomads continued to cultivate all the territory there despite Tabib's resistance. Tabib demanded that they pay rent; Borzu and Khalifeh refused. After the shah's land reform officially ended in 1971, state agencies continued to declare that the government would distribute the territory to those who actually cultivated there, but they never issued any written contracts or deeds, and legal ownership remained uncertain. Tabib died in 1988, and the laws governing inheritance transferred the land deeds to his sons. The Qermezi worried that they might still be forced to divide the land with Tabib's sons to acquire the legal deeds. They had not paid any rent since 1963, when land-reform officials declared that the territory belonged to the Qermezi cultivators.

The agency for natural resources took jurisdiction over Mulleh Balut after the 1979 revolution, and later the Pastures Organization assumed control. Officials surveyed the area and declared it to be pastureland, as it continued to be classified into the early 2000s. The Qermezi users were still unable to obtain legal documents specifying their rights to pastoral and agricultural land there. The Organization for Nomads' Affairs selected 50 hectares at Mulleh Balut for its settlement project in 1998 and transferred that portion from the Pastures Organization to its own authority. The rest of Mulleh Balut remained classified as pastures, despite the continuing use of it by the Qermezi for dry cultivation as well as pastoralism.

Initially ONA selected only those men whose livestock grazed pastures at Dashtak as eligible to build at Mullet Balut. As the Qermezi discussed the issue, some close kinsmen who no longer tended animals at Dashtak also wanted to be included. The government added to the project some men whom it already classified as "nomads" and excluded others who lacked this designation, including several schoolteachers who no longer resided at Dashtak during the winter. One teacher hired a shepherd to care for his herd at Dashtak, the fathers and brothers of other teachers kept the teachers' livestock there, and one or two owned only a few animals.

Husain Ali and his brother Filamarz taught in Kazerun, and each owned a house there. The government classified Filamarz as a nomad because his livestock grazed his legal pastures at Dashtak. He also possessed a coupon book enabling those labeled as nomads to buy flour at state-subsidized rates. Filamarz was one of the first to seize the opportunity to build at Mulleh Balut. The government did not categorize Husain Ali as a nomad, and ONA stated that he was ineligible to build there. Afraid of losing the chance, he wrote to ONA stating that he was indeed a nomad and the son of a nomad who had held pasture rights at Dashtak from the time the Qermezi first lived there. Continuing, he noted that he shared pasture rights with his two brothers, both of whom still tended livestock at Dashtak. Husain Ali completed his file by assembling copies of his family's identity cards and depositing 30,000 tumans in a state bank. Several months later, ONA informed him that his

Facing the future   363

family was now entitled to a coupon book. Officially reclassified as a nomad this way, Husain Ali became eligible for the second stage of construction at Mulleh Balut. Some men with similar statuses took the same approach and also succeeded in changing their official status to nomads.

Some Qermezi men had initially worried that the government would revoke their pasture rights at Dashtak if they joined the Mulleh Balut settlement, but officials declared that they entertained no such intentions. They emphasized that the men could maintain their pastoral livelihood at Dashtak while also enjoying a comfortable residence for their families at a lower elevation at Mulleh Balut.

ONA officials finalized the settlement's broad details in early 1999. An already serviceable road at the site's northwestern border led from the asphalt road and cultivated valley below toward the mountain slopes of Dashtak. Of the 50 hectares, officials allocated five for houses and 45 for agriculture.

The land for houses would initially consist of 44 plots set in eleven rows with lanes between rows. Each lot was 500 square meters, the house to occupy 124 meters and the rest to be used for an enclosed courtyard. These plots were larger than the ones belonging to the Qermezi in Kazerun, which were 250–400 square meters. ONA intended to provide each family with some protected space by its new house at Mulleh Balut for fruit trees, grape arbors, and vegetable gardens. High brick walls would surround each lot there, with neighbors sharing walls on the sides. At first ONA planned for pairs of houses to be back to back, half facing east and the rest west, but later changed to rows of single houses all facing the valley below. Revising plans further, ONA returned to the notion of pairs of houses but permitted all of them to face west.[24] The lanes would run north and south in front of and behind each pair. One house of each pair would face the lane while the other's lane would run behind it. The entrance of the first would be in front while the other's entrance would be from the back and along the side of the house.[25] The potential occupants preferred the first layout to the second. They could sit on their porches, look into the courtyard in front of them, and see the lane (with its human and vehicular traffic) on the other side of the far wall. The downward slope of the land would offer them a beneficial view of the community, the hills and plains below, the road leading from the valley, and the mountains in the distance.

The agency set aside a double plot in the upper section for a school and a single plot for a clinic. Later it would use another space, not yet identified, for a mosque. The potential settlers talked about yet another lot for a small store equipped with a public telephone. They hoped the government would eventually provide electricity. Some noted that, without this utility, the settlement would lack any value. ONA indicated that land above and below the proposed site would be available for other builders in the future, including the sons of the original 44 men who would eventually become independent from their fathers. They spoke of 70 houses possible in the near future. ONA's project for Farsi Madan nomads held 63 houses, some still under construction in 2000, and the agency had also earmarked it for 70.

364   *Facing the future*

ONA officials classified the place as "a community (or neighborhood) for settling nomads" (*shahrak-i iskan-i ashayir*). Attentive to tribal history, Husain Ali Qermezi was considering meaningful Turkish and Qashqa'i-related names. He hoped to avoid having the site named Islamabad ("abode of Islam"), a name bestowed on perhaps thousands of villages throughout Iran since the revolution, including Qermezi's own Atakula.

The government planned the settlement initially for 44 households, 22 each from Aqa Mohammadli and Qairkhbaili lineages. Houses would be built on the slope, and members of both lineages preferred the upper section. By means of a random drawing, representatives of the lineages determined that the upper lots would be for Aqa Mohammadli and the lower ones for Qairkhbaili. Then, each man in the two lineages drew a number for his own house lot. ONA did not permit them to select their locations and neighbors. By chance, some men did draw their closest kinsmen as neighbors (those with plots on either side) while most others did not. The odd arrangements caused by the random selection amused everyone. Long before any construction began, people discussed potential conflicts between neighbors who would not otherwise decide to reside together. The nomads had always valued the principle that those who *chose* to live together would provide mutual support, regardless of the circumstances. The element of choice now gone, many wondered about the nature of their new obligations. They were pleased that they could continue to live with fellow lineage mates. For the Aqa Mohammadli, a lineage mate as a neighbor, whoever he was, was preferable to a Qairkhbaili one. The Qairkhbaili expressed the same notion. Most people married within their own lineages, and few intermarriages connected them.

(Surely, I thought in 1999, intermarriages would occur in the future. The two groups were suddenly aware of the need to create new bonds. When Qairkhbaili families at Kuh Pahn issued wedding invitations that summer, the Aqa Mohammadli at Hanalishah discussed the importance for some of them to travel the long distance there. They rationalized that they would soon be permanent [but seasonal] neighbors and would need to demonstrate the new ties in concrete fashion. Just a year previously, they would not have bothered to attend the rites. Yet, in late 2000, the men in the two groups were not speaking to one another because of ongoing, unresolved disputes over the agricultural land at Mulleh Balut [not the part allocated to the new settlers for orchards], and I reconsidered the inevitability of intermarriage.)

Mindful that the builders would need income in the future, ONA allocated 45 hectares of the 50-hectare project for agriculture. Residents of each house plot were entitled to a hectare of agricultural land across a deep gully to the settlement's south. ONA brought a soil engineer to determine the most appropriate crops, which he declared to be citrus trees (lemon, lime, and orange). Each household could plant an orchard of 400 trees on its assigned hectare, a sufficient number for its labor force and for reasonable productivity. Never before owning any citrus trees, the Qermezi looked forward to diversifying their base of income. Any given year when apple production (the crop in

Facing the future 365

summer pastures for some of them) was poor or market prices low, the quality and price of citrus fruits might be better. Also, citrus fruits in this region matured in the winter and would draw high prices during the New Year's holiday in March, when all commodities temporarily rose in cost to respond to the high demand created by the consumption patterns and elaborate hospitality of Iranians at this celebratory time. Producers and merchants of these low-altitude areas of Iran's south and southwest distributed fresh fruits and vegetables throughout Iran for the holiday and exported it to the Persian Gulf states. ONA declared that it would designate the agricultural plots in early 2000, after it had progressed with the plans for irrigation, without which citrus production was not possible.

ONA planned separate water projects for the dwellings and the orchards. The agency would dig deep wells and install motorized pumps run by fuel oil to supply each house with piped water. Once it introduced electricity, the pumps would run under its power. For irrigation, ONA would dig 150-meter wells, set up pumps, and construct covered concrete reservoirs so the cultivators could run the pumps whenever they needed water, fill the reservoirs, and use concrete channels to direct the water to the orchards. Already a similar irrigation project was in place for the Qairkhbaili families living at lower elevations. Engineers asserted that the groundwater at Mulleh Balut, beginning at 100 meters, would be sufficient for the long term. They cited the proximity of the large sweet-water Lake Famur (called Lake Parishan by the Qashqa'i) just to the south as evidence of adequate water. The lake's northern reaches were visible from Dashtak above. (A victim of a prolonged regional drought, the lake was completely dry in 2008.)

The government promised low-interest loans of one million tumans, possibly one and a half, for each family. After this announcement, 44 potential residents applied for loans from Bank Maskan (the housing bank) and received half a million tumans in cash shortly thereafter. The government earmarked the money for construction. Total costs for building a house would exceed one million, especially because of inflation, but the Qermezi hoped that further loans would be available. Several men remarked that the builders might not have to repay the loans, the government seeming that eager to advance the project. Some men applied for the money on the grounds that no stipulations were attached other than the requirement to build. This enticement more than others created interest in the project and was a powerful incentive for the potential participants.

Qermezi men understood the government's real and potential volatility and the ways that the state introduced projects and then unaccountably abandoned them. They said they should act while the opportunity was ripe. If they waited, they might forfeit the chance and fall behind those who had seized the initiative. Like a warning, tens of thousands of Mohammad Reza Shah's development projects stood unfinished and abandoned throughout Iran 20 years after his flight.

ONA permitted the 44 men to build at Mullah Balut, with other men to follow, during the next three years. At the period's end, those who had not yet

366 *Facing the future*

begun would lose the chance as well as the assigned plot, which ONA would allocate to another. The Pastures Organization would eventually reclaim the land as pastures if people did not build houses and commence agriculture there.

The first group of 37 men began construction at Mulleh Balut in February 1999. (Seven men of the specified 44 chose to wait.) They contracted with two individuals, both Aqa Mohammadli, to build their houses. Burj Ali Qermezi lived in Borujen just north of Qashqa'i summer pastures and worked year-round as a master builder, usually for kinsmen and other Qashqa'i. Living in nearby Naqneh village, Shahriyar Qermezi (not the parliamentary deputy of the same name) was similarly employed. Both men had supervised the construction of reservoirs and irrigation works at Hanalishah for the same Aqa Mohammadli men who were now ready to build houses at Mulleh Balut. Each master builder relied on his sons and other young kinsmen to perform most of the physical labor, for which they were usually paid a daily wage. House owners, depending on their other responsibilities, also contributed their efforts.

ONA required the builders to place the dwellings in straight rows and to use uniform materials, including yellow fired bricks and cement mortar. Its agents held specific notions about the settlement's ultimate physical appearance, which they hoped would showcase their efforts to assist this sector of Iranian society. When the nomads departed for summer pastures in early spring, they had already completed the walls of most of the houses, and kinsmen leaving later oversaw the remaining work. The owners would wait to construct the roofs (from cement) and the courtyard walls (from yellow fired bricks) until their return to winter pastures in the autumn.

House plans allowed from two to five rooms, depending on family needs. The men already owning homes in Kazerun did not require a large house at Mulleh Balut and considered two rooms adequate. Qairkhbaili men whose families lived at lower elevations (below Mulleh Balut) desired larger houses; they could then abandon their existing rudimentary dwellings. Each house would feature a reception room used also for sleeping and one or more sleeping and storage rooms. With piped water, a small kitchen and a small bathing room were not considered "rooms." Residents could also use a hall between rooms for sitting and entertaining. Later, they could build additional rooms in front of the two-roomed houses. An enclosed toilet situated over a pit would be placed in one of the courtyard's far corners. The settlement would have no sewage system or other piped drainage.

State officials, including a few ONA agents, proclaimed that the project would bring these nomads one step further toward permanent settlement. They underestimated the ways these supposed settlers would incorporate the new houses with already existing dwellings, including tents, in different locales. They did not understand the ways the settlers would merge the citrus orchards with their other means of livelihood. In line with other projects to bring services to nomads, state agents assumed that the new settlement would enhance their efforts to control the people politically and integrate them in Iranian society and culture.

Facing the future 367

The nomads approached the government's project differently. Without exception, they were committed to maintaining their current livelihoods and lifestyles. They regarded the potential of a new dwelling and a new source of income (citrus trees) as advantages allowing them to diversify their activities and reduce the risks of any single venture. They talked about how they would combine these new residences and orchards with their existing dwellings and economic pursuits. Men saw the new settlement as an opportunity to provide for their sons when they matured and married. Fathers could continue their current economic activities while at least one son assumed the new responsibilities. Or, as fathers aged, they could live in the new house and their sons could continue as nomadic pastoralists. Even if they adopted this settlement, the nomads saw no reason to change the degree of their political autonomy or the extent of their separation from the wider society and culture.

Other than to joke about the problems they might face with neighbors they did not choose, the nomads did not express any negative sentiments in 1999 about this potentially transforming project. They underestimated the changes that the new settlement would cause. They were eager to receive low-interest bank loans but did not adequately consider the project's added initial costs and ongoing expenses and the pressure to repay the loans. They had not yet worked out the details of citrus production and the ways its schedule would or would not mesh with their other activities. Years would pass before any citrus fruits would be marketable but no one spoke about paying the escalating costs in the meantime. Accustomed to transporting their possessions between winter and summer pastures, they did not worry about a third place of residence complicating their lives. And they misjudged the ways that the project in all its aspects would probably draw them further under the government's control.

The men who taught school in or near Kazerun planned to maintain their primary (but seasonal) residence there and to use the Mulleh Balut house during the agricultural season for themselves, their mature sons, and/or their hired workers. They viewed the new houses and orchards as places for entertaining relatives, a location for recreation and relaxation during the autumn, winter, and spring. Some extolled the climatic advantages of Mulleh Balut, higher in altitude and cooler than Kazerun in the summer and lower in altitude and warmer than Dashtak in the winter. Even if they occupied the new residences only periodically, such as during weekends, they could escape the pressures of Kazerun society and its restrictive norms about behavior and dress. Young unmarried adults were excited to have a place to spend leisure time together, and a few parents began to worry about unsupervised activities.

By the time the nomads returned to Dashtak in the autumn of 1999, some men who were not part of the original 44 were eager to join the Mulleh Balut settlement. They had taken time to consider the venture and now worried that they would lose the opportunity if they did not act. They included a few newly independent sons of men in the first group and some Kazerun residents who were ineligible during ONA's initial selection but whom the state had recently reclassified as nomads. The men laughed, "If we want to settle, we

368   *Facing the future*

have to be designated as nomads first." Nine Aqa Mohammadli and some Qairkhbaili men made up the second group, and most of them began to build houses on new plots opened by ONA, again according to a random selection. A few men took places still unfilled after the original drawing, and several of the original men who decided later not to build gave their places to others or allowed ONA to reassign them.

By early December 2000, the project remained unchanged, at the same stage it had reached by the early spring of 1999. Thirty-nine shells of houses, none with a courtyard wall, sat in neat rows. Only one house had a roof but it too was as unfinished as the rest. The construction site exhibited no evidence of in-progress activity. ONA and the potential residents had ceased all efforts, and their relationship stood at an impasse.

The nomads wanted the government to provide water to their dwellings before they resumed construction, while ONA announced that the nomads needed to complete the houses first, to prove their intentions to live there. The nomads claimed to have depleted the cash loans and needed additional funds to finish the houses. Seven men entitled to build there had not yet begun, their plots vacant, and ONA had not yet started to erect the school, clinic, and mosque on the allocated still-empty lots.

Late in December, after the two parties debated the issues, ONA workers began to dig a trench for the main water line running along the road leading from the valley to the mountain slopes. Later they continued with lateral trenches along the settlement's lanes, and each homeowner would be responsible for connecting his house to the water pipe there. Ramadan, the month of fasting, delayed the work. Still, encouraged by the progress, Aqa Mohammadli men at Dashtak and in Kazerun met to discuss the next stage. The following day, they began negotiations with Persian builders to construct the roofs, a specialized job that the original Qermezi builders would not undertake. The Persian builders were not willing to start until Ramadan was over.

ONA had not yet begun work on the irrigation system necessary for the citrus orchards. Qermezi men of the two lineages continued to cultivate grain and fodder crops in the wider area, without irrigation as they had done since 1945. They made no progress in ending the many escalating land disputes involving the Qermezi cultivators, potential settlers, Persian landowners, and competing state agencies. Aqa Mohammadli and Qairkhbaili men disputed in 1999–2000 about the agricultural land they had shared for half a century, and the two groups of men were not speaking to one another.

At the construction site in late December of 2000, as I sketched the housing layout, my Aqa Mohammadli companion was uncertain about several empty plots in the Qairkhbaili section. When by chance a Qairkhbaili man approached on his tractor, my companion summoned resolve to hail him and inquire about the identities of those who had not yet begun to build. The man answered the question simply, never decreasing his speed, and proceeded on his way, without the pleasantries always uttered whenever two tribesmen meet

Facing the future 369

away from home. Reading the nonverbal signs, I saw that the two men would never have spoken if I had not intruded.

The Aqa Mohammadli and Qairkhbaili men with houses under construction wondered if the government would create an Islamic council (shura) for the new village or if the nomads' existing one would suffice. They speculated that the regime would want a new entity to support the services it was providing to the settlers. Potential residents questioned their ability to choose the council's members, given the widening rift between the two lineages.

The settlement still lacked a name. Husain Ali Qermezi suggested several to ONA officials, who flatly rejected them for obvious political reasons. One was "Qashqa'i," another "Soulat" (for Soulat ed-Douleh, the Qashqa'i ilkhani until 1933 when Reza Shah ordered his execution). Husain Ali noted that a better strategy would have been to offer a list of 50 names, each acceptable by the potential residents, and let the officials choose one. He and the others still hoped for a name related to Qashqa'i or Qermezi history. They lacked any interest in the name of a deceased (usually martyred) revolutionary hero or a generic Islam-related name.

Notes

1 Some sources report 905 or 960 urban councils (720 cities and 240 towns) and 34,205 village councils nationwide, a far cry from the "250,000" settlements often listed in the literature. Sources also mention the 111,000, 115,000, or 190,000 seats available nationwide in these councils, numbers also well below the 250,000 communities (each one having three or more members on its council).

2 In cities and larger towns, parliament's Central Committee for Monitoring Council Elections, parliament's provincial committees, and the Ministry of Interior's election boards vetted candidates. The Guardian Council did not vet candidates in these elections, unlike those for the presidency and parliament. Takeyh (2009: 228) notes that these municipal elections were "the most unregulated contests in Iran" but other sources disagree by describing the heavily politicized vetting process. The vetting handled by parliamentary central and provincial committees favored reformist candidates when reformists were the majority in parliament, and it favored conservatives and neoconservatives when conservatives were the majority.

3 See note 1 in this chapter.

4 Samii (2006).

5 Ehteshami and Zweiri (2007: 35). Gheissari and Sanandaji (2009: 275–98) analyze voting patterns in the presidential elections of 1997, 2001, and 2005, when distinctions between the Persian majority and ethnic minorities, between urban and rural areas, and between the center and the periphery proved essential for understanding electoral results.

6 Some Qashqa'i women were elected, including two to Firuzabad's council. Across Iran, two percent of the electees were women, including 484 in rural areas (Shahidian 2002: 258). Of the 334,000 candidates competing for 115,000 seats, 5,000 were women (Abrahamian 2008: 188).

7 Small, rural Bahai communities are also found elsewhere in southwestern Iran. As in Dezeh, their members usually kept a low profile and tried not to attract the attention of the Islamic regime's agents and fervent supporters. Vigilantes have attacked Bahais and Bahai places of worship since 1979, especially in urban areas.

370 *Facing the future*

8 All members of Semirom's council resigned in 2003 to protest against the state's security forces that had attacked citizens who opposed a redistricting plan. (They probably later rejoined the council.)

9 The government held the next nationwide municipal elections in 2003, and conservatives and neoconservatives won in many cities. Until this election, reformists had not been defeated at the polls since their emergence in the mid-1990s (Takeyh 2003). Ehteshami and Zweiri (2007: 34–36) discuss the 1999 and 2003 municipal elections. Iran's third municipal elections took place in 2006. Reformists viewed a potential victory as a step toward regaining the elected offices lost to conservatives in municipal elections in 2003, parliamentary elections in 2004, and the presidential race in 2005. Conservatives saw a likely victory in the 2006 municipal elections as continuing their winning streak and cementing their hold on power (Samii 2006). Reformists and moderate conservatives won in many locations despite mass disqualifications of reformists in the provinces. Parliament moved the fourth municipal elections from 2010 to 2013, to occur simultaneously with the crucial presidential vote.

10 The Qermezi later replaced these images with photographs of Qashqa'i wedding celebrations.

11 Qermezi men discussed the complicated kinship ties between and among three women who were factors in Mansur's wedding (see Chapter 5). Later, when I asked a few women about these links, so I could record them, they replied, "The three women are *sisters!*"

12 Borzu's sister had married a Shaikh Lur man, but the Qermezi at Hanalishah were not close to his extended family.

13 Azar Nafisi spoke at a conference in Washington, D.C., in 1991 wearing the fully concealing, all-black modest dress that the Islamic Republic mandated (personal observation). She noted privately that she had wanted the audience to understand the restrictions that women in Iran suffered. Her attire, too, served as an act of defiance. Yet many attendees (all academics with interests in Iran) misunderstood her intentions, said she had been brainwashed, or noted that she feared being punished when she returned to Iran.

14 Every year in the 1960s and early 1970s, kinsmen owning apple orchards on either side of Naheed Dareshuri's apple orchard in Mehr-i Gerd village moved the stone-wall borders into her orchard, one row of trees at a time. Her orchard grew steadily smaller until one spring she saw (when she arrived from winter pastures) that it had totally disappeared.

15 The nomads left behind bulky items that were cumbersome to pack and transport and did not have much monetary value (but still cost money to replace). They took their valuables with them to winter pastures.

16 Some urban men brought along low-status preteen or teenage boys who sang and danced for the inebriated revelers. No females were present at these kinds of gatherings. Such semipublic male homosexuality was more socially approved under these circumstances than heterosexual contact with female prostitutes.

17 Amuzegar (1993: 329); the emphasis is mine.

18 Beck and Huang (2006) provide further discussion.

19 The nomads often experienced elaborate codes of politeness (taaruf) among Persians, and they puzzled about the total breech of these norms on such occasions.

20 Cultivators threatened to burn their crops by dropping lighted matches on the ground and bringing the rural police (gendarmes) to witness the charred evidence of the crime that the nomads had allegedly committed.

21 The tree was still visible via satellite imagery in 2011. www.maplandia.com/iran/esfahan/semirom-31-25-0-n-51-34-0-e.

22 I had not known that a qanat could be that short—only 100 meters. Usually qanats stretched from the mountain slopes to villages in the plains many kilometers away. Beaumont et al. (1989) and English (1998) describe qanats.

Facing the future   371

23 The largest of these projects was at Baghan, north of Shiraz, and consisted of four separate settlements in an enormous plain (Azkia and Hooglund 2002: 112–14; Badjian et al. 2009). The World Bank and the UN's Food and Agriculture Organization offered financial assistance and expertise to this project in the mid-1990s.
24 The nomads usually pitched their tents facing northeast, to benefit from the rising sun and to avoid the afternoon's glare. West-facing houses would be too hot, the nomads said.
25 Goodell (1986: 178) describes the development of a model town (shahrak) in Khuzistan under Mohammad Reza Shah and includes a diagram of houses and lanes similar to the plan for the nomads' settlement discussed here.

Conclusion

When confronted with possible alternatives to nomadic pastoralism in 1970, most Qermezi stated that only one other viable livelihood was realistically available for them: village-based agriculture. Agriculture was riskier economically than pastoralism because people were forced to depend on seasonal crops in fixed locations. If environmental conditions were dismal any year or season, people lacked other income-producing activities if their crops failed. By migrating seasonally, nomadic pastoralists dispersed the risks over four seasons and varying ecological zones and could alter their practices quickly if needed. With agriculture, tasks were arduous but seasonal; with nomadic pastoralism, work was unrelenting year-round. Expected profits from agriculture in 1970 matched those of nomadic pastoralism. Yet the nomads said they lost their political and economic independence and their flexible social ties and residential groupings if they chose agriculture over pastoralism. Village-based agriculture sometimes improved living conditions and offered a more comfortable lifestyle. A house, no matter how humble, protected people from the physical elements in ways that an airy goat-hair tent did not.

The alternatives for the Qermezi had expanded by the beginning of the twenty-first century. People said that four routes were now available for those approaching adulthood and uncertain about their choices: literacy (*savad*), cultivation based on landownership, paid labor, and nomadic pastoralism. In distinguishing the relative merits of having literacy or being illiterate (*bisavad*), they said that all youth faced four possibilities. They could be civil servants (*karmand*), land-owning cultivators, low-paid laborers (*kargar*), or nomadic pastoralists. By "literacy," they referred to any work requiring the skill; literacy paved the way for respected, urban-connected occupations. Those without literacy could engage only in physical labor in the agricultural, urban, industrial, or pastoral sectors. Men admonished their sons about their academic performance. If they did not do well in school, they would find themselves digging ditches for less-than-living wages. With literacy, the possibilities were many; without it, only labor for others existed. The Qermezi preferred cultivation based on landownership to paid agricultural labor. Yet both entailed difficult physical work, which some men had grown to disdain.

Conclusion 373

People's value judgments, inherent in these discussions, were muted and ambiguous with regard to nomadic pastoralism. Physical labor was an unavoidable part of the livelihood but the benefits were many, including a high degree of political, economic, and social autonomy for individuals, families, and larger kinship and tribal groups. People said that migratory pastoralism facilitated the continuation of Qashqa'i culture, otherwise under threat if they were dispersed in rural and especially urban settings and subjected to other kinds of influence. If they maintained the livelihood, they ensured the survival of the culture. If they engaged in other work elsewhere, they jeopardized it. Nomadic pastoralism did require physical labor but the nomads performed the work for themselves and their families and not for wealthy individuals elsewhere who would offer them only low-status positions and inadequate remuneration. Profitable nomadic pastoralism meant the hiring of shepherds, who would assume the most arduous tasks.

The struggles of Borzu Qermezi's three sons demonstrate that they and other men valued the land rights to which they were entitled as nomadic pastoralists. They compared the 300 square meters of land they owned or rented in Kazerun or other towns with the vast expanses of mountainous terrain under their control in winter and summer pastures. If they abandoned nomadic pastoralism, they would have to relinquish these territories, which most were loath to do. Many men, deciding to keep one male family member as a pastoralist, were able to preserve the land for the extended family. By hiring shepherds, they found a partial but not fully satisfactory solution because they had to worry about dishonesty, animal neglect, and the workers' desertion.

A Qermezi man commented in 2004 that for every year he and his kinsmen continued as migratory pastoralists, they fell 10 years behind those who had adopted livelihoods requiring literacy. He compared himself to two elementary-school classmates his age. His academic performance had been superior to theirs but they had continued with formal education while he had not. One was poised on the brink of a high-status occupation, and the other one, also a university graduate, was a high-school teacher with a steady income, benefits, and the ability to select his post. Both lived comfortable lives, and members of the wider Persian-dominated society admired them. Their kinsman, still a mountain-dwelling herder of livestock, was not regarded in a similar fashion. Visitors from this wider society praised the territorial expanses under the pastoralist's control and often intruded on him, uninvited, for their leisurely holidays, despite snidely pointing out his low-status livelihood as a shepherd (*chupan*) as compared with that of a property owner (*arbab*). When this pastoralist and others began to invest in apple production, their status as new landowners rose. Outsiders began to view pastoralism as a supplementary means of livelihood that provided, at no cost to the producers (in their view), fresh meat and dairy products (which they coveted for themselves, especially because of escalating inflation in urban areas).

The process of adopting urban-connected livelihoods seemed irreversible. Few of those having literacy and salaried employment returned to nomadic

374   *Conclusion*

pastoralism, and for this reason people cautioned those who were prepared to choose alternative jobs. When someone asked the most highly educated Qermezi person what he would do if he did not pass his upcoming doctoral-candidacy examination, he replied simply, with no obvious displeasure, that he would buy 300 sheep and tend them in winter pastures at Dashtak. No one listening took him seriously; none of them could imagine his settling in a hut that lacked all the modern conveniences. Through the years, they had watched him rise in educational and socioeconomic status and could not imagine a reversal of the stages through which he had passed.

Dichotomies, each pair overlapping with and inherent in the others, arise in these discussions: nomadism and settlement, pastoralism and agriculture, rural life and urban life, and illiteracy and literacy.

Another key dichotomy, also intersecting with the others and emerging in people's discussions, was "Turk" and "Tajik." The Qashqa'i considered the category of "Turks" unambiguously, as those who maintained nomadic pastoralism and held onto Qashqa'i cultural traditions. People who did not perpetuate the livelihood, lifestyle, and culture were in threat of becoming a "Tajik," defined as someone who was not a Turk, who did not practice a Turkish way of life, and who exhibited the traits they despised among Persians.

To stem the tide of this negative association and to benefit in other ways, many Qermezi who did pursue the paths of literacy and urban-connected jobs strove to maintain ties with their nomadic pastoral kin. They cooperated economically with them, as in livestock ownership, even if they did not need the income or want the responsibility. They agreed to share in ventures to establish fruit orchards in winter and summer pastures. They visited their relatives frequently, contributed generously to communal obligations, wore Qashqa'i clothes, cherished the outdoors life, collected and processed useful natural resources, and paid (exaggerated) attention to pastoral conditions and the well-being of the livestock. They watched as the clouds gathered, and they rejoiced when rain fell to nourish the pastures, even though they now lived indoors and pursued indoor jobs. They heralded the advent of the seasons and sub-seasons that were crucial to pastoral and migratory pursuits. They arranged and decorated their village and urban homes in the ways that their nomadic kin outfitted and adorned their tents, and they perpetuated the use of customary technologies, as in weaving, food preparing, and tool assembling. They played and sang Qashqa'i music and recited Qashqa'i poetry. They acknowledged the stages in the life cycle, especially weddings and memorials, in customary ways. They grew attentive to the incursions of Persian and Arabic words in their speech and often corrected themselves. They viewed the process of becoming a Tajik as irreversible and strove to avoid such an identification. Yet they did find themselves caught in a dilemma when members of the wider Persian-dominated society admired their modern livelihood and lifestyle—at the same time as their Qashqa'i relatives rebuked them for trading away and abandoning their culture.

Influences from the state and government lessened the pressures causing fundamental changes for the Qermezi (and other Qashqa'i). The two Pahlavi shahs (1925–79) had aimed their policies toward the pacification, Persianization, integration, and assimilation of Iran's diverse peoples, especially those these rulers had perceived as military and political threats. The ruling clergy of the Islamic Republic (1979–) harbored similar concerns but also tolerated and enhanced existing tribal and ethnic notions, structures, and expressions. The new regime's officials and policies recognized, reinforced, and perpetuated kinship, tribal, socioterritorial, and ethnic entities and sentiments. The Qashqa'i had fought to retain these identities under the shahs, and the new regime validated their efforts. People continued to regard themselves as members of an extended family, a lineage, a subtribe, a tribe, the confederacy, and a unique ethnolinguistic national minority, and these notions were as strong as, if not stronger than, they had been during and perhaps before the reigns of the shahs.

The Islamic Republic's clergymen focused their efforts on Islamization, a broad set of policies endangering some aspects of Qashqa'i culture while allowing others to persist. Yet their efforts to Islamize were aimed at political control over the citizenry (and not at piety and religious observance), and they faced fewer problems with the Qashqa'i than with other sectors of society. Threats to the Islamic regime came primarily from urban populations (especially the middle classes but also the lower ones) and from the youth of all classes, who were now a majority of Iran's citizens. The youngest generations had not experienced the shah's rule, the revolution, Khomeini, the creation of the Islamic Republic, or even the Iraq–Iran war, and they were alienated from Iran's clergy and others who were still motivated by these early associations and experiences. As under previous regimes, the Qashqa'i escaped certain elements of centralized state control due to their often remote residences and their dispersal across vast expanses of land. They avoided many of the constraints that Iran's other citizens often faced. Falling under fewer such pressures, they were less hostile toward the regime.

The Qermezi confronted a variety of choices between 1970 and 2013. Some choices were similar across this 44-year span. Others were caused by accelerating modernization and by distinct policies of one and then another kind of government. Yet the people were certain about the strength of their society and culture if they continued to support and respect the underpinnings. They were less certain about the stability of the state on which their futures seemed to depend. They viewed some trends as irreversible and beyond their control—such as formal education and its importance, technological advances, and increased integration in the nation-state's institutions—but they also understood that they could retain their distinctive cultural, tribal, ethnic, linguistic, and social identities if they persisted with the effort in each of the multiple dimensions of their lives. This volume has detailed these interrelated, ongoing processes.

Glossary

The list contains Persian, Qashqa'i Turkish, and Arabic terms that appear periodically in the text. Other terms, usually used only once in the text, are not included here. The spelling of words corresponds to the usage recommended by the *International Journal of Middle East Studies*, except when other spellings are common in the scholarly literature or the mainstream media.

akhund. Low-ranking clergyman, often a derogatory term. Qashqa'i often use the term as a generic one for any religious figure, from a low-status prayer writer to a grand ayatollah.

ashayir. Nomads; also tribes.

ashayiri. Nomadic.

ayatollah. High-ranking distinguished clergyman; "sign" or "token" of God.

baig. Tribal leader below the level of kikha.

bailay. Patrilineage; section of a subtribe; group.

basij. Volunteer militia; "the mobilized."

basiji. Volunteer in the militia.

bibi. Title of respect for a woman in the families of the tribal khans; a title comparable to khan.

bunku. Patrilineage; section of a subtribe.

bunyad. Parastatal or state foundation.

chadur. Woman's head-to-toe veil-wrap; also tent.

darvish. Sufi; mystic; low-level religious practitioner.

daulat. State; government.

garmsir. Winter zone.

gelim. Hand-woven flatweave used as a blanket or decorative cover.

hajj. Pilgrimage to Mecca.

hezbollahi. Partisan of the party of God; supporter of Khomeini, the revolution, and the Islamic Republic; not part of an organized group (such as Hezbollah in Lebanon).

hijab. Modest dress for a woman according to local standards, government regulations, and/or Islamic values.

hujjat ul-Islam. Religious title for a person below the rank of ayatollah; "proof" of Islam.

Glossary 377

hukumat. Government.

il. Tribe; tribal confederacy.

ilkhani. Paramount tribal leader.

imam. Leader of prayers in a mosque; religious leader. Also, one of 12 men descended from the prophet Mohammad through his daughter Fatemeh and his cousin Ali, the first of the line. As a mark of extreme respect, Iranians often use the term for Khomeini.

imam jumih. Leader of Friday prayers in a town or city mosque, often the preeminent clergyman there; since 1979, a personal appointee of Khomeini and his successor as supreme leader.

inqilab. Revolution.

iskan. Settling; settled.

jajim. Hand-woven flatweave used as a blanket or general utility item.

janbaz. Someone who is willing to sacrifice his life and become a martyr but is only wounded; a term used in the context of the Iraq–Iran war.

jihad. Holy war conducted on behalf of the Muslim community (the lesser jihad); crusade; struggle in the name of God; personal struggle against sin (the greater jihad).

jihad-i sazandigi. Construction Jihad (or Crusade), a government agency and ministry.

kadkhuda. Headman of a tribal group or village; mediator between people and the government.

khan. Tribal leader; also a title of respect for a man.

kikha. Tribal leader below the level of khan.

komiteh. Revolutionary Islamic committee.

majlis. Iran's parliament or assembly.

maktab. Elementary religious school.

mantu (from the French *manteau*). Overcoat used as a woman's modest covering in the Islamic Republic.

maqnai. Hair-concealing hood worn by women and girls in the Islamic Republic.

Muharram. Month of the Islamic calendar during which Shi'i Muslims commemorate the martyrdom of Imam Husain in A.D. 680.

Mujahidin. Leftist movement; holy warriors; freedom fighters.

mulla. Lower-ranking clergyman, often a preacher; a generic term for clergyman; often used derogatorily.

mumin. Faithful; religiously devout.

mustazafin. The deprived, impoverished, and oppressed.

namayandih. Deputy in Iran's parliament.

no ruz. Iranian New Year (beginning on the first day of spring).

pasdar (pasdaran, pl.). Revolutionary guard.

qabilih. Tribe.

qishlaq. Winter zone.

rahbar. Iran's supreme politico-religious leader; Khomeini (1979–89), Khamenei (1989–).

378 *Glossary*

raiyat. Peasant; commoner.

Ramadan (Ramazan). Month of the Islamic calendar during which Muslims fast.

ruhani. Cleric; person educated in religion.

sahib-i zaman. Imam of the Age; the "absent" twelfth Shi'i imam; in occultation.

sarhad. Summer zone.

sayyid. Reputed or presumed descendant of the prophet Mohammad.

shah. King.

shahid. Martyr.

shahrak. Small community; township; neighborhood.

shahristan. Administrative and territorial district within a province (ustan).

shaikh. Religious figure; title of respect for an elderly and wise man, often a leader.

sharia. Religious and sacred law of Islam; revealed, canonical law in Islam.

Shi'i Islam. Minority branch of Islam; the religion of followers of Imam Ali; Iran's official state religion.

shura. Council; consultative body.

sipah. Corps; army.

Sunni Islam. Majority branch of Islam.

tayifih. Tribe or tribal section.

tireh. Subtribe; section of a tribe.

urdu. Tribal gathering or camp for war or other purposes.

vilayat-i faqih. Guardianship or government by an expert in Islamic law.

yailaq. Summer zone.

Bibliography

Abrahamian, Ervand (1980) Structural Causes of the Iranian Revolution. *MERIP Reports* 10 (4): 21–26.

——(1982) *Iran Between Two Revolutions.* Princeton: Princeton University Press.

——(1989) *The Iranian Mojahedin.* New Haven: Yale University Press.

——(1993) *Khomeinism: Essays on the Islamic Republic.* Berkeley: University of California Press.

——(1999) *Tortured Confessions: Prisons and Public Recantations in Modern Iran.* Berkeley: University of California Press.

——(2008) *A History of Modern Iran.* Cambridge: Cambridge University Press.

Abu-Lughod, Lila (1986) *Veiled Sentiments: Honor and Poetry in a Bedouin Society.* Berkeley: University of California Press.

Adelkhah, Fariba (2000) *Being Modern in Iran.* New York: Columbia University Press.

Afkhami, Gholam Reza (2009) *The Life and Times of the Shah.* Berkeley: University of California Press.

Afkhami, Mahnaz, and Erika Friedl (eds.) (1994) 'Appendix 2. The Islamic Penal Code of the Islamic Republic of Iran: Excerpts Relating to Women.' In *In the Eye of the Storm: Women in Post-Revolutionary Iran.* Syracuse: Syracuse University Press.

Afshar, Haleh (1985) 'The Position of Women in an Iranian Village.' In *Women, Work, and Ideology in the Third World.* Haleh Afshar, ed. London: Tavistock.

Aghaie, Kamran (ed.) (2005) *The Women of Karbala: Ritual Performance and Symbolic Discourses in Modern Shi'i Islam.* Austin: University of Texas Press.

Ajami, Amir Ismail (2005) From Peasant to Farmer: A Study of Agrarian Transformation in an Iranian Village, 1967–2002. *International Journal of Middle East Studies* 37 (3): 327–49.

Akhavi, Shahrough (1980) *Religion and Politics in Contemporary Iran: Clergy-State Relations in the Pahlavi Period.* Albany: State University of New York Press.

——(1986) 'Clerical Politics in Iran Since 1979.' In *The Iranian Revolution and the Islamic Republic.* New ed. Nikki Keddie and Eric Hooglund, eds. Syracuse: Syracuse University Press.

Alahmad, Nida, and Arang Keshavarzian (2010) A War on Multiple Fronts. *Middle East Report* 40 (4): 17–28.

Al-Ali, Nadje Sadig (2007) *Iraqi Women: Untold Stories from 1948 to the Present.* London: Zed Books.

Alavi, Nasrin (2005) *We Are Iran: The Persian Blogs.* Brooklyn: Soft Skull Press.

Algar, Hamid (trans. and annotator) (1981) *Writings and Declarations of Imam Khomeini.* Berkeley: Mizan Press.

380　*Bibliography*

Ameri-Siemans, Anne (2009) *Auf bald, Teheran.* Munich: Piper.

Amirahmadi, Hooshang (1990) *Revolution and Economic Transition: The Iranian Experience.* Albany: State University of New York Press.

Amuzegar, Jahangir (1993) *Iran's Economy under the Islamic Republic.* London: I. B. Tauris.

Anonymous (1980) Everything Positive Has Come from the Masses Below. *MERIP Reports* 10 (5): 10–14.

Anonymous (1982) Report from an Iranian Village. *MERIP Reports* 12 (3): 26–29.

Ansari, Ali M. (2007) *Modern Iran: The Pahlavis and After.* 2nd ed. Harlow: Pearson Education.

——(2012) *The Politics of Nationalism in Modern Iran.* Cambridge: Cambridge University Press

Ardalan, Davar (2007) *My Name is Iran: A Memoir.* New York: Henry Holt.

Asayesh, Gelareh (1999) *Saffron Sky: A Life Between Iran and America.* Boston: Beacon Press.

Asgharzadeh, Alireza (2007) *Iran and the Challenge of Diversity: Islamic Fundamentalism, Aryanist Racism, and Democratic Struggles.* New York: Palgrave Macmillan.

Azkia, Mostafa, and Eric Hooglund (2002) Research Note on Pastoral Nomadism in Post-revolution Iran. *Critique* 11 (1): 109–14.

Badjian, Gholam Reza, D. Ismail, M. Othman, and A. Mehrabi (2009) Cost-benefit Analysis of Nomads' Settlement Project: Bakkan Region in Southern Iran. *Livestock Research for Rural Development* 21. www.lrrd.org/lrrd21/5/badj21065.htm.

Bahadori-Kashkuli, Bijan (1985) *Dar an sahargah che gozasht?* (sahargahdan nah gashteh?) (What happened that early morning?). Shiraz, Iran: Afsat Rostamkhaneh.

Bahluli-Qashqa'i, Sohrab (1996–2000) *Seda-yi rasa-yi mardom* (Audible voice of the people) (Bahluli-Qashqa'i's parliamentary speeches). Vols. 1–5. Tehran: Islamic Consultative Assembly.

Bahmanbaigi, Mohammad (1989) *Bokhara-yi man, il-i man* (My Bukhara, my tribe). Tehran: Agah.

——(1995) *Agar Qarehaqaj nabud: gusheh-hai az khaterat* (If Qarehaqaj did not exist: some recollections). Tehran: Bagh-i Aineh.

——(2000) *Be ojaqat qasam: khaterat-i amuzeshi* (I swear on your hearth: an educational memoir). Shiraz, Iran: Navid.

Bahmanbeygi, Mohammad, Naser Mir, and Mohammad Pursartip (1998) Education xii. Rural and Tribal Schools. *Encyclopaedia Iranica* 8 (2): 210–12.

Bakhash, Shaul (1984) *The Reign of the Ayatollahs: Iran and the Islamic Revolution.* New York: Basic Books.

Baktiari, Bahman (1996) *Parliamentary Politics in Revolutionary Iran: The Institutionalization of Factional Politics.* Gainesville: University Press of Florida.

Banuazizi, Ali (1994) Iran's Revolutionary Impasse: Political Factionalism and Societal Resistance. *Middle East Report* 24 (6): 2–8.

Barker, Paul (1981) 'Tent Schools of the Qashqa'i: A Paradox of Local Initiative and State Control.' In *Modern Iran: The Dialectics of Continuity and Change.* Michael Bonine and Nikki Keddie, eds. Albany: State University of New York Press.

Barth, Fredrik (1961) *Nomads of South Persia: The Basseri Tribe of the Khamseh Confederacy.* London: Allen & Unwin.

Basmenji, Kaveh (2005) *Tehran Blues: Youth Culture in Iran.* London: Saqi.

Bayat, Asef (Assef) (1983) Workers' Control after the Revolution. *MERIP Reports* 13 (3): 19–23.

Bibliography 381

——(1988) 'Labor and Democracy in Post-Revolutionary Iran.' In *Post-Revolutionary Iran*. Hooshang Amirahmadi and Manoucher Parvin, eds. Boulder: Westview Press.

——(1997) *Street Politics: Poor People's Movements in Iran*. New York: Columbia University Press.

——(2010) *Life as Politics: How Ordinary People Change the Middle East*. Stanford: Stanford University Press.

Bayat, Kaveh (1986) *Shuresh-i ashayeri-yi Fars, 1307–1309* (Uprising of Fars tribes, 1928–1930). Tehran: Naqareh.

——(2005) The Ethnic Question in Iran. *Middle East Report* 35 (4): 42–45.

——(2008) Iran and the 'Kurdish Question'. *Middle East Report* 38 (2): 28–35.

——(2010) *Nabard Semirom: Ingelesiha, Qashqa'iha va jang-i dovum jehani* (Battle of Semirom: The English, the Qashqa'i and the Second World War). Tehran: Khojasteh Press.

Beaumont, Peter, Michael Bonine, and Keith McLachlan, eds. (1989) *Qanat, Kariz, and Khattara: Traditional Water Systems in the Middle East and North Africa*. London: School of Oriental and African Studies.

Beck, Lois (1978) 'Women among Qashqa'i Nomadic Pastoralists in Iran.' In *Women in the Muslim World*. Lois Beck and Nikki Keddie, eds. Cambridge: Harvard University Press.

——(1980a) Revolutionary Iran and its Tribal People. *MERIP Reports* 10 (4): 14–20.

——(1980b) Tribe and State in Revolutionary Iran: The Return of the Qashqa'i Khans. Special issue, Perspectives on the Iranian Revolution, Farhad Kazemi, ed. *Iranian Studies* 13 (1–4): 215–55.

——(1981a) 'Economic Transformations among Qashqa'i Nomads, 1962–1978.' In *Modern Iran: The Dialectics of Continuity and Change*. Michael Bonine and Nikki Keddie, eds. Albany: State University of New York Press.

——(1981b) Government Policy and Pastoral Land Use in Southwest Iran. *Journal of Arid Environments* 4 (3): 253–67.

——(1982) Nomads and Urbanites, Involuntary Hosts and Uninvited Guests. *Journal of Middle Eastern Studies* 18 (4): 426–44.

——(1986) *The Qashqa'i of Iran*. New Haven: Yale University Press.

——(1990) 'Tribes and the State in Nineteenth- and Twentieth-Century Iran.' In *Tribes and State Formation in the Middle East*. Philip Khoury and Joseph Kostiner, eds. Berkeley: University of California Press.

——(1991) *Nomad: A Year in the Life of a Qashqa'i Tribesman in Iran*. Berkeley: University of California Press.

——(1992a) Clothing xxiv. Clothing of the Qashqa'i Tribes. *Encyclopaedia Iranica* 5 (8): 850–52.

——(1992b) Qashqa'i Nomads and the Islamic Republic. *Middle East Report* 22 (4): 36–41.

——(1993) With My Daughter: In Mountainous Iran, An Anthropologist's Five-Year-Old Child Adapts Quickly to Pastoral Life. *Natural History* 102 (3): 6–10.

——(1995a) Mehman nevazi-yi ashayer-i Iran dokhtaram ra motahayir kard (My daughter was amazed by the hospitality of the nomads of Iran). *Zan-e Ruz* 1511: 8–9.

——(1995b) Qabail va jameh-yi madani (Tribes and civil society). *Iran Nameh* 13 (4): 451–84.

——(1998) Use of Land by Nomadic Pastoralists in Iran, 1970–1998. *Bulletin Series, Yale School of Forestry and Environmental Studies* 103: 58–80.

382 *Bibliography*

——(2000) 'Local Histories: A Longitudinal Study of a Qashqa'i Subtribe in Iran.' In *Iran and Beyond: Essays in Middle Eastern History in Honor of Nikki R. Keddie.* Rudi Matthee and Beth Baron, eds. Costa Mesa: Mazda Publishers.

——(2002) 'Qashqa'i Nomadic Pastoralists and Their Use of Land.' In *Yeki Bud, Yeki Nabud: Essays on the Archaeology of Iran in Honor of William Marvin Sumner.* Naomi Miller and Kamyar Abdi, eds. Monograph 48. Los Angeles: Cotsen Institute of Archaeology, University of California.

——(2004) 'Qashqa'i Women in Postrevolutionary Iran.' In *Women in Iran from 1800 to the Islamic Republic.* Lois Beck and Guity Nashat, eds. Urbana: University of Illinois Press.

——(2013) 'Iran's Ethnic, Religious, and Tribal Minorities.' In *Sectarian Politics in the Persian Gulf.* Lawrence Potter, ed. London: Hurst.

——(n.d. a) *Iran's Minorities.* Unpublished book manuscript.

——(n.d. b) *Lords of the Mountains: Qashqa'i Tribal Insurgency in Post-Revolutionary Iran.* Unpublished book manuscript.

Beck, Lois, and Julia Huang (2006) Manipulating Private Lives and Public Spaces in Qashqa'i Society in Iran. *Comparative Studies of South Asia, Africa and the Middle East* 26 (2): 303–25.

Beck, Lois, and Guity Nashat (eds.) (2004) *Women in Iran from 1800 to the Islamic Republic.* Urbana: University of Illinois Press.

Behdad, Sohrab (1996) 'The Post-Revolutionary Economic Crisis.' In *Iran After the Revolution: Crisis of an Islamic State.* Saeed Rahnema and Sohrab Behdad, eds. London: I. B. Tauris.

——(2000) 'From Populism to Economic Liberalism: The Iranian Predicament.' In *The Economy of Iran: The Dilemmas of an Islamic State.* Parvin Alizadeh, ed. London: I. B. Tauris.

Black-Michaud, Jacob (1986) *Sheep and Land: The Economics of Power in a Tribal Society.* Cambridge: Cambridge University Press.

Borjian, Habib (2008) Isfahan ix. The Pahlavi Period and the Post-Revolution Era. *Encyclopaedia Iranica* 14 (1): 1–6.

Bradburd, Daniel (1990) *Ambiguous Relations: Kin, Class, and Conflict among Komachi Pastoralists.* Washington, DC: Smithsonian Institution Press

——(1998) *Being There: The Necessity of Fieldwork.* Washington, DC: Smithsonian Institution Press.

Bromberger, Christian (1989) *Habitat, Architecture and Rural Society in the Gilan Plain (Northern Iran).* Bonn: Ferd. Dümmlers Verlag

——(2013) *Un autre Iran: Un ethnologue au Gilan.* Paris: Armand Colin.

Buchta, Wilfried (2000) *Who Rules Iran?: The Structure of Power in the Islamic Republic.* Washington, DC: Washington Institute for Near East Policy and Konrad Adenauer Stiftung.

Chehabi, Houchang (1990) *Iranian Politics and Religious Modernism: The Liberation Movement of Iran Under the Shah and Khomeini.* Ithaca: Cornell University Press.

——(1993) Staging the Emperor's New Clothes: Dress Codes and Nation-Building under Reza Shah. *Iranian Studies* 26 (3–4): 209–33.

——(1997) Ardabil Becomes a Province: Center-Periphery Relations in Iran. *International Journal of Middle East Studies* 29 (2): 235–53.

Chelkowski, Peter, and Hamid Dabashi (1999) *Staging a Revolution: The Art of Persuasion in the Islamic Republic of Iran.* New York: New York University Press.

Bibliography 383

Chubin, Shahram, and Charles Tripp (1988) *Iran and Iraq at War*. Boulder: Westview Press.

Cole, Juan (2002) *Sacred Space and Holy War: The Politics, Culture and History of Shi'ite Islam*. London: I. B. Tauris.

Cordesman, Anthony (1987) *The Iran-Iraq War and Western Security 1984–87: Strategic Implications and Policy Options*. London: Jane's Publishing.

Dabashi, Hamid (2007) *Iran: A People Interrupted*. New York: The New Press.

Danishvar Kuhva-Qashqa'i, Nozar (1992) *Naghmehha-yi il-i Qashqa'i* (Melodies of the Qashqa'i tribe). Shiraz, Iran: Naved.

——(1995) *Nasim-i kuhsaran-i Qashqa'i* (Breezes from Qashqa'i mountain ranges). Shiraz, Iran: Mustafavi.

Dareshuri, Naheed, and Lois Beck (2014) 'Bands, Ropes, Braids, and Tassels among the Qashqa'i.' In *Weavings of Nomadic Pastoralists in Iran*. Fred Mushkat, ed. In preparation.

de Brunhoff, Jean (1937) *The Story of Babar: The Little Elephant*. New York: Random House.

Digard, Jean-Pierre, and Asghar Karimi (1989) 'Les Baxtyari [Bakhtiyari] sous influence occidentale: acculturation et deculturation.' In *Entre l'Iran et l'Occident: Adaptation et assimilation des idées et des techniques occidentales en Iran*. Yann Richard, ed. Paris: Maison des Sciences de l'Homme.

Duncan, David Douglas (1982) *The World of Allah*. Boston: Houghton Mifflin.

Dustkhah, Jalil, and Eqbal Yaghmai (1998) Education iii. The Traditional Elementary School (Maktab). *Encyclopaedia Iranica* 8 (2): 180–82.

Duzgun, Hosain (1998) *Qashqa'i lohehlari: sher majmuehsi* (Qashqa'i tablets: a complete set of poems). Zanjan, Iran: Zangan.

Ebadi, Shirin, with Azadeh Moaveni (2007) *Iran Awakening: One Woman's Journey to Reclaim Her Life and Country*. New York: Random House.

Education (1998) 26 entries on education in Iran. *Encyclopaedia Iranica* 8 (2–3): 178–237.

Ehsani, Kaveh (2009) 'The Urban Provincial Periphery in Iran: Revolution and War in Ramhormoz.' In *Contemporary Iran: Economy, Society, Politics*. Ali Gheissari, ed. Oxford: Oxford University Press.

Ehteshami, Anoushiravan (1995) *After Khomeini: The Iranian Second Republic*. London: Routledge.

Ehteshami, Anoushiravan, and Mahjoob Zweiri (2007) *Iran and the Rise of Its Neoconservatives: The Politics of Tehran's Silent Revolution*. London: I. B. Tauris.

Elling, Rasmus Christian (2013) *Minorities in Iran: Nationalism and Ethnicity after Khomeini*. New York: Palgrave Macmillan.

English, Paul (1998) Qanats and Lifeworlds in Iranian Plateau Villages. *Bulletin Series, Yale School of Forestry and Environmental Studies* 103: 187–205.

Esfandiari, Haleh (1997) *Reconstructed Lives: Women and Iran's Islamic Revolution*. Baltimore: Johns Hopkins University Press.

Farhi, Farideh (2004) 'The Antinomies of Iran's War Generation.' In *Iran, Iraq, and the Legacies of War*. Lawrence Potter and Gary Sick, eds. New York: Palgrave Macmillan.

——(2010) The Parliament. *The Iran Primer*. Washington, DC: United States Institute of Peace. http://iranprimer.usip.org/resource/parliament (accessed 17 March 2011).

Farmanfarmaian, Manucher, and Roxane Farmanfarmaian (2005) *Blood and Oil: A Prince's Memoir of Iran from the Shah to the Ayatollah*. 2nd ed. New York: Random House.

Farmanfarmaian, Monir, and Zara Houshmand (2007) *A Mirror Garden*. New York: Random House.

384 *Bibliography*

Farman Farmaian, Sattareh, with Dona Munkir (1992) *Daughter of Persia: A Woman's Journey from her Father's Harem through the Islamic Revolution*. New York: Crown.

Farvar, Mohammad Taghi (2003) Reviving Nomadic Pastoralism in Iran: Facilitating Sustainability of Biodiversity and Livelihoods. Tehran: Centre for Sustainable Development. Unpublished document.

Fazeli, Nematollah (2006) *Politics of Culture in Iran: Anthropology, Politics and Society in the Twentieth Century*. London: Routledge.

Ferdows, Emad (1983) The Reconstruction Crusade and Class Conflict in Iran. *MERIP Reports* 13 (3): 11–15.

Firouz, Eskandar (1998) Environmental Protection. *Encyclopaedia Iranica* 8 (5): 465–72.

Fischer, Michael (1980) *Iran: From Religious Dispute to Revolution*. Cambridge: Harvard University Press.

Fischer, Michael, and Mehdi Abedi (1990) *Debating Muslims: Cultural Dialogues in Postmodernity and Tradition*. Madison: University of Wisconsin Press.

Foran, John (1993) *Fragile Resistance: Social Transformation in Iran from 1500 to the Revolution*. Boulder: Westview Press.

——(1994) 'The Iranian Revolution of 1977–79: A Challenge for Social Theory.' In *A Century of Revolution: Social Movements in Iran*. John Foran, ed. Minneapolis: University of Minnesota Press.

Friedl, Erika (1983) 'State Ideology and Village Women.' In *Women and Revolution in Iran*. Guity Nashat, ed. Boulder: Westview Press.

——(1989) *Women of Deh Koh: Lives in an Iranian Village*. Washington, DC: Smithsonian Institution Press.

——(1997) *Children of Deh Koh: Young Life in an Iranian Village*. Syracuse: Syracuse University Press.

——(1998) Making Mutual Sense: My Daughters and I in a Village in Iran. *Anthropology and Humanism* 23 (2): 157–64.

——(2004) 'Rural Women's History: A Case Study from Boir Ahmad.' In *Women in Iran from 1800 to the Islamic Republic*. Lois Beck and Guity Nashat, eds. Urbana: University of Illinois Press.

——(2014) *The Folktales and Storytellers of Tribal Iran: Culture, Ethos and Identity*. London: I. B. Tauris.

Fromanger, Marine (2013) 'Variations in the Martyrs' Representations in South Tehran's Public and Private Spaces.' In *Unburied Memories: The Politics of Bodies of Sacred Defense Martyrs in Iran*. Pedram Khosronejad, ed. London: Routledge.

Gagon, Glen (1956) 'A Study of the Development and Implementation of a System of Elementary Education for the Ghasghi [sic] and Basseri Nomadic Tribes of Fars Ostan, Iran.' Master's thesis, Brigham Young University.

Garthwaite, Gene (1983) *Khans and Shahs: A Documentary Analysis of the Bakhtiyari in Iran*. Cambridge: Cambridge University Press.

Ghamari-Tabrizi, Behrooz (2008) *Islam and Dissent in Postrevolutionary Iran: Abdolkarim Soroush, Religious Politics and Democratic Reform*. London: I. B. Tauris.

Ghashghai, Malek Mansur (2013) *Khaterat-i Malek Mansur Khan Ghashghai* (Memoirs of Malek Mansur Khan Ghashghai). Tehran: Namak.

Ghashghai, Mohammad Hosain (2005) *Yadmondehha* (Memories). Tehran: Farzan.

Ghashghai, Mohammad Naser Solat (1986) *Salha-yi bohran: khaterat ruzaneh-yi Mohammad Naser Solat Ghashghai, 1329-32* (Crisis years: daily memoirs of Mohammad Naser Solat Ghashghai, 1950–53). Tehran: Maraj.

Bibliography 385

Gheissari, Ali, and Vali Nasr (2006) *Democracy in Iran: History and the Quest for Liberty*. Oxford: Oxford University Press.

Gheissari, Ali, and Kaveh-Cyrus Sanandaji (2009) 'New Conservative Politics and Electoral Behavior in Iran.' In *Contemporary Iran: Economy, Society, Politics*. Ali Gheissari, ed. Oxford: Oxford University Press.

Goodell, Grace (1986) *The Elementary Structures of Political Life: Rural Development in Pahlavi Iran*. New York: Oxford University Press.

Goodey, Chris (1980) Workers' Councils in Iranian Factories. *MERIP Reports* 10 (5): 5–9.

Gruber, Christiane (2013) 'The Martyrs' Museum in Tehran: Visualizing Memory in Post-Revolutionary Iran.' In *Unburied Memories: The Politics of Bodies of Sacred Defense Martyrs in Iran*. Pedram Khosronejad, ed. London: Routledge.

Habibi, Nader (1989) Allocation of Educational and Occupational Opportunities in the Islamic Republic of Iran: A Case Study in the Political Screening of Human Capital. *Iranian Studies* 22 (4): 19–46.

Hakakian, Roya (2004) *Journey from the Land of No: A Girlhood Caught in Revolutionary Iran*. New York: Crown.

Halliday, Fred (1979) *Iran: Dictatorship and Development*. London: Penguin Books.

——(1980) Testimonies of Revolution. *MERIP Reports* 19 (4): 27–29.

——(1989) The Revolution's First Decade. *Middle East Report* 19 (1): 19–21.

——(1990) 'The Iranian Revolution and Great-Power Politics: Components of the First Decade.' In *Neither East nor West: Iran, the Soviet Union, and the United States*. Nikki Keddie and Mark Gasiorowski, eds. New Haven: Yale University Press.

Harris, Kevan (2010) The Imam's Blue Boxes. *Middle East Report* 40 (4): 22–23.

Harun-Mahdavi, Justine (2006) *Nicht ohne meinen Mann: Erinnerungen einer deutschen Frau an ihre Zeit im Iran*. Gernsbach: Katz.

Hegland, Mary (1983) 'Aliabad Women: Revolution as Religious Activity.' In *Women and Revolution in Iran*. Guity Nashat, ed. Boulder: Westview Press.

——(1987) 'Islamic Revival or Political and Cultural Revolution?' In *Religious Resurgence: Contemporary Cases in Islam, Christianity, and Judaism*. Richard Antoun and Mary Hegland, eds. Syracuse: Syracuse University Press.

——(2009) 'Iranian Anthropology—Crossing Boundaries: Influences of Modernization, Social Transformation and Globalization.' In *Conceptualizing Iranian Anthropology: Past and Present Perspectives*. Shahnaz Nadjmabadi, ed. Oxford: Berghahn Books.

——(2014) *Days of Revolution: Political Unrest in an Iranian Village*. Stanford: Stanford University Press.

Hendershot, Clarence (1964) *White Tents in the Mountains: A Report on the Tribal Schools of Fars Province*. Tehran: Communications Resources Branch.

Hiltermann, Joost (2007) *A Poisonous Affair: America, Iraq, and the Gassing of Halabja*. Cambridge: Cambridge University Press.

Hiro, Dilip (1984) Chronicle of the Gulf War. *MERIP Reports* 14 (6–7): 3–14.

——(1985) *Iran Under the Ayatollahs*. London: Routledge & Kegan Paul.

——(1991) *The Longest War: The Iran–Iraq Military Conflict*. New York: Routledge.

——(2005) *The Iranian Labyrinth: Journeys through Theocratic Iran and its Furies*. New York: Nation Books.

Hooglund, Eric (1980) Rural Participation in the Revolution. *MERIP Reports* 10 (4): 3–6.

——(1982a) *Land and Revolution in Iran, 1960–1980*. Austin: University of Texas Press.

——(1982b) Rural Iran and the Clerics. *MERIP Reports* 10 (3): 23–26.

——(1997) Letter from an Iranian Village. *Journal of Palestine Studies* 27 (1): 76–84.

386   *Bibliography*

——(2009) Thirty Years of Islamic Revolution in Rural Iran. *Middle East Report* 39 (1): 34–39.

Hooglund [Hegland], Mary (1980) One Village in the Revolution. *MERIP Reports* 10 (4): 7–12.

——(1982) Religious Ritual and Political Struggle in an Iranian Village. *MERIP Reports* 12 (1): 10–17, 23.

Hourcade, Bernard, Hubert Mazurek, et al. (1998) *Atlas d'Iran*. Paris: RECLUS, La Documentation Française.

Huang, Julia (2006) 'Integration, Modernization, and Resistance: Qashqa'i Nomads in Iran Since the Revolution of 1978–1979.' In *Nomadic Societies in the Middle East and North Africa: Entering the 21st Century*. Dawn Chatty, ed. Leiden: Brill.

——(2009) *Tribeswomen of Iran: Weaving Memories among Qashqa'i Nomads*. International Library of Iranian Studies 15. London: I. B. Tauris.

Hyder, Syed Akbar (2005) 'Sayyedeh Zaynab: The Conquerer of Damascus and Beyond.' In *The Women of Karbala: Ritual Performance and Symbolic Discourses in Modern Shi'i Islam*. Kamran Aghaie, ed. Austin: University of Texas Press.

Irons, William (1975) *The Yomut Turkmen: A Study of Social Organization among a Central Asian Turkic-Speaking Population*. Anthropological Paper No. 58. University of Michigan Museum of Anthropology. Ann Arbor: University of Michigan.

Jahani, Carina (2006) 'State Control and Its Impact on Language in Balochistan.' In *The Role of the State in West Asia*. Annika Rabo and Bo Utas, eds. London: I. B. Tauris.

Jeddi, Hosain Bayat (1999) *Payvastegi-yi qoumi va tarikhi-yi Oghuz va ilha-yi Qashqa'i-yi Iran* (Ethnic and historical affiliation of the Oghuz and the Qashqa'i tribes of Iran). Shiraz, Iran: Navid.

Kar, Mehrangis (2005) 'Shari'a Law in Iran.' In *Radical Islam's Rules: The Worldwide Spread of Extreme Shari'a Law*. Paul Marshall, ed. Lanham: Rowman & Littlefield.

Katouzian, Homa (1981) *The Political Economy of Modern Iran: Despotism and Pseudo-Modernism, 1926–1979*. New York: New York University Press.

——(2009) *The Persians: Ancient, Mediaeval and Modern Iran*. New Haven: Yale University Press.

Kazemi, Farhad (1980) *Poverty and Revolution in Iran: The Migrant Poor, Urban Marginality and Politics*. New York: New York University Press.

Kazemi, Farhad, and Lisa Wolfe (1997) Urbanization, Migration, and Politics of Protest in Iran. In *Population, Poverty, and Politics in Middle East Cities*. Michael Bonine, ed. Gainesville: University Press of Florida.

Keddie, Nikki (2006) *Modern Iran: Roots and Results of Revolution*. Updated ed. New Haven: Yale University Press.

Keddie, Nikki, and Beth Baron (eds.) (1991) *Women in Middle Eastern History: Shifting Boundaries in Sex and Gender*. New Haven: Yale University Press.

Keshavarzian, Arang (2007) *Bazaar and State in Iran: The Politics of the Tehran Marketplace*. Cambridge: Cambridge University Press.

Khomeini, Ruhollah al-Musawi (1989) Matn-i kamel-i vasiyatnameh-yi elahi va siyasi-yi Imam Khomeini (Complete text of Imam Khomeini's divine will and political testament). *Kayhan-e Havai*. 14 June.

——(n.d. [1990]) *Imam Khomeini's Last Will and Testament*. Washington, DC: Interests Section of the Islamic Republic of Iran.

Khosravi, Shahram (2008) *Young and Defiant in Tehran*. Philadelphia: University of Pennsylvania Press.

Bibliography 387

Khosrokhavar, Farhad (1995) *L'islamisme et la mort.* Paris: L'Harmattan.

Khosronejad, Pedram (2013a) 'Introduction: Unburied Memories.' In *Unburied Memories: The Politics of Bodies of Sacred Defense Martyrs in Iran.* Pedram Khosronejad, ed. London: Routledge.

Khosronejad, Pedram (ed.) (2013b) *Unburied Memories: The Politics of Bodies of Sacred Defense Martyrs in Iran.* London: Routledge.

Kian-Thiébaut, Azadeh (1998) *Secularization of Iran: A Doomed Failure? The New Middle Class and the Making of Modern Iran.* Paris: Peeters.

Kiyani, Manuchehr (1993) *Siah chadorha: tahqeqi az zendegi-yi mardom-i il-i Qashqa'i* (Black tents: research on the life of Qashqa'i tribal people). Shiraz, Iran: Kaj.

——(1997) *Garali: dastanha-yi mostanad az il-i Qashqa'i* (Garali [a tribe]: authentic stories from the Qashqa'i tribe). Shiraz, Iran: Kaj.

——(1999) *Kuch ba eshq-i shaqayeq* (Migrating with the love of anemone). Shiraz, Iran: Kiyan.

——(2001) *Tarikh-i mobarezat-i mardom-i il-i Qashqa'i az Safaviyeh ta Pahlavi* (History of combat of the people of the Qashqa'i tribe from the Safavids to the Pahlavis). Shiraz, Iran: Kiyan.

——(2002) *Parchamdar hamaseh-yi junub: Soulat ed-Douleh Qashqa'i* (Flagholder of the battle of the south: Soulat ed-Douleh Qashqa'i). Shiraz, Iran: Kiyan.

Loeffler, Agnes Gertrud (1998) Memories of Difference: From Lur to Anthropologist. *Anthropology and Humanism* 23 (2): 146–56.

Loeffler, Reinhold (1988) *Islam in Practice: Religious Beliefs in a Persian [sic] Village.* Albany: State University of New York Press.

——(2011) The Ethos of Progress in a Village in Iran. *Anthropology of the Middle East* 6 (2): 1–13.

Longinotto, Kim, and Ziba Mir-Hosseini (1998) *Divorce Iranian Style* (film).

Mahdavi, Pardis (2009) *Passionate Uprisings: Iran's Sexual Revolution.* Stanford: Stanford University Press.

Mahdi, Ali Akbar (1998) Ethnic Identity among Second-Generation Iranians in the United States. *Iranian Studies* 31 (1): 77–95.

Mahmoody, Betty, with William Hoffer (1987) *Not Without My Daughter.* New York: St. Martin's Press.

Makhmalbaf, Mohsen, and Mohammad Ahmadi (1996) *Gabbeh: Film Script and Photographs.* M. Ghaed, trans. Tehran: Ney.

Maloney, Suzanne (2000) 'Agents or Obstacles? Parastatal Foundations and Challenges for Iranian Development.' In *The Economy of Iran: The Dilemmas of an Islamic State.* Parvin Alizadeh, ed. London: I. B. Tauris.

Mardani-Rahimi, Asadollah (1999) *Atalar suzu: zarb al-masalha-yi Turki Qashqa'i* (Elders' sayings: proverbs of Qashqa'i Turks). Shiraz, Iran: Kiyan.

Martin, Mary (1989) 'Villages, Agriculture, and the Revolution.' Unpublished manuscript.

Martin, Vanessa (2003) *Creating an Islamic State: Khomeini and the Making of a New Iran.* New ed. London: I. B. Tauris.

Mehran, Golnar (1989) Socialization of Schoolchildren in the Islamic Republic of Iran. *Iranian Studies* 22 (1): 35–50.

——(2002) 'The Presentation of the "Self" and the "Other" in Postrevolutionary Iranian School Textbooks.' In *Iran and the Surrounding World: Interactions in Culture and Cultural Politics.* Nikki Keddie and Rudi Matthee, eds. Seattle: University of Washington Press.

388 *Bibliography*

Menash, Mahdi Lotfi (1996) *Sedai darad* (It has a voice). Shiraz, Iran: Kiyan.

Menashri, David (1990) *Iran: A Decade of War and Revolution*. New York: Holmes and Meier.

——(1992) *Education and the Making of Modern Iran*. Ithaca: Cornell University Press.

——(2001) *Post-Revolutionary Politics in Iran: Religion, Society and Power*. London: Frank Cass.

Middle East Report (2010) 'The Iran-Iraq War 30 Years Later.' Vol. 40, No. 4.

Milani, Abbas (2008) *Eminent Persians: The Men and Women Who Made Modern Iran, 1941–1979*. 2 Vol. Syracuse: Syracuse University Press and Persian World Press.

Milani, Mohsen (1994) *The Making of Iran's Islamic Revolution: From Monarchy to Islamic Republic*. 2nd ed. Boulder: Westview Press.

Mir-Hosseini, Ziba (1994) Inner Truth and Outer History: The Two Worlds of Ahl-e Haqq of Kurdistan. *International Journal of Middle East Studies* 26 (2): 267–85.

——(2009) 'Being From There: Dilemmas of a "Native Anthropologist".' In *Conceptualizing Iranian Anthropology: Past and Present Perspectives*. Shahnaz Nadjmabadi, ed. Oxford: Berghahn Books.

Moaddel, Mansoor (1993) *Class, Politics, and Ideology in the Iranian Revolution*. New York: Columbia University Press.

Moaveni, Azadeh (2005) *Lipstick Jihad: A Memoir of Growing Up Iranian in America and American in Iran*. New York: PublicAffairs.

Moghadam, Valentine (2000) 'Women's Socio-Economic Participation and Iran's Changing Political Economy.' In *The Economy of Iran: The Dilemmas of an Islamic State*. Parvin Alizadeh, ed. London: I. B. Tauris.

Mojab, Shahrzad, and Amir Hassanpour (1996) 'The Politics of Nationality and Ethnic Diversity.' In *Iran After the Revolution: Crisis of an Islamic State*. Saeed Rahnema and Sohrab Behdad, eds. London: I. B. Tauris.

Moslem, Mehdi (2002) *Factional Politics in Post-Khomeini Iran*. Syracuse: Syracuse University Press.

Mosteshar, Cherry (1995) *Unveiled*. New York: St. Martin's Press.

Mottahedeh, Negar (2004) 'Life is Color!' Toward a Transnational Feminist Analysis of Mohsen Makhmalbaf's *Gabbeh*. *Signs: Journal of Women in Culture and Society* 30 (1): 1403–26.

Mottahedeh, Roy (1985) *The Mantle of the Prophet: Religion and Politics in Iran*. New York: Simon & Schuster.

Nadiri-Darrehshuri, Mohammad (2000) *Sayari dar bustan-i Qashqa'i 1: gozedeh-yi asher-i Mazun* (Traveling through the Qashqa'i garden 1: collected poems of Mazun). Shiraz, Iran: Rahgesha.

Nadjmabadi, Shahnaz (1993) Aufbau ohne fremde Hilfe: Die iranische Aufbauorganisation Gehad e Sazandegi. *Sociologus* 43 (2): 168–92.

——(2004) From 'Alien' to 'One of Us' and Back: Field Experiences in Iran. *Iranian Studies* 37 (4): 603–12.

——(2009a) 'The Arab Presence on the Iranian Coast of the Persian Gulf.' In *The Persian Gulf in History*. Lawrence Potter, ed. New York: Palgrave Macmillan.

Nadjmabadi, Shahnaz (ed.) (2009b) *Conceptualizing Iranian Anthropology: Past and Present Perspectives*. Oxford: Berghahn.

——(2010) Cross-Border Networks: Labour Migration from Iran to the Arab Countries of the Persian Gulf. *Anthropology of the Middle East* 5 (1): 18-33.

Bibliography 389

Nafisi, Azar (2003) *Reading Lolita in Tehran: A Memoir in Books.* New York: Random House.

——(2008) *Things I've Been Silent About: Memories.* New York: Random House.

Naipaul, V. S. (1981) *Among the Believers: An Islamic Journey.* New York: Alfred Knopf.

——(1999) *Beyond Belief: Islamic Excursions Among the Converted Peoples.* New York: Little, Brown & Company.

Najmabadi, Afsaneh (2005) *Women with Mustaches and Men without Beards: Gender and Sexual Anxieties of Iranian Modernity.* Berkeley: University of California Press.

Naseri-Tayyibi, Mansur (2002) *Nehzat-i junub: Fars, Qashqa'i va ghaileh-yi Azerbaijan* (Uprising in the south: Fars, Qashqa'i and the struggle in Azerbaijan). Tehran: Shirazeh.

Nashat, Guity, and Lois Beck (eds.) (2003) *Women in Iran from the Rise of Islam to 1800.* Urbana: University of Illinois Press.

Niknam, Azadeh (1999) The Islamization of Law in Iran: A Time of Disenchantment. *Middle East Report* 29 (3): 17–21.

Nomani, Farhad, and Sohrab Behdad (2006) *Class and Labor in Iran: Did the Revolution Matter?* Syracuse: Syracuse University Press.

O'Ballance, Edgar (1988) *The Gulf War.* London: Brassey's Defence Publishers.

Oberling, Pierre (1975) *The Qashqa'i Nomads of Fars.* The Hague: Mouton.

O'Donnell, Terence (1999) *Seven Shades of Memory: Stories of Old Iran.* Washington, DC: Mage.

Omid, Homa (pseudonym of Haleh Afshar) (1994) *Islam and the Post-Revolutionary State in Iran.* New York: St. Martin's Press.

Parsa, Misagh (1989) *Social Origins of the Iranian Revolution.* New Brunswick: Rutgers University Press.

Payami, Babak (2001) *Secret Ballot* (film).

Potter, Lawrence, and Gary Sick (eds.) (2004) *Iran, Iraq, and the Legacies of War.* New York: Palgrave Macmillan.

Qahramani-Abivardi, Mozafar (1994) *Tarikh-i vaqayih-yi ashayeri-yi Fars* (History of events of the nomads of Fars). Tehran: Haidari.

Rahnema, Ali, and Farhad Nomani (1990) *The Secular Miracle: Religion, Politics and Economic Policy in Iran.* London: Zed Books.

Rakel, Eva (2009) *Power, Islam, and Political Elite in Iran: A Study on the Iranian Political Elite from Khomeini to Ahmadinejad.* Leiden: Brill.

Rastegar, Asghar (1996) 'Health Policy and Medical Education.' In *Iran After the Revolution: Crisis of an Islamic State.* Saeed Rahnema and Sohrab Behdad, eds. London: I. B. Tauris.

Rouleau, Eric (1981) The War and the Struggle for the State. *MERIP Reports* 11 (6): 3–8.

Roy, Olivier (1998) Tensions in Iran: The Future of the Islamic Revolution. *Middle East Report* 28 (2): 38–41.

Rubin, Michael (2001) *Into the Shadows: Radical Vigilantes in Khatami's Iran.* Washington, DC: Washington Institute for Near East Policy.

Ruhani, F. (1992) *Chadorha-yi siah: pizuhishi piramun-i jameah va iqtisadi-yi ashayeri-yi il-i Qashqa'i* (Black tents: a socioeconomic study of nomads of the Qashqa'i tribe). Stockholm: n.p.

Sabahi, Farian (2001) *The Literacy Corps in Pahlavi Iran (1963–1979): Political, Social and Literary Implications.* Lugano: n.p.

——(2002a) 'Gender and the Army of Knowledge in Pahlavi Iran, 1968–1979.' In *Women, Religion and Culture in Iran.* Sarah Ansari and Vanessa Martin, eds. Richmond: Curzon Press.

390   Bibliography

——(2002b) The Literacy Corps in Pahlavi Iran, 1963–1979. *ISIM Newsletter* 10: 19.

——(2003) 'The White Tent Programme: Tribal Education Under Muhammad Reza Shah.' In *Tribes and Power: Nationalism and Ethnicity in the Middle East*. Faleh Abdul-Jabar and Hosham Dawod, eds. London: Saqi.

Saeidi, Ali (2004) The Accountability of Para-governmental Organizations (bonyads): The Case of Iranian Foundations. *Iranian Studies* 37 (3): 479–98.

Safari-Kashkuli, Avazollah (2000) *Tavalodi dar atesh* (Birth by fire). Shiraz, Iran: Kiyan.

Safiri, Floreeda (1976) 'The South Persian Rifles.' Doctoral dissertation, University of Edinburgh.

Safizadeh, Fereydoun (1991) 'Peasant Protest and Resistance in Rural Iranian Azerbaijan.' In *Peasants and Politics in the Modern Middle East*. Farhad Kazemi and John Waterbury, eds. Miami: Florida International University Press.

Salzer, Richard (1974) 'Social Organization of a Nomadic Pastoral Nobility in Southern Iran: The Kashkuli Kuchek of the Qashqa'i.' Ph.D. dissertation, Anthropology Department, University of California, Berkeley.

Salzman, Philip (1992) *Kin and Contract in Baluchi Herding Camps*. Vol. 2. Baluchistan Monograph Series. Naples: Dipartimento di Studi Asiatici, Istituto Universitario Orientale.

——(2000) *Black Tents of Baluchistan*. Washington, DC: Smithsonian Institution Press.

Samii, A. William (2000) The Nation and Its Minorities: Ethnicity, Unity, and State Policy in Iran. *Comparative Studies of South Asia, Africa and the Middle East* 20 (1–2): 128–37.

——(2006) 'Iran: Reformists Reportedly Disqualified from Local Elections.' 29 November. www.payvand.com/news/06/nov/1350.html.

Sanandaji, Kaveh-Cyrus (2009) The Eighth Majles Elections in the Islamic Republic of Iran: A Division in Conservative Ranks and the Politics of Moderation. *Iranian Studies* 42 (4): 621–48.

Sanasarian, Eliz (1995) State Dominance and Communal Perseverance: The Armenian Diaspora in the Islamic Republic of Iran, 1979–1989. *Diaspora* 4 (3): 243–65.

——(2000) *Religious Minorities in Iran*. Cambridge: Cambridge University Press.

Sarabi, Farzin (1994) The Post Khomeini Era in Iran: The Elections of the Fourth Islamic Majlis. *Middle East Journal* 48 (1): 89–107.

Schirazi, Asghar (1993) *Islamic Development Policy: The Agrarian Question in Iran*. Philip Ziess-Lawrence, trans. Boulder: Lynne Rienner.

——(1997) *The Constitution of Iran: Politics and the State in the Islamic Republic*. John O'Kane, trans. London: I. B. Tauris.

Sciolino, Elaine (2005) *Persian Mirrors: The Elusive Face of Iran*. New ed. New York: Free Press.

Shaery-Eisenlohr, Roschanack (2008) *Shi'ite Lebanon: Transnational Religion and the Making of National Identities*. New York: Columbia University Press.

Shaghasemi, Ehsan (2011) 'Mohammad Bahmanbeigi.' http://ezinearticles.com/? Mohammad-Bahmanbeigi&id=6102723.

Shahbazi, Shahbaz (n.d.) *Mazun, shaer-i Qashqa'i* (Mazun, Qashqa'i poet). Shiraz, Iran: n.p.

Shahidian, Hammed (2002) *Women in Iran: Gender Politics in the Islamic Republic*. Westport: Greenwood Press.

Shahshahani, Soheila (1995) Tribal Schools of Iran: Sedentarization through Education. *Nomadic Peoples* 36–37: 145–56.

Shariati, Ali (1978) 'Abu Dharr.' In *Collected Works*. Vol. 3. Tehran: Hosainiyyeh Irshad.

Bibliography 391

Shokat, Hamid (2000 [1379]) *Negahi az darun-i be jonbesh-i chop-i Iran: goftegu ba Iraj Kashkuli* (A look inside Iran's leftist movement: discussion with Iraj Kashkuli). Vol. 2. Tehran: Akhtaran.

Shryock, Andrew, and Sally Howell (2001) 'Ever a Guest in Our House': The Emir Abdullah, Shaykh Majid al-Adwan, and the Practice of Jordanian House Politics, as Remembered by Umm Sultan, the Widow of Majid. *International Journal of Middle East Studies* 33 (2): 247–69.

Siavoshi, Sussan (1996) 'Regime Legitimacy and High-school Textbooks.' In *Iran After the Revolution: Crisis of an Islamic State*. Saeed Rahnema and Sohrab Behdad, eds. London: I. B. Tauris.

Sick, Gary (1986) 'General Discussion.' In *The Iranian Revolution and the Islamic Republic*. New ed. Nikki Keddie and Eric Hooglund, eds. Syracuse: Syracuse University Press.

Sigler, John (1990) 'The Legacy of the Iran-Iraq War.' In *Iran at the Crossroads: Global Relations in a Turbulent Decade*. Miron Rezun, ed. Boulder: Westview Press.

Simpson, John (1988) *Inside Iran: Life Under Khomeini's Regime*. New York: St. Martin's Press.

Sohrabi, Ali (1995) *Amuzesh va parvaresh dar ashayer-i Iran* (Education among Iran's nomads). Shiraz, Iran: Shiraz University Press.

Soueif, Ahdaf (2000) *The Map of Love*. New York: Anchor Books.

Spooner, Brian (1984) Anthropology. *Encyclopaedia Iranica* 2 (1–2): 107–16.

——(1998) Ethnography. *Encyclopaedia Iranica* 9 (1): 9–45.

Statistical Centre of Iran (1991) Socioeconomic Census of Nomadic Tribes, 1986. Tehran: Plan and Budget Organization.

——(1999) Selected Tables. National Census of Population and Housing, 1996. Tehran: Plan and Budget Organization.

Supreme Council for the Nomads of Iran (1987 [1366]) *Nomads from Imam Khomeini's Perspective*. Tehran: Ministry of Islamic Guidance.

Swee, Gary (1981) 'Sedentarization: Change and Adaptation among the Kordshuli Pastoral Nomads of Southwestern Iran.' Ph.D. dissertation, Anthropology Department, Michigan State University.

Tabari, Azar (1983) Land, Politics and Capital Accumulation. *MERIP Reports* 13 (3): 26–30.

Takeyh, Ray (2003) 'Iran's Municipal Elections: A Turning Point for the Reform Movement?' 6 March. www.washingtoninstitute.org/templateCO5.php?CID=1599.

——(2009) *Guardians of the Revolution: Iran and the World in the Age of the Ayatollahs*. New York: Oxford University Press.

Talebi, Shahla (2011) *Ghosts of Revolution: Rekindled Memories of Imprisonment in Iran*. Stanford: Stanford University Press.

——(2013) 'From the Light of the Eyes to the Eyes of the Power: State and Dissident Martyrs in Post-Revolutionary Iran.' In *Unburied Memories: The Politics of Bodies of Sacred Defense Martyrs in Iran*. Pedram Khosronejad, ed. London: Routledge.

Tapper, Richard (1979) *Pasture and Politics: Economics, Conflict, and Ritual among Shahsevan Nomads of Northwestern Iran*. London: Academic Press.

——(1994) 'Change, Cognition and Control: The Reconstruction of Nomadism in Iran.' In *When History Accelerates: Essays on Rapid Social Change, Complexity and Creativity*. C. M. Hann, ed. London: Athlone Press.

——(1997) *Frontier Nomads of Iran: A Political and Social History of the Shahsevan*. Cambridge: Cambridge University Press.

392 Bibliography

——(2002) 'Introduction: The Nomads of Iran.' In *The Nomadic Peoples of Iran.* Richard Tapper and Jon Thompson, eds. London: Azimuth Editions.

——(2008) Who are the Kuchi? Nomad Self-Identities in Afghanistan. *Journal of the Royal Anthropological Institute* 14: 97–116.

Tapper, Richard, and Jon Thompson (eds.) (2002) *The Nomadic Peoples of Iran.* London: Azimuth Editions.

Tober, Diane (2004) Children in the Field and Methodological Challenges of Research in Iran. *Iranian Studies* 37 (4): 643–54.

Tohidi, Nayereh (2009) 'Ethnicity and Religious Minority Politics in Iran.' In *Contemporary Iran: Economy, Society, Politics.* Ali Gheissari, ed. Oxford: Oxford University Press.

Warne, William (1956) *Mission for Peace: Point 4 in Iran.* Indianapolis: Bobbs-Merrill.

Wright, Robin (2001) *The Last Great Revolution: Turmoil and Transformation in Iran.* New York: Vintage Books.

Yavari-D'Hellencourt, Nouchine (1988) Ethnies et ethnicité dans les manuels scolaires iraniens. In *Le fait ethnique en Iran et en Afghanistan.* Paris: CNRS.

Youssefzadeh, Ameneh (2000) The Situation of Music in Iran since the Revolution: The Role of Official Organizations. *British Journal of Ethnomusicology* 9 (2): 35–61.

Yusufi, Amrollah (2001) *Qashqa'i dar gozar-i tarikh* (Qashqa'i in the passage of history). Shiraz, Iran: Takht-i Jamshid.

Zakhayer enqilab: A quarterly journal of pastoral nomads in Iran (Treasures of the revolution) (1982–2001) (periodic). Tehran: Organization for Nomads' Affairs, Jihad Sazandegi.

Zekavat, Seid M. (Mohammad) (1997) The State of the Environment in Iran. *Journal of Developing Societies* 13 (1): 49–72.

Index

Members of the Qermezi subtribe are listed under their first names. Other individuals are listed under their last names.

Abbas Qermezi 325–31
Abu Zar 234, 245, 292n2
administrative divisions 293n12
African ancestry: of teacher 264–5, 270
Agricultural Bank 88–9
Agricultural Jihad, Ministry of 73–5
agriculture 32
Agriculture, Ministry of 86–8; dispute over pastureland 178
Ahmadinejad, Mahmud 73, 92, 116, 302n103; and hezbollahis 119; restrictions furthered 352; and revolutionary guards 122; volunteer militia and 101
air force 127
Akbar Qermezi: children of 291–2; as first of two teachers of Qermezi origin 267; retired 282; as teacher among Shahsevan nomads 267–8, 270
akhund 180; as beggars before revolution 81; negative attitude toward 167, 179–80; and war 62
alfalfa 185
Ali Qurban Qermezi: biography of 273–6; daughter's education 276; as teacher among Shahsevan nomads 274
animals: in camps and pastures 12: insurance for sheep and goats 88–9; sacrifice of 346; tax of 45; wild 326
Ansar-i Hezbollah 117, 142n143
anti-Islam activities 352
anti-vice patrols 94
apples: tax on 104–5

Aqa Mohammadli lineage: favored in education 262–3; privileges of 291–2; sociopolitical preeminence 239
Arab Spring 119
Arabic (language) 301n99; prayers in 344
Arabs 92
armed forces 92
army: conscripted soldiers in war 59–60, 110–11; desertion from 190
Atakula (village) 20; council elections in 115, 334–5; disputes in 111; hezbollahis in 335; house-building in 304; school in 263–4, 269–70, 299n71
Atazadeh, Mahmud 87, 90; attends memorial rites 219, 221; and Kachili lineage 237; as parliamentary deputy 237–8, 249
Atazadeh, Murad 168
attire 144–9; appropriation of 149, 171n14; for cultural celebrations 82, 83–4; at cultural festivals 146, 149; endangers Islam 146; men's 144–5; of mourning 207, 217, 227; in town 198; at weddings 148, 149, 159, 346–7; women's and girls' 54, 83–4, 144–9, 205

Bagh-i Eram 193; Qashqa'i headquarters 91; U.S. hostages held at 139n99
Bahais 70, 148, 369n7; in village 337
Bahluli-Qashqa'i, Sohrab 294n25; parliamentary deputy 1996–2000 247; parliamentary deputy 2000–04 255;

394 *Index*

parliamentary election 1992 238; parliamentary election 2000 255
Bahmanbaigi, Mohammad 254, 256; blamed for depoliticizing Qashqa'i 260; celebratory gatherings 261; collective punishment of 265, 270; death of 84; dress of teacher-trainees 296n51; exertion of power 265; father as subordinate of khans 298n67; ignored tribal elite 297n54; inconsistent policies 263; inspections of 297–8n58; positive sentiments toward Qashqa'i 268; program for nomads' education 258–61, 296n47, 296–7n52; selective choices of 262; successes of 298n59
Bahram Qermezi 23–4, 206; head of Islamic council 112–13, 228, 327, 340; as hezbollahi 120, 338, 345; opposed to cultural practices 339–40; opposed to khans 55; wedding of 338–48
Bakhtiar, Shapur 47
Bakhtiyari 78, 131n15; similarities with Qashqa'i 22
Bani-Sadr, Abul Hasan 70; and Iraq-Iran war 59
bathhouse (for nomads) 80–1
Bazargan, Mehdi 70
birthrate: decrease in 269; rise in 91
Bizhan Qermezi 312–31; conflict with Dariush 314, 316–17, 321–2; division of tasks 313; livestock of 314, 319–20, 322
Boir Ahmad Lurs 154, 266, 267, 307; blood feud with 155, 361; conflict with 98; in Dogonbadan 337–8; marriage with 307; in Semirom war 244
Borzu Qermezi: attitude toward Islam 41; boycott of Islamic council 112; and clergymen 222; collector of khans' taxes 53–4; complaints about revolutionary guards 93; conflicts with cultivators 219; and Darrehshuri khans 45–6; death of xi–xii, 14, 211–32; extra-tribal links 231; gravesite of 223–5; as headman 8–9, 23, 25, 108–9, 184, 216, 219, 228, 230, 331n4; hospitality of 186; and khans' defensive resistance 56–7; Khosrow Khan and 212; Land Rover as symbol of networks 318; last view of Hanalishah 358; marriage strategies of 306; photographs of 233n11; in

prison 42–57; problems with regime 178, 179; and Qashqa'i khans 42–57; and Qermezi subtribe 231; rejects revolution 41–2, 57; and revolution 40–2; and revolutionary guards 48–57; seizure of pastureland 178–83; sentiments toward in-laws 228; as supporter of khans 41, 179; and Tang-i Jelo ambush 52; threats against 57, 212; ties to land 174–89; and tribal khans 222, 230; vulnerabilities of 178; weapons of 49, 98
branding of livestock 209
bread: baking of 192, 196; as part of Qashqa'i culture 192
bribery 72, 104, 136n67; to revolutionary guards 56; to teachers 275
burial 141n132, 343, 344

calligraphy 84
camels 27, 170; raise for meat 188
cemetery: Borzu's gravesite 223–5, 225–6, 228–9, 231–2; for Iraq-Iran war martyrs 133n31, 224; in Mehr-i Gerd 215–16, 223, 231–2
censorship 83; attire and 49
chadur 21
Chamran, Mustafa 268, 298–9n69
change: processes for nomads of 3–6, 28–31
chemical warfare 67, 134n52
child custody 173n31
children 12–13, 17n18, 27; attitude toward after revolution 27; costs of 307–8; education of 33, 177, 198–9, 305, 307–8; and Qashqa'i culture 154
civil society 23, 334
clergy 40, 70, 99; alleged power of 179–80; assigned to government agencies 78, 142n149; attitude toward 124, 125, 203, 204; attitude toward prayer 132–3n24; at Borzu's memorial rites 222; and education 131n8; and martyrs 62; negative attitude toward 161, 167; in parliament 142n149; popular abuse of 125; role in revolutionary guards 92; violence against 125
coeducation 263
committees, revolutionary (*komiteh*) 94, 99–100; and Islamic behavior 99; role of revolutionary guards in 99
conspiracy theories 37

Index 395

Construction Jihad, Ministry of 73–5; and Islamic councils 332, 333; religious merit working with 74; services for nomads 74–5; slaughterhouses of 85
continuities: for nomads 30–1
Cooperatives Organization 85
corruption 72, 136n67
councils, Islamic (*shura*) 24, 107–16, 141n124, 141n125, 332–8; for Aqa Mohammadli lineage 111–14; in Atakula 110, 111, 115, 334–5; decrease in power and influence of 116; in Dogonbadan 337–8; elections in 2003–13 370n9; government's vetting of candidates 369n2; hezbollahis not elected to 115; and homicide 327; for Imamverdili and Qasemli lineages 114; and Islam 111; Islamic credentials for 109; in Kazerun 337; in Mehr-i Gerd 336; municipal elections for 116, 332, 333, 369n1, 370n9; for nomads 332–3; in Nurabad 114–15, 335–6; for Qairkhbaili lineage 114; Qashqa'i women elected to 369n6; in Qermezi 109–10; role of Construction Jihad 107, 110, 111; role of Organization for Nomads' Affairs 107, 110, 111; in Semirom 338, 370n8; witnesses of war 60
courts 104, 173n31, 177, 179–80
cultivators: buy fodder from 185; conflict with 86–7, 182, 183, 185–6, 188–9; destructions of 351; government assistance to 356; at Hanalishah 348–60; mediation for 89–90; relationships with nomads 355–6; seizure of pastureland 349–60, 354–6; threats from 201n2; ties with 326
cultural exhibition 171n8
cultural festivals 83–5, 149
cultural revolution 282–3, 300n85
cultural traditions 83–5
culture (Qashqa'i) *see* Qashqa'i culture
Culture and Islamic Guidance, Ministry of 78

Dalai Lama xi
dancing 94, 152–4; forbidden by hezbollahis 162–4, 172–3n28; at weddings 167, 168–9, 170
Dareshuri, Naheed 7–8, 15, 54, 370n14

Dariush Qermezi 312–31; buying house 314–16, 319; conflict with Bizhan 314, 316–17, 321–2; division of tasks 313; job with nomads' committee 100; livestock of 314, 319–20, 322; sale of orchard 314–15
Darrehshuri, Azar Bibi: gravesite of 224; servants' sentiments toward 224
Darrehshuri, Jehangir Khan: death of son 354; economic ties with Borzu 183–4; at memorial rites 221; and paramount khans 44, 45, 47, 51; in prison 54
Darrehshuri, Sohrab Khan 228, 230, 233n14
Darrehshuri, Ziad Khan: gravesite of 224
Darrehshuri khans 41, 230; decline in power of 167–8, 336
Dashtak: pastures at 187–8
Day of the Nomad 66; celebration of 82–3
death: as omen 344; restrictions on entertainment 153; and wedding plans 342, 343
debt 111
defensive resistance of khans *see* khans' defensive resistance
democracy 39
descent: rules of 307
dichotomies 374
discrimination: against nomads 72, 240, 290; against tribes 240; against Turks 240, 290
dissimulation (*taqiyya*) 143n151
Dogonbadan: election of council in 337–8
dowry 170
dwellings 32–3; at Dashtak 190; in Kazerun 190–6

economy: data of 11; of Iran xvi; of nomads 20, 82; and pastoralism 304–5, 313; after revolution 26, 30, 32
education 5, 22, 26, 33, 120, 256–92; fabrication of credentials 288; and government policy 276–7; importance of 242; under Islamic Republic 42, 276–7, 288; and military service 281; under Mohammad Reza Shah 276–7, 288; national system 260; options for women 128, 291; primary level 256–78; and religion 265; secondary level 277–82; and social status 281; university level 282–92

396   *Index*

Education, Ministry of 90–1
elders 164
encampments 21
environmental damage 180–3
ethnic minorities 92, 131n13, 170n1;
    attire of 148–9; defiance among 277;
    and education 276–7, 290–1; and
    parliament 236
ethnolinguistic minorities xv, 39; and
    education 263, 290–1; as voters 248
examinations 278–9, 280–5, 287, 291,
    308, 323; to qualify for university
    300n89
executions 51

facial hair 118; regulations for 102,
    292n5
Falak Qermezi 317–18, 321
family-planning: classes for 91
Fariba Qermezi 314, 318, 324,
    357, 359
Farsi Madan Qashqa'i 51
firewood 196; importance for weddings
    345
Forest Rangers, Organization of 86–7;
    services to nomads 86–7
Foundation for the Oppressed 106–7
foundations (*bunyad*) 105–7, 140–1n123,
    242; part of foreign policy 105

gathering (of natural resources) 82, 350
gelim 225
gendarmerie, rural 92, 93
gender: after revolution 27; segregation
    in schools 298n63, 299n72; at
    wedding 159–63, 167
genealogies 10, 342–3
government: impact of 374–5; parallel
    institutions of 135n56
grazing permits 26, 86–7
Green Movement 101
gum tragacanth 87
Gurginpur, Farhad 83
Gurginpur, Furud 83
gypsies 208

Hanalishah: conflict over land at 330,
    348–60; illegal orchard at 179–83;
    illegal walnut grove at 354–6; orchard
    at 185–6; pastures at 188–9;
    trespassers at 352–4
hat: as Qashqa'i symbol 54, 83, 145
headman (*kadkhuda*) 19; aid to teachers
    257–8; locates teachers 260–1, 262; in

Qermezi subtribe 108; after revolution
    23–4; roles of 108–9; status of 331n4
headscarves: as anti-Islamic 347; under
    Islamic Republic 145–9, 153; as
    symbols of freedom 347; and weddings
    158, 159, 160, 166, 345–6, 347
Health, Ministry of 91
healthcare 151–2
hearth: as family symbol 304; "son of
    the hearth" 312, 317
hezbollahis 39, 117–21; in charge of
    regime 98; cultural prohibitions of 84;
    decrease in power of 340; definition of
    117, 150–1; disruption of weddings
    164–5; dress and appearance of
    118–19, 168; as enforcers 71; networks
    among 117; opportunistic affiliation
    168; opposition to 119; in Qermezi 23,
    24, 39, 117–21; and revolutionary
    guards 118; stifle cultural expressions
    340, 348; and theological students
    121; and volunteer militia 119; and
    women 120, 121
high schools 279–82; diploma from 313;
    females and 281
highway robbery 139n104
Holy Warriors for the Islamic
    Revolution 91
homicide 164; case in 1984 164–5,
    328–9; case in 1999 325–31; under
    Islamic Republic 328; under
    Mohammad Reza Shah 328; and
    Qashqa'i customs 328–9
homosexuality 352, 370n16
honor killing 331n11
hospitality 43, 353; at ceremony 153;
    violations of 353
house: building of 174–6, 177; buying of
    314–15, 316, 319; conflict over 321–2
Huang, Julia xi-xii, xviii, 80, 180,
    302n102, 358; research with 12–13
humor 13, 28, 54, 81, 129, 241–2
hunting 27–8, 82, 325–6, 350
Husain Ali Qermezi 55, 364, 369; as first
    of two teachers of Qermezi origin
    267–8, 272–3; as kin of students 268;
    retired 282; during revolution 42

Ibrahim Qermezi: as advocate for
    Qashqa'i culture 123–4; as speaker at
    memorial rites 222, 231; as theology
    student 123–4
Ibrahim Qermezi (villager): wedding of
    165–70

Index 397

identity xxi-xxii, 21; changes in 30, 31; politicization of 241; strength of 290–1; tribal, subtribal, and lineage 61, 96, 290–1; uphold 375
identity card 110, 177; needed by hospital 214; for voting 238
ilkhani (paramount khan) 19, 24–5; execution of 57; foreign exile 57; imprisoned 57
Imadi, Imad ud-Din 293n17, 295n43; candidate for parliament 1992 237; candidate for parliament 1996 241, 245; won seat in parliament 2000–04 255
imam: as title 210n11
Imam Husain 60
Imamverdili lineage 65, 108, 114, 258, 264–5
interest-taking 26, 137n82
Internet 84, 288, 290
Iranians xv, 146; fleeing Iran 252
Iraq-Iran war 4, 7, 11, 37, 38, 58–69, 82, 129; changes caused to weddings 157; chemical weapons in 67; Construction Jihad in 74; impact on celebrations 340, 341; impact on government and society 71–2; local devastations of 28; nomads' revolutionary-guard corps in 95; prisoners of war in 59, 68–9; Qermezi martyrs in 58; relation to Islam 60; revolutionary guards in 92; and ritual 29; role in uniting Qermezi 61; Shahriyar Qermezi in 234–5, 239; statistics of 133n34; students in 283; volunteer militia in 101; volunteers for 294n24; wounded in 66–7
irrigation 180, 326
Islam: akhund version of 151; "American" version of 129, 143n153; attitude toward 73, 74, 333; benediction of 319–20; changing attitude toward 121; compulsion in 53, 118, 151; conduct and attire 147, 338; financial compensation 329; increasing contact with 202–3; and Iraq-Iran war 60; nomads' attitude toward 28, 41; penalties for crimes 328; politically expedient rituals 53; principles of 347; requirements for animal slaughter 86; taxes of 105
Islamic: calendar 226; uses of term xv–xvi
Islamic law 2; and child custody 104; compulsion in practice 151;

inheritance rights 171–2n18; interest-taking 26; and private property 53, 89–90; and religious duties 53; and tribal codes and customs 150, 331n11
Islamic Republic of Iran 1, 5–6; attitude of nomads to 30; beginning of 36; defiance against 54–5, 158, 338, 339, 347; ethnic minorities and 148–9; fear of tribesmen 83; forced imposition of 169; internal threats to 204–5; lack of state authority 179; no rulings on land reform 348; opposition to pre-Islamic rites 208; parallel governments of 135n56; problem in assimilating tribal and ethnolinguistic minorities 279–80; sentiments against 333; social constraints of 206; society polarized in 284–5; youth resistant to 115
Islamic Republican Party 70, 74
Islamic state: resistance against 54–5
Islamic tribunals 51
Islamization 172n24; forced on society 340; impact on Qashqa'i 375; in names of schools 264; of schools 131n9; in town 192–3, 194
Ismail Khan Soulat ed-Douleh (*ilkhani*) 369; imprisoned by Reza Shah 40–1; name for settlement 369

Jafari, Behruz 330; parliamentary candidate in 1996 242, 245–6; parliamentary candidate in 2000 255
Jahangiri, Allah Qoli 46, 51, 52, 55, 57; death threats issued by 98
Jahangiri, Eshaq 255; as First Vice President 295n44
Janikhani family: use of names by 34n18
Jehangir Qermezi: as council member 113; as teacher-trainee 258
Justice, Ministry of 104

Kachili lineage 237; distribution of members 165
Kashkuli, Bijan Bahadori 84; paintings of 193–4
Kashkuli, Mahmud Khan 214, 227
Kazerun 253–4; attire of women in 198; descriptions of houses in 193–5; economic constraints in 189–90; election of council in 337; incursions of Islam in 192–3; interactions with townspeople 199–200; land in 176–7; living in 189–201; municipal services

398 *Index*

in 196; privacy in 195; revolution in 38; social life in 191, 192, 197–8; thieves in 200–1; visitors to 195; women in 195, 198

Khalifeh Qermezi 120, 257, 262, 362

Khamenei, Ali 204; quotes from 244; and weapons' control 97

Khamseh: similarities with Qashqa'i 22; tribes of 22

khans 19, 24–5; defensive resistance 56–7; gatherings at camps 172n22; livestock tax of 93; pay bribery 56; and relation to Islamic Republic 46, 179; and relation to Mohammad Reza Shah 47; revolt of 131n9; and revolution 39–42; roles of 132n16

khans' defensive resistance (*urdu*) 25, 55, 56–7, 76, 97; humane treatment of captives 235; and nomads' revolutionary-guard corps 95; paramilitary forces against 238; Shahriyar Qermezi's view of 251; weapons in 96, 97

Khatami, Mohammad: council elections in 1999 108, 332, 334, 338; elections of 116, 215; impact of 73

Khomeini, Ahmad: as challenge to regime 203–4, 210n13; illness and death of 203–7

Khomeini, Mustafa: death of 203, 205; rites for 210n12

Khomeini, Ruhollah 70; attitude toward nomads 95; quotes from 244; and revolution 36–42; sons of 15; and war 60

Khosrow Shirin: camp of paramount khans 46, 47, 48, 49, 50

Khunj: councils in 109

kinship: degrees of 342–3; importance in marriage 154–6; and mother's brother 156, 233n8, 321; obligations of 160, 199, 233n8; ties of 370n11

kinship groups: continuing importance of 33

Kurds 92, 140n108

land reform 19, 89–90, 186–7, 357; Islamic principles for 89; shah's program for 90, 354

landowners 89–90

leaders: imprisonment of 42–57

leadership: in Qermezi 23–5

leftists 55; captured 51; Qashqa'i and Persian ones 45; and revolution 39

lineages 63, 109–10, 291–2, 340, 364

literacy: benefits of 372; campaign for 283

Literacy Corps 263–4, 298n65; Qermezi boys served in 264; teachers for Qermezi 269

livestock 85–6; division of 319–20; fluctuation in numbers of 188; insurance for 88–9; purchases of 324; sales of 308–9, 323; tax of 93

local-level studies 1–2, 4–7

Lurs 22, 154–6, 351

magazines (Qashqa'i) 84, 138n88

maktab (religious school) 257; misuse of term 296n47

Mansur Qermezi: cancelled musicians 206–7; wedding of 202–7

manual labor 305

marksmanship: contests of 96

marriage: alliances of 154–6; between close kin 325; and nomadic pastoralism 156; strategies of 338–9; written contract for 346

martyrs: burials of 65; government benefits for families of 66; Islamic notions of 62, 64; memorial services for 66; of revolution 37; treatment of bodies 61–2, 63–4

Martyrs Foundation 63, 64, 65, 66, 106

Masud Qermezi xi, 126–8, 287; age cohort of 273; attitude about career 374; self-identity as 127; sojourn in Russia 128

Meat Marketing Organization 85–6

media: government controlled 84, 345

Mehr-i Gerd: election of council in 336

memorial rites: burial 215–16; donations of livestock 220, 226, 231; fortieth day 217, 226–8; genders separated at 220; of murdered man 328; one year 217, 229–32; printed announcements for 66, 218; second anniversary 232; seventh day 217, 218–23; third day 217; Thursday-afternoon visitations 225–6

merchants 176–7, 196, 305; attend Borzu's memorials 231; Borzu's associates 210n9, 213, 214; debts to 314; deceptions of 347; in Kazerun 200, 206

middle schools 278–9

Index 399

migrations 20, 54, 154, 186, 189, 194, 201, 212, 321, 323; continuing patterns of 198; government assistance for 94; hazards of 88–9; livestock and 308; privations of 322; after revolution 25–6; and schools 262, 269, 286, 289
military service 305
militiamen, volunteer (*basiji*s) 24
minorities 292n8, 299n77
modernization 29–30, 328
modest dress (*hijab*) 27, 30, 31, 94, 205; and Azar Nafisi 370n13; ignored during cultural celebrations 82
Mohammad Karim Qermezi 303–12; choices of 313–14; economic strategies of 14, 15; education of children 307–8; livestock of 308–9, 312; marriage strategies of 306–7; orchard of 309–10; in prison 51, 52, 55–6
Mohammad Quli Qermezi: as council member 113
Mohammad Reza Shah Pahlavi 1, 4, 13; confiscated khans' property 43; failure of regime 29; imperial calendar of 226; land reform of 361–2; nationalization of pastures 348; and revolution 36–41; rural institutions of 107; secret police of 103; Security Force for Nomads of 95; suppressed the Qashqa'i 19; weapons confiscations 96–7
moral squads, mobile 99
Mosaddeq, Mohammad 46–7, 91; and National Front 39
mosque: in Kazerun 192–3, 206; in Mehr-i Gerd 222–3, 227; in Tehran 205; in village 344; women at 223
mourning: attire for 217, 227; practices of 66, 147, 346; restrictions during 227–8; rites of 207, 216–17, 228; rites for deceased's clothing 233n15; women and 216–17
mulla (pejorative label for any religious figure) 62
mulla (teacher) 257–8
Mulleh Balut: Aqa Mohammadli lineage at 360–9; citrus production at 364–5; designation of "nomads" 111, 362–3; disputes over land 90; government attitude to 366; grazing and cultivation at 186–7, 361; houses at 363, 366; intermarriage at 364; and Islamic council 369; land at 186–7;

land reform at 186–7, 361–2; names for 364, 369; new settlement at 81, 187, 360–9; nomads' attitude to 366–7; Qairkhbaili lineage at 360–9; relationships among settlers 364, 368–9; water access at 365
multiculturalism 171n9
Murad Qermezi: political role of 113; in prison 51, 55–6
music: attitude of government toward 138n86; popular Persian forms 202; and Qashqa'i 347–8; restrictions on 172n20; revitalization of culture 324
musicians 152, 157, 160–1, 162–4, 167–9
Muslims 1
mustazafin (the oppressed and deprived) 100, 139–40n106

Nadiri, Mohammad Quli 255; at memorial rite 221–2; as parliamentary candidate 2000 273; as teacher 271, 273
Nadirli subtribe 262, 298n60
naming practices of Qashqa'i 34–5n18, 294n25
Nasir Qermezi: wedding of 154–65
nationalism: and khans 40; as seen by Qashqa'i 39–40
natural resources 86–7, 178
New Year: celebration of 149; nomads and 201; planting for 209; remember deaths beforehand 232; rituals of 197, 201, 207–9; travelers during 201
Nomad: A Year in the Life of a Qashqa'i Tribesman in Iran 2, 4, 14, 15, 18
nomadism 3, 177; and education 289
nomads 3, 299n77; definition of 75–7, 256; in Iran xiii–xiv
nomads': corps of revolutionary guards 60, 94–6; educational program 90–1; process gun permits 97; revolutionary Islamic committees 100; Shahriyar Qermezi as member 234–5; volunteer militia 101–2; volunteer militia, attire of 101;
Not Without My Daughter 8, 17n15
Nurabad (village): council in 114–15; description of 167; school in 264, 270; settling at 165; wedding at 165–70

occupations 11
oil industry 305
opium 232n3, 330, 350

400 *Index*

orchards 309–10; at Hanalishah 185–6, 316; illegal planting at Hanalishah 178–83; at Mehr-i Gerd 183–4; sale of 314–15

Organization for Nomads' Affairs (ONA) 25, 75–83; as ally for nomads 79–83; at Baghan 371n23; definitions of "nomads" 75–7; Farsi Madan settlement 78, 361, 363; functions of 107; government loans 365; and Islamic councils 332; at Mulleh Balut 187, 360–9; plans to settle nomads 360–9; seminar sponsor 102; services offered 79–83

out-marriage 202, 240, 306–7

paramount khans (including *ilkhani*) 19; and land 189; as landowners 354; power of 94

parastatal entities 71, 242

parliament 5, 292n7; 1992 election for 236–8, 294n20; 1996 election for 238–48; 2000 election for 253–5; approval process 293–4n18; candidates for 11; deputies of 293n12; elections of 229; eligibility for 241, 242; factions in 294n20; five Qashqa'i elected in 1996 247; laws concerning land 89, 90; laws for nomads' education 91; merging ministries 88; minority deputies 295n37; negative sentiments toward deputies 295n32; and Qashqa'i 236, 292n7; Qashqa'i khans vote for 246–7; and religious and ethnic minorities 236, 247, 292n8; Shiraz candidates 294n27, 294n28; turnover of deputies 296n45

pastoralists: at Hanalishah 348–60

pastures: nationalization of 178, 348; part of marriage strategies 155–6; rights to 313; seasonal 26; seizure of 178, 179–83

Pastures Organization 86–7; assist at Hanalishah 356, 357; help nomads 181, 182; and settlement 362

peddler: and prayer 28

Persian (language) 40; in nomads' schools 259

Persian calendar 233n12

Persianization 202–3; and Iran's minorities 276–7

Persians xv, 21, 127; attend Borzu's memorials 231; attire of 146; attitude about Qashqa'i culture 207; as

compared with Qashqa'i 27; deceptions of 175–6, 177; in Dogonbadan 337–8; drawn to Qashqa'i weddings 203; equated with "Iranian" 146; land seizures of 179, 180; and nationalism 40; negative attitude toward Turks 351; Qashqa'i attitude toward 146, 169; as revolutionary guards 49–50; speech and actions of 232n4; as teachers among ethnic minorities 263

Perso-Arabic alphabet 84

pilgrimage: to Damascus 105, 130; to Mashhad 66, 105, 130, 151; to Mecca 66, 105, 129–30; to Najaf 105; and tax payment 105

plainclothes paramilitary 119

political factions: in Iran 243, 294n20, 338

political gatherings 131n10

poppy cultivation 330, 350

postrevolutionary society 1–2

prayers 28, 132–3n24, 150–1; in Kazerun 194; in prison 53; and schoolboys' antics 210n7; writer of 114

pregnancy 168–9

presidents: of Iran 29, 73

primary schools 256–78

prime minister 70

prison: and required prayers 53; treatment in 326–8; women visitors 54

prisoners of war 63, 68–9, 133n36, 134n37, 134n49, 134n53

privileged social groups 301n94

"propagating virtue and combating sin" 94, 99; security forces to apply policy 103

Qahramani, Ali: parliamentary deputy 1996–2000 247–8

Qairkhbaili lineage 114, 268, 368–9

qanat (underground aqueduct) 184, 370n22; building of 359–60

Qarachai Qashqa'i 51, 132n18, 169–70

Qasemli lineage 114, 361

Qashqa'i: definitions of 77; history of 18, 23; identity of 144, 156, 184, 237; label of 76–7; major tribes of 33n5; others' attitude toward 127; political role in revolution 130n1; population 1, 18; relation to government 72–3; similarities with Shahsevan 274; as

Index 401

state employees 72; tribal confederacy of 8; as Turks 21; under two shahs 72–3; as urban residents 28

Qashqa'i, Dariush Khan 222

Qashqa'i, Khosrow Khan 25; arrest of 42, 47; Borzu Qermezi's sentiment toward 212; burial of 138n90; defensive resistance of 25, 56; elected to parliament 46, 236, 247; execution of 39, 40, 41, 51, 57, 238, 247; grave of 84; from perspective of Shahriyar Qermezi 251; and punish revolutionary guards 235; return to Iran 41, 42–8, 49–51; video tributes to 84

Qashqa'i, Malek Mansur Khan 44

Qashqa'i, Naser Khan 25; return to Iran 41, 42–8, 49–51; visit Khomeini 40

Qashqa'i culture 21, 83–5, 144–9, 373, 374–5; adoption of 156; attitude of townspeople 207; change among city residents 202–3; change in 27–8; music and 324; nostalgia toward 203, 209; not reconcilable with political Islam 345; part of identity 156; as portrayed in government media 207, 345–6; relation to Islam 207; as represented by fireside gatherings 196; after revolution 27–8, 30, 31; television program about 197; "traditional" versions of 203; as writers on 34n18

Qermezi subtribe: associated families 335; characteristics of 18–19; demographic changes in 31–3; economic changes in 31–3; lineages of 19; in 1970 19–22; reputation as warriors 58; in 2013 22–8

Qubadi, Shapur: parliamentary deputy 1996–2000 247; parliamentary deputy 2000–04 255

Qur'an: benediction of 319–20; as deterrence against thieves 351

Rafsanjani, Ali Akbar Hashemi 73, 83, 122, 251; centralized security forces 100, 102–3

Ramadan: delays construction 368; vows during 200

rebels 50

refugees 74

regime change 4–7

regional groups 83

religion: akhunds' Islam 151; beliefs and practices 149–52; decrees of 142n148; hostility toward 333

religious education: and degrees offered by 142n148; and hezbollahi orientation 265

research methodology xii, xiii-xiv, 3–6, 7–11, 14–15

resistance to regime 71

revolution: experience of 36–42; export of 92

revolutionary guards 24, 38, 91–4, 121–2; under Ahmadinejad 92; attitude toward 122; ban music and dance 152–4, 162–5; disruption of weddings 94; and foreign policy 92; nomads' corps of 94–6; Persians in 93; prison of 132n17, 133n25; Qashqa'i in 93; and Qashqa'i khans 45, 47, 48–57; relation to army 92–3, 122; and revolutionary committees 94; role in Iraq-Iran war 59; seize Bagh-i Eram 91; shave off beards of 235; as "terrorist" organization 92

revolutionary organizations 69–72

Reza Shah Pahlavi 19; assault on nomads 37; imprisoned Qashqa'i ilkhani 40–1

ritual and ceremony 152–4, 159–61

ritual politeness (*taaruf*) 72

Rouhani, Hasan 73, 255

rural Iran 74; importance of education for 275–6; negative attitude toward 295n32; and parliament 295n37

rural migrants 136n73; as compared with Qashqa'i 34n8; efforts to restrict movement of 74

Saddam Hossein 60, 68

Sanjabi, Karim 142n143

Saudi Arabia: massacre of Iranian pilgrims 129

SAVAK 103, 125

sayyid 203, 214; concocted identity of 292–3n10; disdain for 81, 344

schoolchildren: in town 198–9

schoolgirls: attire of 146–7

schools 11; in Atakula 269–70; closed when shah fled Iran 274; coeducational 263, 273; females in 263; named for Chamran 268; and nomads' migrations 261, 268–9; in Qermezi 261–6; use of Persian language required 259

402 Index

schoolteachers 125–6; attire of 147; join volunteer militia 102; livestock of 190; as nomads 76; as settlers 367; status of 190; wages of 189–90
secret police *see* SAVAK
secularism 40
security forces 102–3, 181–2; arrest Abbas 325, 329
Semirom: attitude toward townspeople 169; election of council in 338; land in 174–6; martyrs of 246
Semirom district 236, 238–9, 241, 243–4, 245–7, 293n12; and 1992 parliamentary election 236–8; and 1996 parliamentary election 238–47; and 2000 parliamentary election 254–5; improvements for 249–50
Semirom war 131n7; loss of tanks 244
settlement: process of 79, 81, 250, 360–9
Seven-Person Commissions 89–90
Shah Reza shrine 65
Shahreza district: Shahriyar Qermezi's parliamentary candidacy in 254–5
Shahriyar Qermezi 38, 60, 234–56; accomplishments of 104; appointments of 246, 250; assets as candidate 239–41; attend funeral 344; campaign for Khatami 243, 251–2, 253; campaign posters 244–5; capture of Iraqi tanks 244; conflict between Turks and Persians 246; defend Qashqa'i reputation 251; deputy to Minister of Industries and Mines 255; economic assets of 242, 243; as hezbollahi 240–1, 244; identity as 127, 251; in Iraq-Iran war 60, 66–7, 234–5, 292n2; and Islamic taxes 105; kinship ties of 63, 239–40; loan from foundation 107; national role 250–1; in nomads' volunteer militia 66–7, 234–5; parliamentary candidate for Shahreza 2000 254–5; parliamentary deputy 1996–2000 248–53; parliamentary elections 2004–08 256; as pilgrim 130; recite Qur'an verses 235; role at Qashqa'i level 253; role at Qermezi level 252–3; role in council elections 334; run in parliamentary elections 236, 237, 238–47, 351; seek help from 295n40; service in parliament 85, 129; and settlement 360; speeches of 243–4; as student in Aqa Mohammadli school 239; as teacher 239; training as teacher

292n2; tribal support for 243; tribal ties of 240, 242; views on Iran's international role 252; as war hero 129
Shahsevan 274
Shaikh Lurs 154–6, 159, 163, 230; employed in oil industry 305
shame 344
shepherds, hired 64, 310, 317, 320, 323: scarcity of 189–90; son as 325
Shi'i Islam 22, 60, 149
Shir Mohammad Qermezi: burial site of 215, 224; marriage strategies of 154; as Qermezi martyr 58; and Semirom war 40, 43–4, 184
Shiraz: Qashqa'i parliamentary deputies in 1996–2000 248, 255, 294n27, 294n28
shrines, local 105
social organization: of nomads 20–1; after revolution 26–7
socioeconomic classes 286, 301–2n100
socioterritorial groups 262
Sohrab Qermezi 108; and conflict over teacher 264–5, 270; father of Shahriyar Qermezi 234, 235, 240; fighter in khans' battles 246; and teachers 258; wounds from war 292n4
Sohrabi, Ali: parliamentary deputy 1996–2000 247; parliamentary election 2000 255
soldier-teacher 60, 264
Soroush, Abdolkarim 142n143
Soulat ed-Douleh *see* Ismail Khan Soulat ed-Douleh
state control: over weapons 96–9
states: in Iran xiv
state-tribe relationships 69–107; government fears tribesmen 83; parallel governments 70–2; republican versus unelected Islamic bodies 70
stick fighting 152–3, 160–1, 162, 206, 207, 347
strategies: cultivation versus pastoralism 372–5; from 1970 to 2013 372–5; value judgments 373
students 11; and attitude toward revolution 38; close bonds among 272–3; females among 271; futures of 271–3; hierarchies among 279; motivations of 289–91
subtribes: in Darrehshuri 11, 18–19, 23, 58–9, 163; honor of 340; solidarity within 198, 328, 340

summer pastures: conditions of 175
Supreme Council for Nomads 75, 97

Tahiri, Jalal ud-Din 15; as Friday prayer
leader 132n21; interceded for
Qashqa'i khans 51
Tahmuras Qermezi: as theological
student 124
Tajik 145
Tang-i Jelo: ambush at 49–51, 132n18
taxation 104–5; religious 105
teachers 266–71; before 1959 257–8;
biography of teacher 273–6; females
among 271; for khans 257; of
minority backgrounds 263–4; new
directives after revolution 42; as
nomads 76; other roles of 261; Persian
ones 258–9; of Qermezi origin 267–
71; in Qermezi schools 266–71; as role
models 259–61, 292; tasks as 260–1;
training of 259, 281–2
telephone 84; service for 196–7
television: coverage of attack against
rebels 55; religious content 197
tent 32, 49, 77, 193, 196, 200, 304,
371n24; image of 85; at memorial
services 216, 220; at weddings 166
textiles 52, 53, 77, 193, 194; given to
merchants 309; part of dowries 309;
and stories 274; trade in 190
theological students 121, 123–5; attire of
123–4; expected violence against 125;
status as 124
titles, social 209, 210n14
torture 326–7
transportation 201; jobs in 305
tribal: use of term 132n16, 256
tribal customs 150; and legal
processes 330
tribal groups: continuing importance of
23, 30, 31, 33, 95, 280, 375
tribal high school: excellence of 299n82;
name of 300n83
tribal honor 55
tribal middle schools 260, 270,
278–9, 308
tribal rebellion 171n6
tribal secondary schools 199, 260,
279–80; martyrs in war 59
tribal society: as part of civil society 23
tribal solidarity 56, 61, 328–9
tribal taxes: and khans 53–4
tribal teacher-training school 259, 281–2
tribe-state relationships 4

tribes: of Fars province 101; in Iran
xiii–xiv, 77; misunderstanding about
171n6; urban attitude toward 146; use
of term 76, 256
*Tribeswomen of Iran: Weaving
Memories among Qashqa'i Nomads*
6–7, 13
turban 123
Turkish (Qashqa'i) (language) 54, 84,
156, 208; campaign poster in 251–2;
influenced by Persian and Arabic
274–5; songs of mourning in 214;
speeches at memorial rites in 221; use
by urban residents 248
Turkmans 92
Turks 21, 145, 374; versus Tajiks
338, 374
twelfth Shi'i imam 114, 222

U.S.: shot down Iranian passenger
plane 52
U.S. Peace Corps: as teachers in Iran
260, 297n55
U.S. Point Four program 258, 296n50
universities 282–92; correspondence
ones 285–6, 287; degrees issued by
286–7; free (*azad*) ones 285, 287,
301n97; graduates of 126–8;
privileged social groups 284, 300n91,
300n94; quotas for 284–5; in Semirom
249–50; state ones 67, 283–5, 286,
287; vocational ones 286
university entrance: and "deprived"
students 301n93
university students: activities of 287–8;
attire required of 285; and females
286; later professions of 288–9;
motivations for nomads 289–91;
screening of 283–4; supported by
families 291; surveillance over 285;
unemployment of 289, and war 283
urdu (celebratory gatherings for
students) 261
urdu (defensive resistance) *see* khans'
defensive resistance

Vanak (village): cultivators of 330;
Iraq-Iran war martyrs from 58; role of
citizens in revolution and war 246
vegetation, uncultivated 350–1
vehicles 25–6, 316, 318–19
Veramin district: Qashqa'i
parliamentary deputy for 247
veterinary services 81

404   *Index*

villagers: education important for socioeconomic mobility 276

volunteer (*basij*) militia 24, 38, 100–1; as enforcers 71, 100–1; in Iraq-Iran war 59, 92, 101; organization for 101

voting: age of 141n134; and ethnic minorities 369n5; history of voter 239; rules of 293n13

walnut tree: crisis over 356–60; as symbol of conflict between nomads and cultivators 183, 356–60

water 348, 350; crisis at Hanalishah over 356–60; shortage of 311; and women 360

weapons 46; confiscation of 56; and councils 110; government policies for 325, 329; government seizures of 42, 48, 49; and highway robbery 139n104; importance in Qashqa'i identity 98–9; permits for 96–9; as symbol of 325; used in homicide 325–31; wooden clubs as 52

weaving 12, 84, 299n73; cessation because of mourning 227; in town 195

weddings 121, 152–4, 172n25, 194; Bahram's 338–48; changes in practices of 341–2; changes in schedules of 194, 202, 341–2; disruptions by hezbollahis 164–5; formal invitations for 341; Ibrahim's 165–70; Mansur's 202–7;

and mourning rituals 153; music (with or without) 343, 344, 345, 346, 347; Nasir's 154–65; rituals of 206; in summer 316; timing of 345; unwelcome guests at 202–3; and women's attire 153–4, 159, 166, 167

Wednesday's Celebration 208

westernization 172n24

winter pastures: conditions of 175, 177

wolf 311

women 16n2, 20–1; access to water 360; employed outside the home 128; government benefits for 128; and hezbollahis 120, 121; images of 149; and legal system 104; and restrictions on attire 100

World War I: and Qashqa'i forces against the British 58, 235

youth: activities of 345; among nomads compared with settled people 289–90; social activities of 302n104

Yunus, Muhammad xi

Zahidi family 167–8; attire of women 168

Zain Ali (shrine) 44, 66, 82, 352; camp of paramount khans 44, 102

Zan-e Ruz (magazine) 221–2, 227

Zoroastrianism: rituals of 197, 208